THE

University Guide

2012

John O'Leary

with
Patrick Kennedy
Dr Nicki Horseman

TIMES BOOKS

Published in 2011 by Times Books

HarperCollins Publishers
77–85 Fulham Palace Road
Hammersmith
London W6 8JB

www.harpercollins.co.uk

First published in 1993 by Times Books. Eighteenth edition 2011

© Times Newspapers Ltd 2011

The Times is a registered trademark of Times Newspapers Ltd

ISBN 978-0-00-736455-8

Patrick Kennedy and Dr Nicki Horseman have been lead consultants for Exeter Enterprises Limited, which has compiled the main university league table and the individual subject tables for this guide on behalf of *The Times* and HarperCollins.

Please see chapters 4 and 5 for a full explanation of the sources of data used in the ranking tables. The data providers do not necessarily agree with the data aggregations or manipulations appearing in this book and are also not responsible for any inference or conclusions thereby derived.

Project editor: Christopher Riches
Design, editorial and additional research: Edenside Computing Services Ltd

Printed and bound in Great Britain by Clays Ltd, St Ives plc.

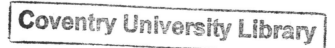

Contents

About the Author

John O'Leary is a freelance journalist and education consultant. He was the Editor of *The Times Higher Education Supplement* from 2002 to 2007 and was previously Education Editor of *The Times*, having joined the paper in 1990 as Higher Education Correspondent. He has been writing on higher education for more than 30 years and is a member of the executive board of the QS World University Rankings. He is the author of *Higher Education in England*, published in 2009 by the Higher Education Funding Council for England. He has a degree in politics from the University of Sheffield.

Acknowledgements

We would like to thank the many individuals who have helped with this edition of *The Times Good University Guide,* particularly Greg Hurst, Education Editor of *The Times*, and Patrick Kennedy and Dr Nicki Horseman, the lead consultants for Exeter Enterprises Limited, which has compiled the main university league table and the individual subject tables for this *Guide* on behalf of *The Times* and HarperCollins Publishers; to the members of *The Times Good University Guide* Advisory Group for their time and expertise: Josie Lewis-Gibbs, Planning Officer, Imperial College, London; Rona Smith, Senior Strategic Planner, University of Edinburgh; Sue Hybart, Director of Planning, Cardiff University; Fidelma Hannah, Director of Planning, Loughborough University; Christine Couper, Head of Planning and Statistics, University of Greenwich; and Janet Isaac, Head of Corporate Information, University of Plymouth; Simon Kemp and Jonathan Waller of HESA for their technical advice; Martin Ince, Mary Bowers, Kaya Burgess and Adam O'Leary for their contributions to the book.

We also wish to thank the publishers of the QS World University Rankings, the Academic Ranking of World Universities and *Times Higher Education* for permission to reproduce some of their main league tables and all the university staff who assisted in providing information for this edition.

How to Use this Book

The Times Good University Guide 2012 will help you to select the subject and university of your choice and to guide you through the whole process of getting to university. The answers to the questions below will help you to get the most out of the information we offer.

How do I choose a course?

» The first half of chapter 1 provides advice on what you should consider when choosing a subject area and relevant courses within that subject.

» The tables near the beginning of chapter 2 give details of the employment prospects for all major subjects.

» Chapter 5 provides details for 62 different subject areas (as listed on page 64).

» For each subject there is a league table that provides our assessment of the ranking of all universities offering courses in the particular subject area.

» For each subject we also provide some background information, details of employment prospects and selected websites where you can find out more about the subject.

» Specific advice for international students is given in chapter 11.

How do I choose a university?

» The second half of chapter 1 provides advice on choosing a university.

» If you are considering studying abroad, chapter 3 provides guidance and practical information.

» Central is the main *Times* league table on pages 57–61. This ranks the universities by assessing their quality not just according to student satisfaction (drawn from the National Student Survey) but also through seven other factors, including research quality, the spending on services and facilities, and graduate employment prospects. This table gives an indication of the overall performance of each university.

» The second half of the book contains two pages on each university, giving a general overview of the institution as well as data on student numbers, how to contact the university, the accommodation provided by the university, and the fees and financial support expected to be available for 2012–13. Note that details given for English universities were still awaiting approval by the Office for Fair Access when this book went to print in spring 2011.

» In addition, chapter 9 provides information on sport and sporting facilities across all the universities.

» For those considering Oxford or Cambridge, details of admission processes and of all the colleges can be found in chapter 12.

» Specific advice for international students is given in chapter 11.

How do I apply?

» Chapter 6 outlines the application procedure for university entry.

» It starts by advising you on how to complete the UCAS application, and then takes you step-by-step through the process that we hope will lead to your university place for autumn 2012.

» Specific information about applying to Oxford and Cambridge is given in chapter 12.

Can I afford it?

» Chapter 7 outlines the costs of studying at university (including the payment of fees) as well as sources of funds (including student loans, grants and bursaries).

» Chapter 8 provides advice on where to live while you are there.

» Accommodation charges for each university are given in the university profiles in chapter 13.

How will university enhance my career?

» The employment prospects and average starting salaries for the main subject groups are given in chapter 2.

» Universities are now doing more to increase the employability of their graduates. Some examples are given in chapter 2 – and check whether your chosen universities provide similar services.

How do I find out more?

» In each university profile (chapter 13) contact details are given (including email addresses and websites), so you can obtain more information on any university you are interested in.

» At the end of each chapter, a selection of useful websites is given.

» A further listing (pages 540–41) provides contact details for higher education institutes and university colleges that are not covered elsewhere within the book.

» *The Times Good University Guide* website **www.thetimes.co.uk/gug** will keep you up to date with developments throughout the year and contains further information and online tables.

Introduction

There have been a number of major changes in the higher education system since this *Guide* was first published in 1993, but none compares with the revolution that will confront both universities and their students in 2012. By removing four fifths of the funding for teaching from universities and colleges in England and allowing institutions to charge up to £9,000 in fees, the Government has embarked on a massive experiment. No one knows whether students will come in the numbers that have swamped universities in the last two years, or whether the new era will turn back the tide of mass higher education, denying opportunities and spelling disaster for institutions that overestimate their appeal.

The Coalition Government's decision, which will have knock-on effects for universities throughout the UK, switches the balance of responsibility for paying for a degree decisively from the state to the individual. That process began when Labour introduced £1,000 fees in 1998 and accelerated when the cost of studying trebled in 2006. On both occasions, predictions of a flight from higher education by students from poor backgrounds were confounded. But those increases came in relatively benign economic conditions and the sums involved were small by comparison with the bills that will now await graduates.

Driven by political compromise, ministers misjudged the cost both to the taxpayer and the student. By imposing a maximum of £9,000, they unwittingly encouraged some universities to charge more than they might have done in a less regulated system or one with a lower ceiling. The new arrangements will certainly be no cheaper for the state in the short or medium term.

Such is the popularity of higher education, however, that the new system may still work – albeit at considerable cost to graduates. Fuelled by the economic downturn and swollen by tens of thousands of repeat candidates who had failed to find places in the previous year, the pool of applicants to UK universities has been growing year by year. Although the anticipated rush for places ahead of the fees rise has not materialised in most universities, there were still record numbers of applicants for courses beginning in 2011.

While this may have been the high-water mark in the demand for full-time degree places, it will be surprising if such a deep-seated trend simply goes into reverse.

No one can predict the eventual impact of the downturn on the jobs market, but few good judges expect the outcome to be an economy in which a degree is less of an advantage than it has been in recent years. International surveys continue to show the salary premium enjoyed by UK graduates over those who choose not to go to university as among the highest in the world, and, with more and more jobs requiring a degree, the financial case for going to university remains compelling, in addition to the wider benefits of an undergraduate education.

However, the new fees surely will encourage prospective students and their parents or advisers to look more closely than ever at the likely benefits of degrees in different subjects at different universities. The institutions certainly expect more intense scrutiny by applicants and greater expectations from those who do enroll – their fee statements are full of promises of employment-related schemes and an improved "student experience". This *Guide* may be one of the weapons in the students' armoury.

The outlook for applicants

Logic suggests that the competition for places in higher education should ease in 2012, except perhaps in Scotland, where there are no fees for Scottish students. The two previous fee rises have been followed by sharp falls in the number of applications before the market has recovered. But, with thousands of applicants certain to be disappointed in 2011, the extent of any fall is difficult to estimate.

Previous editions of this *Guide* have asserted confidently that there would be a place somewhere in higher education for every qualified applicant who wanted one. Although tens of thousands of candidates have always failed to secure a place, most either did not achieve the necessary entrance qualifications or changed their mind about going to university. The last two years have been different, and that is bound to have some effect on 2012. The fact that tens of thousands of last year's candidates reapplied in 2011 demonstrates that the shortage of places was real, despite some extra provision. It is likely that there will be somewhat fewer places available in 2012. Ministers may react to overspending on student loans as a result of universities' higher than expected fees by cutting the number of places they allow to be filled. And some universities are planning their own reductions in order to cut their costs and improve the staffing levels on their remaining courses.

Nevertheless, it will be surprising if the new fees do not put off some people who otherwise would have applied in 2012. Some big employers are stepping up their efforts to recruit bright 18-year-olds and the appetite for repeat applications, in particular, may be reduced by the prospect of much higher costs. In addition, the potential pool of applicants will be somewhat smaller this year because the 18–20 age group, which still produces the largest numbers of students, will be in decline. And the reduced numbers taking a gap year in 2011 will mean that fewer places will be taken by those who deferred applications from the previous year.

How these various factors will translate into the demand for places at individual universities is impossible to predict with accuracy – which is why the new system is such a gamble for the institutions, as well as for applicants. But competition is certain to remain intense in popular subjects and at the most selective universities. The big question is what will happen at universities further down the league tables. They have enjoyed the strongest growth in demand for places over the last two years, with the result that many courses were oversubscribed for the first time. Such universities will not want to go back to the old pattern of applications, when they struggled to fill their places, but some may have to be prepared for that eventuality.

In such uncertain times, it is essential to make every choice count in framing applications. In particular, it makes sense to think seriously about an "insurance choice". Over recent years, the fashion has been for those aiming for the top universities to use up all five of their choices on courses with similar entry requirements, relying on UCAS Extra or Clearing for an alternative, if they ended up with a full set of rejections. Now the pressure on places is such that the leading universities seldom use Clearing and growing numbers of applicants find themselves without an option that they want to take up. Thousands of those who were left without a place in 2010 rejected an offer, rather than being rejected themselves.

Many of those who reapplied from the previous cohort undoubtedly had results that were good enough to have secured a place somewhere in the higher education system. They opted for a second run, rather than accept a place that was not all that they hoped for. Some will end up at universities that could have been their insurance choice in the first place. Applicants for courses beginning in 2012 do not need to lower their sights for their top choices, but they would do well to recognise that the world has changed and to be realistic about their other options.

Nor should applicants pin their hopes on the Adjustment Period, introduced last year to give those with better grades than their highest offer the chance to "trade up" to a more selective university. This opportunity exists for five days immediately after A-level results are published, but there is no obligation on universities to hold back places and many are full by then. Only 377 students out of 487,329 secured their place that way in 2010 and the figure could well be lower in 2012, given the pressure on universities not to over-recruit.

The other factor that is assuming greater importance for those who take A levels is the A* grade. Only Cambridge chose to use the new grade for selection purposes in 2010, but many more universities now require it, at least in some subjects. Most are doing so reluctantly, having opposed its introduction by the Labour Government, but they feel that they cannot continue to ignore an opportunity to distinguish between the growing numbers achieving A grades. Some have followed Cambridge and require at least one A*, without nominating a particular subject; others are more specific. Candidates should look carefully at university prospectuses and websites to see exactly what the policy is because there will be no uniformity, even among the leading universities, in 2012.

Universities and league tables

League tables are seldom popular with those being measured. But the rankings at the heart of this *Guide* have stood the test of time, after 18 years of publication, and are quoted frequently by universities themselves and by those with an interest in higher education, both at home and abroad.

Indeed, favourable results invariably appear prominently on universities' websites. Professor David Eastwood, now the Vice-Chancellor of Birmingham University and chief executive of the Higher Education Funding Council for England at the time of its review of university rankings, reminded universities at a conference to discuss its findings that they often "deplore league tables one day and deploy them the next". He said the tables had become part of the higher education landscape and one of the sources to which prospective students would refer when choosing where and what to study.

Four universities have refused to release information for newspaper league tables this year, although two – London Metropolitan and the West of Scotland – have ended their boycotts. West London University is the latest to join this group, having changed its name from Thames Valley. It argues that the new identity invalidates any comparisons with Thames Valley's performance. The university plans to return in the 2013 *Guide*, although the same argument would apply then.

Wolverhampton, another university (with Liverpool Hope and Swansea Metropolitan) to boycott league tables, says on its website that measures of its quality are available elsewhere – as they are, if you know where to look. But the way in which it quotes existing measures may help to explain why readers value the independent nature of guides such as this. Wolverhampton says, quite accurately, that it is among the top universities in the National Student Survey for the quality of its learning resources and access to specialist equipment, but it neglects to mention that it was barely in the top 90 universities in the 2010 survey for overall satisfaction.

In any case, this *Guide* contains far more than league tables. There are chapters on choosing a course and a university, the application process, managing your money as a student, where to live and what to expect in terms of sport. There are chapters, too, on employment and on going abroad to study. There are also special sections for overseas applicants and for parents, as well as profiles of every university and Oxbridge college.

Changing patterns of demand

The volume of applications for degree places in 2011 may not have matched the unprecedented increases seen in 2010, but the 6.5 per cent increase reported in March would have been regarded as considerable in any other year. Most universities and most subjects have enjoyed increased demand for places, but not all. Many vocational courses have seen a surge in popularity, but applicants were making their own judgements about the prospects for different areas of employment. Building courses were still struggling, for example, while computer science was enjoying a new lease of life.

Not surprisingly, given the economic picture, one discernible pattern appears to be continued growth in home-based study. The longstanding British preference for studying away from home had begun to reassert itself among those who could afford it, after a move in the opposite direction when top-up fees were introduced in 2006. Now, it may be that a change of culture will become established. Several of the big city post-1992 universities have seen the biggest growth in applications both in 2009 and 2010.

There is no consistent pattern of subject choices, however. For several years, students have been more conscious of the need for a marketable qualification to service growing levels of debt among graduates. But the initial rush away from pure academic subjects towards the vocational has not persisted. While some job-related degrees, including most branches of engineering, continue to prove attractive, subjects such as politics, with no direct link to employment, have again increased their popularity in 2011. Some subjects obviously have been affected by the recession, but prospective students seem to recognise that the majority of graduate jobs are open to any discipline. It will be interesting to see if the prospect of much higher fees alters behaviour in 2012.

One significant development will almost certainly be a rise in the popularity of part-time courses, encouraged by the introduction of the first proper system of student support. Although fees will rise, too, part-time education will become much more affordable through the provision of loans on courses that occupy at least 25 per cent of the time taken on an equivalent full-time course. Ministers expect many more students to take the option of spreading out their studies, where possible working at the same time.

What will not change, in all likelihood, is the growing tendency for UK students to remain within national borders. More Scots have applied to Scottish universities, where they no longer pay the graduate endowment; more Welsh are applying to study in Wales, although they will not have to do so to enjoy the advantage of reduced fees; and more English are chasing places at universities in England, with fewer looking further afield. There has been much speculation about increased interest in American and Continental universities as a consequence of higher fees in England, but this will surely be no more than a marginal change in 2012.

The other imponderable about the new fee levels is their impact on working-class participation in higher education, which has been rising – although far less than the Government would have liked. Previous fee changes were not all bad news for students of any background: the requirement to pay upfront was scrapped and grants, bursaries and scholarships made available to bring down the cost for those from poor backgrounds. This will still be the case under the new system, and it will be the fear of future debt, rather than student poverty, that will be the deterrent, if there is one. The institutional profiles include a section outlining the (sometimes complex) arrangements at each university where this information was available before this year's *Guide* went to press in spring 2011.

Finding a place

There were 1.3 applications per place in full-time higher education in every year of the 21st century until 2010, when the ratio was still less than 1.5 to the place. This is a significant change, but still far from impossible odds. More than 90 per cent of those with two A-level passes go on to higher education each year, and almost all of the remainder choose a different career path, rather than being rejected.

Commentators on higher education distinguish between "selecting universities" and "recruiting universities", but these labels underestimate the complexity of the choices facing today's applicants. Even now, there are very few universities where all the courses are heavily selective – there are simply not enough well-qualified candidates to go around in some subjects – and most so-called recruiting universities have areas in which they excel and can attract a strong field of applicants. This *Guide* uses the ratings of academics and students, plus entry standards and graduate employment rates, to differentiate between universities in 62 different subject areas.

When *The Times Good University Guide* first appeared, it helped to explode the myth that any British degree was as good as any other. Since then, the statistics behind the tables have confirmed significant variations in performance within British higher education. Employers distinguish between universities as well as individuals. The need to know the standing of a university, both as an institution and in the various subjects it offers, can only become more important as time goes on.

This year's tables

Unlike most of the rankings that have sprung up in recent years, *The Times Good University Guide* has maintained as much consistency as possible in the methods used to compare universities. The indicators and weightings used in the overall ranking of universities are the same as last year. One marginal change in the main table is a reweighting of the grades awarded in the 2008 Research Assessment Exercise to give universities extra credit for work considered to be world-leading. The previous scores mirrored the official system used to allocate research funds to universities in England and the new ones follow a change in that procedure.

There are four more universities in this year's *Times* league table, although only one is appearing for the first time. That is the University of the Highlands and Islands, which was awarded full university status in February 2011 after a long apprenticeship as the UHI Millennium Institute. Two others – London Metropolitan and the West of Scotland – have sanctioned the release of data after a period boycotting league tables. The final re-entrant – the University of Buckingham – featured in early editions of the *Guide*, but in recent years has not been able to provide sufficient data for a score to be compiled. Although its private status excluded the university from the Research Assessment Exercise, recent growth in student numbers means that it now has scores for every other indicator in the main table. It would almost certainly have finished in the top 20, rather than just outside it, if its research could be assessed.

The first *Times* ranking, in 1993, effectively produced a dead heat between Oxford and Cambridge, with the light blues a fraction of a point ahead. After several years of Cambridge domination, changes in methodology saw the roles reversed in the 2003 edition and Oxford subsequently extended its lead. The current table sees Oxford maintain its leadership, despite playing second fiddle to Cambridge in most of the subject tables. Cambridge has the better record on research, entry standards, completion rates and employment prospects, but Oxford's lead in staffing levels, degree classifications, student satisfaction and particularly in spending on libraries and other student facilities makes the difference. Accurate comparisons of the two are difficult because of the mix of college and central university responsibilities, but Oxford appears to include more college spending in its submission. Cambridge remains well ahead of the London School of Economics, which has moved up to third place this year. St Andrews remains the top university in Scotland and Cardiff the clear leader in Wales.

For most readers, however, the scramble over a handful of points at the top of the overall ranking of universities will be literally academic. The key information is contained in the subject tables, which now cover every area of higher education. One of the strengths of this *Guide*, and others like it, has been to highlight the quality of previously underestimated universities such as York and Bath, and to celebrate the achievements of centres of excellence such as the social sciences at Essex. Universities' own research suggests that well over half of all applicants use newspaper guides, and the proportion may well rise with the introduction of higher fees. Candidates have already become more selective about the courses they choose, as the financial pressures on students and their families have grown.

The benefits of information

Other important changes in higher education in recent years have included the introduction of incentives to extend access to a wider share of the population, and much more selective allocation of research funds. All the main political parties support moves to widen participation in higher education. But alongside the huge expansion in student numbers that has taken place over the last two decades there has been a gradual return to the hierarchical system that seemed to have been abandoned when the polytechnics acquired university status; only this time there are more than two tiers. Although a handful of post-1992 universities appear above one or two older foundations in this year's table, the divisions remain stark.

At the top of the pile, in terms of funding and prestige, is a group of little more than 20 universities, which attract 90 per cent of the resources available for research and also take the lion's share of money for teaching, partly because they offer expensive subjects such as medicine and engineering. A middle group, composed mainly of traditional universities, has been recruiting more undergraduates – especially overseas – while trying to compete on research. The remainder have remained healthy mainly by expanding, or at least maintaining student numbers, while interacting with local companies. The coming year will show whether this pattern is sustainable without the level of Government support that universities have traditionally enjoyed.

There always was a pecking order of sorts. Oxford and Cambridge were world leaders long before most British universities were established, and parts of the University of London have always enjoyed a high status in particular fields. But few outside the higher-education world could discriminate between Keele and Kent, for example.

Employers, careers advisers and certainly academics had their own ideas of which were the leading universities, but there was little hard evidence to back their conclusions. Often they were based on outdated, inaccurate impressions of distant institutions. The expanded higher education system has made such judgements more scientific as well as more necessary. Employers of graduates and those who commit their money to student sponsorship or funding research are comparing institutions department by department.

This has become possible because of a new transparency in what a former Higher Education Minister described as the "secret garden of academe". Official demands for more and more published information may have taxed the patience of university administrators, but they have also given outsiders the opportunity to make more meaningful comparisons. The **unistats.com** website represents the latest attempt to bring together the statistics relevant to applicants, and there are promises of further transparency from the Coalition Government. Universities will be required to publish the employment rates of individual courses and the average salaries of their graduates. But many readers value the more concise nature of guides such as this one, which distil the information displayed on such sites into a more manageable form.

Why university?

Particularly in an economic downturn, some will be tempted, once the cost of living has been added to the growing fees burden and the attractions of university life balanced against loss of potential earnings, to write off higher education. There are plenty of self-made millionaires who still swear by the University of Life as the only training ground for success. Yet even by narrow financial criteria it would be rash to dismiss higher education. With so many more competing for jobs, a degree will never again be an automatic passport to a fast-track career. But graduates' financial prospects remain much brighter than school leavers', as are their prospects in other important areas, such as health.

Even for those who cannot or do not wish to afford three or more years of full-time education after leaving school, university remains a possibility. The modular courses adopted by most universities enable students to work through a degree at their own pace, dropping out for a time if necessary, or switching to part-time attendance. Distance learning is another option, and advances in information technology now mean that some nominally full-time courses are delivered mainly via computers.

For many – perhaps most – students, therefore, the university experience is not what it was in their parents' day. There is more assessment, more crowding, more pressure to get the best possible degree while also finding gainful employment for at least part of the year. The proportion of students achieving first-class degrees has risen significantly, while an upper second (rather than the previously ubiquitous 2:2) has become the norm. Research shows that the classification has a real impact in the labour market.

An uncertain future

Universities are already facing serious cuts to their budgets, although they will more than recoup their losses if they can attract enough students and are allowed to do so by the Government. Already, some campuses have closed where universities are facing financial difficulties, and it is even possible that some institutions will close or merge with stronger neighbours. Every Government has shown a marked reluctance to close universities, but there is talk of private colleges or other companies taking over failing institutions this time.

Universities are often the biggest employers in their area, as well as a source of local pride, and a closure would be a big step, politically as well as educationally.

None of the changes seem unlikely to alter the long-term direction of travel for higher education, however. The system may shrink a little as a result of higher fees and a declining population of 18-year-olds. But numbers will remain more buoyant among the socio-economic groups that provide the bulk of university students than in the population as a whole, so the effects of demographic change may be less dramatic than many commentators have predicted.

In the future it is likely that more students will begin (and some also finish) their degrees at further education colleges, more will opt initially for two-year courses and the range both of subjects and teaching methods will grow still further. The private sector, which is a significant force in higher education in many other countries, may finally develop in the UK. Some predict the rise of the "virtual university" or the demise of the conventional higher-education institution, as companies customise their own courses. However, universities have demonstrated enduring popularity and most show every sign of weathering the current turbulence.

1 What and Where to Study

When the coalition government announced that undergraduate fees at English universities would vary from less than £6,000 to a maximum of £9,000, it appeared that price would become a new and important factor in decisions on what and where to study. Even though payments will not be made up-front, a difference of up to £10,000 in the overall price of a degree would surely be enough to influence many prospective students. In the event, it seems that in most cases the difference between the top and bottom of this intended market will not be sufficiently wide to tip the balance between different universities, although some further education colleges will still offer substantial savings.

That does not mean, of course, that financial considerations will be irrelevant to the decision-making process. Students will want to keep their debts to a minimum and are bound to take the cost of living into account. They will also want the best possible career prospects and may choose their subject accordingly.

But your choice of course and university must be about more than money: these are life-shaping decisions. The outcome will help determine the direction of your career and personal life far beyond the next three or four years (and they are important enough). Many graduates end up living and working near their university; they may make their closest friends in their student days and may even meet their future partner there. So finding the right university demands serious thought and research, and this *Guide* may play an important part.

Setting your priorities

All over the world, career prospects are uppermost in the mind of most people considering a higher education course. As graduate unemployment rises in the UK and the cost of going to university grows dramatically, economic considerations are sure to become even more dominant. Yet there are good reasons not to let fear of the future squeeze out all other considerations.

No one knows which subjects will be in demand when the downturn ends, but graduates will almost certainly be in a stronger position than those who choose not to invest in better qualifications. The majority of graduate jobs are not subject-specific – employers value the transferable skills that higher education confers. Rightly or wrongly, however, most employers are influenced by which university a graduate attended, so the choice of institution remains as important as ever.

Some students may cut their costs by taking a part-time course; others by enrolling on a two-year Foundation degree, which can be converted into an honours degree later. But, at a time of low employment generally, logic suggests that it would be a false economy to dismiss higher education entirely.

Those who want to add value to their degree in the jobs market will find that growing numbers of universities are offering employment-related schemes that are considered in more detail in chapter 2. In many cases, this will involve work experience or extra activities organised by the careers service. Some universities, such as Leicester, now run certificated employability programmes, while others, such as Liverpool John Moores, have built such skills into degree programmes. Such programmes are also highlighted in chapter 2 and in the institutional profiles in chapter 13 and should be described in detail on university websites.

Key reasons for going to university

To improve job opportunities	**74%**
To improve salary prospects	**60%**
To improve knowledge in an area of interest	**58%**
To specialise in a certain subject / area	**47%**
To obtain an additional qualification	**46%**
Essential to my chosen profession	**43%**
To experience a different way of life	**41%**
It's the obvious next step	**40%**
To have a good social life	**31%**
My parents expected me to	**24%**
I didn't want to get a job straightaway	**23%**
I didn't know what else to do	**18%**
All my friends were going	**14%**
Can live at home and still go to university	**9%**

Sodexo University Lifestyle Survey 2008

Is higher education for you?

Before you start, there is one important question to ask yourself: what do you want out of higher education? The answer will make it easier to choose where (and if) to be a student. With more than a third of school-leavers going on to university, it is easy to drift that way without much thought, opting for the subject in which you expect the best grades and looking for a university with a reasonable reputation and a good social life. Your career will look after itself – you hope.

With graduate debt soaring, however, and job prospects varying widely between subjects, now is the time to look at your own motivation. Love of a subject is perhaps the best reason for taking a degree, and one that allows you to focus almost exclusively on the search for a course that corresponds with your passions. If, on the other hand, higher education is a means to an end, you need to think about career ambitions and look carefully at employment rates for any courses you might consider.

Many graduates look back on their student days as the best years of their lives, and there is nothing wrong with wanting to have a good time. Remember, though, that you will be paying for it later (literally) and there will be more studying than partying. If you have not enjoyed sixth-form or college courses, you may be better off in a job and possibly becoming one of the hundreds of thousands each year who return to education later in life.

Narrowing down the field

Once you have decided that higher education is for you, the good news is that, as long as you start early enough, finding the right university can be relatively straightforward. Media attention focuses on the scramble for places on a relatively small proportion of courses where competition is intense, but there are plenty of places at good universities for candidates with the basic qualifications – it's just a matter of finding the one that suits you best. For older applicants, relevant work experience and demonstrable interest in a subject may be enough to win a place.

If anything, the problem is that of too much choice. Students prepared to move away from home will have more than 100 universities and numerous specialist colleges to consider, most with hundreds – even thousands – of course combinations on offer. Institutions come in all shapes and sizes, so there is work to do at the outset narrowing down your options.

Deciding what you want to study may reduce the field considerably – there are only seven institutions offering veterinary medicine for example, although the total is closer to 100 in subjects such as law and English. By the time you have factored in personal preferences about the type or location of your ideal university, the list of possibilities may already be reduced to manageable proportions.

After that, you can take a closer look at what the courses contain and what life is really like for students. Prospectuses and university websites will give you an accurate account of course combinations, and important facts like the accommodation available to new students, but it is their job to sell the university. To get a true picture, you need more – preferably a visit not just to the university, but to the department where you would be studying. If that is not possible, there are plenty of other sources of objective information, such as the National Student Survey (which is available online, with a range of additional data about each institution, at **www.unistats.direct.gov.uk**).

Many students' unions publish alternative prospectuses, giving a "warts and all" view of the university, and those that do not provide this service may be able to arrange a brief discussion with a current student, either by phone or email. Your school or college may put you in contact with someone who went to a university that you are considering. Guides and collections of statistics may give you valuable information about a course or a university, but there is no substitute for personal experience.

What to study?

Most people seeking a place in higher education start by choosing a subject and a course, rather than a university. If you take a degree, you are going to spend at least three years immersed in your subject. It has to be one you will enjoy and can master – not to mention one that you are qualified to study. Many economics degrees require maths, for example, while some medical schools demand chemistry or biology. The UCAS website (**www.ucas.com**) contains course profiles, including entrance requirements, which is a good starting point, while universities' own sites contain more detailed information. In chapter 5, we describe 62 subject areas and provide league tables for each of them.

Your school subjects and the UCAS tariff

The official yardstick by which your results will be judged is the UCAS tariff (see page 18), which gives a score for each grade of most UK qualifications considered relevant for university entrance, as well as for the International Baccalaureate (IB). This tariff has become more controversial as more subjects and types of qualifications have been included in it. Top scores in the new vocational diplomas, for example, attract more points than a full set of A grades at A level, while the most successful IB students already earn considerably more points. If this process continues, it is likely that more of the leading universities will abandon the tariff, as some have done already, choosing instead to frame their offers using actual grades.

A recent change increased the points awarded for high grades in Scottish qualifications. A review raised the number of points awarded for grade A Highers from 72 to 80 points, while an

The UCAS Tariff

Tariffs for selected qualifications are given below.

The full range of acceptable qualifications and their tariff values are given at

www.ucas.com/students/ucas_tariff/tarifftables

GCE AS/AS VCE	GCE AS Double Award	GCE A level/A VCE	A level with additional AS (9 units)	GCE/AVCE Double Award	Points	Advanced Higher	Higher
						GCE/VCE Qualifications	Points	Scottish Qualifications
				A*A*	280		
				A*A	260		
				AA	240		
				AB	220		
			A*A	BB	200		
			AA	BC	180		
			AB		170		
				CC	160		
			BB		150		
		A*	BC	CD	140		
					130	A	
	AA	A	CC	DD	120		
	AB		CD		110	B	
	BB	B		DE	100		
	BC		DD		90	C	
	CC	C	DE	EE	80		A
					72	D	
	CD				70		
					65		B
A	DD	D	EE		60		
B	DE				50		C
C	EE	E			40		
					36		D
D					30		
E					20		

UCAS Tariff for the International Baccalaureate

Points for the International Baccalaureate (IB) are awarded to candidates who achieve the IB Dip.

IB Dip	Points	IB Dip	Points	IB Dip	Points	IB Dip	Points	IB Dip	Points
45	720	40	611	35	501	30	392	25	282
44	698	39	589	34	479	29	370	24	260
43	676	38	567	33	457	28	348		
42	654	37	545	32	435	27	326		
41	632	36	523	31	413	26	304		

A in Advanced Highers has risen from 120 to 130 points – ten points more than a grade A at A level. Grades B and C are also worth more, although a D in an Advanced Higher has stayed at 72 points and a Higher grade D actually dropped from 42 to 36 points.

"Soft subjects"

There is a separate issue for some of the top universities about the subjects studied at A level. The variety of A-level courses now available includes many subjects that they do not consider on a par with traditional academic subjects. For many years, a minority of universities have refused to accept General Studies as a full A level for entrance purposes (although even some leading universities do). The growth of supposedly "soft" subjects, such as media studies and photography, has prompted a few universities to produce lists of subjects that will only be accepted as a third, or fourth, A level. The London School of Economics would prefer to see only one subject from the list shown below in your mix of A levels subjects.

The Russell Group of 20 leading universities, of which Cambridge is one, has now published an extremely useful report, called *Informed Choices* (**http://russellgroup.org/ Informed%20Choices%20final.pdf**), on the post-16 qualifications preferred by its members for a wide range of degrees. Although it names media studies, art and design, photography and business studies among the vocational subjects that would normally be given this label, it does not subscribe to the notion of a single list of "soft" subjects. The report suggests limiting the number of vocational subjects to one, and choosing mainly from a list of "facilitating subjects", which are required for many degrees and welcomed generally at Russell Group universities. The list comprises maths and further maths, English, physics, biology, chemistry, geography, languages (classical and modern) and history. In addition their guide indicates the "essential" and "useful" A-level subjects for 60 different subject areas studied at Russell Group universities.

For most courses at most universities, there are no such restrictions, although those choosing A levels would be wise to bear these lists in mind if they are likely to apply to one or more of the leading universities. At the very least, it is an indication of the subjects that admissions tutors may take less seriously than the rest. Although only the London School of Economics identifies those subjects publicly, others may adopt less formal weightings.

A-level subjects only acceptable as a third or fourth subject at the London School of Economics

» Accounting
» Art and Design
» Business Studies
» Communication and Culture
» Dance
» Design and Technology
» Drama/Theatre Studies
» Environmental Studies

» Film Studies
» Home Economics
» Information and Communication Technology
» Law
» Media Studies
» Music Technology
» Sports Studies
» Travel and Tourism

General Studies and Critical Thinking A levels will only be considered as fourth A level subjects and will not therefore be accepted as part of a conditional offer.

Diplomas

This concern about "soft subjects" also applies to the new diplomas, just as it has to vocational qualifications down the years. Although there has been university involvement in designing the diplomas, there remains confusion about which are accepted by leading universities – especially for admission to degree courses outside the direct scope of the diploma. The engineering diploma has now won near-universal approval (for admission to engineering courses and possibly some science degrees), but some of the other diplomas are in fields that are not on the curriculum of the most selective universities. Regardless of the points awarded under the tariff, it is essential to contact universities direct to ensure that a diploma will be an acceptable qualification for your chosen degree.

Use of tariffs and admission tests

While the majority of universities use the tariff to make offers of places, those that are heavily oversubscribed will tend to demand particular grades at A level, often naming the subjects in

---

Admissions tests

Some of the most competitive courses now have additional entrance tests. The most significant tests are listed below. A few others may also require tests, so check the course details on the UCAS website.

BioMedical Admissions Test (BMAT): for entry to medicine and veterinary medicine at Cambridge, Imperial College London, Oxford, Royal Veterinary College, University College London.
Standard closing date for 2012 admissions is 30 September 2011.
www.admissionstests.cambridgeassessment.org.uk/adt/bmat

English Literature Admissions Test (ELAT): for entry to English at Oxford.
Closing date for 2011 entry is 14 October 2011; test 2 November 2011.
www.admissionstests.cambridgeassessment.org.uk/adt/elat

Graduate Medical School Admissions Test (GAMSAT): for graduate entry to medicine and dentistry at Keele, Nottingham, Peninsula College of Medicine and Dentistry, St. George's University of London, Swansea.
Closing date for registration is 12 August 2011.
www.gamsatuk.org

Health Professions Admissions Test (HPAT): for certain medical courses at Ulster.
Closing date for 2012 registration not confirmed. For 2011 admissions it was 12 January 2011.
www.hpat.org.uk

National Admissions Test for Law (LNAT): for entry to law courses at Birmingham, Bristol, Durham, Glasgow, King's College London, Nottingham, Oxford, University College London.
Registration opens 2 August 2011; tests between 1 September and 20 October 2011.
www.lnat.ac.uk

Modern and Medieval Languages Test (MML): for entry to modern and medieval languages at Cambridge, taken at Cambridge during interview process.
www.cam.ac.uk/admissions/undergraduate/courses/mml/tests.html

which the highest grades are required. There are no set rules about using the tariff. Some universities will give credit for qualifications in key skills, for example, while others exclude them from candidates' points totals. In certain universities, some departments, but not others, will use the tariff to set offers. The university's prospectus or website should show which does what. In addition, some universities now require applicants in particular subject areas that are heavily oversubscribed, such as medicine and law, to take an entrance test. The details are listed in the boxes below.

Making a choice

Your A levels, or Scottish Highers, may have chosen themselves, but the range of subjects across the whole university system is vast. Even subjects that you have studied at school may be quite different at degree level – some academic economists actually prefer their undergraduates not to have taken economics A level because they approach the subject so differently. Other students are disappointed because they appear to be going over old ground when they

---

Oxford tests: Oxford university administers its own tests for: classics II, computer science, history, joint courses including history, mathematics, joint courses including mathematics, modern languages (if course includes linguistics), physics, physics and philosophy. Test taken on 2 November 2011, usually at candidate's educational institution.
www.ox.ac.uk/admissions/undergraduate_courses/how_to_apply/tests

Sixth Term Examination Papers (STEP): for entry to mathematics at Cambridge and Warwick (also encouraged by Bristol, Bath, Imperial College London, and Oxford).
Standard closing date for 2011 entry is 29 April 2011. Date for 2012 entry to be announced in September 2011.
http://www.admissionstests.cambridgeassessment.org.uk/adt/step

Thinking Skills Assessment (TSA) Cambridge: mainly for computer science, economics, engineering, land economy (some colleges) and natural sciences at most Cambridge colleges, taken at Cambridge during interview process.
www.admissionstests.cambridgeassessment.org.uk/adt/tsacambridge

Thinking Skills Assessment (TSA) Oxford: for economics and management, experimental psychology, philosophy, politics and economics (PPE), and psychology and philosophy.
Last date for entry is 14 October 2011; test taken 2 November 2011.
www.admissionstests.cambridgeassessment.org.uk/adt/tsaoxford

Thinking Skills Assessment (TSA) UCL: for entry to European social and political studies at University College London; the test is arranged in the interview process
www.admissionstests.cambridgeassessment.org.uk/adt/tsaucl

UK Clinical Aptitude Test (UKCAT): for entry to medical and dental schools at Aberdeen, Brighton and Sussex Medical School, Barts and the London School of Medicine and Dentistry, Cardiff, Dundee, Durham, East Anglia, Edinburgh, Glasgow, Hull York Medical School, Imperial College London (graduate entry), Keele, King's College London, Leeds, Leicester, Manchester, Newcastle, Nottingham, Oxford (graduate entry), Peninsula College of Medicine and Dentistry, Queen's University, Belfast, Sheffield, Southampton, St Andrews, St George's University of London, Warwick (graduate entry).
Registration deadline for candidates for 2012 entry is 23 September 2011; tests from 5 July to 7 October 2011.
www.ukcat.ac.uk

continue with a subject that they enjoyed at school. Universities now publish quite detailed syllabuses, and it is a matter of going through the fine print.

The greater difficulty comes in judging your suitability for the many subjects that are not on the school or college curriculum. Philosophy and psychology sound fascinating (and are), but you may have no idea what degrees in either subject entail – for example, the level of statistics that may be required. Forensic science may look exciting on television – more glamorous than plain chemistry – but it opens fewer doors, as the type of work portrayed in *Silent Witness* or *Raising the Dead* is very hard to find.

Vocational subjects

The introduction of top-up fees encouraged more students into job-related subjects, rather than traditional academic disciplines, in the hope of improving their employment prospects. It will be no surprise if the new, much higher fees accelerate the trend. This is understandable and, if you are sure of your future career path, possibly also sensible. But much depends on what that career is – and whether you are ready to make such a long-term commitment. Some of the programmes that have attracted public ridicule, such as surf science or golf course management, may narrow graduates' options to a worrying extent, but there is nothing wrong with their employment records. Jibes about so-called "Mickey Mouse" courses have become less frequent, although there are some who are yet to accept that the higher education curriculum has moved into new areas since they were students.

Many vocational courses are tailored to particular professions. If you choose one of these, make sure that the degree is recognised by the relevant professional body (such as the Engineering Council or one of the institutes) or you may not be able to use the skills that you acquire. Most universities are only too keen to make such recognition clear in their prospectus; if no such guarantee is published, contact the university department running the course and seek assurances.

Even where a course has professional recognition, bear in mind that a further qualification may be required to practise. Both law and medicine, for example, demand additional training to become a fully qualified solicitor, barrister or doctor. Nor is either degree an automatic passport to a job: only about half of all law graduates go into the profession and the UK is now training more medical students than the National Health Service can afford. Both law and medicine also provide a route into the profession for graduates who have taken other subjects.

The ten most popular subject groups by applications		The ten most popular subject groups by acceptances	
1 Nursing	145,092	1 Nursing	27,079
2 Business and management studies	141,840	2 Business and management studies	25,187
3 Subjects allied to medicine	133,298	3 Subjects allied to medicine	22,643
4 Law	108,487	4 Law	21,913
5 Design studies	95,461	5 Computer science subjects	19,072
6 Psychology	91,509	6 Design studies	18,819
7 Pre-clinical medicine	83,948	7 Psychology	16,138
8 Computer science subjects	74,867	8 Social work	11,204
9 English studies	55,775	9 Sports science	10,974
10 Training teachers	54,415	10 English studies	10,116

UCAS 2011 (number of applicants to 21 February 2011)   UCAS acceptances in 2010

Law conversion courses, though not cheap, are increasingly popular, and there is a growing number of graduate-entry medical degrees.

One way to ensure that a degree is job-related is to take a "sandwich" course, which involves up to a year in business or industry. Students often end up working for the organisation which provided the placement, while others gain valuable insights into a field of employment – even if only to discount it. The drawback with such courses is that, like the year abroad that is part of most language degrees, the period away from university inevitably disrupts living arrangements and friendship groups. But most of those who take this route find that the career benefits make this a worthwhile sacrifice.

Academic or vocational courses?

Employers' organisations calculate that more than half of all graduate jobs are open to applicants from any subject, and recruiters for the most competitive graduate training schemes often prefer traditional academic subjects to apparently relevant vocational degrees. Newspapers, for example, often prefer a history graduate to one with a media studies degree; computing firms take a disproportionate number of classicists. A good degree classification and the right work experience are more important than the subject for most non-technical jobs. But it is hard to achieve a good result on a course that you do not enjoy, so scour prospectuses, and email or phone university departments to ensure that you know what you are letting yourself in for. Their reaction to your approach will also give you an idea of how responsive they are to their students.

If you are not sure whether you will be suited to a particular subject, you can take an online aptitude test through the UCAS website. The "Choosing courses" section gives you access to the Stamford Test, which uses an online questionnaire to match your interests and strengths to possible courses and careers (**www.ucas.com/students/choosingcourses/ choosingcourse//stamfordtest**).

Studying more than one subject

You may find that more than one subject appeals, in which case you could consider Joint Honours – degrees that combine two subjects – or even Combined Honours, which will cover several related subjects. Such courses obviously allow you to extend the scope of your studies, but they should be approached with caution. Even if the number of credits suggests a similar workload to Single Honours, covering more than one subject inevitably involves extra reading and often more essays or project work.

However, there are advantages. Many students choose a "dual" to add a vocational element to make themselves more employable – business studies with languages or engineering, for example, or media studies with English. Others want to take their studies in a particular direction, perhaps by combining history with politics, or statistics with maths. Some simply want to add a completely unrelated interest to their main subject, such as environmental science and music, or archaeology and event management – both combinations that are available at UK universities.

At most universities, however, it is not necessary to take a degree in more than one subject in order to broaden your studies. The spread of modular programmes ensures that you can take courses in related subjects without changing the basic structure of your degree. You may not be able to take an event management module in a single-honours archaeology degree, but it should be possible to study some history, or a language. The number and scope of the combinations offered at many of the larger universities is extraordinary. Indeed, it has been criticised by academics who believe that "mix-and-match" degrees can leave a graduate without a rounded view of a subject. But for those who seek breadth and variety, close scrutiny of university prospectuses (whether online or on paper) is a vital part of the selection process.

What type of course?
Once you have a subject, you must decide on the level and type of course. Most readers of this *Guide* will be looking for full-time degree courses, but higher education is much broader than that. You may not be able to afford the time or the money needed for a full-time commitment of three or four years at this point in your life.

Part-time courses
Tens of thousands of people each year opt for a part-time course – usually while holding down a job – to continue learning and improve their career prospects. But, with little or no financial support available from the Government, the numbers have been dropping over recent years. That may well change in 2012 both because of the high fees for full-time courses and the introduction of a much more generous system of student support for part-time students.

Under the new arrangements, loans will be available for students whose courses occupy between a quarter and three-quarters of the time expected on a full-time course. Repayments will be on the same conditions as those for full-time courses, except that repayments will begin after three years of study even if the course has not been completed by then. The downside is that universities may increase their fees in the knowledge that part-time students will be able to take out student loans to cover fees, but the change should still be beneficial.

Part-time study can be exhausting unless your employer gives you time off, but if you have the stamina for a course that will usually take twice as long as the full-time equivalent, this route should still make a degree more affordable. Part-time students tend to be highly committed to their subject, and many claim that the quality of the social life associated with their course makes up for the quantity of leisure time enjoyed by full-timers.

Distance learning
Another option, if you are confident that you can manage without regular face-to-face contact with teachers and fellow students, is distance learning. Courses are delivered mainly or entirely online or through correspondence, although some programmes offer a certain amount of local tuition. The process might sound daunting and impersonal, but students of the Open University (OU), all of whom are educated in this way, are the most satisfied in the country, according to the results of the annual National Student Survey. Attending lectures or oversized seminars at a conventional university can be less personal than regular contact with your tutor at a distance. Of course, not all universities are as good at communicating with their distance-learning students as the OU, or offer such high-quality course materials, but this mode of study does give students ultimate flexibility to determine when and where they study. Distance learning is becoming increasingly popular for the delivery of professional courses, which are often needed to supplement degrees. The OU now takes students of all ages, including a growing number of school-leavers, not just mature students.

Foundation degrees
Even if you are set on a full-time course, you might not want to commit yourself for three or more years. Growing numbers are taking two-year Foundation degrees – vocational courses which the Government would like to be the main source of expansion in universities and

colleges. Many other students take longer-established two-year courses, such as Higher National Diplomas or other diplomas tailored to the needs of industry or parts of the health service. Those who do well on such courses usually have the option of converting their qualification into a full degree with further study, although many are satisfied without immediately staying on for the further two or more years that completing a BA or BSc will require.

Other short courses

A number of universities are experimenting with two-year degrees, squeezing more work into an extended academic year. The so-called "third semester" makes use of the summer vacation for extra teaching, so that mature students, in particular, can reduce the length of their career break. Several universities are offering accelerated degrees as part of a pilot project initiated under the last Government. But the pattern has really only caught on at the University of Buckingham, the UK's only established private university, where it has had a small but enthusiastic following for more than 30 years.

Other short courses – usually lasting a year – are designed for students who do not have the necessary qualifications to start a degree in their chosen subject. Foundation courses in art and design have been common for many years, and are the chosen preparation for a degree at leading departments, even for many students whose A levels would win them a degree place elsewhere. Access courses perform the same function in a wider range of subjects for students without A levels, or for those whose grades are either too low or in the wrong subjects to gain admission to a particular course. Entry requirements are modest, but students have to reach the same standard as regular entrants if they are to progress to a degree.

Yet more choice

No single guide can allow for personal preferences in choosing a course. You may want one of the many degrees that incorporate a year at a partner university abroad, or to try a six-month exchange on the Continent through the European Union's Erasmus Programme. Either might prove a valuable experience and add to your employability. You might prefer a January or February start to the traditional autumn start – there are plenty of opportunities for this, mainly at new universities. In some subjects – particularly engineering and the sciences – the leading degrees may be Masters courses, taking four years rather than three (in England).

Subjects with the highest ratio of applications to acceptances 2010

1	Dentistry	10.3
2	Medicine	10.2
3	Veterinary medicine	8.6
4	Anatomy, physiology and pathology	8.4
5	Training teachers	7.5
6	Aural and oral sciences	7.4
7	Social Work	7.3
8	Nursing	7.2
9	Drama	7.0
10	Architecture	6.9

UCAS 2010

Universities with the highest application to place ratio 2010

1	Brighton and Sussex Medical School	19.5
2	London School of Economics	14.5
3	Edinburgh	11.9
4	Bristol	10.2
5	St George's University of London	9.9
6	King's College London	9.1
7	City	8.7
8	Warwick	8.3
8	Peninsula College of Medicine & Dentistry	8.3
10	Hull York Medical School	8.2

UCAS 2010

Job prospects

Even before the recession, job prospects were the key element in choosing a subject for many (probably most) students. Chapter 2 examines this topic in detail, providing information on employment prospects by subject and initial starting salaries by subject, as well as giving advice on how to enhance your chances in the jobs market.

Where to study

Once you have decided what to study, there are still several factors that might influence your choice of university or college. Obviously, you need to have a reasonable chance of getting in, you may want reassurance about the university's reputation, and its location will probably also be important to you. On top of that, most applicants have views about the type of institution they are looking for – big or small, old or new, urban or rural, specialist or comprehensive. You may surprise yourself by choosing somewhere that does not conform to your initial criteria, but working through your preferences is another way of narrowing down your options.

Non-academic factors considered when choosing a university

Good impression from open days	**51%**
Friendly atmosphere	**46%**
Attractive university environment	**42%**
Active social life and good social facilities	**31%**
Campus university	**31%**
Close to transport links	**28%**
Living away from home, but sufficiently close if support needed	**27%**
City centre university	**26%**
Recommendation from friends	**23%**
Quality of accommodation	**22%**
Close to home/able to live at home	**21%**
Internet research favourable to university	**18%**
Advice from teachers	**16%**
Low cost of living	**14%**
Cost of accommodation	**13%**
Advice from parents	**11%**
Good sporting facilities	**10%**
Opportunities for part-time jobs	**8%**

Sodexo University Lifestyle Survey 2008

Entry standards

Unless you are a mature student or have taken a gap year, your passport to your chosen university will be a conditional offer based on your predicted grades, previous exam performance, personal statement and school or college reference. A lucky few may get an offer that is so low that success is a foregone conclusion – because the university considers them outstanding and needs no further evidence of their potential. But only those who already have their grades receive unconditional offers.

Supply and demand dictate whether you will receive an offer – the odds may be slightly better this year if there is a reaction to the imposition of higher fees, but large numbers will still apply. Beyond the national picture, your chances will be affected both by the university and the subject you choose. A few universities (but not many) at the top of the league tables are heavily oversubscribed in every subject; others will have areas in which they excel, but may make relatively modest demands for entry to other courses. Even in many of the leading universities, the number of applicants for each place in languages or engineering is still not high. Conversely, three As at A level will not guarantee a place on one of the top English or law degrees, but there are enough universities running courses to ensure that three Cs will put you in with a chance somewhere. The difference in the last two years has been that the pressure on places in popular subjects is greater than before at the more lowly ranked universities.

University prospectuses and the UCAS website will give you the "standard offer" for each course, but in some cases this is pitched deliberately low in order to leave admissions staff extra flexibility. The standard A-level offer for medicine, for example, is often two As and a B, but nearly all successful applicants have three As or more.

The average entry scores in our subject tables give the actual points obtained by successful applicants – many of which are far above the offer made by the university, but which give an indication of the pecking order at entry. The subject tables (in chapter 5) are, naturally, a better guide than the main table (in chapter 4), where average entry scores are influenced by the range of subjects available at each university.

Location

The most obvious starting point is the country you study in. Most degrees in Scotland take four years, rather than the UK norm of three. It is possible, but not normal, for A-level candidates to go straight into the second year of a Scottish degree course. Otherwise, four years obviously cost more than three, especially given the loss of the year's salary you might have been earning after graduation. A later chapter will go into the details of the system, but suffice to say that students from Scotland pay no fees (a situation expected to continue when arrangements for 2012 are confirmed), while those from the rest of the UK do. Nevertheless, Edinburgh and St Andrews remain particularly popular with English students, and more than 1,000 students from Northern Ireland entered Scottish universities in 2010.

Close to home

Far from crossing national boundaries, however, growing numbers of students choose to study near home, whether or not they continue to live with their family. This may be to cut costs or for personal reasons, such as family circumstances, a girlfriend or boyfriend, continuing employment, or religion. Some simply want to stick with what they know. But the trend for full-time students who do go away to study, is to choose a university within about two hours' travelling time. The assumption is that this is far enough to discourage parents from making unannounced visits, but close enough to allow for occasional trips home to get the washing done and have a decent meal. The leading universities recruit from all over the world, but most still have a regional core.

The ten most popular universities for living at home		
1	Wolverhampton	8,900
2	Glasgow Caledonian	7,845
3	Ulster	7,210
4	London Metropolitan	6,800
5	Westminster	6,635
6	Manchester Metropolitan	6,505
7	Glasgow	6,170
8	Northumbria	6,080
9	Kent	6,040
10	Glamorgan	5,905

HESA 2008

The ten most popular universities by applications for degree courses		
1	Manchester	51,627
2	Manchester Metropolitan	51,493
3	Leeds	48,539
4	Nottingham	44,396
4	Sheffield Hallam	42,408
6	Leeds Metropolitan	39,965
7	Birmingham	39,628
8	Nottingham Trent	39,374
9	Edinburgh	38,073
10	Bristol	37,404

UCAS applications to 15 January 2011

University or college?

This guide is primarily concerned with universities, the destination of choice for the vast majority of higher education students. But there are other options – and not just for those searching for lower fees. A number of specialist higher education colleges offer a similar, or sometimes superior, quality of course in their particular fields. The subject tables in Chapter 5 chart the successes of various colleges in art, agriculture, music and teacher training in particular. Some colleges of higher education are not so different from the newer universities and may acquire that status themselves in future years.

The second group of colleges offering degrees are further education colleges. These are often large institutions with a wide range of courses, from A levels to vocational subjects at different levels, up to degrees in some cases. Although their numbers of higher education students have been falling in recent years, the new fee structure presents them with a fresh opportunity because they tend not to bear all the costs of a university campus. For that reason, too, they may not offer a broad student experience of the type that universities pride themselves on, but the best colleges respond well to the local labour market and offer small teaching groups and effective personal support.

FE colleges are a local resource and tend to attract mature students who cannot or do not want to travel to university. Many of their higher education students apply nowhere else. But, as competition for university places has increased, they have become more of an option for school-leavers, and for their own students, to continue their studies, as they always have done in Scotland. Ministers hope that they will now also become more attractive by virtue of price.

Both further and higher education colleges are audited by the Quality Assurance Agency and appear in the National Student Survey, where their results often show wide variation. Some demonstrate higher levels of satisfaction among their students than most universities.

The final group of colleges that present an alternative to university has been insignificant in terms of size until now, but may also prosper under the new fee regime. This is the private sector, seen mainly in business and law but also in some other specialist fields. The best-known currently is BPP University College, which was given that title in 2010 and offers degrees, as well as shorter courses, in both law and business subjects. Like Buckingham, the only private university in the UK, BPP runs two-year degrees with short vacations to maximise teaching time – a model that other private providers are likely to follow. In 2011, fees for an entire BPP

The ten universities that scored highest in the 2012 *Times* table for student satisfaction		The ten universities that scored highest in the 2012 *Times* table for graduate prospects	
1	Buckingham	88%	1	Buckingham	87.5%
2	Oxford	86%	2	Imperial College	86.7%
3	Loughborough	85%	3	Cambridge	85.5%
=4	Aberystwyth	84%	4	Oxford	85.0%
=4	Cambridge	84%	5	London School of Economics	84.1%
=4	Leicester	84%	6	King's College London	82.6%
=7	East Anglia	83%	7	University College London	81.1%
=7	Exeter	83%	8	Durham	80.4%
=7	Glasgow	83%	=9	Bath	77.9%
=7	St Andrews	83%	=9	Nottingham	77.9%

degree were £10,800 and, while they are expected to rise in 2012, they will remain "competitively priced", according to the college's website.

City universities
The most popular universities, in terms of total applications, are nearly all in big cities – generally with other major centres of population within that two-hour travelling window. For those looking for the best nightclubs, top sporting events, high-quality shopping or a varied cultural life – in other words, most young people, and especially those who live in cities already – city universities are a magnet. The big universities also, by definition, offer the widest range of subjects, although that does not mean that they necessarily have the particular course that is right for you. Nor does it mean that you will actually use the array of nightlife and shopping that looks so alluring in the prospectus, either because you cannot afford to, because student life is focused on the university, or even because you are too busy working.

Campus universities
City universities are the right choice for many young people, but it is worth bearing in mind that the National Student Survey shows that the highest satisfaction levels tend to be at smaller universities, often those with their own self-contained campuses. It seems that students identify more closely with institutions where there is a close-knit community and the social life is based around the students' union rather than the local nightclubs.

Few UK universities are in genuinely rural locations, but some – particularly among the newly promoted – are in relatively small towns. Several longer-established institutions in Wales and Scotland also share this type of setting, where the university dominates the town.

Importance of Open Days
The only way to be certain if this, or any other type of university, is for you is to visit. Schools often restrict the number of open days that sixth-formers can attend in term-time, but some universities offer a weekend alternative. The full calendar of events is available at **www.opendays.com** and on universities' own websites. Bear in mind, if you only attend one or two, that the event has to be badly mismanaged for a university not to seem an exciting place to someone who spends his or her days at school, or even college. Try to get a flavour of several institutions before you make your choice.

How many universities to pick?
When that time comes, of course, you will not be making one choice but five; four if you are applying for medicine, dentistry or veterinary science. (Full details of the application process are given in chapter 6.) Tens of thousands of students each year eventually go to a university that did not start out as their first choice, either because they did not get the right offer or because they changed their mind along the way. UCAS rules are such that applicants do not list universities in order of preference anyway – indeed, universities are not allowed to know where else you have applied. So do not pin all your hopes on one course; take just as much care choosing the other universities on your list.

The value of an "insurance" choice
Until recently, nearly all applicants included at least one "insurance" choice on that list – a university or college where entry grades were significantly lower than at their preferred institutions. This practice has been in decline, presumably because candidates expecting high

grades think they can pick up a lower offer either in Clearing or through UCAS Extra, the service that allows applicants rejected by their original choices to apply to courses that still have vacancies after the first round of offers. However, it is easy to miscalculate and leave yourself without a place that you want. You may not like the look of the options in Clearing, leaving yourself with an unwelcome and potentially expensive year off at a time when jobs are thin on the ground.

If you are at all uncertain about your grades, including an insurance choice remains a sensible course of action – especially since entry requirements have risen in response to increased demand for places. Indeed, even if you are sure that you will match the standard offers of your chosen universities, there is no guarantee that they will make you an offer. Particularly for degrees demanding three As at A level, there may simply be too many highly qualified applicants to offer places to all of them, for example, UCAS estimates that the odds against winning a place on one of the top ten English degrees for those who made no other choices was 10:1 in 2009. The main proviso for insurance choices, as with all others, is that you must be prepared to take up that place. If not, you might as well go for broke with courses with higher standard offers and take your chances in Clearing, or even retake exams if you drop grades. Thousands of applicants each year end up rejecting their only offer when they could have had a second, insurance, choice.

Reputation

The reputation of a university is something intangible, usually built up over a long period and sometimes outlasting reality. Before universities were subject to external assessment and the publication of copious statistics, reputation was rooted in the distant past. League tables are partly responsible for changing that, although employers are often influenced by what they remember as the pecking order of higher education institutions when they were students.

The fragmentation of the British university system into groups of institutions is another factor: the Russell Group (**www.russellgroup.ac.uk**) represents 20 research-intensive universities, nearly all with medical schools; the 1994 Group (**www.1994group.ac.uk**) a similar number of smaller research universities; and the Million+ Group (**www.millionplus.ac.uk**) containing many of the former polytechnics and newer universities. To these have been added the University Alliance (**www.university-alliance.ac.uk**), which provides a home for 23 universities, both old and new, that did not fit into the other categories. In addition there is GuildHE (**www.guildhe.ac.uk**), an organisation mainly for specialist colleges, but including five of the newest universities, and the Cathedrals Group: an affiliation of church-based universities and colleges (**www.cathedralsgroup.org.uk**). The university profiles in chapter 13 give the affiliation of each university.

Many of you will barely have heard of a polytechnic, let alone be able to identify which of today's universities had that heritage, but you will know which of two universities in the same city has the higher status. While that should matter far less than the quality of a course, it would be naïve to ignore institutional reputation entirely if that is going to carry weight with a future employer. Some big firms restrict their recruitment efforts to a small group of leading universities, for example (see chapter 2), and, however shortsighted that might be, it is something to bear in mind if a career in the City or a big law firm is your ultimate aim.

Cost

Quite apart from the level of fees, the cost of studying in different parts of the UK inevitably varies. Some cities – notably London – are notoriously expensive for students and non-students alike. But even these comparisons can be complicated by the availability of part-time employment – an important factor for a growing number of students today. The NatWest survey rates London as the cheapest place in the UK to study once earning opportunities are taken into account. If you intend to take part-time employment while studying, check that your chosen university has a "job shop", or some other organisation to help students find reasonably paid work.

Accommodation costs listed alongside the university profiles in this *Guide* are probably the nearest proxy for a cost-of-living indicator. The *Guide* also includes a summary of the bursaries available at each university where this information is known. The size of bursaries varies enormously, as do the rules governing eligibility. Scholarships are awarded for other achievements, regardless of family income.

Facilities

Universities compete for the best students not only through their courses but, increasingly, also through non-academic facilities. Accommodation is the main selling point for those living away from home, but sports facilities, libraries and computing equipment also play an important part. Even campus nightclubs have become part of the facilities race that has coincided with the introduction of top-up fees.

Many universities guarantee first-year students accommodation in halls of residence or university-owned flats. But it is as well to know what happens after that. Are there enough places for second or third-year students who want them, and if not, what is the private market like? Rents for student houses vary quite widely across the country and there have been tensions with local residents in some cities. All universities offer specialist accommodation for disabled students – and are better at providing other facilities than most public institutions. Their websites give basic information on what is provided, as well as contact points for more detailed inquiries.

Special-interest clubs and recreational facilities, as well as political activity, tend to be based in the students' union – sometimes knows as the guild of students, especially in Scotland. In some universities, the union is the focal point of social activity, while in others the attractions of the city seem to overshadow the union to the point where facilities are underused. Students' union websites are included with the information found in the university profiles (chapter 13).

Sources of information

With nearly 120 universities to choose from, the Unistats and UCAS websites, as well as guides such as this one, are the obvious places to start your search for the right course. But once you have narrowed down the list of candidates, you will want to go through undergraduate prospectuses. Most are available online, where you can select the relevant sections rather than waiting for an account of every course to arrive in the post. Beware of generalised claims about the standing of the university, the quality of courses, friendly atmosphere and legendary social life. Stick, if you can, to the factual information, which is generally accurate.

If the material that the universities publish about their own qualities is less than objective, much of what you will find on the internet is equally unreliable, for different reasons. A simple search on the name of a university will turn up spurious comparisons of everything from the standard of lecturing to the attractiveness of the students. These can be seriously misleading and are usually based on anecdotal evidence, at best. Make sure that any information you may take into account comes from a reputable source and, if it conflicts with your impression of a university, try to cross-check it with this *Guide* and the institution's own material.

Checklist

Choosing a subject and a place to study is a major decision. Make sure you can answer these questions:

Choosing a course:

» What do I want out of higher education?
» Which subjects do I enjoy studying at school?
» Which subject or subjects do I want to study?
» Do I have the right qualifications?
» What are my career plans and does the subject and course fit these?
» Do I want to study full-time or part-time?
» Do I want to study at a university or a college?

Choosing a university:

» What type of university do I wish to go to: campus, city or smaller town?
» How far is the university from home?
» Is it large or small?
» Is it specialist or general?
» Does it offer the right course?
» How much will it cost?
» Have I arranged to visit the university?

Useful websites

The following websites will help you find out more about the topics discussed in this chapter. The best starting point is the UCAS website (**www.ucas.com** or **www.ucas.ac.uk**). On the site there's lots of information on courses, universities and the whole process of applying to university. In addition UCAS has an official presence
on Facebook (**www.facebook.com/ucasonline**)
and Twitter (**http://twitter.com/UCAS_online**)
and now also has a series of video guides (**www.ucas.tv**) on the process of applying, UCAS resources and comments from other students on higher education.

Within the UCAS site, useful but not immediately obvious pages include:
The Stamford Test
www.ucas.com/students/choosingcourses/choosingcourse//stamfordtest
The UCAS tariff (and especially its use with vocational qualifications)
www.ucas.com/students/ucas_tariff/tarifftables

For statistical information which allows limited comparison between universities (and for full details of the National Student Survey), visit:
http://unistats.direct.gov.uk

For information on Foundation degrees: Foundation Degree Forward
www.fdf.ac.uk

For an official listing of recognised degrees and recognised higher education institutions:
www.dcsf.gov.uk/recognisedukdegrees

UK Course Finder:
www.ukcoursefinder.com

Unofficial Guides to universities:
www.unofficial-guides.com

For a full calendar of university and college open days:
www.opendays.com

Students with disabilities: SKILL, the National Bureau for Students with Disabilities:
www.skill.org.uk

University groupings
1994 Group, a group of medium and small research-intensive universities:
www.1994group.ac.uk
GuildHE, a group of higher education colleges, specialist institutions and some universities:
www.guildhe.ac.uk
Million+ Group, a group of newer universities:
www.millionplus.ac.uk
Russell Group: a group of large research-intensive universities:
www.russellgroup.ac.uk
The University Alliance, a group of old and new universities:
www.university-alliance.ac.uk
The Cathedrals Group: an affiliation of church-based universities and colleges
www.cathedralsgroup.org.uk

2 Graduate Employment Prospects

The graduate labour market is still coping with the aftermath of the banking crisis and the continuing worldwide recession, both of which have depressed graduate recruitment. In the UK, a pickup in optimism among private sector employers has been accompanied by the realisation that the public sector, the destination of many UK graduates, is about to lose hundreds of thousands of jobs.

The recession has been especially tough for new graduates. Early in 2011, the UK government's Office for National Statistics reported that people who had graduated between two and six years earlier were experiencing slightly higher unemployment than before, but were still less likely to be unemployed than members of the working-age population overall. But by contrast, unemployment among those who had graduated up to two years earlier reached nearly 20 per cent in the third quarter of 2010, up from 10.6 per cent at the start of the recession. These figures are produced by a different methodology from that used by the Higher Education Statistics Agency, whose findings are discussed below. In the light of the growing cost of higher education, they are bound to be a concern. But the low unemployment of more established graduates is evidence that a degree continues to be economically beneficial.

No one can predict the changes that may take place in the three or four years before those starting a degree in 2012 begin their careers. But those choosing a course now will want to know what they can do to insulate themselves against the possibility of joining the growing band of unemployed or underemployed graduates after they leave university.

The good news is that in the private sector at least, the worst may be over. Leading employers planned to increase their recruitment targets by 9.4 per cent in 2011, after a 12.6 per cent increase in 2010, according to the annual *Graduate Market* survey by High Fliers. This follows deep cuts of 19.8 per cent in 2009 and 7.6 per cent in 2008. However the public sector – a huge employer of graduates – is only just starting to feel the pinch.

The UK may never return to the days of plentiful, well-paid graduate jobs that it enjoyed only a few years ago. That era is certainly not going to return in the immediate future and graduates will need to do all they can to make themselves attractive to employers. They will still be in a much better position than young people without higher education, but there are going to be a lot of graduates chasing a more limited number of opportunities than in the past.

Subject choice and career opportunities

The tables on pages 36–37 will help you assess whether your prospective course will pay off in career terms, at least to start with. They date from 2008–09, the early phase of the downturn in graduate employment, so the picture today may be a little less gloomy than these figures suggest. But there is no reason to believe that the pattern of success rates will have changed.

The Higher Education Statistics Agency (HESA) collects data on what graduates do straight after graduation (sometimes called graduate destinations) and on their average salaries. The results are to be treated with caution because they represent only the first six months of a graduate's career – not even that if he or she has gone on to postgraduate study – and they make no allowances for the variety of entry routes into different areas of employment. Dentists are virtually guaranteed a job if they complete a degree successfully, whereas those going into art and design know that periods of freelance or casual work may be an occupational hazard at the start of their career, and perhaps later on as well. Degrees in social work can sometimes involve a placement after final exams, so people doing these courses can seem to be unemployed when they might in fact have reasonable job prospects.

This table does reveal some unexpected results, such as unemployment of over 10 per cent for graduates in physics and various engineering disciplines, and hitting 17 per cent for librarians. By contrast, it shows that a course in education is the most certain route to a graduate job apart from various

Universities targeted by the largest number of top employers in 2010–11

1	(4)	Cambridge
2	(3)	Warwick
3	(1)	Manchester
4	(2)	London
5	(5)	Oxford
6	(6)	Nottingham
7	(8)	Bristol
8	(7)	Bath
9	(11)	Durham
10	(9)	Leeds
11	(14)	Edinburgh
12	(10)	Birmingham
13	(13)	Loughborough
14	(12)	Sheffield
15	(15)	Southampton
16	(17)	Cardiff
17	(–)	Aston
18	(–)	Strathclyde
19	(16)	Newcastle
20	(–)	Exeter

Last year's position in brackets
Source: Graduate Market in 2011

branches of medicine, with 4 per cent unemployment. The table also shows that some subjects, especially sciences such as physics and chemistry, have a higher expectation than others, such as art and design, that their graduates will undertake further study, probably for a doctorate.

We use classifications developed at the universities of Warwick and the West of England to distinguish between "graduate-level" work and jobs that do not normally require a degree. Subjects are ranked on "positive destinations" which include postgraduate study and other forms of training, whether or not they are combined with a job. Some similar tables do not make a distinction between different types of job. These tend to give the impression that all universities and subjects have uniformly high employment rates.

The second table, on pages 38–39, gives average earnings six months after graduation. It contains interesting – and in some cases surprising – information about early career pay levels. Few would have placed social work or Middle Eastern studies in the top ten fields for graduate pay, while accounting and business studies appear in 20th and 22nd place respectively. Those

What graduates do by subject studied

Times Subject (ranked by the total of the first four columns on the right)	Employed in graduate job	Employed in graduate job and studying	Studying and not employed	Employed in non-graduate job and studying	Employed in non-graduate job	Unemployed
1 Medicine	92%	3%	5%	0%	0%	0%
2 Dentistry	91%	8%	0%	0%	0%	0%
3 Nursing	90%	5%	1%	0%	2%	2%
4 Veterinary Medicine	86%	3%	2%	1%	3%	6%
5 Pharmacology and Pharmacy	61%	17%	12%	1%	5%	4%
6 Other Subjects Allied to Medicine	68%	6%	8%	1%	12%	5%
7 Social Work	66%	7%	5%	2%	13%	7%
8 Chemical Engineering	49%	5%	26%	0%	9%	11%
9 Education	60%	5%	10%	2%	18%	4%
10 Physics and Astronomy	24%	6%	45%	1%	12%	12%
11 Chemistry	27%	5%	42%	1%	16%	9%
12 Civil Engineering	51%	6%	15%	1%	12%	14%
13 Law	18%	5%	43%	7%	21%	6%
14 General Engineering	47%	8%	16%	1%	17%	10%
15 Celtic Studies	20%	5%	42%	5%	22%	6%
16 Mathematics	28%	11%	30%	2%	18%	10%
17 Anatomy and Physiology	22%	3%	42%	4%	22%	7%
18 Mechanical Engineering	49%	4%	16%	1%	16%	13%
19 Russian	39%	7%	25%	0%	21%	9%
20 Theology and Religious Studies	26%	5%	34%	5%	23%	7%
21 Architecture	42%	9%	17%	1%	17%	14%
22 Food Science	48%	5%	15%	2%	24%	7%
23 French	35%	5%	26%	3%	24%	6%
24 Economics	36%	10%	21%	3%	20%	11%
25 Iberian Languages	38%	4%	23%	4%	25%	6%
26 Land and Property Management	57%	3%	9%	0%	18%	13%
27 German	35%	6%	24%	3%	23%	9%
28 Electrical and Electronic Engineering	43%	4%	18%	2%	18%	15%
29 Town and Country Planning and Landscape	36%	5%	23%	3%	22%	11%
30 Building	54%	5%	7%	1%	19%	14%
31 Music	32%	6%	26%	3%	24%	9%
32 Materials Technology	48%	3%	14%	1%	24%	10%
33 Biological Sciences	24%	4%	34%	3%	24%	10%
34 East and South Asian Studies	41%	6%	15%	3%	23%	12%
35 Geology	26%	3%	33%	2%	23%	12%

Times Subject (ranked by the total of the first four columns on the right)	Employed in graduate job	Employed in graduate job and studying	Studying and not employed	Employed in non-graduate job and studying	Employed in non-graduate job	Unemployed
36 Politics	31%	4%	25%	4%	25%	10%
37 Aeronautical and Manufacturing Engineering	39%	5%	18%	2%	21%	15%
38 Middle Eastern and African Studies	30%	5%	24%	4%	25%	11%
39 Italian	37%	3%	22%	1%	27%	10%
40 Classics and Ancient History	24%	3%	32%	4%	27%	10%
41 Geography and Environmental Sciences	28%	4%	27%	4%	29%	8%
42 Accounting and Finance	27%	17%	12%	5%	26%	12%
43 Computer Science	43%	4%	13%	2%	21%	17%
44 Philosophy	27%	3%	27%	4%	28%	12%
45 Anthropology	29%	3%	25%	3%	30%	10%
46 Librarianship and Information Management	44%	2%	11%	2%	23%	17%
47 Agriculture and Forestry	38%	7%	11%	3%	31%	9%
48 History	23%	3%	28%	5%	32%	9%
49 Sports Science	33%	5%	17%	4%	35%	7%
50 Business Studies	41%	5%	10%	3%	31%	11%
51 English	26%	3%	24%	5%	33%	9%
52 Linguistics	29%	3%	21%	4%	32%	10%
53 Psychology	26%	5%	19%	6%	37%	8%
54 History of Art, Architecture and Design	28%	4%	18%	4%	35%	10%
55 American Studies	31%	2%	16%	5%	36%	9%
56 Art and Design	38%	3%	8%	4%	34%	14%
57 Archaeology	24%	2%	22%	4%	34%	13%
58 Social Policy	29%	5%	14%	4%	39%	10%
59 Sociology	27%	4%	15%	5%	40%	10%
60 Drama, Dance and Cinematics	34%	3%	9%	5%	39%	11%
61 Hospitality, Leisure, Recreation and Tourism	36%	2%	6%	3%	43%	9%
62 Communication and Media Studies	34%	2%	7%	3%	40%	14%
Overall	**40%**	**5%**	**18%**	**3%**	**25%**	**9%**

Source: HESA 2008–09 DLHE return

What graduates earn by subject studied

	Subject	Graduate employment or self employment	Non-graduate employment or self employment
1	Dentistry	£30,143	..
2	Medicine	£29,129	..
3	Chemical Engineering	£27,151	..
4	Veterinary Medicine	£25,807	..
5	Economics	£25,637	£16,249
6	Middle Eastern and African Studies	£25,004	..
7	General Engineering	£24,937	£24,246
8	Social Work	£24,655	£15,669
9	Mechanical Engineering	£24,337	£14,764
10	Civil Engineering	£23,720	£15,501
11	Aeronautical and Manufacturing Engineering	£23,478	£14,697
12	Librarianship and Information Management	£23,246	£15,889
13	Mathematics	£23,160	£15,807
14	Electrical and Electronic Engineering	£22,993	£18,640
15	Physics and Astronomy	£22,946	£15,778
16	Building	£21,979	£15,500
17	Nursing	£21,911	£19,415
18	Theology and Religious Studies	£21,749	£14,043
19	Computer Science	£21,712	£16,465
20	Accounting and Finance	£21,551	£16,157
21	Geology	£21,182	£13,950
22	Business Studies	£21,006	£15,774
23	Education	£20,867	£14,191
24	Other Subjects Allied to Medicine	£20,866	£15,419
25	Classics and Ancient History	£20,864	£15,013
26	Politics	£20,831	£16,135
27	East and South Asian Studies	£20,750	£14,190
28	Sociology	£20,744	£14,272
29	German	£20,657	£15,207
30	Iberian Languages	£20,573	£15,645
31	Food Science	£20,505	£15,880
32	Anatomy and Physiology	£20,420	£14,248
33	Anthropology	£20,223	£14,985
34	History of Art, Architecture and Design	£20,103	£15,196
35	Philosophy	£20,097	£14,853
36	Pharmacology and Pharmacy	£20,059	£14,236
37	French	£20,034	£14,979
38	Materials Technology	£20,006	£13,888
39	Land and Property Management	£19,993	£14,707
40	Town and Country Planning and Landscape	£19,956	£15,198
41	Chemistry	£19,948	£14,550
42	History	£19,909	£14,534

Subject	Graduate employment or self employment	Non-graduate employment or self employment
43 Geography and Environmental Sciences	£19,856	£14,659
44 Social Policy	£19,570	£14,709
45 Agriculture and Forestry	£19,394	£13,934
46 Russian	£19,358	£14,862
47 Biological Sciences	£19,265	£14,248
48 Law	£18,911	£14,826
49 Italian	£18,745	£16,583
50 English	£18,343	£14,303
51 Sports Science	£18,319	£14,238
52 Psychology	£18,176	£14,119
53 Linguistics	£18,074	£14,131
54 Architecture	£17,873	£14,526
55 Celtic Studies	£17,779	..
56 Hospitality, Leisure, Recreation and Tourism	£17,680	£14,840
57 Archaeology	£17,675	£13,884
58 American Studies	£17,511	£14,304
59 Drama, Dance and Cinematics	£17,477	£14,158
60 Communication and Media Studies	£17,351	£14,481
61 Art and Design	£17,326	£13,853
62 Music	£17,040	£13,928
Total	**£21,405**	**£14,855**

NOTE: .. indicates a suppressed mean salary based on 7 or less graduates
Source: HESA 2008–09 DLHE return

positions underline the differences between starting salaries and long-term prospects in different jobs. In future years, this data will improve as information emerges on salary levels for specific courses at each university. Incidentally, the top non-City pay for a graduate is with supermarket group Aldi. Despite its budget image, it pays graduates training to be area managers £40,000 in their first year.

But HESA's research also shows that graduate prospects improve in the first few years after graduation. Looking late in 2008 at graduates from 2005, HESA found that after three and a half years, overall unemployment had dropped from 5 per cent, six months after graduation, to under 3 per cent. Most of the rest (76 per cent) were in full-time employment and the others were in some combination of work and study. Of those in full-time employment, 81 per cent were in graduate occupations compared with 71 per cent in the initial survey. Corresponding differences emerged when the sample was broken down by subject. This data is now several years old and a new edition is planned for September 2011.

Enhancing your employability
Universities are well aware of the difficulties in the graduate employment market and have been introducing all manner of schemes to try to give their graduates an advantage in the

labour market. Many have incorporated specially designed employability modules into degree courses; some are certificating extra-curricular activities to improve their graduates' CVs; others are stepping up their efforts to provide work experience to complement degrees.

Opinion is divided on the value of such schemes. Some of the biggest employers restrict their recruitment activities to a small number of universities, believing that these institutions attract the brightest minds, and that trawling more widely is not cost-effective. These companies, often big payers from the City of London and including some of the top law firms, are not likely to change their ways at a time when they are more anxious than ever to control costs. Widening the pool of universities from which they recruit is costly, and unnecessary in a buyers' market like the one we see today. As before, they will expect to pick up outstanding candidates who went to other universities later in their careers.

Most graduates do not work in the City, and most students do not go to universities at the top of the league tables. The best advice for those looking to maximise their employment opportunities (and who isn't?) must be to go for the best university you can.

University schemes

If a university offers extra help towards employment, it is worth considering whether its scheme is likely to work for you. Some are too new to show results in the labour market, but they may have been endorsed by big employers or introduced at an institution whose graduates already have a record of success in the jobs market. In time, these extras may turn into mandatory parts of degree study, complete with course credit.

At Liverpool John Moores University, for example, the World of Work (WoW) programme was devised with the help of the CBI, Shell, Sony, and Marks and Spencer. Taken by students in all subjects, including postgraduates, it offers classes in CV writing, interview skills, finance, entrepreneurship and negotiation skills, among many other topics. There are guest lectures and demonstrations related to the eight employment-related skills that WoW is intended to develop, and employers carry out mock interviews to assess students' strengths and weaknesses.

Hertfordshire is another university to have demonstrated a sustained focus on its students' job prospects. It was arguably the first of many universities to describe itself as "business-facing". Employer groups are consulted on the curriculum, and often supply guest lecturers on degree courses. Like some other universities, such as Derby, it offers career development support to graduates throughout their working life.

Other universities, such as Exeter, have taken a different tack and are helping students make the most of their voluntary and extra-curricular activities by certificating them. The Exeter Award gives credit for attendance at skills sessions and training courses, active participation in sporting and musical activities, engagement in work experience and voluntary work. The university already claimed to have more students than any other involved in voluntary activities. It believes that the award will encourage employers to take more notice of them.

The York Award is another well-established example of this type of scheme that has the involvement of organisations from the public, private and voluntary sectors. The university has found that employers value a combination of academic study, work experience and leisure interests. The scheme offers York students a framework to gain recognition for activities that are not formally recognised through the degree programme. Among the subjects on an extensive list of courses are networking, time management, counselling and understanding different cultures.

The value of work experience

As the table earlier in this chapter showed, there are big differences in the average employment prospects for different subjects. But the majority of graduate jobs are open to applicants from any discipline. For those general positions, employers tend to be more impressed by a good degree from what they consider a prestigious university than by an apparently relevant qualification. Here numeracy, literacy and communications – the arts needed to function effectively in any organisation – are of vital importance.

Specialist jobs – for example in engineering or design – are a different matter. Employers may be much more knowledgeable about the quality of individual courses and less influenced by a university's overall position in league tables when the job relies directly on knowledge and skills acquired as a student. That goes for the likes of medicine and architecture as well as the new vocational areas such as computer games design or environmental management.

In either case, however, work experience has become increasingly important. The High Fliers survey mentioned above shows that a third of the jobs taken by 2011 graduates will go to people who have already worked in the organisation that employs them, whether in holiday jobs or via placements or sponsored degrees. Sandwich degrees, extended programmes that include up to a year at work, have always boosted employment prospects. Graduates often end up working where they undertook their placement. And while a sandwich year will make your course longer, it will not be subject to a full year's fees.

Many conventional degrees now include shorter work placements that should offer some advantages in the labour market. Not all are arranged by the university so, unless you have an opening that you would like to pursue, that is something to establish and weigh in the balance when choosing a course. The majority of big graduate employers offer some provision of this nature, although access to it can be competitive.

If your chosen course does not include a work placement, you may still want to consider the possibilities for arranging your own part-time or temporary employment. The majority of supposedly full-time students now take jobs during term time, as well as in vacations, to make ends meet. But such jobs can also boost your CV – even working in a bar or a shop shows some experience of dealing with the public and coping with the disciplines of the workplace. Inevitably, the more prosperous cities are likely to offer more employment opportunities than rural areas or conurbations that have been hard hit in the recession.

Of course, the ultimate work-related degree is one sponsored by an employer or even taken in the workplace – something that Government ministers have encouraged recently. Middlesex University provides tailored programmes for Dell and Marks and Spencer, among other organisations, and has more than 1,000 students taking courses run by its Institute of Work Based Learning. Most such courses are provided for people already employed by the companies concerned, rather than as a route into the company. But they may come to be considered as an alternative to entering full-time higher education straight from school or college.

Consider part-time degrees

Another option, also favoured by ministers, is part-time study. Although the low level of financial support had deterred many prospective students, the number taking part-time degrees has been rising, and more younger people are doing degrees with the Open University. Of the extra 20,000 university and college places announced by Lord Mandelson before the 2010 general election, 5,000 were earmarked for part-timers. Under new arrangements for 2012–13, for the first time, part-time students will be able to apply for a tuition fees loan.

Part-time study requires a high degree of commitment – knuckling down to an essay or an assignment after a hard day at work is not easy – but it does reduce the cost of higher education for those in work. Bear in mind, however, that most part-time courses take twice as long to complete as the full-time equivalent. If your earning power is linked to the qualification, it will take that much longer for you to enjoy the benefits.

Plan early for your career

Whatever type of course you choose, it is sensible to start thinking about your future career early in your time at university. There has been a growing tendency in recent years for students to convince themselves that there would be plenty of time to apply for jobs after graduation, and that they were better off focusing entirely on their degree while at university. In the current employment market, all but the most obviously brilliant graduates need to offer more than just a degree, whether it be work experience, leadership qualities demonstrated through clubs and societies, or commitment to voluntary activities. Many students finish a degree without knowing what they want to do, but a blank CV will not impress a prospective employer.

The recession had the effect of reducing the number of vacancies for graduate-level jobs – while increasing the number of applications to 45 per graduate-level job in 2010, according to High Fliers. Employers also told High Fliers that they are not interested in applicants with no previous work experience.

Useful websites

Prospects, the UK's official graduate careers website:
prospects.ac.uk

For information on internships, graduate schemes and career advice:
www.milkround.com

3 Going Abroad to University

For several years, a steady stream of British people have been going abroad to study – mainly at postgraduate level, but some for a first degree. The hike in undergraduate fees in England, Wales and Northern Ireland has led to suggestions that what began as a trickle will now become a torrent. There are no fees in some Continental countries, after all, and even many American universities are not so much more expensive than staying at home now.

The logic of the argument is impeccable, but there are several reasons for thinking that the torrent is still some way off. Where Europe is concerned, the main issue concerns the language barrier. Although there are now thousands of postgraduate courses taught in English at Continental universities, first degree programmes are much thinner on the ground. A few universities, like Maastricht, in the Netherlands, have made a serious pitch for business from the UK and are offering a wide range of subjects in English at a fraction of the cost of a UK degree. But most European universities teach undergraduates in the host language – and, up to now, that has always deterred UK students.

The obvious alternative lies in US, Australian and Canadian universities, all of which are keen to attract more international students. Here, cost and distance are the main obstacles. Four-year courses add considerably to the cost of affordable-looking fees, while the state of the pound has been another serious disadvantage. Add in the natural reluctance of most 18-year-olds to commit to life on the other side of the world (or even just the Atlantic) and the prospect of a significant increase in student emigration lessens considerably.

Nevertheless, in an age of global job mobility, it will be surprising if the new fees do not prompt more interest in studying abroad this year. This chapter examines some of the pros and cons, as well as suggesting further sources of information.

Where students go to

The last official estimate, published by the UK International Higher Education Unit put the number of Britons studying abroad at 33,000, modest by comparison with the 370,000 international students in UK universities. By far the largest number go to the USA – about 9,000 in 2008 – with Canada, France and Germany (in that order) the next most popular destinations. A few find their way to unexpected locations like South Korea or Slovakia, but usually for family reasons or to study the language.

Many of these students have an abiding interest in some foreign culture that means they want to immerse themselves in it instead of studying it in the UK and making occasional visits. But the figures suggest that British students are more attracted to countries that are familiar or close at hand, and where they can speak English, than they are to the exotic. Many are doubtless planning to stay in, say, Canada, the USA or Australia after they graduate, although visa regulations may make this difficult. Often they are already in the country where they will study – perhaps because their parents live and/or work there – and they may well have been to school there.

Studying in Europe

Particularly with fees rising so steeply in most of the UK, you may be able to save considerable sums by studying abroad, especially in another EU nation. You are entitled to study there for the same fees as a local resident. This will be much lower for most undergraduates than in the UK, or may even be zero for some courses. In the EU, you will also be able get a job while studying. Farther afield, your student visa might not allow you to take on paid work.

Undergraduates can study at a French university for £150 a year but, not surprisingly, nearly all first degrees are taught in French. The Campus France website (**www.campusfrance.org/en**) lists 299 business or economics programmes taught in English, but only 20 of them are at undergraduate level – and only one of them at a state university. Germany is much the same, despite attracting large numbers of international students. The DAAD website (**www.daad.de/en**) lists 31 undergraduate programmes in economics or management taught wholly or mainly in English, but most are at private universities like Jacobs University in Bremen, which charges more than £15,000 a year.

Any potential saving has to be considered with care. Despite the Bologna process – an inter-governmental agreement which means that degrees across Europe are becoming more similar in content and duration – many continental courses are longer than their UK equivalents, adding to the cost and to your lost earnings from university attendance. And, of course, you will have higher travel costs. It is harder to generalise about the cost of living. It can be lower than the UK in southern Europe, but eyewateringly high in Scandinavia.

You can cut down the cost of an international experience and hedge your bets about committing yourself to a full course overseas by opting instead for an exchange scheme. UK universities have exchange partners all over the world, providing opportunities for everything from a summer school of less than a month to a full year abroad.

The most common offering is the EU's Erasmus scheme, which funds exchanges of between three months and a year, the work counting towards your degree. More than 2 million students throughout Europe have used the scheme, and there are 2,000 universities to choose from in 30 countries. Applications, which are made through universities' international offices, must be approved by the UK university as well as by the Erasmus administrators. Erasmus students do not pay any extra fees and they are eligible for grants to cover the extra expense of travelling and living in another country.

For those who opt for more than an exchange, there is still the chance of financial support. Many universities in the developed world offer their own grants or loans to selected international students, especially postgraduates, as some countries do to their nationals. The best way to find out what is available is to decide what course you want to take and where, and then investigate possible fees, scholarships and subsistence packages. You may have a good experience here. But bear in mind that for most universities in any country, foreign students are a source of big fees. You must assume that you will be seen in this light.

Which countries are best?

Anyone going abroad to study will be in search of a good experience. In early 2010 the British Council completed a detailed analysis of how well countries around the world work to attract foreign students, as well as how well-regarded the degrees they award are internationally.

The report shows that, relative to their student population, smaller countries send the most people abroad to study. Almost 11 per cent of Moroccan students are outside Morocco, and 10 per cent of Irish students are outside Ireland. The equivalent for the UK would be about 0.5 per cent. The proportion in China may be similarly low but, as it is the world's most populous country, it is much the biggest exporter of students.

The British Council report, prepared by the Economist Intelligence Unit, went on to look in detail at which countries have the most developed approach to welcoming international students. It began by looking at which countries have a proper strategy in place to internationalise their universities, at their policies on migration and at their international presence, including their ability to negotiate student exchange agreements with other nations. The authors then looked at the international acceptability of degrees from a range of countries, and finally at access, the steps which countries take to make their university systems open to students and academics from around the world.

The UK itself scores highly on these measures, no doubt to the British Council's relief. Britain comes third in the world as a destination for international students. The top place goes to Germany, with Australia second. China is in fourth place, while Malaysia, the USA, Japan, Russia, Nigeria, Brazil and India (these two in joint tenth place) complete the top eleven.

The report says that Germany is one of the few nations that does not allow public universities to increase fees for foreign students, and a German student visa lasts until a year after graduation, to help you look for a permanent job there. In Australia, universities can charge foreign students big fees, but other aspects of its system are highly rated. The quality of Australian degrees is generally regarded as high, and despite the high cost of getting there, life in Australia costs less than in the UK once you arrive.

Some Asian countries are looking to recruit more foreign students, both as part of a broader internationalisation agenda and to compensate for falling numbers of potential students at home. Japan is a case in point. The high cost of living may put off many potential students, as may the unfamiliarity of its language, but more support is being offered to attract foreign students and more courses are being taught in English. However, as with any non-English speaking country, the language of instruction is only part of the story. You will need to know enough of the local language to manage the shops and the transport system, and, of course, to make friends and get the most out of being there.

Another option of growing interest is China. While you may not believe the whole of the story that China is about to take over the world, it has already grown massively in importance. Its university system is growing in quality, especially at the C9 group of international institutions, which have become known as the Chinese Ivy League. Familiarity with China is unlikely to be a career disadvantage for anyone in the 21st century.

It seems that the USA will always be the top overseas destination, however. Its high-prestige universities, its use of English and its massive economy, make the country a magnet for footloose British students. The Ivy League and other world-famous universities dominate global league tables, and many students hope to stay on the other side of the Atlantic to work after graduation, rather than coming straight home.

The individual systems of each state and the importance of private universities means that practices in relation to international students vary from university to university in the USA.

There are only a few thousand state-funded places for overseas students in the whole country. On the other hand, many US universities have some sort of student support package on offer, and big institutions spend millions on supporting students.

The sheer depth of the US university system means that if you are thinking of studying abroad, the USA is almost bound to be on the list of possibilities. Outside the Ivy League, the fee gap is narrowing: at Texas A&M University, for example, ranked in the top 200 in the world, international students paid $10,000 a year, about £6,225 at the time of writing. Fees are lower than that at the State University of New York, but around £8,000 a year at the University of Florida. If the State University of North Dakota takes your fancy, you can get away with little more than £4,000 a year.

Will my degree be recognised?

Even in the era of globalisation, you need to bear in mind that not all degrees are equal. At one extreme is the MBA, which has an international system for accrediting courses, and a global admissions standard. But with many professional courses, study abroad is a potential hazard. To work as a doctor, engineer or lawyer in the UK, you need a qualification which the relevant professional body will recognise. It is understandable that to practise law in England, you need to have studied the English legal system. For other subjects, the issues are more to do with the quality and content of courses outside UK control.

There are ways of researching this issue in advance. One is to contact Naric, the National Recognition Centre for the UK (**www.naric.org.uk**). Naric exists to examine the compatibility and acceptability of qualifications from around the world. The other approach is to ask the UK professional body in question – maybe an engineering institution, the Law Society or the General Teaching, Medical or Dental Councils – about the qualification you propose to study for.

The British Council report suggests that Australian and German degrees are the most internationally acceptable from its Top 11 countries, with Brazil at the bottom. The USA comes fifth. While it is home to the world's top universities, the USA also has many less prestigious institutions whose qualifications are less likely to be welcomed around the world.

Which are the best universities?

Going abroad to study is a big and expensive decision, and you want to get it right. But a 2009 survey of UK students who were studying abroad or planning to do so suggested that excitement, adventure and glamour were more important in their choice than career positioning. Many have family money and have been privately educated. Their approach contrasts with that of international students coming to the UK, most of whom are highly tactical and career-minded about the choice they are making.

But let's assume that you are more thoughtful in your approach than this survey suggests. Especially if you plan to study abroad to establish yourself as an internationally mobile high-flyer, you will want to know that the university you are going to is taken seriously around the world. Systems for global university ranking offer one avenue for researching this problem.

At the moment there are three main systems for ranking universities on a world scale. One is run by QS (Quacquarelli Symonds), an educational research company based in London (**www.topuniversities.com**). Another is by Shanghai Ranking Consultancy, a company set up by Shanghai Jiao Tong University in China and is called the Academic Ranking of World Universities (ARWU) (**www.arwu.org**). These two have been joined by *Times Higher Education* (**www.timeshighereducation.co.uk**), a weekly newspaper with no connection to *The*

The top 50 universities in the world in 2010 according to QS World University Ranking (QS), the Academic Ranking of World Universities (ARWU) and *Times Higher Education* (THE)

QS Rank	Institution	Country	ARWU Rank	Institution	Country	THE Rank	Institution	Country
1	University of Cambridge	UK	1	Harvard University	USA	1	Harvard University	USA
2	Harvard University	USA	2	University of California, Berkeley	USA	2	California Institute of Technology	USA
3	Yale University	USA	3	Stanford University	USA	3	Massachusetts Institute of Technology	USA
4	University College London	UK	4	Massachusetts Institute of Technology	USA	4	Stanford University	USA
5	Massachusetts Institute of Technology	USA	5	University of Cambridge	UK	5	Princeton University	USA
6	University of Oxford	UK	6	California Institute of Technology	USA	6	University of Cambridge	UK
7	Imperial College London	UK	7	Princeton University	USA	6	University of Oxford	UK
8	University of Chicago	USA	8	Columbia University	USA	8	University of California, Berkeley	USA
9	California Institute of Technology	USA	9	University of Chicago	USA	9	Imperial College London	UK
10	Princeton University	USA	10	University of Oxford	UK	10	Yale University	USA
11	Columbia University	USA	11	Yale University	USA	11	University of California, Los Angeles	USA
12	University of Pennsylvania	USA	12	Cornell University	USA	12	University of Chicago	USA
13	Stanford University	USA	13	University of California, Los Angeles	USA	13	Johns Hopkins University	USA
14	Duke University	USA	14	University of California, San Diego	USA	14	Cornell University	USA
15	University of Michigan	USA	15	University of Pennsylvania	USA	=15	ETH Zurich (Swiss Federal Institute of Technology)	Switzerland
16	Cornell University	USA	16	University of Washington	USA	=15	University of Michigan	USA
17	Johns Hopkins University	USA	17	University of Wisconsin, Madison	USA	17	University of Toronto	Canada
18	ETH Zurich (Swiss Federal Institute of Technology)	Switzerland	=18	Johns Hopkins University	USA	18	Columbia University	USA
19	McGill University	Canada	=18	University of California, San Francisco	USA	19	University of Pennsylvania	USA
20	Australian National University	Australia	20	The University of Tokyo	Japan	20	Carnegie Mellon University	USA

The top 50 universities in the world in 2010 according to QS World University Ranking (QS), the Academic Ranking of World Universities (ARWU) and Times Higher Education (THE)

QS Rank	Institution	Country	ARWU Rank	Institution	Country	THE Rank	Institution	Country
21	King's College London	UK	21	University College London	UK	21	University of Hong Kong	Hong Kong
22	University of Edinburgh	UK	22	University of Michigan, Ann Arbor	USA	22	University College London	UK
23	University of Hong Kong	Hong Kong	23	ETH Zurich (Swiss Federal Institute of Technology)	Switzerland	23	University of Washington	USA
24	University of Tokyo	Japan	24	Kyoto University	Japan	24	Duke University	USA
25	Kyoto University	Japan	25	University of Illinois, Urbana-Champaign	USA	25	Northwestern University	USA
26	Northwestern University	USA	26	Imperial College London	UK	26	University of Tokyo	Japan
27	University of Bristol	UK	27	University of Toronto	Canada	27	Georgia Institute of Technology	USA
28	University of California, Berkeley	USA	28	University of Minnesota, Twin Cities	USA	28	Pohang University of Science and Technology	South Korea
29	University of Toronto	Canada	29	Northwestern University	USA	29	University of California, Santa Barbara	USA
30	The University of Manchester	UK	30	Washington University, St. Louis	USA	=30	University of British Columbia	Canada
31	National University of Singapore	Singapore	31	New York University	USA	=30	University of North Carolina, Chapel Hill	USA
=32	Ecole Polytechnique Fédérale de Lausanne	Switzerland	=32	University of California, Santa Barbara	USA	32	University of California San Diego	USA
=32	École Normale Supérieure, Paris	France	=32	University of Colorado, Boulder	USA	33	University of Illinois, Urbana-Champaign	USA
34	Carnegie Mellon University	USA	34	Rockefeller University	USA	34	National University of Singapore	Singapore
35	University of California, Los Angeles	USA	35	Duke University	USA	35	McGill University	Canada
=36	École Polytechnique	France	=36	University of British Columbia	Canada	36	University of Melbourne	Australia

37	University of Sydney	Australia
38	University of Melbourne	Australia
39	Brown University	USA
40	Hong Kong University of Science and Technology	Hong Kong
41	New York University	USA
42	Chinese University of Hong Kong	Hong Kong
43	University of Queensland	Australia
44	University of British Columbia	Canada
45	University of Copenhagen	Denmark
=46	University of New South Wales	Australia
=46	Peking University	China
=46	University of Wisconsin, Madison	USA
49	Osaka University	Japan
50	Seoul National University	South Korea

=36	University of Maryland, College Park	USA
38	University of Texas, Austin	USA
39	Pierre and Marie Curie University – Paris 6	France
40	University of Copenhagen	Denmark
41	University of North Carolina, Chapel Hill	USA
42	Karolinska Institute	Sweden
43	Pennsylvania State University, University Park	USA
44	The University of Manchester	UK
45	University of Paris Sud (Paris 11)	France
=46	University of California, Davis	USA
=46	University of California, Irvine	China
=46	University of Southern California	USA
49	The University of Texas Southwestern Medical Center, Dallas	USA
50	Utrecht University	Netherlands

37	Peking University	China
38	Washington University, Saint Louis	USA
39	Ecole Polytechnique	France
40	University of Edinburgh	UK
41	Hong Kong University of Science and Technology	Hong Kong
42	Ecole Normale Superieure, Paris	France
=43	Australian National University	Australia
=43	University of Göttingen	Germany
=43	Karolinska Institute	Sweden
=43	University of Wisconsin	USA
47	Rice University	USA
48	École Polytechnique Federale de Lausanne	Switzerland
=49	University of Science and Technology of China	China
=49	University of California, Irvine	USA

We gratefully acknowledge permission to reproduce these three rankings. The full QS World University Rankings 2010 can be consulted at www.topuniversities.com and the full Academic Ranking of World Universities 2010 at www.arwu.org. The full *Times Higher Education* rankings can be viewed at www.timeshighereducation.co.uk.

Times, which produced its own ranking for the first time in 2010, having previously published the QS version.

The QS system uses a number of measures including academic opinion, employer opinion, international orientation, research impact and staff/student ratio to create its listing, while the ARWU uses measures such as Nobel Prizes and highly cited papers, which are more related to excellence in scientific research. The *Times Higher* has added a number of measures to the QS model, including research income and a controversial global survey of teaching quality. Despite these different approaches, many universities appear in all three rankings. If you go to a university that features highly on any of the tables, you will be at a place that is well-regarded around the world. After all, even the 200th university on any of these rankings is an elite institution in a world with 4,000 universities. The top 50 universities in all three rankings are listed here.

These systems tend to favour universities which are good at science and medicine. Places that specialise in the humanities and the social sciences, such as the London School of Economics, can appear in deceptively modest positions. In addition, the rankings tend to look at universities in the round, and contain only limited information on specific subjects.

One advantage of the QS ranking system is that 10 per cent of a university's possible score comes from a global survey of recruiters. So you can look at this column of the table for an idea about where the major employers like to hire. Note that the author of this *Guide* has a role in developing the QS Rankings.

Other options for overseas studies

If you decide that studying abroad for a complete degree is too much, other options remain open. A language degree will typically involve a year abroad, but a look at the UCAS website will show many options for studying another subject alongside your language of choice. UK universities offer degrees in information technology, science, business and even journalism with a major language such as Chinese.

Another possibility is a joint degree awarded by more than one university. Here you would be admitted to a UK institution but would spend about half of your time at the partner organisation, and be awarded a degree from both. Many British universities now work this way and the Bologna process means that it is becoming simpler for European universities to offer them.

The best approach is to decide what you want to study and then see if there is a UK university that offers it as a joint degree. Then you should ask some searching questions. Employers and academics alike sometimes look askance at these degrees. In principle they should match the quality control systems of both the nations involved – or all, as some have up to five awarding universities. In practice, some have been criticised for inadequate standards. They are also an unfamiliar concept for employers. At least make sure that all the universities involved are well-regarded, for example by looking at their rankings on one or other of the websites mentioned above.

Useful websites

The following websites will help you find out more about the topics discussed in this chapter.

Association of Commonwealth Universities: **www.acu.ac.uk**
College Board (USA): **www.collegeboard.org**
Education Ireland: **www.educationireland.ie**
Erasmus Programme (EU): **www.britishcouncil.org/erasmus**
Finaid (USA): **www.finaid.org**
Fulbright Commission: **www.fulbright.co.uk**
Study in Australia: **www.studyinaustralia.gov.au**
Study in Canada: **www.studyincanada.com**
Campus France: **www.campusfrance.org/en**
DAAD (for Germany): **www.daad.de/en**

Recognition of international degrees

National Recognition Centre for the UK (Naric): **www.naric.org.uk**

Global university ranking tables

QS World University Rankings: **www.topuniversities.com**
Academic Ranking of World Universities: **www.arwu.org**
Times Higher Education World University Rankings: **www.timeshighereducation.co.uk/world-university-rankings**

4 The Top Universities

What distinguishes a top university? And who is to say that one course is better than another – especially when the university system is so reluctant to make any such comparison?

Higher education now publishes copious statistics, but resists combining them in a way that might answer applicants' questions. Critics of league tables insist that this is because every university has different priorities, and every course different ways of approaching a subject. Students must choose the one that suits them best.

So they must. However, the sheer range of universities and courses in the UK is such that most applicants need some help paring down the options to create a shortlist for their five application choices. For 18 years, *The Times Good University Guide* has been assisting students and their parents with that process, using the statistics that universities themselves employ to measure their own performance.

Every element of the table in this chapter has been chosen for the light it shines on the undergraduate experience and a student's future prospects. The selection of these eight measures and the way in which they are combined give a particular view of universities' overall strengths, but it is one that has stood the test of time. Unlike some others, *The Times Good University Guide* has placed a premium on consistency, confident that the measures are the best available for the task.

Some changes have been forced upon us. Universities stopped assessing teaching quality subject by subject, when this was the most heavily weighted measure in the table. Spending on libraries, which was a measure in virtually all university league tables, is no longer collected separately from that relating to museums, galleries and observatories. There have been developments, too, such as the National Student Survey, which was first used in the table five years ago.

The basic information that applicants need, however, in order to judge universities and their courses does not change. A university's entry standards, staffing levels, completion rates, degree classifications and graduate employment rates are all vital pieces of intelligence for anyone deciding where to study. Research grades, while not directly involving undergraduates, bring with them considerable funds and enable a university to attract top academics. Leading researchers in any subject may deliver the most inspiring lectures.

Most of the measures in *The Times Good University Guide*'s table have been used since it was first published and, while any element can be discounted by the individual, the package has struck a chord with readers. The ranking is the most-quoted of its type both in Britain and overseas, and has built a reputation as the most authoritative arbiter of changing fortunes in higher education.

The measures used in the ranking are kept under review by a group of university administrators and statisticians, which meets annually. The raw data that go into the table in this chapter and the subject tables in chapter 5 are all in the public domain and are sent to universities for checking before any scores are calculated.

Indeed, while the various official bodies concerned with higher education do not publish league tables, several produce system-wide statistics in a format that encourages comparison. The Higher Education Funding Councils' Research Assessment Exercise was one early example of this, with universities trumpeting their successes almost as soon as the grades had been announced. The Higher Education Statistics Agency (HESA), which supplies most of the figures used in our tables, also publishes annual "performance indicators" on everything from completion rates and research output to the proportion of under-represented social groups at each university.

Any scrutiny of league table positions is best carried out in conjunction with an examination of the relevant subject table – it is the course, after all, that will dominate your undergraduate years and influence your subsequent career.

How *The Times* League Table works

The table is presented in a format that displays the raw data, wherever possible. In building the table, scores for student satisfaction and research quality were weighted by 1.5; all other measures were weighted by 1. The indicators were combined using a common statistical technique known as Z-scores, to ensure that no indicator has a disproportionate effect on the overall total for each university, and the totals were transformed to a scale with 1000 for the top score.

For entry standards, student–staff ratio, good honours and graduate prospects, the score was adjusted for subject mix. For example, it is accepted that engineering, law and medicine graduates will tend to have better graduate prospects than their peers from English, psychology and sociology courses. Comparing results in the main subject groupings helps to iron out differences attributable simply to the range of degrees on offer. This subject-mix adjustment means that it is not possible to replicate the scores in the table from the published indicators because the calculation requires access to the entire dataset.

The Z-score technique makes it impossible to compare universities' total scores from one year to the next, although their relative positions in the table are comparable. Individual scores are dependent on the top performer, so a university might drop from 60 per cent of the top score to 58 per cent but still have improved, if the leading university had done better still.

Only where data are not available from HESA are figures sourced directly from universities. Where this is not possible – for example, in the case of those Scottish universities that are not part of the National Student Survey – scores are generated according to a university's average performance on other indicators.

The organisations providing the raw data for the tables are not involved in the process of aggregation, so are not responsible for any inferences or conclusions we have made. Every care has been taken to ensure the accuracy of the tables and accompanying information, but no responsibility can be taken for errors or omissions.

The Times league table uses eight important measures of university activity, based on the most recent data available at the time of compilation:

» Student satisfaction
» Research quality
» Entry standards
» Student–staff ratio

» Services and facilities spend
» Completion
» Good honours
» Graduate prospects

Student satisfaction

This is a measure of students' views of the quality of their courses. The National Student Survey (NSS) was the source of this data. The NSS is an initiative undertaken by the Funding Councils for England, Northern Ireland and Wales. It is designed, as an element of the quality assurance for higher education, to inform prospective students and their advisers in choosing what and where to study. The survey encompasses the views of final-year students on the quality of their courses. Data from the surveys published in 2009 and 2010 were used.

» The National Student Survey covers six aspects of a course: teaching, assessment and feedback, academic support, organisation and management, learning resources and personal development, with an additional question gauging overall satisfaction. Students answer on a scale from 1 (bottom) to 5 (top) and the measure is the percentage of positive responses (4 and 5) in each section, averaged to produce the final score.

» The survey is based on the opinion of final-year students rather than directly assessing teaching quality. Most undergraduates have no experience of other universities, or different courses, to inform their judgements. Although all the questions relate to courses, rather than the broader student experience, some types of university – notably medium-sized campus universities – tend to do better than others.

» Scottish universities were not automatically included in the survey, although 11 out of 15 have so far opted in.

» Where a university did not have sufficiently high response rates to publish results for one of the two years used to compile this measure, a single year's data have been used.

Research quality

This is a measure of the quality of the research undertaken in each university. The information was sourced from the 2008 Research Assessment Exercise (RAE), a peer-review exercise used to evaluate the quality of research in UK higher education institutions undertaken by the UK Higher Education funding bodies. Additionally, academic staffing data for 2007–08 from the Higher Education Statistics Agency have been used.

» A research quality profile was given to every university department that took part. This profile used the following categories: 4* world-leading; 3* internationally excellent; 2* internationally recognised; 1* nationally recognised; and unclassified. The Funding Bodies decided to direct more funds to the very best research by applying weightings. The English, Scottish and Welsh funding councils have slightly different weightings. Those adopted by HEFCE (the funding council for England) for funding in 2011–12 are used in the tables: 4* is weighted by a factor of 9, 3* is weighted by a factor of 3 and 2* weighted by a factor of 0.294. Outputs of 1* carry zero weight.

» Universities could choose which staff to include in the RAE, so, to factor in the depth of the research quality, each quality profile score has been multiplied by the number of staff returned in the RAE as a proportion of all eligible staff.

» Estimations of the eligible staff for each university were made drawing from publicly available data that have been quality assured by universities themselves. The eligible staff data include all staff directly responsible for teaching and research (excluding those on part-time contracts of less than 20 per cent of a full-time position as they were not eligible), with an adjustment made to remove more junior staff on research-only contracts. An adjustment has also been made to reflect patterns of staffing in those institutions which carry out further education as well as higher education. The calculations were checked against the figures published by a number of universities that declared the proportion of eligible staff entered for assessment.

Estimation was necessary because, as you will see from the note on page 56, HESA decided not to publish data on numbers of staff in university departments who were eligible to be submitted in the RAE. The proportion of staff entered by each university had been considered sufficiently important to be included in the grades used in every previous RAE to give an indication of the ethos and overall quality of departments. The methodology used in *The Times* league table attempts to replicate that process as accurately as possible, given the restrictions imposed by HESA.

Entry standards

This is the average score, using the UCAS tariff (see page 18), of new students under the age of 21 who took A and AS Levels, Highers and Advanced Highers and other equivalent qualifications (e.g. International Baccalaureate). It measures what new students actually achieved rather than the entry requirements suggested by the universities. The data comes from HESA for 2009–10. The original sources of data for this measure are data returns made by the universities themselves to HESA.

» Using the UCAS tariff, each student's examination results were converted to a numerical score. HESA then calculated an average for all students at the university. The results have then been adjusted to take account of the subject mix at the university.

» A score of 360 represents three As at A level. Although all of the top 30 universities in the table have entry standards of at least 360, it does not mean that everyone achieved such results – let alone that this was the standard offer. Courses will not demand more than three subjects at A level and offers are pitched accordingly. You will need to reach the entry requirements set by the university, rather than the scores represented here.

Student–staff ratio

This is a measure of the average number of students to each member of the academic staff, apart from those purely engaged in research. In this measure a low score is better than a high score. The data comes from HESA for 2009–10. The original sources of data for this measure are data returns made by the universities themselves to HESA.

» The figures, as calculated by HESA, allow for variation in employment patterns at different universities. A low value means that there are a small number of students for each academic member of staff, but this does not, of course, ensure good teaching quality or contact time with academics.

» Student–staff ratios vary by subject, for example the ratio is usually low for medicine. In building the table, the score is adjusted for the subject mix taught by each university.

Services and facilities spend

The expenditure per student on staff and student facilities, including library and computing facilities. The data comes from HESA for 2008–09 and 2009–10. The original data sources for this measure are data returns made by the universities to HESA.

» This is a measure calculated by taking the expenditure on student facilities (sports, grants to student societies, careers services, health services, counselling, etc.) and library and computing facilities (books, journals, staff, central computers and computer networks, but not buildings) and dividing this by the number of full-time-equivalent students. Expenditure is averaged over two years to even out the figures (for example, a computer upgrade undertaken in a single year).

Completion

This measure gives the percentage of students expected to complete their studies (or transfer to another institution) for each university. The data comes from the HESA performance indicators, based on data for 2009–10 and earlier years.

» This measure is a projection, liable to statistical fluctuations.

Good honours

This measure is the percentage of graduates achieving a first or upper second class degree. The results have been adjusted to take account of the subject mix at the university. The data comes from HESA for 2009–10. The original sources of data for this measure are data returns made by the universities themselves to HESA.

» Four-year first degrees, such as an MChem, are treated as equivalent to a first or upper second.
» Scottish Ordinary degrees (awarded after three years of study) are excluded.
» Universities control degree classification, with some oversight from external examiners. There have been suggestions that since universities have increased the numbers of good honours degrees they award, this measure may not be as objective as it should be. However, it remains the key measure of a student's success and employability.

Graduate prospects

This measure is the percentage of the total number of graduates who take up graduate-level employment or further study. The results have been adjusted for subject mix. The data come from HESA for 2009 graduates.

» HESA surveys graduates six months after graduation to find out what they are doing and the data are based on this survey.

Statement from the Higher Education Statistics Agency (HESA) regarding the use of staffing data in looking at Research Assessment Exercise performance:

This analysis of the results of the Research Assessment Exercise 2008 makes use of contextual data supplied under contract by the Higher Education Statistics Agency (HESA). It is a contractual condition that this statement should be published in conjunction with the analysis. HESA holds no data specifying which or how many staff have been regarded by each institution as eligible for inclusion in RAE 2008, and no data on the assignment to Units of Assessment of those eligible staff not included. Further, the data that HESA does hold is not an adequate alternative basis on which to estimate eligible staff numbers, whether for an institution as a whole, or disaggregated by Units of Assessment, or by some broader subject-based grouping.

		Student satisfaction (%)	Research quality	Entry standards	Student–staff ratio	Services and facilities spend per student (£)	Completion (%)	Good honours (%)	Graduate prospects (%)	Total
1	Oxford	86	4.0	536	10.8	3249	97.9	91.2	85.0	1000
2	Cambridge	84	4.1	559	11.7	2895	98.7	88.3	85.5	968
3	London School of Economics	74	3.6	513	11.8	2583	95.7	79.0	84.1	870
4	Imperial College	77	3.0	519	10.9	3971	91.2	76.2	86.7	835
5	University College London	78	3.0	477	9.7	2207	94.9	83.2	81.1	819
=6	Durham	81	2.8	487	15.3	2231	96.7	79.4	80.4	815
=6	St Andrews	83	2.6	485	13.3	2108	93.8	86.7	76.3	815
8	Warwick	80	2.7	480	14.1	1998	95.5	80.7	72.5	779
9	Lancaster	81	2.7	407	13.8	1825	93.8	73.6	71.8	766
10	Exeter	83	2.6	439	19.0	1948	96.5	82.8	70.3	762
11	York	82	2.7	437	14.9	1946	95.4	75.6	68.2	759
12	Bath	80	2.2	459	16.1	1682	96.4	76.6	77.9	745
13	Bristol	77	2.8	467	13.5	2055	96.0	80.8	77.7	740
14	Sussex	81	2.4	380	16.1	1569	91.7	82.7	69.3	731
15	Edinburgh	76	3.0	442	14.4	2043	92.5	81.3	72.4	725
16	Nottingham	79	2.2	428	14.2	1604	94.5	73.0	77.9	717
=17	Sheffield	81	2.5	426	14.9	1534	94.0	73.1	73.6	715
=17	Leicester	84	1.9	399	14.7	1891	92.7	66.8	71.5	715
19	Southampton	79	2.1	427	13.6	1966	93.0	75.3	68.3	714
20	Loughborough	85	2.3	390	17.1	1486	89.2	69.6	69.2	710
21	Buckingham	88	..	273	8.9	1041	90.8	43.6	87.5	708
22	Glasgow	83	2.3	408	14.5	2085	86.8	73.7	72.1	705

	Student satisfaction (%)	Research quality	Entry standards	Student–staff ratio	Services and facilities spend per student (£)	Completion (%)	Good honours (%)	Graduate prospects (%)	Total
23 School of Oriental and African Studies	74	2.0	423	11.1	1961	86.8	75.0	68.7	703
24 King's College London	77	2.2	447	12.0	1924	93.7	75.3	82.6	700
25 Newcastle	80	2.0	410	15.3	1742	94.2	75.5	75.4	695
26 Birmingham	79	2.2	421	15.4	1969	93.9	72.9	71.8	693
27 East Anglia	83	2.0	386	14.9	1688	90.2	69.6	66.1	686
28 Royal Holloway	77	2.6	381	15.7	1505	92.3	68.8	63.1	665
29 Surrey	77	1.9	388	19.0	1870	91.6	66.0	76.4	663
30 Leeds	78	2.1	408	14.9	1416	92.1	76.7	65.8	660
31 Liverpool	77	1.9	401	13.2	2088	90.8	71.5	70.3	658
32 Manchester	73	2.6	422	15.4	1802	93.6	70.6	70.4	652
33 Reading	79	2.1	370	15.5	1243	91.0	67.3	66.3	649
34 Strathclyde	78	1.6	394	18.0	1608	83.3	76.2	73.0	640
35 Cardiff	78	1.9	406	15.0	1374	93.0	68.5	73.6	638
36 Aston	77	1.3	370	17.1	1525	91.7	66.0	74.8	630
37 Queen Mary London	78	2.1	387	13.6	1582	89.4	64.4	71.7	628
38 Queen's, Belfast	77	1.8	362	14.8	1911	85.1	71.8	69.4	619
39 Kent	79	1.6	329	14.4	1311	88.6	61.9	60.7	613
40 Dundee	81	1.5	353	14.3	1355	81.9	68.5	68.9	610
41 Essex	78	2.1	307	15.6	1594	86.7	59.3	58.6	607
42 Aberdeen	81	1.9	332	15.8	1421	80.6	67.4	69.4	606
43 Aberystwyth	84	1.9	298	18.1	1404	86.3	58.5	55.1	604
44 Heriot-Watt	76	1.7	335	19.1	1732	85.4	68.0	68.8	594

Rank	University								
45	Keele	80	1.2	310	14.5	1185	90.2	61.6	67.5	589
46	Stirling	79	1.3	305	19.3	1198	86.6	63.6	66.2	576
47	City	73	1.4	361	17.6	1578	88.1	64.5	70.6	571
48	Oxford Brookes	79	0.6	314	18.1	1287	88.5	67.1	62.0	557
49	Swansea	77	1.5	314	16.5	1259	89.4	57.7	60.3	555
50	Goldsmiths College	74	2.3	327	17.6	935	82.8	66.5	53.8	549
51	Brunel	73	1.6	325	20.2	1558	87.8	65.7	59.3	547
52	Robert Gordon	78	0.5	295	19.0	1286	82.2	60.2	76.7	543
53	Hull	81	1.1	309	20.1	1244	83.4	52.0	64.6	539
54	Chichester	81	0.2	290	16.6	1148	88.8	54.0	54.4	530
55	Lincoln	79	0.5	289	19.7	1202	86.1	57.7	55.9	523
56	Ulster	78	1.1	266	17.0	1515	84.4	60.4	53.9	522
57	Bangor	79	1.5	288	20.7	1091	81.1	57.1	59.7	520
58	Plymouth	75	0.7	297	16.4	1306	84.9	61.4	64.3	518
59	Huddersfield	77	0.2	273	17.6	1439	77.6	56.1	69.5	511
60	Northumbria	77	0.3	300	19.7	1183	81.8	58.6	68.0	508
61	Central Lancashire	78	0.4	260	18.4	1642	80.9	52.8	59.6	505
=62	Bradford	77	1.0	268	17.5	1258	78.6	57.5	69.4	503
=62	Bournemouth	74	0.4	297	23.6	1260	87.0	63.6	61.1	503
64	Hertfordshire	76	0.3	244	18.5	1636	83.9	62.1	59.7	501
65	Gloucestershire	76	0.2	264	20.6	1320	84.2	63.0	57.8	495
66	Nottingham Trent	74	0.4	287	19.3	1402	84.1	54.8	60.6	493
=67	West of England	76	0.5	278	20.7	1317	82.1	62.2	61.4	492
=67	Portsmouth	79	0.5	283	20.5	1188	84.4	50.9	56.7	492
=69	Brighton	76	0.9	290	18.8	959	82.5	61.4	55.5	490
=69	Winchester	75	0.4	280	17.7	1017	83.9	60.5	54.0	490
=71	Chester	76	0.1	273	17.2	1085	79.2	57.9	63.4	485
=71	Edinburgh Napier	76	0.3	296	21.6	1133	75.5	61.3	69.3	485

		Student satisfaction (%)	Research quality	Entry standards	Student–staff ratio	Services and facilities spend per student (£)	Completion (%)	Good honours (%)	Graduate prospects (%)	Total
=71	Sheffield Hallam	74	0.4	289	19.8	1056	84.0	61.6	61.8	485
=71	UWIC, Cardiff	76	0.3	267	20.7	1354	84.7	55.3	55.3	485
75	Glasgow Caledonian	77	0.3	302	20.9	1257	79.7	68.4	57.3	484
76	Coventry	74	0.2	298	15.7	1158	77.6	61.4	59.9	482
77	Edge Hill	79	0.1	260	18.5	1107	79.1	51.1	63.2	481
78	Queen Margaret Edinburgh	..	0.3	309	21.7	1082	80.7	68.7	61.8	479
79	Roehampton	73	0.8	259	18.8	1369	82.0	54.7	59.9	477
=80	Sunderland	78	0.5	246	15.8	1113	78.6	49.8	54.8	475
=80	Teesside	79	0.2	271	19.5	1186	78.0	52.6	61.9	475
=82	University of the Arts, London	64	1.9	276	20.2	1148	89.0	64.8	53.1	473
=82	Cumbria	71	0.0	263	16.3	1361	84.8	55.8	66.2	473
84	Bath Spa	75	0.3	293	21.1	741	89.0	69.0	46.5	471
85	De Montfort	78	0.6	259	17.5	1080	81.8	49.8	52.8	469
86	York St John	76	0.1	282	21.2	1199	85.6	58.3	51.8	463
87	Birmingham City	73	0.2	263	20.9	1554	78.7	53.7	67.7	458
88	Canterbury Christ Church	74	0.2	247	18.6	1067	84.5	54.5	63.3	457
89	Staffordshire	77	0.1	241	21.7	1143	79.4	52.4	60.7	456
90	Trinity St David	75	0.9	251	18.7	1170	76.6	48.8	59.7	450
91	Salford	74	0.9	280	23.8	1013	86.4	55.3	55.1	447
92	Northampton	77	0.2	238	22.9	1198	83.1	60.9	52.9	446
93	Glamorgan	74	0.4	279	20.2	1362	74.4	57.6	54.3	445
=94	Middlesex	71	0.5	207	21.0	2305	72.4	55.8	57.8	444

=94	Worcester	74	0.1	271	21.9	956	84.4	54.4	60.8	444
96	Westminster	69	0.5	273	17.1	1273	79.5	56.1	55.1	439
97	Kingston	74	0.3	243	19.9	1155	80.4	61.9	52.3	435
98	Manchester Metropolitan	72	0.4	271	20.6	1133	78.7	57.0	57.1	433
99	Greenwich	79	0.3	215	23.3	1290	79.8	46.7	54.7	432
100	Liverpool John Moores	74	0.4	263	20.9	1200	80.8	59.2	50.5	429
101	Abertay	..	0.3	252	19.4	1268	74.2	51.0	57.7	425
=102	Glyndŵr	74	0.1	231	22.5	1598	76.1	49.4	65.5	420
=102	University for Creative Arts	66	0.5	269	21.6	1583	85.2	53.3	50.8	420
=104	Newport, University of Wales	74	0.3	252	22.5	1061	79.5	49.3	54.5	418
=104	Leeds Metropolitan	71	0.2	267	20.6	941	82.6	52.9	55.5	418
106	Bedfordshire	74	0.2	187	19.1	1368	76.2	44.4	61.2	417
107	Derby	75	0.1	250	20.5	1373	73.2	50.1	52.3	412
108	Anglia Ruskin	70	0.2	254	22.7	1101	82.4	56.9	55.5	398
109	Southampton Solent	73	0.1	266	21.5	1079	74.3	42.7	46.2	384
110	Buckinghamshire New	69	0.1	212	22.3	1467	81.8	49.3	48.8	376
111	Highlands and Islands	..	0.2	269	..	888	57.2	63.0	49.5	361
112	West of Scotland	..	0.1	241	20.1	1232	67.9	43.1	58.3	351
113	London South Bank	74	0.3	201	23.3	1021	76.1	33.9	49.3	337
114	Bolton	73	0.2	222	20.4	625	66.2	45.7	45.4	332
115	East London	70	0.4	200	23.3	998	74.5	44.4	48.6	328
116	London Metropolitan	65	0.3	221	19.7	885	68.3	49.8	45.5	304

Liverpool Hope, Swansea Metropolitan, West London (formerly Thames Valley) and Wolverhampton have refused to allow the release of data, and so do not appear in this year's League Table.

Where needed, data from Lampeter and Trinity College Carmarthen have been amalgamated for Trinity St David. Last year's figures for Completion have been used for Glasgow Caledonian and York St John. The Student Satisfaction figure for Highlands and Islands has been suppressed by HESA.

5 The Top Universities by Subject

Knowing where a university stands in the pecking order of higher education is a vital piece of information for any prospective student, but the quality of the course is what matters most. As the latest Research Assessment Exercise (RAE) in 2008 confirmed, the most modest institution may have a centre of specialist excellence, and even famous universities have mediocre departments. This section offers some pointers to the leading universities in a wide range of subjects. With a number of universities reviewing the courses they will offer in the future, it is possible that not all institutions listed in a particular subject area will be running courses in 2012.

The subject tables in this *Guide* also include scores from the National Student Survey (NSS). These distil the views of final-year undergraduates on several aspects of their course, including teaching quality, assessment and feedback, and the quality of learning resources. The three other measures used are research quality, students' entry qualifications and graduate employment prospects. None of the measures are weighted.

The tables include the research grades drawn from the deliberations of expert assessors in the 2008 RAE. No data have been released on the proportion of academics entered for assessment, for example, so it has not been possible to mirror the approach adopted in the main institutional ranking (see pages 57–61). Data supplied by the Higher Education Statistics Agency (HESA) are used to calculate average entry qualifications and the employment prospects of graduates. The prospects information draws a distinction between different types of employment: graduate employment, where a degree is normally required, and non-graduate employment. The tables give the percentage of "positive destinations" by adding those undertaking further study to the total in graduate employment.

Many subjects, such as dentistry or sociology, have their own table, but others are grouped together in broader categories, such as subjects allied to medicine, which includes such specialisms as physiotherapy and radiology. Not all universities in Scotland participate in the National Student Survey, so to qualify for inclusion in the table a university has to have data for at least two of the other measures. Scores are not published where the number of students is too small for the outcome to be statistically reliable. In the NSS, a 50 per cent response rate is required from a minimum of 30 students.

Cambridge is again the most successful university. It tops 31 of the 62 tables. Oxford has the next highest number of top places with 14, while 12 other universities also gain top spots.

The subject rankings demonstrate that there are "horses for courses" in higher education. Thus the London School of Economics is more than a match for its rivals in social policy, while Loughborough remains a force in sports science and librarianship, and this year adds a top spot in building. In their own fields, table-toppers such as Warwick in American studies, drama, and accounting and finance, Durham in history, Nottingham in agriculture and Aberystwyth in Celtic studies, are equally well-known. But the tables contain less obvious success stories, such as King's College London in communication and media studies, Edinburgh in nursing and Bath in social work.

Research quality

This is a measure of the quality of the research undertaken in the subject area. The information was sourced from the 2008 Research Assessment Exercise (RAE), a peer-review exercise used to evaluate the quality of research in UK higher education institutions, undertaken by the UK Higher Education Funding Bodies.

For each subject, a research quality profile was given to those university departments that took part, showing how much of their research was in various quality categories. These categories were: 4* world-leading; 3* internationally excellent; 2* internationally recognised; 1* nationally recognised; and unclassified. The funding bodies decided to direct more funds to the very best research by applying weightings. The English, Scottish and Welsh funding councils have slightly different weightings. Those adopted by HEFCE (the funding council for England) for funding in 2011–12 are used in the tables: 4* is weighted by a factor of 9, 3* is weighted by a factor of 3 and 2* weighted by a factor of 0.294. Outputs of 1* carry zero weight.

Staffing data to show how many of a department's academics were submitted in the RAE are not currently available. Some research ratings shown could relate to a relatively low proportion of the academic staff in the department.

Entry standards

This is the average UCAS tariff score for new students under the age of 21, based on A and AS Levels and Highers and Advanced Highers and other equivalent qualifications (including the International Baccalaureate), taken from HESA data for 2009–10. Each student's examination grades were converted to a numerical score using the UCAS tariff (see page 18 for details) and added up to give a total score. HESA then calculated an average score for each university.

Student satisfaction

This measure is taken from the National Student Survey results published in 2009 and 2010. A single year's figures are used when that is all that is available, but an average of the two years' results is used in all other cases. The score for each university represents the percentage of final-year undergraduates declaring themselves satisfied or very satisfied with their course, averaged over the seven sections of the survey (teaching, assessment and feedback, academic support, organisation and management, learning resources, personal development and overall satisfaction).

Graduate prospects

This is the percentage of graduates undertaking further study or in a graduate job, in the annual survey by HESA six months after graduation. Two years of data (2008 and 2009 graduates) are aggregated to make the data more reliable. A low score on this measure does not necessarily indicate unemployment – some graduates may have taken jobs that are not categorised as graduate work. The averages for each subject are given close by the relevant subject table in this chapter and in a table in chapter 2 (see pages 36–37).

The Education table uses a fifth measure: teaching quality, as measured by the outcomes of Ofsted inspections of teacher training courses.

The subjects listed below are covered in the tables in this chapter:

Accounting and Finance
Aeronautical and Manufacturing
  Engineering
Agriculture and Forestry
American Studies
Anatomy and Physiology
Anthropology
Archaeology
Architecture
Art and Design
Biological Sciences
Building
Business Studies
Celtic Studies
Chemical Engineering
Chemistry
Civil Engineering
Classics and Ancient History
Communication and Media Studies
Computer Science
Dentistry
Drama, Dance and Cinematics
East and South Asian Studies
Economics
Education
Electrical and Electronic Engineering
English
Food Science
French
General Engineering
Geography and Environmental Sciences
Geology

German
History
History of Art, Architecture and Design
Hospitality, Leisure, Recreation and Tourism
Iberian Languages
Italian
Land and Property Management
Law
Librarianship and Information Management
Linguistics
Materials Technology
Mathematics
Mechanical Engineering
Medicine
Middle Eastern and African Studies
Music
Nursing
Other Subjects Allied to Medicine
  (see page 161 for included subjects)
Pharmacology and Pharmacy
Philosophy
Physics and Astronomy
Politics
Psychology
Russian and East European Languages
Social Policy
Social Work
Sociology
Sports Science
Theology and Religious Studies
Town and Country Planning and Landscape
Veterinary Medicine

Accounting and Finance

There have been big rises in applications for both accounting and (especially) finance in 2011, despite the fact that the subjects remain relatively low in the graduate employment table. Although those who found graduate jobs in 2009 were in the top 20 for graduate salaries, averaging more than £21,500, the 12 per cent unemployment rate was considerably higher than the average for all subjects. There are contrasting fortunes for last year's joint leaders in the latest table: Warwick is now the clear leader, while Exeter has dropped to seventh. Warwick has the highest entry standards and establishes a lead with good scores across the board. Lancaster jumps from sixth to second and Bath, a previous leader, takes third place.

Good scores are dotted around the table. Lincoln, for example, has the most satisfied students, despite being only 39th overall. Salford, Portsmouth and De Montfort also do well on this measure, although none is in the top 20. For the fourth year in a row, Robert Gordon is both the top post-1992 university and the best for graduate prospects. Manchester's courses are run by Manchester Business School.

Strathclyde remains well clear of its rivals in Scotland, however, and is fourth overall. Cardiff, the leader in Wales, had the best grade in the 2008 Research Assessment Exercise, but is again restricted to eighth place because a third of its graduates were without a graduate-level job or a training place six months after completing their degrees.

As in many of the subject tables, higher entry scores and research grades make the difference for the old universities. Entry grades have risen again since the 2011 *Guide*: 19 universities (rather than 16) averaged more than 400 points at A level, while only four had averages below 200 points, two fewer than last year.

In the latest survey, 17 per cent were continuing to study while in a graduate job six months after leaving university – a proportion matched by only one other subject. This reflects the professional structure of accountancy and shows that a high proportion of graduates are going on to practise accountancy. However, more than a quarter of all leavers start work in a non-graduate job and the 12 per cent unemployment rate is well above average for all subjects.

Employed in graduate job:	27%	Employed in non-graduate job and studying:	5%
Employed in graduate job and studying:	17%	Employed in non-graduate job:	26%
Studying:	12%	Unemployed:	12%
Average starting graduate salary:	£21,551	Average starting non-graduate salary:	£16,157

Accounting and Finance	Research quality	Entry standards	Student satisfaction %	Graduate prospects %	Overall rating
1 Warwick	3.8	489	84	77	100.0
2 Lancaster	3.8	401	85	89	99.5
3 Bath	4.0	450	80	84	98.1
4 Strathclyde	3.5		85	81	97.8
=5 Loughborough	2.8	414	85	85	95.8
=5 London School of Economics	4.0	488	74	82	95.8
7 Exeter	2.4	446	85	81	94.7
8 Cardiff	4.3	404	81	66	93.8
9 Leeds	3.4	430	78	80	93.5

	Research quality	Entry standards	Student satisfaction %	Graduate prospects %	Overall rating
10 Glasgow	2.1	450	84	78	92.4
11 City	2.7	415	83	76	91.9
12 Newcastle	2.2	426	83	78	91.5
13 Nottingham	3.4	410	77	75	90.7
14 Bristol	2.4	434	78	80	89.7
15 Southampton	2.7	442	78	71	88.9
16 Robert Gordon	1.0	338	86	94	88.8
17 Durham	2.7	399	77	77	88.1
18 Reading	2.2	407	77	84	88.0
19 Edinburgh	2.2	418	77	79	87.5
20 East Anglia	2.1	388	84	67	87.4
21 Queen's, Belfast	2.7	395	75	79	87.3
=22 Birmingham	3.0	403	79	62	86.9
=22 Kent	2.6	343	80	75	86.9
24 Manchester	3.5	422	72	63	86.2
25 Liverpool	2.2	414	78	66	85.5
26 Sheffield	2.8	376	78	60	84.5
27 Dundee	1.6	338	85	67	84.3
28 Stirling	1.5	316	82	73	82.7
29 Queen Mary, London	2.7	390	75	54	81.9
30 De Montfort	1.8	264	86	65	81.8
31 Northumbria	0.7	328	82	80	81.4
32 Bangor	2.9	274	83	50	81.3
33 Ulster	1.5	304	83	66	81.2
34 Heriot-Watt	2.1	333	77	67	81.1
35 Aberdeen	1.9	321	77	70	80.8
36 Hull	1.8	294	83	61	80.6
37 Portsmouth	1.5	277	87	58	80.3
38 Aberystwyth	1.3	272	86	63	79.8
39 Lincoln		291	94	56	79.5
=40 West of England	1.9	261	81	64	79.1
=40 Essex	2.4	313	74	64	79.1
42 Brighton	2.6	271	78	57	78.9
43 Surrey	2.2	354	73		78.6
=44 Sheffield Hallam	1.2	282	81	68	78.3
=44 Bradford	2.4	293	76	58	78.3
46 Huddersfield	1.0	266	82	69	78.2
47 Salford	1.3	273	88	45	77.5
48 Keele	2.1	292	76	61	77.3
49 Bournemouth	1.3	300	80	59	76.7
50 Glamorgan	0.9	239	85	59	76.1
51 Oxford Brookes		306	85	59	75.5
52 Nottingham Trent	1.3	270	74	70	74.8

53	Glasgow Caledonian	0.6	305	81	54	74.1
54	Leeds Metropolitan		259	86	55	73.2
55	Plymouth	1.3	294	78	46	72.8
56	Edinburgh Napier	0.6	258	75	72	72.4
57	Greenwich	1.0	228	81	49	71.4
58	Manchester Metropolitan	1.5	262	72	60	71.3
59	Hertfordshire	1.5	234	78	49	71.2
60	Northampton		213	84	56	70.5
61	Gloucestershire		306	75	55	68.7
62	Coventry		300	75	56	68.5
63	Central Lancashire	1.3	291	69	51	68.4
64	Birmingham City	1.1	242	66	69	67.6
65	Staffordshire		215	73	71	67.2
66	Kingston		256	79	46	66.9
67	UWIC, Cardiff		254	77	44	65.3
68	Southampton Solent		227	77	47	65.0
69	Liverpool John Moores	0.3	254	77	38	64.8
70	Middlesex		192	78	48	64.5
71	East London		172	83	31	62.9
72	Derby		208	78	37	62.5
73	London South Bank	1.0	180	77	25	61.4
74	London Metropolitan		209	71	39	58.9
75	Bedfordshire		155	76	31	58.0
76	West of Scotland	1.3	243		9	57.3
77	Anglia Ruskin		213	52	62	52.9

» Actuarial Profession: **www.actuaries.org.uk**
» Association of Chartered Certified Accountants: **www.accaglobal.com**
» Careers in accounting: **www.careers-in-accounting.com**
» Chartered Institute of Public Finance and Accountancy: **www.cipfa.org.uk**
» Institute of Chartered Accountants: **www.icaew.co.uk**
» Institute of Chartered Accountants of Scotland: **www.icas.org.uk**
» Institute of Financial Services: **www.ifslearning.ac.uk**

Aeronautical and Manufacturing Engineering

Aeronautical and manufacturing engineering have plunged down the employment table this year, with a higher proportion of jobless graduates than most other subjects. Although salaries have held up in graduate jobs, averaging nearly £23,500 and taking the subjects to the verge of the top ten, the effects of the recession have left the subjects in the bottom half of the table for graduate prospects.

Most of the courses in this ranking focus on aeronautical or manufacturing engineering, but it includes some with a mechanical title. To add to the confusion, manufacturing degrees often go under the rubric of production engineering (*see* General Engineering *and* Mechanical Engineering). The number of institutions in the table now appears to have stabilised after a period of decline.

Aeronautical and Manufacturing Engineering cont.

Bristol and Sheffield, in joint second place, have closed the gap a little on Cambridge this year. But Cambridge still has by far the highest entry grades and easily the best performance in the latest Research Assessment Exercise (RAE), when some of the university's work in this field was submitted in other engineering categories. Only fourth-placed Surrey has more satisfied students, while only Newcastle, in sixth place, has a better score for graduate prospects.

Imperial College London makes the most progress at the top of the table, while further down, Plymouth is the main success story, moving up seven places. However, De Montfort is the only new university in the top half of the table. Swansea is the clear leader in Wales, while Glasgow has pulled further ahead of Strathclyde in Scotland.

Applications for degrees in aerospace engineering were up by nearly 4 per cent in March 2011, following two successive increases of more than 20 per cent. The smaller area of manufacturing and production engineering saw slightly more modest growth, as it did in 2010. Many graduates go on to further study or training to meet professional requirements.

Entry grades have been rising, with Cambridge posting a particularly high average, Imperial also averaging more than 500 points and both Southampton and Bath coming close. But three Cs at A level has been enough secure a place at most universities outside the top 20.

Employed in graduate job:	39%	Employed in non-graduate job and studying:	2%
Employed in graduate job and studying:	5%	Employed in non-graduate job:	21%
Studying:	18%	Unemployed:	15%
Average starting graduate salary:	£23,478	Average starting non-graduate salary:	£14,697

Aeronautical and Manufacturing Engineering	Research quality	Entry standards	Student satisfaction %	Graduate prospects %	Overall rating
1 Cambridge	5.4	567	84	92	100.0
=2 Bristol	3.9	489	79	91	90.0
=2 Sheffield	4.1	433	84	87	90.0
4 Surrey	3.2	382	94	83	89.5
5 Imperial College	4.2	538	71	82	86.7
6 Newcastle	2.9		78	97	85.3
7 Southampton	2.8	493	81	80	85.0
8 Bath	2.4	476	83	83	84.3
9 Loughborough	3.4	411	81	78	83.6
10 Nottingham	3.8	356	81	82	83.3
11 Leeds	3.6	385	78	59	77.4
12 Manchester	3.4	412	68	74	76.2
13 Glasgow	2.1	391	79	73	76.0
14 Queen's, Belfast	2.9	378	75	65	74.9
15 Swansea	2.1	325	77	81	74.8
16 Queen Mary, London	2.0	330	80	71	74.2
17 Liverpool	3.3	406	65	72	73.5
18 De Montfort	1.9		76	73	72.1
19 Aston	1.8	317	82	61	71.6

20 Strathclyde	2.5	362	74	61	71.2
21 Brunel	2.2	364	71	63	69.7
22 Hertfordshire	2.5	237	75	68	68.7
23 Plymouth	0.9		79	68	68.6
24 West of England	2.4	290	70	70	68.5
25 Sussex		340	81	68	67.3
26 Salford	2.2	290	78	49	67.0
27 Portsmouth	1.8	231	83	52	66.8
28 Liverpool John Moores	3.1	241	70	60	66.7
29 Coventry	0.8	284	71	70	63.4
30 City	2.1	313	70	45	62.7
31 Glamorgan	2.2	253	61	58	59.6
32 Kingston	1.2	269	65	61	59.0
33 London South Bank	2.2		71	34	58.8
34 Sheffield Hallam	1.5	267	74	33	58.6
35 Manchester Metropolitan	1.2	220	68	50	56.5
36 Glasgow Caledonian		264	72	43	54.9
37 Ulster		178	67	65	53.8

» Manufacturing Institute: **www.makeit.org.uk**
» Royal Aeronautical Society: **www.aerosociety.com**
» Why Aeronautical engineering?:
   www.science-engineering.net/aeronautical_engineering.htm

Agriculture and Forestry

Nottingham is the clear leader in agriculture and forestry this year, having shared top place with Reading in the 2011 *Guide*. The main movement is further down the table, with Plymouth moving into the top ten and becoming the top post-1992 university. It is joined there by Lincoln, which was second from bottom last year.

There are generally low scores on all measures in these subjects, although satisfaction levels have been improving. Only Nottingham averages more than 350 points at entry, while Aberdeen's top score for research is lower than in most subjects.

Three universities tied for the best student satisfaction score: Aberystwyth, Newcastle and Harper Adams University College, in Shropshire, which was also one of only two institutions to see 80 per cent of leavers go straight into graduate jobs or further training. Queen's University, Belfast was the other. But for a low research score, Harper Adams would have challenged the top two.

Aberystwyth is the top in Wales, while Aberdeen is the clear leader in Scotland, although it will be offering only forestry and not agriculture degrees in 2012. The Scottish Agricultural College, which does not qualify for this table, will then be the only place to take a full degree in agriculture north of the border. Nevertheless, the number of institutions in the ranking has risen to 19, three more than in the 2010 *Guide*. A 22 per cent increase in demand for places on courses in agriculture, following an equally large rise last year, may mean higher 2012 entry requirements. Forestry is a much smaller area, with only 300 applications in March 2011.

Agriculture and Forestry cont.

A quarter of those enrolling for degrees in agriculture and more than a third in forestry do so without A levels, often coming with relevant work experience. About one in seven has been arriving through the Clearing system, although this may be reduced this year. Entry grades have been rising from a low base: no university now averages less than 200 points.

The definition of a graduate job does no favours to agriculture or forestry in the employment statistics, but the figures are still low in several universities. Half of the institutions in the table saw fewer than 50 per cent of leavers go straight into graduate jobs or training courses. More than a third of graduates start in lower-level jobs, although the unemployment rate is not high. The subjects are never going to lead to big starting salaries, but they are only just in the bottom 20 this year.

Employed in graduate job:	38%	Employed in non-graduate job and studying:	3%
Employed in graduate job and studying:	7%	Employed in non-graduate job:	31%
Studying:	11%	Unemployed:	9%
Average starting graduate salary:	£19,394	Average starting non-graduate salary:	£13,934

Agriculture and Forestry	Research quality	Entry standards	Student satisfaction %	Graduate prospects %	Overall rating
1 Nottingham	2.8	385	81	62	100.0
2 Reading	2.1	345	80	76	96.2
3 Harper Adams	0.9	310	86	80	91.4
4 Newcastle	1.8	329	86	52	90.2
5 Aberdeen	3.0			36	88.5
6 Aberystwyth	2.1	253	86	43	82.7
7 Queen's, Belfast	1.4	303	55	80	78.7
=8 Plymouth	0.5	324	80	43	78.5
=8 Bangor	1.8			38	78.5
10 Lincoln	0.7	327	71	53	78.3
=11 West of England	1.8	279		34	76.5
=11 Royal Agricultural College	0.5	265	82	49	76.5
13 Greenwich	1.3	202		52	71.4
14 Cumbria	0.1	304			71.2
15 Nottingham Trent		259	76	45	69.3
16 Sheffield Hallam		271	75	35	67.6
17 Bournemouth		216		52	65.8
18 Worcester		227		43	63.7
19 Highlands and Islands	0.3			18	53.7

» Institute of Chartered Foresters: **www.charteredforesters.org**

» Royal Agricultural Society of England: **www.rase.org.uk**

» Royal Forestry Society: **www.rfs.org.uk**

» Royal Scottish Forestry Society: **www.rsfs.org**

» Sector Skills Council for the Environmental and Land-Based Sector (LANTRA): **www.lantra.co.uk**

American Studies

American studies may never repeat the surge in popularity that it experienced as a result of the huge interest in the election of Barack Obama. But a small increase in applications, following a larger one in 2010, will mean that the level of competition for places remains higher than in previous years. About 550 students started degree courses in 2010.

Warwick remains well clear of the field, sharing the lead for research quality, while boasting the highest entry standards and the best graduate employment record. Manchester was the other research star in the 2008 assessments, while the most satisfied students are at Leicester.

American Studies	Research quality	Entry standards	Student satisfaction %	Graduate prospects %	Overall rating
1 Warwick	4.1	450	88	74	100.0
2 Leicester	2.8	389	91	62	92.8
3 Lancaster	4.0		83	58	90.3
4 Birmingham	2.7	373	85	58	87.1
5 Sussex	3.7	384	76	65	86.8
6 Manchester	4.1	402	79	41	85.8
7 Nottingham	3.0	374	79	64	85.5
8 East Anglia	2.8	366	83	49	84.2
9 King's College London	2.5		78	70	82.9
=10 Kent	3.8	294	86	28	82.2
=10 Hull	2.4	288	90	42	82.2
12 Keele	2.2	319	84	53	81.7
13 Liverpool	2.1	332	79	52	78.7
14 Essex	2.4	276	79	56	77.9
15 Dundee		343	85	44	74.5
16 Portsmouth	2.4	252	84	28	74.4
17 Swansea	1.6	299	76	42	72.1
18 Lincoln		273	82	54	71.9
19 Goldsmiths College		360	76	52	71.0
20 Winchester		256	83	33	67.6
21 Derby		223	80	40	65.6
22 Canterbury Christ Church		210	79	35	63.8

Employed in graduate job:	31%	Employed in non-graduate job and studying:	5%
Employed in graduate job and studying:	2%	Employed in non-graduate job:	36%
Studying:	16%	Unemployed:	9%
Average starting graduate salary:	£17,511	Average starting non-graduate salary:	£14,304

No university saw three quarters of leavers go straight into graduate-level jobs or continue their studies, although Warwick came close to that mark. Just King's College London, of the other 21 universities in the ranking, recorded a success rate of 70 per cent or over on this measure. Birmingham has made the most progress up the table, taking fourth place, behind Leicester and Lancaster, thanks to improved satisfaction levels.

American Studies cont.

Portsmouth is the top-rated new university and the only one to enter the latest Research Assessment Exercise. Dundee and Swansea are the only universities from outside England.

Entry scores are more bunched than in many subjects, with only Warwick and Manchester averaging more than 400 points and only two university slipping below 250. Nine out of ten students taking American Studies have A levels or equivalent qualifications and there is an impressive level of firsts and 2:1s. The downside is in the employment statistics, with four universities reporting success rates in the graduate jobs market of less than 40 per cent, two of them falling below 30 per cent. The subject is in the bottom four for graduate earnings, averaging little more than £17,500, and the bottom 10 for employment prospects.

» British Association for American Studies: **www.baas.ac.uk**

Anatomy and Physiology

Over the past three years, anatomy, physiology and pathology have recovered their popularity after a period of decline. Applications were up by 11 per cent in March 2011. It was already a competitive field, with more than six applications for every place, although average entry scores at some of the universities towards the bottom of the table remain below 300 points. At Oxford the average is more than 500 points, while Cambridge's score is close to 600. Grades are boosted by the fact that the subjects are often a fall-back for candidates whose real target was medical school.

Oxford, which achieved much the best grades in the 2008 Research Assessment Exercise, has regained one of the places it lost last year, with an improved employment score. However, it has been overtaken by Cardiff, which takes second place with by far the best employment record among the leading universities. Cambridge retains overall leadership.

Loughborough had the most satisfied students, although scores in the National Student Survey were generally high, with only three universities registering less than 75 per cent satisfaction among final-year undergraduates. Ironically, the least satisfied were at East London, where every graduate from the previous year's cohort was in a graduate job or a higher-level course within six months of completing the course. Dundee remains the top university in Scotland, while Cardiff is the only provider of these subjects in Wales. Huddersfield is the best-placed of six post-1992 universities in the ranking.

Anatomy and physiology are in the top 25 for employment prospects, with one of the lowest unemployment rates, at 7 per cent. Four out of ten students go on to full-time postgraduate training – one of the highest proportions for any group of subjects. Average earnings in graduate jobs have improved since the last survey, but at £20,400, are still below average.

This ranking covers degrees in cell biology, neurosciences and pathology, as well as anatomy and physiology. Universities often demand at least two science subjects – usually biology and chemistry, although some new universities will accept just one science.

Employed in graduate job:	22%	Employed in non-graduate job and studying:	4%
Employed in graduate job and studying:	3%	Employed in non-graduate job:	22%
Studying:	42%	Unemployed:	7%
Average starting graduate salary:	£20,420	Average starting non-graduate salary:	£14,248

Anatomy and Physiology	Research quality	Entry standards	Student satisfaction %	Graduate prospects %	Overall rating
1 Cambridge	3.1	595	85	82	100.0
2 Cardiff	2.7		86	92	96.8
3 Oxford	4.2	515	77	70	94.5
4 Sussex	2.9	393	89	80	93.1
5 Newcastle	2.8	429	89	73	92.2
6 Loughborough	3.0	393	92	66	91.7
7 Dundee	3.5	472	87	56	91.3
8 Manchester	3.3	424	84	68	90.1
9 Bristol	2.7	449	80	81	89.8
10 University College London	3.2	478	76	72	89.3
11 King's College London	3.0	423	79	74	87.7
12 Nottingham	1.6	428	85	79	86.9
=13 Queen's, Belfast	2.8	362	79	81	86.6
=13 Edinburgh	2.6		90	54	86.6
15 Leeds	2.8	419	83	61	86.0
16 Glasgow	2.7	413	84	63	85.9
17 Liverpool	2.4	393	87	63	85.5
18 Aberdeen	1.6	338	86	84	85.3
19 Huddersfield		339	90	89	82.3
20 St Andrews		520		69	82.1
21 Bradford	1.6		84	70	81.7
22 Leicester		433	84	78	79.7
23 East London	1.6		66	100	79.5
24 Plymouth	0.7	347	89		78.0
25 Nottingham Trent	2.8		76	54	77.7
26 Reading	1.5	347	78	58	74.2
=27 Keele		267	89	61	72.0
=27 Salford	1.5		83	44	72.0
29 Ulster		310	72	78	68.9
30 Westminster		243	75	51	61.2
31 Northampton		221	73	57	60.8

» Anatomical Society of Great Britain and Ireland: **www.anatsoc.org.uk**
» British Association of Clinical Anatomists: **www.liv.ac.uk/HumanAnatomy/phd/baca**
» Physiological Society: **www.physoc.org**

Anthropology

The relatively small numbers taking anthropology – fewer than 750 started degrees in 2010 – make for substantial swings in average performance. The unemployment rate was 5 per cent in last year's *Guide*, for example, but 10 per cent in this edition. A quarter of all graduates go on

Anthropology cont.

to take a higher degree or some form of postgraduate training, but a third were in non-graduate jobs when the last survey was carried out.

Cambridge has retained the top position that it lost to second-placed Oxford three years ago. It has slightly higher entry standards and ties with Oxford for the top score on student satisfaction. It is on graduate destinations that Cambridge really pulls ahead, although it does not have the best score on this indicator. That distinction goes to Trinity St David, University of Wales, where 87 per cent of leavers went straight into graduate jobs or on to further study. However, Cambridge was the only other university to top 75 per cent.

The London School of Economics (LSE), in fifth place, eclipsed both Oxford and Cambridge in the 2008 Research Assessment Exercise, with 40 per cent of its work judged to be world-leading. The LSE also improved its student satisfaction rating this year, but still lagged behind the leaders on this measure.

Anthropology tends to be the preserve of old universities. East London is the highest-placed of four post-1992 universities in this year's table. Third-placed St Andrews is the top university in Scotland; Trinity St David the only representative of Wales.

Entry standards are high: nine of the 21 universities in the table averaged more than 400 points and none slipped below 200. There had been a small drop in applications in March 2011, but this followed a big increase in 2010. Clearing usually accounts for a significant share of the places in anthropology. There are no subject-specific requirements at most universities.

Employed in graduate job:	29%	Employed in non-graduate job and studying:	3%
Employed in graduate job and studying:	3%	Employed in non-graduate job:	30%
Studying:	25%	Unemployed:	10%
Average starting graduate salary:	£20,223	Average starting non-graduate salary:	£14,985

Anthropology	Research quality	Entry standards	Student satisfaction %	Graduate prospects %	Overall rating
1 Cambridge	4.2	514	88	80	100.0
2 Oxford	3.2	506	88	74	94.8
3 St Andrews	3.2	447	86	62	89.1
4 School of Oriental and African Studies	4.0	438	75	68	87.2
5 London School of Economics	4.4	415	72	68	86.6
6 Durham	2.9	413	77	74	84.2
7 University College London	3.7	453	72	61	83.1
8 Edinburgh	3.4	431	72	61	81.5
9 Sussex	3.3	373	71	68	79.4
10 Queen's, Belfast	3.8	346	76	41	78.1
11 Aberdeen	3.5	321	80	38	77.4
12 Trinity St David	2.5	218		87	77.2
13 Goldsmiths College	3.2	327	76	47	76.3
14 Brunel	2.8	306	72	70	76.2
15 Glasgow	1.9	406	83	38	76.0
16 East London	1.9		75	68	75.4
17 Kent	2.5	340	76	47	73.9

	2.8	399	70	45	73.6
18 Manchester	2.8	399	70	45	73.6
19 Liverpool John Moores	2.1	224	76	61	70.6
20 Roehampton	3.3	248	67	42	67.8
21 Oxford Brookes	1.5	311	77	38	66.9

» Royal Anthropological Institute: **www.therai.org.uk**

Archaeology

The number of universities offering degrees in archaeology continues to grow by leaps and bounds, confounding predictions that the economic downturn would produce a flight from non-vocational subjects. The total of 50 universities in this year's ranking is twice that in the 2005 *Guide*. New universities are mainly responsible, their numbers growing from three to 22 over the same period. Many of those attracted onto courses are mature students – often retired – who are studying the subject out of interest and not for career progression. Archaeology is in the bottom six both for employment prospects and graduate salaries.

Cambridge holds on to first place in archaeology, with the highest entry standards and good scores on the other indicators. University College London has moved up to second place, with the most satisfied students and one of the best employment scores. The very best was at Huddersfield, the leading post-1992 university and the only other institution in the table to see more than 80 per cent of leavers go straight into graduate jobs or onto postgraduate courses.

Archaeology	Research quality	Entry standards	Student satisfaction %	Graduate prospects %	Overall rating
1 Cambridge	3.7	514	88	80	100.0
2 University College London	3.7	433	92	81	98.0
3 Oxford	4.1	500	86	64	95.5
4 Durham	4.4	419	87	71	95.1
5 Leicester	3.5	380	87	60	87.1
6 Exeter	2.9	418	82	65	86.2
7 York	3.4	382	91	50	85.8
8 Southampton	3.4	362	83	65	85.3
9 Reading	4.4	333	86	45	83.5
10 Liverpool	3.5	345	80	58	81.6
11 Glasgow	2.2	375	89	53	81.2
12 Edinburgh	3.1	444	74	50	80.1
13 Nottingham	3.1	351	78	58	79.6
=14 Cardiff	2.7	356	77	62	79.1
=14 Newcastle	2.5	342	85	54	79.1
16 Birmingham	2.2	381	76	59	77.4
17 Aberdeen	2.2	348	81		76.5
18 Sheffield	3.4	371	73	46	76.2
19 Manchester	2.8	341	79	49	76.1
20 Queen's, Belfast	3.3	311	84	34	74.8

Archaeology cont.	Research quality	Entry standards	Student satisfaction %	Graduate prospects %	Overall rating
21 Huddersfield		242	86	84	74.2
22 Hull		302	88	65	72.7
23 Dundee		385	86	52	72.6
24 Kent	0.8	305	84	60	72.5
25 Nottingham Trent	1.3	290	75	63	70.6
26 Trinity St David	2.5	236	79	47	69.3
27 Bristol	2.5	368	60	55	69.2
28 Bradford	2.8	230	70	59	69.1
29 Robert Gordon		332	72	71	68.5
=30 Keele		276	85	59	68.4
=30 Staffordshire		246	87	60	68.4
32 Central Lancashire	1.0	267	82	51	68.1
33 West of England		281	83	57	67.2
34 Chester		259	83	55	65.6
35 Lincoln		297	79	49	64.2
36 Derby		256	81	51	63.9
37 Swansea		338	81	36	63.7
38 Bournemouth	1.8	246	72	46	63.5
39 Winchester	0.8	275	86	23	62.0
40 Glasgow Caledonian		279	74	50	61.1
41 Glamorgan		261	74	45	59.3
=42 Anglia Ruskin		279	70	44	57.9
=42 Teesside		263	74	40	57.9
=44 Liverpool John Moores		242	70	50	57.5
=44 London South Bank		244	67	55	57.5
46 Worcester		266	68	45	56.6
47 De Montfort		222	70	44	55.4
48 Coventry		299	64	36	53.9
49 West of Scotland		258		29	52.1
50 Canterbury Christ Church		237	71	28	51.9

» Council for British Archaeology: **www.britarch.ac.uk**

» TORC (Training Online Resource Centre for Archaeology): **www.torc.org.uk**

Fourth-placed Durham has the best record for research, with three quarters of its work rated as world-leading or internationally excellent in 2008. But it is pipped to third place by Oxford, the only university to approach Cambridge's entry standards. Glasgow remains the top university in Scotland; Cardiff the leader in Wales.

Archaeology has produced consistently high levels of satisfaction. Only two universities in the ranking failed to satisfy at least two thirds of their final-year undergraduates in the results published in 2010. The increase in the number of universities offering the subject has had the effect of spreading out entry scores, which now range from 220 points to more than 500. Applications for pure archaeology degrees lag well behind those for forensic and archaeological science, which had seen another healthy increase in the early part of 2011.

Unemployment six months after graduation remains higher than average, at 13 per cent, with another 34 per cent taking non-graduate jobs. The average starting salary in graduate jobs had been improving, but had dropped by £700 in the latest survey, when the average for non-graduate employment was the lowest in any subject. At a third of the universities in the table, more than half of the graduates were either unemployed or in non-graduate jobs six months after completing their course.

Employed in graduate job:	24%	Employed in non-graduate job and studying:	4%
Employed in graduate job and studying:	2%	Employed in non-graduate job:	34%
Studying:	22%	Unemployed:	13%
Average starting graduate salary:	£17,675	Average starting non-graduate salary:	£13,884

Architecture

With more than six applications for every place, architecture is one of the most competitive of the major subjects. Entry grades at the leading universities reflect this, with a dozen averaging over 400 points. Some universities ask candidates to produce a portfolio of work if they have not taken an art or design-based A level. An average of more than 540 points helps to take Cambridge to the top of this year's table, overtaking Bath, which still has the most satisfied students. Sheffield occupies third place on its own, having shared it with University College London, which has the best research grades, last year.

Training in architecture is a long haul – usually seven years, in which the first degree is but one step on the way. Until now, the graduate employment rate has been some compensation, but the recession saw unemployment shoot up to 11 per cent in the last year's *Guide* and rise again to 14 per cent in the latest edition. The subject has dropped out of the employment top 20 as a result. Only two universities reached the 90 per cent mark, compared with 13 in last year's *Guide* and 30 the year before. Glasgow Caledonian only managed 31 per cent positive destinations, and just over half the other universities reached at least 70 per cent.

Edinburgh is the top university in Scotland, while fifth-placed Cardiff remains the leader in Wales. Ulster outperforms Queen's, Belfast, in Northern Ireland. New universities take up more than half the table, with Brighton the highest-placed of eight in the top 20.

A third of all undergraduates enter architecture degrees with qualifications other than A level or Advanced Highers. A series of increases in applications continued in the spring of 2011, when there was another 3 per cent rise. Satisfaction rates are higher after graduation than during the course itself – three years into their careers, architects were among the least likely of all graduates to say that they wished they had taken a different degree or chosen a different profession.

This cannot be a matter of money: architecture is in the bottom ten subjects for graduate starting salaries, averaging less than £18,000, compared with more the £19,000 a year earlier.

Employed in graduate job:	42%	Employed in non-graduate job and studying:	1%
Employed in graduate job and studying:	9%	Employed in non-graduate job:	17%
Studying:	17%	Unemployed:	14%
Average starting graduate salary:	£17,873	Average starting non-graduate salary:	£14,526

Architecture

	Research quality	Entry standards	Student satisfaction %	Graduate prospects %	Overall rating
1 Cambridge	4.3	542		87	100.0
2 Bath	3.7	515	85	92	98.9
3 Sheffield	4.0	452	79	80	91.0
4 University College London	4.4	470	73	79	90.0
5 Cardiff	3.2	484	78	74	87.5
6 Nottingham	1.9	458		89	85.8
7 Edinburgh	3.7	454	66	82	84.6
8 Liverpool	4.1	423	74	67	84.4
9 Manchester School of Architecture	2.3	444	74	83	83.9
10 Brighton	4.1	380	72	70	82.3
11 Newcastle	3.4	429	63	82	81.0
12 Northumbria	1.9	355	79	78	79.5
13 Liverpool John Moores	2.8	302	81	59	76.0
14 Sheffield Hallam	1.8	309	83	67	75.7
15 Plymouth	2.3	357	69	74	75.1
16 Dundee	1.6	393	77	63	75.0
17 Ulster	2.9	292	73	69	74.6
18 West of England	1.8	290	78	71	73.9
19 Robert Gordon	1.6	333	64	88	73.6
=20 Westminster	3.1	332	70	61	73.5
=20 Strathclyde	1.6	423	54	91	73.5
22 Lincoln	1.4	330	79	61	72.3
23 Oxford Brookes		406	75	70	71.6
24 Salford	3.5	292	61		69.9
=25 Kent		351	69	82	69.6
=25 De Montfort	2.9	279	59	76	69.6
27 Portsmouth	0.4	322	74	72	69.4
=28 Huddersfield		295	76	77	69.1
=28 Greenwich	1.9	256	78	57	69.1
30 Queen's, Belfast		347	71	77	69.0
31 Nottingham Trent	1.0	341	67	72	68.9
32 Central Lancashire	1.6	319	65		66.0
33 University for Creative Arts		294	74	68	65.8
34 London Metropolitan	2.2	291	63	60	65.4
35 Glasgow Caledonian	2.8		71	31	62.4
36 Kingston		306	69	61	62.0
37 East London		274	70	63	61.7
38 Leeds Metropolitan		291	64	70	61.3
39 London South Bank		213	75	56	59.1
40 Birmingham City		309	59	62	57.7
41 Arts University College, Bournemouth	0.3	297			56.4
42 Southampton Solent		244	64	54	54.8
43 Derby		242	64	51	54.1

44 UWIC, Cardiff		222	60	60	53.9
45 Glamorgan	2.2		54	42	53.5

» Design Council (now incorporating CABE): **www.designcouncil.org.uk**
» Royal Institute of British Architects: **www.architecture.com**
» Royal Incorporation of Architects in Scotland: **www.rias.org.uk**

Art and Design

Applications for places in art and design were up by more than a third in 2010 and there has been another increase of close to 10 per cent by the spring of 2011.

Increases have continued despite employment rates and average starting salaries that are both in the bottom ten for all subjects. Artists and designers accept that they are likely to have a period of self-employment early in their career while they find a way to pursue their vocation, but two thirds of those surveyed three years after graduation said they would make the same choice again. More than 40 per cent of all leavers went straight into graduate-level jobs, but only 8 per cent went on to take another full-time course – one of the lowest proportions for any subject. Only four subjects have a higher unemployment rate than the 14 per cent for art and design in the latest survey.

Most courses in art and design are at new universities – often in former art colleges – but the top 11 places in this year's ranking are all filled by older institutions. Oxford, the oldest of them all, where fine art is taught at the Ruskin School of Drawing, regains top place this year. It has the highest entry standards and among the most satisfied students in the UK. Last year's leader, University College London, where students attend the Slade School of Fine Art, is back in second place, sharing the best research score with Kent. The two universities benefited from the revaluation of grades in the 2008 Research Assessment Exercise to reward world-leading submissions, mirroring the system used to allocate research grants.

The best employment prospects – a rare 100 per cent score in a difficult year for the graduate jobs market – were at Roehampton, the top post-1992 university. Edge Hill was the only other university to see more than 80 per cent of leavers go straight into graduate jobs or further study. Aberystwyth has overtaken Bangor to become the top university in Wales, while Edinburgh remains in third place, fractionally ahead of Glasgow as the top university in Scotland.

Falmouth University College, in 19th place, finishes higher than most of the former polytechnics. However, the college has slipped behind Bournemouth, as well as Roehampton, this year. Low entry grades and research scores count against many of the new universities and colleges, although most artists would argue that these are of less significance than in other subjects.

Employed in graduate job:	38%	Employed in non-graduate job and studying:	4%
Employed in graduate job and studying:	3%	Employed in non-graduate job:	34%
Studying:	8%	Unemployed:	14%
Average starting graduate salary:	£17,326	Average starting non-graduate salary:	£13,853

Art and Design	Research quality	Entry standards	Student satisfaction %	Graduate prospects %	Overall rating
1 Oxford	3.8	441	83	67	100.0
2 University College London	4.3	360		70	95.7
3 Edinburgh	2.8	438	73	76	94.9
4 Glasgow	3.3		83	65	91.4
5 Brunel	1.2	374	85	73	91.0
6 Lancaster	4.0	360	78	61	90.5
7 Loughborough	4.0	324	82	56	88.7
8 Newcastle	4.1	358	75	57	88.4
9 Reading	4.2	368	63	69	86.8
10 Leeds	3.3	380	69	58	85.2
11 Dundee	3.8	330	75	53	84.5
12 Roehampton		301	71	100	83.3
13 Goldsmiths College	3.5	337	73	51	83.1
14 Kent	4.3	342	59	69	83.0
15 Bournemouth	3.1	281	78	60	82.6
16 Heriot-Watt	2.5	306	66	80	82.4
17 Aberystwyth		347	84	55	80.9
18 Bangor		294	78	79	80.7
19 Falmouth University College	1.4	289	82	56	79.5
20 Brighton	4.1	318	72	40	79.4
21 Edge Hill		253	78	84	79.1
22 Robert Gordon	1.7	319	72	57	77.9
23 Nottingham Trent	1.4	304	72	62	77.7
24 Westminster	3.5	304	71	44	77.6
25 UWIC, Cardiff	2.8	287	78	41	77.5
26 Lincoln	0.9	300	78	54	77.0
27 Kingston	1.0	313	74	56	76.4
28 Arts University College, Bournemouth	0.3	294	77	58	75.3
=29 Northumbria	2.3	292	68	55	75.2
=29 West of England	2.5	277	75	45	75.2
31 University of the Arts, London	3.1	277	64	56	74.5
=32 Birmingham City	3.7	282	66	44	74.0
=32 Teesside		285	82	49	74.0
34 Edinburgh Napier	0.9	324	62	64	73.0
35 Norwich University College of the Arts	1.5	294	73	44	72.9
36 Coventry	1.7	320	66	48	72.4
=37 Southampton	1.2	350	66	44	72.2
=37 Sheffield Hallam	2.7	282	67	45	72.2
=37 Manchester Metropolitan	2.1	287	70	45	72.2
40 Oxford Brookes	2.0	260	76	40	72.0
41 De Montfort	1.7	260	70	54	71.8
42 Ulster	2.6	265	70	41	71.5
=43 Plymouth	2.3	287	67	44	71.2

=43 Derby	1.2	275	74	45	71.2
45 Essex		228	77	60	70.9
46 Bath Spa	1.1	289	72	44	70.8
47 Sunderland	1.6	242	74	45	70.2
48 Chester	0.2	278	71	53	69.6
49 Huddersfield		262	75	52	69.5
50 Hull		243	81	44	69.2
51 Newport	2.8	257	64	43	69.0
52 Leeds Metropolitan	0.9	251	74	45	68.9
53 Canterbury Christ Church		260	74	50	68.8
54 Central Lancashire	0.5	234	74	51	68.4
55 Greenwich		201	75	62	68.1
56 Portsmouth	0.4	262	77	39	68.0
57 Anglia Ruskin	1.3	263	69	42	67.7
=58 Middlesex	1.2	221	71	51	67.6
=58 Buckinghamshire New	1.3	263	68	44	67.6
60 Glamorgan		280	69	49	67.2
61 Hertfordshire	2.5	213	68	44	67.0
62 University for Creative Arts	1.3	254	66	47	66.8
=63 Salford	1.1	251	71	41	66.7
=63 Gloucestershire	0.8	273	69	41	66.7
=63 Staffordshire	0.3	226	74	48	66.7
66 Northampton	0.2	261	71	44	66.2
67 Cumbria	0.4	304	62	47	65.7
68 Southampton Solent	1.0	283	62	43	64.6
69 Bedfordshire		219	75	41	64.0
70 Chichester		275	74	29	63.8
71 Glasgow Caledonian		316	66	30	63.1
72 East London	1.9	222	60	46	62.7
73 Glyndŵr	0.3	228	66	47	62.4
74 London South Bank		233	66	44	61.1
75 Liverpool John Moores	1.2	236	60	43	61.0
76 Bolton	0.1	235	62	42	58.9
77 Worcester		261	54	51	58.8
78 York St John		245	59	44	58.5
79 London Metropolitan	0.4	215	59	41	56.2

» Design Council: **www.designcouncil.org.uk**
» National Society for Education in Art and Design: **www.nsead.org**
» Sector Skills Council for Creative Media: **www.skillset.org**

Biological Sciences

While other science subjects have struggled to attract applicants in recent years, biological subjects have thrived. The various combinations all registered increases in applications at the start of 2011 – more than 8 per cent in the case of biology itself, which remained well ahead of

Biological Sciences cont.

chemistry and physics in the demand for places. Two thirds of all entrants arrive with A levels or their equivalent, and more than half of the undergraduates are awarded firsts or 2:1s. More than four in ten go on to take postgraduate courses, either full or part-time.

The top five in the table are unchanged since last year. Cambridge has maintained its lead with some of the highest entry grades in any subject – the equivalent of almost five As at A level. Not even second-placed Oxford comes close, although its entrants, too, average more than 500 points. The two ancient rivals also share the best graduate employment record. Sheffield remains third, while Dundee is the leader in Scotland and Cardiff remains well clear of the competition in Wales.

Manchester, Oxford and Dundee achieved the best grades in the 2008 Research Assessment Exercise, while Dundee and East Anglia have the most satisfied students. At 32nd, West of England is the highest-placed post-1992 university.

Entry standards have been rising: in addition to Oxford and Cambridge, another 20 universities, compared with 13 last year, average 400 points or more. Only four universities have an average below 200 points, even though a relatively high proportion of the entrants (11 per cent in 2009) win places through Clearing.

Graduate employment prospects nationally are slightly below average for all subjects. Starting salaries are in the bottom 20 and are particularly low for those who fail to find a graduate-level job.

Employed in graduate job:	24%	Employed in non-graduate job and studying:	3%
Employed in graduate job and studying:	4%	Employed in non-graduate job:	24%
Studying:	34%	Unemployed:	10%
Average starting graduate salary:	£19,265	Average starting non-graduate salary:	£14,248

Biological Sciences	Research quality	Entry standards	Student satisfaction %	Graduate prospects %	Overall rating
1 Cambridge	3.1	594	85	82	100.0
2 Oxford	3.5	522	84	82	98.4
3 Sheffield	3.4	464	88	71	94.8
4 York	3.4	432	89	67	93.2
5 Manchester	3.5	437	84	69	91.4
6 Lancaster	3.1	408	84	75	90.8
7 Imperial College	3.2	494	75	78	90.6
8 Bristol	2.7	472	85	66	89.9
9 Dundee	3.5	361	90	61	89.7
10 Leicester	2.1	436	85	75	89.6
11 Bath	2.2	464	82	72	88.3
12 East Anglia	2.2	379	90	66	88.0
13 University College London	3.2	461	76	71	87.9
=14 Durham	2.2	468	76	78	87.1
=14 St Andrews	2.2	445	81	72	87.1
=16 Sussex	2.3	387	84	72	86.9
=16 Surrey	3.1	384	74	81	86.9

18 King's College London	3.2	414	78	68	86.5
19 Glasgow	2.7	392	88	59	86.2
20 Edinburgh	2.8	443	80	65	85.8
21 Leeds	2.8	385	82	67	85.6
22 Cardiff	2.7	418	81	64	85.2
=23 Nottingham	2.6	409	81	66	85.1
=23 Liverpool	1.9	405	83	70	85.1
=25 Birmingham	2.2	413	83	62	84.1
=25 Warwick	2.2	435	79	67	84.1
27 Newcastle	2.8	372	80	66	83.7
28 Brunel	1.4	328	83	77	83.2
29 Aston	2.5	329	82	67	83.0
30 Exeter	2.2	411	80	64	82.8
31 Southampton	2.2	423	79	63	82.3
32 West of England	2.6	266	86	60	81.5
33 Royal Holloway	3.1	339	76	64	81.4
34 Nottingham Trent	2.8	258	82	64	81.0
35 Queen Mary, London	1.6	386	76	72	80.5
36 Aberdeen	2.7	322	82	56	79.9
=37 Strathclyde	2.6	322	78	62	79.7
=37 Queen's, Belfast	1.3	352	80	68	79.7
39 Portsmouth	2.4	292	84	57	79.6
40 Reading	1.5	358	79	68	79.3
41 Heriot-Watt	1.6	309	83	63	79.2
42 Kent	1.5	349	81	63	78.9
43 UWIC, Cardiff	0.9	272	80	80	78.6
44 Abertay	2.1	228		73	78.5
45 Keele	0.6	282	85	67	76.9
46 Salford	1.5	253	82	65	76.7
47 Huddersfield	0.9	249	87	63	76.5
=48 Plymouth	1.5	334	79	60	76.3
=48 Essex	1.6	260	80	66	76.3
=48 Hull	0.9	316	81	65	76.3
=48 Hertfordshire	1.5	269	76	72	76.3
52 Staffordshire		229	86	73	75.6
53 Bradford	1.6	267	74	70	75.1
54 Sheffield Hallam	0.9	290	78	69	74.9
55 Glasgow Caledonian	1.3	286	80	57	73.8
56 Coventry		307	78	71	73.7
57 Brighton	1.8	273	75	61	72.9
=58 Northumbria	1.3	282	69	71	72.1
=58 Swansea	0.8	326	77	58	72.1
=58 Stirling	1.8	321	76	49	72.1
61 Edinburgh Napier	0.7	285	80	55	71.5
62 Manchester Metropolitan	1.5	261	77	55	71.4
63 Liverpool John Moores	1.4	275	77	54	71.2
64 Ulster		244	81	63	70.7

Biological Sciences cont.	Research quality	Entry standards	Student satisfaction %	Graduate prospects %	Overall rating
65 Greenwich		227	82	63	70.6
66 Aberystwyth		294	84	52	70.4
67 Sunderland		164	82	69	70.3
=68 Oxford Brookes	1.0	301	78	50	70.2
=68 Bath Spa		262	75	70	70.2
70 Chester	0.5	279	80	53	69.9
71 Derby	0.6	243	82	53	69.8
72 Edge Hill		195	74	79	69.7
73 Bournemouth		233	80	60	68.7
74 Gloucestershire		287	77	55	67.4
75 Bolton		193	69	78	67.1
76 Bangor	1.2	298	73	47	66.8
77 Robert Gordon		294	68	67	66.3
78 Leeds Metropolitan		245	70	65	65.1
79 Worcester		268	72	57	64.9
80 Central Lancashire		263	69	62	64.4
81 Kingston	1.2	243	72	44	63.7
82 Westminster		244	72	52	62.5
83 Glamorgan	0.4	302	76	33	61.8
84 Roehampton	0.3	207	64	65	61.5
85 London South Bank		196	73	48	60.0
86 Anglia Ruskin		258	74	38	59.7
87 East London		224	65	49	57.2

» Biochemical Society: **www.biochemistry.org**
» British Society for Cell Biology: **www.bscb.org**
» Society of Biology: **www.societyofbiology.org**
» Society for Experimental Biology: **www.sebiology.org**

Building

The recession did less damage than might have been expected to the employment prospects of graduates with building degrees. Although only four subjects had a higher unemployment rate when the latest survey was conducted, more than half of the leavers had gone straight into graduate jobs and building remains (just) in the top half of the table overall. However, average starting salaries had dropped by nearly £3,000, taking the subject down to 16th on this measure. The decline is reflected in individual universities' employment scores: while only two universities slipped below 70 per cent positive destinations last year, 15 are in that position in the latest table.

Applications were down by 5 per cent early in 2011, following further declines in the two previous years. Entry grades have always been comparatively modest, but the standard at

Building	Research quality	Entry standards	Student satisfaction %	Graduate prospects %	Overall rating
1 Loughborough	3.8	351	89	90	100.0
2 University College London	4.4	395	72	90	98.0
3 Nottingham	1.9	457			95.4
4 Reading	3.7	330	70	78	86.9
5 Manchester	3.1		69	89	86.5
6 Glasgow Caledonian	2.8	319	72	74	82.2
7 Westminster	3.1	263	74	76	81.0
8 Plymouth	2.3	274	83	63	79.4
9 Robert Gordon	1.6	263	71	93	79.0
10 Northumbria	1.9	271	74	80	78.4
11 West of England	1.8	263	76	81	78.3
12 Salford	3.5	316	59	68	77.9
13 Heriot-Watt	2.5	313	65	69	76.1
14 Sheffield Hallam	1.8	296	71	70	75.5
15 Edinburgh Napier	1.5	292	70	72	73.9
16 Aston	1.8	319	73	55	73.5
17 Liverpool John Moores	2.8	246	67	65	72.8
18 Ulster	2.9	239	65	65	72.4
19 Brighton	1.3	246	77	68	72.3
20 Oxford Brookes		257	76	85	72.2
21 Nottingham Trent	1.0	275	68	79	72.0
22 Central Lancashire	1.6	244	66	74	70.4
23 Glamorgan	2.2	271	54	72	68.8
24 Greenwich	1.9	172	71	71	68.3
25 Coventry		261	77	67	67.6
26 Portsmouth		244	76	70	67.0
27 Bolton	1.9		79	31	63.8
=28 Kingston		253	68	66	63.2
=28 Anglia Ruskin		282	69	58	63.2
30 Leeds Metropolitan		245	66	66	61.8
31 London South Bank		230	64	65	59.9
32 Southampton Solent		237	59	53	54.7
33 Birmingham City		213	46	63	50.7

» Chartered Institute of Building: **www.ciob.org.uk**

several universities has dropped in the new table. Only third-placed Nottingham averages more than 400 points, although second-placed University College London (UCL) comes close. Just eight of the 33 universities in the table reach 300 points and one averages less than 200.

Loughborough's lead at the top of the table has shrunk, but it still has by far the most satisfied students and among the best employment prospects. UCL recorded the best grades in the 2008 Research Assessment Exercise, while Robert Gordon, in ninth place, again had the best employment score. Glasgow Caledonian is the leading post-1992 university and top in

Building cont.

Scotland. It is joined in the top ten by Westminster, Plymouth and Northumbria. Glamorgan is the only representative of Wales in the ranking.

Building has been one of the best prospects for a place in Clearing and may be so again if places in other subjects are restricted in 2012. Almost half of all building students come with qualifications other than A level.

Employed in graduate job:	54%	Employed in non-graduate job and studying:	1%
Employed in graduate job and studying:	5%	Employed in non-graduate job:	19%
Studying:	7%	Unemployed:	14%
Average starting graduate salary:	£21,979	Average starting non-graduate salary:	£15,500

Business Studies

Taken together, the various branches of business and management represent by far the most popular area of higher education. Even without the many dual or combined honours degrees that are common for both of the main areas, there were more than 120,000 applications by the official deadline for courses beginning in 2011. That represented an increase of over 8 per cent on the previous year for both business studies and management. The subjects are the biggest recruiters in many of the new universities, although some of the most famous business schools are absent from this ranking because they do not offer undergraduate courses, Manchester Business School provides Manchester's courses.

There is no change in the top two in this year's table, although Oxford's lead over Cambridge has narrowed. The two universities can only be compared on two measures because neither had sufficient responses to produce a student satisfaction score and there are no separate entry scores for Cambridge. Neither Cambridge's Judge School of Management, nor Oxford's Said Business School qualify for the table, being exclusively postgraduate institutions, so both universities are assessed on courses offered by other colleges. Oxford has the best employment score and the highest entry standards in the ranking. Fourth-placed Imperial produced the best research score in the 2008 assessments, while Loughborough, in seventh place, has the most satisfied students.

Even before the recession, employment scores were surprisingly varied. Overall, the subjects are in the bottom half of the employment table, even though nearly half of those completing courses go straight into graduate-level jobs. Three years after graduation, this proportion rises to nearly three quarters. Those who do find graduate-level work enjoy average starting salaries of just over £21,000 – nearly £500 less than last year.

St Andrews has maintained its position as the top university in Scotland, while Cardiff remains the clear the leader in Wales. More than half of the institutions are new universities, of which Robert Gordon is the highest-placed and the only one in this year's top 40.

Up to now, about 10 per cent of those securing places in business and management have done so through Clearing. Entrance qualifications vary widely, with 20 universities averaging more than 400 points and seven less than 200. Satisfaction levels have been improving in the National Student Survey: 14 universities managed to satisfy more than 80 per cent of final-year undergraduates, compared with only nine in 2009. They are spread throughout the table, with Newport, in equal 82nd place, recording one of the top scores despite also registering the lowest employment prospects.

Employed in graduate job:	41%	Employed in non-graduate job and studying:	3%
Employed in graduate job and studying:	5%	Employed in non-graduate job:	31%
Studying:	10%	Unemployed:	11%
Average starting graduate salary:	£21,006	Average starting non-graduate salary:	£15,774

Business Studies

		Research quality	Entry standards	Student satisfaction %	Graduate prospects %	Overall rating
1	Oxford	4.0	560		89	100.0
2	Cambridge	4.4			81	95.4
3	Warwick	3.8	490	81	83	92.2
4	Imperial College	4.7	479		66	92.0
5	Bath	4.0	471	79	86	91.7
6	Lancaster	3.8	418	82	83	90.3
7	Loughborough	2.8	428	88	75	89.4
8	St Andrews	2.5	522	83	71	88.3
9	London School of Economics	4.0	487	72	85	88.0
10	Exeter	2.8	455	85	70	87.3
11	Strathclyde	3.5	420	81	67	85.5
12	Nottingham	3.4	410	77	81	85.4
13	King's College London	4.0	465	73	74	85.3
14	York	2.2	394		79	83.0
=15	Cardiff	4.3	377	75	68	82.7
=15	City	2.7	402	79	73	82.7
17	Leeds	3.4	420	74	74	82.6
18	Durham	2.7	431	77	72	82.5
19	Leicester	2.6	368	79	73	81.6
20	Sussex	2.8	356	77	77	81.3
21	Aston	2.8	388	76	75	81.2
22	Glasgow	2.3	394	80	66	80.8
=23	Manchester	3.5	408	72	67	79.7
=23	Sheffield	2.8	382	77	65	79.7
25	Birmingham	3.0	407	73	71	79.4
26	Reading	2.2	383	77	71	79.3
27	Southampton	2.7	415	76	61	78.6
28	Liverpool	2.2	375	78	66	78.3
29	Aberdeen	1.9	326	81	66	77.5
30	Edinburgh	2.2	423	74	66	77.4
31	Newcastle	2.2	384	72	75	77.2
32	Kent	2.3	293	79	65	76.6
33	East Anglia	2.1	339	79	60	76.0
=34	Heriot-Watt	2.1	344	74	70	75.8
=34	Surrey	2.2	374	71	74	75.8
36	School of Oriental and African Studies	1.6	382			75.6
37	Bangor	2.9	252	79	62	75.4
38	Robert Gordon	1.6	273	78	75	75.3

Business Studies cont.	Research quality	Entry standards	Student satisfaction %	Graduate prospects %	Overall rating
39 Buckingham		257	84	82	75.2
40 University College London		451	80	63	75.0
41 Royal Holloway	2.7	387	70	62	74.6
42 De Montfort	1.8	236	85	59	74.5
43 Queen's, Belfast	2.7	357	74	54	74.1
=44 Oxford Brookes	1.2	321	79	63	73.4
=44 Hull	1.8	278	78	64	73.4
46 Lincoln	0.7	273	84	62	73.2
47 Bournemouth	1.3	316	75	67	72.7
48 Aberystwyth	1.3	275	78	64	72.3
49 Queen Mary, London	2.7	364	70	52	71.6
50 Keele	2.1	273	73	66	71.5
51 Stirling	1.9	306	75	57	71.1
52 Brighton	2.6	275	74	54	71.0
53 Nottingham Trent	1.3	280	71	75	70.9
54 Central Lancashire	1.3	253	77	63	70.6
55 Bradford	2.4	236	77	52	70.4
56 Sheffield Hallam	1.2	285	75	63	70.3
57 Edinburgh Napier	0.6	267	74	74	70.2
58 Northumbria	0.7	315	73	68	70.1
=59 Essex	2.4	280	73	54	69.8
=59 Portsmouth	1.5	273	77	55	69.8
=59 Salford	2.2	268	75	53	69.8
62 Plymouth	1.3	276	75	62	69.6
63 Royal Agricultural College		270	81	61	69.4
=64 Glamorgan	0.9	290	76	55	68.3
=64 Swansea	1.9	312	72	51	68.3
66 Brunel	2.1	341	66	59	68.1
67 Ulster	1.5	250	78	47	68.0
=68 West of England	1.1	267	73	60	67.4
=68 Greenwich	1.0	194	82	49	67.4
70 Hertfordshire	1.5	228	76	50	66.8
=71 Dundee		316	83	38	66.6
=71 Manchester Metropolitan	1.5	254	70	61	66.6
73 Trinity St David		272		63	66.5
74 Huddersfield	1.0	252	69	69	66.4
75 Kingston	2.1	222	74	44	65.4
=76 Leeds Trinity		251	75	60	65.0
=76 St Mary's College, Twickenham		220	80	52	65.0
78 Birmingham City	1.1	231	71	58	64.8
79 Bath Spa		274	78	47	64.5
80 Glasgow Caledonian	0.9	295	75	40	64.3
81 Westminster	1.3	269	70	51	64.2

=82	Newport		252	83	35	64.1
=82	Southampton Solent		262	75	54	64.1
84	Sunderland		241	79	47	64.0
85	York St John		255	75	54	63.8
86	Chester		259	72	60	63.7
87	Northampton	0.8	223	77	44	63.6
88	Teesside	1.2	243	73	45	63.5
=89	Gloucestershire	0.4	255	69	63	63.4
=89	Winchester		263	76	50	63.4
=91	Coventry	0.7	292	72	46	63.2
=91	Staffordshire	1.4	222	68	57	63.2
93	London South Bank	1.0	176	79	38	62.7
94	Worcester		255	74	49	62.0
=95	UWIC, Cardiff	0.4	228	71	56	61.8
=95	Chichester		233	80	37	61.8
=97	Roehampton		208	78	44	61.5
=97	Canterbury Christ Church		214	74	52	61.5
=97	West of Scotland	1.3	242		42	61.5
100	Bolton	0.4	172	75	51	61.2
101	Abertay	0.6	197		54	60.6
102	University College Birmingham		224	72	51	60.5
103	Liverpool John Moores	0.3	254	71	44	59.9
104	Leeds Metropolitan	0.7	262	62	59	59.7
105	Glyndŵr		230		49	59.4
106	Edge Hill		206	70	54	59.3
107	Middlesex	1.3	171	71	39	59.0
108	Bedfordshire	0.6	141	74	44	58.8
109	Anglia Ruskin		225	69	50	58.5
110	Derby		212	72	41	57.6
111	Queen Margaret Edinburgh	0.2	242		41	57.2
112	Cumbria		230	71	36	56.8
113	Buckinghamshire New	0.7	181	67	43	56.1
114	East London		211	69	40	55.5
115	London Metropolitan	0.6	217	61	35	51.8
116	University of the Arts, London		238	54	48	49.6

» Chartered Management Institute: **www.managers.org.uk**
» Confederation of British Industry: **www.cbi.org.uk**
» Institute of Business Consulting: **www.iconsulting.org.uk**

Celtic Studies

Applications for places on Celtic studies degrees were up by almost 8 per cent in March 2011, following a much larger rise in 2010, but there were still fewer than 800 in total. Most of the successful candidates have good A levels, or equivalent qualifications: only two of the nine

Celtic Studies cont.

universities in the table averaged less than 300 points. Students seem to enjoy their courses: no university failed to satisfy at least three quarters of their final-year undergraduates.

Aberystwyth, the new leader of the table, overtakes Cardiff by a fraction of a point, thanks to the best employment score. Cardiff has the highest entry standards, since Cambridge did not have enough entrants to compile a reliable score. Third-placed Bangor has the most satisfied students, while Cambridge, in fourth, achieved by far the best results in the 2008 Research Assessment Exercise, when almost half of its submission was judged to be world-leading.

The ranking is split between four universities from Wales, which naturally major in Welsh, and the remaining six, which focus on Irish or Gaelic studies. Ulster has overtaken Queen's, Belfast this year as the top university in Northern Ireland. Glasgow has been joined by the University of the Highlands and Islands as the Scottish representatives this year.

Only 160 students started degrees in 2010 and the small numbers play havoc with the employment data. Celtic studies appears in this year's top 20 for graduate employment, with more than half of the leavers going on to take postgraduate courses. Only 6 per cent are unemployed, although 22 per cent start their career in lower-level employment. However, Celtic studies remains in the bottom ten for graduate salaries – and even that is an improvement on last year, when it was at the bottom.

Employed in graduate job:	20%	Employed in non-graduate job and studying:	5%
Employed in graduate job and studying:	5%	Employed in non-graduate job:	22%
Studying:	42%	Unemployed:	6%
Average starting graduate salary:	£17,779	Average starting non-graduate salary:	n/a

Celtic Studies	Research quality	Entry standards	Student satisfaction %	Graduate prospects %	Overall rating
1 Aberystwyth	3.5	334	90	82	100.0
2 Cardiff	2.6	427	86	80	99.8
3 Bangor	2.4	371	91	74	97.3
4 Cambridge	5.0		88	56	96.1
5 Glasgow	2.5		87	68	92.0
6 Swansea	3.2	299	77	79	89.5
7 Ulster	4.4	251	84	63	88.5
8 Queen's, Belfast	1.6	347	78	74	87.4
9 Liverpool	2.5	354	79	62	86.6
10 Highlands and Islands	0.9			57	75.4

» You can find out more about Celtic studies directly from the universities listed.

Chemical Engineering

Only medicine and dentistry produce higher starting salaries than chemical engineering. The £27,151 average in graduate-level jobs has fallen since the *Guide*'s previous edition, but it is

Chemical Engineering

	Research quality	Entry standards	Student satisfaction %	Graduate prospects %	Overall rating
1 Cambridge	4.4	583	84	88	100.0
2 Imperial College	4.4	525	77	92	95.9
3 Loughborough	3.4	433	85	90	93.0
4 Birmingham	3.2	469	86	80	91.7
5 University College London	3.2	459	87	75	90.1
6 Manchester	4.1	485	72	87	89.5
7 Newcastle	2.5	418	85	86	88.4
8 Nottingham	3.8	442	76	82	88.2
9 Surrey	3.2	410	83	79	88.0
10 Edinburgh	2.7	463	76	88	86.9
11 Sheffield	2.7	419	80	84	86.4
=12 Bath	2.4	474	76	85	85.4
=12 Heriot-Watt	2.9	336	83	83	85.4
14 Leeds	3.7	432	69	73	80.9
15 Aston	1.8	324	84	77	80.2
16 Queen's, Belfast	1.8	369	75	84	79.0
17 Aberdeen	2.9	339	75		78.9
18 Strathclyde	1.6	419	78	74	78.7
19 Swansea	3.4	280	77	64	76.8
20 London South Bank	2.2	227	71	52	64.6

Employed in graduate job:	49%	Employed in non-graduate job and studying:		0%
Employed in graduate job and studying:	5%	Employed in non-graduate job:		9%
Studying:	26%	Unemployed:		11%
Average starting graduate salary:	£27,151	Average starting non-graduate salary:		n.a

still almost twice the average for lower-level work. This may help to explain the continuing popularity of the subject, which has been growing for several years. Although it is still one of the smaller branches of engineering, applications were up by almost 15 per cent in March 2011, the latest in a series of substantial rises, which took the total over 11,000.

Cambridge tops the chemical engineering table for the tenth year in a row, with much the highest entry standards and one of the two top research scores. It was ranked second only to the Massachusetts Institute of Technology in world rankings published in 2011. Imperial College London, which remains at second, has the best employment score and matched Cambridge's rating for research, both universities having 30 per cent of their work rated as world-leading.

The most satisfied students were at University College London, just ahead of Birmingham, one place above, and the biggest climber among the leading universities this year. Edinburgh remains the highest-placed Scottish institution. Swansea is the only representative of Wales and London South Bank the only post-1992 university left in the ranking.

Two thirds of the universities in the table registered "positive destinations" for at least 80 per cent of those graduating. Nationally, more than half of students go straight into graduate jobs, although the 11 per cent unemployment rate is above average for all subjects.

Chemical Engineering cont.

Four out of five students have A levels or equivalent qualifications, and average entry grades are the highest for any engineering subject – 14 of the 20 universities in the table average more than 400 points at entry. This helps produce engineering's largest proportion of firsts and 2:1s. Most courses offer industrial placements in the final year and lead to Chartered Engineer status.

» Institution of Chemical Engineers: **www.icheme.org**
» Royal Society of Chemistry: **www.rsc.org**

Chemistry

Applications for chemistry degrees were up by nearly 10 per cent early in 2011, the latest in a series of increases, but the number of universities in the ranking has dropped below 50 again this year after reaching this mark 12 months ago when the subject appeared to have recovered from a much-publicised series of departmental closures. Forensic science has become an attractive alternative to the pure subject but, for many, chemistry remains the classic science. There are now more than five applications for every place.

Cambridge remains well clear of Oxford at the top of the table, with the highest entry standards and the best research grades. Both universities had average entry scores of more than four As at A level, and 40 per cent of Cambridge's research was rated world-leading. The most satisfied students are at Loughborough, which has jumped ten places this year from outside the top 20.

Chemistry	Research quality	Entry standards	Student satisfaction %	Graduate prospects %	Overall rating
1 Cambridge	4.9	595	85	82	100.0
2 Oxford	4.1	548	83	86	96.3
3 Durham	3.2	536	84	87	94.2
4 St Andrews	4.0	469	83	82	92.3
5 Nottingham	4.4	435	83	77	90.9
6 Southampton	2.5	461	89	82	90.8
7 York	3.2	466	87	77	90.6
8 Strathclyde	2.8	400	89	83	89.8
9 Sheffield	3.1	432	85	80	89.0
10 Bristol	3.8	474	81	74	88.8
11 Edinburgh	4.0	450	82	73	88.4
12 Sussex	2.2	432	85	85	87.6
13 Warwick	3.2	452	80	80	87.4
14 Loughborough	1.0	366	94	85	86.4
15 Queen's, Belfast	1.8	351	90	84	86.2
16 Hull	1.9	298	91	86	85.7
17 Liverpool	3.4	405	81	74	85.2
18 Imperial College	3.5	501	70	80	85.0

19 Manchester	3.3	429	80	73	84.9
=20 Heriot-Watt	2.2	349	84	84	84.1
=20 Leeds	3.4	397	80	74	84.1
22 Bath	2.2	425	81	80	83.9
23 Leicester	1.7	336	88	80	83.1
24 Surrey	3.1	369	74	83	82.4
25 Glasgow	2.8	371	79	75	81.8
26 University College London	3.0	455	75	71	81.6
27 Cardiff	2.5	384	79	74	80.9
28 Birmingham	2.5	376	77	76	80.0
29 Keele	2.2	301	86	68	79.1
30 Plymouth	1.5	306	83	81	79.0
31 Queen Mary, London	2.0	348	75	83	78.7
32 Aston	1.8	349		77	78.4
33 Newcastle	1.8	375	74	80	77.6
34 Aberdeen	1.7	330	80	75	77.3
35 East Anglia	2.1	404	77	66	77.2
36 Nottingham Trent	2.7	239	78	76	76.5
37 Bangor	2.1	270	76	77	75.1
38 Reading	0.9	337	79	73	74.5
39 Sheffield Hallam	0.9	289	77	74	72.0
40 Bradford	2.6	267	70		70.2
41 Brighton	1.8	240	77	62	69.6
42 Huddersfield	0.9	241	78	68	69.2
43 Kent		288	85	56	68.4
44 Northumbria	1.3	272	74	59	67.2
45 Manchester Metropolitan	1.0	236	71	71	66.6
46 Kingston		241	72	59	61.2
47 Glamorgan		264	73	51	60.2
48 University of the Arts, London		309		47	59.0
49 Abertay		328		43	58.5

Employed in graduate job:	27%	Employed in non-graduate job and studying:		1%
Employed in graduate job and studying:	5%	Employed in non-graduate job:		16%
Studying:	42%	Unemployed:		9%
Average starting graduate salary:	£19,948	Average starting non-graduate salary:		£14,550

The best employment record was at third-placed Durham, although no university satisfied 90 per cent of final-year undergraduates. There were good employment scores throughout most of the ranking, as chemistry moved up the subject table to just outside the top ten. Almost half of all graduates continue their studies, either full or part-time. However, starting salaries have dropped by about £1,500 since last year's *Guide*, leaving chemistry well down the earnings table.

Chemistry is old university territory, with Plymouth the only former polytechnic in the top 30. There are only 11 post-1992 universities in the table and they struggle to compete on research or entry grades. Almost 20 of the 49 universities average more than 400 points at entry, four of them topping 500 points. Nearly nine out of ten undergraduates have A levels or

Chemistry cont.

their equivalent, although entry requirements are not far above the average for all subjects.

» European Association for Chemical and Molecular Sciences: **www.euchems.org**
» Royal Society of Chemistry: **www.rsc.org**
» Society of Dyers and Colourists: **www.sdc.org.uk**

Civil Engineering

Civil engineering has dropped out of the top ten subjects for employment prospects this year, but it is still there (just) for graduate starting salaries. The unemployment rate has shot up from 8 to 14 per cent, although considerably more than half of all leavers go straight into graduate jobs. Those in such employment were paid a little less than last year, at £23,700, but the drop was less dramatic than in some other subjects. Graduate destinations remain good throughout most of the table, with Aberdeen replacing Imperial College London and Dundee this year as the only university to achieve 100 per cent positive destinations.

Cambridge maintains its lead in civil engineering after four years at the top. The university enjoys a predictably enormous lead over the rest on entry standards and has by far the best research grades. Imperial and Bath remain in second and third place respectively. Greenwich, although only just in the top 30, is again the only university where 90 per cent of final-year civil engineers were satisfied with their course. However, Plymouth just pips Greenwich to become the top-placed new university.

Civil Engineering	Research quality	Entry standards	Student satisfaction %	Graduate prospects %	Overall rating
1 Cambridge	5.4	567	84	92	100.0
2 Imperial College	5.3	521	77	94	95.0
3 Bath	3.7	475	88	85	92.5
4 Bristol	3.9	493	80	89	91.0
5 Sheffield	3.8	450	82	89	89.9
6 Cardiff	4.2	416	82	85	89.2
7 Loughborough	2.9	416	88	88	89.1
8 Surrey	3.2	398	81	92	87.0
9 Durham	2.5	524	76	93	86.8
10 Nottingham	4.1	394	82	80	86.6
11 Southampton	4.0	487	75	82	86.4
12 Swansea	5.0	331	78	81	85.1
13 Warwick	3.4	442	77	81	83.9
14 Newcastle	3.9	400	76	79	82.8
15 Aberdeen	2.9	319	75	100	82.1
16 Edinburgh	2.7	444	74	82	81.2
17 Exeter	2.4	416	80	75	80.4
18 Queen's, Belfast	3.5	364	70	87	79.4
19 Dundee	3.5	359	77	73	79.3

20 City	2.1	328	80	85	79.1
21 Heriot-Watt	2.1	336	83	78	78.9
22 University College London	2.7	454	71	76	78.0
23 Leeds	2.4	405	73	79	77.4
24 Birmingham	2.6	400	72	79	77.3
25 Manchester	3.4	418	68	74	76.8
26 Plymouth	2.4	299	79	76	76.2
27 Salford	3.5	294	79	65	76.1
28 Greenwich	1.4	235	90	73	75.9
29 Liverpool	3.0	376	69	76	75.2
30 Glasgow	2.6	358	69	81	75.1
31 Nottingham Trent	1.0	289	77	87	74.0
32 Portsmouth		270	83	84	72.4
33 Edinburgh Napier	1.3	284	75	80	71.4
34 Bradford	2.1	282	74	72	71.1
35 Strathclyde	1.6	391	69	73	70.9
36 Glamorgan	2.2		61	90	70.0
37 Northumbria	1.9		65	78	67.8
38 Glasgow Caledonian		297	72	80	67.1
39 Brighton	1.3	277	73	61	65.6
40 Coventry	0.7	310	71	66	65.3
41 West of Scotland		242		79	64.9
42 Kingston	1.2	206	75	59	63.0
43 East London		265	80	51	62.8
44 Ulster		233	67	82	62.5
45 Teesside		274	74	58	61.8
46 London South Bank		188	71	63	58.2
47 Liverpool John Moores		242	70	50	56.3
48 Leeds Metropolitan		264	69	41	54.6
49 Abertay		232		53	54.5

Employed in graduate job:	51%	Employed in non-graduate job and studying:	1%
Employed in graduate job and studying:	6%	Employed in non-graduate job:	12%
Studying:	15%	Unemployed:	14%
Average starting graduate salary:	£23,720	Average starting non-graduate salary:	£15,501

Dundee is again the top university in Scotland and Cardiff the leader in Wales. There has been more movement in the civil engineering table than many others. Aberdeen, for example, has jumped nine places – mainly thanks to that rare 100 per cent employment record – to become the top university in Scotland. Dundee, last year's leader north of the border, has dropped from sixth place almost out of the top 20 after failing by some distance to repeat last year's full employment.

Entry scores have been rising in civil engineering, with 15 universities averaging more than 400 points this year. Fewer than half of all undergraduates are admitted with A levels or equivalent qualifications, reflecting the large numbers of mature students who are upgrading their qualifications. Applications were up by 9 per cent at the start of 2011, a second successive increase of this magnitude. Some of the top degrees in civil engineering are four-year courses

Civil Engineering cont.

leading to an MEng; others are sandwich courses incorporating a period at work. The leading departments will expect physics and maths A levels, or their equivalent.

» EngineeringUK: **www.engineeringuk.com**
» Institution of Civil Engineers: **www.ice.org.uk**
» Institution of Structural Engineers: **www.istructe.org**

Classics and Ancient History

Oxford and Cambridge are locked together at the top of the classics table once more. They are slightly farther apart this year than last, when only the revaluation of grades in the 2008 Research Assessment Exercise kept Cambridge ahead. The new scoring system, mirroring the one used to distribute research grants, gives extra credit for world-leading research, of which Cambridge had slightly more than Oxford. Oxford still has the highest entry standards in the table, but Cambridge has pulled ahead with one of the two top student satisfaction scores. Glasgow, in 11th place, shares this distinction.

Satisfaction levels are generally high in classics, but employment prospects are much more mixed. Fourth-placed Durham was the only university to see more than 80 per cent of leavers go straight into graduate jobs or on to postgraduate courses. Classicists are often said to be favourite recruitment targets of computer companies and management consultants, but there is little sign of it in the latest results. The subject is in the bottom half of the employment table, with 10 per cent unemployment, just above average. Starting salaries have risen since the last edition of the *Guide*, but classics remains well outside the top 20 by this measure.

St Andrews remains the clear leader in Scotland, Swansea the better-placed of two universities in Wales, while Roehampton is the only post-1992 university in the ranking, rooted to the bottom of the table. There has been a slight drop in applications by March 2011, but the total still reached 5,000 – more than might be expected in the light of the subject's decline in comprehensive schools. Several universities teach the subjects as part of a modular degree scheme, but not as a degree in its own right. A-level grades in classics are among the highest for any group of subjects, but most universities offering classics teach the subject from scratch, as well as to more practised students.

There are more than five applications for every place in both classics and ancient history. Almost a third of graduates opt for postgraduate courses, but the proportion in non-graduate work is also relatively high.

Classics and Ancient History	Research quality	Entry standards	Student satisfaction %	Graduate prospects %	Overall rating
1 Cambridge	4.9	533	90	73	100.0
2 Oxford	4.6	550	86	79	98.7
3 University College London	3.9	464	85	78	93.1
4 Durham	3.5	473	83	84	92.4
5 Warwick	3.5	458	86	71	91.2
6 Exeter	3.7	438	86	63	88.9

7 St Andrews		2.8	462	85	68	88.2
8 King's College London		3.8	411	85	55	85.9
9 Bristol		3.0	438	78	69	83.5
10 Birmingham		2.8	388	84	59	83.0
11 Glasgow		1.5	384	90	50	81.0
12 Edinburgh		2.1	445	76	70	80.6
13 Manchester		3.3	378	83	46	80.3
14 Liverpool		2.2	356	82	58	79.0
15 Nottingham		2.4	407	78	57	78.8
16 Royal Holloway		1.8	361	80	61	77.2
17 Newcastle		2.1	372	82	46	76.5
18 Kent		0.8	331	80	58	73.3
19 Reading		2.2	339	80	38	73.1
20 Leeds		1.3	387	75	51	72.4
21 Swansea		1.2	298	88	30	72.1
22 Trinity St David		1.0	216	81	54	69.4
23 Roehampton			249	69	35	56.8

Employed in graduate job:	24%	Employed in non-graduate job and studying:	4%
Employed in graduate job and studying:	3%	Employed in non-graduate job:	27%
Studying:	32%	Unemployed:	10%
Average starting graduate salary:	£20,864	Average starting non-graduate salary:	£15,013

» Classical Association: **www.classicalassociation.org**
» Society for the Promotion of Roman Studies: **www.romansociety.org**

Communication and Media Studies

Students flock to degrees in this area, despite carping in mainstream media about their currency in the employment market. Applications for journalism and media studies were up again in the spring of 2011 after another big increase in the previous year. Together with mass communication courses, the subjects attracted more applications than mathematics.

The division of jobs into graduate and non-graduate fields of employment hits communication and media studies harder than most other subjects. Academics in the field argue that it is normal for students completing media courses to take "entry level" work that is not classified as a graduate job. Nevertheless, the subjects are bottom of this year's employment league, with 14 per cent unemployment, and in the bottom three for graduate starting salaries.

Communication and media studies are mainly the preserve of the new universities, but older universities have been moving in and now fill the top 15 places. King's College London has taken over from Warwick at the top of the table after climbing from sixth place in the last *Guide*. Warwick's outstanding performance in the 2008 Research Assessment Exercise ensures that it falls no further than second. The university, which also has the highest entry standards, achieved one of the highest grades in any subject for its film and television studies, but an unusually low employment score cost it the lead this year. Westminster matched Warwick's 60 per cent of world-leading research in media studies, but is restricted to 16th place by relatively low scores for graduate employment and entry standards.

Communication and Media Studies cont.

Queen Mary, University of London, is the only university to have satisfied 90 per cent of final-year undergraduates, but it remains behind Sheffield and East Anglia, in fifth place. No university saw 70 per cent of their leavers go straight into graduate-level jobs or continue their studies within six months of graduation, but City came closest, and the proportion dropped below 50 per cent at well over half of the universities in the table.

Westminster is the highest-placed new university this year, firmly inside the top 20, where it is joined by Birmingham City and Central Lancashire. Cardiff remains the top university in Wales, while Strathclyde maintains its advantage over Stirling as the leader in Scotland. Entry grades have started to rise again: four universities (compared with last year's two) average more than 400 points, while three average less than 200 points.

Employed in graduate job:	34%	Employed in non-graduate job and studying:	3%
Employed in graduate job and studying:	2%	Employed in non-graduate job:	40%
Studying:	7%	Unemployed:	14%
Average starting graduate salary:	£17,351	Average starting non-graduate salary:	£14,481

Communication and Media Studies.	Research quality	Entry standards	Student satisfaction %	Graduate prospects %	Overall rating
1 King's College London	5.0	443	84	61	100.0
2 Warwick	6.3	456	84	40	96.7
3 Sheffield	2.0	406	89	63	93.8
4 East Anglia	5.7	373	83	48	93.0
5 Queen Mary, London	3.7	370	90	50	92.1
6 Leicester	4.2	364	82	59	92.0
7 Southampton	3.5	392	89	40	88.7
8 Nottingham Trent	3.6	309		65	88.1
9 Cardiff	5.0	390	74	49	87.8
10 Loughborough	2.9	378	81	55	87.7
11 Goldsmiths College	5.1	356	70	58	87.5
12 Sussex	3.2	346	78	60	87.1
13 Royal Holloway	3.5	376	79	50	85.9
14 Lancaster	4.0	361	76	51	85.5
15 Strathclyde		366		64	84.1
16 Westminster	6.3	303	68	50	83.7
17 Leeds	2.5	393	69	61	83.4
18 Birmingham City	3.7	295	80	52	83.2
19 Central Lancashire	2.1	307	82	57	82.8
20 Stirling	2.8	340	79	49	82.4
21 Bournemouth	2.5	335	73	59	81.9
22 Lincoln	3.1	307	75	56	81.4
23 Liverpool		380	84	46	79.4
24 De Montfort	3.4	264	77	49	78.2
25 City		367	67	69	77.7
26 Leeds Metropolitan	2.6	273	71	57	76.8

27	Birmingham		425	71	50	76.5
28	West of England	2.8	276	80	41	76.2
29	Glasgow Caledonian	1.6	335	75	46	75.9
30	Staffordshire	1.1	258	75	61	75.8
31	Keele		285	80	56	75.2
32	Sunderland	2.9	248	74	49	74.6
33	Brunel	1.8	300	67	57	74.5
34	Hull	2.4	296		46	74.4
35	Oxford Brookes		315	78	50	73.7
36	Brighton	1.5	302	76	43	73.4
37	Aberystwyth		242		64	73.3
38	Hertfordshire	1.5	263	76	50	73.2
39	Teesside		253	82	51	72.7
40	Edinburgh Napier		335	64	63	72.4
41	Surrey	1.3	349	61	54	71.8
42	Portsmouth	1.7	285	79	36	71.6
43	Manchester		390	68	44	71.3
44	Queen Margaret Edinburgh	2.0	307		39	71.0
45	Bangor		278		53	70.9
46	Robert Gordon		263	76	52	70.6
47	Salford	2.5	307	65	42	70.4
48	Kingston	1.0	243	74	49	70.0
49	Northumbria	2.2	291	64	46	69.6
50	Ulster	2.9	257	73	33	69.3
51	East London	3.6	194	76	32	68.5
52	Bradford	1.0	253	70	47	67.8
=53	Southampton Solent		277	74	44	67.7
=53	Coventry	2.2	271	63	46	67.7
55	Chester		248	69	56	67.5
56	Bath Spa	1.3	278	73	35	67.4
=57	Swansea	1.7	274	71	36	67.2
=57	University of the Arts, London		290	63	57	67.2
59	Queen's, Belfast		341	73	33	67.0
60	Marjon, Plymouth		211	79	46	66.9
61	Falmouth		279	68	49	66.5
62	Winchester	1.5	273	65	43	66.2
63	Middlesex	1.4	225	69	46	66.0
64	Derby	2.8	239	70	30	65.7
=65	Worcester		269	69	46	65.6
=65	Chichester		263	80	32	65.6
67	Bedfordshire	2.2	195	67	44	65.1
68	Roehampton	1.5	287	68	32	65.0
69	Greenwich	0.4	221	77	37	64.6
70	UWIC, Cardiff		224	75	43	64.5
=71	St Mary's College, Twickenham		235	74	42	64.4
=71	Liverpool John Moores		287	71	37	64.4
73	Leeds Trinity		238	69	49	64.3

	Research quality	Entry standards	Student satisfaction %	Graduate prospects %	Overall rating
=74 London Metropolitan	2.2	233	65	39	64.1
=74 University for Creative Arts		253	67	48	64.1
76 York St John		268	71	38	63.3
77 Huddersfield		241	69	43	63.0
=78 Gloucestershire	0.1	268	66	41	62.4
=78 Cumbria		270	72	32	62.4
80 Canterbury Christ Church		231	70	41	62.1
81 London South Bank	2.2	200	70	30	62.0
82 West of Scotland	1.6	233		33	61.5
83 Manchester Metropolitan	1.4	256	66	29	60.9
84 Sheffield Hallam	1.7	288	57	34	60.4
=85 Trinity St David	0.6	226		39	60.3
=85 Anglia Ruskin		247	71	31	60.3
87 Northampton		224	76	27	60.1
88 Buckinghamshire New		199	72	36	59.6
89 Glamorgan	1.6	313	56	28	59.0
90 Essex		225		37	58.4
91 Edge Hill		242	68	30	57.6

» Broadcast Journalism Training Council: **www.bjtc.org.uk**
» Chartered Institute of Journalists: **www.cioj.co.uk**
» National Union of Journalists: **www.nuj.org.uk**
» Sector Skills Council for Creative Media: **www.skillset.org**

Computer Science

Computer science, once seen as the guarantee of a lucrative career, again has the highest unemployment rate in this year's *Guide*, an unwanted distinction it shares with librarianship and information management, at a worrying 17 per cent. However, it is not all bad news in the computing world: the subject is still among the top 20 for graduate salaries and almost half of those completing degrees do go straight into graduate-level jobs.

Applications for degree places were up by 9 per cent early in 2011 – the second substantial increase in a row after a prolonged decline. With more than 55,000 degree applications, plus 2,000 for Foundation degrees, computer science remains among the 20 most popular subjects.

The top three in the computing table are unchanged since last year, with Cambridge still clear of Oxford in first place, thanks to the best research grades, by far the highest entry scores and the top employment score. Cambridge's computer scientists average nearly five As at A level, one of the highest scores in any subject, while 45 per cent of the university's research was considered world-leading in the 2008 assessments.

St Andrews, in sixth place, was the only university to satisfy 90 per cent of its final-year undergraduates in the 2010 National Student Survey. It also remains ahead of Edinburgh in the race to be the top university in Scotland. Three years after graduation, more than a quarter of computing students said they would be "very likely" to choose a different course if they had their time again – the second-highest total among 19 groups of subjects.

Aberystwyth has overtaken Cardiff to become the leader in Wales. Only five post-1992 universities, headed by Plymouth, feature in the top 50. The others are Bournemouth, De Montfort, Oxford Brookes and Robert Gordon. Entry standards are spread more widely than in any other subject, average scores on the UCAS tariff ranging from 581 points to only 99, the only entry score below 100 points in any subject. Fourteen universities average more than 400 points, while 11 have an average of less than 200, four fewer than last year.

Employed in graduate job:	43%	Employed in non-graduate job and studying:	2%
Employed in graduate job and studying:	4%	Employed in non-graduate job:	21%
Studying:	13%	Unemployed:	17%
Average starting graduate salary:	£21,712	Average starting non-graduate salary:	£16,465

Computer Science	Research quality	Entry standards	Student satisfaction %	Graduate prospects %	Overall rating
1 Cambridge	5.4	581	84	95	100.0
2 Oxford	4.6	526		92	96.6
3 Imperial College	4.7	506	83	91	94.3
4 Bristol	4.0	492	84	89	92.2
5 Southampton	4.7	459	83	82	90.8
6 St Andrews	2.8	449	90	85	90.0
7 University College London	4.6	421	80	88	88.7
8 York	3.8	471	82	84	88.4
9 Edinburgh	4.7	437	79	81	87.8
10 Glasgow	4.3	381	86	77	87.4
11 Warwick	2.9	485	80	87	86.3
12 Birmingham	4.1	403	85	71	86.1
13 Bath	3.8	404	78	89	85.5
14 Newcastle	3.4	357	82	86	84.5
15 Sussex	3.4	351	84	78	83.6
16 Manchester	4.4	401	77	76	83.5
17 Loughborough	2.7	340	87	78	82.8
18 Leeds	4.0	360	80	78	82.7
19 Nottingham	4.3	354	76	83	82.3
20 Surrey	2.2	397	81	85	81.9
21 Royal Holloway	3.5	321	77	90	81.5
22 Aberdeen	3.4	317		85	81.4
=23 Sheffield	2.9	386	81	75	81.1
=23 Leicester	3.2	350	83	72	81.1
25 Durham	3.2	429	76	78	81.0
26 Aberystwyth	3.7	264	80	83	80.3
=27 East Anglia	3.2	347	80	72	79.6
=27 Lancaster	4.0	373	74	76	79.6
29 Liverpool	4.1	331	78	69	79.3

	Research quality	Entry standards	Student satisfaction %	Graduate prospects %	Overall rating
30 Swansea	3.7	295	77	75	78.1
31 Cardiff	3.4	354	80	63	77.8
=32 Kent	2.9	317	76	81	77.4
=32 Dundee	2.9	309	80	72	77.4
34 King's College London	2.8	380	75	73	76.8
35 Exeter	2.9		77	74	76.4
36 Queen's, Belfast	2.8	327	76	72	75.6
37 Essex	2.9	352	79	57	75.0
38 Reading	1.3	360	74	85	74.2
39 Queen Mary, London	3.8	312	75	58	74.1
40 Strathclyde	2.5	340	75	70	74.0
41 Hull	1.4	254	84	72	73.6
42 Heriot-Watt	2.8	294	78	61	73.1
43 City	2.7	315	72	73	72.3
44 Plymouth	3.8	270	71	67	72.2
45 Oxford Brookes	2.5	234	76	71	71.3
=46 Brunel	2.8	302	75	59	71.1
=46 Aston	1.8	330	74	68	71.1
48 Robert Gordon	1.8	248	77	72	70.6
=49 Bournemouth	1.5	263	74	78	70.3
=49 De Montfort	2.1	236	79	62	70.3
51 Glyndŵr	1.6	226	81	65	70.2
52 Lincoln	2.5	285	74	59	69.1
53 Ulster	2.4	232	77	56	68.2
54 Teesside	2.3	278	75	49	67.1
55 Newman		237		78	66.9
56 Bangor	2.5	243		55	66.7
=57 Stirling	1.8	271		59	66.5
=57 Huddersfield	1.2	256	72	70	66.5
59 Staffordshire	1.0	245	75	67	66.4
60 Portsmouth	1.2	238	79	53	65.9
=61 Edinburgh Napier	1.1	273		64	65.7
=61 Glamorgan	1.6	269	73	58	65.7
63 Northumbria		248	74	76	65.5
64 West of England	2.1	232	70	64	65.4
65 Brighton	2.7	261	67	57	64.9
=66 Sunderland	1.2	234	75	59	64.7
=66 Salford	2.9	220	67	59	64.7
68 Goldsmiths College	3.1	229	71	47	64.6
69 Sheffield Hallam	1.2	253	73	59	64.5
=70 Keele		246	76	67	64.4
=70 Hertfordshire	2.4	182	71	60	64.4
72 Abertay		302		60	64.2

73 Nottingham Trent	1.1	248	67	72	63.7
74 Chester		242	75	66	63.5
75 Greenwich	0.7	182	80	49	62.9
=76 Southampton Solent		253	74	61	62.3
=76 Manchester Metropolitan	1.5	236	72	51	62.3
78 Kingston	1.5	209	73	52	62.2
=79 Central Lancashire		237	74	61	61.6
=79 Liverpool John Moores	1.9	216	70	51	61.6
81 Derby		262	73	58	61.3
82 Gloucestershire		233	71	66	61.2
83 Glasgow Caledonian	0.6	268		52	60.5
84 Middlesex	1.8	150	73	48	60.4
=85 Bradford	1.8	222	68	48	59.7
=85 Coventry	1.4	260	64	57	59.7
87 Northampton		193	75	55	59.4
88 Worcester		214	74	53	59.1
89 Newport		231	76	42	58.9
90 Roehampton		184	75	52	58.7
91 Bolton		226		53	58.0
92 Leeds Metropolitan		193	73	52	57.9
93 London South Bank	1.3	99	74	47	57.8
94 West of Scotland	1.0	255		39	57.5
=95 Birmingham City		230	67	59	57.1
=95 Cumbria		256	64	61	57.1
97 East London		205	73	43	56.3
98 Anglia Ruskin		225	70	47	56.2
99 Westminster	1.2	206	66	45	56.1
100 Canterbury Christ Church		182	69	53	55.7
=101 Bedfordshire	1.0	131	70	45	55.5
=101 Edge Hill		219	61	67	55.5
103 UWIC, Cardiff		203		45	54.5
104 Buckinghamshire New		160	72	37	53.3
105 London Metropolitan	0.4	156	66	32	49.4

» BCS, The Chartered Institute for IT: **www.bcs.org**

Dentistry

The average starting salary of more than £30,000 for dentists is the highest in any subject. Only medicine has a fractionally better graduate employment rate than dentistry. At nearly half of the 13 undergraduate dental schools in this ranking, every leaver was in a graduate job or studying six months after finishing the course when the latest survey was carried out. As a result, not even medicine can match the level of competition for places in dentistry: more than ten applications to the place in 2010, significantly more than in the previous year. However, there was a little relief for aspiring dentists early in 2011, when applications were down by almost 4 per cent.

Dentistry cont.

Most degrees last five years, although several universities offer a six-year option for those without the necessary scientific qualifications. The number of places has been increased in recent years to tackle shortages in the profession, but entry standards are still high: none of the schools averages less than 440 points on the UCAS tariff. Most demand chemistry and many give preference to candidates who also have biology; some also demand maths or physics.

Scores in the subject are so close that the ranking changes frequently. Since last year, employment scores have not been used as a measure (although they are included for guidance) to avoid very small differences distorting positions. Glasgow was top two years ago, but is down to sixth in this edition of the *Guide*. Newcastle is the new leader, having moved up from fifth place to take over from Manchester. Newcastle has the highest entry standards, while third-placed Bristol has the most satisfied students.

Manchester recorded the best performance in the 2008 Research Assessment Exercise. There are no post-1992 universities in the ranking, although that will change when there are data for Central Lancashire, which opened a purpose-built dental school in 2007. The Peninsula Dental School, a partnership of Exeter and Plymouth, also had its first intake in 2007. Glasgow remains the leader in Scotland and Cardiff offers the only dentistry degree in Wales.

Employed in graduate job:	91%	Employed in non-graduate job and studying:		0%
Employed in graduate job and studying:	8%	Employed in non-graduate job:		0%
Studying:	0%	Unemployed:		0%
Average starting graduate salary:	£30,143	Average starting non-graduate salary:		n/a

Dentistry	Research quality	Entry standards	Student satisfaction %	Graduate prospects %	Overall rating
1 Newcastle	2.8	499	86	99	100.0
2 Manchester	4.1	471	84	100	99.3
3 Bristol	3.1	473	90	100	98.9
4 King's College London	4.0	484	76	100	97.9
5 Sheffield	3.1	472	86	100	97.3
6 Glasgow	2.8	470	89	99	97.2
7 Birmingham	2.5	474	89	100	96.9
8 Queen Mary, London	3.8	464	77	100	95.0
9 Cardiff	2.9	471	80	99	94.6
10 Dundee	2.2	476	82	99	94.2
11 Leeds	3.1	462	75	99	92.5
12 Liverpool	2.0	474	78	99	91.9
13 Queen's, Belfast	2.3	441	85	99	91.0

» British Dental Association: **www.bda.org**
» Dental Professionals Association: **www.uk-dentistry.org**

Drama, Dance and Cinematics

Drama has become one of the most popular subjects in UK higher education – consistently in the top 20 for degree applications. Another small increase at the start of 2011 took the number of applications for Honours or Foundation degrees past 50,000. The various degrees categorised as cinematics, which include photography as well as film studies, are not far behind, with a 10 per cent increase taking total applications past 40,000. Even the smaller area of dance has attracts almost 9,000 applications. But the subjects' popularity is not reflected in high entry grades: only six of the 87 universities offering them average more than 400 points at entry. Three average less than 200 points, with most bunched around the 250–300 mark.

Warwick retains the top position for drama, dance and cinematics that it won back last year. It has the second highest entry standards after Bristol and is among the leaders on the other measures. Queen Mary, University of London, holds on to second place, with much the best results in the 2008 Research Assessment Exercise, when half of its submission was rated world-leading. Roehampton's research in dance achieved an even higher score, but it was not sustained over the whole group of subjects in this category.

The most satisfied students are at third-placed Glasgow, the leading university in Scotland. And for the third year in a row, by far the best graduate destinations score is at the Central School of Speech and Drama, part of the University of London. Other employment scores remain low: even at some top-20 universities more than half of the leavers were unemployed or in low-level work six months after graduation. Specialist colleges do well in the ranking, with both the Central School and the Royal Scottish Academy of Music and Drama (RSAMD) finishing in the top 20.

There are no post-1992 universities in the top 20, although Roehampton, Middlesex and Huddersfield all appear in the top 30. This is another table where the gulf in qualifications between entrants to new and old universities is evident, although for drama and dance in particular, this is unlikely to be the main criterion for selection. Some drama courses do demand English literature A level, however.

Drama, dance and cinematics is back in the bottom five both for employment prospects and graduate salaries this year. Freelancing and periods of temporary employment are common throughout the performing arts, but this is yet to deter prospective students.

Employed in graduate job:	34%	Employed in non-graduate job and studying:	5%
Employed in graduate job and studying:	3%	Employed in non-graduate job:	39%
Studying:	9%	Unemployed:	11%
Average starting graduate salary:	£17,477	Average starting non-graduate salary:	£14,158

Drama, Dance and Cinematics	Research quality	Entry standards	Student satisfaction %	Graduate prospects %	Overall rating
1 Warwick	4.4	431	85	67	100.0
2 Queen Mary, London	5.7	389	84	57	97.2
3 Glasgow	5.0	401	87	50	95.5
4 Exeter	4.4	417	86	51	94.4
5 Lancaster	4.0	362	73	75	91.6
=6 Royal Holloway	4.4	391	77	58	91.2

Drama, Dance and Cinematics cont	Research quality	Entry standards	Student satisfaction %	Graduate prospects %	Overall rating
=6 Central School of Speech and Drama	2.6	330	80	80	91.2
8 Manchester	5.3	412	70	58	91.0
9 Birmingham	2.9	390	78	68	90.7
10 Bristol	5.0	444	57	59	86.2
11 Sussex		377	84	69	86.0
12 Loughborough	2.2	384	82	53	85.9
13 Surrey	3.0	361	64	74	84.7
14 Kent	4.3	329	76	53	84.6
15 RSAMD, Glasgow		318		74	83.5
16 East Anglia		428	86	46	83.1
=17 Leeds	3.4	369	69	57	82.7
=17 Hull	2.4	309	83	55	82.7
19 Aberystwyth	3.7	287	81	48	81.1
20 Reading	3.6	338	76	45	80.9
21 Goldsmiths College	3.2	377	69	48	80.0
22 Essex	2.4	292	78	56	79.8
23 Aberdeen	3.0	290	83	44	79.5
24 Queen's, Belfast	2.6	356	76	41	78.4
25 Roehampton	4.2	284	71	47	77.4
26 Middlesex	2.9	261	72	60	77.2
27 Huddersfield		277	76	72	76.8
28 Nottingham	3.0	339	77	35	76.6
29 Arts University College, Bournemouth	0.3	330	76	57	76.3
=30 Brighton	4.1	271	69	49	76.0
=30 Trinity St David		284	82	59	76.0
32 Queen Margaret Edinburgh	0.1	348		58	75.6
33 Coventry	2.2	299	66	58	74.6
34 De Montfort	2.8	263	75	47	74.5
35 Chichester	1.3	330	77	42	74.3
36 Glamorgan	1.3	300	72	53	73.6
37 Teesside		266	82	54	73.3
38 Chester	1.4	271	72	57	73.0
39 Gloucestershire		282	83	47	72.7
40 Nottingham Trent		312	72	57	72.2
=41 Cumbria		297	76	52	71.9
=41 Bishop Grosseteste		213		70	71.9
43 Staffordshire	1.1	240	81	46	71.4
=44 Greenwich		222	80	58	70.8
=44 UWIC, Cardiff		227	78	60	70.8
46 Plymouth	1.9	282	69	47	70.4
47 Edge Hill		292	77	46	70.1
48 Liverpool John Moores		277	77	48	70.0
49 Brunel	2.2	308	69	38	69.8

50	Winchester	1.5	270	72	44	69.7
51	Birmingham City		198	83	53	69.2
=52	Northumbria		286	71	52	68.9
=52	Manchester Metropolitan	1.4	246	74	45	68.9
=54	Hertfordshire	0.9	244	71	54	68.6
=54	Kingston	1.4	248	77	40	68.6
56	Bath Spa		294	73	47	68.5
57	West of England		285	77	42	68.3
58	Newport		261	69	58	68.0
59	West of Scotland		281		47	67.1
60	Falmouth		279	70	47	66.1
61	University for Creative Arts		273	69	48	65.4
62	Westminster		276	69	45	64.9
63	Anglia Ruskin		259	73	42	64.7
=64	Lincoln	1.0	284	63	44	64.4
=64	Bolton		258	81	29	64.4
66	Salford	1.1	280	63	44	64.3
=67	Sunderland	0.9	238	76	33	63.9
=67	Bedfordshire	2.2	197	71	37	63.9
69	University of the Arts, London		267	62	55	63.8
70	Worcester		297	73	32	63.7
71	Newman		212	78	39	63.4
72	Northampton	0.9	241	72	35	63.0
73	Portsmouth	0.4	270	69	36	62.8
74	London South Bank		226	66	53	62.7
75	Central Lancashire		242	70	43	62.4
76	Leeds Metropolitan		253	61	54	62.3
77	St Mary's College, Twickenham		251	71	38	62.0
78	York St John	1.5	289	63	31	61.8
79	Sheffield Hallam		269	71	33	61.5
80	Canterbury Christ Church		272	72	30	61.3
81	Southampton Solent		283	63	42	61.2
82	Ulster		258	70	34	60.7
83	London Metropolitan	0.8	258	62	39	60.2
84	Glyndŵr		214	67	38	57.9
85	Derby		258	65	33	57.8
86	Buckinghamshire New		203	62	36	54.2
87	East London	1.5	186	44	40	49.4

» The Stage: **www.thestage.co.uk**
» UKP-Arts: **www.ukperformingarts.co.uk**

East and South Asian Studies

Two more universities have joined the East and South Asian studies ranking since last year, doubling the total only four years ago, when these subjects were identified as officially

East and South Asian Studies cont.

"vulnerable". Universities come in and out of the table because small numbers of students mean that reliable averages cannot always be compiled, even though courses are still running.

Numbers may well grow in future years, with the clamour for more interaction with China and India. However, fewer than 500 students began degrees in these subjects in 2010. Around half those completing degrees go straight into graduate jobs, but the small numbers make for exaggerated swings in some of the data. Last year's *Guide* showed a huge rise in starting salaries, for example. An average of almost £25,000 propelled the subjects into the top ten on this measure, but the latest figure is below £21,000.

Japanese is still the biggest draw, with more than 1,600 applications by the official deadline for courses beginning in 2011 – twice the numbers applying for Chinese studies. Competition was still high for the 221 places awarded in 2010, with seven applications to the place. The well-publicised growth in the number of schools now teaching Mandarin may be beginning to have an effect since applications for Chinese were up by 15 per cent this year.

Cambridge is just ahead of Oxford at the top of the table, with the highest entry standards and the most satisfied students. Cardiff, which has surrendered second place this year, has the best research score. Newcastle, in sixth place, had much the best of an extremely variable set of employment scores. Edinburgh is the only Scottish university in the ranking, while Oxford Brookes and Liverpool John Moores are the only post-1992 institutions.

Four out of five students enter with tariff scores that are above average for all subjects, so degree classifications are also high. Most learn their chosen language from scratch, although universities expect to see evidence of potential in other modern language qualifications.

Employed in graduate job:	41%	Employed in non-graduate job and studying:	3%
Employed in graduate job and studying:	6%	Employed in non-graduate job:	23%
Studying:	15%	Unemployed:	12%
Average starting graduate salary:	£20,750	Average starting non-graduate salary:	£14,190

East and South Asian Studies	Research quality	Entry standards	Student satisfaction %	Graduate prospects %	Overall rating
1 Cambridge	2.5	555	88	81	100.0
2 Oxford	3.2	548	87	69	99.6
3 Cardiff	4.3	408	84		97.7
4 School of Oriental and African Studies	3.8	436	76	69	91.0
5 Sheffield	1.3	427	82	57	80.4
6 Newcastle		380	79	91	79.2
7 Leeds	1.8	417	72	63	78.1
8 Nottingham	1.6	425	63	81	77.6
9 Manchester	1.8	411	71		75.4
10 Edinburgh	1.7	448	61	63	74.1
11 Oxford Brookes		342	76	31	62.2
12 Liverpool John Moores		221	79	35	58.7

» Association of South-East Asian Studies (UK): **http://aseasuk.org.uk**

» British Association for Chinese Studies: **www.bacsuk.org.uk**

» British Association for Japanese Studies: **www.bajs.org.uk**
» British Association for Korean Studies: **www.baks.org.uk**
» British Association for South Asian Studies: **www.basas.org.uk**
» Royal Asiatic Society: **www.royalasiaticsociety.org**
» Royal Society for Asian Affairs: **www.rsaa.org.uk**

Economics

Economics was one of the few major subjects to see a drop in applications in the boom year of 2010, but it is back on the rise in 2011 with an increase of more than 6 per cent. Competition for places is stiff, with more than six applications for every degree place, and the subject remains in the top 20 in terms of popularity. Economics is also in the top five for graduate starting salaries, reflecting the value that employers place on a subject that they see combining the skills of the sciences and the arts.

Indeed, many prospective students underestimate the mathematical skills required for an economics degree. Many universities demand maths at A level, or its equivalent, as part of offers that are consistently high. Entry standards in this year's table reflect that, with the top three universities all averaging over 550 points – the equivalent of more than four As at A level and another at AS level. Another 12 universities (compared with seven last year) have averages of at least 450 points, while only four of the 68 institutions in the ranking average less than 200 points.

Employed in graduate job:	36%	Employed in non-graduate job and studying:	3%
Employed in graduate job and studying:	10%	Employed in non-graduate job:	20%
Studying:	21%	Unemployed:	11%
Average starting graduate salary:	£25,637	Average starting non-graduate salary:	£16,249

Economics	Research quality	Entry standards	Student satisfaction %	Graduate prospects %	Overall rating
1 Cambridge	4.1	575		93	100.0
2 Oxford	5.3	554	83	87	99.0
3 London School of Economics	6.5	558	74	86	95.8
4 University College London	6.2	508	76	83	94.4
5 Warwick	5.3	519	76	88	93.9
6 Nottingham	4.4	489	78	84	91.6
7 Durham	2.7	507	81	86	90.1
8 Bath	4.0	487	76	87	89.6
9 Glasgow	3.8	425	81	80	89.0
=10 Surrey	3.0	387	88	73	88.8
=10 St Andrews	2.7	515	77	88	88.8
=12 Exeter	3.5	459	82	73	88.7
=12 Bristol	4.4	467	76	82	88.7
14 York	3.4	459	80	75	87.5
15 Essex	5.3	336	82	67	87.1

Economics cont

	Research quality	Entry standards	Student satisfaction %	Graduate prospects %	Overall rating
16 Kent	3.2	339	87	69	86.2
=17 Edinburgh	3.7	455	75	78	85.8
=17 Lancaster	3.8	418	77	76	85.8
=17 Heriot-Watt	2.1	345	89	73	85.8
20 Birmingham	2.9	439	80	71	85.0
21 Southampton	3.7	463	75	75	84.8
22 Newcastle	2.2	412	81	76	84.5
23 East Anglia	2.9	396	83	64	84.2
24 Sheffield	3.1	394	82	67	84.1
25 Leicester	3.4	385	79	68	83.4
26 Cardiff	4.3	413	76	64	83.1
27 Leeds	3.4	446	74	74	82.8
28 Stirling	2.8	314	80	76	81.9
29 Sussex	2.5	384	79	72	81.8
30 Royal Holloway	3.7	400	72	71	80.7
31 Liverpool	2.2	389	80	66	80.4
32 Loughborough	1.8	412	79	69	80.3
33 Queen Mary, London	4.4	403	76	50	79.8
=34 Aberdeen	3.3	334	78	64	79.6
=34 Swansea	2.8	312	84	55	79.6
36 Manchester	4.0	426	70	64	79.2
37 Queen's, Belfast	2.7	364	77	63	78.3
38 Hull	1.8	322	77	73	77.4
39 Central Lancashire	1.3	301	79	70	76.2
40 School of Oriental and African Studies	1.9	465	68	70	76.0
41 Reading	2.2	377	73	60	74.8
=42 Oxford Brookes		292	82	68	74.7
=42 Coventry		323	81	67	74.7
=42 West of England	1.1	280	83	57	74.7
45 Aberystwyth	1.3	292	81	56	74.3
46 Keele	2.1	288	73	66	73.1
=47 Brighton	2.6	268	74		72.8
=47 Portsmouth	1.5	290	79	54	72.8
=49 Nottingham Trent	1.3	278	78	58	72.3
=49 Bradford	2.2	234	81	48	72.3
51 Northumbria	0.7		77	63	72.1
=52 Greenwich	1.0	227	85	48	71.9
=52 Salford	1.3		79	50	71.9
54 Hertfordshire	1.5	250	79	51	71.1
55 City	2.4	373	66	60	70.7
=56 Plymouth	1.3	276	76	55	70.2
=56 Ulster		259	80	58	70.2
58 Dundee	1.8	342	76	38	69.4

59 Staffordshire	1.4	187	73	69	69.0
60 Brunel	2.5	326	67	50	67.5
61 Birmingham City	1.1	252	70		64.3
62 Manchester Metropolitan	0.4	263	69	54	63.6
63 Kingston	1.1	231	71	47	63.3
64 Leeds Metropolitan		268	69	54	62.7
65 London Metropolitan	1.2	192	70	48	62.2
66 Liverpool John Moores	0.3	261	73	24	58.5
67 Middlesex		191	67	49	58.1
68 East London		161	74	33	57.8

Cambridge has regained the lead from Oxford after two years in second place. It has the highest entry standards and the best employment score. Both Oxford and Cambridge were eclipsed by the third-placed London School of Economics (LSE) and also by University College London, in fourth, in the 2008 Research Assessment Exercise. Heriot-Watt, which is in a three-way tie for 17th place, has the most satisfied students, with Surrey and Kent close behind.

Glasgow is the leading university in Scotland, replacing St Andrews in the top ten, while Cardiff remains the leader in Wales. Central Lancashire is the only post-1992 university in the top 40.

Economics is not the sure-fire bet for a good job that many assume it to be: more than three graduates in ten are in non-graduate jobs or unemployed after six months, leaving the subject outside the top 20 in the employment table. But starting salaries in the latest survey averaged more than £25,600 for graduate-level jobs and the £16,250 average for other types of employment is also among the highest for any subject.

» Economics, Business and Enterprise Association: **www.ebea.org.uk**
» Royal Economic Society: **www.res.org.uk**
» Why Study? Economics: **www.whystudyeconomics.ac.uk**

Education

Education is the only ranking that still contains teaching scores – because teacher training assessments by Ofsted at English universities remain current. Northumbria, Warwick and Birmingham University College, only six places off the bottom of the table, tie for the best performance in those assessments this year. But Cambridge, which has entry standards that are more than 80 points ahead of its nearest challenger and much the best research grades, retains an extremely comfortable lead in the overall table.

For the third year in a row, Huddersfield is the only university to register 100 per cent positive destinations, although Glasgow comes within two percentage points of matching this feat, and nine others reach the 90 per cent mark. Education is in the top ten for employment, with two thirds of graduates going straight into schools and only 4 per cent unemployed. However, the average starting salary of less than £21,000 is outside the top 20 for all subjects.

Employment scores at different universities reflect to some extent the variations in demand for new staff between primary and secondary schools and between different parts of the UK.

Education cont.

But even in the bottom ten, there are universities where at least eight out of ten leavers went straight into graduate jobs or further study – and others where less than half did so.

The most satisfied students are at Northumbria, in fifth place, and Derby, which is only just in the top 50. Satisfaction levels are high generally, not only among the final-year undergraduates who complete the National Student Survey, but also in the early stage of careers. Three years after graduation, those with education degrees were among the most satisfied at work and least inclined to wish they had taken a different subject.

Some of the leading universities are absent from the education table because they offer only the postgraduate courses that have become the normal route into secondary teaching and an increasingly popular choice for those wanting a career in primary schools. As such, they are not included in the National Student Survey for the subject and neither entry scores nor graduate destinations are comparable. The University of London's Institute of Education, which achieved the top grades in the 2008 research assessments, is one example; Oxford and King's College London, which ran it close, are others.

Low entry scores have been a concern to successive governments, but only two universities average less than 200 points in the latest table, while most score more than 250. Teacher training courses have become more selective of late and there are now more than seven applications to the place – considerably more than the average for all subjects. The economic downturn helped to encourage a big increase in 2010 and there had been further growth in the demand for places early in 2011, when education was only just outside the ten most popular subjects.

Employed in graduate job:	60%	Employed in non-graduate job and studying:	2%
Employed in graduate job and studying:	5%	Employed in non-graduate job:	18%
Studying:	10%	Unemployed:	4%
Average starting graduate salary:	£20,867	Average starting non-graduate salary:	£14,191

Education	Research quality	Teaching quality/5	Entry standards	Student satisfaction %	Graduate prospects %	Overall rating
1 Cambridge	3.8	3.8	488	84	86	100.0
2 Stirling	2.7		330	83	93	90.8
3 Durham	2.9	3.0	402	81	91	90.0
4 Glasgow	1.6		334	84	98	89.4
5 Northumbria		4.0	321	87	91	85.8
6 Edinburgh	2.3		367	71	94	85.5
7 Sussex	2.9	3.0			87	85.1
=8 Warwick	3.1	4.0	359	74	66	84.9
=8 Reading	1.6	3.7	332	82	81	84.9
10 Brighton	1.7	3.7	319	79	85	84.1
=11 Dundee	1.0		309	85	86	83.8
=11 Leeds	3.1	3.0	325	84	68	83.8
13 York	2.8	3.7	364	77	60	83.5
14 Keele	2.9	3.7	292	83	61	83.3
15 West of Scotland	1.3		291		96	82.9

Rank	University						
16	Oxford Brookes	1.3	3.8	304	80	76	81.6
17	Brunel	0.9	3.3	318		91	81.2
18	Manchester Metropolitan	3.0	3.5	278	73	82	81.1
19	Manchester	2.9	3.7	307	78	55	80.7
=20	Canterbury Christ Church	1.8	3.7	324	68	89	80.5
=20	Strathclyde	1.3		352	73	85	80.5
22	Huddersfield	0.9	3.0	291		100	80.1
=23	Aberdeen	1.2		281	76	95	79.9
=23	Cardiff	3.3		355	75	48	79.9
25	Birmingham City	1.2	3.7	288	76	84	79.7
26	Birmingham	2.1	3.3	353	77	61	79.6
=27	Bangor	1.6		280	85	65	79.4
=27	Bath	2.4	3.3			68	79.4
=29	East Anglia	2.5	3.8	312		48	78.9
=29	Sunderland	0.8	3.3	296	78	85	78.9
31	Plymouth	1.6	3.7	295	76	70	78.8
32	Northampton	0.9	3.7	275	80	70	77.8
33	Chichester		3.0	304	82	86	77.7
34	Leeds Trinity		3.0	272	82	94	77.6
35	Gloucestershire	1.5	3.0	273	78	80	77.1
36	Goldsmiths College	1.6	3.0	210	83	82	77.0
37	West of England	0.9	3.3	260	82	71	76.5
=38	Aberystwyth			253	86	72	76.2
=38	York St John		3.3	305	79	77	76.2
=40	Edge Hill	0.2	3.3	302	74	87	76.1
=40	Sheffield Hallam	1.2	3.0	289	74	85	76.1
42	St Mary's, Twickenham	0.4	3.0	286	76	90	75.9
43	UWIC, Cardiff	0.1		270	79	85	75.7
44	Kingston	0.8	3.0	264	81	75	75.4
45	Roehampton	1.3	3.2	269	74	78	75.2
=46	Hull	1.2	3.2	267	72	82	74.6
=46	Winchester	1.6	2.7	283	75	77	74.6
=48	Worcester		3.5	284	76	75	74.4
=48	Hertfordshire	0.7	3.0	272	79	73	74.4
=48	Derby		3.0	253	87	69	74.4
51	Bishop Grosseteste	0.3	2.7	274	79	84	74.2
52	Leeds Metropolitan	0.7	3.0	290	75	77	74.1
53	Ulster	1.5		239	83	55	73.7
54	Newport	0.1		269	74	87	73.2
55	Marjon, Plymouth	0.2	3.2	261	71	85	72.3
56	Newman	0.9	3.2	249	74	72	72.0
57	Chester	0.6	3.0	281	72	76	71.8
58	Bath Spa	0.5	2.8	289	75	68	71.3
=59	De Montfort			266	83	56	70.9
=59	Nottingham Trent		2.8	282	74	77	70.9
61	Central Lancashire	0.2		200	81	74	70.5
62	Cumbria	0.2	3.5	261	65	81	70.1

Education cont	Research quality	Entry standards	Student satisfaction %	Graduate prospects %	Overall rating
63 Liverpool John Moores	0.7	3.2	265	71	64	69.6
64 Bedfordshire		3.3	211	70	83	69.0
65 Anglia Ruskin		3.0	290	65	78	68.2
66 Greenwich	0.7	3.0	215	70	74	67.8
67 University College Birmingham		4.0	210	74	51	67.7
68 Trinity St David			249	72	67	67.2
69 Glyndŵr	0.2		255	72	64	66.5
70 Middlesex		3.3	199	63	82	65.3
71 Teesside			239	80	45	65.0
72 East London	1.1	3.2	180	67	46	62.0

» Graduate Teacher Training Registry (GTTR): **www.gttr.ac.uk**

» Training and Development Agency for Schools: **www.tda.gov.uk**

Electrical and Electronic Engineering

Cambridge has extended its lead in electrical and electronic engineering, with Surrey overtaking Southampton to become the nearest challenger. Cambridge, which was ranked third in the world in these subjects in 2011, has by far the best research grades and a lead of nearly 70 points on entry standards. Newcastle has the best employment record, with an impressive 97 per cent of leavers finding graduate work or a postgraduate course within six months of graduating, while the most satisfied students are at Kent, in 18th place.

Applications were in decline nationally for much of the last decade, but a recovery that started in 2009 showed no sign of flagging in 2011, when there had been another 8 per cent rise in the demand for places. In its heyday at the start of the decade, electronic and electrical engineering used to attract far more applications than civil or mechanical engineering. It is now the least popular of the three, partly because some natural applicants have been diverted into subjects such as computer games design, but its recovery has brought it close to the total applying for civil engineering. Most of the top courses demand maths and physics at A level, or the equivalent.

Glasgow remains fractionally ahead of Edinburgh as the top university in Scotland, while Bangor has overtaken Cardiff to take the honours in Wales. Staffordshire is the leading post-1992 institution, in equal 33rd place in a table where old universities predominate.

Employment rates have slipped a little since last year's *Guide*, when they already varied considerably between universities. Half of the top 30 saw at least 80 per cent of leavers go straight into graduate jobs or further training, but the proportion drops below 60 per cent at 13 institutions in the bottom half.

About half of the students – more in electrical engineering – come with qualifications other than A levels. Yet it is electrical engineering which has the higher proportion of firsts and 2:1s. Two thirds of the graduates nationally go straight into graduate jobs or continue their studies, but the 15 per cent unemployment rate is one of the highest in any subject. For those who do find graduate work, the average starting salary of nearly £23,000 is in the top 15 of all subjects. Those in lower-level jobs are the second-best paid of any subject's graduates, averaging more than £18,500.

Employed in graduate job:	43%	Employed in non-graduate job and studying:	2%
Employed in graduate job and studying:	4%	Employed in non-graduate job:	18%
Studying:	18%	Unemployed:	15%
Average starting graduate salary:	£22,993	Average starting non-graduate salary:	£18,640

Electrical and Electronic Engineering	Research quality	Entry standards	Student satisfaction %	Graduate prospects %	Overall rating
1 Cambridge	5.4	567	84	92	100.0
2 Surrey	4.0	448	84	89	90.1
3 Southampton	3.5	435	85	93	89.6
=4 Sheffield	3.0	376	89	92	87.4
=4 Imperial College	3.5	498	78	87	87.4
6 University College London	3.4	439	79	88	85.6
7 Bath	3.4	442	79	85	84.8
8 Newcastle	2.8	366	83	97	84.4
9 Queen's, Belfast	3.1	375	83	86	83.3
10 Loughborough	2.8	364	85	87	83.2
11 Manchester	3.7	395	82	76	83.1
12 Essex	3.1		87	74	82.5
13 York	2.4	362	90	79	82.1
14 Bristol	2.6	423	78	88	81.8
15 Nottingham	2.6	371	79	91	81.2
16 Glasgow	3.2	369	82	76	81.0
17 Edinburgh	2.7	399	83	78	80.8
18 Kent	2.2	288	92	82	80.4
19 Leeds	4.2	403	71	72	79.6
20 Strathclyde	2.5	400	80	76	79.0
21 Exeter	2.4	416	80	75	78.6
22 Sussex	2.5		81	78	77.6
23 Birmingham	2.5	382	79	76	77.1
24 Bangor	4.0	201		81	76.8
25 Lancaster	2.4	388	77	77	76.4
26 Cardiff	2.2	357	79	78	76.3
27 Reading	1.6	360	79	81	74.8
28 Aston	1.8	342	84	71	74.6
29 Hull	1.4	292	89		74.2
30 Aberdeen	2.9		73	74	73.3
31 Heriot-Watt	2.4	305	77	77	73.1
32 Salford	2.9	264	78	68	72.0
=33 Liverpool	2.7	382	72	64	71.8
=33 Staffordshire	1.9		72	85	71.8

Electrical and Electronic Engineering cont	Research quality	Entry standards	Student satisfaction %	Graduate prospects %	Overall rating
35 Brunel	1.9	314	80	63	70.3
36 Queen Mary, London	2.5	298	76	62	69.6
37 King's College London	1.6	334	77	64	69.0
38 Portsmouth	1.2	218	85	73	68.8
39 Liverpool John Moores	3.1	262	69	68	68.3
40 Robert Gordon		347	77	80	68.2
41 Swansea	1.6	294	78	64	67.9
=42 Hertfordshire	2.5	195	79	63	67.2
=42 Huddersfield	1.5	291	76	66	67.2
44 Plymouth	1.0	280	79	68	67.1
45 Coventry	1.9	283	74	67	66.9
46 West of England	2.4	268	69	69	66.4
47 Northumbria	1.9	252	72	70	65.9
48 De Montfort	1.5	276	76	62	65.1
49 City	2.1	297	70	58	64.4
50 London South Bank	2.2		71	52	62.0
51 Sheffield Hallam	1.5	245	72	56	61.0
52 Central Lancashire	1.0	241	77	52	60.9
53 Bradford	0.4	262	78	55	60.8
=54 Manchester Metropolitan	1.2	263	69	60	60.3
=54 Southampton Solent		252	76	64	60.3
=54 Westminster	0.6	248	77	55	60.3
57 Dundee		262	77	53	58.3
58 Derby		250	69	68	57.5
59 Ulster		242	67	68	56.4
60 Greenwich		189	75	59	56.2
61 Birmingham City		249	70	58	55.8
62 Glasgow Caledonian		254	72	53	55.6
63 Teesside		261	78	39	55.3
64 Bolton		241	63	52	50.7
65 Glamorgan	1.8	180	53	37	46.5

» Institute of Electrical and Electronics Engineers, UK section: **www.ieee.org.uk**

» Institution of Engineering and Technology: **www.theiet.org**

English

Nothing, it seems, can dent the popularity of English among undergraduates: more than 10,000 of them began degrees in 2009. The subject is not in the top 50 for employment levels and barely any higher for starting salaries, but it remains among the top seven choices by applicants. The number of applications was down in March 2011, but this followed a series of increases and there were still six applications for each place. High entry grades reflect this, with 27 universities averaging more than 400 points and, for the first time, none dropping below 200. Only 15 of the 101 institutions in the ranking average less than 250 points on the UCAS tariff.

Oxford has hung on to top place in English after three years of changes of leader. It does not lead on any of the four indicators but is strong across the board. Cambridge, in second place, has the highest entry standards, while third-placed University College London is the only institutions to see more than 80 per cent of leavers go straight into graduate jobs or onto postgraduate courses. Loughborough, in 13th place, has the most satisfied students, closely followed by Chester, Chichester and Sunderland, all of which are much further down the table. Seventh-placed York produced the best results in the 2008 Research Assessment Exercise, when three quarters of its work was judged to be world-leading or internationally excellent.

Durham, the leader in 2009, is in fourth this year. St Andrews remains the top university in Scotland, while Cardiff has the same status in Wales. De Montfort is easily the top post-1992 university, holding on to its place in the top 30 and finishing above the likes of Birmingham and Manchester in the table. Leeds Trinity University College also does well to finish in the top 40.

Almost a third of English graduates continue their studies – more than go into graduate-level jobs. Unemployment is no higher than the average for all subjects, but approaching four out of ten graduates start out in lower-level jobs. However, English has produced consistently good scores in the National Student Survey. In the results published in 2010, only three universities out of 97 failed to satisfy at least 70 per cent of the final-year undergraduates.

Employed in graduate job:	26%	Employed in non-graduate job and studying:	5%
Employed in graduate job and studying:	3%	Employed in non-graduate job:	33%
Studying:	24%	Unemployed:	9%
Average starting graduate salary:	£18,343	Average starting non-graduate salary:	£14,303

English	Research quality	Entry standards	Student satisfaction %	Graduate prospects %	Overall rating
1 Oxford	4.4	504	87	78	100.0
2 Cambridge	4.4	529	87	70	98.6
3 University College London	3.8	486	85	81	97.5
4 Durham	3.7	497	86	76	96.9
5 Warwick	4.1	487	84	74	95.6
6 Exeter	4.7	459	86	67	95.5
7 York	5.0	490	80	74	95.1
8 St Andrews	4.3	480	81	69	92.9
9 Queen Mary, London	4.6	401	85	64	91.8
10 Nottingham	4.3	459	79	71	91.1
11 Leicester	2.8	416	87	68	91.0
12 Leeds	4.1	449	83	61	90.5
13 Loughborough	2.2	398	89	68	90.1
14 Lancaster	3.1	425	84	69	89.9
15 Liverpool	3.8	425	83	62	89.6
16 Southampton	3.5	429	84	60	89.1
=17 Glasgow	4.3	402	85	54	88.8

English cont.

	Research quality	Entry standards	Student satisfaction %	Graduate prospects %	Overall rating
=17 Edinburgh	4.6	438	79	62	88.8
19 Sussex	3.0	415	82	70	88.7
20 Newcastle	3.7	444	79	61	87.2
=21 Sheffield	3.6	437	79	62	87.0
=21 Aberdeen	3.8	330	87	56	87.0
23 Cardiff	4.0	425	80	57	86.8
24 East Anglia	3.2	421	84	54	86.7
25 Bristol	3.4	503	72	69	86.4
26 Kent	3.8	345	82	60	85.3
27 Reading	3.5	381	83	52	84.4
28 Hull	2.4	320	83	65	83.3
29 De Montfort	4.3	279	83	53	83.0
=30 Strathclyde	2.4	368	79	67	82.9
=30 Royal Holloway	3.8	426	74	59	82.9
32 King's College London	3.1	450	72	65	82.6
33 Dundee	2.1	361	86	50	82.1
=34 Manchester	4.1	426	73	53	81.4
=34 Birmingham	3.4	429	72	60	81.4
36 Queen's, Belfast	4.1	363	77	48	81.0
37 Keele	2.2	329	80	61	80.4
38 Leeds Trinity	1.1	239	81	79	80.2
39 Chester	1.0	305	88	54	79.9
=40 Stirling	2.4	317	81	54	79.3
=40 Aberystwyth	2.0	311	84	51	79.3
=42 Essex	2.4	325	79	56	78.8
=42 Sunderland	1.9	229	88	52	78.8
44 Roehampton	1.8	300	81	56	77.8
=45 Portsmouth	2.4	298	84	44	77.7
=45 Nottingham Trent	2.3	297	80	54	77.7
47 Oxford Brookes	1.7	342	81	50	77.6
48 Goldsmiths College	2.9	360	76	48	77.5
49 Huddersfield	1.0	312	80	61	77.2
50 Lincoln		294	85	61	77.1
=51 Edge Hill	0.7	262	81	68	77.0
=51 Anglia Ruskin	2.8	258	77	58	77.0
53 Newman		264	81	71	76.6
54 Brunel	2.4	310	74	60	76.1
55 Swansea	2.5	338	78	45	76.0
56 Cumbria	0.4	255		72	75.8
57 Sheffield Hallam	1.4	323	81	48	75.7
=58 Northumbria	1.2	317	79	54	75.6
=58 Teesside		275	85	58	75.6
60 Hertfordshire	2.1	280	79	50	75.3

61	Glamorgan	2.2	268	84	38	75.0
62	Bath Spa	1.3	310	78	53	74.8
63	Bishop Grosseteste	0.2	265		69	74.7
=64	Central Lancashire	0.7	279	82	52	74.6
=64	Edinburgh Napier	1.1	307	80		74.6
66	Staffordshire	1.1	235	77	66	74.3
67	Bangor	2.4	295	79	42	74.1
68	Bedfordshire	2.2	207	80	52	74.0
69	Plymouth	1.6	293	78	50	73.9
70	Winchester		311	84	46	73.7
71	Chichester	0.9	294	88	31	73.6
72	St Mary's College, Twickenham	1.3	238	82	49	73.5
73	Worcester	1.2	292	77	54	73.4
74	West of England	1.4	298	81	40	72.8
75	Gloucestershire	1.5	267	80	44	72.7
=76	Manchester Metropolitan	2.1	320	75	43	72.3
=76	Ulster	1.5	253	83	38	72.3
78	York St John	0.4	298	79	49	72.1
79	Birmingham City	1.1	241	70	72	71.7
80	Salford	1.8	292	74	49	71.6
=81	Aston	1.0	333	76	45	71.5
=81	Kingston	1.9	261	77	45	71.5
83	Canterbury Christ Church	0.7	268	78	50	71.2
=84	Liverpool John Moores	1.3	281	83	31	71.1
=84	Middlesex	1.5	220	75	56	71.1
86	Trinity St David	0.6	256	74	59	70.5
=87	Greenwich	0.8	215	80	49	70.4
=87	Northampton	0.6	255	82	40	70.4
89	Falmouth University College		286	80	45	70.1
90	Westminster	0.7	272	72	59	69.6
91	Brighton	1.5	314	73	42	69.1
92	Derby		242	81	43	68.7
93	Marjon, Plymouth	0.1	218	80	44	67.8
94	Leeds Metropolitan		281	72	55	67.6
95	Coventry	0.7	284	69	53	66.7
96	Bradford	1.2	219	76	38	66.1
97	Bolton	0.4	223		45	65.3
98	East London		206	78	36	63.8
99	London Metropolitan		230	66	59	63.3
100	UWIC, Cardiff		277	69	29	59.1
101	London South Bank		208		25	56.4

» Poetry Society: **www.poetrysociety.org.uk**
» Royal Society of Literature: **www.rslit.org**
» Society of Authors: **www.societyofauthors.org**
» Society for Editors and Proofreaders: **www.sfep.org.uk**
» Teaching English as a Foreign Language: **www.eflweb.com**

Food Science

The lead enjoyed by King's College London at the head of the food science table has narrowed slightly since last year, but there is little threat to its position. King's had the best grades in the 2008 Research Assessment Exercise, when two thirds of its submission in nutritional sciences was considered world-leading or internationally excellent, and the highest entry standards in this table. Coventry, in seventh place, is the only university to offer better employment prospects. Coventry also shares with Ulster the distinction of having the most satisfied students and is clearly the leading post-1992 institution.

Surrey has moved up a place into second position. The majority of the 29 institutions in the ranking are new universities, although higher entry standards and research grades ensure that their older counterparts fill the top six places. Ulster is the highest-placed institution outside England. Heriot-Watt is the top university in Scotland, while University of Wales Institute Cardiff (UWIC) is the only representative in the Principality.

Entry standards have been rising – no university in this year's ranking averages less than 225 points – but there were still fewer than four applications per place in 2010. Almost a third of entrants to food science courses arrive with alternative qualifications to A levels. The subjects had been in the doldrums in the latter part of the last decade, but have enjoyed big increases in applications both this year and last. An 18 per cent rise at the start of 2011 was among the biggest in any subject.

Career prospects are good, with more than half of those completing courses going straight into graduate-level jobs and only 7 per cent without work six months after graduation. Food science is mid-way in the graduate salaries league, with an average starting rate of more than £20,500.

Employed in graduate job:	48%	Employed in non-graduate job and studying:	2%
Employed in graduate job and studying:	5%	Employed in non-graduate job:	24%
Studying:	15%	Unemployed:	7%
Average starting graduate salary:	£20,505	Average starting non-graduate salary:	£15,880

Food Science	Research quality	Entry standards	Student satisfaction %	Graduate prospects %	Overall rating
1 King's College London	3.8	434	81	95	100.0
2 Surrey	3.1	422	75	88	92.0
3 Leeds	3.0	393	81	80	91.0
4 Nottingham	2.8	367	81	85	89.7
5 Newcastle	1.8	431	85	67	87.8
6 Reading	2.1	368	84	76	86.5
7 Coventry		325	86	97	83.3
8 Ulster	1.2	317	86	67	79.5
9 Leeds Metropolitan		347	84	75	77.9
10 Harper Adams	0.9	290	85		77.1
11 Heriot-Watt	1.6	326		67	77.0
12 Plymouth	0.5	304	76	89	76.8
=13 Greenwich	1.3		80	64	75.9

=13 Robert Gordon		362	70	89	75.9
15 Northumbria	1.1	290	75	74	74.1
16 Oxford Brookes		327	84	61	73.5
17 Queen's, Belfast	1.4	331	71	63	72.8
18 Chester	0.5	310	64	87	71.6
19 Sheffield Hallam		291	81	68	71.5
20 Bath Spa		304	79	65	70.8
21 Queen Margaret Edinburgh		332		63	70.6
22 Lincoln	0.7	266	76		68.6
23 Bournemouth		269	76	68	68.2
24 Manchester Metropolitan	1.0	264	70	66	67.7
25 Liverpool John Moores	1.2	273	68	63	67.0
26 UWIC, Cardiff	0.9	258	71	59	65.8
27 Kingston		226	82	50	63.7
28 University College Birmingham		266	81	40	63.4
29 London Metropolitan	0.3	238	58	59	56.5

» Institute of Food Science and Technology: **www.ifst.org**
» Society of Food Hygiene and Technology: **www.sofht.co.uk**

French

French at degree level has weathered the problems that have afflicted the teaching of modern languages in secondary schools: there are more applications and more places than there were five years ago. But a small drop in applications at the start of 2011 followed roughly static demand for places in 2010, when other subjects enjoyed big increases. Nevertheless, a ratio of well over five applications for every place is close to the average for all subjects and is reflected in the usual high entry grades. Almost half of the 49 universities in the table averaged more than 400 points and none had an average of less than 250 points.

Oxford retains the slim lead over Cambridge that it established two years ago, thanks to the best performance in the 2008 Research Assessment Exercise, when 30 per cent of its submission was rated world-leading. Cambridge is ahead on all the other indicators and has the highest entry grades in the table. Northumbria, in 34th place, has the most satisfied students, while Lancaster, in 27th, again boasts the top employment score.

Glasgow and Birmingham have made the most progress in the upper reaches of the table, but St Andrews remains easily the top university in Scotland after holding on to third place. Cardiff has widened its lead over Swansea in Wales. Portsmouth is clearly the leading post-1992 university and one of only two in the top 40, the other being Northumbria.

French still attracts nearly twice as many degree applications as any other language, although there were barely 4,000 at the start of 2011. Nine out of ten undergraduates enter with A levels or their equivalents, almost 10 per cent securing their place in Clearing in 2009.

Seven out of ten of those completing a degree in French go on to graduate jobs or further study within six months and the 6 per cent unemployment rate is better than average for all subjects and one of the few to be lower than last year. Only three universities dipped below the 50 per cent success mark for graduate destinations. Graduate starting salaries had dropped a little in the latest survey and remain below the average for all subjects.

French cont.

Employed in graduate job: 35%
Employed in graduate job and studying: 5%
Studying: 26%
Average starting graduate salary: £20,034

Employed in non-graduate job and studying: 3%
Employed in non-graduate job: 24%
Unemployed: 6%
Average starting non-graduate salary: £14,979

French	Research quality	Entry standards	Student satisfaction %	Graduate prospects %	Overall rating
1 Oxford	3.8	518	86	79	100.0
2 Cambridge	3.0	534	90	81	99.8
3 St Andrews	2.5	472	88	81	94.7
4 Southampton	3.5	431	89	66	92.9
5 Sheffield	3.1	419	83	79	91.9
=6 Durham	2.5	488	82	77	91.2
=6 Warwick	3.2	462	84	67	91.2
8 King's College London	3.5	442	81	66	89.6
9 Glasgow	2.4	428	83	77	89.0
10 Bath	2.1	449	83	77	88.9
11 Birmingham	2.1	421	91	69	88.8
12 Leeds	2.7	424	83	72	88.6
13 University College London	2.4	470	80	72	87.9
14 Exeter	2.5	441	83	67	87.1
15 Hull	2.4	312	87	78	86.4
16 Leicester	0.9	379	90	80	86.2
17 Nottingham	2.9	408	79	69	85.9
18 Newcastle	2.5	416	82	66	85.1
19 Cardiff	2.4	405	88	59	85.0
20 Edinburgh	2.3	466	72	73	83.8
21 Bristol	1.5	481	75	77	83.7
22 Manchester	2.5	427	78	61	82.3
23 Kent	2.5	332	86	59	82.1
24 Aston	1.0	382	84	74	81.8
25 Aberdeen	3.0	312	83	61	81.7
26 Queen's, Belfast	1.9	369	80	70	81.5
27 Lancaster	1.5	435	69	83	80.9
28 Queen Mary, London	2.3	392	75	68	80.8
29 Reading	2.7	359	81	55	79.5
30 East Anglia		351	87	76	79.0
31 Portsmouth	2.4	267	83		78.5
32 Liverpool	2.2	375	77	60	78.3
33 Heriot-Watt	1.6	372	77	66	77.8
34 Northumbria		306	92	69	77.4
35 Royal Holloway	2.4	391	79	49	77.3
36 Strathclyde		383	83	71	76.6
37 Ulster	1.2	300	90	55	76.3

38 Stirling	1.3	301	82	64	75.6
39 Salford	1.3	312	80	57	72.7
40 York		410	80	59	72.6
41 Chester		274	79	77	72.4
42 Nottingham Trent	1.0	279	87	49	71.4
43 Oxford Brookes	1.5	296	76	57	71.2
44 Sussex		385	71	63	68.5
45 Bangor		286	83	55	68.2
46 Swansea	1.5	281	77	48	68.0
47 Manchester Metropolitan	0.7	268	77	56	67.7
48 Liverpool John Moores		291	72	61	64.8
49 Westminster	0.8	263	64	56	61.1

» Alliance Française: **www.alliancefrancaise.org.uk**
» Chartered Institute of Linguists: **www.iol.org.uk**
» National Centre for Languages (CILT): **www.cilt.org.uk**
» Society for French Studies: **www.sfs.ac.uk**

General Engineering

Cambridge's lead over Oxford in general engineering has narrowed slightly since last year, but remains substantial. Cambridge has the highest entry standards, the best employment record and the top grades in the 2008 Research Assessment Exercise (RAE), when 45 per cent of the university's work was classified as world-leading. Greenwich had the best results in the 2010 National Student Survey, and was the only university to satisfy more than 85 per cent of final-year undergraduates.

Nottingham remains in third place, where it entered the ranking last year. Greenwich has joined this year in 12th place, making it the leading post-1992 university. Cardiff, in fourth place, remains the top university in Wales, while Aberdeen is the leader in Scotland.

As in the specialist branches of engineering, there is an enormous spread of entry grades, from more than 550 points at Oxford and Cambridge to less than 200 at De Montfort and Birmingham City.

Applications were down a little in 2011, but the total was still more than 12,000. There were fewer than four applications per place in 2010, making admissions the least competitive of any of the main branches of engineering.

Nationally, the subject is in the top 20 for employment, with more than 70 per cent of all those completing a degree going straight into graduate jobs or further study. The subject is also among the most rewarding financially. Average starting salaries close to £25,000 for graduate-level jobs place general engineering seventh on this measure, while those in lower-level jobs are the best-paid in any subject.

Employed in graduate job:	47%	Employed in non-graduate job and studying:	1%
Employed in graduate job and studying:	8%	Employed in non-graduate job:	17%
Studying:	16%	Unemployed:	10%
Average starting graduate salary:	£24,937	Average starting non-graduate salary:	£24,246

General Engineering	Research quality	Entry standards	Student satisfaction %	Graduate prospects %	Overall rating
1 Cambridge	5.4	567	83	92	100.0
2 Oxford	4.1	560		89	96.5
3 Nottingham	3.8	454	81		88.8
4 Cardiff	3.3	325	82	90	85.6
5 Warwick	3.4	460	77	78	84.0
6 Exeter	2.4	416	84	75	83.1
7 Leicester	2.4	347	81	85	81.8
8 Durham	2.5	513	76	68	80.4
9 Queen Mary, London	2.0	291	80	87	79.0
10 Swansea	3.4	283	77		78.1
11 Aberdeen	2.9	314	75		75.5
12 Greenwich	0.7		90	58	74.9
13 Strathclyde	2.8		74	67	73.8
14 Central Lancashire	1.0	278	80	71	72.2
15 Edinburgh Napier	1.3	280	80	66	71.9
16 Liverpool John Moores	3.1	289	70		71.4
17 Bournemouth	1.6	269		71	70.3
18 De Montfort	1.4	147	76	83	69.5
19 West of England	2.4	298	79	43	69.4
20 Sheffield Hallam	1.5	241	76	64	68.6
21 Bradford	1.7	211	73		65.4
22 London South Bank	2.2	211	73	47	64.4
23 Glamorgan	2.2		65	58	62.2
24 Glasgow Caledonian	0.7	242	73	49	61.2
25 Ulster		232	67	68	59.4
26 Oxford Brookes	1.7	207	65		59.3
27 Birmingham City		164	71	63	58.5
28 Coventry	0.7		71	44	56.4

» Engineering Council: **www.engc.org.uk**
» EngineeringUK: **www.engineeringuk.com**
» Institution of Engineering and Technology: **www.theiet.org**

Geography and Environmental Sciences

Geography and environmental sciences have been benefiting from growing interest in "green" issues among potential students. Physical geography and environmental sciences have become notably more popular than human and social geography, with physical courses up by 3 per cent in the spring of 2011 and social down by 10 per cent. However, competition for places in the human and social branch of the discipline remains more competitive than in physical geography, with almost six applications to the place in 2010, rather than 5.5.

Cambridge has maintained its lead in this year's ranking, with the highest entry standards and one of the best research scores, but Oxford has won back second place. The top four all had

30 per cent of their research rated as world-leading in the 2008 assessments. Edge Hill, which does not make the top 40 overall, has the most satisfied students, while the fifth-placed London School of Economics again has by far the best of generally mediocre set of employment scores. Only eight of the 75 universities saw more than 70 per cent of leavers go straight into graduate jobs or further study and the proportion dropped below 40 per cent at five of them.

Staffordshire is the leading post-1992 university, a fraction ahead of Chester, but neither reaches the top 30. St Andrews has opened up a big lead as the top Scottish university, while Cardiff has overtaken Aberystwyth in Wales.

Entry grades are not as high as they are in some other popular subjects. Although 15 universities average more than 400 points at entry, only Cambridge tops 500 and even some old universities have averages of less than 300 points. The subjects are in the bottom half of the employment and salaries tables. In the latest survey, a third of graduates were in low-level jobs six months after completing their courses, although the unemployment rate was slightly better than average for all subjects.

Employed in graduate job:	28%	Employed in non-graduate job and studying:	4%
Employed in graduate job and studying:	4%	Employed in non-graduate job:	29%
Studying:	27%	Unemployed:	8%
Average starting graduate salary:	£19,856	Average starting non-graduate salary:	£14,659

Geography and Environmental Sciences	Research quality	Entry standards	Student satisfaction %	Graduate prospects %	Overall rating
1 Cambridge	4.0	530	89	79	100.0
2 Oxford	4.0	500	86	80	96.9
3 Durham	4.0	476	83	77	93.8
4 Bristol	4.0	473	86	70	93.6
5 London School of Economics	3.4	482	74	87	89.8
=6 Lancaster	3.1	394	83	75	88.3
=6 East Anglia	3.6	407	85	65	88.3
8 St Andrews	3.1	463	80	71	87.8
9 University College London	3.5	474	77	71	87.7
=10 Nottingham	3.1	425	82	70	87.5
=10 Queen Mary, London	3.8	379	86	60	87.5
12 Royal Holloway	3.2	400	83	67	87.0
13 Cardiff	3.5	346	86	64	86.4
14 Sheffield	3.4	435	81	63	86.0
15 Loughborough	2.2	385	88	63	85.8
16 Exeter	3.1	419	83	62	85.6
17 Birmingham	2.7	405	82	67	85.2
18 Glasgow	2.1	385	86	67	85.1
19 Southampton	3.2	424	79	65	85.0
20 Aberystwyth	3.2	325	88	58	84.7
=21 Leicester	1.9	378	89	60	84.3
=21 Sussex	2.9	372	82	66	84.3
=23 Leeds	3.7	393	80	61	84.2

Geography and Environmental Sciences cont.	Research quality	Entry standards	Student satisfaction %	Graduate prospects %	Overall rating
=23 Edinburgh	2.9	424	77	70	84.2
=25 King's College London	3.4	395	78	67	84.0
=25 Reading	3.5	390	80	62	84.0
27 Dundee	2.8	339	83	67	83.5
28 Newcastle	2.4	378	83	62	82.8
29 Manchester	2.9	406	76	62	81.0
30 Hull	2.7	304	84	58	80.6
31 Liverpool	2.4	375	80	61	80.2
32 Sheffield Hallam	2.8	301	84	57	80.0
33 York	2.5	391	76	64	79.8
34 Aberdeen	2.2	311	81	61	78.6
35 Swansea	2.8	321	81	53	78.5
36 Staffordshire		236	87	76	77.7
37 Chester	0.4	280	87	65	77.5
38 Strathclyde	0.8	362	83	57	76.7
39 Highlands and Islands	1.6	344			76.6
=40 Coventry	0.7	317	83	62	76.4
=40 Queen's, Belfast	2.2	323	80	54	76.4
=42 Plymouth	2.1	285	81	56	76.1
=42 Edge Hill	0.2	239	91	58	76.1
44 Keele		282	85	64	75.1
45 Stirling	1.6	309	76	61	74.2
=46 Northumbria		281	85	58	73.4
=46 Brighton	1.3	272	87	42	73.4
48 Ulster	1.6	244	81	52	72.7
49 West of England	0.7	281	84	49	72.2
50 Central Lancashire		251	88	47	71.6
51 Portsmouth	1.4	286	84	38	71.3
52 Bath Spa	0.5	277	79	56	70.6
53 Manchester Metropolitan	1.6	259	79	47	70.3
=54 Bradford	2.8	241		39	69.9
=54 Gloucestershire	0.6	282	80	50	69.9
=56 Greenwich		253		60	69.8
=56 Northampton	0.8	231	84	46	69.8
58 Glamorgan		242	83	50	69.1
59 Nottingham Trent	0.3	275	77	57	69.0
60 Canterbury Christ Church		274	86	39	68.7
61 Hertfordshire		261	72	69	68.4
=62 Oxford Brookes		311	78	49	68.3
=62 Sunderland	0.4	263		54	68.3
64 St Mary's College, Twickenham		262		55	68.2
=65 Salford	1.3	272		41	67.1
=65 Kingston	1.4	233	72	55	67.1

67 Liverpool John Moores		251	81	45	66.6
68 Worcester	0.4	252	77	46	66.0
69 Bangor		273	75	48	64.8
70 Bournemouth	2.1	214	65	59	64.6
71 Cumbria		231	76	43	63.0
=72 Leeds Metropolitan		254		39	62.0
=72 Southampton Solent		256		39	62.0
74 Marjon, Plymouth	0.2			41	60.3
75 Derby		246	71	43	60.2

» British Cartographic Society: **www.cartography.org.uk**
» Royal Geographical Society (with the Institute of British Geographers): **www.rgs.org**
» Royal Scottish Geographical Society: **www.rsgs.org**

Geology

Cambridge remains well clear of Oxford in geology, with better scores than its ancient rival on all four indicators. Cambridge registered the best performance in the 2008 Research Assessment Exercise and has the highest entry standards in the table. Imperial College London, fourth-place, has clearly the best employment score.

Geologists are generally satisfied with their courses, if the National Student Survey of 2010 is any guide – none more so than at Leicester, which produced the top score for the fourth year in a row. In fact, satisfaction levels were above 70 per cent for the subject across the board.

All but six of the 29 institutions in this year's ranking are pre-1992 universities. Plymouth is again the highest-placed of the newer foundations, while Cardiff is the leading university in Wales, and third-placed St Andrews is the clear leader in Scotland.

Applications to study geology have fluctuated in recent years, but the subject has seen strong growth in the last three. A small rise in 2011 followed two years with increases in applications of more than 10 per cent. Extra places were allocated in 2009, but the subject will have to fend for itself from 2012 onwards.

Outside Cambridge, Oxford and Imperial, there is less contrast in entry standards in geology than in many other subjects. The average is above 230 points at all but one university in the ranking, and only the bottom nine average less than 300. Some of the leading universities expect candidates to have two, or even three, scientific or mathematical subjects at A level. Relatively few places are filled in Clearing.

Two thirds of geologists go on to graduate jobs or further study within six months of graduation, although the unemployment level is above the average for all subjects, at 12 per cent. Average salaries for graduate-level jobs have dropped since the last survey, but geology is only just outside the top 20 for all subjects, at more than £21,000. By contrast, the 25 per cent of geologists who go into lower-level jobs are among the worst-paid of all new graduates, averaging less than £14,000 a year.

Employed in graduate job:	26%	Employed in non-graduate job and studying:	2%
Employed in graduate job and studying:	3%	Employed in non-graduate job:	23%
Studying:	33%	Unemployed:	12%
Average starting graduate salary:	£21,182	Average starting non-graduate salary:	£13,950

Geology

Geology	Research quality	Entry standards	Student satisfaction %	Graduate prospects %	Overall rating
1 Cambridge	5.1	595	85	82	100.0
2 Oxford	4.7	569	83	77	95.5
3 St Andrews	3.1	460	85	84	89.6
4 Imperial College	3.7	491	79	87	89.5
5 Durham	3.1	431	86	80	88.1
6 Southampton	3.4	394	89	69	87.3
7 Leicester	2.6	411	94	63	86.6
8 East Anglia	3.7	409	82	74	86.1
9 Royal Holloway	3.4	329	88	74	85.7
10 Bristol	3.8	447	79	67	84.4
11 Birmingham	2.9	367	87	72	84.3
12 University College London	4.0	484	72	76	83.9
13 Leeds	3.1	386	81	74	82.5
14 Manchester	3.4	371	84	62	82.3
15 Glasgow	2.1	385	88	70	82.2
16 Exeter	1.5	414	84	81	81.2
17 Cardiff	3.1	385	81	63	80.5
18 Edinburgh	3.1	422	76	70	80.3
19 Aberdeen	2.5	312	79	82	79.0
20 Liverpool	3.2	401	73	66	77.5
21 Plymouth	2.1	281	87	61	76.8
22 Portsmouth	1.8	263	83	44	69.1
23 Keele		273	85	63	68.7
24 Brighton	1.3	242	78	62	67.9
25 Bangor	2.5	288	78	33	67.3
26 Aberystwyth		282	83	40	62.9
27 Liverpool John Moores		249	74	50	58.9
28 Kingston		232	72	52	58.0
29 Derby		215	76	33	55.8

» Geological Society: **www.geolsoc.org.uk**

German

The number of universities in the German ranking has stabilised after 16 dropped out in two years. This reflected a worldwide decline in the language that has been worrying the German government, as well as academic linguists. There was a small decline in applications in 2010, but universities will hope that a 2 per cent increase at the start of 2011 means that the corner has been turned at last.

Cambridge makes it six years in a row as the leader in German. Indeed, the top two are the same as last year but Southampton, which had the best results in the 2008 Research Assessment Exercise (RAE), has continued its rise up this ranking as far as third place. It was only just in the top ten two years ago. Oxford has the highest entry standards and Cambridge the most satisfied students. Satisfaction levels remained generally high in the 2010 National Student Survey and, although Cambridge was the only university to satisfy 90 per cent of final-year undergraduates, every university secured at least 70 per cent approval.

The best employment score was at Hull, which is relegated to the bottom half of the table because it did not enter the RAE in German. Queen's, Belfast, which is also outside the top 20, was only one percentage point behind. Fourth-placed St Andrews remains the leading university in Scotland, while Cardiff has overhauled Swansea in Wales. Portsmouth is one of just three post-1992 universities left in the ranking and the only one in the top 30.

Despite the recruitment difficulties in German departments, there are still more than five applications for every place. Nine out of ten undergraduates enter with A levels or equivalent qualifications, and entry standards are relatively high, especially at the leading universities. At more than half of the universities in the table, entrants average more than 400 points.

As in other modern languages, career prospects are reasonable: two thirds of leavers go straight into graduate jobs or further study, and the unemployment rate is on the average for all subjects. German is only just in the top half of the table for starting salaries, which were slightly below the average at the time of the latest survey. Most universities in the table offer German *ab initio* as part of a languages package.

Employed in graduate job:	35%	Employed in non-graduate job and studying:	3%
Employed in graduate job and studying:	6%	Employed in non-graduate job:	23%
Studying:	24%	Unemployed:	9%
Average starting graduate salary:	£20,657	Average starting non-graduate salary:	£15,207

German	Research quality	Entry standards	Student satisfaction %	Graduate prospects %	Overall rating
1 Cambridge	3.2	534	90	81	100.0
2 Oxford	3.3	551	85	79	97.4
3 Southampton	3.5	467	87		97.2
4 St Andrews	3.1	481	85	84	95.5
5 Durham	3.1	488	82	77	92.2
6 Warwick	2.4	455	89	68	90.7
7 Birmingham	2.8	432	88	63	89.3
8 Leeds	3.1	402	85	66	88.1
9 Bristol	2.5	442	78	78	87.1
10 Manchester	2.9	396	83	68	87.0
11 Cardiff	2.4	400	81	79	86.9
12 Newcastle	2.7	423	81	71	86.6
13 King's College London	3.4	380	80	71	86.5
14 University College London	3.2	461	75	71	86.4
15 Nottingham	1.9	408	85	72	86.3
16 Bath	2.1	450	82	71	86.1
17 Exeter	2.6	442	83	62	86.0
18 Glasgow	1.7	428	83	67	84.3
19 Edinburgh	3.1	438	73	68	83.6

	Research quality	Entry standards	Student satisfaction %	Graduate prospects %	Overall rating
20 Sheffield	1.6	434	77	76	82.8
21 Queen's, Belfast	0.9	369	79	85	81.4
22 Hull		312	87	86	80.9
23 Portsmouth	2.4	287	83	63	80.0
=24 Lancaster	1.5	421	75	65	78.3
=24 Reading	1.6	341	81		78.3
26 Heriot-Watt	1.6	372	77	66	78.0
27 Kent	1.0	292	82	·71	77.7
28 Swansea	2.2	300	78	66	77.6
29 Aston	1.0	372	78	64	76.1
30 Queen Mary, London	1.6	360	77		76.0
31 Aberdeen	0.9	335	83	59	75.8
32 Liverpool	2.1		73	60	74.6
33 Royal Holloway	3.0	378	71	43	73.6
34 East Anglia		377	87	43	73.2
35 Bangor		302	83	57	71.4
36 Nottingham Trent		279	87	49	70.6
37 Manchester Metropolitan	0.7	268	77	56	69.2

» Chartered Institute of Linguists: **www.iol.org.uk**

» Goethe-Institut: **www.goethe.de/enindex.htm**

» National Centre for Languages (CILT): **www.cilt.org.uk**

History

History's currency in the graduate jobs market has been a matter of debate. Surveys have shown a strong representation of historians among business leaders, celebrities and senior politicians, but more are in non-graduate jobs than those categorised as graduate occupations six months after completing a degree. Only two subjects have a lower proportion of leavers going straight into graduate jobs.

Nevertheless, history remains only just outside the top ten subjects as a degree choice, despite not enjoying in the level of applications common in most subjects over the last two years. The increase in 2011 was less than 1 per cent, but the subject was already among the most competitive at entry, with almost six applications to every place.

Durham has overtaken Cambridge at the top of this year's history table. Although it does not lead on any of the four measures, it is second for entry standards, student satisfaction and employment prospects. Cambridge shares the best research score with fourth-placed University College London. In fact, Imperial College London's work on the history of science won the top grade in the 2008 Research Assessment Exercise, but history is not an undergraduate subject at Imperial so it does not appear in this table.

The London School of Economics, in fifth place, again has by far the best employment score, a full ten points ahead of its nearest rival. While the LSE saw 91 per cent of historians go straight into graduate jobs or onto postgraduate courses, the proportion was below 50 per cent at more than a third of the 91 universities in the ranking.

Average entry scores at the top three universities are all over 500 points, the equivalent of more than four As at A level, with Cambridge leading the way. Other leading universities' entry standards are closer to the top three than in many other subjects: all the top ten – and another 14 universities further down the ranking – average at least 400 points.

The most satisfied students are at Derby, which is not among the top 50 universities in the ranking. Satisfaction levels are high at most of the universities in the ranking: only one fails to achieve a 70 per cent approval rating. Two post-1992 universities appear in the top 30, ahead of such luminaries as Bristol and Manchester, largely thanks to high satisfaction levels. Huddersfield just pulls ahead of Teesside. St Andrews remains the top university in Scotland, while Cardiff does the same in Wales.

Employed in graduate job:	23%	Employed in non-graduate job and studying:	5%
Employed in graduate job and studying:	3%	Employed in non-graduate job:	32%
Studying:	28%	Unemployed:	9%
Average starting graduate salary:	£19,909	Average starting non-graduate salary:	£14,534

History	Research quality	Entry standards	Student satisfaction %	Graduate prospects %	Overall rating
1 Durham	3.1	536	92	81	100.0
2 Cambridge	4.4	541	88	75	99.8
3 Oxford	4.3	518	86	75	97.4
4 University College London	4.4	462	82	77	93.8
5 London School of Economics	4.1	497	74	91	93.2
6 St Andrews	3.1	478	87	68	91.6
7 Warwick	4.1	478	82	66	91.4
8 King's College London	3.4	472	84	67	90.5
9 York	3.3	480	83	67	89.9
10 Exeter	3.1	450	86	66	89.7
11 Sussex	3.5	381	85	71	89.3
12 Sheffield	4.1	445	82	61	88.8
13 Queen Mary, London	3.7	392	83	70	88.4
14 Southampton	4.0	420	83	61	88.0
15 East Anglia	3.1	400	88	55	86.9
=16 Nottingham	2.5	432	81	74	86.8
=16 Glasgow	3.4	410	89	49	86.8
=16 Lancaster	2.7	419	85	65	86.8
19 Leeds	2.9	446	82	63	86.5
=20 Kent	4.3	346	84	58	85.9
=20 Royal Holloway	3.1	409	83	63	85.9
22 Liverpool	4.3	384	83	52	85.8
23 Leicester	2.8	379	87	55	85.0
24 Essex	4.3	332	86	50	84.7
25 Hull	2.9	342	88	57	84.6

	Research quality	Entry standards	Student satisfaction %	Graduate prospects %	Overall rating
26 School of Oriental and African Studies	3.7	397	78	59	83.3
27 Huddersfield	1.8	340	86	67	82.9
28 Teesside	2.2	272	92	57	82.6
29 Bristol	2.7	451	73	71	82.5
30 Birmingham	3.1	408	79	57	82.1
31 Aberdeen	3.7	324	81	57	81.8
32 Keele	2.9	311	83	60	81.6
33 Oxford Brookes	3.5	324	82	54	81.4
34 Dundee	2.9	335	86	49	81.3
35 Manchester	3.4	416	73	61	81.0
36 Strathclyde	1.6	369	83	63	80.9
37 Newcastle	2.2	412	79	59	80.8
38 Edinburgh	3.4	438	74	57	80.6
39 Cardiff	2.1	406	82	55	80.5
40 Winchester	2.7	284	85	54	79.8
=41 Portsmouth	2.4	304	88	46	79.5
=41 Stirling	2.5	313	83	57	79.5
=43 Reading	2.2	358	82	52	78.8
=43 Aberystwyth	2.1	297	85	56	78.8
45 Chester	2.4	290	80	57	76.8
46 Chichester	1.0	293	89	48	76.7
47 Hertfordshire	3.7	257	79	48	76.6
48 Edge Hill	1.5	226	87	56	76.0
49 Queen's, Belfast	2.8	341	79	43	75.6
50 Swansea	2.5	310	80	46	75.2
51 Bangor	2.5	279	83	43	75.0
=52 Central Lancashire	1.8	258	83	51	74.3
=52 De Montfort	1.5	265	87	44	74.3
54 Leeds Trinity	1.2	242		67	74.2
=55 Brighton	4.1	239	80	33	74.1
=55 Derby		219	93	52	74.1
57 West of England	1.6	285	84	44	73.7
58 Goldsmiths College	1.6	334	76	53	73.3
59 Northampton	1.6	233	89	34	72.6
60 Lincoln	1.3	263	80	55	72.5
61 Northumbria	0.7	329	78	57	72.4
=62 Staffordshire		231	83	64	71.9
=62 Newman	0.2	224	82	64	71.9
=64 Ulster	2.6	244	80	39	71.7
=64 Trinity St David	1.6	260	81	46	71.7
66 Coventry		306	76	68	71.5
67 Newport	0.7	216	82	57	71.2
68 Bath Spa	1.8	289	81	35	70.7

69 Greenwich		1.8	239	81	42	70.6
70 Nottingham Trent		1.3	287	80	43	70.3
71 Brunel			304	81	51	70.1
=72 St Mary's College, Twickenham			243	85	49	69.8
=72 Cumbria		0.8	267		54	69.8
=72 Anglia Ruskin		3.1	239	76	39	69.8
75 Bradford		1.2	253	85	32	69.5
76 Glamorgan		2.2	273	80	29	69.2
77 Plymouth		0.9	281	80	41	69.1
78 Gloucestershire		1.2	287	76	48	69.0
79 Sunderland		2.1	234	73	51	68.6
=80 Sheffield Hallam		1.6	299	75	40	68.3
=80 Salford		1.2	291	76	44	68.3
82 Canterbury Christ Church		1.0	253	82	36	68.2
83 Kingston		1.3	249	72	56	67.6
84 York St John			283	87	26	67.1
85 Roehampton		1.8	276	69	52	66.9
86 Liverpool John Moores		0.6	243	79	36	65.2
=87 Manchester Metropolitan		0.7	285	73	34	63.1
=87 Westminster		0.7	266		34	63.1
89 Worcester		0.1	271	70	42	60.6
90 Leeds Metropolitan			247	71	40	60.1

» Historical Association: **www.history.org.uk**

» Institute of Historical Research: **www.history.ac.uk**

» Royal Historical Society: **www.royalhistoricalsociety.org**

History of Art, Architecture and Design

The only tie at the top of any table this year sees London's Courtauld Institute make up a significant gap on Cambridge in the history of art. The Courtauld, a previous ranking leader, does not have the top score in any of the four indicators, but performs consistently well. Most unusually, Cambridge is let down by a research score that is low by its own standards, despite having much the highest scores in the table for both entry standards and graduate prospects.

The two top universities are the only ones where 70 per cent of leavers went straight into graduate jobs or on to further study, and the proportion dropped below 50 per cent at a third of the universities in the table. The subject has dropped into the bottom ten for employment prospects this year. Although unemployment was not far above average, at 10 per cent, at the time of the last survey, nearly 40 per cent of graduates went into lower-level jobs. The specialised nature of the jobs market has always made for uncertain prospects immediately after graduation, but the subject is only slight below mid-way in the earnings table.

Glasgow did best in the 2008 Research Assessment Exercise, which classified 85 per cent of its work as world-leading or internationally excellent, and it also has the most satisfied students. There were good scores in art history for most universities in the 2010 National Student Survey: all 26 institutions in the ranking satisfied at 70 per cent of their final-year undergraduates.

History of Art, Architecture and Design cont.

Only five post-1992 universities are left in the ranking, with Oxford Brookes the highest-placed, just outside the top 20. Glasgow remains just ahead of St Andrews as the top university in Scotland, but Wales has lost its former representative, Aberystwyth, in this year's table.

Fewer than 4,000 undergraduates take full-time degrees in the history of art, although another 1,000 are registered on part-time courses. The majority of students are female. Entry standards are high, with ten universities averaging over 400 points and none less than 250.

Employed in graduate job:	28%	Employed in non-graduate job and studying:	4%
Employed in graduate job and studying:	4%	Employed in non-graduate job:	35%
Studying:	18%	Unemployed:	10%
Average starting graduate salary:	£20,103	Average starting non-graduate salary:	£15,196

History of Art, Architecture and Design	Research quality	Entry standards	Student satisfaction %	Graduate prospects %	Overall rating
=1 Cambridge	2.5	506	88	82	100.0
=1 Courtauld	4.9	452	83	74	100.0
3 Oxford	4.3	481	86	64	98.6
4 Glasgow	5.3	384	89	58	97.5
5 Sussex	4.9	381	85	67	96.5
6 St Andrews	3.2	457	87	69	96.4
7 York	4.9	405	85	62	95.8
8 University College London	4.2	435	81	65	94.3
9 East Anglia	5.2	372	88	36	91.5
=10 Warwick	3.1	423	82	58	89.0
=10 Birmingham	4.0	413	79	57	89.0
12 Nottingham	3.5	383	81	58	87.6
13 Leeds	3.0	383	82	61	87.5
14 School of Oriental and African Studies	3.4	393	78	57	86.1
15 Edinburgh	2.8	430	74	62	85.1
16 Manchester	4.8	347	74	54	84.9
17 Leicester	1.9	326	87	58	84.1
18 Reading	2.8	351	83	47	82.8
19 Aberdeen	3.0	306	81	53	81.7
20 Bristol	2.4	433	70	61	81.0
21 Oxford Brookes	2.6	328	82	35	78.3
22 Sheffield Hallam	2.7		75	46	76.8
23 Brighton	4.1	251	78	34	76.7
24 Goldsmiths College	2.8	317	76	32	74.1
25 Plymouth	2.1	275	80	36	73.4
26 Kingston	2.2	252	72	47	70.4

» Association of Art Historians: **www.aah.org.uk**
» Society of Architectural Historians of Great Britain: **www.sahgb.org.uk**

Hospitality, Leisure, Recreation and Tourism

The demand for places in this wide-ranging group of subjects was very slightly down in March 2011, but this followed an increase of nearly 20 per cent in 2010, which reflected their position among the 20 most popular undergraduate choices. The category covers a variety of courses, most directed towards management in the leisure and tourism industries.

Three additional institutions in this year's ranking make a total of 50, most of which are post-1992 universities. But the two leaders are older foundations, with Surrey well ahead of Stirling at the top. Surrey's 40-year reputation in hotel and tourism management helps to give it an eight-point lead. It is one of only five universities with average entry grades of more than 300 points and it achieved the best of an extremely modest set of results in the 2008 Research Assessment Exercise (RAE). Fifth-placed Birmingham leads on employment prospects, but did not enter the RAE in this category while the University of the Arts, London, has the highest entry standards (its poor satisfaction score places it at equal 34th).

As last year, the most satisfied students are at Ulster, which is at 26th place because it has a low employments score and was another university not to enter the RAE. Satisfaction rates are generally high, which is more than can be said of the employment record in this area. Birmingham and Surrey were the only universities to manage "positive destinations" for two thirds of their graduates.

The 9 per cent unemployment rate is no worse than the average for all subjects, but the unusually large numbers – nearly half – going into lower-level jobs relegate hospitality, leisure, recreation and tourism to second from bottom of the employment table. The subjects fare a little better in terms of starting salaries, although the average of £17,680 for graduate-level jobs had dropped in each of the last two years.

Central Lancashire, in third place, is the highest-placed post-1992 university and is joined in the top ten by Bournemouth, Brighton, Plymouth and Hertfordshire. Second-placed Stirling is the top university in Scotland, while UWIC has that distinction in Wales.

Employed in graduate job:	36%	Employed in non-graduate job and studying:	3%
Employed in graduate job and studying:	2%	Employed in non-graduate job:	43%
Studying:	6%	Unemployed:	9%
Average starting graduate salary:	£17,680	Average starting non-graduate salary:	£14,840

Hospitality, Leisure, Recreation and Tourism	Research quality	Entry standards	Student satisfaction %	Graduate prospects %	Overall rating
1 Surrey	2.2	336	80	68	100.0
2 Stirling	2.0	309	78	56	92.1
3 Central Lancashire	2.1	244	82	62	90.8
4 Sheffield Hallam	1.8	278	78	48	85.0
5 Birmingham		346	77	83	84.6
6 Bournemouth	1.3	299	70	58	82.1
7 Brighton	1.7	255	74	43	80.0
8 Manchester		331	85	55	79.2
9 Hertfordshire	1.5	249	77	41	78.1
10 Plymouth	1.4	259	75	43	78.0

Hospitality, Leisure, Recreation and Tourism cont.	Research quality	Entry standards	Student satisfaction %	Graduate prospects %	Overall rating
11 Arts University College, Bournemouth		279	81	62	75.1
12 Manchester Metropolitan	1.5	252	62	49	74.0
13 UWIC, Cardiff	1.2	253	73	39	73.7
14 Salford	1.3	204	78	42	73.5
15 Oxford Brookes		300	80	49	73.3
16 Queen Margaret Edinburgh		262		61	73.1
17 Chester	1.2	237	66	49	71.6
18 Sunderland	1.3	189	79	36	71.2
19 Edinburgh Napier		279	72	60	71.0
20 Robert Gordon		243	77	62	70.7
21 Gloucestershire		234	76	65	70.0
=22 Glamorgan		259	85	41	69.7
=22 Leeds Metropolitan		273	73	57	69.7
24 Bath Spa		274	77	47	68.8
25 West of England	0.7	242	79	27	68.2
26 Ulster		226	89	37	67.6
27 Coventry		292	66	52	67.0
28 Lincoln		224	82	45	66.6
=29 Portsmouth		232	78	47	66.0
=29 Glasgow Caledonian		283	76	35	66.0
31 Huddersfield		227	74	54	65.7
32 Greenwich		227	77	49	65.6
33 Southampton Solent		249	75	42	64.9
=34 University of the Arts, London		348	55	44	64.5
=34 University College Birmingham		216	79	45	64.5
36 Canterbury Christ Church		206	72	56	63.6
37 Bedfordshire	1.0	156	78	28	63.5
38 Westminster		253	79	29	63.3
39 Hull		206	79	39	62.4
40 Chichester		260	79	18	61.0
41 Derby		220	72	38	59.9
42 St Mary's College, Twickenham		160	80	31	56.5
43 West of Scotland		230		29	56.4
44 Liverpool John Moores		251	64	26	55.8
45 Winchester		256	53	42	55.7
46 Middlesex		167	71	38	55.2
47 Anglia Ruskin		206	67	31	54.8
48 Buckinghamshire New		225	65	28	54.6
49 London South Bank		216	63	32	54.3
50 London Metropolitan		226	52	44	53.2

» Association for Tourism in Higher Education: **www.athe.org.uk**

» Council for Hospitality Management Education: **www.chme.org.uk**

» Institute of Hospitality: **www.instituteofhospitality.org**

» Leisure Studies Association: **www.leisure-studies-association.info**

Iberian Languages

Spanish has been growing in popularity as an alternative to French in schools, and is a common choice as an element of a broader modern languages degree. The positive trend was continuing at the start of 2011, when an increase in applications of nearly 9 per cent contrasted favourably with a smaller rise in German and a decline in French. It was the second successful year in a row for the language, but total applications were still not far above 2,400, well behind the figure for French. The table also includes Portuguese, which had only ten applications at degree level at the start of 2011, although it is still offered at 17 universities, at least as part of a broader languages programme.

Cambridge's lead at the top of the table has narrowed, with Oxford overtaking Durham to move into second place. Cambridge has the highest entry standards, but Oxford pips it to the best employment score. The most satisfied students are at Northumbria, in joint 17th position, while Nottingham and Manchester tie for the best performance in the 2008 Research Assessment Exercise. The 2010 National Student Survey showed high levels of satisfaction in most universities. Only four failed to satisfy at least 70 per cent of final-year undergraduates.

All but eight of the 45 institutions in the ranking are pre-1992 universities. Northumbria is by far the highest-placed of the newer foundations and the only one in the top 20, but, for the fourth year in a row, Portsmouth makes the top 30.

Entry standards have risen after levelling off last year: 16 universities average over 400 points and only one slips below 250.

The languages have moved into the top half of the employment table this year and the 6 per cent unemployment rate is among the lowest in any subject. Average starting salaries have risen to around £20,500, also just in the top half of the table. Employment prospects appear to be more evenly spread than in many subjects, although four universities (rather than two last year) saw fewer than half of their leavers go into graduate jobs or further training in 2009.

Employed in graduate job:	38%	Employed in non-graduate job and studying:	4%
Employed in graduate job and studying:	4%	Employed in non-graduate job:	25%
Studying:	23%	Unemployed:	6%
Average starting graduate salary:	£20,573	Average starting non-graduate salary:	£15,645

Iberian Languages	Research quality	Entry standards	Student satisfaction %	Graduate prospects %	Overall rating
1 Cambridge	4.0	534	90	81	100.0
2 Oxford	2.8	526	89	82	95.6
3 Durham	3.2	488	82	77	90.7
4 Bath	2.1	449	87	81	89.3
5 St Andrews	2.6	489	82	75	88.4
6 King's College London	3.5	424	85	64	86.9

Iberian Languages cont.

	Research quality	Entry standards	Student satisfaction %	Graduate prospects %	Overall rating
7 Nottingham	4.1	399	77	72	86.3
=8 Southampton	3.5	440	85	50	84.1
=8 Newcastle	2.5	436	77	77	84.1
10 Bristol	1.6	455	79	79	83.7
11 Manchester	4.1	398	76	65	83.6
=12 Leeds	3.1	431	79	63	83.1
=12 Leicester	1.9	365	86	76	83.1
14 University College London	2.1	451	81	69	82.9
15 Sheffield	3.2	413	73	67	80.7
16 Exeter	2.4	440	76	63	79.7
=17 Queen Mary, London	3.4	369	73	68	79.5
=17 Northumbria		300	91	86	79.5
19 Lancaster	1.5	402	75	79	79.4
20 Aberdeen	2.1	324	83	70	78.8
21 Cardiff	2.4	388	78	64	78.4
22 Birmingham	1.9	386	75	72	77.8
23 Aston	1.0	389	83		76.6
24 Kent	1.2	297	82	73	75.8
25 Heriot-Watt	1.6	372	77	66	75.6
26 Portsmouth	2.4	287	83	60	75.5
27 Glasgow	1.3	419	67	78	75.3
28 Edinburgh	2.5	466	65	61	75.2
29 Stirling	1.3	292	82	70	74.8
30 Queen's, Belfast	2.7	366	73	58	74.6
31 Strathclyde	0.8	389	76	67	73.5
32 Royal Holloway	2.3	383	68	63	73.4
33 Swansea	2.1	298	81	56	72.9
34 Liverpool	2.5	369	70	54	71.8
35 Sussex		381	73	74	71.4
36 Hull		303	82	71	71.3
37 Ulster	0.4	302	88	53	70.7
38 East Anglia		377	87	46	70.1
39 Chester		289	79	71	69.3
40 Salford	1.3	329	77	50	68.5
41 Roehampton	1.3	283	81	43	66.7
42 Nottingham Trent		279	87	49	66.4
43 Manchester Metropolitan	0.7	268	77	56	65.9
44 Westminster		290	66	68	62.3
45 Liverpool John Moores		242	72	43	56.3

» Association for Contemporary Iberian Studies: **www.iberianstudies.net**
» Association of Hispanists of Great Britain and Ireland: **www.dur.ac.uk/hispanists**
» Instituto Cervantes: **http://londres.cervantes.es/en/default.shtm**

Italian

Cambridge continues to lead a group of 21 universities qualifying for the ranking in Italian – 13 fewer than five years ago. It has the top score on three of the four measures, but Oxford's high entry standards deny it the clean sweep it enjoyed last year. Both of the ancient universities average more than 500 points at entry, but Cambridge managed a much better score in the 2008 Research Assessment Exercise, when 80 per cent of its submission was judged to be world-leading or internationally excellent.

Fifth-placed Manchester ties with Cambridge for the most satisfied students. As in previous years, student satisfaction was generally high in the 2010 National Student Survey. Only one university (just) failed to satisfy at least three quarters of final-year undergraduates. Manchester and Warwick, in fourth position, have made the most progress this year, each moving up five places.

St Andrews has dropped out of the table this year, leaving Glasgow a fraction ahead of Strathclyde as the top university in Scotland, while Cardiff remains ahead of Swansea in Wales. There are only three post-1992 universities left in the table, with Portsmouth much the best-placed, in 12th position.

Employment scores are variable: Cambridge was the only university to see over 80 per cent of leavers go straight into graduate-level jobs or postgraduate courses, while at two universities, the proportion slipped below 50 per cent.

There were only 295 applications to study Italian as a separate subject at the start of 2011, but this still represented a substantial increase on the previous year and many more students include the language in combined degree programmes. Only 62 started degrees in 2010, but the language remains widely available at degree level, with 37 universities offering courses involving Italian. A high proportion secure places in Clearing. Most students have no previous knowledge of the language, but there is a high completion rate.

The low numbers can make for big swings in the annual statistics: last year, for example, starting salaries were only just outside the top 30, whereas in this year's *Guide* they are in the bottom 15, averaging less than £19,000.

Employed in graduate job:	37%	Employed in non-graduate job and studying:		1%
Employed in graduate job and studying:	3%	Employed in non-graduate job:		27%
Studying:	22%	Unemployed:		10%
Average starting graduate salary:	£18,745	Average starting non-graduate salary:		£16,583

Italian	Research quality	Entry standards	Student satisfaction %	Graduate prospects %	Overall rating
1 Cambridge	5.1	534	90	81	100.0
2 Oxford	3.7	548	87	70	93.2
3 Leeds	3.8	416	84	75	89.0
4 Warwick	3.7	445	80	67	85.2
5 Manchester	3.0	376	90	59	85.1
6 Durham	1.2	488	82	77	84.7
7 Bath	2.1	439	81	74	83.6
=8 Bristol	3.0	435	81	64	82.9

Italian cont.

	Research quality	Entry standards	Student satisfaction %	Graduate prospects %	Overall rating
=8 University College London	2.7	446	80	66	82.9
10 Exeter	1.8	444	82	67	82.1
11 Birmingham	2.5	357	84	53	78.8
12 Portsmouth	2.4	287	83	60	77.5
13 Reading	3.5	354	81	44	77.2
14 Glasgow	1.3		83	56	76.8
15 Strathclyde	0.8		79	70	76.6
=16 Cardiff	2.4	344	78	59	75.8
=16 Edinburgh	0.9	434	73	71	75.8
18 Royal Holloway	1.6	384	78	51	73.4
19 Nottingham Trent		279	87	49	71.8
20 Swansea	1.3	280	78		70.1
21 Manchester Metropolitan	0.7	268	77	56	69.3

» Chartered Institute of Linguists: **www.iol.org.uk**

» National Centre for Languages (CILT): **www.cilt.org.uk**

» Society for Italian Studies: **www.sis.ac.uk**

Land and Property Management

Another university has joined the land and property management table this year, adding to the two which rejoined in the *2011 Guide*. But there are still only eight in the ranking, compared with 23 in 2005 edition. The subject tends to have small intakes, making it impossible to compile reliable scores for some universities, even though they are still offering one or more of the subjects. More than 25 universities and colleges are advertising degrees in this field starting in 2012.

Cambridge maintains the lead, with entry standards that are more than 100 points higher than at second-placed Reading and 200 points above the other universities in the table. Cambridge also has by far the highest employment score and registered the best performance in the 2008 Research Assessment Exercise.

The response to the 2010 National Student Survey was too low to produce a score for Cambridge. Greenwich, which occupies last place in the table, has the most satisfied students, with Ulster close behind.

Land and property management had been enjoying considerable success in the graduate jobs market, but it has dropped out of the top 20 for "positive destinations" this year. The unemployment rate, which was below 3 per cent in the *2010 Guide*, has now reached 13 per cent. Graduate salaries have followed the same trend, declining from an average of almost £22,000 in the last *Guide* to below £20,000 in this edition. Graduates' prospects inevitably depend to a large extent on the state of the property market, which had gone into decline when these statistics were collected.

Only about 2,000 students are taking the subject at degree or diploma level, although the subjects are often included in wider environmental programmes.

Employed in graduate job:	57%	Employed in non-graduate job and studying:	0%
Employed in graduate job and studying:	3%	Employed in non-graduate job:	18%
Studying:	9%	Unemployed:	13%
Average starting graduate salary:	£19,993	Average starting non-graduate salary:	£14,707

Land and Property Management	Research quality	Entry standards	Student satisfaction %	Graduate prospects %	Overall rating
1 Cambridge	4.1	513		96	100.0
2 Reading	3.4	408	78	87	90.4
3 Sheffield Hallam	2.8	292	76		82.0
4 Queen's, Belfast	1.6	293	75		76.9
5 Birmingham City	1.4	238	72	84	75.5
6 Ulster		282	81	57	75.4
7 Westminster	1.2	246	70	76	72.1
8 Greenwich		167	82	33	69.5

» Chartered Institute of Housing: **www.cih.org**

» Institute of Residential Property Management: **www.irpm.org.uk**

» Royal Institution of Chartered Surveyors: **www.rics.org/uk**

Law

Law is in the top four subjects for applications – more than 90,000 by March 2011, after a 4 per cent rise in the demand for places. Entry standards reflect its popularity: nine subjects have higher average entry scores, but only in medicine do so many universities make such testing demands. Six universities average more than 500 points and almost a third of the 95 universities have average entry scores of more than 400 points. There are now only three universities where the average is less than 200 points, but the 5.6 applications to each place in 2010 was no more than the average for all subjects.

Oxford retains the top place it won from Cambridge last year, despite not leading the table on any of the measures. Cambridge has the highest entry standards and, like last year, equal 11th-placed Aberdeen the best record for graduate destinations. Law has moved up the employment table since last year, but is still not in the top ten because of some low scores at the bottom of the ranking. Most of the top 20 universities saw at least 80 per cent of graduates go straight into graduate-level jobs or continue studying.

Aspiring solicitors go on to take the Legal Practice Course, while those aiming to be barristers take the Bar Vocational Course, so it is no surprise that law has by far the highest proportion engaged in postgraduate study. Many law graduates opt for careers in other areas, but the 6 per cent unemployment rate shows that they are still in demand.

Once more, the most satisfied students are not at one of the top universities. That distinction goes to Greenwich, in 42nd place, with Sunderland, not even in the top 50, sharing the next-best score with Newcastle. There were good scores in law throughout the 2010

Law cont.

National Student Survey. Only eight universities – and only one of the top 50 – failed to satisfy at least 70 per cent of the undergraduates.

The London School of Economics, in third place, achieved the best grades in the 2008 Research Assessment Exercise, when three quarters of its submission was rated world-leading or internationally excellent. Glasgow has overtaken Aberdeen as the top university in Scotland, while Cardiff is now well clear of the rest in Wales. Buckingham holds the highest position outside the traditional universities while Oxford Brookes is the leading post-1992 university.

Average starting salaries are not as high as many might believe, partly because of training salaries in law firms and also because only about half of all law graduates find their way into the profession. At less than £19,000, the average for graduate-level jobs is in the bottom 15 and substantially lower than in the previous survey.

Employed in graduate job:	18%	Employed in non-graduate job and studying:	7%
Employed in graduate job and studying:	5%	Employed in non-graduate job:	21%
Studying:	43%	Unemployed:	6%
Average starting graduate salary:	£18,911	Average starting non-graduate salary:	£14,826

Law	Research quality	Entry standards	Student satisfaction %	Graduate prospects %	Overall rating
1 Oxford	4.3	528	87	91	100.0
2 Cambridge	3.4	547		87	97.5
3 London School of Economics	5.0	536	76	87	95.2
4 University College London	4.4	522	78	88	94.8
5 Nottingham	3.8	488	85	84	94.4
6 Durham	3.8	512	80	84	92.6
7 Queen Mary, London	3.1	442	85	82	90.8
8 Reading	3.1	419	84	87	90.2
9 Newcastle	1.3	436	91	81	88.5
10 Glasgow	2.7	489	79	84	88.3
=11 Aberdeen	1.5	369	86	93	87.0
=11 Leicester	1.6	440	86	83	87.0
13 Edinburgh	3.6	451	73	86	86.8
14 Birmingham	2.8	446	80	79	86.7
15 Strathclyde	3.1	436	75	88	86.5
16 King's College London	2.5	505	77	81	86.3
=17 Bristol	2.7	494	76	81	86.1
=17 School of Oriental and African Studies	1.8	465	80	85	86.1
=19 Warwick	2.1	484	80	77	85.4
=19 Lancaster	1.8	411	81	88	85.4
21 Exeter	2.0	441	82	79	85.1
22 Southampton	1.9	457	82	76	85.0
23 Sussex	2.1	380	83	80	84.3
=24 Leeds	2.6	432	79	73	83.7

=24 Dundee		1.9	397	86	71	83.7
26 East Anglia		1.6	407	83	78	83.3
27 Kent		3.8	350	79	71	83.2
28 Cardiff		3.4	415	78	67	82.6
29 Manchester		2.2	447	73	82	81.9
30 Sheffield		2.5	438	74	78	81.8
31 Buckingham			279	89	89	80.5
32 Hull		1.8	355	80	79	80.2
33 Queen's, Belfast		3.4	397	72	71	80.1
34 Brunel		1.9	366	78	77	79.5
35 Stirling		1.6	336	84	70	79.4
=36 Aberystwyth		1.4	302	81	77	78.0
=36 Liverpool		2.3	415	72	72	78.0
38 Oxford Brookes		2.1	329	78	70	76.9
39 Keele		2.2	320	75	72	76.1
40 Swansea		1.8	329	79	66	75.7
41 Glamorgan		0.5	289	82	77	75.4
42 Greenwich		0.3	248	94	60	75.3
=43 Surrey		1.3	384	69	82	75.1
=43 Northumbria			347	80	76	75.1
45 Robert Gordon		0.3	301	77	85	74.8
46 Salford		0.7	340	80		74.6
47 Edinburgh Napier		0.2	347	77	79	74.3
48 Essex		1.9	321	74	69	74.2
49 Nottingham Trent		0.4	318		80	74.1
50 Portsmouth		1.5	318	80	63	74.0
51 Lincoln		0.4	289	85	66	73.9
52 West of England		1.0	309	79	68	73.6
53 De Montfort		0.7	251	83	69	73.0
=54 Sunderland		0.1	253	91	56	72.9
=54 Ulster		3.0	304	80	44	72.9
56 Hertfordshire		1.5	243	83	61	72.8
57 Manchester Metropolitan		1.5	324	72	73	72.7
58 City		1.5	393	65	78	72.5
59 Huddersfield			319	74	83	72.3
=60 Central Lancashire		0.6	243	80	75	72.2
=60 Chester			306	78	77	72.2
62 Teesside			282	84	65	72.1
63 Brighton		2.6	270	72	62	71.2
64 Coventry		0.2	321	78	67	71.1
=65 Heriot-Watt			326		70	71.0
=65 Bradford		2.4	249	78	53	71.0
67 Glasgow Caledonian		0.5	354	79	55	70.7
=68 Bournemouth		0.1	324	73	75	70.0
=68 Derby			260	85	59	70.0
=68 Abertay		0.8	287		68	70.0
71 Staffordshire			235	78	75	69.5

Law cont.

	Research quality	Entry standards	Student satisfaction %	Graduate prospects %	Overall rating
72 East London	1.5	191	77	65	68.9
73 Sheffield Hallam	0.3	299	75	65	68.4
74 Birmingham City		291	68	83	68.2
75 Buckinghamshire New		217	77	73	68.1
76 Plymouth	1.5	286	74	55	67.7
77 Westminster	1.2	316	65	70	67.3
78 Gloucestershire		268	74	68	66.9
79 St Mary's College, Twickenham		203		75	66.5
80 Liverpool John Moores		275	78	56	66.4
81 Kingston	0.4	280	70	67	65.9
=82 Middlesex	0.6	232	69	71	65.2
=82 Anglia Ruskin		266	73	64	65.2
84 Edge Hill		241	80	51	64.8
85 Leeds Metropolitan		267	68	66	63.1
86 Bangor		284	72	55	62.9
87 Bolton		220	70	67	62.8
88 Northampton		229	78	49	62.7
89 Southampton Solent		242	74	51	61.4
90 London Metropolitan	0.4	242	65	59	60.0
=91 Bedfordshire		196	71	57	59.9
=91 London South Bank		195	69	63	59.9
93 Canterbury Christ Church		246	76	37	59.4
94 Newport		207		52	58.0
95 West of Scotland		236		21	49.0

» Law Society of England and Wales: **www.lawsociety.org.uk**
» Law Society of Northern Ireland: **www.lawsoc-ni.org**
» Law Society of Scotland: **www.lawscot.org.uk**

Librarianship and Information Management

The top three universities for librarianship and information are unchanged for the third year in a row, but Northumbria has taken fourth place for the first time, overhauling Aberystwyth. Second-placed Sheffield has the best score for research, but Loughborough is the leader on the other three indicators. King's College London actually produced the top results in the 2008 Research Assessment Exercise but does not have undergraduate courses in this field so does not appear in the table. Sheffield was close behind, with two thirds of its work classed as world-leading or internationally excellent, followed by University College London, which also third in *The Times* table.

Employment prospects, even among such a small group of universities, are extremely variable. While three quarters of Loughborough graduates found graduate–level work or further courses within six months of completing a degree, the rate in half of the universities with scores on this measure was well below 50 per cent. This contributes to an unemployment rate of 17 per cent, the highest in any subject this year.

Student numbers are low – three universities in the table did not recruit enough undergraduates for entry grades to be published. Barely 600 candidates had applied to study information sciences at the start of 2011, representing a small decline on the previous year. There are five fewer universities than there were in the 2006 edition of the *Guide*. There is no representative in Scotland and only Aberystwyth from Wales. Northumbria's rise up the table has made it clearly the leading post-1992 university.

Librarianship and information management are not the poor payers that their reputation might suggest, however. Average starting salaries in graduate-level jobs of more than £23,000 place them just outside the top ten.

Employed in graduate job:	44%	Employed in non-graduate job and studying:	2%
Employed in graduate job and studying:	2%	Employed in non-graduate job:	23%
Studying:	11%	Unemployed:	17%
Average starting graduate salary:	£23,246	Average starting non-graduate salary:	£15,889

Librarianship and Information Management	Research quality	Entry standards	Student satisfaction %	Graduate prospects %	Overall rating
1 Loughborough	2.6	347	87	76	100.0
2 Sheffield	3.8	339	82	68	97.3
3 University College London	3.6		80	67	93.6
4 Northumbria	0.7	259	80	65	84.0
5 Aberystwyth	2.2	257	81	42	83.4
6 Brighton	1.9		79	44	81.2
7 London South Bank	0.5		77	44	75.4
8 Manchester Metropolitan	0.7	219	78	39	74.6
9 Liverpool John Moores	1.1	222	71		70.8

» Association for Information Management: **www.aslib.com**
» Chartered Institute of Library and Information Professionals: **www.cilip.org.uk**

Linguistics

Applications for linguistics have fluctuated in recent years, veering from a 15 per cent drop in 2009 to an even larger increase in the following year. In March 2011, they seemed to have stabilised at more than 2,500. Entry standards remain comparatively high: only one university averages less than 250 points and about a third of the ranked universities have an average of more than 400 points. Eight out of ten students arrive with A levels or their equivalent.

Oxford has overtaken Cambridge at the top of the table, despite a surprisingly low set of grades in the 2008 Research Assessment Exercise. Oxford has the highest entry standards and the best employment score, while the two ancient universities tie for the most satisfied students, as they did last year.

Linguistics cont.

Third-placed Lancaster was the only university, apart from Oxford, to see 70 per cent of their linguists go straight into graduate-level work or further study. Six universities, compared with only two last year, dropped below 50 per cent on this measure. Cardiff, which has dropped out of the top ten, produced the best grades in the 2008 Research Assessment Exercise. Queen Mary, London, was close behind, holding on to a place in the top five as a result.

Edinburgh is Scotland's only representative in the table, while Cardiff is well ahead of Bangor in Wales. Portsmouth is the highest-placed post-1992 university, having moved up to sixth in a ranking that is dominated by the older foundations. Hertfordshire is the only other post-1992 university in the top 20.

Linguistics is close to the bottom ten subjects for immediate employment prospects, with an unemployment rate above average at 10 per cent. Starting salaries for graduate jobs are in the bottom ten, but still better than last year when the average was less than £17,500.

Employed in graduate job:	29%	Employed in non-graduate job and studying:	4%
Employed in graduate job and studying:	3%	Employed in non-graduate job:	32%
Studying:	21%	Unemployed:	10%
Average starting graduate salary:	£18,074	Average starting non-graduate salary:	£14,131

Linguistics	Research quality	Entry standards	Student satisfaction %	Graduate prospects %	Overall rating
1 Oxford	1.9	531	87	78	100.0
2 Cambridge	2.8		87	64	94.4
3 Lancaster	2.7	429	83	70	93.5
4 University College London	2.8	467	84	59	92.7
5 Queen Mary, London	3.9	387	85	55	92.3
6 Portsmouth	2.4		84	63	90.1
7 Edinburgh	3.7	453	71	66	89.6
8 York	3.2	403	81	57	88.9
9 Essex	3.4	330	76	69	87.4
10 Sheffield	3.1	429	75	59	87.2
11 Newcastle	2.2	410	79	60	86.1
12 Cardiff	4.0	382	78	44	85.1
13 Leeds	1.9	396	77	64	84.7
14 Ulster	2.2	284	83	59	82.9
15 Sussex	1.0		81	64	82.5
16 Hertfordshire	2.1	263	80	57	79.6
17 School of Oriental and African Studies	1.8	384	75		79.5
18 Manchester	2.4	379	73	49	78.8
19 King's College London		403	77	55	76.1
20 Bangor	1.5	286	83	34	73.2
21 West of England	2.1	280	71	50	73.0
22 York St John		316	80	48	72.4
23 Salford	1.5	290	67	46	67.9

24 Brighton	0.4	287	73	43	66.6
25 Westminster	0.7	240	72		64.8

» British Association for Applied Linguistics: **www.baal.org.uk**
» Linguistics Association of Great Britain: **www.lagb.org.uk**

Materials Technology

There had been only 800 applications to study materials technology by March 2011, but this represented 4 per cent rise, following much stronger growth in 2010. Courses in this category cover three distinct areas: materials science, mining and engineering; textiles technology and printing; and marine technology. The leading universities demand chemistry and sometimes also physics, maths or design technology at A level or its equivalent.

There is more movement than usual in this year's table. Although Cambridge retains the leadership it won from Oxford three years ago, the next ten places have all changed. Nottingham has moved up to second place, while Imperial College London has slipped to fifth, behind Sheffield. Cambridge achieved the best grades in the 2008 Research Assessment Exercise, when only 5 per cent of the university's research was considered less than

Employed in graduate job:	48%	Employed in non-graduate job and studying:	1%
Employed in graduate job and studying:	3%	Employed in non-graduate job:	24%
Studying:	14%	Unemployed:	10%
Average starting graduate salary:	£20,006	Average starting non-graduate salary:	£13,888

Materials Technology	Research quality	Entry standards	Student satisfaction %	Graduate prospects %	Overall rating
1 Cambridge	5.3	595	84	82	100.0
2 Nottingham	3.8		85	91	92.0
3 Oxford	3.9			88	91.7
4 Sheffield	3.0	371	84	95	86.2
5 Imperial College	3.0	474	79	82	85.1
6 Leeds	3.7		74	77	80.2
7 Birmingham	3.2	376	78	75	79.4
8 Loughborough	3.4	358	82	68	78.9
9 Swansea	2.8	296	78	87	77.9
10 Queen Mary, London	2.7	344	85	69	77.3
11 Exeter	1.5	415	72	87	76.3
12 Sheffield Hallam	1.5	302	87		73.6
13 Manchester	3.6	381	65	55	70.3
14 De Montfort	1.7	284	77	63	66.4
15 Manchester Metropolitan	1.0	296	68	65	62.2
16 London Metropolitan	0.1		59	48	46.2
17 University of the Arts, London		251	52	49	46.0

Materials Technology cont.

world-leading or internationally excellent. It also has by far the highest entry standards – more than 100 points ahead of Imperial. Other entry scores are tightly bunched, with only six universities averaging less than 350 points and none less than 250.

Sheffield graduates had the best employment prospects at the end of 2009, when 95 per cent found a graduate-level job or were on a more advanced course six months after completing a degree. Nottingham also did well on this measure, but there were mixed scores elsewhere in the table.

Like last year, the most satisfied students are at Sheffield Hallam, the leading post-1992 university but still not a member of the top ten. Swansea is the only Welsh university in the table and there is no representative from Scotland.

Employment prospects are about average for all subjects: more than half of those completing a degree go straight into graduate-level work, but the unemployment rate is no longer below the norm for all subjects. Average starting salaries for those who find graduate jobs are also below average, at almost exactly £20,000.

» Institute of Materials, Minerals and Mining: **www.iom3.org**
» UK Centre for Materials Education (materials science): **www.materials.ac.uk**

Mathematics

Maths has been enjoying a renaissance as a degree subject since sixth-form numbers began to recover from a slump in the last decade. Another 3 per cent increase in applications at the start of 2011 brought the total back above 40,000 – about 15,000 more than there were six years ago. The number of places has grown as well – about 7,300 started degrees in 2010, a rise of nearly 6 per cent on the previous year – but the ratio of applications to places is still well over 5:1.

This shows in the high entry grades. Ten universities (compared with seven last year) had average entry grades of more than 500 points, a number exceeded only in medicine, while another 18 averaged more than 400 points. The totals are boosted by the fact that many candidates for the leading universities take two A levels in the subject, as well as two or three others.

Oxford remains in first place, but its lead over Cambridge is even slimmer this year. Oxford has the best grades in two of the three of the subjects grouped together as mathematics in the 2008 Research Assessment Exercise, sharing that distinction with Cambridge in applied maths. Ninety per cent of Oxford's work in statistics and operational research was considered world-leading or internationally excellent. Imperial was top for pure mathematics, helping it to third place in *The Times* maths table, with Warwick managing the next-best grades, although it has slipped to fourth this year.

Cambridge still has the highest entry standards, but the most satisfied students are at Northumbria, which finishes just inside the top 20. None of the top three universities have satisfaction rates and there are gaps, too, further down the table, but where there were sufficient responses to compile a score, mathematicians appear well satisfied with their courses. No university fell below a 70 per cent approval rating.

Oxford pips Cambridge to the top employment score. Employment levels are generally good – maths is among the top 20 subjects for positive destinations – but three universities do fall below 50 per cent on this measure in the latest table. Maths is often cited as one of the subjects most likely to lead to a lucrative career, and the earnings table seems to bear this out. Average salaries in graduate jobs have dropped slightly since the last *Guide*, but were still £23,000 at the time of the latest survey.

St Andrews is the top university in Scotland, despite dropping one place this year, while Cardiff retains the lead in Wales. Northumbria is by far the highest-placed post-1992 university, but London Metropolitan and Greenwich also make the top 40.

Employed in graduate job:	28%	Employed in non-graduate job and studying:	2%
Employed in graduate job and studying:	11%	Employed in non-graduate job:	18%
Studying:	30%	Unemployed:	10%
Average starting graduate salary:	£23,160	Average starting non-graduate salary:	£15,807

Mathematics	Research quality Pure Mathematics	Research quality Applied Mathematics	Research quality Statistics	Entry standards	Student satisfaction %	Graduate prospects %	Overall rating
1 Oxford	4.4	4.1	5.1	568		87	100.0
2 Cambridge	4.1	4.1	4.1	598		86	99.5
3 Imperial College	5.0	3.3	3.8	543		86	96.5
4 Warwick	4.6	3.7	3.7	541	80	81	91.6
5 Durham	3.1	3.2	1.9	550	78	81	87.8
6 St Andrews	1.5	3.7	2.5	520	82	79	87.6
7 Bath	3.4	3.4	3.1	507	77	83	87.5
8 Nottingham	2.5	3.2	3.4	493	82	75	87.2
9 Lancaster	2.2		2.8	452	84	77	86.3
10 East Anglia	2.8	1.8		393	86	74	84.2
11 Bristol	4.0	3.7	3.7	527	70	76	84.1
12 Loughborough	2.4	2.2		439	83	74	83.9
13 Edinburgh	3.7	2.9	2.1	478	77	71	83.7
14 London School of Economics	1.8		2.7	521	73	85	83.4
15 University College London	3.1	2.2	2.2	518	75	77	83.2
16 Surrey		3.1		440	80	67	82.9
17 Exeter	2.4	2.5		484	84	61	82.7
=18 Northumbria		1.9		322	91	67	82.4
=18 King's College London	3.4	2.9		462	77	69	82.4
20 Sussex		2.2		386	81	78	82.1
=21 York	2.1	2.2		486	79	68	81.3
=21 Southampton	1.9	3.1	2.9	461	77	70	81.3
23 Heriot-Watt	3.7	2.9	2.1	385	76	79	81.1
=24 Leicester	2.2	1.8		431	84	64	81.0
=24 Glasgow	2.7	2.2	2.5	403	82	68	81.0
=26 Sheffield	2.7	2.1	2.5	437	78	72	80.9
=26 Birmingham	2.7	2.1		457	82	63	80.9
28 Aberdeen	3.3			328		68	80.2
29 Newcastle	1.5	2.8	2.4	435	78	69	80.0

Mathematics cont.

	Research quality Pure Mathematics	Research quality Applied Mathematics	Research quality Statistics	Entry standards	Student satisfaction %	Graduate prospects %	Overall rating
30 Manchester	3.1	3.4	2.9	462	73	67	79.9
31 Queen's, Belfast	1.8			388	82	70	79.8
32 London Metropolitan	1.8		1.2	213	90	76	79.7
33 Greenwich			1.3	226	90	75	79.5
34 Cardiff	1.6			455	78	72	79.4
35 Kent	1.2	2.1	3.2	315	75	84	79.2
36 Reading		1.6	1.5	379	83	67	78.6
37 Royal Holloway	0.9			384	83	73	77.9
38 Leeds	2.4	2.7	3.5	443	72	68	77.8
39 Strathclyde		2.2	1.9	397	76	70	77.6
40 Aston	1.8	1.8	1.8	356	74	82	77.2
=41 Liverpool	2.1	2.8	1.2	409	74	69	77.0
=41 Keele		2.8		342	80	59	77.0
43 Cumbria				347		83	76.3
44 Aberystwyth	1.6			333		74	76.2
45 Swansea	1.6			328	77	74	75.9
46 Glamorgan		0.7		306	84	70	75.6
47 Sheffield Hallam	1.2	1.2	1.2	289		81	75.4
48 Plymouth		0.9	1.1	347	81	67	75.2
49 Stirling		1.6		303		71	74.4
=50 Nottingham Trent	1.3	1.3	1.3	292	87	54	74.0
=50 Queen Mary, London	2.5	2.2	1.9	359	73	66	74.0
52 Brighton		0.6		278	82	72	73.7
53 Essex				342	79	78	73.6
54 Edge Hill				269		83	73.2
55 Hertfordshire	2.7			245	75	61	71.8
56 Brunel		2.2	2.5	300	76	57	71.5
57 Manchester Metropolitan	1.8			300	75	64	71.3
58 Portsmouth		3.2		304	77	43	71.1
59 Dundee		2.1		357		49	70.1
60 Chester		0.6		295		71	69.9
61 Coventry	0.7	0.8		284	74	71	69.6
62 West of England		0.4		314	80	54	68.5
63 City		1.1		342	73	58	68.3
64 Kingston				251	82	56	66.8
65 Central Lancashire				297		60	65.4
66 Oxford Brookes		0.5		284		55	63.6
67 Liverpool John Moores				274		44	58.2

» London Mathematical Society: **www.lms.ac.uk**
» Maths Careers: **www.mathscareers.org.uk**
» Royal Statistical Society: **www.rss.org.uk**

Mechanical Engineering

Cambridge's lead in mechanical engineering has narrowed since last year, but it still considerable. Imperial College London has moved into second, but is nearly ten points behind. Cambridge, which was ranked second in the world in mechanical engineering in 2011, has by far the highest entry standards, the best research grades and the top employment record.

Hull, in 20th place, has the most satisfied students. High satisfaction scores are spread through most of the table, with only seven universities failing to win the approval of at least 70 per cent of final-year undergraduates. Entry scores vary widely. Imperial, Bath and Durham all join Cambridge with average entry scores of more than 500 points, but three universities still average less than 200 points.

Imperial was Cambridge's nearest challenger in the 2008 Research Assessment Exercise, while Surrey comes closest to emulating the 92 per cent positive destinations among Cambridge graduates in 2009. Cardiff remains the top university in Wales and Strathclyde does the same in Scotland. The University of the West of England is the leading post-1992 university and is joined in the top 30 by Robert Gordon. The large numbers of mature students upgrading their qualifications in mechanical engineering mean that more than a third of the entrants at post-1992 universities are admitted without A levels or their equivalent.

Mechanical Engineering	Research quality	Entry standards	Student satisfaction %	Graduate prospects %	Overall rating
1 Cambridge	5.4	567	83	92	100.0
2 Imperial College	4.2	518	77	87	90.1
3 Sheffield	4.1	431	83	88	89.8
4 Loughborough	3.4	430	84	85	87.3
5 Surrey	3.2	377	87	89	87.1
6 Bristol	3.6	496	80	81	87.0
7 Nottingham	3.8	418	83	82	86.8
8 Southampton	2.8	488	82	82	85.7
9 Liverpool	3.3	388	82	82	83.9
10 Bath	2.4	503	84	74	83.6
11 Newcastle	2.9	400	79	86	82.6
12 Birmingham	3.4	426	80	74	82.0
13 Strathclyde	2.5	448	79	83	81.9
14 Cardiff	3.2	404	82	70	81.3
15 Exeter	2.4	416	84	75	81.2
16 University College London	3.0	458	79	71	81.0
17 Leeds	3.5	389	75	79	80.5
18 Glasgow	2.1	370	88	74	80.2
19 Edinburgh	2.7	423	74	75	77.3
20 Hull	1.4	312	89	76	76.9
21 Queen's, Belfast	2.9	370	75	74	76.5
22 Queen Mary, London	2.0	339	85	66	75.5
23 Heriot-Watt	2.4	333	76	80	75.3
24 Lancaster	2.2	372	77	73	74.9

	Research quality	Entry standards	Student satisfaction %	Graduate prospects %	Overall rating
25 Aberdeen	2.9	313	72	80	74.6
26 Durham		514	76	82	74.5
27 Manchester	3.4	410	65	74	74.4
28 Sussex	2.5	299	79	71	74.2
29 West of England	2.4	295	76	79	73.9
=30 Swansea	2.1	313	79	74	73.6
=30 Robert Gordon		326	85	88	73.6
=32 Brighton	2.5	306	81	62	72.9
=32 Brunel	2.2	359	71	78	72.9
=34 Warwick		442	82	74	72.8
=34 King's College London	2.1	408	73	70	72.8
36 Liverpool John Moores	3.1	323	71	67	71.6
37 Northumbria	1.9	265	77	73	70.3
38 Glyndŵr	1.5			76	70.2
39 Portsmouth	1.8	267	76	76	70.0
40 Greenwich	4.0	179	82	45	69.7
41 Dundee		330	77	85	69.2
42 Harper Adams		255	82	81	68.3
=43 Plymouth	0.9	267	83	62	67.4
=43 Bradford	1.9	251	78	60	67.4
45 Central Lancashire		258	84	72	67.2
46 Aston	1.8	340	67	71	67.0
47 Teesside		313	76	80	66.9
48 City	2.1	299	78	44	65.6
49 Staffordshire	1.9	247	73	62	65.2
50 Manchester Metropolitan	1.2	260	70	74	64.9
51 Coventry	0.8	316	75	59	64.2
52 Birmingham City		249	79	69	63.9
53 Sheffield Hallam	1.5	246	69	70	63.6
=54 Hertfordshire	2.5	264	64	59	62.7
=54 Huddersfield	1.5	259	62	78	62.7
56 Sunderland	1.0	275		63	62.1
57 Kingston	1.2	238	71	60	60.7
58 Oxford Brookes		328	65	66	58.6
=59 De Montfort	1.9	243	70	40	58.1
=59 Ulster		238	64	77	58.1
61 London South Bank	2.2	191	75	31	57.5
62 Bolton	1.7	172	75	36	56.4

Employed in graduate job:	49%	Employed in non-graduate job and studying:	1%
Employed in graduate job and studying:	4%	Employed in non-graduate job:	16%
Studying:	16%	Unemployed:	13%
Average starting graduate salary:	£24,337	Average starting non-graduate salary:	£14,764

Mechanical engineering now attracts more applicants than any other branch of the wider discipline. Indeed, it was among the 20 most popular subjects at the start of 2011, following a third successive rise in applications of more than 10 per cent. The number of places has also been rising, allowing more than 6,500 students to start degrees in 2010. Most universities demand maths – preferably with a strong component of mechanics – and another science subject (usually physics) at A level or its equivalent.

The recession did not hit graduate employment prospects as it did other branches of engineering, although it has dropped six places in the latest table of positive destinations. The subject remains in the top 20 for graduate destinations, but unemployment was well above average, at 13 per cent in the latest survey. The subject is still in the top ten in the earnings league: starting salaries in graduate jobs averaged more than £24,000 at the end of 2009.

» Engineering UK: **www.engineeringuk.com**
» Institution of Mechanical Engineers: **www.imeche.org**

Medicine

The number of universities in the ranking has been growing year by year, as graduates emerge from the medical schools established after 2000. The new medical schools were expected to ease this pressure, but entry standards have risen again this year. No subject has such high entry standards – nine schools average more than 500 points and only one drops below 450. Cambridge has the highest, its entrants averaging close to five As at A level.

The top five remain the same as last year, with Oxford ahead of Cambridge thanks largely to much the highest satisfaction levels anywhere in the table. Cambridge recorded the best results in the 2008 Research Assessment Exercise. At least 80 per cent of its research was considered world-leading or internationally excellent in all but one of the eight specialisms in which it submitted work. In the 2008 Research Assessment Exercise, universities were able to submit research in up to 12 areas (called units of assessment, UoA). Full details can be seen for UoA 1–9, 12, 14 and 15 at **www.rae.ac.uk/results**.

There were more than ten applications to the place in medicine in 2010 – only dentistry was fractionally more competitive. And a 4 per cent increase by the deadline for courses beginning in 2011 ensured that this ratio would go higher still. Even though candidates are restricted to four medical schools, the subject was once more among the top five in terms of total applications at the start of 2011.

Employment scores have been dropped as a measure (although they are still shown for guidance) to avoid small differences distorting positions in a subject where virtually all graduates become junior doctors or researchers.

Undergraduates have to be prepared to work long hours, particularly towards the end of the course. But student satisfaction is generally high, even if it does not reach the levels seen in some subjects. Just Oxford managed to satisfy 90 per cent of undergraduates, but only four dropped below 70 per cent on this measure. Medicine is also second in the earnings league, with average starting salaries of more than £29,000 in 2009.

Nearly all schools demand chemistry and most biology. Physics or maths is required by some, either as an alternative or addition to biology Universities will want to see evidence of commitment to the subject through work experience or voluntary work. Almost all schools interview candidates, and several use one of the two specialist aptitude tests (see chapter 1).

Medicine

Medicine	Research quality	Entry standards	Student satisfaction %	Graduate prospects %	Overall rating
1 Oxford	4.3	555	92	100	100.0
2 Cambridge	4.7	585	82	99	99.9
3 Edinburgh	4.0	530	84	100	93.6
4 University College London	3.9	536	79	100	91.6
5 Imperial College	3.7	530	79	100	90.4
6 Newcastle	2.6	497	85	100	86.2
7 St Andrews	2.2	504	86	99	85.9
8 Hull-York	3.0	497	80	100	85.4
9 Aberdeen	3.3	454	84	100	84.2
10 Queen Mary, London	3.4	499	71	100	83.8
=11 Birmingham	2.7	517	72	100	83.3
=11 Dundee	2.3	490	82	100	83.3
=11 Leeds	2.6	490	79	100	83.3
14 Leicester	1.9	498	83	100	83.2
15 Peninsula Medical School	2.2	487	83	100	83.1
16 Southampton	2.7	487	78	99	82.9
17 Sheffield	2.2	495	79	100	82.6
18 Nottingham	1.5	519	79	99	82.2
19 Glasgow	2.6	509	71	100	82.1
=20 Manchester	3.1	495	66	100	80.2
=20 King's College London	2.8	487	70	100	80.2
=22 St George's	1.8	482	75	100	78.3
=22 East Anglia	1.8	475	77	100	78.3
24 Bristol	2.7	488	65	100	78.1
=25 Warwick	2.1		73	100	78.0
=25 Liverpool	2.5	488	66	100	78.0
27 Queen's, Belfast	2.1	461	75	99	77.3
28 Brighton & Sussex Medical School	1.5	430	84	100	76.2
29 Cardiff	2.2	487	61	100	74.8
30 Keele	1.5	457	70	99	72.9

Employed in graduate job:	92%	Employed in non-graduate job and studying:	0%
Employed in graduate job and studying:	3%	Employed in non-graduate job:	0%
Studying:	5%	Unemployed:	0%
Average starting graduate salary:	£29,129	Average starting non-graduate salary:	n/a

» British Medical Association: **www.bma.org.uk**

» NHS Careers: **www.nhscareers.nhs.uk**

» Student BMJ: **http://student.bmj.com**

Middle Eastern and African Studies

Cambridge has re-entered the ranking for Middle Eastern and African Studies for the first time in six years, but finishes a fraction of a point behind Oxford, the long-established leader. Cambridge has the highest entry standards and the most satisfied students, but Oxford's lead in research and employment prospects is enough to ensure that it is not toppled. Durham drops to third place, while St Andrews remains ahead of Edinburgh in fourth.

Like last year, the School of Oriental and African Studies, in London, has the best employment record in the table, as the only institution to have seen over 80 per cent of those completing a degree go straight into graduate-level work or continue their studies in 2009. There are no universities in the ranking from Wales or Northern Ireland, and the last post-1992 university dropped out last year.

The small numbers make for big swings even in the national statistics. Middle Eastern and African studies had by far the highest unemployment rate three years ago, but that figure dropped to just 4 per cent the following year. Now it is just above average, at 11 per cent, but the subject is back in the bottom half of the table for "positive destinations". However, the subjects are back in the top ten of the earnings league, with average graduate starting salaries about £25,000, compared with less than £21,000 in the last *Guide*.

Middle Eastern Studies is the larger of the two subjects in terms of student numbers. Fewer than 100 applications had been made for African studies at the start of 2011, but there were 500 for Middle Eastern subjects, which had been growing in popularity. Most students come with A levels or their equivalent. Entry standards are high, with no university averaging less than 330 points, and at least 70 per cent of students are satisfied at all but two of the universities in the table. Completion rates are good, and a high proportion graduate with a first or 2:1.

Employed in graduate job:	30%	Employed in non-graduate job and studying:	4%
Employed in graduate job and studying:	5%	Employed in non-graduate job:	25%
Studying:	24%	Unemployed:	11%
Average starting graduate salary:	£25,004	Average starting non-graduate salary:	n/a

Middle Eastern and African Studies	Research quality	Entry standards	Student satisfaction %	Graduate prospects %	Overall rating
1 Oxford	4.6	515	87	78	100.0
2 Cambridge	4.4	555	88	71	99.9
3 Durham	3.2	488	85	77	91.0
4 St Andrews	3.1		84	78	89.2
5 Edinburgh	3.7	507	63	73	85.4
6 School of Oriental and African Studies	3.4	399	73	81	84.3
7 Birmingham	3.1	337	79	59	76.2
8 Exeter	2.2	433	84	40	73.2
9 Manchester	2.8	383	58	47	66.1
10 Leeds		365	84	61	64.3

» African Studies Association of the UK: **www.asauk.net/**
» British Society for Middle Eastern Studies: **www.brismes.ac.uk**

Music

Music continues to grow in popularity as a degree subject and six more institutions have joined the ranking this year as a result. A 16 per cent increase in applications took the total past 25,000 for the first time in 2010, and 2011 saw another 6 per cent rise. Growing numbers are seeking places on Foundation degrees as well. Nine out of ten degree applicants come with A levels and most university departments expect music to be among them, although they may accept a distinction or merit in Grade 8 music exams.

There is considerable variation in the character of courses, from the practical and vocational programmes in conservatoires to the more theoretical degrees in some of the older universities. But entry standards tend to be high throughout: a dozen of the 72 universities in this year's ranking average at least 400 points, while only three slip below 200.

Music	Research quality	Entry standards	Student satisfaction %	Graduate prospects %	Overall rating
1 Oxford	5.3	474	86	84	100.0
2 Bristol	3.2	442	89	85	95.7
3 Cambridge	5.3	485	76	87	95.6
4 Manchester	5.6	424	85	74	95.2
5 Sheffield	5.2	382	83	85	93.8
6 York	5.3	424	80	79	92.8
7 King's College London	5.3	479	76	75	92.4
8 Newcastle	4.5	358	87	80	92.2
9 Birmingham	5.6	440	81	63	91.3
10 Durham	3.7	462	79	79	90.9
11 Royal Academy of Music	3.7		78	95	90.8
12 Southampton	5.4	384	79	73	89.9
13 Royal Holloway	6.3	380	78	64	88.7
14 Sussex	3.2	361	84	80	87.9
15 School of Oriental and African Studies	4.5	389		70	87.6
16 Nottingham	4.1	438	76	64	85.6
=17 Edinburgh	3.2	446	76	71	85.4
=17 Surrey	3.2	419	76	76	85.4
19 RSAMD, Glasgow	2.2	342		89	83.9
20 Glasgow	4.1	407	78	57	83.6
21 Cardiff	3.1	383	81	63	83.4
22 Bangor	3.7	300	81	74	83.2
23 Lancaster	4.0	370	71	80	82.9
24 Leeds	3.2	371	80	64	82.8
=25 Keele	3.2	286	81	72	81.0
=25 Royal College of Music	2.5	331	71	93	81.0
27 Queen's, Belfast	4.3	355	74	64	80.8
28 East Anglia	1.3	354	86	64	80.5
29 Huddersfield	3.5	286	78	69	79.7
30 Liverpool	2.5	345	81	60	79.4

31 Goldsmiths College	4.0	329	71	71	79.1
32 Birmingham City	2.2	310	73	87	78.9
33 Royal Northern College of Music	1.5	325	73	87	78.2
34 Hull	1.6	275	83	70	77.4
35 Strathclyde		394		66	76.0
36 City	3.8	369	65	63	75.3
37 Bath Spa	1.6	297	81	58	75.0
38 Aberdeen	1.9	287	83	52	74.8
39 De Montfort	2.6	291	78	52	73.9
40 Cumbria		331	76	72	73.0
41 Oxford Brookes	2.1	284	74	63	72.5
42 Edinburgh Napier	0.2	366	68	76	71.7
43 Glamorgan		319	73	71	70.7
44 Gloucestershire		246	76	78	70.4
45 Plymouth	2.3	225	73	64	70.0
46 Chester	1.4	225	72	73	69.7
47 Canterbury Christ Church	1.6	212	78	58	69.1
48 Ulster	1.0	273	70	67	68.3
49 Hertfordshire	0.9	252	79	49	68.1
50 Derby		271	78	52	67.2
51 Middlesex		294	65	79	67.0
52 Brighton	4.1	269	69	33	66.6
53 Coventry	2.2	287	65	58	66.4
54 Brunel	2.4	309	59	63	65.8
55 Salford	0.9	290	68	56	65.2
56 Manchester Metropolitan		236	73	62	64.9
57 Chichester		274	73	54	64.6
58 Bournemouth		249	75	50	64.0
59 Central Lancashire		222	78	47	63.6
60 Westminster	1.5	252	66	56	63.5
61 Essex		192	78	51	63.3
62 Kent		247	75	47	62.8
63 Falmouth University College		246	71	56	62.7
64 Kingston	0.4	234	68	60	62.5
65 Anglia Ruskin	0.9	248	70	40	61.1
66 Sunderland	0.9	242	74	29	60.2
67 West of Scotland		304		35	59.2
68 Southampton Solent		259	69	37	57.8
69 Liverpool John Moores		181	78	29	57.2
70 Buckinghamshire New		230	67	39	56.0
71 Northampton	0.9	153	65	43	54.6
72 East London		226	58	45	52.4

Employed in graduate job:	32%	Employed in non-graduate job and studying:	3%
Employed in graduate job and studying:	6%	Employed in non-graduate job:	24%
Studying:	26%	Unemployed:	9%
Average starting graduate salary:	£17,040	Average starting non-graduate salary:	£13,928

Music cont.

Oxford has widened its lead in the music ranking, despite not leading on any individual measure, but there has been considerable movement below it. Bristol has shot up ten places to second with the most satisfied students and one of the best scores for employment prospects. The Royal Academy of Music has the best employment score and it is noticeable that the specialist institutions do far better than even the leading university departments on this measure. While the four specialists registered positive destinations for between 87 per cent and 95 per cent of their leavers, eight of the bottom ten universities fell below 50 per cent.

Royal Holloway, although no longer in the top ten overall, had the best grades in a high-scoring set of research assessments, with no less than 90 per cent of its research considered world-leading or internationally excellent. Third-placed Cambridge has the highest entry standards. Huddersfield is the top post-1992 university and the only one in the top 30. As in most subjects, the new universities suffer for their lower entry grades, although selection is more a matter of musical ability than academic achievement.

The 9 per cent unemployment rate in the latest survey remains no worse than the average for all subjects, despite the fact that career prospects for musicians are notoriously uncertain. Music finishes mid-way in the employment table, although nearly 30 per cent of leavers were in non-graduate jobs six months after graduation. However, the subject is at the bottom this year for starting salaries, averaging barely more than £17,000 in graduate jobs.

» Incorporated Society of Musicians: **www.ism.org**
» Royal Musical Association: **www.rma.ac.uk**

Nursing

Nursing has been one of the main growth points of higher education since moving towards becoming a graduate profession, and the impending withdrawal of the diploma option has produced another surge in applications. There were more than 100,000 degree applications for the first time in 2010, representing growth of over 60 per cent and making nursing the most popular choice of all. By March 2011, the total was almost 150,000 after further growth of 48 per cent. There were another 47,000 applications for the last diplomas and over 6,000 for Foundation degrees – by far the largest number in any subject at that level, too. It is all a far cry from 2008, when well-publicised stories of nurses finishing their training to face the dole led to a decline in the demand for places.

The number of places has expanded significantly in recent years, with 2,000 more enrolments on degree courses in 2010. But there was no prospect of universities keeping pace with such massive growth in demand, so an already competitive selection process – there were more than seven applications to the place in 2010 – is certain to tighten further. Nevertheless, only six universities averaged more than 350 points for A levels and Highers in 2010. Entry scores are more closely bunched than in many tables: just three universities average less than 200 points.

Edinburgh has regained the lead in the table, overtaking York, as the only university with average entry standards of more than 400 points. Glasgow, in sixth place, has the most satisfied students, while fourth-placed Manchester produced the best grades in the 2008 Research Assessment Exercise, with 85 per cent of its submission considered world-leading or internationally excellent.

Lincoln, only just outside the bottom five in the table, is one of nine universities with 100 per cent employment records. The others are Bedfordshire, East Anglia, Liverpool, Sheffield Hallam, Surrey, Manchester Metropolitan, York and the joint school at Kingston and St George's, in south London. The subject is in the top three for employment, with only 2 per cent of 2008 graduates unemployed at the end of the year. However, it is only just in the top 20 for starting salaries, which average less than £22,000 in graduate-level jobs.

Northumbria, which shares eighth place with East Anglia, is the only post-1992 university in the top ten of a ranking where less than a third of the institutions are older foundations. Teesside, Hertfordshire, Kingston and St George's, and Huddersfield join it in the top 20. Cardiff is the top university in Wales, while Ulster outperforms Queen's, Belfast in Northern Ireland.

Almost two thirds of the students arrive without A levels, many of them upgrading other health-related qualifications. A quarter of those who join pre-registration programmes drop out, but the rate is nearer 10 per cent thereafter.

Employed in graduate job:	90%	Employed in non-graduate job and studying:	0%
Employed in graduate job and studying:	5%	Employed in non-graduate job:	2%
Studying:	1%	Unemployed:	2%
Average starting graduate salary:	£21,911	Average starting non-graduate salary:	£19,415

Nursing	Research quality	Entry standards	Student satisfaction %	Graduate prospects %	Overall rating
1 Edinburgh	3.8	401	91	98	100.0
2 York	4.3	370		100	99.8
3 Southampton	5.3	371	77	99	97.6
4 Manchester	5.6	353	77	98	96.9
5 Liverpool	1.9	344	92	100	96.5
6 Glasgow	2.8	377	94	92	95.8
7 Ulster	4.9	276	81	99	95.1
=8 East Anglia	1.9	334	79	100	92.4
=8 Northumbria	2.5	306	84	98	92.4
10 Leeds	3.4	315	76	99	92.3
11 Nottingham	3.0	340	75	97	91.7
12 Surrey	0.3	341	83	100	91.5
13 Cardiff	2.4	317	77	99	91.2
14 King's College London	2.2	360	74	97	91.0
15 Teesside		325	86	99	90.7
16 Salford	1.9	297	81	97	90.3
17 Hertfordshire	3.3	261	75	97	89.1
=18 City	3.9	291	67	98	89.0
=18 Kingston/St George's	2.3	247	76	100	89.0
20 Huddersfield		311	86	96	88.5
21 De Montfort	1.6	305	74	98	88.3
22 Birmingham		332	81	96	88.2
23 Queen's, Belfast	1.9	270	78	97	88.1

Nursing cont.

	Research quality	Entry standards	Student satisfaction %	Graduate prospects %	Overall rating
24 Bangor		284	82	99	88.0
=25 Edinburgh Napier	1.6	304	78	95	87.9
=25 Swansea	1.8	287	75	97	87.9
=27 Birmingham City		298	81	97	87.5
=27 Bradford	1.8	284	73	98	87.5
29 Manchester Metropolitan	1.0	256	76	100	87.4
=30 Oxford Brookes		271	81	99	87.2
=30 West of England	1.6	280	71	99	87.2
=30 Sheffield Hallam	1.7	285	68	100	87.2
33 Greenwich	1.3	269	85	93	87.1
=34 Edge Hill	1.3	273	86	92	87.0
=34 Glyndŵr	0.8	251	83	96	87.0
=36 Bedfordshire		244	81	100	86.8
=36 Queen Margaret Edinburgh		313		96	86.8
=38 Hull		308	76	98	86.5
=38 Brighton	0.6	293	74	98	86.5
=40 Glasgow Caledonian	2.8	285	86	86	86.3
=40 Staffordshire		251	81	98	86.3
42 Plymouth	1.6	277	70	98	86.2
43 Cumbria		296	79	96	86.1
44 Keele		227	88	95	85.8
45 Worcester		257	82	96	85.6
=46 Canterbury Christ Church		254	75	99	84.8
=46 Coventry		307	77	94	84.8
48 Glamorgan	1.8	265	83	89	84.6
49 Dundee	2.2	179	77	96	84.2
50 Chester	0.6	262	68	99	84.0
51 Stirling	2.8	139	78	96	83.9
52 Northampton		276	74	96	83.8
=53 Central Lancashire	2.2	259	77	89	83.7
=53 London South Bank	1.5	204	78	95	83.7
55 Anglia Ruskin		252	77	95	83.4
56 Liverpool John Moores	1.6	242	71	94	83.1
57 Lincoln		292	62	100	83.0
58 Leeds Metropolitan		257	78	93	82.9
59 Middlesex	1.5	236	70	94	82.5
60 Bournemouth	1.9	285	75	86	81.9
61 Robert Gordon		160	77	98	81.7
62 Abertay		220		88	75.3

» NHS Careers: **www.nhscareers.nhs.uk**
» The Royal British Nurses' Association: **www.rbna.org.uk**
» Royal College of Nursing: **www.rcn.org.uk**

Other Subjects Allied to Medicine

The "allied to medicine" category covers audiology, complementary therapies, counselling, health services management, health sciences, nutrition, occupational therapy, optometry, ophthalmology, orthoptics, osteopathy, physiotherapy, podiatry, radiography and speech therapy. Traditional universities dominate the top ten, but big names such as Durham and Imperial College London find themselves outside the top 20.

The top two in the table are unchanged, despite the fact that neither first-placed Aston nor Cardiff, in second place, lead on any of the four indicators. Newcastle, which has moved up two places to third, is one of three universities tying for the best satisfaction score. The others are Oxford Brookes and Keele, both just outside the top ten.

Cambridge, in sixth place, has by far the highest entry grades – nearly 90 points ahead of Imperial College – but, like a number of universities in the ranking, neither entered the 2008 Research Assessment Exercise in this category. Fourth-placed Leeds and University College London, which is in a tie for seventh place, share the best of a mediocre set of research grades. Leeds also has the best employment score, having seen all its leavers go straight into graduate-level work or further study in 2009, as it did in 2008.

Stiff competition for places in subjects such as optometry and physiotherapy has been pushing up entry grades, with 11 universities averaging at least 400 points on the UCAS tariff, while only one dropped below 200 in the latest survey. The choice of specialism also affects graduate employment rates, which range from better than 90 per cent positive destinations at 17 universities to less than 50 per cent at other universities around the bottom of the table.

The table is more mixed than most in terms of the performance of new and old universities. Oxford Brookes is the highest-placed post-1992 institution, while Glasgow Caledonian, Portsmouth, Robert Gordon and the West of England all join it in the top 20. Across the whole range of subjects, almost half of the students arrive without A levels.

Applications were up by 18 per cent in March 2011, following a similar increase in 2010, making the subjects among the most popular choices at degree level. They have also shot up the employment table in the last two years, finishing in the top six in this edition, with more than 80 per cent going straight into graduate jobs or continuing their studies and only 5 per cent unemployed. Starting salaries have improved but are still not in the top 20.

Other Subjects Allied to Medicine	Research quality	Entry standards	Student satisfaction %	Graduate prospects %	Overall rating
1 Aston	2.5	410	86	96	100.0
2 Cardiff	3.0	399	84	92	98.5
3 Newcastle	2.8	437	88	75	98.2
4 Leeds	3.4	358	79	100	97.2
5 Lancaster	3.1	378	84	86	96.7
6 Cambridge		595	85	82	96.2
=7 Sheffield	2.8	414	85	76	95.7
=7 Exeter	2.8	395	78	98	95.7
=7 University College London	3.4	419	76	88	95.7
10 Manchester	2.8	414	75	92	93.8
11 Oxford Brookes	1.6	341	88	89	92.9

		Research quality	Entry standards	Student satisfaction %	Graduate prospects %	Overall rating
12	Portsmouth	2.6	371	75	98	92.8
13	King's College London	1.5	408	81	90	92.1
14	Keele	2.2	322	88	80	91.6
15	Strathclyde	2.8	378	81	75	91.1
16	West of England	2.9	307	80	88	90.6
17	Bradford	1.6	354	81	94	90.5
18	Nottingham	1.9	350	80	91	90.3
19	Glasgow Caledonian	2.8	359	78	81	89.9
20	Robert Gordon	1.0	349	83	94	89.7
21	Liverpool	1.9	347	75	98	89.0
22	East Anglia	0.6	345	84	94	88.5
23	Glamorgan		350	82	98	86.8
24	Durham		407	85	80	86.4
25	Bournemouth		324	84	96	85.9
26	City	1.7	343	72	95	85.6
27	Hull	3.1		77	64	85.4
=28	Ulster	2.9	331	76	69	85.3
=28	Anglia Ruskin	0.9	315	86	78	85.3
30	Northumbria	1.3	372	75	85	85.1
31	Hertfordshire	2.5	267	78	82	84.9
32	Birmingham		415	83	74	84.6
33	Imperial College		508	70	86	84.4
=34	Teesside	0.7	310	82	86	83.9
=34	Bangor		328	80	96	83.9
=34	Nottingham Trent	2.8	294	72	82	83.9
37	Kent	1.6	322	83	67	83.7
=38	Swansea	3.0	330	69	78	83.4
=38	Kingston	1.2		85	67	83.4
40	Coventry	0.7	316	80	85	83.1
41	Brunel	1.4	333	76	80	82.5
42	Sheffield Hallam	0.9	332	75	88	82.2
43	Southampton	0.9		75	90	82.0
44	Brighton	0.6	349	75	85	81.1
45	Salford	1.5	281	76	78	80.1
46	Reading		412	68	89	79.7
47	Cumbria		298	77	91	79.5
=48	De Montfort	1.2	251	79	78	79.3
=48	Manchester Metropolitan	1.3	313	76	72	79.3
=48	York St John	0.2	296	81	78	79.3
51	London South Bank		246	79	94	79.0
52	Queen Margaret Edinburgh	0.2	352		78	78.7
=53	Huddersfield		257	82	77	76.9
=53	Central Lancashire	1.3	270	77	66	76.9

=55 Birmingham City		293	74	88	76.8
=55 London Metropolitan	1.3	206	77	79	76.8
57 Lincoln	0.3	270	79	75	76.3
58 St George's		342	70	85	76.1
59 Plymouth	0.4	313	70	85	76.0
=60 Edinburgh Napier	0.7		77	68	75.9
=60 Essex		254	79	81	75.9
=60 UWIC, Cardiff	0.9	310	70	77	75.9
63 Leeds Metropolitan	0.4	327	73	72	75.4
64 Derby		275	77	76	74.6
65 Middlesex	1.3	232	68	86	74.4
=66 Canterbury Christ Church	0.2	232	69	93	73.4
=66 St Mary's College, Twickenham		217	81	73	73.4
68 Bristol		347	62	89	73.3
=69 Chester	0.5	269	80	56	73.2
=69 Marjon, Plymouth		358	69	72	73.2
=71 Northampton	0.7	263	65	90	73.1
=71 Liverpool John Moores	1.2	265	74	63	73.1
73 Sunderland	0.5	260	79	60	72.8
74 Westminster	1.8	251	62	82	72.7
75 Bedfordshire		229	72	87	72.2
76 East London	1.6	241	63	76	70.9
77 Greenwich		246	83	48	70.2
78 Worcester	0.3		82	41	68.6
79 West of Scotland	2.2	212		46	68.4
80 Abertay	0.4	252		62	68.0
81 University College Birmingham		197	77	47	64.4
82 Roehampton	0.7		79	29	64.2

Employed in graduate job:	68%	Employed in non-graduate job and studying:	1%
Employed in graduate job and studying:	6%	Employed in non-graduate job:	12%
Studying:	8%	Unemployed:	5%
Average starting graduate salary:	£20,866	Average starting non-graduate salary:	£15,419

» Association of Health Professions in Ophthalmology: **www.ahpo.org**
» British Association and College of Occupational Therapists: **www.cot.org.uk**
» British Society of Audiology: **www.thebsa.org.uk**
» Chartered Society of Physiotherapy: **www.csp.org.uk**
» General Chiropractic Council: **www.gcc-uk.org**
» General Osteopathic Council: **www.osteopathy.org.uk**
» General Optical Council: **www.optical.org**
» Health Professions Council: **www.hpc-uk.org**
» NHS Careers: **www.nhscareers.nhs.uk**
» Royal College of Radiologists: **www.rcr.ac.uk**
» Royal College of Speech and Language Therapists: **www.rcslt.org**
» Society of Chiropodists and Podiatrists: **www.feetforlife.org**
» Society of Radiographers: **www.sor.org**

Pharmacology and Pharmacy

Pharmacology and pharmacy have been among the big successes of higher education in recent years. The numbers of applications and places have grown significantly and the subjects are in the top five for "positive destinations". There were still considerably more than six applications for every place in 2010, despite another increase in places for first-year students, and the start of 2011 saw further growth of almost 15 per cent in the demand for places. Only 4 per cent of graduates were unemployed at the end of 2009, when 91 per cent were already in graduate-level jobs or continuing their studies.

Cambridge is top of the table for the first time in five years, having been outside the top ten in the 2011 *Guide*. The university's normal high entry standards make the difference – it did not enrol enough students to compile a reliable score in the previous year. Nottingham, last year's leader, has dropped to fourth, overtaken by Edinburgh, which has the best research score, and East Anglia, which is one of eight universities with 100 per cent employment records, the others being Aston, Cardiff, Kent, Queen's Belfast, Reading, Robert Gordon and the University of London's School of Pharmacy. The recession seems to have had no impact on graduates' employment prospects: only one university saw less than two thirds of leavers go on to "positive destinations". The most satisfied students are at Greenwich.

Entry standards are high: almost half of the universities in the table average more than 400 points and none less than 250. Cardiff, in fifth place, is again the only representative of Wales in a table that contains seven more institutions than there were four years ago. Brighton is the highest-placed post-1992 university and is joined by Robert Gordon, Huddersfield and Greenwich in the top 20.

Departments in England are evenly split between those specialising in pharmacy and pharmacology. Only four cover both. Since 1997, pharmacy degrees have been converted to the four-year MPharm, whereas pharmacology is available either as a three-year BSc or as an extended course. Most courses require chemistry and another science or maths at A level or the equivalent. Surprisingly, given graduates' success in the labour market, the subjects are not high in the earnings league: average starting salaries of just over £20,000 for graduate-level jobs place them 36th out of the 62 subjects.

Employed in graduate job:	61%	Employed in non-graduate job and studying:	1%
Employed in graduate job and studying:	17%	Employed in non-graduate job:	5%
Studying:	12%	Unemployed:	4%
Average starting graduate salary:	£20,059	Average starting non-graduate salary:	£14,236

Pharmacology and Pharmacy	Research quality	Entry standards	Student satisfaction %	Graduate prospects %	Overall rating
1 Cambridge	3.1	595	85	82	100.0
2 Edinburgh	4.9		90	71	99.3
3 East Anglia	2.6	403	93	100	99.0
4 Nottingham	4.5	462	78	99	98.8
5 Cardiff	2.6	421	87	100	96.4
6 Manchester	4.0	430	79	96	96.0
7 Bath	3.1	468	80	96	95.4

8 Queen's, Belfast	2.7	410	83	100	94.4
9 Aston	2.5	432	81	100	93.3
10 Liverpool	2.8	413	89	75	92.3
11 King's College London	2.6	428	81	93	91.9
12 University College London	3.2	486	81	69	90.6
13 Strathclyde	2.6	435	78	89	89.7
=14 Brighton	1.8	355	83	95	87.8
=14 School of Pharmacy	3.5	401	67	100	87.8
16 Bradford	2.6	347	78	95	87.6
17 Reading	2.1	359	78	100	87.4
18 Robert Gordon		408	85	100	87.2
=19 Huddersfield	0.9	354	90		87.0
=19 Greenwich	1.1	292	95	83	87.0
21 Leeds	2.8	391	84	68	86.8
22 Glasgow	2.7	355	83	78	86.7
23 Dundee	3.5	355	89	50	86.0
24 Bristol	2.7	434	79	68	85.4
25 Portsmouth	2.6	310	78	90	84.8
26 Kent	1.5	250	83	100	84.0
27 Hertfordshire	1.5	313	86	82	83.9
28 Liverpool John Moores	1.2	345	79	95	83.4
29 Sunderland	0.7	368	80	94	83.0
30 De Montfort	1.8	314	76	90	80.9
31 Nottingham Trent	2.8	276	76		79.9
32 Aberdeen		327	85	83	79.6
33 Glasgow Caledonian	1.3	274	82	80	79.3
34 Kingston	1.2	280	77	72	73.9

» Association of Pharmacy Technicians UK: **www.aptuk.org**
» British Pharmacological Society: **www.bps.ac.uk**
» General Pharmaceutical Council: **www.pharmacyregulation.org**
» Royal Pharmaceutical Society: **www.rpharms.com**

Philosophy

Many expected philosophy to struggle in the era of top-up fees, with perceptions of employability dominating subject choices. But there were still more than six applications to the place in 2010 – one of the highest ratios in the arts and social sciences – when the demand for places grew by another 6 per cent. There had been a small decline early in 2011, but entry requirements were still high. More than a third of the 47 universities in the latest ranking average at least 400 points on the UCAS tariff.

Oxford holds on to the top place in philosophy that it took from Cambridge last year, albeit by a narrower margin. Oxford has the highest entry standards (although Cambridge is within three points) and by far the best employment score. It was the only university where 80 per cent of the graduates went straight into graduate-level work or further study in 2009. Other employment scores are extremely variable, with the 13 per cent positive destinations at

Philosophy cont.

Central Lancashire among the lowest in any subject. Philosophy is among the bottom 20 subjects in the employment table, with nearly a third of leavers starting their working life in non-graduate jobs.

Like last year, the best of a generally high set of scores in the 2009 National Student Survey came at Aberdeen, where almost nine out of ten undergraduates were satisfied with their course. Also like last year, only Manchester failed to satisfy at least 70 per cent of its students.

University College London, in third place, produced the best results in the 2008 Research Assessment Exercise, when three quarters of its submission was rated world-leading or internationally excellent. St Andrews was close behind on research and remains the top university in Scotland. Cardiff remains top in Wales, while Brighton records the highest finish outside the old universities.

Relatively few philosophy undergraduates studied the subject at A level – indeed, Bristol warns that even an A in the subject is "not necessarily evidence of aptitude for philosophy at university". Degrees can require more mathematical skills than many candidates expect, especially when there is an emphasis on logic in the syllabus. The subject remains in the bottom half of the earnings table, with an average of little more than £20,000 for graduate-level work.

Employed in graduate job:	27%	Employed in non-graduate job and studying:	4%
Employed in graduate job and studying:	3%	Employed in non-graduate job:	28%
Studying:	27%	Unemployed:	12%
Average starting graduate salary:	£20,097	Average starting non-graduate salary:	£14,853

Philosophy	Research quality	Entry standards	Student satisfaction %	Graduate prospects %	Overall rating
1 Oxford	4.1	553	85	83	100.0
2 Cambridge	3.9	550	86	68	96.9
3 University College London	5.0	473	81	73	94.7
4 King's College London	4.4	459	83	69	93.1
5 London School of Economics	4.1	508	77	78	92.4
6 St Andrews	4.7	520	82	51	91.8
7 Sheffield	4.3	432	83	63	90.9
8 Bristol	3.8	479	77	78	90.7
9 Durham	2.7	502	79	77	90.2
10 Essex	3.5	323	86	75	89.9
11 Exeter	3.0	425	81	73	88.5
12 York	2.7	446	82	67	87.6
13 Sussex	2.5	362	88	62	87.1
14 Newcastle	2.5	378	86	63	86.4
15 Dundee	2.1	335	86	67	85.4
16 Edinburgh	3.2	447	76	65	84.9
17 Glasgow	2.1	397	84	58	83.9
18 Lancaster	2.0	395	81	68	83.8
19 Warwick	2.7	479	75	64	83.7
20 Stirling	3.7	313	88	39	83.4

21	Nottingham	3.4	409	74	63	82.0
22	Reading	4.1	352	79	48	81.9
23	Southampton	1.7	404	81	56	81.1
24	East Anglia	1.5	377	82	57	80.7
25	Leeds	3.2	405	75	53	80.0
26	Aberdeen	1.0	305	89	52	79.8
27	Queen's, Belfast	2.3	361	78	54	78.7
28	Liverpool	0.9	382	78	63	78.4
29	Brighton	4.1	260	81	35	77.2
30	Birmingham	1.8	389	75	55	76.7
31	Hull	1.5	321	82	49	76.6
32	Cardiff	1.4	359	82	43	76.5
33	Marjon, Plymouth	0.7		73	77	76.3
34	Middlesex	3.2	235			75.8
35	Keele	1.6	291	74	60	73.6
36	Kent	1.8	315	76	47	73.1
=37	Manchester Metropolitan	1.7	271	83	34	72.9
=37	Staffordshire	0.8	240	83		72.9
=39	Hertfordshire	1.2	275	79	48	72.5
=39	West of England	0.5	291	78	55	72.5
=39	Trinity St David	0.6	271	79	55	72.5
=42	Manchester	2.1	432	64	54	72.0
=42	Newport		266	82	50	72.0
44	Heythrop College	0.3	329	72	60	70.6
45	Greenwich		234	82	48	70.1
46	Oxford Brookes	0.2	323	80	36	69.7
47	Central Lancashire		241	83	13	63.6

» British Philosophical Association: **www.bpa.ac.uk**
» Philosophical Society of England:
   http://atschool.eduweb.co.uk/cite/staff/philosopher/philsocindex.htm
» Royal Institute of Philosophy: **www.royalinstitutephilosophy.org**

Physics and Astronomy

There has been constant concern about the state of physics in recent years, with sixth-form numbers dropping and university departments closing. But two universities have joined the ranking this year and applications were up by an astonishing 18 per cent in March 2011. There was a big increase in 2010 as well, when the competition for places was more intense than in 2009, with 5.5 (generally high-grade) applications to the place.

Indeed, physics is one of the most competitive tables, with high scores on all the indicators among the leading universities. No fewer than seven universities, led by top-placed Cambridge, average more than 500 points at entry. Cambridge now has the slimmest possible lead and, as it did last year, the rest of the table shows substantial changes. St Andrews has become Cambridge's nearest challenger, and Lancaster has jumped seven places to take third place.

Physics and Astronomy cont.

St Andrews and Oxford, in fifth place, share the best employment record in a subject where more than half of all graduates continue their studies, either full or part-time. Physics has moved up the employment table again this year and is in the top ten – all but six of the universities in the ranking saw at least 70 per cent of those completing degrees go straight into graduate-level jobs or further study.

Physics has also produced consistently high scores in the National Student Survey, with every university satisfying at least three quarters of their undergraduates in the 2010 results. Lancaster, Birmingham and Kent, which only just makes the top 30, share the top satisfaction score. By contrast, physics was one of the lowest-scoring subjects in the 2008 Research Assessment Exercise, when only Lancaster had more than 20 per cent of its work rated world-leading. Cardiff is the leading university in Wales. Hertfordshire is the highest-placed of the four post-1992 universities in the table.

Most universities demand physics and maths at A level for both physics and astronomy, as well as good grades overall. The profile of undergraduates is among the most traditional: only one in five is female and a similar proportion arrives without A levels or their equivalent. About 5 per cent transfer to other courses or drop out, usually at the end of the first year, but over half of those who remain get firsts or 2:1s. The subjects are in the top 20 for starting salaries, averaging almost £23,000 in graduate-level jobs.

Employed in graduate job:	24%	Employed in non-graduate job and studying:	1%
Employed in graduate job and studying:	6%	Employed in non-graduate job:	12%
Studying:	45%	Unemployed:	12%
Average starting graduate salary:	£22,946	Average starting non-graduate salary:	£15,778

Physics and Astronomy	Research quality	Entry standards	Student satisfaction %	Graduate prospects %	Overall rating
1 Cambridge	3.5	595	85	82	100.0
2 St Andrews	3.5	505	87	86	99.9
3 Lancaster	3.7	444	91	79	99.3
4 Birmingham	3.1	490	91	77	97.7
5 Oxford	3.0	570	81	86	96.5
6 Durham	3.1	555	82	82	96.0
7 Nottingham	3.5	456	85	78	95.4
8 Glasgow	3.1	401	87	83	94.9
9 Manchester	2.9	499	87	74	94.6
10 Sussex	2.8	426	85	83	93.6
11 Sheffield	3.1	440	87	72	93.3
12 Imperial College	3.2	549	76	83	93.1
13 Bristol	3.0	510	81	80	92.6
14 Warwick	2.5	517	84	77	92.4
15 Bath	3.4	461	81	76	92.0
=16 York	2.7	401	86	79	91.5
=16 Southampton	2.7	452	84	77	91.5
=18 Exeter	2.8	475	86	69	91.2

=18 Surrey	2.4	437	84	81	91.2
20 Edinburgh	3.2	454	81	74	90.7
21 Liverpool	3.0	424	84	73	90.5
22 Queen's, Belfast	2.2	406	87	75	90.0
23 Loughborough	2.5	383	86	75	89.8
24 Leeds	2.5	458	83	73	89.4
=25 King's College London	2.2	460	81	79	89.2
=25 Royal Holloway	2.4	374	88	71	89.2
27 Leicester	2.6	408	82	78	89.0
28 Kent	2.5	329	91	64	88.5
29 University College London	3.1	465	78	73	88.3
30 Strathclyde	1.6	344	87	77	86.6
31 Heriot-Watt	2.7	342	81	75	86.2
32 Aberdeen	2.9	327	80	75	86.1
33 Hertfordshire	2.7	293		75	85.8
34 Hull	1.9	329	90	64	85.6
35 Nottingham Trent	2.7	269	78	83	84.9
36 Salford	2.2	316	82	76	84.7
37 Cardiff	1.9	411	81	66	82.9
38 Keele	1.6	287	85	70	82.2
39 Swansea	2.2	301	76	73	80.4
40 Queen Mary, London	2.6	370	83	46	79.6
41 Central Lancashire	1.6	280	82		78.7
42 Aberystwyth	1.0	272	81	52	72.1
43 West of Scotland	0.7	253			68.5

» British Astronomical Association: **http://britastro.org**
» Institute of Physics: **www.iop.org**

Politics

Politics has been enjoying a boom as a degree subject. Having grown substantially in the last decade, applications rose by 14 per cent in 2010 and by another 8 per cent in 2011. With six applications for every place, entry scores have been rising. Twenty-two universities, four more than last year and almost twice as many as in the 2009 *Guide*, average over 400 points and only one less than 200 points.

Oxford holds onto top place with the highest entry grades, but its lead over second-placed Sheffield has narrowed since last year. Sheffield shares the best score from the 2008 Research Assessment Exercise with Essex, in eleventh place. Both had three quarters of their research rated world-leading or internationally excellent. Aberystwyth is the top university in Wales, while Brighton is the only post-1992 university in the top 40.

For the second year in a row, the most satisfied students are at Leicester, which retains its place in the top 20 as a result. Scores in politics were generally high in the 2010 National Student Survey: only five of the 71 universities failed to satisfy at least 70 per cent of their final-year undergraduates.

Politics cont.

The best employment prospects are at University College London, in fourth place. Scores elsewhere are variable, with ten universities failing to see half of their politics graduates go straight into graduate-level jobs or continue their studies. The subject is now in the top half of the earnings league, but has yet to make the same progress in the comparison of positive destinations. Unemployment is just above average, at 10 per cent, and almost 30 per cent of graduates start off in lower-level jobs.

Employed in graduate job:	31%	Employed in non-graduate job and studying:	4%
Employed in graduate job and studying:	4%	Employed in non-graduate job:	25%
Studying:	25%	Unemployed:	10%
Average starting graduate salary:	£20,831	Average starting non-graduate salary:	£16,135

Politics	Research quality	Entry standards	Student satisfaction %	Graduate prospects %	Overall rating
1 Oxford	4.0	550	84	85	100.0
2 Sheffield	5.0	447	85	69	96.0
3 Cambridge	2.8	524	86	74	94.4
4 University College London	3.2	518	74	89	92.2
5 Bath	2.1	482	80	86	90.3
6 London School of Economics	3.7	508	75	76	90.1
7 Warwick	3.1	479	80	74	89.8
8 St Andrews	2.1	513	80	77	89.3
9 Exeter	2.9	443	84	69	89.2
10 Durham	2.5	489	78	80	88.9
11 Essex	5.0	329	83	59	88.0
12 Aberystwyth	4.4	342	83	63	87.5
13 York	2.3	456	77	76	85.8
14 King's College London	2.3	459	78	72	85.4
15 Nottingham	2.5	429	76	76	85.1
16 School of Oriental and African Studies	2.8	469	73	75	84.9
17 Sussex	2.7	385	79	68	83.7
18 Leicester	0.9	352	89	67	82.7
19 Bristol	1.9	453	73	76	82.2
20 Queen Mary, London	1.8	398	79	68	81.4
21 Newcastle	2.2	394	79	63	81.3
22 Loughborough	1.9	356	83	62	81.2
23 Birmingham	1.8	419	81	58	81.0
24 Glasgow	2.3	407	81	54	80.9
=25 Hull	1.8	348	81	64	80.0
=25 Cardiff	2.4	405	77	60	80.0
27 Lancaster	1.0	400	80	66	79.6
28 East Anglia	1.5	381	82	58	79.3
29 Dundee	1.6	347	84	55	79.0
30 Edinburgh	2.3	450	68	69	78.8

31	Leeds	0.9	410	75	72	78.5
32	Brighton	4.1	277	71		77.8
=33	Southampton	1.3	418	76	62	77.6
=33	Surrey	1.3	337	73	79	77.6
35	Strathclyde	1.0	366	83	53	77.2
36	Bradford	2.5	254	79	62	76.9
37	Keele	1.6	299	79	64	76.6
38	Manchester	2.8	429	64	65	76.1
39	Reading	1.8	342	77	56	75.6
=40	Liverpool	0.6	366	80	59	75.4
=40	Royal Holloway	1.3	376	71	69	75.4
42	Aston	1.0	360	76	63	75.2
43	Brunel	1.2	301	80	60	75.1
=44	Queen's, Belfast	2.2	350	73	57	74.6
=44	Kent	1.2	326	77	61	74.6
=44	Stirling	0.9	319	79	61	74.6
=47	Portsmouth	2.4	283	80	44	73.8
=47	Plymouth	1.9	269	79	53	73.8
49	Aberdeen	1.2	329	78	51	73.0
50	Huddersfield	0.1	295	77	68	72.5
51	Swansea	1.1	312	75	60	72.4
52	Northumbria	1.5	296	74	60	72.3
53	Ulster	1.8	248	78	52	71.8
54	Oxford Brookes	0.8	310	77	50	69.9
55	West of England	0.5	266	80	48	69.4
56	Goldsmiths College	1.6	322	69	53	69.2
57	De Montfort	1.0	244	79	49	69.1
58	City		365	68	67	69.0
59	Westminster	1.0	263	70	59	67.7
60	Salford	1.2	263	75	45	66.9
61	Birmingham City	1.1		73	48	66.7
62	Manchester Metropolitan	0.7	251	76	45	66.0
63	Lincoln	1.0	256	77	36	65.4
64	Kingston	1.0	243	70	52	65.1
65	Nottingham Trent		253	74	51	64.6
66	London Metropolitan	1.0	239	71	49	64.3
67	Liverpool John Moores		244	70	54	62.5
68	Leeds Metropolitan		241	70	52	62.2
69	Central Lancashire	0.2	241	71		62.1
70	Greenwich	0.1	185	76	42	61.0
71	Coventry	0.7	304	61	43	58.9

» Political Studies Association: **www.psa.ac.uk**
» Study Politics: **www.studypolitics.org**

Psychology

Psychology is now the biggest table in the *Guide*, two more universities having joined the ranking this year. Only nursing and design attracted more applications at the start of 2011. An increase of more than 16 per cent in the demand for places took the number of applications close to 94,000 in 2010 and there had been another small rise by March 2011. The subject's popularity has continued to rise in spite of its relatively poor record in the graduate employment market: it is in the bottom ten for the proportion of graduates with "positive destinations" and only one place higher for average starting salaries in graduate-level jobs. Although unemployment is below average at 8 per cent, 43 per cent of graduates begin their careers in low-level jobs.

Most undergraduate programmes are accredited by the British Psychological Society, which ensures that key topics are covered, but the clinical and biological content of courses still varies considerably. Some universities require maths and/or biology A levels among an average of at least three Bs, but others are much less demanding. The contrast is obvious in the ranking, with 24 universities averaging more than 400 points at entry but 18 below 250 points. There was only a relatively small increase in the number of first-year places for psychology in 2010, so entry standards were forced up for the second year in a row.

Employed in graduate job:	26%	Employed in non-graduate job and studying:	6%
Employed in graduate job and studying:	5%	Employed in non-graduate job:	37%
Studying:	19%	Unemployed:	8%
Average starting graduate salary:	£18,176	Average starting non-graduate salary:	£14,119

Psychology	Research quality	Entry standards	Student satisfaction %	Graduate prospects %	Overall rating
1 Cambridge	4.7	595	86	81	100.0
2 Oxford	4.5	547	84	79	96.5
3 University College London	4.1	490	85	66	90.1
4 Bath	4.4	460	76	71	86.4
5 Sheffield	2.8	444	80	75	85.1
6 Sussex	2.8	389	85	69	84.3
7 Glasgow	3.1	407	85	63	83.8
8 York	3.2	470	82	58	83.4
9 Bristol	2.5	473	79	68	82.6
10 Durham	2.8	434	78	69	82.1
11 Exeter	2.7	429	83	59	81.4
12 Warwick	2.3	439	80	66	81.3
13 Southampton	2.8	432	84	54	80.7
=14 Cardiff	3.7	434	78	56	80.6
=14 Royal Holloway	3.1	395	83	57	80.6
16 St Andrews	3.3	487	77	53	80.5
17 Edinburgh	2.8	434	77	63	80.1
18 Lancaster	1.9	411	78	73	80.0
19 Kent	1.9	385	81	70	79.8
20 Loughborough	3.4	413	81	52	79.7

21	Nottingham	2.5	431	75	68	79.4
22	Bangor	3.2	324	85	55	79.1
23	Aston	2.5	381	81	62	79.0
24	Birmingham	4.0	423	74	55	78.6
25	Newcastle	1.9	430	77	61	77.0
26	Surrey	1.9	418	73	70	76.9
27	Leeds	2.2	425	74	62	76.4
28	Dundee	1.5	344	86	53	75.4
29	Strathclyde	1.0	386	81	60	74.9
30	Leicester	0.9	392	77	67	74.6
31	Northumbria	0.9	332	80	66	74.3
32	Essex	2.4	326	80	52	73.7
33	Stirling	0.9	314	84	59	73.6
34	Hull	1.5	349	82	52	73.1
35	City	1.9	359	74	62	73.0
36	Cumbria		227		82	72.9
37	Central Lancashire	1.0	288	82	62	72.6
38	Aberdeen	1.9	306	81	51	72.3
=39	Lincoln	1.2	311	83	54	72.1
=39	Goldsmiths College	2.2	331	75	57	72.1
=39	Reading	2.5	403	73	50	72.1
42	Bournemouth	1.5	297	79	60	72.0
43	East Anglia	0.6	379	82	50	71.3
44	Bradford	2.2	227	79	57	70.4
45	Liverpool	1.3	393	76	48	70.2
46	Plymouth	1.4	320	78	54	70.1
=47	Keele	0.9	308	80	55	69.9
=47	Chester	0.5	291	81	58	69.9
49	Nottingham Trent	0.6	313	82	52	69.8
=50	Manchester	2.2	420	68	50	69.7
=50	Edinburgh Napier	0.2	292	82	58	69.7
52	Hertfordshire	1.4	263	79	57	69.4
53	Queen's, Belfast	1.3	366	77	47	69.3
54	Anglia Ruskin	1.8	290	77	51	68.7
55	Swansea	1.5	351	76	47	68.6
56	Brunel	1.5	337	75	49	68.4
57	Portsmouth	0.9	331	80	45	68.3
=58	Staffordshire	1.0	267	78	56	68.0
=58	St Mary's College, Twickenham		261	84	54	68.0
60	Oxford Brookes	0.9	341	81	40	67.7
61	Teesside		282	83	50	67.4
62	Manchester Metropolitan	1.7	326	73	48	67.1
63	Huddersfield		277	82	50	66.7
=64	West of England	1.6	302	77	43	66.6
=64	Coventry	0.6	302	79	48	66.6
66	Sunderland	0.2	264	84	42	65.7
67	Newman		246	79	57	65.5

Psychology cont.	Research quality	Entry standards	Student satisfaction %	Graduate prospects %	Overall rating
68 De Montfort		249	83	47	65.4
69 Sheffield Hallam	0.4	317	76	46	64.9
70 Heriot-Watt	0.2	297	81	41	64.8
=71 Salford	1.5	314	72	45	64.6
=71 York St John	0.1	296	81	42	64.6
73 Ulster	1.2	253	81	37	64.5
74 Leeds Trinity	0.2	259	75	56	64.0
75 Leeds Metropolitan		326	68	61	63.4
76 Bath Spa	0.3	307	75	44	63.0
77 Derby	0.4	262	73	53	62.9
78 Westminster	0.6	274	70	55	62.7
79 UWIC, Cardiff	0.9	269	71	50	62.6
=80 Brighton	1.2	297	72	40	61.9
=80 Roehampton	0.7	249	68	57	61.9
=82 Queen Margaret Edinburgh		300		45	61.8
=82 Liverpool John Moores	1.2	264	76	36	61.8
84 Bedfordshire		179	79	50	61.5
85 Winchester		296	74	44	61.2
86 Greenwich	0.6	224	71	53	61.1
87 Glamorgan	0.4	275	74	42	60.8
88 Bolton	0.2	225	68	60	60.6
=89 Glasgow Caledonian	0.4	307	70	43	60.4
=89 Northampton		246	78	39	60.4
91 Middlesex	0.4	224	64	65	60.2
92 Abertay	0.6	233		45	59.6
93 Gloucestershire	0.4	297	68	45	59.5
94 Buckinghamshire New		246	72	46	59.0
=95 Kingston	0.7	243	71	40	58.8
=95 East London	0.8	200	71	46	58.8
97 Southampton Solent		261	76	33	58.4
98 Worcester		280	65	52	58.3
99 Canterbury Christ Church		278	71	38	57.6
100 Newport		246	63	58	57.3
101 London Metropolitan	0.4	236	70	41	57.1
102 London South Bank	0.7	241	69	38	56.9
103 Edge Hill		251	67	40	55.0
104 West of Scotland		237		31	52.6

Cambridge has retained its lead over Oxford at the top of the table. Cambridge leads on all four measures, although it shares the top satisfaction score with Dundee, in 28th place. It also registered the top performance in the 2008 Research Assessment Exercise, when 80 per cent of its work was considered world-leading or internationally excellent. Cambridge has pulled well ahead of Oxford on entry standards, having been no more than one point ahead for the last two years.

Cambridge and Cumbria, in 36th place, were the only universities to see eight out of ten psychologists go straight into graduate-level work or further study.

The top four in the table are unchanged since last year, but there has been considerable movement further down. Sussex has moved up seven places to sixth and Southampton ten places to 13th, for example. Glasgow remains the top university in Scotland and Cardiff the same in Wales. Northumbria is again the highest-placed post-1992 university and is joined in the top 40 by Cumbria, Central Lancashire and Lincoln.

» British Psychological Society: **www.bps.org.uk**

Russian and Eastern European Languages

Oxford remains ahead of Cambridge at the top of the ranking for Russian and Eastern European languages but, as in the previous three editions of the *Guide*, there is little to separate them. Oxford heads the table for entry standards and research, while Cambridge has the most satisfied students and shares the best employment score with fourth-placed Exeter. The two ancient rivals are a long way ahead of St Andrews, in third place, which has re-entered the ranking after an absence of three years.

Russian has been growing in popularity in schools, although most undergraduates learn the language from scratch, and two more universities have joined the table this year. Applications

Employed in graduate job:	39%	Employed in non-graduate job and studying:	0%
Employed in graduate job and studying:	7%	Employed in non-graduate job:	21%
Studying:	25%	Unemployed:	9%
Average starting graduate salary:	£19,358	Average starting non-graduate salary:	£14,862

Russian and Eastern European Languages	Research quality	Entry standards	Student satisfaction %	Graduate prospects %	Overall rating
1 Oxford	4.2	579	87	75	100.0
2 Cambridge	3.3	534	90	81	99.7
3 St Andrews	0.7	574	85		90.9
4 Exeter	2.2	430	82	81	89.4
5 Durham	1.6	488	82	77	88.7
6 Birmingham	2.7		82	70	88.3
7 University College London	2.1	433	80	77	87.0
8 Bristol	2.8	451	77	74	86.5
9 Nottingham	3.1	380	77	79	86.4
10 Manchester	4.3	368	74		83.5
11 Sheffield	3.7	374	80	58	83.1
12 Bath	2.1		83	54	81.6
13 Glasgow	0.2	392	85	65	81.1
14 Edinburgh	1.6	453	75		80.3
15 Leeds	0.9	415	77	59	76.8
16 Portsmouth		287	83	65	76.5

rose by 17 per cent in 2010, although the total still only reached 550. The early part of 2011 saw a reversal in fortunes, as applications dropped by nearly 20 per cent.

Portsmouth is the sole representative of the post-1992 universities and there are no institutions from Wales or Northern Ireland. Entry standards are high throughout the table: only Portsmouth averages less than 350 points on the UCAS tariff. Nationally, there were 5.5 applications for each place in 2010. Satisfaction levels were high in the 2010 National Student Survey. Nearly every university in the table satisfied at least three quarters of its final-year undergraduates.

The small numbers make for exaggerated swings in institutional and national statistics, but Russian and Eastern European languages showed considerable improvement in terms of employment prospects in the latest survey. Having been around the middle of the table in last two editions of the *Guide*, the languages are now in the top 20. Seven out of ten graduates went straight into graduate-level employment of further study in 2009. Unfortunately, this success coincided with a drop in average starting salaries for these jobs from more than £22,500 to less than £19,500.

» British Association for Slavonic and East European Studies: **www.basees.org.uk**
» National Centre for Languages (CILT): **www.cilt.org.uk**

Social Policy

The London School of Economics (LSE) has retained its accustomed position at the head of the social policy ranking, with much the highest research score and an even bigger lead on employment prospects. Last year's surprise runner-up, Bolton, has dropped two places, but still has the most satisfied students, while Edinburgh, which has moved up five places to second, has the highest entry standards.

The LSE is very much the exception in a generally mediocre set of employment statistics. Although nine percentage points down on last year, its 85 per cent positive destinations were 13 points ahead of the only other university to reach 70 per cent on this measure. Social policy is among the bottom five subjects for employment, although it does a little better in the earnings table. Manchester Metropolitan's 14 per cent in graduate jobs or further study six months after graduation is one of the worst figures in any subject.

Satisfaction levels are better. There were good scores for most universities in the 2010 National Student Survey, only four failing to satisfy at least 70 per cent of their final-year undergraduates. Entry standards are comparatively modest – only the top two average 400 points this year. This reflects the fact that there were only three applications to the place in 2010, one of the lowest ratios for any subject. Although two thirds of entrants come with A levels or their equivalent, some courses cater very largely for mature students.

In the 2008 Research Assessment Exercise, 80 per cent of the LSE's submission in the wider category of social work and policy and administration was rated world-leading or

Employed in graduate job:	29%	Employed in non-graduate job and studying:	4%
Employed in graduate job and studying:	5%	Employed in non-graduate job:	39%
Studying:	14%	Unemployed:	10%
Average starting graduate salary:	£19,570	Average starting non-graduate salary:	£14,709

Social Policy	Research quality	Entry standards	Student satisfaction %	Graduate prospects %	Overall rating
1 London School of Economics	5.5	420	74	85	100.0
2 Edinburgh	3.8	435	76	67	92.5
3 Bath	4.4	370	76	63	90.6
4 Bolton	1.7		87	72	90.5
5 Bristol	3.1	394	78	61	87.9
6 Glasgow	2.6		85	49	85.4
=7 Leeds	4.1	329	76	50	85.0
=7 Cardiff	3.3	361	77	55	85.0
=7 Kent	4.0	299	79	53	85.0
=10 Loughborough	2.9	371	81	45	84.6
=10 Stirling	2.4	322	80	66	84.6
12 York	3.5	315	75	57	83.4
13 Queen's, Belfast	2.9		73	68	83.0
=14 Leicester	1.4	390	81	54	82.8
=14 Northumbria	1.5		82	64	82.8
16 Birmingham	2.8	354	76	55	82.7
=17 Sheffield	3.2	355	73	55	82.3
=17 Keele	2.9	302	79	54	82.3
19 Central Lancashire	1.9		78	57	80.0
=20 Lincoln	1.5	258	85		78.7
=20 Nottingham Trent	2.8	239	73	68	78.7
=22 Nottingham	2.2	375	70	55	78.5
=22 Hull	1.9		79	51	78.5
24 Swansea	2.5	312	76	43	77.2
25 Sheffield Hallam	2.8	294	76	43	77.0
26 Birmingham City	1.1	275	82		75.8
=27 Manchester	2.4		65	63	73.0
=27 Salford	1.9	190	78	52	73.0
29 London South Bank	2.8	145	84	34	72.9
30 Aston	1.0	352	71		71.9
31 Ulster	2.5	229	77	24	69.6
32 Brighton	1.2	293	67	39	65.8
33 Plymouth	2.1		71	26	65.1
34 Leeds Metropolitan		277	65	60	65.0
35 Anglia Ruskin	1.4	207	64	42	61.1
36 Manchester Metropolitan	1.0	209	75	14	60.2

internationally excellent. Cardiff leads Swansea in Wales. A third of the 36 universities in the table are post-1992. Bolton is by far the highest-placed, but Northumbria, Central Lancashire, Lincoln and Nottingham Trent also make the top 20.

Demand for places in social policy has fluctuated in recent years, but there was a 20 per cent increase in applications in March 2011, following another big rise in 2010. A significant proportion of the places have been filled in Clearing in recent years.

» National Institute of Economic and Social Research: **www.niesr.ac.uk**

» UK Social Policy Association: **www.social-policy.org.uk**

Social Work

Despite some bad publicity in recent years, social work is now among the ten most popular choices for higher education candidates. That may be partly because it is also in the top dozen for employment prospects and – even more surprisingly – also in the top ten for starting salaries, which averaged more than £24,500 in 2009. Almost three quarters of those completing social work degrees go straight into graduate-level work and only 7 per cent are unemployed.

Social work used to be unusual for having more students taking certificate or diploma courses than degrees, but the diploma was withdrawn in the move to a graduate profession. Extra places at undergraduate level brought 46 more universities into the table in the last three years, and another three have been added in this edition of the *Guide*. A 27 per cent increase in applications for degree courses in 2010 left more than seven applications for every place. Even so, entry grades are still the lowest in the *Guide*. Edinburgh, in 21st place, has the highest grades, but no university averages more than 375 points.

Employed in graduate job:	66%	Employed in non-graduate job and studying:	2%
Employed in graduate job and studying:	7%	Employed in non-graduate job:	13%
Studying:	5%	Unemployed:	7%
Average starting graduate salary:	£24,655	Average starting non-graduate salary:	£15,669

Social Work	Research quality	Entry standards	Student satisfaction %	Graduate prospects %	Overall rating
1 Bath	4.4	366	71	95	100.0
2 York	3.5	368	79	88	98.5
3 Sussex	2.8		86	98	98.3
4 Kent	4.0	279	83	88	95.4
5 Queen's, Belfast	3.0	340	79	91	95.2
6 Sheffield	3.2	373	70	88	93.7
7 Keele	2.9	300	79	95	93.1
=8 Lancaster	3.1	366	61	98	91.7
=8 Glamorgan	1.8		82	100	91.7
10 Leeds	4.1	343	77	63	91.1
11 Strathclyde	1.6	331	83	88	90.2
12 Bristol	3.1	356	74	75	90.1
13 Stirling	2.4		78	88	88.2
14 Middlesex	1.9		72	100	86.4
15 Bradford	2.2	271	76	92	86.3
16 Hull	1.9	276	76	92	85.7
17 Birmingham	2.8	302	77	70	85.2
18 Reading	1.9		72	95	84.6

19 East Anglia	2.4	277	80	75	84.5
20 Ulster	2.5	254	78	80	83.9
=21 Chester	0.6	262	84	95	83.7
=21 Bedfordshire	1.9		80	78	83.7
23 Northumbria	1.5	264	85	80	83.6
24 Edinburgh	3.8	375	46	80	83.2
25 Huddersfield	2.1	256	77	83	82.8
=26 Swansea	2.5		63	96	82.3
=26 Lincoln	1.5	254	78	89	82.3
28 Glasgow Caledonian		289	83	91	82.1
29 Robert Gordon		276	85	90	82.0
30 Newport	1.7		74	86	81.8
31 Coventry	1.2	281	76	84	81.5
32 West of England	0.9		77	91	81.3
33 Dundee	1.5	275	67	96	81.0
34 Southampton Solent		279	77	98	80.8
=35 West of Scotland	1.9	296		75	80.6
=35 Goldsmiths College	1.8		79	75	80.6
37 De Montfort	1.3	222	75	95	79.9
38 Oxford Brookes		310	83	76	79.7
39 Nottingham Trent	2.8	207	70	84	78.9
40 Sheffield Hallam	1.7	265	67	87	78.6
41 London South Bank	2.8		67	73	78.1
42 Hertfordshire	0.6	228	70	97	75.8
43 Manchester	2.4		59	84	75.7
44 UWIC, Cardiff		208	79	93	75.3
45 Central Lancashire	1.9	226	67	81	75.1
46 Teesside		281	79	72	74.6
47 Salford	1.9	282	63	69	74.1
48 Brunel	1.5	277	57	86	73.7
49 Kingston		232	71	93	73.0
50 Portsmouth		275	62	92	72.0
51 Anglia Ruskin	1.4	239	63	80	71.9
=52 Gloucestershire	0.4	240	72	78	71.5
=52 London Metropolitan	2.2		69	60	71.5
54 Plymouth	2.1	250	57	73	70.6
55 Marjon, Plymouth		204	81	72	69.9
=56 Chichester		262	76	64	69.8
=56 Staffordshire		230	67	88	69.8
58 Birmingham City	1.1	225	60	83	69.5
59 Derby		211	73	79	69.1
60 Manchester Metropolitan	1.0	228	67	69	68.5
61 Northampton		210	69	83	68.0
62 Leeds Metropolitan		203	72	78	67.4
63 Sunderland		219	72	72	66.9
64 East London	1.2	145	71	76	66.6
=65 Bournemouth		216	66	81	66.5

Social Work cont.	Research quality	Entry standards	Student satisfaction %	Graduate prospects %	Overall rating
=65 Worcester		240	72	65	66.5
67 Canterbury Christ Church		237	70	67	65.8
68 Liverpool John Moores		218	74	61	64.9
69 Bishop Grosseteste		257		63	64.6
70 Greenwich		190	69	76	64.5
71 Winchester		278		56	64.1
72 Edge Hill	0.5	224	76	42	63.2
73 Glyndŵr	0.7	218	57	71	62.8
74 Bangor	1.4	239	59	50	61.7
75 Cumbria		226	64	64	61.6
76 Roehampton		223	66	42	56.5

The ranking has had new leaders in each of the last three years. In the latest table, Bath has taken over from Queen's, Belfast, which has dropped to fifth. Bath achieved the best results in the 2008 Research Assessment Exercise and high scores on the other three measures. The most satisfied students are at third-placed Sussex, closely followed by Northumbria and Robert Gordon, both of which are outside the top 20.

Two universities – Glamorgan and Middlesex – have 100 per cent employment records. Several others topped 90 per cent, but scores further down the table are surprisingly variable, with more than half of the graduates at two universities in low-level work or unemployed six months after completing their degrees.

Strathclyde had taken over from Edinburgh as the top university in Scotland, while Glamorgan, in equal eighth place, is the leader in Wales, and is joined by Middlesex as the two post-1992 universities in the top 20. The majority of the institutions in the table are new universities, but most are in the bottom half. Entry grades are largely responsible: most of the older universities in the table have average entry scores of more than 300 points, whereas only Oxford Brookes of the post-1992 universities, reaches that threshold.

» British Association of Social Workers: **www.basw.co.uk**
» General Social Care Council: **www.gscc.org.uk**
» Social Care Association: **http://socialcareassociation.co.uk**

Sociology

Sociology has been growing in popularity, but the competition for places is less intense than in most of the social sciences. Applications were up by 7 per cent early in 2011, following a 16 per cent increase in 2010, but there are fewer than five applications to the place and entry grades are manageable. Numbers have remained buoyant despite an employment record that is in the bottom four for all subjects. More than half of those graduating in 2009 were in low-level jobs or unemployed at the end of the year.

Cambridge is well clear in first place, despite uncharacteristically low grades for research. The sociology panel for the 2008 assessments was no respecter of reputations: neither

Cambridge nor the London School of Economics is among the top 15 universities on this measure. Bath, which has dropped three places to sixth this year, did best for research, with three quarters of the university's work judged to be world-leading or internationally excellent. Grades in sociology were not as high as in many subjects, but Southampton, in eleventh place, also did well, with 70 per cent of research in the top two categories.

Employed in graduate job:	27%	Employed in non-graduate job and studying:	5%
Employed in graduate job and studying:	4%	Employed in non-graduate job:	40%
Studying:	15%	Unemployed:	10%
Average starting graduate salary:	£20,744	Average starting non-graduate salary:	£14,272

Sociology	Research quality	Entry standards	Student satisfaction %	Graduate prospects %	Overall rating
1 Cambridge	3.0	524	86	74	100.0
2 Warwick	3.5	417	81	62	90.6
3 Surrey	3.6	356	85	64	90.4
4 Lancaster	4.0	362	82	63	89.7
5 Durham	2.8	428	77	70	89.3
6 Bath	4.4	364	76	65	88.8
7 Edinburgh	3.6	429	81	54	88.7
8 London School of Economics	2.7	431	72	77	88.2
9 Sussex	3.2	351	81	59	85.7
10 York	3.7	351	81	54	85.6
11 Southampton	4.3	382	84	39	85.4
12 Essex	4.0	322	81	54	85.1
13 Exeter	3.0	376	84	48	84.7
14 Strathclyde	0.8	377	84	63	83.4
=15 Leeds	4.1	368	75	51	83.0
=15 Loughborough	2.9	364	77	58	83.0
17 Sheffield	3.2	369	76	55	82.9
18 Cardiff	3.3	359	77	50	81.5
19 Portsmouth	2.4	297	79	62	81.2
20 Glasgow	1.9	405	83	44	81.0
21 Kent	4.0	306	76	52	80.9
22 Leicester	1.6	343	82		79.8
23 Newcastle	2.5	368	78	48	79.4
24 Stirling	2.4	321	79	52	79.2
25 Aberdeen	2.7	300	82	47	79.1
=26 Keele	2.9	288	75	56	78.4
=26 Goldsmiths College	4.0	287	76	46	78.4
=28 Birmingham	1.3	359	77	57	78.2
=28 East Anglia		353	86	53	78.2
30 Edinburgh Napier	0.4	278	82	66	77.9
31 Northumbria	1.5	288	82	52	77.1
32 Bristol	2.2	365	68	60	77.0

Sociology cont.

	Research quality	Entry standards	Student satisfaction %	Graduate prospects %	Overall rating
=33 Manchester	4.3	395	61	46	75.5
=33 Nottingham	2.2	345	70	54	75.5
35 Hull	1.9	260	82	46	75.1
36 Queen's, Belfast	2.9	312	71	47	74.0
37 Birmingham City	1.1	235	82	53	73.9
38 Liverpool	1.3	351	79	40	73.8
39 Lincoln		268	85	52	73.7
40 Aston	1.0	339	71	57	73.4
=41 Robert Gordon	0.5	226	83	54	72.9
=41 East London	1.9	185	80	53	72.9
=43 Glasgow Caledonian	1.1	284	80	44	72.5
=43 Brunel	2.2	291	73	47	72.5
45 City	2.3	334	68	48	72.1
46 Huddersfield	0.8	235	79	55	71.9
47 Chester	0.6	275	75	58	71.8
48 Salford	2.1	281	75	40	71.1
49 Staffordshire	1.1	207	78	54	71.0
50 Brighton	1.4	283	77	41	70.4
=51 Bedfordshire	1.9	193	81	39	69.8
=51 Bath Spa		290	79	47	69.8
53 Teesside	1.2	230	76	50	69.5
54 Central Lancashire		259	82	43	69.2
=55 Plymouth	1.5	283	71	47	69.0
=55 Canterbury Christ Church		217	75	61	69.0
57 Bangor		274	78	46	68.8
58 Manchester Metropolitan	1.5	266	75	41	68.7
59 West of Scotland		230		56	68.5
60 Nottingham Trent		250	74	56	68.2
61 Coventry		272	77	47	68.1
62 Worcester		272	73	53	67.6
63 Bradford	2.2	189	74	42	67.5
64 Edge Hill		245	76	50	67.3
=65 Southampton Solent		252	82	38	67.2
=65 Abertay		236		52	67.2
67 Ulster		248	83	35	66.9
68 Sheffield Hallam		266	72	53	66.8
69 West of England	0.6	277	75	38	66.3
70 Leeds Metropolitan		262	75	45	66.2
71 Oxford Brookes		327	75	35	66.0
72 Westminster		241	71	49	64.3
73 Northampton		219	80	34	63.6
74 Glamorgan		234	70	49	63.4
=75 Middlesex		190	74	48	63.0

=75	Liverpool John Moores		241	79	30	63.0
77	Greenwich		196	72	49	62.7
=78	Kingston	1.0	221	71	39	62.6
=78	Derby		231	77	35	62.6
80	Buckinghamshire New		209	72	42	61.3
81	Roehampton	1.3	223	67	35	60.4
82	Gloucestershire		268	66	38	59.5
83	Anglia Ruskin		233	70	35	59.3
84	London South Bank		167	70	43	58.4
85	Sunderland		224	71	31	58.0
86	London Metropolitan		214	66	39	57.2
87	UWIC, Cardiff		304	61	32	56.2
88	St Mary's College, Twickenham		243		25	55.5

Cambridge, however, has by far the highest entry standards, 80 points ahead of the field, and, jointly with East Anglia, the most satisfied students. Third-placed Surrey was only one percentage point behind in the 2010 National Student Survey, which showed generally high levels of satisfaction.

Sociology's low standing in the employment table is naturally reflected in the performance of individual universities. It is one of the few subjects in which not a single university saw 80 per cent of leavers to straight into graduate-level jobs or continue their studies. The London School of Economics, in eighth place, came closest to that mark, but at University of Wales Institute, Cardiff, Liverpool John Moores, Sunderland and St Mary's College, Twickenham, there were "positive destinations" for fewer than one student in three.

Edinburgh remains the leading university in Scotland, while Cardiff is best-placed in Wales. Portsmouth is the top post-1992 university and the only one in the top 20. Edinburgh Napier makes the top 30.

Other subjects such as criminology, urban studies, women's studies and some communication studies are included in the category of sociology and a large number of institutions teach the subject as part of a combined studies or modular programme. The subject's poor performance in the employment ranking is not repeated in the comparison of graduate earnings: it is in the top half of the table, with an average starting salary of £20,750 in graduate-level jobs.

» The British Sociological Association: **www.britsoc.co.uk**

Sports Science

This is the third appearance of a separate table for the growing range of courses listed under the category of sports science. In earlier editions of the *Guide*, they appeared in the broader ranking that covers hospitality, leisure, recreation and tourism, but the popularity of sport as a degree subject demands more detailed scrutiny. A 16 per cent increase in applications in 2010 took sports science to the verge of the top ten subjects and another 3 per cent rise in 2011 has kept it there.

The subject covers more than 40 specialisms at degree level, from sports therapy to equestrian sport studies and marine sport technology. Many contain more science and less

Sports Science cont.

physical activity than candidates may expect. Brunel, for example, requires at least an AS level in one of the sciences. Many universities now offer sports scholarships for elite performers, but most are not tied to a particular course and, officially at least, do not mean that the normal entry requirements are waived.

Loughborough, the most famous name in university sport, tops the table, as it did in both previous years of the ranking and when the broader classification was used. It is the only university where entrants average more than 400 points on the UCAS tariff. Loughborough also shares with fifth-placed Birmingham the best record in the 2008 Research Assessment

Employed in graduate job:	33%	Employed in non-graduate job and studying:	4%
Employed in graduate job and studying:	5%	Employed in non-graduate job:	35%
Studying:	17%	Unemployed:	7%
Average starting graduate salary:	£18,319	Average starting non-graduate salary:	£14,238

Sports Science	Research quality	Entry standards	Student satisfaction %	Graduate prospects %	Overall rating
1 Loughborough	3.4	424	85	69	100.0
2 Exeter	1.8	393	90	72	95.4
3 Edinburgh	2.3	374	79	82	94.6
4 Durham	2.8	389	78	72	93.2
5 Birmingham	3.4	377	83	58	92.8
6 Bath	2.1	363	87	66	91.5
=7 Leeds	1.6	384	85	62	88.9
=7 Glasgow	2.9	395	83	48	88.9
=7 Stirling	2.2	345	82		88.9
10 Sheffield Hallam	1.8	312	81	69	86.0
11 East Anglia		358	87	73	85.8
12 Brighton	1.7	276	83	69	84.7
13 Leeds Metropolitan	2.2	311	75	69	84.4
=14 Brunel	2.1	326	75	64	83.3
=14 Liverpool John Moores	3.1	265	81	54	83.3
16 Portsmouth	2.6	262	86	49	82.3
17 Bangor	1.8	266	81	61	81.0
18 Aberystwyth	0.6	225	95	61	80.9
=19 Strathclyde	2.6		80	51	80.8
=19 Chester	1.2	245	80	73	80.8
21 Hertfordshire	1.5	235	81	68	79.8
22 Chichester	1.0	288	85	57	79.7
23 Essex	1.6	303	83	49	79.3
24 UWIC, Cardiff	1.2	292	82	57	78.9
25 Kent	2.3	267	70	66	78.6
26 Aberdeen	1.3	265	82	58	78.3
27 Cumbria		232		76	78.1
28 Heriot-Watt	1.5	293	72	64	77.4

29 Northumbria	1.0	286	74	67	77.2
=30 Nottingham Trent	0.2	283	83	61	76.5
=30 Ulster	1.3	241	81	57	76.5
=30 Dundee		353	86	46	76.5
33 Swansea	0.1	296	87	53	76.3
=34 Staffordshire	0.7	207	85	63	76.0
=34 Bournemouth		275	81	65	76.0
36 Hull	0.4	226	79	68	74.9
37 Lincoln		259	85	57	74.6
38 Manchester Metropolitan	1.3	213	74	66	74.2
39 Edinburgh Napier		272	81	58	73.3
40 Newman	0.1	207	78	71	73.1
41 Sunderland	1.3	223	80	51	73.0
42 Leeds Trinity		192	76	77	72.9
43 Winchester		246	84	55	72.7
44 Salford	1.5	250	81	42	72.5
45 St Mary's College	0.4	220	79	62	72.4
46 Central Lancashire		233	80	61	72.1
47 Worcester		286	76	58	72.0
=48 Middlesex		190	74	76	71.4
=48 Greenwich		182	79	70	71.4
50 Glyndŵr		178	97	43	71.1
51 Coventry	0.6	281	71	56	70.4
52 Teesside		279	83	44	70.3
=53 West of Scotland		216		62	70.0
=53 Gloucestershire	0.4	236	79	52	70.0
55 Abertay		221		60	69.4
56 Roehampton	0.1	195	76	65	69.3
57 Derby		251	72	61	69.0
58 Edge Hill		261	78	48	68.4
59 Glamorgan	1.0	246	76	41	67.9
60 Plymouth		260	80	42	67.6
61 West of England		241	77	48	66.6
62 London Metropolitan		235	72	56	66.5
63 London South Bank	1.2		73	45	66.3
64 Marjon, Plymouth	0.1	215	78	49	66.1
65 Southampton Solent		234	81	40	66.0
66 York St John	0.1	215	76	49	65.7
67 Northampton		211	78	48	65.5
68 Bedfordshire	1.0	178	65	59	64.5
69 Canterbury Christ Church	0.7	188	75	45	64.2
70 Newport		178	78	48	63.5
71 Kingston		225	67	53	62.6
72 East London		160	69	58	61.8
73 Buckinghamshire New	0.3	202	62	51	58.8
74 Bolton		248	64	41	58.6
75 Robert Gordon		283	55	32	53.0

Sports Science cont.

Exercise. Both had 60 per cent of their research rated world-leading or internationally excellent. Entry standards are modest throughout the table: nine universities average less than 200 points.

The most satisfied students are at Glyndŵr, in Wrexham, where 97 per cent of final-year undergraduates gave their stamp of approval although other results restrict the university to 50th place. Aberystwyth, in 18th, is the only other university to come close to this level of satisfaction.

Exeter, another university with an illustrious sporting pedigree, moves up to second, while Edinburgh finishes third, moving clear of Glasgow as the top university in Scotland. Bangor is the leader in Wales and Sheffield Hallam is the highest-placed post-1992 university, the only one in the top ten. Edinburgh has easily the best employment score and Leeds Trinity University College, Cumbria and Middlesex are the only other institutions in the table to see three quarters of leavers go straight into graduate jobs or another course.

Sports science has moved out of the bottom ten subjects for starting salaries this year, but the average was still only £18,300 at the time of the last survey. Although the unemployment rate among graduates is low, at only 7 per cent, more than a third begin their working life in low-level jobs

» British Association of Sport and Exercise Sciences: **www.bases.org.uk**
» English Institute of Sport: **www.eis2win.co.uk**
» London 2012: **www.london2012.com**
» Scottish Institute of Sport: **www.sisport.com**
» Sport Wales National Centre: **www.sportwales.org.uk**

Theology and Religious Studies

Applications for theology and religious studies dropped in 2011, but this followed a series of increases, culminating in an 11 per cent rise in 2010. It remains one of the least competitive subjects in the arts and social sciences: there were little more than four applications to the place in 2010. This is not fully reflected in the entry grades, however. Although only eight of the 37 institutions in the table average more than 400 points, only three (compared with four last year) has an average of less than 250.

Oxford has taken over at the top of the table and Durham, too, has overtaken Cambridge, last year's leader. Oxford has much the highest entry standards, while Durham produced the best results in the 2008 Research Assessment Exercise, when two thirds of its work was considered world-leading or internationally excellent.

The order has also changed in the competition between the top universities in Scotland, which occupy the next three places. Aberdeen has leapfrogged St Andrews and Edinburgh, largely thanks to the best employment record in the table. Seventh-placed Exeter has the most satisfied students in these subjects.

Cardiff has retaken the top position in Wales from Trinity St David, while Leeds Trinity University College is the highest-placed institution outside the old universities. It is joined in the top 20 by St Mary's College, Twickenham.

Surprisingly, theology and religious studies are now in the top 20 in the graduate destinations table, with an unemployment rate of only 7 per cent. By no means all graduates go

Employed in graduate job:	26%	Employed in non-graduate job and studying:			5%
Employed in graduate job and studying:	5%	Employed in non-graduate job:			23%
Studying:	34%	Unemployed:			7%
Average starting graduate salary:	£21,749	Average starting non-graduate salary:			£14,043

Theology and Religious Studies	Research quality	Entry standards	Student satisfaction %	Graduate prospects %	Overall rating
1 Oxford	3.8	512	85	83	100.0
2 Durham	4.4	465	86	80	99.8
3 Cambridge	4.0	489	81	86	98.3
4 Aberdeen	3.4	362	89	90	95.9
5 St Andrews	2.8	441	91	69	93.8
6 Edinburgh	3.7	416	80	72	90.1
7 Exeter	2.2	413	92	62	89.5
8 Glasgow	2.1	410	83	74	87.8
9 Lancaster	2.7	376	81	78	87.3
10 Sheffield	3.3		88	56	86.7
11 Kent	1.9	334	87	77	86.6
12 Nottingham	3.1	381	79	71	86.0
13 Birmingham	2.8	371	81	72	85.9
14 Stirling	1.3	310	87	83	85.8
15 Manchester	3.5	377	76	66	84.3
16 Leeds Trinity	1.2	294		86	82.6
=17 Bangor	1.3	301	87	66	80.9
=17 Bristol	2.4	384	73	71	80.9
=19 St Mary's College, Twickenham	1.9	276	85	66	79.9
=19 King's College London	2.6	418	70	64	79.9
21 Cardiff	1.5	369	83	57	79.7
22 Chester	1.1	281	81	79	79.1
23 Leeds	2.4	382	76	56	78.4
24 Queen's, Belfast		339	85	67	78.0
25 Chichester	0.6		90	52	77.6
26 Newman		235	83	85	77.1
27 Trinity St David	1.5	267	83	64	76.9
=28 Roehampton	1.1	293	79	71	76.8
=28 School of Oriental and African Studies	2.9	347	69	64	76.8
30 Cumbria	0.9	254		77	75.8
31 York St John	0.3	293	86	56	74.2
32 Heythrop College	0.4	323	80	59	73.4
33 Hull		346	80	57	73.1
34 Bath Spa	0.3	288	75	63	70.3
35 Winchester	0.4	316	71	52	66.8
36 Gloucestershire	1.3	239	76	38	64.8
37 Canterbury Christ Church	0.7	235	74	46	64.0

Theology and Religious Studies cont.

into the church, but the vocation helps to maintain this record. The new table contains more variation between institutions in employment prospects than has been the case in previous years, when more than half of the leavers at every university had graduate jobs or were continuing their studies six months after graduation. In this edition, two universities have slipped below that threshold, while one, Aberdeen, managed 90 per cent positive destinations.

Starting salaries had improved to such an extent since the survey used in last year's *Guide* was compiled that the subjects are now also in the top 20 for graduate starting salaries. The average rate in graduate jobs leapt from little more than £18,000 to £21,750 in a year.

» British Association for the Study of Religions: **http://basr.open.ac.uk**
» Society for the Study of Theology: **www.theologysociety.org.uk**

Town and Country Planning and Landscape

The demand for places on planning courses fell alarmingly during and after the recession, but there was a recovery in 2011, when applications rose slightly. The subjects were among the few to see a decline in applications in 2010, when numbers fell by 17 per cent for the second year in a row. Only the much smaller area of landscape design saw an increase in both years. About 12 per cent of places across the whole category tend to be filled through Clearing.

Cambridge remains at the head of the ranking for town and country planning and landscape studies, with the best research grades and entry standards that are nearly 80 points higher than the nearest challenger. Second-placed Reading and University College London, in fifth, are the only other universities to top 400 points at entry. Most of the remaining entry scores are tightly bunched, with only Birmingham City averaging less than 200 points.

Competition was tight in the 2008 Research Assessment Exercise: Cambridge had the most work placed in the top two categories, but Sheffield – which drops to third this year – had a higher proportion judged to be world-leading.

Employment scores are down on last year, but there are good results throughout the table. None comes close to Reading's, which, for the third year in a row, shows every graduate finding

Town and Country Planning and Landscape	Research quality	Entry standards	Student satisfaction %	Graduate prospects %	Overall rating
1 Cambridge	4.1	513		96	100.0
2 Reading	3.4	407	70	100	85.1
3 Sheffield	3.9	361	82	83	85.0
4 Cardiff	3.8	351	81	82	83.5
5 University College London	3.1	415	72	85	81.1
6 Birmingham	2.2	397	92	63	80.0
7 Newcastle	3.5	338	76	80	79.4
8 Loughborough	3.8	332	84	65	79.3
9 Queen's, Belfast	1.6	332	73	82	72.3
10 Liverpool	2.2	333	76	70	72.2
11 Aberdeen	3.1	299		65	71.8

12 Gloucestershire	1.6	309		78	70.8
13 Dundee	1.6	306	80	67	70.2
14 Northumbria	1.9	301	75		69.1
=15 Manchester	3.1	333	71	53	68.8
=15 Oxford Brookes	1.6	321	73	70	68.8
17 Heriot-Watt	2.8	346	61	70	68.7
18 Leeds Metropolitan		273	91	69	68.6
19 West of England	1.9	281	77	67	68.4
=20 Sheffield Hallam	2.8	229	78	61	67.7
=20 Manchester Metropolitan	1.5	279	75	72	67.7
22 Glasgow Caledonian	2.8	276	71	63	67.5
23 Nottingham Trent	1.0	281	75	67	65.0
24 Liverpool John Moores	1.1		69	63	60.7
25 Birmingham City	1.4	195	59	78	58.6
26 Kingston	0.4	225	67	68	57.3
27 Ulster		201	68	43	48.9

high-level work or continuing to study within six months of completing a degree. Only two universities recorded positive destinations for less than 60 per cent of those graduating in 2009.

Birmingham, which has jumped 13 places to sixth in this year's table, has the most satisfied students, closely followed by Leeds Metropolitan. Cardiff, in fourth place, is the top university outside England, while Aberdeen has overtaken Dundee to become the leader in Scotland. Gloucestershire, in twelfth place, has become the leading post-1992 university, with Northumbria its nearest challenger.

Job prospects have mirrored the fall in student recruitment, as subjects have dropped from inside the top ten two years ago to mid-way in the new employment table. Despite this, two thirds of graduates were in graduate-level jobs or still studying at the end of 2009. Average starting salaries in graduate-level jobs had dropped slightly in the latest survey, dipping just below £20,000.

Employed in graduate job:	36%	Employed in non-graduate job and studying:	3%
Employed in graduate job and studying:	5%	Employed in non-graduate job:	22%
Studying:	23%	Unemployed:	11%
Average starting graduate salary:	£19,956	Average starting non-graduate salary:	£15,198

» Royal Town Planning Institute: **www.rtpi.org.uk**
» Planning Officers Society: **www.planningofficers.org.uk**
» Landscape Institute: **www.landscapeinstitute.org**

Veterinary Medicine

Only medicine itself compares with veterinary medicine for high entry standards and the level of competition for places. There was another small rise in the demand for places in 2011, following an increase of more than 13 per cent in the previous year. There were then more than eight applications for each place and, with veterinary numbers strictly controlled, there is no likelihood of an easing in 2012.

Veterinary Medicine cont.

Veterinary medicine is another of the rankings from which employment scores have been removed from the calculations that determine universities' positions. The scores are still shown in the table, but the review group of academic planners consulted on *Guide* agreed that employment rates in the subject were so tightly bunched that small differences could distort the overall ranking.

Cambridge, which actually has the lowest employment score, remains ahead of the field, despite having a surprisingly low research grade. Its high entry standards and the top score for student satisfaction more than make up for this. Nottingham does not yet have a full set of statistics because it only opened in 2006, so its first students will graduate in summer 2011, but its other scores were enough to take the university up to second place. There are no degrees in veterinary medicine in Wales or Northern Ireland.

Veterinary medicine has moved back up to fourth place for employment this year. More than nine out of ten vets were in graduate jobs or still studying six months after graduating. The subject is in the same position for starting salaries, which averaged close to £26,000 at the time of the latest survey. Most courses demand high grades in chemistry and biology, with some accepting physics or maths as one alternative subject. Cambridge and the Royal Veterinary College also set applicants a specialist aptitude test that is used by a number of medical schools. Few candidates win places without evidence of practical commitment to the subject, through work experience, either in veterinary practices or laboratories.

The five-year courses have to meet the requirements of the Royal College of Veterinary Surgeons. Vets' final qualifications are not classified, but between 5 and 15 per cent are awarded a commendation.

Employed in graduate job:	86%	Employed in non-graduate job and studying:	1%
Employed in graduate job and studying:	3%	Employed in non-graduate job:	3%
Studying:	2%	Unemployed:	6%
Average starting graduate salary:	£25,807	Average starting non-graduate salary:	n/a.

Veterinary Medicine	Research quality	Entry standards	Student satisfaction %	Graduate prospects %	Overall rating
1 Cambridge	1.8	532	82	88	100.0
2 Nottingham	2.8	477			96.8
3 Edinburgh	2.9	496	68	91	95.0
4 Liverpool	1.8	480	81	94	93.9
5 Glasgow	2.1	478	78	94	93.6
6 Royal Veterinary College	2.4	491	70	91	92.8
7 Bristol	1.3	454	77	91	87.4

» Royal College of Veterinary Surgeons: **www.rcvs.org.uk**

6 Making Your Application

One of the few things that will not change about higher education in 2012 is the process of making an application. There is talk of a new system here, too, with only two choices and later deadlines. But, for the moment, applicants will continue to have five choices of course, and to make decisions well before they have their results. You do not have to take advantage of all five – some people make only a single application, perhaps because they do not want to leave home or they have very particular requirements – but you will give yourself the best chance of success if you go for the maximum.

Too many people take their eye off the ball in actually making the application. Surprising numbers of applicants each year spell their own name wrongly, or enter an inaccurate date of birth, or the wrong course code. And that is to say nothing of the damage that can be done in the personal statement and teachers' references.

In an era when there are relatively few interviews and more candidates each year achieve high A-level grades, what goes on your UCAS form is becoming more and more important – too important, many would say. The art of conveying knowledge of, and enthusiasm for, your chosen subject – preferably with supporting evidence from your school or college – can make all the difference. While UCAS will decode misspelt names, other errors in grammar or spelling present admissions officers with an easy starting point in cutting applications down to a more manageable number.

The application process

Most applications for full-time higher education courses go through UCAS, although specialist admissions bodies still handle applications to the music conservatoires (Conservatoires UK Admissions Service: **www.cukas.ac.uk**) and some postgraduate courses, including teacher training (Graduate Teacher Training Registry: **www.gttr.ac.uk**). The trend is towards the UCAS model even among specialist providers, however: recruitment to nursing and midwifery diploma and degree courses in Scotland switched to the UCAS system in 2010 and the art and design courses that used to recruit using the separate "Route B" scheme also moved to the main system in 2010.

Universities that have not filled all their places, even during Clearing, will accept direct applications up to and after the start of the academic year, but UCAS is both the official route and the only way into the most popular courses.

Since 2006, all UCAS applications have been made online. The Apply electronic system is accessed via the UCAS website and is straightforward to use. For those who do not have the internet at home and prefer not to use school or college computers, the UCAS website lists 900 libraries, all over the UK, where you can make your application. Apply is available 24 hours a day, and, when the time comes, information on the progress of your application may arrive at any time.

Registering with Apply

The first step in the process is to register. If you are at a school or college, you will need to obtain a "buzzword" from your tutor or careers adviser – it is used when you log on to register. It links your application to the school or college so that the application can be sent electronically to your referee (usually one of your teachers) for your reference to be attached. If you are no longer at a school or college, you do not need a "buzzword" but you will need details of your referee. More information is given on the UCAS website.

To register, go to the UCAS website and click on "Apply". The system will guide you through the business of providing your personal details and generating a username and password, as well as reminding you of basic points, such as amending your details in case of a change of address. You can register separate term-time and holiday addresses – a useful option for boarders, who could find offers and, particularly, the confirmation of a place, going to their school when they are miles away at home. Remember to keep a note of your username and password in a safe place.

Throughout the process, you will be in sole control of communications with UCAS and your chosen universities. Only if you nominate a representative and give them your unique nine-digit application number (sent automatically by UCAS when your application is submitted), can a parent or anyone else give or receive information on your behalf, perhaps because you are ill or out of the country.

Once you are registered, you can start to complete the Apply screens. The details required cover the following areas:

» Personal details and some additional non-educational details for UK applicants.
» Your university choices.
» Details of your education so far, including examination results and examinations still to be taken.
» Details of any jobs you have done.
» Your personal statement.
» A reference from one of your teachers.
» A declaration that you confirm that the information is correct and that you will be bound by the UCAS rules.
» Payment details (in 2011 applications cost £21, or £11 to apply to just one course).

The sections that follow cover the most important sections.

Personal details

This information is taken from your initial registration, and you will be asked for additional information, for example, on ethnic origin and national identity, used to monitor equal opportunities in the application process.

Choices

Since 2007–08, you have been restricted to a maximum of five, rather than six, courses on your UCAS form. The switch met remarkably little resistance – perhaps because most applicants, having set their heart on one or two courses with genuine appeal, were going through the motions by the time it came to choosing a sixth. Applicants in medicine, dentistry and veterinary science were already restricted to four choices in their chosen subject, so they now have the option of only one additional choice in another subject.

The other important restriction concerns Oxford or Cambridge, because you can only apply to one or the other; you cannot apply to both Oxford and Cambridge. For both Oxford and Cambridge you may need to take a written test (see pages 20–21) and submit examples of your work (depending on the course selected) and, in addition, for Cambridge, you will be asked to complete a Supplementary Application Questionnaire once Cambridge has received your application from UCAS. The deadline for Oxbridge applications – and for all medicine, dentistry and veterinary science courses – is 15 October. For all other applications the deadline is 15 January (or 24 March for some specified art and design courses).

Most applicants use all five choices. But if you do choose fewer than five courses, you can still add another to your form up to 30 June, as long as you have not accepted or declined any offers. Nor do you have to choose five different universities if more than one course at the same institution attracts you – perhaps because the institution itself is the real draw and one course has lower entrance requirements than the other. Universities are not allowed to see where else you have applied, or whether you have chosen the same subject elsewhere. But they will be aware of multiple applications within their own institution. It is, in any case, more difficult to write a convincing personal statement if it has to cover more than one subject.

For each course you select, you will need to put the UCAS code on the form – and you should check carefully that you have the correct code and understand any special require-ments that may be detailed on the UCAS description of the course. You will also need to indicate whether you are applying for a deferred entry (for example, if you are taking a gap year – see page 201).

Education

In this section you will need to give details of the schools and colleges you have attended, and the qualifications you have obtained or are preparing for. The UCAS website gives plenty of advice on the ways in which you should enter this information, to ensure that all your relevant qualifications are included with their grades. While UCAS does not need to see qualification certificates, it can double-check results with the examination boards to ensure that no-one is tempted to modify their results.

Personal statements

As the competition for places on popular courses has become more intense, so the value attached to the personal statement has increased. Admissions officers look for a sign of potential beyond the high grades that growing numbers of applicants offer. Many (but not all) value success in extracurricular activities such as drama, sport or the Duke of Edinburgh's Award scheme. But your first priority should be to demonstrate an interest in and understand-ing of your chosen subject beyond the confines of the exam syllabus.

This is not easy in a relatively short statement that can readily sound trite or pretentious. You should resist any temptation to lie, particularly if there is any chance of an interview. A claim to have been inspired by a book that you have not read will backfire instantly under questioning and, even without an interview, experienced academics are likely to see through grandiose statements that appear at odds with a teacher's reference. Genuine experiences of after-hours clubs, lectures or visits – better still, work experience or actual reading around the syllabus – are much more likely to strike the right note. Take advice from teachers and, if there is still time before you make your application, look for some subject-related activities that will help fill out your statement.

Admissions officers are also looking for evidence of character that will make you a productive member of their university and, eventually, a successful graduate. Taking responsibility in any area of school or college life suggests this – leading activities outside your place of learning even more so. Evidence of initiative and self-discipline is also valuable, since higher education involves much more independent study than sixth-formers are used to.

Your overall aim in writing your personal statement is to persuade the admissions officer to pick you out of the piles of applications on his or her desk. That means trying to stand out from an often rather dull and uniform set of statements based around the curriculum and the more predictable sixth-form activities. Everyone is going to say they love reading, for example; narrow your interest down to an area of (real) interest. Don't be afraid to include the unusual, but bear in mind that an academic's sense of humour may not be the same as yours.

Give particular thought to why you want to study your chosen subject – especially if it is not one you have taken at school or college. You need to show that your interests and skills are well-suited to the course and, if it is a vocational degree, that you know how you envisage using the qualification. Admissions officers want to feel that you will be committed to their subject for the length of the course, which could be three, four or even five years, and capable of achieving good results.

Your school or college should be the best source of advice, since they see personal statements every year, but there are others. The UCAS website has a useful checklist of themes that you may wish to address, while sites such as **www.studential.com** also provide tips. But do not fall into the trap of cutting and pasting from the model statements included on such sites – both UCAS and individual universities have software that will spot plagiarism immediately. In one year, no fewer than one in twenty applicants came to grief in this way, and more than 200 applicants claimed to trace a passion for science back to setting their pyjamas on fire when experimenting with a chemistry set that they received as a birthday present. Plagiarists of this type are unlikely to be disqualified, but they destroy the credibility of their application.

Try not to cram in more than the limited space will allow – admissions officers will have many statements to go through, and judicious editing may be rewarded. As long as you write clearly – preferably in paragraphs and possibly with sub-headings – it will be up to you what to include. It is a personal statement. But consider these points:

» What attracts you to this subject (or subjects, in the case of dual or combined honours)?
» Have you undertaken relevant work experience or voluntary activities, either through school or elsewhere?
» Have you taken part in other extra-curricular activities that demonstrate character – perhaps as a prefect, on the sports field or in the arts?
» Have you been involved in other academic pursuits, such as Gifted and Talented programmes, widening participation schemes, or courses in other subjects?
» Which aspects of your current courses have you found particularly stimulating?
» Are you planning a gap year? If so, explain what you intend to do and how it will affect your studies. Some subjects – notably maths – actively discourage a break in studies.

» What other outside interests might you include that show that you are well-rounded?

The Apply system allows 4,000 characters (including spaces), or 47 lines for your statement. While there is no requirement to fill all the space, it should not look embarrassingly short. UCAS recommends using a word-processing package to compile the statement before pasting it into the application system. This is because Apply will time-out after 35 minutes of inactivity, so there is a danger of losing valuable material. Working offline also has the advantage of leaving you with a copy and making it easier to show it to others.

References
Hand in hand with your personal statement goes the reference from your school, college or, in the case of mature students, someone who knows you well but is not a friend or family member. The reference has to be independent – you are specifically forbidden to change any part of it if you send off your own application – but that does not mean you should not try to influence what it contains. Most schools and colleges conduct informal interviews before compiling a reference, but it does no harm to draw up a list of the achievements that you would like to see included, and ensure your referee knows what subject you are applying for. Referees cannot know every detail of a candidate's interests and most welcome an aide-memoire.

The UCAS guidelines skirt around the candidate's right to see his or her reference, but it does exist. Schools' practices vary, but most now show the applicant the completed reference. Where this is not the case, the candidate can pay UCAS £10 for a copy, although at this stage it is obviously too late to influence the contents. Better, if you can, to see it before it goes off, in case there are factual inaccuracies that can be corrected.

Timing
The general deadline for applications through UCAS is 15 January but even those received up to 30 June will be considered if the relevant courses still have vacancies. After that, you will be limited to Clearing, or an application for the following year. In theory – and usually in practice – all applications submitted by the January deadline are given equal consideration. But the best advice is to get your application in early: before Christmas, or earlier if possible. Applications are accepted from September onwards, so the autumn half-term is a sensible target date for completing the process. While no offers are made before the deadline, many admissions officers look through applications as they come in and may make a mental note of promising candidates. If your form arrives with the deadline looming, you may appear less organised than those who submitted in good time; and your application may be one of a large batch that receives a more cursory first reading than the early arrivals. Under UCAS rules, last-minute applicants should not be at a disadvantage, but why take the risk?

UCAS has acknowledged that the funding changes imposed by the Government may delay some universities in planning and confirming the courses to be offered in 2012. At the time of writing, however, there was no suggestion that any of the deadlines for application or universities' responses would alter.

Next steps
Once your application has been processed by UCAS, you will receive a welcome letter confirming your choices and summarising what will happen next. The letter will contain a reminder of your identification number and the username and password that you used to

Timetable for applications (based on 2010–11 dates)

May onwards	Find out about courses and universities. Attend university open days.
September	Registration starts for UCAS Apply.
15 October	Final day for applications to Oxford and Cambridge, and for all courses in medicine, dentistry and veterinary science.
15 January	Final day for all other applications from UK and EU students to ensure that your application is given equal consideration with all other applicants. Now also the deadline for all art and design courses except those which have a 24 March deadline (specified in UCAS Course Search).
16 January–30 June	New applications continue to be accepted by UCAS, but only considered by universities if the relevant courses have vacancies.
25 February	Start of applications through UCAS Extra.
24 March	Final day for applications for those art and design courses that specify this date.
31 March	Universities should have sent decisions on all applications received by 15 January, but decisions may be later than this.
5 May	Final day by which applicants have to decide on their choices if application submitted by 15 January and all decisions received by 31 March (exact date for each applicant will be confirmed by UCAS). **If you do not reply to UCAS, they will decline your offers.**
6 May	UCAS must receive all decisions from universities if you applied by 15 January.
7 June	Final day by which applicants have to decide on their choices if all decisions received by 6 May (exact date for each applicant will be confirmed by UCAS).
1 July	Any new application received from this date held until Clearing starts.
6 July	Final day for applications through UCAS Extra.
19 July	Universities must give decisions on all applications submitted by 30 June. You must make a decision on these offers by 26 July.
4 August	SQA results published. Scottish Clearing starts.
18 August	GCE results published. Full Clearing and Adjustment starts.
31 August	Adjustment closes.
20 September	Last day UCAS will accept applications for courses about to start.
30 September	Clearing vacancy service closes. Contact universities directly about vacancies.
24 October	Last date by which a university can accept you through Clearing. Last day to add a Clearing choice.

apply. These will also give you access to Track, the online system that allows you to follow the progress of your application. Check all the details carefully: you have 14 days to contact UCAS to correct any errors. Since 2010 universities have been able to make direct contact with you through Track, including arranging interviews.

After that, it is just a matter of waiting for universities to make their decisions, which can take days, weeks or even months, depending on the university and the course. Some obviously see an advantage in being the first to make an offer – it is a memorable moment to be reassured that at least one of your chosen institutions wants you – and may send their response almost immediately. Others take much longer, perhaps because they have so many good applications to consider, or maybe because they are waiting to see which of their applicants withdraw when Oxford and Cambridge make their offers. Universities are asked to make all their decisions by the end of March, and most have done so long before that.

Interviews

Unless you are applying for a course in health or education that brings you into direct contact with the public, the chances are you will not have a selection interview. For prospective medics, vets, dentists or teachers, a face-to-face assessment of your suitability will be crucial to your chances of success. Likewise in the performing arts, the interview may be as important as your exam grades. Oxford and Cambridge still interview applicants in all subjects, and a few of the top universities see a significant proportion. But the expansion of higher education has made it impractical to interview everyone, and many admissions experts are sceptical about interviews.

What has become more common, however, is the "sales" interview, where the university is really selling itself to the candidate. There may still be testing questions, but the admissions staff have already made their minds up and are actually trying to persuade you to accept an offer. Indeed, you will probably be given a clear indication at the end of the interview that one is on its way. The technique seems to work, perhaps because you have invested time and nervous energy in a sometimes lengthy trip, as well as acquiring a more detailed impression of both the department and the university.

The difficulty can come in spotting which type of interview is which. The "real" ones require lengthy preparation, revisiting your personal statement and reading beyond the exam syllabus. Dress smartly and make sure that you are on time. Impressions count for a lot at interviews, so have a question of your own ready, as well as being prepared to give answers.

While you would not want to appear ignorant at a "sales" interview, lengthy preparation might be a waste of valuable time during a period of revision. Naturally, you should err on the side of caution, but if your predicted grades are well above the standard offer and the subject is not one that normally requires an interview, it is likely that the invitation is a sales pitch. It is still worth going, unless you have changed your mind about the application.

Offers

When your chosen universities respond to your application, there will be one of three answers:

» Unconditional Offer (U): This is a possibility only if you applied after satisfying the entrance requirements – usually if you are applying as a mature student, while on a gap year, after resitting exams or, in Scotland, after completing Highers.

» Conditional Offer (C): The university offers a place subject to you achieving set grades or points on the UCAS tariff.

» Rejection (R): You do not have the right qualifications, or have lost out to stronger competition.

If you have chosen wisely, you should have more than one offer to choose from, so you will be required to pick your favourite as your firm acceptance – known as UF if it was an unconditional offer and CF if it was conditional. Candidates with conditional offers can also accept a second offer, with lower grades, as an Insurance choice (CI). You must then decline any other offers that you have.

You do not have to make an Insurance choice – indeed, you may decline all your offers if you have changed your mind about your career path or regret your course decisions. But most people prefer the security of a back-up route into higher education if their grades fall short. You must be sure that your firm acceptance is definitely your first choice because you will be allocated a place automatically if you meet the university's conditions. It is no good at this stage deciding that you prefer your Insurance choice because UCAS rules will not allow a switch.

The only way round those rules – if your personal circumstances have changed, or you do much better than expected and are determined to "trade up" to another university – is through direct contact with the universities concerned. Your firm acceptance institution has to be prepared to release you so that your new choice can award you a place in Clearing. Neither is under any obligation to do so but, in practice, it is rare for a university to insist that a student joins against his or her wishes. Admissions staff will do all they can to persuade you that your original choice was the right one – as it may well have been, if your research was thorough – but it will almost certainly be your decision in the end.

UCAS Extra

If things do go wrong and you receive five rejections, that need not be the end of your higher education ambitions. From the end of February until the end of June, you have another chance through UCAS Extra, a listing of courses that still have vacancies after the initial round of offers. Extra is sometimes dismissed (wrongly) as a repository of second-rate courses. In fact, even in the boom year for applications of 2010, most Russell Group universities still had hundreds of courses listed in a wide variety of subjects.

You will be notified if you are eligible for Extra and can then select courses marked as available on the UCAS website. Applications are made, one at a time, through UCAS Track. If you do not receive an offer, or you choose to decline one, you can continue applying for other courses until you are successful. About half of those applying through Extra normally find a place.

Results Day

Rule Number One on results day is to be at home, or at least in communication. Places are filled extremely rapidly with the newest electronic admissions systems, and you cannot afford to be on some remote beach if there are complications. If you get the grades stipulated in your conditional offer, the process should work smoothly and you can begin celebrating. You don't need to do anything – Track will let you know as soon as your place is confirmed and the paperwork will arrive in a day or two. You can phone the university to make quite sure, but it should not be necessary and you will be joining a long queue of people doing the same thing.

If the results are not what you hoped – and particularly if you just miss your grades – you need to be on the phone and taking advice from your school or college. In a year when results are better than expected, some universities will stick to the letter of their offers, perhaps refusing to accept your AAC grades when they had demanded ABB. Others will forgive a dropped grade to take a candidate who is regarded as promising, rather than go into Clearing to recruit an unknown quantity. Admissions staff may be persuadable – particularly if there are extenuating personal circumstances, or the dropped grade is in a subject that is not relevant to your chosen course. Try to get a teacher to support your case, and be persistent if there is any prospect of flexibility.

One option, if your results are lower than predicted, is to ask for papers to be re-marked, as growing numbers do each year. The school may ask for a whole batch to be re-marked, and you should ensure that your chosen universities know this if it may make the difference to whether or not you satisfy your offer. If your grades improve, the university will review its decision, but if by then it has filled all its places, you may have to wait until next year to start the course.

Results Day is bound to be stressful, unless you are absolutely confident that you achieved the required grades – more of a possibility in an era of modular courses with marks along the way. But for thousands of students Track has removed the agony of opening the envelope or scanning a results noticeboard. From midnight on the eve of A-level results day, the system informs those who have already won a place on their chosen course. You will not learn your grades until later, but at least your immediate future is clear.

If you took Scottish Highers, you will have had your results for more than a week by the time the A-level grades are published. If you missed your grades, there is no need to wait for A levels before you begin approaching universities. Admissions staff at English universities may not wish to commit themselves before they see results from south of the border, but Scottish universities will be filling places immediately and all should be prepared to give you an idea of your prospects.

Adjustment

If your grades are better than those demanded by your first-choice university, there is now an opportunity to "trade up". Introduced in 2009, the Adjustment Period runs for only five days after you have received your results, so there is no time to waste. First, go into the Track system and click on "Register for Adjustment" and then contact your preferred institutions to find another place. If none is available, or you decide not to move, your initial offer will remain open. Only 382 students switched places in the first year of adjustment and the figure was down to 377 in 2010. UCAS is yet to publish a breakdown of which universities were involved, but it is known that many students successfully went back to institutions that had rejected them at the initial application stage. The numbers using the system may well rise as it becomes better known, particularly if students become more cautious with their applications in response to the increased demand for places.

Clearing

If you have the opposite problem and do not have a place on Results Day, there will still be plenty of options through the UCAS Clearing scheme. Almost 47,000 people – close to 10 per cent of all applicants – found a place through this route in 2010, despite widespread predictions of a Clearing drought. There is no reason to think there will be fewer places filled through Clearing in 2012, particularly if high fees put off some potential applicants. Although the most popular courses fill up quickly, many remain open up to and beyond the start of the academic year. And, at least at the start of the process, the range of courses with vacancies is much wider than in Extra. You will not find Oxford or Cambridge, but most universities will list some courses, and most subjects will be available somewhere.

Clearing runs from Results Day until late September, matching students without places to full-time courses with vacancies. As long as you are not holding any offers and you have not withdrawn your application, you are eligible automatically. You will be sent a Clearing number via Track to quote to universities.

After that, it is just a matter of trawling through the lists on the UCAS website, and elsewhere, before making a direct approach to the university offering the course that appeals most, and where you have a realistic chance of a place. Tens of thousands of hopefuls will be doing the same thing, so do not waste time on courses where the standard offer is far above your grades. Universities run Clearing hotlines and have become adept at dealing with a large number of calls in a short period, but you can still spend a long time on the phone at a time when the most desirable places are beginning to disappear. If you can't get through – or even if you can – send an email setting out your grades and detailing the course that interests you. The best advice is to plan ahead and not to wait for Results Day to draw up a list of possible Clearing targets. Many universities publish lists of courses that are likely to be in Clearing on their websites from the start of August. Think again about some of the courses that you considered when making your original application, or others at your chosen universities that had lower entrance requirements. But beware of switching to another subject simply because you have the right grades – you still have to sustain your interest and be capable of succeeding over three or more years. Many of the students who drop out of degrees are those who chose the wrong course in a rush during Clearing.

In short, you should start your search straight away if you do find yourself in Clearing, and act decisively, but do not panic. Apply the same criteria that you used in choosing courses initially: look at the syllabus and satisfy yourself that you will enjoy the course, that the university is one which you are happy to attend, and that the qualification will take you where you want to go in your career. You can make as many approaches as you like, until you are accepted on the course of your choice.

Most of the available vacancies will appear in Clearing lists, but some of the universities towards the top of the league tables may have a limited number of openings that they choose not to advertise – either for reasons of status or because they do not want the administrative burden of fielding large numbers of calls to fill a handful of places. If there is a course that you find particularly attractive – especially if you have good grades and are applying late – it may be worth making a speculative call. Sometimes a number of candidates holding offers drop grades and you may be on the spot at the right moment.

What are the alternatives?

If your results are lower than expected and there is nothing you want in Clearing, there are several things you can do. The first is to resit one or more subjects. The modular nature of most courses means that you will have a clear idea of what you need to do to get better grades. You can go back to school or college, try a "crammer" or take a job and revise in the evenings. Although some colleges have a good success rate with re-takes, you have to be highly focused and realistic about the likely improvements. Some of the most competitive courses, such as medicine, may demand higher grades for a second application, so be sure you know the details before you commit yourself to a year's delay.

Other options are to get a job and study part-time, or to take a break from studying and return later in your career. The part-time route can be arduous – many young people find a job enough to handle without the extra burden of academic work. But others find it just the combination they need for a fulfilling life. It all depends on your job, your social life and your commitment to the subject you will study. It may be that a relatively short break is all that you need to rekindle your enthusiasm for studying. Many universities now have a majority of mature students, so you need not be out of place if this is your chosen route.

Taking a gap year

The other increasingly popular option – despite the economic downturn – is to take a gap year. About 7 per cent of applicants now defer their entry until the following year while they travel, or do voluntary or paid work. A whole industry has grown up around tailor-made activities, many of them in Asia, Africa or Latin America. Some have been criticised for doing more for the organisers than the underprivileged communities that they purport to assist, but there are programmes that are useful and character-building, as well as safe. Most of the overseas programmes are not cheap, but raising the money can be part of the experience. The alternative is to stay closer to home and make your contribution through organisations like Community Service Volunteers (**www.csv.org.uk**) or to take a job that will make higher education more affordable when the time comes.

Many admissions staff are happy to facilitate gap years because they think it makes for more mature, rounded students than those who come straight from school. The right programme may even increase your chances of winning a place, if it is relevant to your course. But there are subjects – maths in particular – that discourage a break because it takes too long to pick up study skills where you left off. From the student's point of view, you should also bear in mind that a gap year postpones the moment at which you embark on a career. This may be important if your course is a long one, such as medicine or architecture.

If you are considering a gap year, it makes sense to apply for a deferred place, rather than waiting for your results before applying. The application form has a section for deferments. That allows you to sort out your immediate future before you start travelling or working, and leaves you the option of changing your mind if circumstances change.

Useful websites

The essential website for making an application is, of course, that of UCAS:
www.ucas.com/students/applying
For applications to music conservatoires: **www.cukas.ac.uk**
For applications for graduate teacher training: **www.gttr.ac.uk**
For advice on your personal statement:
www.ucas.com/students/applying/howtoapply/personalstatement
www.studential.com

Gap years

To help you consider options and start planning: **www.gapadvice.org**
For links to volunteering opportunities in the UK: **www.do-it.org.uk**
For links to many gap year organisations: **www.yearoutgroup.org**
For work placements relevant to university courses: **www.yini.org.uk**
Also consult: Community Service Volunteers: **www.csv.org.uk**
v (the national young volunteers service): **www.vinspired.com**

7 The Cost of Studying

The mountain of publicity surrounding increased tuition fees at English universities is certain to make this year's applicants think twice about how they will afford higher education. There is no denying that going to university had already become an expensive business – and will be much more expensive now – but funding is available, especially for those from less affluent backgrounds, to make it affordable.

No one knows what the long-term effects of the economic downturn will be, but most independent research continues to show that it is worth investing in a degree – as long as you pick the right course and work hard enough to ensure that you at least gain your qualification. The extra amount you earn, over and above what you would have made without a degree, should far outstrip the cost of your higher education in most subjects at most universities.

Funding help

Even under the new fees regime, there will be enough sources of funding to enable most students to meet the costs of higher education and live reasonably – albeit building up considerable debts in the process. But it will take perseverance to put together the best possible package. Depending on your family income and where you live in the UK, you may be entitled to a range of grants, bursaries or scholarships. There are further calculations to do on fee levels, the length of courses and the cost of living at different universities. With many families feeling the pinch, it has never been more important to get it right. Getting into debt is now a fact of life for almost all students. Graduates and students still on courses now owe more than £30 billion between them in England alone – and those figures are about to rise dramatically. Most research now puts average graduate debt at around £20,000. The good news is that most of it is in the form of student loans, which have been pegged to inflation and are repayable only when a graduate is earning at least £15,000 a year. Under the new system in England, interest rates will rise, but repayments will not begin until you are earning £21,000 a year.

Forewarned is forearmed, and a little bit of careful financial planning and research into help that is available can go a long way to helping you emerge from your university education with a level of debt that is not going to become a millstone for life. As well as student loans, which will still be provided at relatively generous rates and under very favourable terms and conditions, you can shop around for university bursaries and scholarships and other sponsorship packages, and seek out any supplementary support to which you may be entitled. The latter may include a maintenance grant: despite recent changes in eligibility, these are available to a much larger slice of the population than was the case in the early years of tuition fees.

However, even with a grant, you will need to gather together all the resources you can to survive. Analysis by the National Union of Students (NUS) suggests that it is not possible to get by on student loans and grants alone. Savings, earnings, and help from family and friends have to be added to the pot. The information provided below should at least help you understand how big your pot needs to be, and what you can expect to be added and taken away from it.

University tuition fees

As everyone now knows, tuition fees for new British and EU undergraduates on full-time courses will rise to a maximum of £9,000 a year in 2012 at universities and colleges in England. Part-timers will pay a maximum of £6,750. But the May elections delayed decisions in Northern Ireland, Scotland and Wales. An already complicated situation is likely to become more difficult to navigate, as the devolved administrations try to protect their own students from the fee increases without subsidising those from the rest of the UK.

Students from other EU countries will pay the same rate as home students. Those from outside the EU are not affected by the changes, although universities may still raise their fees after a normal review. The new fees for UK undergraduates will narrow the gap with international students, but those from outside the EU will still pay more.

With changes, large or small, becoming almost an annual occurrence, it is essential to consult the latest information provided by Government agencies. It is worth checking the following websites for the latest information:
» England: **www.direct.gov.uk/yourfuture**
» Wales: **www.studentfinancewales.co.uk**
» Scotland: **www.saas.gov.uk**
» Northern Ireland: **www.studentfinanceni.co.uk**

What follows is a summary of the position for British students at the spring of 2011. While there are substantial differences across the four countries of the UK, there is one important piece of common ground. Up-front payment of fees is not compulsory, as students can take out a fee loan (see below) to cover them. This is repayable in instalments after graduation, when your earnings reach the threshold set by the Government.

Fees in England

In England, the maximum tuition fee for full-time undergraduates will be £9,000 a year in 2012–13. Private colleges and some further education colleges may charge considerably less than this, particularly for Foundation degrees, but very few university degrees will be available for the £6,000 fee that ministers hoped would be the norm. Individual universities' fees are listed at the end of this chapter and alongside their profiles in chapter 13, where announcements were made ahead of the official confirmation of approved fee levels in July 2011.

Most universities have opted for fees of £9,000, or close to it, in order to recoup the money removed from Government grants and leave room for further investment and student support. But this is only the headline figure and almost all universities will offer bursaries and scholarships that make the actual cost lower for students from less affluent backgrounds. In many cases, these will reduce the cost by up to a third for those from homes where the combined salaries are less than £25,000.

The lowest fees in public universities will be for Foundation degrees and Higher National Diplomas. Although some universities have chosen to charge the same for all courses, in many of them these two-year courses will remain a cost-effective stepping stone to a full degree.

Fees in Scotland

At Scottish universities and colleges, students from Scotland and those from other EU countries outside the UK pay no fees. The universities' vice-chancellors and principals have appealed for some charges to be introduced to save their institutions from falling behind their English rivals, but Alex Salmond, Scotland's First Minister, famously declared that the "rocks will melt with the sun" before this happens.

The students who do pay are those from England, Wales and Northern Ireland, who for the last three years have been charged £1,820 (£2,895 for medical students). These students can also avoid having to pay up front by applying for a student loan administered by their funding agency. Students whose home is in Scotland and are studying at a Scottish university apply to the Student Awards Agency for Scotland (SAAS) to have their fees paid for them.

The new SNP government was deciding on its fees policy as this *Guide* went to press, but a similar system was expected to emerge, with higher charges for non-Scots to reflect the increases in England.

Fees in Wales

The Welsh Assembly Government has announced that it will protect students whose homes are in Wales against the fee increases announced in Westminster, whether or not they attend universities in the Principality. Universities in Wales will increase their fees for 2012 – Aberystwyth has already announced charges of £9,000 a year.

At least some other universities in Wales are expected to follow Aberystwyth's lead with fees of £9,000 that will be paid by students from other parts of the UK. But undergraduates who live in Wales will be able to apply for a New Fee Grant, wherever they study. Details had not been announced when this *Guide* went to press and the Student Finance Wales website guaranteed only that this would "offset some of the cost", but the political commitment was to make up the difference between fees in 2011–12 and those in 2012–13.

Fees in Northern Ireland

Until now, the two universities in Northern Ireland have charged the same fees as those in England, but a consultation was under way as the *Guide* went to press on whether to follow the same pattern in 2012.

Student loans

Around 80 per cent of students take out a student loan, and it is not difficult to see why. First of all, as noted earlier, it is very difficult to get by financially without one. If you don't take out a loan to cover your fees, then you will have to pay for them up front, and with living costs estimated to average more than £10,500 a year (over £11,700 in London), most students find it impossible to cover everything on savings and earnings alone. The only reasons to consider paying your fees up front might be if your parents are offering to meet the costs, or if a university is offering a discount if you do so. There are two types of student loan – one to cover the cost of tuition fees and another to help you cover the cost of living.

Tuition fees loan

In the case of fees loans, everyone can borrow up to the full amount needed to cover the cost of their tuition fees. Scots studying in Scotland are even better off, as there are no tuition fees for them to pay so no need for a loan.

Maintenance loan

The second type of student loan, a maintenance loan, is means-tested. The amount you can borrow therefore depends on a number of factors, including your family income, where you intend to study, and whether you expect to be living at home. Final-year students receive less than those in earlier years.

The maximum maintenance loan for students starting in 2012 will be £5,500 outside London for those who leave home to study; £7,675 if you live away from home and study in London; and £4,375 for those living at home.

Sixty-five per cent of the maintenance loan is available to you regardless of your family circumstances, while the remaining quarter is means-tested. If your parents are separated, divorced or widowed, then only the parent with whom you normally live will be assessed. However, if that parent has married again, entered into a civil partnership, or has a partner of the opposite sex, then both their incomes will be taken into account.

Maintenance loans in Scotland

In Scotland, the rules and regulations for maintenance loans are different. The loans available are lower than the rest of the UK, particularly in the case of students going to study in London, and the proportion that is means-tested is higher. In 2010–11 the maximum loan available was £5,710. All the latest details can be found at **www.saas.gov.uk**.

Loans for mature students

Mature students (those who are over the age of 25, married, or have supported themselves for at least three years before entering university) are assessed for loan and grant entitlements on their own income plus that of their spouse or partner. Grants are also available for those with

---

Maintenance grant and loan example for a first-year English student 2012

The mixture of grant and loan for a first-year English student in 2012–13 who is studying full-time and living away from home (but not in London). The maximum loan is £5,500, payable when the household income is £42,600. The loan thereafter declines to a minimum of £3,575 by £62,500.

Household income	Non-repayable grant	Maintenance loan	Total
£25,000 or less	£3,250	£3,875	£7,125
£30,000	£2,341	£4,330	£6,671
£35,000	£1,432	£4,784	£6,216
£40,000	£523	£5,239	£5,762
£45,000	£0	£5,288	£5,288
£50,000	£0	£4,788	£4,788
Over £62,500	£0	£3,575	£3,575

Department for Business, Innovation and Skills

children, for single parents, and for students with adult dependents. Further support is available for students with children through the Childcare Grant, the Parents' Learning Allowance, the Adult Dependants' Grant and Child Tax Credit system.

Payment of loans

Maintenance loans are usually paid in three instalments into your bank or building society account. English students should apply for grants and loans through Student Finance England, Welsh students through Student Finance Wales, Scottish students through the Student Awards Agency for Scotland, and those in Northern Ireland through Student Finance NI or their Education and Library Board. You should make your application as soon as you have received an offer of a place at university. European Union students from outside the UK will usually be sent an application form by the university that has offered them a place.

Repaying loans

The terms and conditions for student loans will change in 2012, but they will still be more favourable than anything available from banks, not least because the amount you pay back is linked to how much you earn, not how much you owe. In England at least – and possibly in the rest of the UK, depending on the decisions of the devolved administrations – interest rates will rise, but repayment will only start when graduates are earning £21,000 a year, rather than the current £15,000.

Full-time students will begin accumulating interest during their course and will start repaying in the April after graduation, if they earn over £21,000. They will then pay 9 per cent of income above £21,000, but repayments will stop during any period in which annual income falls below the threshold. Repayments are normally taken automatically through tax and National Insurance. If the loan has not been paid off after 30 years, no further repayments will be required.

During repayment periods, the amount of interest will vary according to how much you earn. If you earn less than £21,000, interest will be at the rate of inflation; between £21,000 and £41,000 you will be charged inflation plus up to three per cent; and if you earn over £41,000, interest will be at inflation plus the full three per cent. The Government website set up to guide prospective students through the changes includes a repayments calculator based on starting salaries for a range of careers, at **http://yourfuture.direct.gov.uk/calculate** .

Grants

In the good old days, most students didn't have to pay fees and many received relatively generous maintenance grants to help them cover day-to-day costs. After a brief disappearance, these non-repayable grants have made a comeback, and are particularly significant if you come from a low-income family. The size and type of grants available, and the rules and regulations governing their distribution, are different for each country of the UK. To receive a grant, students whose home is in England must apply through Student Finance England, in Wales to Student Finance Wales, those from Scotland must apply to the Student Awards Agency for Scotland, and those from Northern Ireland to Student Finance NI or their Education and Library Board. In addition, there are various types of bursaries and scholarships you can apply for, and other types of grants or support in each country to help students in particular circumstances, such as those that have a disability. What follows is a description of the maintenance grant arrangements country-by-country.

England

Students from England can apply for a maintenance grant from the Government and a bursary from their university. Those on full-time courses are entitled to a full grant of £3,250 in 2012-13 if their household income is £25,000 or less, or a partial grant if household income is between £25,000 and £42,600. Grants are paid into the student's bank account at the beginning of each term.

From 2012, there will be also a new £150-million National Scholarship Programme to help students from lower income families. Assistance may include reduced tuition fees or accommodation discounts. Each university will determine its own pattern of support. Some examples are given alongside the university profiles in Chapter 13 and details will be available on university and college websites from summer 2011.

One important rule to bear in mind is that for every £1 you receive in maintenance grant, the amount you can borrow in student loans falls by £1. Thus, it is not possible to have both a full grant and a maximum student loan. Bursaries and scholarships on offer from universities are discussed in a separate section below.

Northern Ireland

Arrangements for applying for and receiving means-tested maintenance grants and university bursaries and scholarships have been very similar in Northern Ireland to those in England, and are likely to remain so. The main difference so far has been a more generous upper limit (£3,475 for 2010–11) on grants in Northern Ireland. Up to £1,887 of the maintenance grant has been paid in substitution for an element of the student loan for maintenance. There is also a

---

Funding timetable

It is vital that you sort out your funding arrangements before you start university. Each funding agency has its own arrangements, and it is very important that you find out the exact details from them. The dates below give general indications of key dates.

March/April

» Online and paper application forms become available from funding agencies.

» You must contact the appropriate funding agency to make an application. For funding in England contact **www.studentfinanceengland.co.uk** rather than your LEA, as was the case before 2009.

» Complete application form as soon as possible. At this stage select the university offer that will be your first choice.

» Check details of bursaries and scholarships available from your selected universities.

May/June

» Funding agencies will give you details of the financial support they can offer.

» Last date for making an application to ensure funding is ready for you at the start of term (exact date varies significantly between agencies).

August

» Tell your funding agency if the university or course you have been accepted for is different from that originally given them.

September

» Take letter confirming funding to your university for registration.

» After registration, the first part of funds will be released to you.

Special Support Grant of the same value for full-time students who may be eligible to receive benefits such as Income Support or Housing Benefit while they are studying. However, you cannot receive both the maintenance grant and the Special Support Grant.

Wales

In addition to the normal loans, students from low-income backgrounds in Wales will also be able to apply for Assembly Learning Grants of up to £5,000. They will be scaled according to household income, which in 2011–12 ranged from £18,370 for a full grant to £50,000 for the smallest payment.

Scotland

In Scotland, the maintenance grant is known as a Young Students' Bursary (YSB), and is also means-tested and does not have to be repaid. For 2010–11, the maximum bursary is £2,640 if you come from a family with an annual income of £19,310 or less. If your family income is between this amount and £34,195 you will be entitled to a partial bursary, but if it is higher than £34,195 you will receive nothing. You can get an additional student loan if your family income is £21,760 or less. If you qualify for the YSB then you may also qualify for an additional loan of up to £605.

Part-time students

In 2012-13, part-time students in England will enjoy much-improved financial support, although they may have to pay higher fees into the bargain. The most that universities or colleges can charge for part-time courses is between £4,500 and £6,750 a year, and this cannot be more than 75 per cent of the full-time course fee.

New part-time students will be able to apply for a tuition fee loan that is not dependent on household income. Eligibility depends on the "intensity" of the course being at least 25 per cent of a full-time course, so that if a course takes six years to complete and the full-time equivalent takes three, the intensity will be 50 per cent.

Extra financial help will be available to disabled students studying on a part-time basis through Disabled Students' Allowances, which are paid in addition to the standard student finance package. They do not depend on income and do not have to be repaid.

Bursaries and scholarships

Bursaries and scholarships offered by universities and colleges are an important part of the student financial support system ushered in by the Labour Government to try to ensure that no one was excluded from university because they could not afford it. Virtually all institutions will be stepping up their offer when the fees go up in 2012.

Most support is targeted on students from poor backgrounds, but many scholarships are available (for academic achievement or sporting prowess) purely on merit. Some combine eligibility by family circumstances with academic excellence. Most schemes focus on entrants to degree courses, but some also reward performance at university.

Finding out about bursaries

There is now a bewildering variety of bursaries and scholarships on offer at UK universities, but it is worth shopping around to see what you can get. The full details are due for publication by the Universities and Colleges Admissions Service (UCAS) in July 2011 at **www.ucas.com**. The websites of individual institutions also carry details of scholarships, bursaries and other financial support available.

The whole system of bursaries and scholarships is overseen for England by the Office for Fair Access. It requires all universities to submit what are called "Access Agreements" that contain details of what fees they intend to charge and what scholarships and bursaries they are offering. Access Agreements also describe other kinds of financial support, such as "hardship funds". Some awards are guaranteed depending on your personal circumstances, while others are available through open competition. Copies of access agreements can be found at **www.offa.org.uk**.

Applying for bursaries and scholarships

Do take note of the application procedures for scholarships and bursaries, as these vary from institution to institution, and even from course to course within individual institutions. There may be a particular deadline you have to meet to apply for an award, or in some cases the university will work out for you whether you are entitled to an award by referring to your funding agency's financial assessment. If your personal circumstances change part way through a course then your entitlement to a scholarship or bursary may be reviewed.

If you feel you still need more help or advice on scholarships or bursaries, you can get this in most cases by referring to a university's website or prospectus. Some institutions also maintain a helpline. Some questions you will need answered include whether the bursary or scholarship is automatic or conditional and, if the latter, when you will find out whether your application has been successful. For some awards, you won't know whether you have qualified until you get your exam results.

Another obvious question is how the scholarship or bursary on offer compares with awards made by another university you might consider applying to. Watch out for institutions that list entitlements that others don't mention but you would get anyway.

Some institutions offer "fee remission" (a lower tuition fee) rather than scholarships or bursaries, which means you will have no more cash in hand during your course, but will owe less after you have graduated.

Living in one country, studying in another

As each of the countries of the UK develops its own distinctive system of student finance, there has been a need to address the question of how students leaving home in one country to go and study in another are affected. UK students who cross borders to study pay the tuition fees of their chosen university and are eligible for a fee loan to cover these. They are also entitled to apply for the scholarships or bursaries on offer from that institution. Any maintenance loan or grant will still come from the awarding body of their home country. The detailed arrangements for 2012–13 have not yet been announced. You must check for the latest information, as the funds available may differ from those for home students.

European Union laws stipulate that EU students from outside the UK must be charged the same tuition fees as those paid by nationals of the country where they are studying, rather than the higher fees paid by students from outside the EU. They can also apply for a fee loan and may be considered for some of the scholarships and bursaries offered by individual institutions. Only students who have been living and studying in the UK for at least three years can apply for a maintenance loan or grant. If you haven't, then you will need to apply for such assistance from the authorities in your own country. Tuition fee rules for non-UK European Union students are the same in Scotland as for Scottish students – that is, you do not have to pay a tuition fee. There are also no fees to pay for exchange students coming to the UK, including those on the Socrates Programme.

Further sources of income

If you are feeling daunted by the potential costs, you can take some comfort from this section which outlines just some of the ways you can raise additional funds.

Taking a gap year

Gap years have become increasingly popular both for travelling and to begin the process of earning money to help pay for higher education. They became an expensive proposition in 2011 because of the difference in fees for those deferring for a year, but normal service is likely to be resumed in 2012. Many students will want to travel, but others will be more focused on boosting the bank balance in preparation for beginning life as a student. Of course, there is still potentially much more to taking a gap year than short-term financial gain. The longer-term benefits of taking part in cultural exchanges and courses, expeditions, volunteering or structured work placements may extend to advantages in the graduate employment market. Both university admissions officers and employers look for evidence in candidates that they have more about them than academic ability. The experience you gain on a gap year can help you develop many of the attributes they are looking for, such as interpersonal, organisational and teamwork skills, leadership, creativity, experience of new cultures or work environments, and enterprise.

Various organisations can help you find voluntary work, if this is the way you prefer to spend at least some of your year out. Some examples include v (**www.vinspired.com**), Lattitude Global Volunteering (**www.lattitude.org.uk**) and Volunteer Africa (**www.volunteerafrica.org**).

Work placements can be structured or casual. An example of the structured variety is the Year in Industry Scheme (**www.yini.org.uk**). Sponsorship is also available mainly to those wishing to study engineering or business. To find out more, visit **www.everythingyouwantedto-know.com**.

Further Government support

There are various types of support available from Government sources for students in particular circumstances, other than the main loans, grants and bursaries.

» Undergraduates in financial difficulties can apply for help from the Access to Learning Fund (Financial Contingency Fund in Wales, Hardship Fund in Scotland, Support Funds in Northern Ireland). These are allocated by universities to provide support for anything from day-to-day study and living costs to unexpected or exceptional expense. The university decides which students need help and how much money to award them. These funds are often targeted at older or disadvantaged students and finalists.

» Students with children can apply for a Childcare Grant, worth £148.75 a week if you have one child and £225 a week if you have two or more children; and a Parents' Learning Allowance, for help with course-related costs, of between £50 and £1,508 a year.

» Students with disabilities can apply for a Disabled Students' Allowance, worth up to £20,520 a year for full-time students.

» Any students with a partner, or another adult such as a family member who is financially dependent on them, can apply for an Adult Dependants' Grant of up to £2,642 a year.

If you do not qualify for any of this kind of financial support you may still be able to apply for a Professional and Career Development Loan available from certain banks, in partnership with the Young People's Learning Agency. Students on a wide range of vocational courses can borrow from £300 to £10,000 at a fixed rate of interest to fund up to two years of learning.

Part-time work

The need to hold down a part-time job during term time is now a fact of life for more than half of students. Unsurprisingly, students from a working-class background are more likely to need to earn while they learn. A report by UNITE showed that 51 per cent of students from low-income families worked during term time, compared with just over a third of those from higher-income families. If you need or want to earn during term time, it is important to try to ensure that you do not work so many hours that it starts to affect your studies. A survey by the NUS found that 59 per cent of students who worked felt it had an impact on their studies, with 38 per cent missing lectures and over a fifth failing to submit coursework because of their part-time jobs.

Student employment agencies, which can now be found on many university campuses, can help you get the balance right. These introduce employers with work to students seeking work, sometimes even offering jobs within the university itself. But they also abide by codes of practice that regulate both minimum wages and the maximum number of hours worked in term time (typically 15 hours a week).

According to the Halifax bank, the average working student puts in about 18 hours a week, and makes around £6,000 a year out of this. Some firms, such as the big supermarkets, offer continuing part-time employment to their school part-time employees when they go to university. Some students make use of their expertise in areas like web design to earn some extra money, but most take on casual work in retail stores, restaurants, bars and call centres.

Most students, including those who don't work during term time, get a job during vacations. A Government survey found that 86 per cent of students in their second year of study or above worked during their summer vacation. Most of this kind of work is casual, but some is formalised in a scheme like STEP (**www.step.org.uk**) or may be part of a sponsorship programme. Many vacation jobs are fairly mundane, but with a bit of imagination and get-up-and-go, it is possible to find more interesting work. Some students broaden their experience by working abroad, others work as film extras, or do a variety of jobs at big events such as festivals. It is also a good idea to try to use the summer holidays to get some work experience in a field that has some relevance to your career aspirations. Even if you don't get paid, this can significantly enhance your chances of finding employment after graduation.

Total average weekly term-time costs by region	
London	**£247.90**
South East England	**£207.10**
Eastern England	**£206.50**
South West England	**£203.10**
Scotland	**£191.50**
West Midlands	**£186.20**
North West England	**£176.30**
Wales	**£175.50**
Yorkshire and Humberside	**£167.80**
East Midlands	**£166.50**
Northern Ireland	**£159.80**
North East England	**£157.50**
UK Average	**£193.50**

Information from the 2009 *Halifax Student Cost of Living Survey*

What you will need to spend money on
Living costs

The NUS estimated that in 2010–11 the average student living outside London would spend £10,500 a year on regular living costs, including rent, food, personal items, travel and leisure. For those living in the capital, the estimated average expenditure was £11,700, not including tuition fees, books or equipment. Little surprise, then, that a growing number of students are choosing to live at home and study at a local university. However, even this option is not necessarily low cost, once travel to and from the university is taken into account.

Certain costs are unavoidable. You have to have a roof over your head, eat enough, clothe yourself, and probably do a certain amount of travelling. But the cost of even these essential items can be cut down significantly through a mixture of shopping around and careful budgeting. If you set aside a certain amount of money a week for food, you will find it goes much further if you keep takeaways and ready-meals to a minimum, and stick to a shopping list when you go to a supermarket. Some catering outlets at your university or in the students' union may well offer good value meals, but probably the most economical way to eat is to cook and share meals with fellow students with whom you may be living in a shared house. Make sure you make full use of student travel cards and other offers and facilities available locally to help you cut the cost of travel. In certain locations, a bicycle is a very worthwhile investment (as is buying a lock for it).

If you can keep your essential costs down, then this will leave more money for what you would probably prefer to spend your money on – going out and personal items. Most students spend a good proportion of their budget on socialising, and this is certainly an important part of the university experience. You can have plenty of fun and keep your leisure costs down by making the most of your students' union's facilities and events.

Studying costs

The latest NUS survey estimated that the average student spent over £1,000 a year on costs associated with course work and studying, but the amount you spend will be determined largely by the nature of your course and what you study. Additional financial support may be available for certain expenditure, but this is unlikely to cover you fully for spending on books, stationery, equipment, fieldwork or electives. A long reading list could prove very expensive if you tried to buy all of the required books brand new. Find out as soon as possible which books are available either in your university library or local libraries. Another approach is to buy books second hand from students who no longer need them. Your students' union or your university may run second-hand book sales or offer a service helping students to buy and sell books.

Other costs

The first thing to say about any other costs you may incur is that you should do everything you can to keep them as low as possible. This may sound trite, but it is easy to let "other costs" get out of hand to the extent that they start to eat into your budget for day-to-day living. Mobile phone bills are a case in point. Look at your previous bills, or think carefully about your usage, and then shop around for the best deal to cover this. Remember that extras like downloading games or music, or sending pictures, can add significantly to your bill. Most of all, try to avoid getting tied up with an expensive and inflexible contract.

Overdrafts and credit cards

Other costs it is best to avoid are the more expensive forms of debt. Many banks offer free overdraft facilities for students, but if you go over that limit without prior arrangement, you can end up paying over the odds for your borrowing. Credits cards can be useful if managed properly. The best way to manage a credit card is to set up a direct debit to pay off your balance in full every month, which means you will avoid paying any interest. One of the worst ways is just paying the minimum charge each month, which can cost you a small fortune over a long period. If you are the kind of person that spends impulsively and doesn't keep track of that spending, then you are probably better off without a credit card.

Insurance

One kind of additional spending that can actually end up saving you money is getting insurance cover for your possessions. Most students arrive at university with a number of items, such as digital cameras, mobile phones, laptops and iPods, that are tempting to petty thieves. It is estimated that around a third of students fall victim to crime at some point during their time at university. If you shop around, you should be able to get a reasonable amount of cover for these kinds of items without it costing you an arm and a leg. It may be possible to add cover cheaply or for free to your parents' policy.

Planning your budget

University websites and many other sites offer guidance on preparing a budget, usually with the basic headings provided for you to complete. First, list out your likely income (grants, bursaries, loans, part-time work, savings, parental support) and then see how this compares with what you will spend. Try to be realistic and not too optimistic about both sides of the equation. Hopefully, you will end up either only slightly in the red, or preferably far enough in the black for you to be able to afford things you would really like to spend your money on.

Above all, keep track of your finances so that your university experience isn't ruined by money worries or finding you can't go to the ball because the cash machine has eaten your card.

Useful websites

This government website covers the basics of fees, loans, grants and other allowances: **www.direct.gov.uk/studentfinance**.
For details of the changes in England in 2012–13: **www.direct.gov.uk/yourfuture**

UCAS provides helpful advice: **www.ucas.com/students/studentfinance**
For England, visit Student Finance England through : **www.direct.gov.uk/studentfinance**
Office for Fair Access: **www.offa.org.uk**
For Wales, visit Student Finance Wales: **www.studentfinancewales.co.uk**
For Scotland, visit the Student Awards Agency for Scotland: **www.saas.gov.uk**
For Northern Ireland, visit Student Finance Northern Ireland: **www.studentfinanceni.co.uk**
All UK student loans are administered by the Student Loan Company: **www.slc.co.uk**
Educational Grants Advisory Service (EGAS): **www.family-action.org.uk/section.aspx?id=1924**
HM Revenue and Customs: **www.hmrc.gov.uk/students**
NHS Student Bursaries for students on pre-registration health professional and social work training courses: **www.nhsbsa.nhs.uk/students**

University tuition fees for UK/EU and international students

England

The fees given for UK/EU undergraduates are those proposed by universities for **2012–13**. At the time of going to press in spring 2011, these proposed fees were awaiting approval from the Office for Fair Access. Where universities have not announced their proposed fees, we have indicated this by "t.b.a". When there is a price range, this may include lower costs for Foundation degrees. See the individual university profile for details. The fees for International students are for **2011–12**.

	Undergraduate fees UK / EU students 2012–13	Undergraduate fees International students 2011—12
Anglia Ruskin	£8,300	£9,500–£10,500
Aston	£9,000	£11,700–£14,700
Bath	£9,000	£11,600–£14,800
Bath Spa	£9,000	£9,690–£10,315
Bedfordshire	t.b.a.	£9,300
Birkbeck	£4,500–£6,750[1]	£11,334
Birmingham	£9,000	£11,340–£14,650; £26,590 (clinical)
Birmingham City	£7,500–£9,000	£9,600–£11,050; £13,750 (Conservatoire)
Bolton	£6,300–£8,400	£8,400
Bournemouth	£8,200–£9,000	£9,500–£11,500
Bradford	£9,000	£9,800–£12,350
Brighton	£9,000	£9,960–£11,580; £23,678 (medicine)
Bristol	£9,000	£12,400–£15.550 ; £28,700 (dentistry, medicine)
Brunel	£9,000	£10,300–£12,600
Buckingham	£9,360[3]	£15,285[3]
Buckinghamshire New	£6,000–£8,000	£8,500–£9,300
Cambridge	£9,000[4]	£10,829–£18,000; £26,632 (medicine)[5]
Canterbury Christ Church	t.b.a	£9,150–£9,405
Central Lancashire (UCLan)	£9,000	£9,450–£10,450
Chester	£9,000	£7,920–£9,270
Chichester	£8,500	£8,775–£9,990
City	£9,000	£10,000–£11,500
Coventry	£7,500–£9,000	£9,060–£9,380
Cumbria	£8,400	£8,550
De Montfort	£9,000	£9,250
Derby	£6,995–£7,995	£9,250–£9,500
Durham	£9,000	£11,970–£15,300
East Anglia	£9,000	£11,000–£13,700; £23,250 (medicine)
East London	£9,000	£9,300–£13,200
Edge Hill	£9,000	£9,900
Essex	£9,000	£10,750–£12,750
Exeter	£9,000	£12,200–£14,500; £13,200–£21,500 (medicine)[2]
Gloucestershire	£8,250	£8,800
Goldsmiths	£9,000	£10,500–£14,100
Greenwich	t.b.a.	£9,375
Hertfordshire	£7,400–£8,500	£9,000–£10,000
Huddersfield	£7,950	£10,750–£11,750

	Undergraduate fees UK / EU students 2012–13	Undergraduate fees International students 2011—12
Hull	£9,000	£10,290–£12,495; £23,268 (medicine)
Imperial	£9,000	£22,450–£23,800; £26,250–£39,150 (medicine)
Keele	£9,000	£9,990–£11,800; £19,570–£22,900 (medicine)
Kent	£9,000	£11,230–£13,400
King's College London	£9,000	£13,250–£16,800; £31,150 (medicine)
Kingston	£8,500–£9,000	£9,950–£11,000
Lancaster	£9,000	£11,425–£14,580
Leeds	£9,000	£11,800–£15,600; £29,750 (medicine)
Leeds Metropolitan	£8,500	£10,500–£11,500
Leicester	£9,000	£10,750–£13,750; £24,895 (medicine)
Lincoln	£9,000	£10,395–£11,460
Liverpool	£9,000	£10,500–£13,500 ; £20,500 (dentistry & medicine)
Liverpool Hope	less than £9,000	£7,120–£8,400
Liverpool John Moores	£9,000	£10,050–£10,750
London Metropolitan	£4,500–£9,000	£10,080
London School of Economics	t.b.a.	£14,592
London South Bank	£8,450	£9,000–£9,240[2]
Loughborough	£9,000	£10,990–£14,400[2]
Manchester	£9,000	£11,700–£14,700; £26,800 (medicine)
Manchester Metropolitan	£8,000–£9,000	£9,030–£14,700
Middlesex	£9,000	£10,400
Newcastle	£9,000	£10,840–£13,905; £25,735 (medicine)
Northampton	t.b.a.	£9,100
Northumbria	£8,500	£9,450–£10,150; £11,350 (physiotherapy)
Nottingham	£9,000	£11,420–£14,970; £14,970–£20,420 (veterinary medicine) £15,780–£27,430 (medicine)
Nottingham Trent	t.b.a.	£9,950–£10,950
Oxford	£9,000[4]	£12,700–£14,550[5]; £26,500 (medicine)
Oxford Brookes	£9,000	£10,600–£11,300; £12,150 (physiotherapy)
Plymouth	£9,000	£9,104; £14,000–£21,500 (medicine)[2]
Portsmouth	£8,500	£9,600–£11,000
Queen Mary	£9,000	£11,300–£13,250; £16,442–£26,224 (medicine)
Reading	£9,000	£10,896–£12,996
Roehampton	£7,900–£8,250	£9,900
Royal Holloway	£9,000	£11,855–£13,780
Salford	£8,000–£9,000	£9,410–£11,700
Sheffield	£9,000	£11,490–£15,100; £27,290 (medicine)
Sheffield Hallam	£8,500	£10,080–£11,520
SOAS	£9,000	£13,230
Southampton	£9,000	£10,820–£13,840; £25,500 (medicine)
Southampton Solent	£7,800	£9,100
Staffordshire	t.b.a.	£9,385
Sunderland	£7,800–£8,500	£8,800
Surrey	£9,000	£11,000–£13,750
Sussex	£9,000	£10,900–£14,640; £23,678 (medicine)[2]

	Undergraduate fees UK / EU students 2012–13	Undergraduate fees International students 2011—12
Teesside	£8,500	£9,750
University of the Arts London	£9,000	£12,700
University College London	£9,000	£13,410–£7,560; £26,190 (medicine)
University for the Creative Arts	t.b.a.	£10,660
Warwick	£9,000	£12,325–£16,000
West of England	t.b.a.	£10,000–£10,500
West London	t.b.a.	£8,150–£9,540
Westminster	£9,000	£10,500
Winchester	£8,500	£9,200
Wolverhampton	£8,500	£9,450
Worcester	£8,100	£9,000
York	t.b.a.	£12,000–£15,600; £23,268 (medicine)
York St John	£8,500	£8,500–£11,600

1   On the basis of students studying for four years at 75 per cent intensity, equivalent to £6,000 to £9,000 full-time fees
2   Figures for 2010–11
3   Duration of degree course is two years
4   UK & EU students eligible for tuition fee support not liable for College fees (Cambridge and Oxford)
5   Plus College fees (£5,920, Oxford; £4,400–£5,200, Cambridge)

Wales

For **2012–13**, universities can to charge up to £9,000 (with the Welsh Assembly paying fees above £3,375 for most Welsh students; details to be confirmed). At the time of going to press in spring 2011, only Aberystwyth had announced its fees, subject to approval by the Higher Education Funding Council for Wales. The fees for International students are for **2011–12**.

	Undergraduate fees UK / EU students 2012–13	Undergraduate fees International students 2011—12
Aberystwyth	£9,000	£8,500–£9,500
Bangor	t.b.a.	£9,600–£11,800
Cardiff	t.b.a.	£10,700–£13,750; £24,500 (medicine, dentistry)
Cardiff (UWIC)	t.b.a.	£8,200–£9,400; £11,400 (podiatry)
Glamorgan	t.b.a.	£9,800
Glyndŵr	t.b.a.	£7,500
Newport	t.b.a.	£8,250–£9,250
Swansea	t.b.a.	£9,800–£12,600
Swansea Metropolitan	t.b.a.	£8,000
Trinity Saint David	t.b.a.	£9,348

Northern Ireland

The fee policy for **2012–13** was not confirmed at the time of going to press in spring 2011, so no UK/EU fees can be given.

	Undergraduate fees UK / EU students 2012–13	Undergraduate fees International students 2011–12
Queen's, Belfast	t.b.a.	£10,730–£13,145; £14,534–£26,534 (medicine)
Ulster	t.b.a.	£9,225

Scotland

The Scottish Government had not confirmed its policy for **2012–13** at the time of going to press in spring 2011. However, it is expected that there will continue to be no fees for Scottish and EU students, but that charges for students from elsewhere in the UK will increase. The figures given here are for **2011–12**. The fees for International students are for **2011–12**.

	Fees for Scottish students and eligible non-UK EU students 2011–12	Fees for students from else-where in the UK 2011–12	Undergraduate fees International students 2011–12
Aberdeen	Tuition fee paid by SAAS	£1,820	£10,500–£13,200
		£2,895 (medicine)	£24,000 (medicine)
Abertay	Tuition fee paid by SAAS	£1,820	£9,500
Dundee	Tuition fee paid by SAAS	£1,820	£9,200–£13,700
		£2,895 (medicine)	£16,750–£25,500 (medicine)
Edinburgh	Tuition fee paid by SAAS	£1,820	£12,050–£15,850
		£2,895 (medicine)	£15,850–£33,200 (medicine)
Edinburgh Napier	Tuition fee paid by SAAS	£1,820	£9,310–£10,820
Glasgow	Tuition fee paid by SAAS	£1,820	£11,500–£15,000
		£2,895 (medicine)	£22,500 (veterinary medicine)
			£27,000 (medicine)
			£32,000 (dentistry)
Glasgow Caledonian	Tuition fee paid by SAAS	£1,820	£9,700–£14,500
Heriot-Watt	Tuition fee paid by SAAS	£1,820	£10,120–£12,760
Highlands and Islands	Tuition fee paid by SAAS	£1,820	£7,200–£8,580
Queen Margaret	Tuition fee paid by SAAS	£1,820	£10,170–£11,230
Robert Gordon	Tuition fee paid by SAAS	£1,820	£9,550–£11,500
St Andrews	Tuition fee paid by SAAS	£1,820	£13,500
		£2,895 (medicine)	£20,500 (medical science)
Stirling	Tuition fee paid by SAAS	£1,820	£10,200–£12,250
Strathclyde	Tuition fee paid by SAAS	£1,820	£11,330–£15,400
West of Scotland	Tuition fee paid by SAAS	£1,820	£10,000–£10,500

Scholarships

Each university in the United Kingdom has its own selection of scholarships. Consult university websites. Course-related scholarships are included on the UCAS site in the description of a course (**www.ucas.com**).

8 Finding Somewhere to Live

The first decision of your university life – even before choosing which courses to take – is where to live. With the number of students continuing to rise all over the UK, the search for affordable and acceptable housing is becoming tougher every year. The property bubble may have burst, but rents are continuing to rise, particularly in the student market. The National Union of Students (NUS) reports that average rents shot up 22 per cent in three years at the end of the last decade, with the average student now paying more than £100 a week.

Living at home

For a growing number of undergraduates, the solution to this problem is to live at home – particularly now that fees are rising so steeply. With repayments starting only after graduation, the new fee regime will leave students no worse off during their time at university. But many undergraduates will be more careful about the debts they run up, and housing is the biggest single item in the student budget.

The pattern of recent applications shows that the trend towards studying from home is accelerating, and there is no reason to think that will change while the downturn continues. Indeed, it may be a permanent shift, given the rising costs and the willingness of many young people to live with their parents well into their twenties. More than one student in five now lives at home – a figure that is inflated by the large number of mature students, but still a sign of the times.

Living away from home

Yet most of those who can afford it still see moving away to study as integral to the rite of passage that student life represents. Some have little option because, in spite of the expansion of higher education, the course they want is not available locally. Others are happy to travel to secure their ideal place and widen their experience.

For the lucky majority, the search for accommodation will be over quickly because the university can offer a place in one of its halls of residence or self-catering flats. The choice may come down to the type of accommodation and whether or not to do your own cooking. For others, however, the offer of a degree place will be the start of an anxious search for a room in a strange city.

Going to university will oblige those who take the "away" route to think for the first time about practicalities of living independently. This can make the decision about where to live – both in terms of location and the type of accommodation – doubly difficult, but vital to get right. It may even influence your choice of university, since there are big differences across the sector in the cost and standard of accommodation – and your choice will have a significant impact on the quality of your life as a student.

How much will it cost?

Students in the UK are estimated to spend almost twice as much on rent as their combined spending on food, going out, books and music. The NUS survey found that even in 2009–10 students were paying a weekly rent of nearly £100, with those living in London paying more than £150 a week and those at the cheaper end of the spectrum in Belfast and Lancaster paying around £70 a week. But in this case, averages are becoming meaningless because the range of rents is so wide, particularly in London. Research by Drivers Jonas Deloitte suggested that the average in London was actually £134 a week but that some students were paying £300.

There is undoubtedly a growing luxury end to the student market, even while others live in much cheaper, often sub-standard accommodation. Most universities with a range of accommodation find that their most expensive rooms fill up first and students appear to have higher expectations – almost half of all the rooms in the NUS survey had en-suite facilities. The privately run blocks, which the union blames for pushing up prices, certainly tend to be well-appointed as well as popular. The Deloitte survey found that 2,500 purpose-built residential places had been added in London in 2009–10, with another 4,000 under construction.

Generally speaking, the cost of student accommodation is highest in London and the southeast of England and lowest in the Midlands and North of England, Wales, Scotland and Northern Ireland. But the NUS survey shows considerable variations within those regions.

NatWest Student Living Index 2010

The NatWest Student Living Index was calculated as follows: for each town listed, average local weekly student expenditure on living and accommodation costs was divided by average local weekly income for working students. This provided a value, by which 25 university towns were ranked. At the top is London, where an average student earns £167.48 from part-time work during terms. At the bottom was York, not least because students study for longer than the UK average and so have less time for work.

1	(NE)	London	14	(19)	Nottingham
2	(17)	Dundee	15	(12)	Leeds
3	(5)	Manchester	16	(4)	Reading
4	(13)	Plymouth	17	(10)	Edinburgh
5	(3)	Glasgow	18	(14)	Cardiff
6	(11)	Birmingham	19	(1)	Brighton
7	(15)	Portsmouth	20	(18)	Norwich
8	(8)	Cambridge	21	(NE)	Exeter
9	(9)	Oxford	22	(NE)	Southampton
10	(16)	Newcastle	23	(7)	Leicester
11	(6)	Bristol	24	(NE)	Belfast
12	(NE)	Sheffield	25	(20)	York
13	(2)	Liverpool		NE indicates a new entry in 2010	

Renting in new blocks of flats – and especially those that are en suite – is often more expensive than sharing a house with friends, but the latter is a lot more common after the first year.

It is important to remember that both your living costs and your potential earnings should be factored into your calculations when deciding where to live. While living costs in London are, unsurprisingly, the highest, potential earnings are nearly double those in other parts of the country. Students in London were earning more than £5,000 a year on average in 2009–10, according to the NatWest Student Living Index, making it the most cost-effective place to study in the bank's estimation. Of course, those earnings figures may be lower this year, whereas student rents undoubtedly have risen.

The choices you have

No longer are you faced with a straightforward choice between a university hall of residence and a poor quality rented house. A report from the NUS puts accommodation into 16 categories, ranging from luxurious university halls to a bedsit in a shared house. The choices include:

» University hall of residence, with individual study bedrooms and a full catering service; many will have en-suite accommodation.
» University halls, flats or houses where you have to provide your own food.
» Private, purpose-built student accommodation.
» Rented houses or flats, shared with fellow students.
» Living at home.
» Living as a lodger in a private house.

This chapter will provide you with more information to help you decide where you would like to live and whether you can afford it.

Making your choice

Financial considerations are not the only factor you should consider when deciding where to live. Feeling comfortable and happy in your student home is of crucial importance to your success at university and to the quality of your experience. It is therefore worth investing some time to find the right place, and to avoid the false economy of choosing somewhere cheap where you may end up feeling depressed and isolated. Most students who drop out of university do so in the first few months, when homesickness and loneliness can be felt most acutely. Being warm and well fed is likely to have a positive effect on your studies.

Perhaps for these reasons, most undergraduates in their first year plump for living in university halls, which offer a convenient, safe and reliable standard of accommodation, along with a supportive community environment. If meals are included, then this adds further peace of mind both for students and their parents. But nowadays most are self-catering, with groups of students sharing a kitchen. The sheer number of students – especially first years – in halls also makes this form of accommodation an easy way of meeting people from a wide range of courses and making friends.

Wherever you chose to live, there are some general points you will need to consider, such as how safe the neighbourhood seems to be, and how long it might take you to travel to and from the university – especially during rush hour. A recent survey of travel time between term-time accommodation and the university found that most students in London can expect a commute of at least 30 minutes and often over an hour, while students living in Wales are usually much less than 30 minutes away from their university. Be sure to make use of any local or national

Student Travel Card and any university or students' union transport system that may be provided to help you get back to your accommodation cheaply and safely.

Information to help you
In the university profiles (which are in the second half of this book), we provide details of what accommodation each university offers. You will be able to find the following:

» The number of university-provided places. A quick check against the number of undergraduates will show you how well provided for the university is.
» The percentage of places that are catered.
» The percentage of places that are self-catered.
» The weekly cost of catered and self-catered accommodation.
» A summary of the offer of accommodation that can be made to first years.
» A summary of the offer of accommodation that can be made to international students.
» The web address for details of the university's accommodation provision.

Continuing to live at home
The first decision must be whether to move at all. If the course you want is within reasonable travelling time and you are happy in the family home, you may decide to stay there – particularly if money is tight. You can always move out later, as many students do when they have met others with whom they want to share.

The number of students living at home has been rising for several years. The Sutton Trust published a report in 2008 which found that those choosing this option tended to be state school or college students, and usually not those with the highest grades. There was also a strong representation of Asian students in the sample. But it is reasonable to assume that, in future, more applicants of all backgrounds will be considering student life at home.

The potential financial benefits of this are obvious, and there may also be advantages in terms of academic work if the alternative involves shopping, cooking and cleaning, as well as the other distractions of a student flat. The obvious downside is that you may miss out on a lot of the student experience, especially the social scene and the opportunity to make new friends.

There is no evidence that students living at home do any worse academically. The quality of your home environment should influence your decision when weighing up whether or not to

---

Money paid weekly for accommodation

Average weekly spend

	Overall	Catered halls	Self-catered halls/flats houses	Rented flats/ houses off campus	Own flats/ houses off campus	Home parents/family off campus
	£90.70	£156.70	£104.60	£106.60	£76.80	£14.30

Distribution of average weekly spend as a percentage

£0	£1–£60	£61–£80	£81–£100	£101–£150	Over £150
19%	12%	27%	22%	13%	7%

Adapted from Sodexo University Lifestyle Survey 2010

take this option. If it is stressful or not conducive to studying, then you are probably better off moving out, even if it means having to take a job to make ends meet. On the other hand, there is a lot to be said for making use of supportive and flexible home conditions where these exist. If you are studying at a "new" university, you are more likely to have fellow students who also live at home.

What universities offer

You might think that opting to live in university accommodation is the most straightforward choice, especially since first-year students are invariably given priority in the allocation of places in halls of residence. Certainly if you go for university residences you benefit from being able to make arrangements in advance and at a distance, rather than having to be in the right place at the right time, as is often the way when searching for private housing. However, you may still need to select from a range of options because some universities will have a variety of accommodation on offer. You will need to consider which best suits your pocket and your preferred lifestyle.

New university accommodation

At the top end of the market, partnerships between universities and private firms have recently begun to lead the way. Private organisations such as UNITE plc (**www.unite-students.com**) and LibertyLiving (**www.libertyliving.co.uk**) have been paid by universities to build and manage some of the most luxurious student accommodation the UK sector has ever seen. Rooms in these complexes are typically en suite and include facilities such as your own phone line, satellite TV and internet access. Shared kitchens are also top quality and fitted out with all the latest equipment. This kind of accommodation naturally comes at a higher price, but offers the advantages of flexibility both in living arrangements and through a range of payment options. Private companies have invested more than £5 billion into new student flats in recent years, continuing to do so even while the recession brought the rest of the construction business to a halt

Halls of residence

Many new or recently refurbished university-owned halls offer a standard of accommodation that is not far short of the privately built residences. One of the reasons for this is that rooms in these halls can be offered to conference delegates during vacations. Even though these halls are also at the pricier end of the spectrum, you will probably find that they are in great demand, and you may have to get your name down for one quickly to secure one of the fancier rooms. That said, you can often get a guarantee of some kind of university accommodation if you give a firm acceptance of an offered place by a certain date in the summer. This may not be the case if you have gained your place through Clearing – although rooms in private halls might still be on offer at this stage.

While a few halls are single-sex, most are mixed, and often house over 500 students. They are therefore great places for making friends and becoming part of the social scene. One possible downside is that they can also be noisy places where it can be difficult at times to get down to some work. The more successful students learn, before too many essay deadlines and exams start to loom, to get the balance right between all-night partying and escaping to the library for some undisturbed study time. Some libraries, especially new ones, are also now open 24 hours a day. If you feel in need of either personal or study support, this is often at hand either through a counselling service or from fellow students.

University self-catering accommodation

An alternative to halls, offered particularly by some older universities, are smaller, self-catering properties fitted out with a shared kitchen and other living areas. Students looking for a more independent and flexible lifestyle may prefer this option. Remember that if you choose this kind of university housing, you will be responsible for feeding yourself, and you may also have heating and lighting bills to pay. University properties are often on campus or nearby, and so travel costs should not pose a problem.

Catering in university accommodation

Many universities have responded to a general increase in demand from students for a more independent lifestyle, by providing more flexible catering facilities. A range of eateries, from fast food outlets to more traditional refectories, can usually be found on campus. Students in university accommodation may now be offered pay-as-you-eat deals as an alternative to full-board packages.

What after the first year?

After your first year of living in university residences you may well wish, and will probably be expected, to move out to other accommodation. The only exceptions are in collegiate universities – particularly Oxford and Cambridge – which may allow you to stay on in college halls for another year or two, and particularly for your final year. Students from outside the EU are also sometimes guaranteed accommodation. There are also some universities, such as Loughborough, where it is not uncommon for students to move back in to halls for their final year.

Practical details

If you have decided to start out in university accommodation, then you will probably be expected to sign an agreement to cover rent. Contract lengths vary. They can be for around 40 weeks, which includes the Christmas and Easter holiday periods or for just the length of the three university terms. These term-time contracts are common when a university uses its rooms for conferences during vacations, and you will be required to leave your room empty during these weeks. It is therefore advisable to check whether the university has secure storage space for you to leave your belongings – otherwise you will have to make arrangements to take all your belongings home between terms. Depending on where you are in the country, it may be possible to pay to store your belongings somewhere privately, such as Big Yellow Self

---

Type of accommodation by year of study

1st year		2nd year onwards	
Self-catered halls	27%	Privately let flats/houses	52%
University self-catered flats/houses	19%	At home with parents/family	12%
At home with parents/family	15%	Commercially let flats/houses	10%
Privately let flats/houses	14%	Own flat/house	9%
Catered halls	13%	University self-catered flats/houses	8%
Own flat/house	10%	Self-catered halls	7%
Commercially let flats/houses	3%	Catered halls	3%

Sodexo University Lifestyle Survey 2008

Storage, but this will not necessarily be cheap. International students may be offered special arrangements, in which they can stay in halls during the short vacation periods. Organisations like **www.hostuk.org** can also arrange for international students to stay in a UK family home at holiday times such as the Christmas break.

Being a lodger or staying in a hostel

A small number of students live as a lodger in a family home, an option most frequently taken up by international students. The usual arrangement is for a study bedroom and some meals to be provided, while other facilities such as a washing machine are shared. Students with particular religious affiliations or those from certain countries may wish to consider living in one of a number of hostels run by charities catering for certain groups. Most of these can be found in London.

Renting from the private sector

Every university city or town is awash with privately owned accommodation available via agencies or direct from landlords. Indeed, there has been so much of it that so-called "student ghettoes", where local residents feel outnumbered, have become hot political issues. Into this traditional market in rented flats and houses have come the new private-sector complexes and residences, often created in partnership with universities, adding considerably to the private-sector options. Some are on university campuses. Others are in city centres and usually open to students of more than one university. Examples can be seen online through sites such as **www.accommodationforstudents.com**, which are listed at the end of this chapter.

While there are always exceptions, a much more professional attitude and approach to managing rented accommodation has emerged among smaller providers, thanks to a combination of greater regulation and increasing competition. Nevertheless, it is wise to take certain precautions when seeking out private residences.

How to start looking for rented property

Contact your university's accommodation service and ask for their list of approved rented properties. Some have a Student Accommodation Accreditation Scheme, run in collaboration with the local council. To get onto an approved list under such schemes, landlords must show they are adhering to basic standards of safety and security, such as having an up-to-date gas and electric safety certificate. University accommodation officers should also be able to advise you on any hidden charges. For instance, you may be asked to pay a booking or reservation fee to secure a place in a particular property, and fees for references or drawing up a tenancy agreement are also sometimes charged. The practice of charging a "joining fee", however, has been outlawed. It would also be wise to speak to older students with first-hand experience of renting in the area. Certain companies in the area will often be notorious among second and third years and therefore you can seek to avoid them.

Making a choice

Once you have made an initial choice on the area you would like to live in and the size of property you are looking for, the next stage is to look at possible places. If you plan to share, it is important that you all have a look at the property. If you will be living by yourself, take a friend with you when you go to view a property, since he or she can help you assess what you see objectively, and avoid any irrational or rushed on-the-spot decisions. Don't let yourself be pushed into signing on the dotted line there and then. Take time to visit and consider a number of options. It is often helpful to spend some time in the area in which you may be living, to check out the local facilities, transport, and the general environment at various times of the day and different days of the week. If you can stay in the area for a few days, this will help you get a more accurate idea of what living in the district will be like.

If you are living in private rented accommodation, it is likely that at least some of your neighbours will not be students. Local people often welcome students, but resentment can build up, particularly in areas of towns and cities that are dominated by student housing. It is important to respect your neighbours' rights, and not to behave in an anti-social manner.

Preparing for sharing

The people you are planning to share a house with may not be as unsavoury as the characters in the TV comedy *The Young Ones,* but you can be sure they will have some habits that you find at least mildly irritating. How well you cope with some of the downsides of sharing will be partly down to the kind of person you are – where you are on the spectrum between laid back and highly strung – but it will help a lot if you are co-habiting with people whose outlook on day-to-day living is not too far out of line with your own. Some students sign for their second year houses as early as November and while it is good to be ahead of the rush, in such a short time at the university you may not have met your best friends yet. If you have not already selected your own group of friends, universities and landlords can help by taking personal preferences and lifestyle into account when grouping tenants together. You can make this task easier if you give full details about yourself when filling in accommodation application forms.

Potential issues to consider when deciding whether to move into a shared house include whether any of the housemates smoke, own a loud musical instrument that they may decide to play at any time of the day or night, or have a habit of spending hours on the telephone. With most students owning a mobile phone, the latter should not be a problem unless someone decides to save on their mobile bills by using a landline in your shared house instead. If this is the case, then you should arrange for individual billing, provided by a number of phone companies. It will also be important to sort out broadband arrangements that will work for everyone in the house, and that you will be able to arrange access to the university system. It may seem like a drag, but it is usually a good idea to agree from the outset a rota for everyone to share in the household cleaning chores. Otherwise it is almost certain that you will live in a state of permanent unhygienic squalor or that one or two individuals will be left to clear up everyone else's mess.

The practical details about renting

It is a good idea to ask whether your house is covered by an accreditation scheme or code of standards. Such codes provide a clear outline of what constitutes good practice as well as the responsibilities of both landlords and tenants. Adhering to schemes like the National Codes of Standards for Larger Student Developments compiled by Accreditation Network UK (**www.anuk.org.uk**) may well become a requirement for larger properties, including those managed by universities, now that the Housing Act is in force.

At the very least, make sure that if you are renting from a private landlord, you have his or her telephone number and home address. Some can be remarkably difficult to contact when repairs are needed or deposits returned.

Multiple occupation

If you are renting a private house it may be subject to the 2004 Housing Act in England and

Wales (similar legislation applies in Scotland and Northern Ireland). Licenses are compulsory for all private Houses in Multiple Occupation (HMOs) with three or more stories that house five or more unrelated residents. The provisions of the Act also allow local authorities to designate whole areas in which HMOs of all sizes must be licensed. The good news is that these regulations are likely to be applied in sections of university towns and cities where most students live. This means that a house must be licensed, well-managed and must meet various health and safety standards, and its owner subject to various financial regulations. The bad news is that this could lead to a reduction in the number and range of privately rented properties on the market, or an increase in rental prices. Oxford City Council is the first authority to require HMOs of all sizes within the city to be licensed by January 2012.

Tenancy agreements

Whatever kind of accommodation you go for, you must be sure to have all the paperwork in order and be clear about what you are signing up to before you move in. If you are taking up residence in a shared house, flat or bedsit, the first document you will have to grapple with is a tenancy agreement or lease offering you an "assured shorthold tenancy". Since this is a binding legal document you should be prepared to go through every clause with a fine-tooth comb. Remember that it is much more difficult to make changes or overcome problems arising from unfair agreements once you are a tenant than before you become one.

You would be well advised to seek help, in the likely event of your not fully understanding some of the clauses. Your university accommodation office or students' union are a good place to start – they should know all the ins and outs, and have model tenancy agreements to refer to. A Citizens Advice Bureau or Law Advice Centre should also be able to offer you free advice. In particular, watch out for clauses that may make you jointly responsible for the actions of others with whom you are sharing the property. If you name a parent as a guarantor to cover any costs not covered by you, then they may also be liable for charges levied on all tenants for any damage that might not be your fault. A rent review clause could allow your landlord to increase the rent at will, whereas without such a clause, they are restricted to one rent rise a year. Make sure you keep a copy of all documents, and get a receipt (and keep it somewhere safe) for anything you have had to pay for that is the landlord's responsibility.

Contracts tend to be longer than for university accommodation – they will frequently commit you to paying rent for 52 weeks of the year. There are probably more advantages than disadvantages to this kind of arrangement. It means you don't have to move out during vacation periods, which you might have to in university halls to make way for conference delegates. You can store your belongings in your room when you go away (but don't leave anything really valuable behind if you can help it). You may be able to negotiate a rent discount for those periods when you are not staying in the property. The other advantage, particularly important for cash-strapped students, is that you have a base from which to find work and hold down a job during the vacations. Term dates are also not as dictatorial as they might be in halls; if you rent your own house then you can come back when you wish.

Deposits

On top of the agreed rent, you will need to provide a deposit or bond to cover any possible breakages or damage. This will probably set you back the equivalent of another month's rent. The deposit should be returned, less any deductions, at the end of the contract. However, be warned that disputes over the return of deposits are quite common, with the question of what constitutes reasonable wear and tear often the subject of disagreements between landlords and tenants. To protect students from unscrupulous landlords who withhold deposits without good reason, the 2004 Housing Act has introduced a National Tenancy Deposit Scheme under which deposits are held by an independent body rather than by the landlord. This is designed to ensure that deposits are fairly returned, and that any disputes are resolved swiftly and cheaply.

Inventories and other paperwork

You should get an inventory and schedule of condition of everything in the property. This is another document that you should check very carefully – and make sure that everything listed is as described. Write on the document anything that is different. The National Union of Students even suggests taking photographs of rooms and equipment when you first move in (putting the date on the pictures if you are using a digital camera), to provide you with additional proof should any dispute arise when your contract ends and you want to get your deposit back. If you are not offered an inventory, then make one of your own. You should have someone else witness and sign this, send it to your landlord, and keep your own copy. Keeping in contact with your landlord throughout the year and developing a good relationship with him or her will also do you no harm, and may be to your advantage in the long run.

You should ask your landlord for a recent gas safety certificate issued by a qualified CORGI engineer, a fire safety certificate covering the furnishings, and a record of current gas and electricity meter readings. Take your own readings of meters when you move in to make sure these match up with what you have been given, or make your own records if the landlord doesn't supply this information. This also applies to water meters if you are expected to pay water rates (although this isn't usually the case).

If you are sharing a house only with other full-time students, then you will not have to pay Council Tax. However, you may be liable to pay a proportion of the Council Tax bill if you are sharing with anyone who is not a full-time student. You may need to get a Council Tax exemption certificate from your university as evidence that you do not need to pay Council Tax or should pay only a proportion, depending on the circumstances.

Security in rented accommodation

As students living in private housing are twice as likely to be burgled as those in university halls, it is worth running through this security checklist provided by the NUS:

» Check that the front and back doors are fitted with five-lever mortise locks in addition to standard catch locks.
» Make sure the door to your room has a lock, and always lock up when you leave it, especially for long periods such as during vacations.
» Check the locks and catches on accessible windows, especially those at ground-floor level.
» Before you move in, try to talk to neighbours about how safe the area is and whether there have been many instances of burglary or car crime.
» Ask your landlord to ensure that all previous tenants and holders of keys no longer have copies.
» If you find a property that you are keen to rent, but you are unsure about some of the security aspects, discuss your concerns with the letting agency or landlord . They may be able to make the necessary changes to make the property more secure before you move in.

Safety and security

Once you have arrived and settled in, remember to take care of your own safety and the security of your possessions. You are particularly vulnerable as a fresher, when you are still getting used to your new-found independence. This may help explain why a fifth of students are burgled or robbed in the first six weeks of the academic year. Take care with valuable portable items such as mobile phones, iPods and laptops, all of which are tempting for criminals. Ensure you don't have them obviously on display when you are out and about. If your mobile phone is stolen, call your network or 08701 123 123 to immobilise it. Students' unions, universities and the police will provide plenty of practical guidance when you arrive. Following their advice will reduce the chance of you becoming a victim of crime, and so able to enjoy living in the new surroundings of your chosen university town.

Insurance

It is a false economy not to have adequate insurance to cover you for the loss or theft of valuable items. Your students' union will probably be able to advise you on where to go for the best deals and there may even be a shop on campus that can help you. It may be that your parents' insurance will cover you when you are a student, and you should certainly check this. You should also keep a record somewhere safe of the serial and model numbers of expensive electrical equipment. If you have to claim on your insurance for these items you will need these details. Remember that courting the notion that "it won't happen to me" is one of the best ways to ensure that it probably will.

Useful websites

In the university profiles later in this book, we give an indication of costs for university-provided accommodation and details of university accommodation websites.

For advice on a range of housing issues, visit:
www.nus.org.uk/en/Student-Life/Housing-Advice
The 2009–10 Accommodation Costs Survey carried out by the NUS and Unipol can be read downloaded from the NUS website (**www.nusconnect.org.uk)** or the Unipol website (**www.unipol.org.uk).**
The Shelter website has separate sections covering different housing regulations in England, Wales, Scotland and Northern Ireland: **www.shelter.org.uk**

Private accommodation

As examples of providers of private hall accommodation, visit:
www.unite-students.com or **www.libertyliving.co.uk**

There are a number of sites that will help you find accommodation and/or potential housemates. Among the best-known are:
www.accommodationforstudents.com
www.homesforstudents.co.uk
www.studentaccommodation.org
www.studentpad.co.uk
www.let4students.com
www.studentbunk.com

9 Sporting Opportunities

Sports facilities in universities have improved out of all recognition over the past decade. Such has been the scale of investment that some of the biggest multi-sports developments in recent years have been on university campuses, where facilities nationally are said to be worth an astonishing £20 billion. As a result, half of all universities were chosen as pre-Olympics training bases for Great Britain squads and a number will host other nations' teams in the run-up to the Games themselves.

University sport may not be big business, as it is in the USA, but it has become increasingly important in the student experience. Gone are the days when physical exercise was a minority pursuit on campus and regarded as not cool. Today it is said that at least 1.7 million students take part in regular physical activity, from gym sessions to competitive individual or team sports.

Some of the new facilities are so specialist that they are reserved for elite (often international) performers. It is expected that, as in the Beijing Olympics, more than half of Team GB at London 2012 will be either students or relatively recent graduates. But most campus facilities are available for everyday use by students.

Where universities have been able to attract Lottery funding or have made sport a priority in their portfolio of subjects, the amenities can be breathtaking. Naturally, not all can aspire to those heights, but most now offer resources to compare with the best available commercially – and usually at a fraction of the price. So many facilities are also available to local communities that a recent survey of usage found that more than 20 per cent of bookings were by non-students.

Sporting opportunities

Being a full-time student offers unrivalled opportunities to discover and play a vast range of sports. Many universities still encourage departments not to schedule lectures and seminars on Wednesday afternoons, to give students free time for sport. Even those who spend long hours in the laboratory have more time for leisure activities as a student than they will be able to spare later in life.

There are student-run clubs for all the major sports and – particularly at the larger universities – a host of minor ones. Or you can content yourself with high-quality gyms, with staff on hand to devise personalised training regimes. The cost varies widely between universities, and membership fees can represent a large amount to lay out at the start of the year, but most provide good value if you are going to be a regular user.

The course is rightly still top of most students' priorities when choosing a university, but sporting options play a growing role in the process. More and more students want to keep fit, even if they don't play competitive sport, and universities have joined a race of their own to provide the best facilities. Sport may still be a secondary consideration for most applicants, but particularly good (or particularly poor) facilities can sometimes tip the balance.

Sport for all

For most universities, it is in the area of "sport for all" that most attention has been focused. Beginners are welcomed and coaching provided in a range of sports, from ultimate Frisbee to tai-chi, that would be difficult to match outside the higher education system. Check on university websites to see whether your usual sport is available, but don't be surprised if you come across a new favourite when you have the opportunity to try out some new sports as a student. Many universities have programmes designed to encourage students to take up a new sport, with expert coaching provided.

All universities are conscious of the need to provide for a spread of ability. Sports scholarships for elite performers are now commonplace, but there will be plenty of opportunities, too, for beginners. University teams demand a hefty commitment in terms of training and practice sessions – often several times a week – and in many sports standards are high. University teams often compete in local and national leagues.

For those who don't aspire to such heights, or whose interests are primarily social, there are thriving internal, or intramural, leagues. These provide opportunities for teams from halls of residence or faculties, or even a group of friends, to participate on a regular basis. Nor is university sport a male preserve – student teams were among the pioneers in mixed sport and are still strong in areas such as women's cricket, football and rugby.

First year student-run sport

Halls of residence and university-owned flats will generally offer an array of sports teams. These are normally organised by the Sports Captain, elected the year previously as part of the Junior Common Room, whose responsibility it is to organise trials and pick the teams, as well as to arrange fixtures for the year. Hall sport is a great way of meeting like-minded people from your accommodation and over the course of the years, friendly rivalries often develop with other halls or flats. These competitions will take place over all three terms and will culminate with a winning team in each sport so, while it may start as a great way of playing sport and making friends, it will end very competitively. In the summer term, there is also often a Sports Day that is either restricted to your particular hall of residence, or one that is organised against another hall.

Generally there will be teams for football (both five- and 11-a-side), hockey, netball, cricket, tennis, squash, badminton and even golf. If your lodgings are smaller then don't worry, they are often twinned with similar flats to enable as many first-year students as possible to get involved in freshers' sport. The number and variety of teams will often depend on what has gone on in years gone by, as well as on the enthusiasm and dedication of the Sports Captain, so it is also up to you to make sure that he or she is doing a good job.

Intramural sport

As university numbers have increased, so has the standard of student sports teams. And, while there are many keen sportsmen and women in higher education, most won't quite have the ability to play for a university team. This is where intramural (Latin for "inside the wall") competitions come in. Intramural sport allows students to compete against their fellow students in an organised league, something that has proved massively popular. From hall, subject and society teams, to corridor, house and simply "mates' teams", intramural sport can be taken as seriously as you wish, but offers everybody the opportunity to get out there and play.

Unsurprisingly, the main winner in this set-up has been football. Most teams will offer both a five-a-side and 11-a-side option, with the former proving particularly popular. In large universities, the big departments have been known to field as many as 15 five-a-side teams. The competitions tend to span all three terms, giving you a lot of playing time over the year. If you want to get involved, there should be little to stop you and the cost is generally very reasonable.

For women, hockey and netball have led the way and there are also many unisex hockey and football leagues. Whilst each university will vary, badminton, basketball, cricket, tennis and squash are also all common in most campuses' intramural set-ups.

Other opportunities

You may even end up wanting to coach, umpire or referee – and this is another area in which higher education has much to offer. Many university clubs and sports unions provide subsidised courses for students to gain qualifications that may be of use to the individual in later life, as well as benefiting university teams in the short term. Or you might want to try your hand at some sports administration, with an eye to your career. In most universities there is a sports (or athletic) union, with autonomy from the main students' union, which organises matches and looks after the wider interests of those who play. There are plenty of opportunities for those seeking an apprenticeship in the art of running a club, or larger organisation.

Universities that excel

A few universities are known particularly for sport – the University of London women's volleyball team has won the English Volleyball Championships, for example, and Bath University's "Team Bath" have tasted success in the FA Cup. Institutions are benefiting from the increasing popularity of sport as a degree subject, as well as an extra-curricular activity. Several of this elite group had a head start as former physical education colleges. Loughborough is probably the best-known of them, but Leeds Metropolitan and Brunel are others with a similar pedigree. Other universities with different traditions, such as Bath and the University of East Anglia, also have a variety of outstanding facilities, while the likes of Stirling and UWIC have the same in a narrower range of sports.

As in so much else, Oxford and Cambridge are in a category of their own. The Boat Race and the Varsity Match (in rugby union) are the only UK university sporting events with a big popular following, and there is a high standard of competition in other sports. But you should not assume that success in school sport will be a passport to an Oxbridge place. While star rowers and rugby players do turn up on postgraduate diploma courses, the days of special consideration for sporty undergraduates appear to be over, and there are few of the sports scholarships offered at other universities.

Representative sport

Competitive standards have been rising in university sport. British Universities and Colleges

Sport (BUCS) runs competitions in almost 50 sports, and ranks participating institutions. There is also international competition in a number of sports, and numerous examples of students being selected for Olympic and professional teams. The World Student Games have become one of the biggest occasions in the international sporting calendar.

Formed in 2008, BUCS has brought together the administration of university sport and the job of lobbying for the best possible facilities. The new organisation has a student membership, but also plays a role in the wider sporting community, as well as negotiating with the Government and other national and international bodies to promote, develop and enable participation in sport and active recreation.

University sports facilities

Even the smallest university should provide reasonable indoor and outdoor sports facilities – a sports hall, modern gym equipment and outdoor pitches (usually including an all-weather surface and floodlights). Most will also have a swimming pool and extras such as climbing walls, but some smaller universities make arrangements for students to use local sports centres and clubs when it is not feasible to provide for minority sports. The same goes for the really expensive sports, like golf, which is usually the subject of an arrangement with one or more local clubs that give students a discount. Specialist facilities, like boat houses and climbing huts, obviously depend on location, but the most landlocked university is likely to have a sailing club that organises regular activities away from campus, and a skiing club that runs at least annual trips to the mountains.

Many of the larger universities have spent millions of pounds improving their sports facilities, sometimes in partnership with local authorities, national sporting bodies or the Lottery. University campuses are ideal locations for national coaching centres, and many have been established in recent years. Although elite coaching generally takes place in closed sessions, students can occasionally find themselves rubbing shoulders with star players – and not just in the bar.

It is estimated that close to £500 million has been spent on new or upgraded sports facilities at UK universities over the past decade. Universities now boast a significant proportion of the UK's 50-metre pools, for example, and more are planned. One opened at Surrey University only this year. Other innovative schemes include Leeds Metropolitan's development of the Headingley cricket and rugby league grounds, providing teaching space for students during the week and improved facilities for players and spectators on match days.

Both the scale of investment and the emphasis on sport has increased as the 2012 Olympics have come closer. The legacy for students – not just in London - should be considerable, as it was at the Commonwealth Games in Manchester and the World Student Games in Sheffield.

Beyond scrutinising the prospectus for the extent of university facilities, there are two important questions to ask: how much do they cost and where are they? Neither is easy to track down on the average university website.

How much?

Students who are used to free (if inferior) facilities at school often get a nasty surprise when they find that they are expected to pay to join the Athletic Union and then pay again to use the gym or play football. Because most university sport is subsidised, the charges are reasonable compared to commercial facilities, but the best deal may require a considerable outlay at the start. Some campus gyms and swimming pools now charge more than £300 a year, for example, which is still considerably cheaper than paying per visit if you intend to use the facilities regularly (and provides an incentive to carry on doing so). Most universities offer a variety of peak and off-peak membership packages – some for the entire length of your course.

Outdoor sports are usually charged by the hour, although clubs will also charge a membership fee. You may be required to pay up to £25 for membership of the Athletic Union (although not all universities require this). Fees for intramural sport are seldom substantial; teams will usually pay a fee for the season, while courts for racket sports tend to be marginally cheaper per session than in other clubs.

How far away?

University prospectuses tend to major on the quality of the sports facilities without being as forthcoming about the prices or location. The common complaint by students is that the playing fields are too far from the campus – understandable in the case of city centre universities, but still aggravating if you have to arrange your own transport. This is where campus universities have a clear advantage.

For the rest, there has to be some trade-off between the quality of outdoor facilities and the distance you have to travel to use them. But universities are beginning to realise that long journeys depress usage of important (and expensive) facilities, and some have tried to find suitable land closer to lectures and halls of residence. Indoor sports centres should all be within easy reach.

Sport as a degree subject

Sports science and other courses associated with sport have seen big increases in recent years – so much so that the subject was in the top dozen in terms of popularity, with more than 52,000 applications at the start of 2011. A separate ranking for the subject is published on pages 183–86.

As those who have taken sports science at A level will know, an interest in sport is invaluable but far from sufficient. The same goes for sporting excellence. If you are hoping to be rewarded with an academic qualification for three years on the sports field, you will be disappointed because there is serious science involved. However, sport is a growing employment field and one that demands qualifications like any other. Entrance requirements vary widely, with some of the top courses asking for 360 points on the UCAS tariff, while others ask half this number or less.

Other degrees in the sports area are more closely focused on management, with careers in the leisure industry in mind – golf course management, for example, has proved popular with students despite being a target of those who see anything beyond the traditional academic portfolio as "dumbing down". Such courses are usually no less rigorous than general management degrees. The question is not whether the courses are up to standard, but whether a less specialised one will offer more career flexibility if a decline in popularity for the particular sport limits future opportunities. The chance to combine work and play for three years holds obvious attractions, but there will be opportunities to pursue your chosen sport at university in any case.

Sports scholarships

The number and range of sports scholarships have expanded just as rapidly as courses in the subject, but the two are usually not connected. Sports scholarships are for elite performers, regardless of what they are studying – indeed, they exist at universities with barely any degrees in the field. Imported from the USA, scholarships now exist in an array of sports. At

Birmingham University, for example, there are specialist golf awards (as there are at ten other universities) and a scholarship for triathletes, as well as others open to any sport.

The value of scholarships varies considerably – sometimes according to individual prowess. The Royal and Ancient scholarships for golfers, for example, range from £500 for promising handicap golfers to £10,000 for full internationals. All of them demand that you meet the normal entrance requirements for your course and maintain the necessary academic standards, as well as progressing in your sport. In practice, most departments will be flexible about attendance and deadlines, as long as you make your requests well in advance.

Many sports scholarships offer benefits in kind, in the form of coaching, equipment or access to facilities. The Government-funded Talented Athlete Scholarship Scheme (TASS), which is restricted to students at English universities who have achieved national recognition at under-18 level and are eligible to represent England, is one such example. No fewer than 21 of the medallists in the Beijing Olympics were current or former TASS athletes. The scholarships are worth £3,500 a year and can be put towards costs such as competition and training costs, equipment or mentoring. Further details are available at **www.tass.gov.uk**.

Part-time work

University sports centres are an excellent source of term-time (and out-of-term) employment. They beat other campus jobs, such as bar work, in terms of enjoyment and healthiness. Depending on your qualifications, you could earn up to £17 an hour for coaching, or more like £7 an hour as a receptionist or for other forms of assistance. You may also be trained in first aid, fire safety, customer care and risk assessment – all useful skills for future employment. The experience will help you secure employment in commercial or local authority facilities – and even for jobs such as stewarding at football grounds and music venues.

Administrative work within the Athletic Union or university sports organisation, is more likely to be unpaid, but may still provide useful experience that will add to your CV. So, indeed, does a position of responsibility in a club, or even captaining a team. Many employers value sport as an indication of self-confidence and team-working qualities. Most universities also have a sabbatical post in the Athletic Union or similar body, a paid position with responsibility for organising university sport and representing the sporting community within the university.

Useful websites

BUCS (British Universities and Colleges Sports)
www.bucs.org.uk
UK Sport
www.uksport.gov.uk
London 2012
www.london2012.com
Talented Athlete Scholarship Scheme
www.tass.gov.uk

Table of university sporting facilities

The following six pages outline the sporting facilities at each of the universities covered in this book, based on a survey undertaken by University and College Sport (now absorbed into BUCS) in 2007 and updated where possible. The information only covers the facilities that universities provide centrally for all their students, and not those in halls of residence or colleges. At Oxford and Cambridge, for example, many colleges have facilities that are not reflected in the table. The table also contains the most recent BUCS League Ranking and websites correct as of April 2011.

The table provides the following information:
» British Universities and Colleges Sports (BUCS) League Rankings 2009–10, based on all sports. Teams get points each year for their success in inter-university competitions and BUCS uses them to compile an annual league table. The universities with the highest rankings (eg, Loughborough, Bath and Birmingham) are therefore the most successful competitively overall. A number of institutions with teams in BUCS are not universities and so do not appear in the following table. The BUCS rankings are based on all teams in the leagues.
» An indication of whether the university has (Y for "yes") or does not have (N for "no") the following facilities:
   Sports hall
   Swimming pool
   Squash courts
   Climbing wall
   Indoor tennis courts
   Fitness facilities
   Winter grass pitches (eg, for football, rugby, etc.)
   Cricket pitches
   Artificial turf pitches
» The number of different sports with student clubs.
» The number of indoor sports with intramural competitions.
» The number of outdoor sports with intramural competitions.
» Whether instruction classes are available to encourage new participants (Y = yes; N = no).
» Whether sports scholarships or bursaries are available. Full details will need to be checked on university websites.
» Details of university websites devoted to sports. Students' unions websites usually have sports information as well. Where the main university website is given, visit that site and search for sports. The full web address is too long to include in this table.

Grey boxes show where information is not available.

University sporting facilities

Universities	BUCS ranking 2009–10	Sports hall?	Swimming pool?	Squash courts?	Climbing wall?	Indoor tennis court(s)?	Fitness facilities?	Winter grass pitch(es)?
Aberdeen	31	Y	Y	Y	N	N	Y	Y
Abertay	99	N	N	N	N	N	Y	N
Aberystwyth	62	Y	Y	Y	Y	Y	Y	Y
Anglia Ruskin	104	Y	Y	Y	Y	Y	Y	Y
Aston	84	Y	Y	Y	Y	N	Y	Y
Bangor	70	Y	N	Y	Y	N	Y	Y
Bath	4	Y	Y	Y	Y	Y	Y	Y
Bath Spa	133	No further information reported						
Bedfordshire	66	Y	Y	N	Y	Y	Y	Y
Birmingham	3	Y	Y	Y	Y	N	Y	Y
Birmingham City	109	N	N	N	N	N	N	Y
Bolton	136	Y	Y	Y	Y	N	Y	N
Bournemouth	33	Y	Y	Y	Y	N	Y	Y
Bradford	89	Y	Y	Y	Y	Y	Y	Y
Brighton	34	Y	N	N	Y	N	Y	Y
Bristol	12	Y	Y	Y	N	Y	Y	Y
Brunel	18	Y	N	Y	Y	N	Y	Y
Buckinghamshire New	87	No further information reported						
Cambridge	14	N	Y	Y	N	Y	Y	Y
Canterbury Christ Church	79	Y	N	N	N	N	Y	Y
Cardiff	15	Y	N	Y	N	N	Y	Y
Cardiff, UWIC	13	Y	Y	Y	N	Y	Y	Y
Central Lancashire	37	Y	Y	N	N	Y	Y	Y
Chester	74	Y	Y	Y	N	N	Y	Y
Chichester	66	Y	N	N	Y	Y	Y	Y
City	117	Y	N	Y	N	N	Y	N
Coventry	73	Y	N	N	N	N	Y	Y
Cumbria	100	Y	N	N	N	N	Y	N
De Montfort	94	Y	N	Y	N	N	Y	N
Derby	98	No further information reported						
Dundee	43	Y	Y	Y	N	Y	Y	Y
Durham	6	Y	N	Y	Y	N	Y	Y
East Anglia	60	Y	Y	Y	Y	N	Y	Y
East London	124	No further information reported						
Edge Hill	81	Y	Y	Y	N	N	Y	Y
Edinburgh	5	Y	Y	Y	Y	N	Y	Y
Edinburgh Napier	56	No further information reported						
Essex	39	Y	N	Y	Y	N	Y	Y
Exeter	10	Y	Y	Y	Y	Y	Y	Y
Glamorgan	49	Y	N	Y	Y	N	Y	Y

Cricket pitch(es)?	Artificial turf pitch(es)?	Number of different sports with student clubs	Number of indoor sports with intra-mural competitions	Number of outdoor sports with intra-mural competitions	Instruction classes available?	Sports scholarships or bursaries available?	Sport website
Y	Y	53	0	2	Y	Y	www.abdn.ac.uk/sportandexercise
N	N	16	3	3	Y	Y	http://sport.abertay.ac.uk
Y	Y	50	0	1	Y	N	www.aber.ac.uk/en/sportscentre
N	N	60	5	5	Y	Y	www.anglia.ac.uk
Y	Y	37	0	0	Y	Y	www.aston.ac.uk/sport
N	Y	39	3	3	Y	Y	www.bangor.ac.uk/maesglas
Y	Y	47	8	6	Y	Y	www.teambath.com
							www.bathspa.ac.uk
Y	N	11	4	2	Y	Y	www.beds.ac.uk/studentlife/town/sport
Y	Y	43	3	4	Y	Y	www.sport.bham.ac.uk
N	Y	20	1	1	Y	N	www.birminghamcitysu.com/sports
N	N	9	3	0	Y	N	www.bolton.ac.uk/sport
Y	N	15	7	3	Y	Y	www.bournemouth.ac.uk/sports
Y	Y	34	13	14	Y	N	www.brad.ac.uk/sports
Y	N	24	0	4	Y	Y	www.brighton.ac.uk/sport
Y	Y	56	7	4	Y	Y	www.bris.ac.uk/sport
N	Y	39	3	2	Y	Y	www.brunel.ac.uk/life/sport
							www.bucks.ac.uk
Y	Y	53	12	7	Y	Y	www.sport.cam.ac.uk
N	N	15	0	4	Y	Y	www.canterbury.ac.uk/sport
Y	Y	59	0	3	Y	Y	www.cardiff.ac.uk/sport
Y	Y	19	0	0	Y	Y	www3.uwic.ac.uk/English/sport
Y	Y	35	0	1	Y	Y	www.uclan.ac.uk/uclansport
N	Y	33	3	3	Y	Y	www.chester.ac.uk
N	Y	17	0	1	Y	Y	www.chi.ac.uk/SportAtChichester.cfm
N	N	16	5	0	Y	N	www.city.ac.uk/studentcentre
Y	Y	34	4	2	Y	Y	www.coventry.ac.uk/cu/sport
N	N	12	8	2	Y	Y	www.cumbria.ac.uk
N	N	26	0	0	Y	N	www.dmu.ac.uk
							www.derby.ac.uk/sports
Y	N	44	5	3	Y	Y	www.dundee.ac.uk/ise
Y	Y	51	8	9	Y	Y	www.teamdurham.com
Y	Y	46	18	8	Y	Y	www.sportspark.co.uk
							www.uel.ac.uk/sports
N	Y	12	0	0	Y	Y	www.edgehill.ac.uk/sportingedge
Y	Y	59	3	5	Y	Y	www.eusu.ed.ac.uk
							www.napier.ac.uk
Y	Y	45	15	7	Y	Y	www.essex.ac.uk/sport
Y	Y	47	6	6	Y	Y	www.sport.ex.ac.uk
N	Y	25	6	1	Y	Y	http://sport.glam.ac.uk

University sporting facilities cont.

Universities	BUCS ranking 2008–09	Sports hall?	Swimming pool?	Squash courts?	Climbing wall?	Indoor tennis court(s)?	Fitness facilities?	Winter grass pitch(es)?
Glasgow	30	Y	Y	Y	N	N	Y	Y
Glasgow Caledonian	77	Y	N	N	N	N	Y	N
Gloucestershire	35	No further information reported						
Glyndŵr	136	No further information reported						
Goldsmiths College	126	Y	N	N	N	N	Y	Y
Greenwich	110	Y	N	N	N	Y	Y	Y
Heriot-Watt	50	Y	N	Y	Y	N	Y	Y
Hertfordshire	48	Y	Y	Y	Y	N	Y	Y
Highlands and Islands	132	No further information reported						
Huddersfield	114	Y	N	Y	N	N	Y	N
Hull	68	Y	N	Y	Y	N	Y	Y
Imperial College	17	Y	Y	Y	Y	N	Y	Y
Keele	72	Y	Y	Y	Y	N	Y	Y
Kent	41	Y	N	Y	Y	Y	Y	Y
King's College	58	N	N	Y	N	N	Y	Y
Kingston	71	N	N	N	N	N	Y	Y
Lampeter (Trinity Saint David)	146	No further information reported						
Lancaster	46	Y	Y	Y	Y	N	Y	Y
Leeds	16	Y	N	Y	Y	N	Y	Y
Leeds Metropolitan	2	Y	Y	Y	Y	Y	Y	Y
Leicester	85	Y	N	Y	N	Y	Y	Y
Lincoln	61	Y	N	Y	N	N	Y	Y
Liverpool	32	Y	Y	Y	Y	N	Y	Y
Liverpool Hope	118	No further information reported						
Liverpool John Moores	64	Y	Y	N	Y	N	Y	Y
London Metropolitan	42	No further information reported						
London School of Economics	54	No further information reported						
London South Bank	90	Y	N	N	N	N	Y	Y
Loughborough	1	Y	Y	Y	Y	Y	Y	Y
Manchester	9	Y	Y	Y	N	N	Y	Y
Manchester Metropolitan	63	Y	N	Y	N	N	Y	N
Middlesex	80	Y	N	N	N	N	Y	Y
Newcastle	11	Y	N	Y	N	N	Y	Y
Northampton	95	Y	Y	N	N	N	Y	Y
Northumbria	20	Y	Y	Y	N	N	Y	Y
Nottingham	7	Y	Y	Y	Y	Y	Y	Y
Nottingham Trent	27	Y	Y	Y	Y	N	Y	Y
Oxford	8	Y	Y	Y	Y	N	Y	Y
Oxford Brookes	38	Y	N	Y	Y	N	Y	Y
Plymouth	45	Y	Y	Y	N	N	Y	N

Cricket pitch(es)?	Artificial turf pitch(es)?	Number of different sports with student clubs	Number of indoor sports with intra-mural competitions	Number of outdoor sports with intra-mural competitions	Instruction classes available?	Sports scholarships or bursaries available?	Sport website
Y	Y	46	2	2	Y	Y	www.gla.ac.uk/services/sport
N	N	24	0	0	Y	Y	www.gcal.ac.uk/arc
							www.yourstudentsunion.com
							www.glyndŵr.ac.uk
Y	N	17	1	1	Y	N	www.gold.ac.uk/sports
N	N	7	0	0	N	Y	www.gre.ac.uk/about/sports
N	Y	32	3	2	Y	Y	www.hw.ac.uk/sports
N	Y	24	1	2	Y	Y	http://student.hertssportsvillage.co.uk
							www.uhi.ac.uk
N	N	28	0	0	Y	N	www2.hud.ac.uk/estates/sports
Y	Y	38	1	1	Y	N	www.hullstudent.com/au
Y	Y	73	5	4	Y	Y	www3.imperial.ac.uk/sports
Y	Y	32	2	1	Y	N	www.kususport.net
Y	Y	40	5	4	Y	Y	www.kent.ac.uk/sports
Y	N	51	0	0	Y	N	www.kclsu.org
Y	N	27	0	1	Y	Y	www.kingston.ac.uk/sport
							www.lampetersu.co.uk
Y	Y	30	7	7	Y	N	www.sportscentrelancaster.co.uk
Y	Y	63	9	6	Y	Y	www.leeds.ac.uk/sport
N	Y	40	1	2	Y	Y	www.leedsmet.ac.uk/sport
Y	Y	32	8	4	Y	Y	www.le.ac.uk/sports
N	Y	40	2	1	Y	Y	www.lincoln.ac.uk
Y	Y	43	3	3	Y	Y	www.liv.ac.uk/sports
							www.hope.ac.uk/hopeparksports
N	Y	30	0	3	Y	Y	www.ljmu.ac.uk/sport
							www.londonmet.ac.uk/sports
							www.lsesu.com
Y	N	13	1	0	Y	Y	www.lsbu.ac.uk/sports
Y	Y	53	28	14	Y	Y	http://sdc.lboro.ac.uk
Y	Y	44	5	7	Y	Y	www.manchester.ac.uk/sport
N	N	35	2	2	Y	N	www.mmu.ac.uk/sport
Y	N	12	2	2	Y	Y	www.mdx.ac.uk/sport
Y	Y	65	2	4	Y	Y	www.ncl.ac.uk/cprs
N	N	15	0	1	Y	Y	www.northamptonunion.com/clubs
Y	Y	27	4	2	Y	Y	www.teamnorthumbria.com
Y	Y	73	4	6	Y	Y	www.nottingham.ac.uk/sport
Y	Y	38	3	1	Y	Y	www.ntu.ac.uk/sport
Y	Y	81	28	18	Y	Y	www.sport.ox.ac.uk
Y	Y	30	1	1	Y	Y	www.brookes.ac.uk/sport
N	N	57	2	3	Y	Y	www.plymouth.ac.uk/recreation

University sporting facilities cont.

Universities	BUCS ranking 2008–09	Sports hall?	Swimming pool?	Squash courts?	Climbing wall?	Indoor tennis court(s)?	Fitness facilities?	Winter grass pitch(es)?
Portsmouth	24	Y	N	Y	N	N	Y	Y
Queen Margaret, Edinburgh	112	Y	N	N	N	N	Y	N
Queen Mary, London	86	Y	N	Y	N	N	Y	N
Queen's, Belfast	93	Y	Y	Y	Y	N	Y	Y
Reading	28	Y	N	Y	N	N	Y	Y
Robert Gordon	59	Y	Y	Y	Y	Y	Y	N
Roehampton	95	Y	N	N	N	N	Y	Y
Royal Holloway	52	Y	Y	Y	N	N	Y	Y
St Andrews	26	Y	N	Y	Y	N	Y	Y
Salford	107	No further information reported						
Sheffield	23	Y	Y	Y	Y	N	Y	Y
Sheffield Hallam	29	Y	N	N	N	N	Y	Y
SOAS	129	No further information reported						
Southampton	19	Y	Y	Y	Y	N	Y	Y
Southampton Solent	55	Y	N	N	N	N	Y	Y
Staffordshire	82	Y	N	N	Y	Y	Y	Y
Stirling	22	Y	Y	Y	N	Y	Y	Y
Strathclyde	47	Y	Y	Y	N	N	Y	Y
Sunderland	102	Y	Y	N	N	N	Y	N
Surrey	75	Y	Y	Y	Y	Y	Y	Y
Sussex	51	Y	N	Y	N	N	Y	Y
Swansea	25	Y	Y	Y	Y	N	Y	Y
Swansea Metropolitan	128	No further information reported						
Teesside	76	Y	N	Y	Y	N	Y	Y
Ulster	134	Y	N	Y	N	Y	Y	Y
University of the Arts London	130	N	N	N	N	N	N	N
University College London	40	Y	N	Y	N	N	Y	Y
University for the Creative Arts	141	No further information reported						
UWE, Bristol	36	Y	N	N	N	N	N	Y
Wales, Newport	108	Y	Y	N	N	N	Y	N
Warwick	21	Y	Y	Y	Y	Y	Y	Y
West London	121	No further information reported						
Westminster	138	No further information reported						
West of Scotland	116	No further information reported						
Winchester	111	Y	N	Y	N	N	Y	Y
Wolverhampton	88	Y	N	Y	N	N	Y	N
Worcester	57	Y	Y	N	N	N	Y	Y
York	44	Y	N	Y	N	N	Y	Y
York St John	91	Y	N	N	Y	N	Y	Y

Cricket pitch(es)?	Artificial turf pitch(es)?	Number of different sports with student clubs	Number of indoor sports with intra-mural competitions	Number of outdoor sports with intra-mural competitions	Instruction classes available?	Sports scholarships or bursaries available?	Sport website
N	Y	49	6	3	Y	Y	www.port.ac.uk/sport
N	Y	12	0	0	Y	N	www.qmu.ac.uk/sports
N	N	30	4	7	Y	N	www.qmsu.org
Y	Y	53	6	5	Y	Y	www.qub.ac.uk/sport
Y	Y	50	5	2	Y	Y	www.sport.reading.ac.uk
N	N	30	0	0	Y	Y	www.rgu.ac.uk/rgusport
N	N	20	0	3	Y	N	www.roehampton.ac.uk
Y	N	36	0	0	Y	Y	www.rhul.ac.uk/sports
Y	Y	46	7	7	Y	Y	www.st-andrews.ac.uk/sport
							www.salfordstudents.com
Y	Y	48	4	4	Y	Y	www.usport.co.uk
Y	Y	38	3	2	Y	Y	www.shu.ac.uk/sporthallam
							http://soasunion.org
Y	Y	70	7	9	Y	Y	www.sportrec.soton.ac.uk
Y	N	27	16	5	Y	Y	www.solent.ac.uk/sport
N	Y	35	0	0	Y	N	www.staffs.ac.uk
Y	Y	38	0	7	Y	Y	www.stir.ac.uk/sport
Y	Y	36	3	0	Y	Y	www.strath.ac.uk/sport
N	N	33	3	0	Y	N	www.unisportsunderland.com
Y	Y	35	7	1	Y	Y	www.unisport.co.uk
Y	Y	20	5	1	Y	Y	www.sussex.ac.uk/sport
Y	Y	50	6	1	Y	Y	www.swan.ac.uk/sport
							www.metsu.org
N	Y	40	0	1	Y	Y	www.tees.ac.uk/sections/sport
Y	Y	42	2	0	Y	Y	www.uusport.com
N	N	17	0	0	N	N	www.suarts.org
Y	N	33	3	0	Y	Y	www.uclunion.org/sport-fitness
							http://ucasu.com
Y	N	40	2	0	Y	Y	www.uwe.ac.uk/sport
N	N	0	2	1	Y	N	www.newport.ac.uk
Y	Y	75	2	5	Y	Y	warwicksport.warwick.ac.uk
							www.tvu.ac.uk/students
							ww.westminster.ac.uk
							www.sauws.org.uk
Y	N	27	3	2	Y	N	www.winchesterstudents.co.uk
N	N	28	7	0	Y	Y	www.wlv.ac.uk/sport
Y	Y	42	0	0	Y	Y	www.worc.ac.uk/student/sports
Y	Y	58	5	9	Y	N	www.york.ac.uk/univ/sports
N	Y	23	1	0	Y	Y	www.yorksj.ac.uk

10 What Parents Should Do

When upfront fees were abolished in 2006 and responsibility for repayment shifted to
graduates, some thought that parents would become less involved in their children's higher
education. Far from it: spiralling student debt left parents feeling just as obliged as before to
help their children through university, even though they no longer had to find the initial £1,000
in fees. The shift to much higher fees may, if anything, spark even more parental interest –
particularly in the selection process, but also in the continuing question of value for money in
the student experience. This chapter looks at where to draw the line between constructive
involvement and unwelcome interference. Nearly all students are adults, and university offers
an environment where they can begin to make their own decisions and develop as individuals.

A good starting point is to offer advice only when it is sought, and to leave direct contact
with university administrators and academics to the student. Of course, throughout the *Guide*,
all references to parents apply equally to guardians and step-parents.

Student finance and parental involvement

No matter how independent students are meant to be, most parents will still want to help out
when they can. The new student finance system is designed to enable undergraduates to pay
their own way through a degree course – albeit building up considerable debts along the way.
Student loans are repayable after graduation, only when the graduate's salary reaches £21,000,
a £6,000 increase on the previous threshold. Parents will not even know when repayments
begin, let alone be required to make a contribution. However, remember that part of the
maintenance loan is income-assessed and you may need to contribute to living expenses,
especially in Scotland, where loans are less generous.

Students still have to live, however, and the combination of loans and bursaries that
comprises the new system will seldom be enough to make ends meet. Hundreds of thousands
of students – particularly mature students – do pay their own way through university. But every
survey shows that families play an important financial (and, until now, growing) role where
students move straight from school to higher education.

"Helicopter parents"

Universities have found that anxious mothers and fathers are more inclined than ever to
question what their children are getting for their increasingly substantial fees. There have been

stories of parents challenging not just the amount and quality of tuition, but even the marking of essays and exams. The phenomenon, first reported in the USA, has given rise to the phrase "helicopter parents" – so called because they hover over their children's education when they should be letting go. No one wants to think of themselves in that category, but it is not surprising – or reprehensible – that parents are taking more of an interest. Many more of today's parents have been to university themselves, so have the knowledge and confidence to offer advice, both in choosing where and what to study, and in the decisions facing students at university. One of the reasons that some then overstep the mark is that they are shocked that the amount of teaching and size of seminar groups are not what they recall from their own "free" higher education. The new fees are meant to herald improvements in the student experience, including more contact hours, but it remains to be seen if these materialise. Few universities will have any more money to spend on teaching, and it may be that fewer and larger seminars are here to stay in the arts and social sciences, where almost all state support has been withdrawn.

An associated reason for greater parental involvement is that family relationships have changed. Many teenage applicants are happy to accept a lift to an open day to get a second opinion on a university and their prospective course. They are also more likely than previous generations of students to come home at the weekend – or to live there in the first place – and to air any grievances.

Laying the ground

The first thing any parent can do to smooth the path to university is to be encouraging about the value of higher education. Ideally, this should have started long before the application process, but it is especially important at this point. Particularly now that student debt has become a frequent media topic and the economic downturn has hit graduate employment prospects, it is only natural for sixth-formers and others thinking of higher education to have second thoughts.

The lure of a regular wage packet will be tempting, and there are plenty of young people who are not suited to full-time higher education. Even after the years of rapid university expansion, most people still do not go to university, but those who are capable of going generally do not regret the decision. Many people look back on their student days as the best period of their life, as well as the one that shaped their personality and their career.

Time as a student should still pay off for the individual in terms of lifetime earnings, as well as personal development. A little reassurance at this stage may make all the difference.

Making the choice

Any parent wants to help a son or daughter through the difficult business of choosing where and what to study. How big a role you play will depend on a number of factors, not the least of which is the extent to which your advice is wanted. In the end, it is the student's decision, and you can do no more than offer relevant information.

One important factor is the quality of advice available at school or college. If this is good, parental involvement should be marginal. But often that is not the case, and you may have to call on other resources, including your own research.

A second factor is your own level of expertise: you may have opinions about particular universities or subjects, but are they up-to-date and based on evidence? Try not to give advice that is coloured by memories of your own student days. That was probably a quarter of a century ago, and higher education has changed out of all recognition in the intervening years.

Avoid second-hand opinions gleaned through the media or dinner party gossip. You may think that some subjects are a sure-fire route to lucrative employment, while others are shunned by employers, but are you right? And do you really know the strengths and weaknesses of more than 100 universities? The tables in chapters 2 and 4 offer a reality check, but even they cannot take account of the differences within institutions. The subject tables in chapter 5 show that the best graduate employment rates are often not at the obvious universities. Above all, do not try to rewind your own career decisions through your children. The fact that you enjoyed – or hated – a subject or a university does not mean that they will. You may have always regretted missing out on the chance to go to Oxbridge or to become a brain surgeon, for example, but they have their own lives to lead. Students who switch courses or drop out of university frequently complain that they were pressured into their original choice by their parents.

Check that choices are being made for sensible reasons, not on the basis of questionable gossip or trivial criteria. But beyond that, you should stay in the background unless there is a very good reason to play a more substantive role. Make a point of looking for important aspects of university life that the applicant might miss. Security, for example, usually does not feature near the top of a teenager's list of priorities, and likewise other practical issues, such as the proximity of student accommodation to lectures, the library and the students' union.

Many universities now publish guides specifically for parents and put on programmes for them at Open Days. The latter may be a way of separating prospective applicants from their more demanding "minders", but the programmes themselves can be interesting and informative. Do not worry that you will be an embarrassment by attending Open Days – thousands of parents do so, and you may add a critical edge to the proceedings. Like prospectuses, Open Days are part of the sales process, and it is easy for a sixth former to be carried away by the excitement surrounding a lively university. You are much more likely to spot the defects – even if they are ignored in the final decision.

Finding a place

Once the choices have been made, get to know the UCAS system and quietly ensure that deadlines are being met. The school should be doing this, but there is no harm in providing a little back-up, especially on parts of the process that take time and thought, such as writing the personal statement. There is little a parent can do as the offers and/or rejections come rolling in, other than to be supportive. If the worst happens and there are five rejections, you may have to start the advice process all over again for a new round of applications through UCAS Extra. If so, a cool head is even more necessary, but the same principles apply.

Results day

Then, before you know it, results day is upon you. Make sure you are at home, rather than in some isolated holiday retreat. Your son or daughter needs to have access to instant advice at school or college, and to be able to contact universities straight away if Clearing or Adjustment is required. And your moral support will be much more effective face to face, rather than down a telephone line. Whatever happens, try not to transmit the anxiety that you will inevitably be feeling to your son or daughter, especially if the results are not what was wanted. It is easy to make rash decisions about re-sitting exams or rejecting an insurance offer in the heat of the moment. Try to slow the process down and encourage clear and realistic thinking. As at other stages in the application, make sure you know in advance what might be required, such as where to access Clearing lists. After that, if it is Clearing or Adjustment, you will need to be on hand to offer advice and help with for visits to possible universities. Clearing or Adjustment is all but over in a week, so the agony should be short-lived.

Before they go

Little more than a month after the tension of results day, everything should be ready for the start of term. Unless your son or daughter is one of the growing band choosing to stay at home to study, there will be forms to fill in to secure university accommodation, as well as student loans to sort out and registration to complete. You can perform useful services, like supplying recipe books if the first year is to be spent in self-catering accommodation, but now is the time for independence to become reality. Make sure that important details like insurance are not forgotten, but otherwise stand clear.

Then it is just a matter of agreeing a budget, assuming you are in a position to make a financial contribution. How large that contribution is will depend on family circumstances and your attitude to independent living. Some parents want to ensure that their children leave university debt-free; others could never afford to do that, while yet others believe that paying your own way is part of the learning experience. The important thing is that students and parents know where they stand.

After they've left

Any new student is going to be nervous if they are leaving home for the first time and having to settle into a strange environment. But in most cases it isn't going to last long because everyone is in the same boat and freshers' weeks hardly leave time for homesickness. In any case, they won't want to let their apprehension show. The people who are most likely to be emotional are the parents – especially if they are left with an empty nest for the first time. It can take a while to get used to an orderly, quiet house after all those years of mayhem.

Resist any temptation to decorate their bedroom and turn it into an office – it is more common than you might think, and psychologists say it can do lasting damage to family relationships. Keep in touch by phone, text or email, but try not to pry. You're not going to be told everything anyway – which is probably just as well. They will be back soon enough and, just as you were getting used to having the place to yourself, a weekend visit or the Christmas vacation will remind you of how things used to be. If things are not going smoothly at university, this may be the time for more reassurance – more students drop out at Christmas of their first year than at any other time.

Lastly, do not become a helicopter parent. Your son or daughter may well seek your advice if they are dissatisfied with the course, their accommodation or some other aspect of university life. By all means, give advice, but leave them to sort the problem out. Universities will cite the Data Protection Act, in any case, to say they can only deal with students, not parents. What they really mean is that students are adults and should look after themselves.

Useful websites

Many universities have sections on their websites for parents of prospective students.
UCAS has a Parents section and newletter on its website: **www.ucas.com/parents**
On this site, you can register for a regular newsletter designed to keep parents informed during the application process.
To find out more about open days, visit: **www.opendays.com**
There is helpful information: **www.direct.gov.uk/parentsguidetohe**

11 Coming to the UK to Study

Only the USA, with its vast higher education system, attracts more international students than the UK. Global surveys have shown that UK universities are seen as offering high quality in a relatively safe environment compared with those in most other countries. And, while their Achilles heel in such research is the perceived cost, there are compensations in the recent state of the pound and in the reduced living expenses offered by courses that are relatively short by international standards.

UK universities have been growing in popularity among international students for many years, although their "market share" has dropped as countries such as Australia and Germany have competed aggressively. Numbers have risen further as the value of the pound has made courses more affordable, while higher visa charges and changes in immigration regulations seem not to have dimmed global enthusiasm for UK higher education. The country's international student population rose by nearly 10 per cent in 2009–10 and overseas applications for undergraduate places were up by another 9 per cent at the start of 2011.

Both EU students (who pay the same fees as their British counterparts) and those from the rest of the world (who pay considerably more) have shared in the boom. There was a disproportionately large increase in applications from EU countries for first degree courses starting in 2011, but that may have been to escape the fee increase due in 2012. When postgraduates are included, much the largest numbers continue to come from China and India.

There have been suggestions, even from the Prime Minister, that fees for non-EU students may fall (or at least rise more slowly) when British students are paying more. The logic behind the argument is that if the new rates for UK and other EU undergraduates reflect the full cost of teaching, international applicants and their sponsors will not expect to pay more. There is little sign as yet, however, of universities moving towards a single fee.

Applicants from some EU countries may come to see the new fee regime as a good deal, however. They still will not be required to pay fees upfront and at £21,000 rather than the current £15,000, the threshold for beginning loan repayments is double the average wage in some countries. Aside from the well-publicised difficulties in collecting loan repayments outside the UK, many graduates will never qualify to repay.

Popularity of UK for studying

Nearly all UK universities are cosmopolitan places that welcome international students in large numbers. The latest survey by i-graduate, the student polling organisation, put the country close behind the USA among the world's most attractive study destinations. More than 400,000 international students were taking higher education courses in the UK in 2009–10. They now make up over 16 per cent of all students at UK universities and colleges. More full-time postgraduates – the fastest-growing group – come from outside the UK than within it. In many UK universities you can expect to have fellow students from over 100 countries from around the world.

More than 80 per cent of international students declare themselves satisfied with their experience of UK universities. Satisfaction has increased by 8 percentage points in four years, according to i-graduate, reflecting greater efforts to keep ahead of the global competition. International students were particularly complimentary about students' unions, multiculturalism, teaching standards and places of worship. Their main concerns were financial, with the UK considered the second-most expensive study location in the world (after the USA), partly because of a lack of employment opportunities (only 56 per cent were satisfied with the ability to earn money while studying).

One way round this in a growing number of countries is to take a UK degree through a local institution or a full branch campus of a UK university. Indeed, there are now more international students taking UK degrees in their own country than in Britain, 340,000 of them

The top countries for sending international students to the UK

EU countries (Top 20)		%	Non-EU countries (Top 20)		%
France	7,678	11.7	China	23,701	23.2
Germany	7,079	10.8	Malaysia	9,854	9.7
Ireland	6,364	9.7	Hong Kong	7,350	7.2
Poland	5,291	8.0	India	5,365	5.3
Greece	4,666	7.1	Nigeria	4,768	4.7
Cyprus (EU)	4,349	6.6	United States of America	3,866	3.8
Cyprus (Other*)	3,024	4.6	Pakistan	2,860	2.8
Spain	2,643	4.0	Singapore	2,546	2.5
Bulgaria	2,553	3.9	Saudi Arabia	2,507	2.5
Lithuania	2,449	3.7	Norway	2,234	2.2
Italy	2,386	3.6	Sri Lanka	2,137	2.1
Sweden	2,195	3.3	Canada	2,112	2.1
Romania	2,168	3.3	South Korea	1,895	1.9
Belgium	1,733	2.6	Bangladesh	1,615	1.6
Netherlands	1,376	2.1	Russia	1,441	1.4
Portugal	1,303	2.0	Kenya	1,334	1.3
Latvia	1,288	2.0	United Arab Emirates	1,305	1.3
Finland	1,181	1.8	Brunei	1,296	1.3
Slovakia	933	1.4	Japan	1,256	1.2
Estonia	749	1.1	Switzerland	1,168	1.1
All EU students	65,808		All non-EU students	102,092	

Note: First degree non-UK students

* Includes students from northern Cyprus and all students from Cyprus entering prior to domicile coding change of 2007–08.

outside the EU. The numbers have grown by 70 per cent in the past decade and are likely to rise further if the UK Government prevents universities increasing the number of students coming to Britain.

Where to study in the UK

The UK is made up of three countries: England, Scotland and Wales – which collectively may be referred to as Great Britain – plus the province of Northern Ireland. The vast majority of the UK's universities and other higher education institutions are in England. Of the 120 universities covered in *The Times Good University Guide*, 93 are in England, 15 in Scotland, ten in Wales and two in Northern Ireland.

It is now over a decade since Scotland gained its own parliament and Wales formed a National Assembly Government. Each has devolved powers and sets fee limits for higher education, which in some cases has brought benefits for EU students. All undergraduates from other EU countries are charged the same fees as those from the part of the UK where their chosen university is located, so EU students currently pay no tuition fees in Scotland, for example.

Within the UK, the cost of living varies by geographical area. Although London is the most expensive, accommodation costs in particular can also be high in many other major cities. You should certainly find out as much as you can about what living in Britain will be like. Further advice and information is available through the British Council at its offices worldwide, at more than 60 university exhibitions that it holds around the world every year, or at its Education UK website (**www.educationuk.org**). Another useful website for international students is provided by the UK Council for International Student Affairs (UKCISA) at **www.ukcisa.org.uk**. We recommend some further websites at the end of the chapter.

Universities in all parts of the UK have a worldwide reputation for high quality teaching and research, as evidenced in global rankings such as those shown on pages 47–9. They maintain this standing by investing heavily in the best academic staff, buildings and equipment, and by taking part in rigorous quality assurance monitoring. The main regulatory bodies include the Quality Assurance Agency for Higher Education (QAA), higher education funding councils for each country of the UK, and the Office for Standards in Education, all of which publish reports on their websites. Professional bodies also play an important role, and there is an Independent Adjudicator for Higher Education who handles student complaints that have not been resolved by universities' own internal complaints procedures.

Although many people from outside the UK associate British universities with Oxford and Cambridge, in reality most higher education institutions are nothing like this. Some universities do still maintain a traditional culture, but most are modern institutions that place at least as much emphasis on teaching as research and offer many vocational programmes, often with close links with business, industry and the professions. The table below shows the universities that are most popular with international students at undergraduate level. Although some of those at the top of the lists are among the most famous names in higher education, others achieved university status only in the last 20 years.

What subjects to study?

One of the reasons for such diversity is that strongly vocational courses are favoured by international students. Many of these in professional areas such as architecture, dentistry or medicine take one or two years longer to complete than most other degree courses. Traditional first degrees are mostly awarded at Bachelor level (BA, BEng, BSc, etc.) and last three to four years. There are also some "enhanced" first degrees (MEng, MChem, etc.) that take four years to complete. The relatively new Foundation degree programmes are almost all vocational and take two years to complete as a full-time course, with an option to study for a further year to gain a full degree. The tables at the end of this chapter select the 20 most popular subjects and show which universities for each subject have the greatest numbers of students. Remember, though, that you need also to consider the details of any course that you wish to study and to look at the ranking of that university in our main league table in chapter 4 and in the subject tables in chapter 5.

English language proficiency

The universities maintain high standards partly by setting high entry requirements, including proficiency in English. For international students, this usually includes a score of 6 or 7 in the International English Language Testing System (IELTS), which assesses English language ability through listening, speaking, reading and writing tests. Under new visa regulations introduced in 2011, universities will be able to vouch for a student's ability in English. This proficiency will need to be equivalent to an "upper intermediate" level (level B2) of the CEFR (Common European Framework of Reference) for studying at an undergraduate level.

There are many private and publicly funded colleges throughout the UK that run courses designed to bring the English language skills of prospective higher education students up to the required standard. However, not all of these are Government approved. The web address for the list of Tier 4 Register of Sponsors in the UK is given at the end of this chapter. Some

The universities most favoured by EU and non-EU students

Institution (Top 20)	EU students	Institution (Top 20)	Non-EU students
Edinburgh Napier	1,682	Manchester	3,637
London Metropolitan	1,492	University of the Arts, London	2,752
Coventry	1,372	Nottingham	2,750
Aberdeen	1,339	University College London	2,376
Manchester	1,329	Imperial College	2,159
University of the Arts, London	1,312	Warwick	2,095
Edinburgh	1,297	Hertfordshire	1,945
Westminster	1,211	Northumbria	1,879
Middlesex	1,114	Edinburgh	1,848
University College London	1,081	Greenwich	1,822
Anglia Ruskin	1,050	East London	1,589
Glasgow	1,014	Sheffield	1,577
Brighton	981	Sheffield Hallam	1,487
Kingston	974	St Andrews	1,448
Ulster	963	London School of Economics	1,445
Salford	950	Liverpool	1,420
King's College London	949	Middlesex	1,402
Robert Gordon	948	Coventry	1,396
Surrey	937	Leeds	1,383
Portsmouth	917	London Metropolitan	1,350

private organisations such as INTO (**www.into.uk.com**) have joined with universities to create centres running programmes preparing international students for degree-level study. The British Council also runs English language courses at its centres around the world.

Tougher student visa regulations will be introduced in April 2012. Although universities' international students will not be denied entry to the UK, some lower-level preparatory courses taken by international students will be affected. It is, therefore, doubly important to consult the official UK government list of approved institutions before lodging an application.

How to apply

You should read the information below in conjunction with that provided in chapter 6, which deals with the application process in some detail.

Some international students apply directly to a UK university for a place on a course, and others make their applications via an agent in their home country. But most applying for a full-time first degree course do so through the Universities and Colleges Admissions Service (UCAS). If you take this route, you will need to fill in an online UCAS application form at home, at school or perhaps at your nearest British Council office. There is lots of advice on the UCAS website about the process of finding a course and the details of the application system (**www.ucas.com/students/wheretostart/nonukstudents**).

Whichever way you apply, the deadlines for getting your application in are the same. For those applying from within an EU country, application forms for 2012 must be received at UCAS by 15 January 2012 for most courses. Note that applications for Oxford and Cambridge

The most popular subjects for international students

Subject group	EU students	Non-EU students	Total	%
Business and administrative studies	15,766	31,061	46,828	28%
Engineering and technology	6,658	16,525	23,183	14%
Social studies	6,471	8,858	15,329	9%
Creative arts and design	5,540	5,754	11,294	7%
Subjects allied to medicine (including pharmacy and nursing)	4,240	5,656	9,895	6%
Law	3,398	6,190	9,589	6%
Biological sciences	5,002	3,785	8,787	5%
Computer science	3,275	5,401	8,675	5%
Languages	4,079	2,371	6,450	4%
Architecture, building and planning	2,262	2,491	4,754	3%
Mathematical sciences	1,076	3,323	4,400	3%
Physical sciences	2,069	2,326	4,395	3%
Medicine and dentistry	1,039	3,295	4,334	3%
Mass communications and documentation	2,114	1,912	4,026	2%
Historical and philosophical studies	1,631	1,416	3,046	2%
Education	566	511	1,077	1%
Veterinary science	101	548	649	0%
Agriculture and related subjects	286	311	597	0%
Total	**65,572**	**101,736**	**167,308**	**100%**

Note: First degree non-UK students

and for all courses in medicine, dentistry and veterinary science have to be received at UCAS by 15 October 2011. Some art and design courses also have a later deadline of 24 March 2012.

If you are applying from a non-EU country to study in 2012, you can submit your application to UCAS at any time between 1 September 2011 and 30 June 2012. Most people will apply well before the 30 June 2012 deadline to make sure that places are still available and to allow plenty of time for immigration regulations, and to make arrangements for travel and accommodation.

Entry and employment regulations

Visa regulations have been the subject of frequent controversy in the UK since the tightening that followed the terrorist attacks of 2001. Until then, the Labour Government had tried to streamline the system for students as part of a global campaign to promote the UK's universities. More recently, however, many new rules and regulations have been introduced, often hotly contested by universities. The Government was criticised for increasing visa fees, doubling the cost of visa extensions, and ending the right to appeal against a refusal of a visa. It also introduced a points system for entry – known as Tier 4 – which came into effect in March 2009. Under this scheme, prospective students can check whether they are eligible for entry against published criteria, and so assess their points score. Universities are also required to provide a Certificate of Acceptance for Study to their international student entrants and they must have "Highly Trusted" status on the Register of Sponsors (details of where to find this list are given at the end of the chapter). Prospective students have to demonstrate that, as well as the necessary qualifications, they have English language proficiency and enough money for the first year of their specified course. This is set at £800 a month in inner London and £600 a month elsewhere. Under new visa requirements, details of financial support will be checked in more detail.

Since September 2007, all students wishing to enter the UK to study have been required to obtain entry clearance before arrival. The only exceptions are British nationals living overseas, British overseas territories citizens, British Protected persons, British subjects, and non-visa national short-term students who may enter under a new Student Visitor route. Visa fees have been increased again under the Coalition Government and the details of the regulations have been reviewed by the UK Border Agency. Further changes are likely in 2011. You can find more about all the latest rules and regulations for entry and visa requirements at **www.ukba.homeoffice.gov.uk/studyingintheuk**.

The rules and regulations governing permission to work vary according to your country of origin. If you are from a European Economic Area (EEA) country (the EU plus Iceland, Liechtenstein and Norway), you don't need permission to work in the UK, although you will need to be ready to show an employer your passport or identity card to prove you are a national of an EEA country. Students from outside the EEA who are here as Tier 4 students are allowed to work part-time for up to 20 hours a week during term time and to work full-time during vacations. These arrangements apply to students of degree courses; stricter limits were introduced in 2010 for lower-level courses. If you wish to stay on after you have graduated, you can apply for permission under Tier 2 under the new points-based immigration system, but you will need a sponsor and the work must be considered "graduate level". The latest reforms abolished the Tier 1 two-year post-study period for graduates who do not have such a sponsor. They will be required to apply for a new visa from scratch. Full details are on the UK Border Agency website.

Bringing your family

Since 2010, international students on courses of six months or less have been forbidden to bring a partner or children into the UK, and the latest reforms in 2011 extend this prohibition to all undergraduates except those who are government sponsored. Postgraduates will still be able to bring dependants to the UK and most universities can help to arrange facilities and accommodation for families as well as for single students. The family members you are allowed to bring with you are your husband or wife, civil partner (a same-sex relationship that has been formally registered in the UK or your home country) and dependent children.

If you are a national of any country from outside the EEA, your family will be subject to immigration policy. Those who are eligible to bring dependants will need to show that they can support them financially, arrange appropriate accommodation, and that they will leave the UK when the student has finished his or her studies. Such family members will usually be able to study (children under 16 are required to attend full-time education), and any over the age of 16 should be able to work as long as you have permission to stay for over 12 months and are following a degree or Foundation degree course. You can find out more about getting entry clearance for your family at **www.ukcisa.org.uk/student/info_sheets/your_family.php**.

Support from British universities

Support for international students is more comprehensive than in many countries, and begins long before you arrive in the UK. Many universities have advisers in other countries. Some will arrange to put you in touch with current students or graduates who can give you a first-hand account of what life is like at a particular university. Pre-departure receptions for students and their families, as well as meet-and-greet arrangements for newly arrived students, are common. You can also expect an orientation and induction programme in your first week, and many universities now have "buddying" systems where current students are assigned to new arrivals to help them find their way around, adjust to their new surroundings, and make new friends. Each university also has a students' union that organises social, cultural and sporting events and clubs, including many specifically for international students. Both the university and the students' union are likely to have full-time staff whose job it is to look after the welfare of students from overseas.

International students also benefit from free medical and subsidised dental and optical care and treatment under the UK National Health Service, plus access to a professional counselling service and a university careers service.

At university, you will naturally encounter people from a wide range of cultures and walks of life. Getting involved in student societies, sport, voluntary work, and any of the wide range of social activities on offer will help you gain first-hand experience of British culture, and, if you need it, will help improve your command of the English language.

The 20 most popular subjects and universities for international students

1 Business Studies

	EU	Non-EU
Aston	235	676
Westminster	480	366
Middlesex	264	568
Manchester	203	521
Coventry	318	396
Northumbria	204	498
Anglia Ruskin	469	228
London Metropolitan	372	317
UWIC, Cardiff	126	553
Bedfordshire	232	400
All overseas students	**11,606**	**18,520**

4 Computer Science

	EU	Non-EU
East London	27	549
Greenwich	36	403
Middlesex	52	295
Coventry	146	127
Portsmouth	71	164
Imperial College	121	95
Manchester	94	115
Edinburgh Napier	160	44
Teesside	57	135
Edinburgh	151	35
All overseas students	**3,275**	**5,401**

2 Accounting and Finance

	EU	Non-EU
West of England	14	671
Manchester	87	467
City	100	392
Essex	79	376
Lancaster	96	308
Warwick	71	299
Bangor	4	347
Sheffield Hallam	22	312
Hull	49	247
Kent	24	240
All overseas students	**1,903**	**10,267**

5 Economics

	EU	Non-EU
University College London	96	486
London School of Economics	83	446
Warwick	91	364
Manchester	64	304
Essex	109	174
Royal Holloway	72	209
York	66	175
Leicester	19	214
St Andrews	56	134
Bath	40	148
All overseas students	**2,133**	**5,456**

3 Law

	EU	Non-EU
Northumbria	11	495
King's College London	230	219
Leicester	190	226
Kent	116	218
Manchester	79	244
Warwick	61	231
Essex	185	86
London School of Economics	38	218
Buckingham	21	230
University College London	88	134
All overseas students	**3,398**	**6,190**

6 Art and Design

	EU	Non-EU
University of the Arts, London	712	1,923
Nottingham Trent	49	168
Birmingham City	82	128
University for Creative Arts	137	59
Kingston	49	146
Middlesex	128	62
Northumbria	26	134
London Metropolitan	97	60
Coventry	60	94
West of England	66	67
All overseas students	**2,766**	**3,922**

The 20 most popular subjects and universities for international students cont.

7 Electrical and Electronic Engineering

	EU	Non-EU
Imperial College	85	312
Manchester	40	207
Birmingham City	28	204
Sheffield	22	208
Strathclyde	18	204
Northumbria	15	201
Birmingham	15	193
Liverpool	12	168
Hertfordshire	3	139
Liverpool John Moores	18	123
All overseas students	**1,117**	**5,267**

10 Biological Sciences

	EU	Non-EU
Edinburgh	220	115
Imperial College	82	188
University College London	62	123
Manchester	63	89
Aberdeen	119	28
Cambridge	57	72
Glasgow	80	39
Nottingham	36	82
Oxford	47	61
St Andrews	43	61
All overseas students	**2,284**	**2,283**

8 Mechanical Engineering

	EU	Non-EU
Imperial College	91	175
Nottingham	28	179
Coventry	34	143
Hertfordshire	23	143
Birmingham	10	154
Bath	67	94
Sheffield	12	138
Bradford	41	100
Loughborough	38	98
King's College London	28	104
All overseas students	**1,257**	**3,754**

11 Mathematics

	EU	Non-EU
Imperial College	79	304
University College London	65	285
Warwick	57	225
Manchester	77	187
London School of Economics	16	230
Oxford	37	174
Cambridge	83	118
Liverpool	10	182
Southampton	22	114
Bath	43	80
All overseas students	**1,076**	**3,323**

9 Politics

	EU	Non-EU
St Andrews	82	304
Kent	231	52
London School of Economics	58	135
Aberdeen	144	32
Edinburgh	37	136
Warwick	59	99
London Metropolitan	96	52
Aberystwyth	100	33
University College London	96	36
Sussex	81	47
All overseas students	**2,676**	**1,966**

12 Hospitality, Leisure, Recreation and Tourism

	EU	Non-EU
West London	155	253
University College Birmingham	167	195
University of the Arts, London	45	183
Edinburgh Napier	54	171
Brighton	177	42
Surrey	68	114
London Metropolitan	112	45
Bournemouth	68	88
Oxford Brookes	77	56
Sheffield Hallam	18	106
All overseas students	**2,161**	**2,104**

The 20 most popular subjects and universities for international students cont.

13 Civil Engineering

	EU	Non-EU
Edinburgh Napier	315	6
Bradford	147	47
East London	42	128
Imperial College	61	108
Nottingham	44	124
Cardiff	48	103
Coventry	70	78
Salford	72	58
Surrey	86	36
Birmingham	17	96
All overseas students	**1,960**	**2,146**

16 Communication and Media Studies

	EU	Non-EU
University of the Arts, London	94	137
Liverpool John Moores	13	191
Westminster	117	69
Goldsmiths College	61	123
London Metropolitan	96	55
Middlesex	87	49
Southampton Solent	86	16
Coventry	51	47
Central Lancashire	26	71
Anglia Ruskin	76	16
All overseas students	**1,980**	**1,632**

14 Medicine

	EU	Non-EU
Manchester	49	225
King's College London	80	186
Nottingham	36	181
Imperial College	55	153
Leicester	32	149
Birmingham	27	145
Edinburgh	29	138
Glasgow	45	119
University College London	57	105
Cambridge	41	115
All overseas students	**969**	**3,035**

17 Other Subjects Allied to Medicine

	EU	Non-EU
Bournemouth	175	157
Queen Margaret Edinburgh	133	99
Imperial College	52	132
Greenwich	87	64
Cambridge	59	74
Cardiff	15	107
Salford	81	29
Robert Gordon	101	1
Bedfordshire	54	43
East London	54	33
All overseas students	**1,921**	**1,619**

15 Psychology

	EU	Non-EU
Aberdeen	130	27
Glasgow	124	18
University College London	38	96
St Andrews	59	63
York	15	95
Royal Holloway	69	37
Nottingham	31	74
Middlesex	55	39
London Metropolitan	57	24
East London	40	31
All overseas students	**2,246**	**1,381**

18 Architecture

	EU	Non-EU
Nottingham	57	215
Manchester Metropolitan	51	92
London Metropolitan	80	54
Greenwich	86	38
Portsmouth	81	40
Plymouth	111	8
Robert Gordon	77	41
East London	69	40
University College London	12	89
Westminster	60	35
All overseas students	**1,622**	**1,479**

The 20 most popular subjects and universities for international students cont.

19 Pharmacology and Pharmacy	EU	Non-EU
Sunderland	115	208
Nottingham	20	244
Brighton	162	71
Robert Gordon	216	10
Liverpool John Moores	33	153
Manchester	29	137
Bath	22	128
Strathclyde	6	128
Kingston	59	64
School of Pharmacy	16	97
All overseas students	**1,004**	**1,944**

20 English	EU	Non-EU
Portsmouth	110	286
Central Lancashire	85	210
St Andrews	18	86
Edinburgh	30	66
Salford	50	33
Anglia Ruskin	48	25
Glasgow	57	6
Bedfordshire	49	13
Canterbury Christ Church	34	26
Aberdeen	45	11
All overseas students	**1,283**	**1,367**

Useful websites

The British Council, with its dedicated Education UK site designed for those wishing to find out more about studying in the UK:
www.educationuk.org

The UK Council for International Student Affairs (UKCISA) produces a wide range of factsheets on all aspects of studying in the UK:
www.ukcisa.org.uk

UCAS, for full details of courses available and an explanation of the application process:
www.ucas.com/students/wheretostart/nonukstudents

For the latest information on entry and visa requirements, visit the UK Border Agency:
www.ukba.homeoffice.gov.uk/studyingintheuk

Register of Sponsors for Tier 4 educational establishments:
www.ukba.homeoffice.gov.uk/sitecontent/documents/employersandsponsors/pointsbasedsystem/registerofsponsorseducation

UK Student Life, a guide designed to explain British daily life and culture to international students:
www.ukstudentlife.com

For a general guide to Britain, available in many languages:
www.visitbritain.com

12 Applying to Oxbridge

Oxbridge (as Oxford and Cambridge are called collectively) not only dominates UK higher education; the two universities are recognised as among the best in the world, regularly featuring among the top five in global rankings. But that is not why they merit a separate chapter in this *Guide*.

The two ancient universities have different admissions arrangements to the rest of the higher education system. Although part of the UCAS network, they have different deadlines from other universities, you can only apply to one or the other, and selection is in the hands of the colleges rather than the university centrally. Most candidates apply to a specific college, although you can make an open application if you are happy to go anywhere.

There have been reforms to the admissions system at both universities in recent years, in order to make the process more user-friendly to those who do not have school or family experience to draw upon. In particular, the business of choosing a college has been intimidating for many prospective applicants. Candidates are now distributed around colleges more efficiently, regardless of the choices they make initially.

There is little to choose between the two universities in terms of entrance requirements, and a formidable number of successful applicants have the maximum possible grades. However, that does not mean that the talented student should be shy about applying: both have fewer applicants per place than many less prestigious universities, and admissions tutors are always looking to extend the range of schools and colleges from which they recruit. For those with a realistic chance of success, there is little to lose except the possibility of one wasted space out of five on the UCAS application.

Overall, there are about five applicants to every place at Oxford and Cambridge, but there are big differences between subjects and colleges. As the tables in this chapter show, competition is particularly fierce in subjects such as medicine and English, but those qualified to read geology or classics have a much better chance of success. The pattern is similar to that in other universities, although the high degree of selection (and self-selection) that precedes an Oxbridge application means that even in the less popular subjects the field of candidates is certain to be strong.

The two universities' power to intimidate prospective applicants is based partly on myth. Both have done their best to live down the *Brideshead Revisited* image, but many sixth-formers still fear that they would be out of their depth there, academically and socially. In fact, the state sector produces nearly 55 per cent of entrants to Oxford and over 59 per cent to Cambridge, and the dropout rate is lower than at almost any other university. The "champagne set" is still present and its activities are well publicised, but most students are hard-working high achievers with the same concerns as their counterparts on other campuses. A joint poll by the two universities' student newspapers showed that undergraduates were spending much of their time in the library or worrying about their employment prospects, and relatively little time on the river or even in the college bar.

State school applicants

Both universities and their student organisations have put a great deal of effort into trying to encourage applications from state schools, and many colleges have launched their own campaigns. Such has been the determination to convince state school pupils that they will get a fair crack of the whip that a new concern has grown up of possible bias against independent school pupils. In reality, however, the dispersed nature of Oxbridge admissions rules out any conspiracy. Some colleges set relatively low standard offers to encourage applicants from the state sector, who may reveal their potential at interview. Some admissions tutors may give the edge to well-qualified candidates from comprehensive schools over those from highly academic independent schools because they consider theirs the greater achievement in the circumstances. Others stick with tried and trusted sources of good students. The independent sector still enjoys a degree of success out of proportion to its share of the school population.

Choosing the right college

Simply in terms of winning a place at Oxford or Cambridge, choosing the right college is not quite as important as it used to be. Both universities have got better at assessing candidates' strengths and finding a suitable college for those who either make an open application or are not taken by their first-choice college.

Cambridge: The Tompkins Table 2010

College	2010	2009	College	2010	2009
Emmanuel	1	2	Jesus	16	11
Trinity	2	1	Queens'	17	12
Churchill	3	7	Sidney Sussex	18	22
Trinity Hall	4	9	Robinson	19	19
Magdalene	5	8	St John's	20	14
Selwyn	6	3	Girton	21	20
Peterhouse	7	16	Fitzwilliam	22	21
Clare	8	18	Murray Edwards	23	23
St Catharine's	9	5	Wolfson	24	27
Pembroke	10	6	Newnham	25	24
Gonville and Caius	11	4	Homerton	26	25
Christ's	12	13	Hughes Hall	27	26
Corpus Christi	13	10	St Edmund's	28	28
King's	14	17	Lucy Cavendish	29	29
Downing	15	15			

At Oxford, subject tutors from around the university put candidates into bands at the start of the selection process, using the results of admissions tests as well as exam results and references. Applicants are spread around the colleges for interview and may not be seen by their preferred college if the tutors think their chances of a place are better elsewhere. Almost a quarter of last year's successful candidates were offered places by a college other than the one they applied to.

Cambridge relies on the "pool", which gives the most promising candidates a second chance if they were not offered a place at the college to which they applied. Those placed in the pool are invited back for a second round of interviews early in the new year. The system lowers the stakes for those who apply to the most selective colleges – in 2010 over 18 per cent of offers came via the pool. Cambridge still interviews about 90 per cent of applicants, whereas the new system at Oxford has resulted in more immediate rejections in some subjects. In medicine, fewer than a third of Oxford's applicants were interviewed in 2010, while in biochemistry almost all were.

However, most Oxbridge applicants still apply direct to a particular college, not only to maximise their chances of getting in, but because that is where they will be living and socialising, as well as learning. Most colleges may look the same to the uninitiated, but there are important differences. Famously sporty colleges, for example, can be trying for those in search of peace and quiet.

Thorough research is needed to find the right place. Even within colleges, different admissions tutors may have different approaches, so personal contact is essential. The tables in this chapter give an idea of the relative academic strengths of the colleges, as well as the varying levels of competition for a place in different subjects. But only individual research will suggest where you will feel most at home. For example, women may favour one of the few remaining single-sex colleges (Murray Edwards, Newnham and Lucy Cavendish at Cambridge). Men have no such option.

Oxford: The Norrington Table 2010

College	2010	2009	College	2010	2009
Magdalen	1	3	Queen's	16	10
Corpus Christi	2	4	Pembroke	17	23
Merton	3	2	St Anne's	18	20
St John's	4	1	St Hugh's	19	22
New	5	5	Lady Margaret Hall	20	21
University	6	7	St Hilda's	21	29
Christ Church	7	12	Brasenose	22	26
Worcester	8	15	St Edmund Hall	23	27
Balliol	9	14	Somerville	24	19
Jesus	10	17	Trinity	25	11
Oriel	11	24	St Peter's	26	25
Hertford	12	6	Exeter	27	18
Wadham	13	9	Keble	28	13
St Catherine's	14	16	Mansfield	29	28
Lincoln	15	8	Harris Manchester	30	30

Oxford applications and acceptances by course

Arts	Applications		Acceptances		Acceptances to Applications %	
	2010	2009	2010	2009	2010	2009
Ancient and Modern History	84	69	23	13	27.4	18.8
Archaeology and Anthropology	83	73	26	24	31.3	32.9
Classical Archaeology and Ancient History	82	95	22	18	26.8	18.9
Classics	294	267	122	110	41.5	41.2
Classics and English	34	23	6	5	17.6	21.7
Classics and Modern Languages	31	25	9	12	29.0	48
Economics and Management	1,169	1,171	89	92	7.6	7.9
English	1,307	1,122	224	242	17.1	21.6
English and Modern Languages	158	153	24	25	15.2	16.3
European and Middle Eastern Languages	56	51	26	13	28.6	25.5
Fine Art	156	155	25	20	16.0	12.9
Geography	389	310	86	82	22.1	26.5
Modern History	1,035	890	224	242	21.6	27.2
Modern History and Economics	73	75	14	13	19.2	17.3
Modern History and English	85	79	9	6	10.6	7.6
Modern History and Modern Languages	119	92	18	14	15.1	15.2
Modern History and Politics	344	282	45	46	13.1	16.3
History of Art	88	77	14	14	15.9	18.2
Law	1,153	1,078	192	191	16.7	17.7
Law with Law Studies in Europe	345	321	31	30	9.0	9.3
Mathematics and Philosophy	104	86	16	24	15.4	27.9
Modern Languages	584	554	170	175	29.1	31.6
Modern Languages and Linguistics	73	75	24	16	32.9	21.3
Music	210	158	67	68	31.9	43
Oriental Studies	151	163	40	42	26.5	25.8
Philosophy and Modern Languages	88	73	18	17	20.5	23.3
Philosophy and Theology	86	105	21	21	24.4	20
Physics and Philosophy	126	86	17	14	13.5	16.3
PPE	1,668	1,503	238	248	14.3	16.5
Theology	112	114	45	42	40.2	36.8
Theology and Oriental Studies	7	–	2	–	28.6	–
Total Arts	*10,294*	*9,325*	*1,877*	*1,879*	*18.2*	*20.2*

The findings in the Tompkins Table (see page 258) are not officially endorsed by Cambridge University itself. However, since 2007 we have been able to publish the "official" Norrington Table from Oxford. Sanctioned or not, both tables give an indication of where the academic powerhouses lie – information which can be as useful to those trying to avoid them as to those seeking the ultimate challenge. Although there can be a great deal of movement year by year, both tables tend to be dominated by the rich, old foundations. Both tables are compiled from the degree results of final-year undergraduates. A first is worth five points; a 2:1, four; a 2:2,

Oxford applications and acceptances by course cont.

Sciences	Applications		Acceptances		Acceptances to Applications %	
	2010	2009	2010	2009	2010	2009
Biochemistry	329	315	91	105	27.7	33.3
Biological Sciences	382	344	107	108	28.0	31.4
Chemistry	573	474	181	192	31.6	40.5
Computer Science	148	126	19	16	12.8	12.7
Earth Sciences (Geology)	123	69	35	31	28.5	44.9
Engineering Science	757	606	150	134	19.8	22.1
Engineering, Economics and Management	125	140	10	16	8.0	11.4
Experimental Psychology	270	215	50	57	18.5	26.5
Human Sciences	106	111	25	31	23.6	27.9
Materials Science (including MEM)	125	78	31	31	24.8	39.7
Mathematics	1,046	917	173	174	16.5	19
Mathematics and Computer Science	91	78	20	18	22.0	23.1
Mathematics and Statistics	194	166	22	23	11.3	13.9
Medicine	1,469	1,293	154	156	10.5	12.1
Physics	841	765	162	175	19.3	22.9
Physiological Sciences	95	79	24	23	25.3	29.1
PPP	176	176	23	33	13.1	18.8
Total Sciences	**6,850**	**5,952**	**1,277**	**1,323**	**18.6**	**22.2**
Total Arts and Sciences	**17,144**	**15,277**	**3,154**	**3,202**	**18.4**	**21**

Note: the dates refer to the year in which the acceptances were made.

three; a third, one point. The total is divided by the number of candidates to produce each college's average.

In both universities, teaching for most students is based in the colleges. In practice, however, this arrangement holds good in the sciences only for the first year. One-to-one tutorials, which are Oxbridge's traditional strength for undergraduates, are by no means universal. However, teaching groups remain much smaller than in most universities, and the tutor remains an inspiration for many students. Both Oxford and Cambridge give applicants the option of leaving the choice of college to the university. For those with no ready source of advice on the colleges, this would seem an attractive solution to an intractable problem, but it is also a risky one: a slightly lower proportion succeeds in this way than by applying to a particular college and, inevitably, you may end up somewhere that you hate.

The applications procedure

Both universities have set a UCAS deadline of 15 October 2011 for entry in 2012. You may also need to take a written test and submit examples of your work – the exact requirements vary depending on the course you select, so check this carefully. See pages 20–21 for details of application tests. In addition, once Cambridge receives your UCAS form, you will be asked to complete an online Supplementary Application Questionnaire (SAQ). The deadline for this

Cambridge applications and acceptances by course

Arts	Applications 2010	Applications 2009	Acceptances 2010	Acceptances 2009	Acceptances to Applications % 2010	Acceptances to Applications % 2009
Anglo-Saxon, Norse and Celtic	47	52	21	25	44.7	48.1
Archaeology and Anthropology	181	163	66	69	36.5	42.3
Architecture	464	499	37	43	8.0	8.6
Asian and Middle Eastern Studies	149	188	48	61	32.2	32.4
Classics	148	173	71	88	48.0	50.9
Classics (4 years)	33	34	13	11	39.4	32.4
English	875	1,035	204	221	23.1	21.4
Geography	337	332	101	99	30.0	29.8
History	731	772	199	210	27.2	27.2
History of Art	139	126	31	34	22.3	27
Linguistics	86	–	23	–	26.7	–
Modern and Medieval Languages	580	605	164	191	28.3	31.6
Music	157	182	56	71	35.7	39
Philosophy	254	312	45	52	17.7	16.7
Theology and Religious Studies	111	124	46	58	41.4	46.8
Total Arts	**4,292**	**4,597**	**1,125**	**1,233**	**26.2**	**26.8**
Social Science						
Economics	1,342	1,396	169	178	12.6	12.8
Land Economy	230	261	56	56	24.3	21.5
Law	1,143	1,062	213	219	18.6	20.6
Social and Political Sciences	798	689	124	110	15.5	16
Total Social Sciences	**3,513**	**3,408**	**562**	**563**	**16.0**	**16.5**
Science and Technology						
Computer Science	272	329	76	69	27.9	21
Engineering	1,798	1,546	336	307	18.7	19.9
Mathematics	1,196	1,177	232	244	19.4	20.7
Medical Sciences	1,968	1,857	304	299	15.4	16.1
Natural Sciences	2,378	2,278	637	647	26.8	28.4
Veterinary Medicine	446	414	78	75	17.5	18.1
Total Science and Technology	**8,058**	**7,601**	**1,663**	**1,641**	**20.6**	**21.6**
Education	103	98	44	42	42.7	42.9
Total	**15,966**	**15,704**	**3,394**	**3,479**	**21.3**	**22.2**

Note: the dates refer to the year in which the acceptances were made.

Mathematics includes mathematics and mathematics with physics. Medical sciences includes medicine and the graduate course in medicine.

The Tripos courses in chemical engineering, management studies and manufacturing engineering can be taken only after Part 1 in another subject. Applications and acceptances for these courses are recorded under the first year subjects taken by the applicants involved.

Linguistics could only be taken after Part 1 of another Tripos for 2009 entry. From 2010 entry onwards, however, this subject became available as a full three-year degree programme.

will be 22 October 2011 in most cases. For international applications to Cambridge you must also submit a Cambridge Online Preliminary Application (COPA), in some cases by 9 September 2011.

You may apply to either Oxford or Cambridge (but not both) in the same admissions year, unless you are seeking an Organ award at both universities. Interviews take place in December for those short-listed (for international applicants, Cambridge hold some interviews overseas while Oxford holds some interviews over the internet, though medicine interviewees must come to Oxford). Applicants to Oxford will receive either a conditional offer or a rejection by Christmas, while in Cambridge the news arrives early in the new year.

For more information about the application process and preparation for interviews, visit **www.cam.ac.uk/admissions** and **www.ox.ac.uk/admissions**.

Oxford College Profiles

Balliol

Balliol College, Oxford OX1 3BJ
01865 277777   undergrad.admissions@balliol.ox.ac.uk   www.balliol.ox.ac.uk
Undergraduates: 385   Postgraduates: 321

Famous as the *alma mater* of many prominent post-war politicians, Balliol has maintained a strong presence in university life and is usually well represented in the Union and most other societies. Academic standards are formidably high, as might be expected in the college of Wycliffe and Adam Smith, notably in the classics and social sciences. PPE is notoriously oversubscribed. Library facilities are good and include the Tylor law library. Balliol began admitting overseas students in the 19th century and has cultivated an attractively cosmopolitan atmosphere. It is now the only college to have an entirely student-run bar, the focal point for evening socialising. Most undergraduates are offered accommodation in college for three years, with second year accommodation off-site. Graduate students are usually lodged in the Graduate Centre at Holywell Manor. Centrally located, with a JCR pantry that is open all day, Balliol is convenient as well as prestigious.

Brasenose

Brasenose College, Oxford OX1 4AJ
01865 277510 (admissions)   admissions@bnc.ox.ac.uk   www.bnc.ox.ac.uk
Undergraduates: 351   Postgraduates: 212

Brasenose may not be the most famous Oxford college, but it makes up for its discreet image with an advantageous city-centre position, nestled beside the stunning Radcliffe Camera. The *alma mater* of David Cameron, Brasenose was one of the first colleges to admit women in the 1970s, and now usually has a near-even split within each year. BNC, as the college is often known, has a strong rugby reputation, though relinquished the rugby crown to St Edmund Hall this year, and also has among the lowest proportions of students from state schools in the university. Named after the door knocker on the 13th-century Brasenose Hall, the college has a pleasant, intimate ambience which most find conducive to study. Law, PPE, medicine and modern history are traditional strengths, and competition for places in these subjects is intense.

The library is open 24 hours a day and there is a separate law library. All undergraduate rooms have internet connections. Sporting standards are as high as at many much larger colleges and the college's rowing club is one of the oldest in the university. The annexe at Frewin Court means nearly all undergraduates can live in, and many graduates can also live in the St Cross Building.

Christ Church

Christ Church, Oxford OX1 1DP
01865 276181 (admissions) admissions@chch.ox.ac.uk www.chch.ox.ac.uk
Undergraduates: 435 Postgraduates: 212

The college founded by Cardinal Wolsey in 1525 and affectionately known as "The House" has come a long way since Evelyn Waugh mythologised its aristocratic excesses in *Brideshead Revisited*, and a little under half of offers tend to be made to state school pupils, although this still leaves Christ Church with among the highest proportion of private school students. Academic pressure is reasonably relaxed, although natural high-achievers prosper and the college's history and law teaching is highly regarded. The college is now seventh in the Norrington Table, rising from twelfth last year. The magnificent 18th-century library is one of the best in Oxford and is supplemented by a separate law library. Christ Church has its own art gallery, which holds over 2,000 works of mainly Italian Renaissance art. Sport, especially rugby and football, is an important part of college life. The college has good squash courts and the river is close by for the aspiring oarsman, with the men's crew retaining its position at Head of the River this year. Accommodation for all three years is rated by Christ Church undergraduates as excellent and includes flats off Iffley Road as well as a number of beautifully panelled shared sets (double rooms) in college. The modern bar adds to the lustre of a college justly famous for its imposing architecture and bowler-hatted porters. Its chapel is also the cathedral of the Diocese of Oxford – England's smallest medieval cathedral.

Corpus Christi

Corpus Christi College, Oxford OX1 4JF
01865 276693 (admissions) admissions.office@ccc.ox.ac.uk www.ccc.ox.ac.uk
Undergraduates: 247 Postgraduates: 108

Corpus, one of Oxford's smallest colleges, is naturally overshadowed by its Goliath-like neighbour, Christ Church, but makes the most of its intimate, friendly atmosphere and exquisite beauty. Like "The House", it has an exceptional view across the Meadows. Although the college has only around 350 students including postgraduates, it has an admirable library open 24 hours a day. Academic expectations are high and English, Classics, PPE and medicine are especially well-established. Perhaps unsurprising, then, that Corpus has stormed to victory in University Challenge twice in recent years, although after their 2008 win the team were subsequently disqualified and stripped of their title. Corpus is able to offer accommodation to all its undergraduates, one of its many attractions to those seeking a smaller community in Oxford. The college is also one of the most generous with bursaries, giving travel, book and vacation grants at an almost unparalleled level across the university. Scholars are particularly well rewarded and the college came second in the Norrington Table last year.

Exeter

Exeter College, Oxford OX1 3DP
01865 279648 (academic secretary)   admissions@exeter.ox.ac.uk   www.exeter.ox.ac.uk
Undergraduates: 344   Postgraduates: 221

Exeter is the fourth oldest college in the university and was founded in 1314 by Walter de Stapeldon, Bishop of Exeter. Nestling between the High Street and Broad Street, site of most of the city's bookshops, it could hardly be more central. The college boasts handsome buildings, the exceptional Fellows' garden and attractive accommodation for most undergraduates for all three years of their university careers, although many second year students currently live out in college hostels or flats. The college has recently refurbished its graduate accommodation in the east of the city. Exeter does have academic pedigree, but has slipped down the Norrington Table in recent times, coming in 27th out of 30 last year. It is, however, often accused of being rather dull. Given its glittering roll-call of alumni, which includes Martin Amis, J.R.R. Tolkien, Alan Bennett, Richard Burton, Imogen Stubbs and Tariq Ali, this seems an accusation that, on the face of it at least, is hard to sustain. The arrival of Frances Cairncross, the former managing editor of *The Economist*, in 2004 has created a new dynamic at the college, with regular, high-profile, speaker events and the incorporation of a college careers service. The college recently took over the buildings of Ruskin College in Walton Street, which will provide further accommodation, although complete occupation is not expected until 2014. Exeter has strong links with the USA and takes around 25 students each year from Williams College in Massachusetts

Harris Manchester

Harris Manchester College, Oxford OX1 3TD
01865 271009 (admissions tutor)   enquiries@hmc.ox.ac.uk   www.hmc.ox.ac.uk
Undergraduates: 94   Postgraduates: 99

Founded in Manchester in 1786 to provide education for non-Anglican students, Harris Manchester finally settled in Oxford in 1889 after spells in both York and London. A full university college since 1996, its central location with fine buildings and grounds in Holywell Street is very convenient for the Bodleian, although the college itself does have an excellent library. Harris Manchester admits only mature students of mostly 25 years and above to read for both undergraduate and graduate degrees, predominantly in the arts. The average age has come down slightly in recent years, but all students must be 21 or older. There are also groups of visiting students from American universities and some men and women training for the ministry. Most of its members live in and all meals are provided, indeed the college encourages its members to dine regularly in hall. The college has few sporting facilities (a croquet lawn and a college punt), but members can use two central Oxford gyms without charge and can play football, cricket, swimming and chess as well as playing on other college or university teams. Other outlets include the college Drama Society, the popular Wine Society, and also the chapel, a focal point to many there.

Hertford

Hertford College, Oxford OX1 3BW
01865 279404 (admissions)   admissions@hertford.ox.ac.uk   www.hertford.ox.ac.uk
Undergraduates: 387   Postgraduates: 179

Though tracing its roots to the 13th century, Hertford is determinedly modern. It was one of the first colleges to admit women (in 1975). Hertford also helped set the trend towards offers of places conditional on A-levels, which paved the way for the abolition of the entrance examination. It is still popular with state school applicants, and is one of the least stuffy colleges, with a reputation for attracting students from a broad range of backgrounds. The college lacks the grandeur of Magdalen, of which it was once an annex, but has its own architectural trademark in the Bridge of Sighs. It is also close to the History Faculty library (Hertford's neighbour), the Bodleian and the King's Arms, perhaps Oxford's most popular pub. Academic pressure at Hertford is relaxed, but the quality of teaching, especially in English, is generally thought admirable. Accommodation has improved, thanks in part to the Abingdon House and Warnock House complex close to the Thames near Folly Bridge, and the college can now lodge all of its undergraduates at any one time, often at subsidised rates, albeit in disparate parts of the city. The bar, offering some notorious cocktails, serves as a central social hub, and is popular with students across the university. Like most congenial colleges, Hertford is often accused of being claustrophobic and inward-looking – a charge most Hertfordians would ascribe simply to jealousy.

Jesus

Jesus College, Oxford OX1 3DW
01865 279721 (admissions)   admissions.officer@jesus.ox.ac.uk   www.jesus.ox.ac.uk
Undergraduates: 344   Postgraduates: 176

Jesus, the only Oxford college to be founded in the reign of Elizabeth I, suffers from something of an unfair reputation for insularity. Its students, whose predecessors include T.E. Lawrence and Harold Wilson, describe it as "friendly but gossipy" and shrug off the legend that all its undergraduates are Welsh. Close to most of Oxford's main facilities, Jesus has three compact quads, the second of which is especially enticing in the summer. The college's JCR is well-equipped, with a pool table, large projector screen television, and a hatch serving tea and toast throughout the day. Academic standards are high and most subjects are taught in college. Physics, chemistry and engineering are especially strong. Rugby and rowing also tend to be taken seriously. Accommodation is almost universally regarded as excellent and relatively inexpensive, and the new Ship Street Centre was opened this academic year with 33 new en-suite rooms for first-year students (all with Wi-Fi) and a new lecture theatre. Self-catering flats in north and east Oxford have enabled every graduate to live in throughout his or her Oxford career. The range of accommodation available to undergraduates is similarly good and is available for the full length of any course. The college's Cowley Road development, also the site of the college's sports ground, has been described by the students' union as "some of the plushest student housing in Oxford".

Keble

Keble College, Oxford OX1 3PG
01865 272711 (admissions)   college.office@keble.ox.ac.uk   www.keble.ox.ac.uk
Undergraduates: 426   Postgraduates: 211

Keble is one of Oxford's most distinct colleges, with its unmistakable Victorian Gothic architecture and newly cleaned brickwork walls gleaming around the grand quads. Named after John Keble, the leader of the Oxford Movement, Keble was founded in 1870 with the intention of making Oxford education more accessible, and the college remains proud of "the legacy of a social conscience". With around 400 undergraduates, Keble is one of the biggest colleges in Oxford, although the college's academic performance varies from year to year. It is strong in the sciences, where it benefits from easy access to the Science Area, the Radcliffe Science Library and the Mathematical Institute. The college's sporting record remains exemplary, with the rugby team regularly dominating university competitions, winning both the league and cup competitions this year, and it was once famous for the special privileges it extended to rowers. Though the overflow of the sporting ethos into the college's social life can be a little overbearing, it by no means dominates the life of a college with one of the longest bars in the university and numerous music and drama societies as well as a highly successful annual Arts Week. Undergraduates are guaranteed accommodation in their first two years and the college can also accommodate most undergraduates in their final year. The cosy, wood-panelled library is open 24 hours a day and all rooms have internet connections. The college hall, where students wishing to dine must wear gowns six nights a week, has recently been intensively cleaned to restore it to its former glory and is one of the most impressive in the university – the original choice for the Harry Potter filmmakers, who eventually chose the hall at Christ Church. The refurbished "spaceship" bar and Café Keble are particular attractions. The college also has a well-equipped gym and the modern O'Reilly theatre, the acoustics of which are rated the best in the university.

Lady Margaret Hall

Lady Margaret Hall, Oxford OX2 6QA
01865 274310 (admissions)   admissions@lmh.ox.ac.uk   www.lmh.ox.ac.uk
Undergraduates: 395   Postgraduates: 195

Lady Margaret Hall, Oxford's first college for women, has been co-educational since 1978 and now enjoys an equal gender balance. For many students, LMH's comparative isolation – the college is three quarters of a mile north of the city centre – is a real advantage, ensuring a clear distinction between college life and university activities, and a refuge from tourists. For others it means a long journey to central library facilities. Although the neo-Georgian architecture is not to everyone's taste, the college's beautiful gardens back onto the Cherwell river, allowing LMH to have its own punt house and 12 acres of land. The students' union describes life at the college as "relaxed". It generally hovers around the lower reaches of the Norrington Table (20th out of 30 this year), although English is strong, producing a high proportion of firsts each year, as did maths, physics and history last year. Accommodation is guaranteed for first, second and third years since the opening of the new Pipe Partridge building, which has considerably enlarged undergraduate accommodation and houses a new JCR, dining hall and lecture theatre. Ongoing building works aim to provide further graduates rooms as well as a new gym. LMH shares most of its sports facilities with Trinity College, though it has tennis courts on site and has become a leading rowing college. The library is open 24 hours and is well-stocked for English and classics, with a separate law library. It has long been one of Oxford's dramatic centres, with at least five student productions a year put on at the Simpkins Lee lecture theatre, and has recently attained a strong presence in student journalism and the Oxford Union.

Lincoln

Lincoln College, Oxford OX1 3DR
01865 279836 (admissions)   admissions@lincoln.ox.ac.uk   www.lincoln.ox.ac.uk
Undergraduates: 312   Postgraduates: 307

Small, central Lincoln cultivates a lower profile than many other colleges with comparable assets. The college's 15th-century buildings and beautiful library – a converted Queen Anne church – combine to produce a delightful environment in which to spend three years. Academic standards are high, particularly in arts and social science subjects, although the college's relaxed atmosphere is justly celebrated. City-centre accommodation is provided by the college for all undergraduates throughout their careers and includes rooms above the Mitre, a medieval inn. Students parade around Oxford in sub fusc (formal wear) on Ascension Day (an entirely optional tradition) while choristers from the University Church beat the parish bounds. The college has a healthy rivalry with neighbouring Brasenose. Historically, Lincoln students must invite their Brasenose counterparts into the bar for free drinks every Ascension Day, in recognition of a time when a Lincoln and Brasenose student were both being chased by a town mob and the Brasenose student was denied access to Lincoln, leaving him to be killed by the mob. Graduate students have their own centre a few minutes' walk away in Bear Lane and at the EPA Science Centre close to the university science area. Finalists live in a recently refurbished complex on Museum Road, by Keble and the University Parks. Lincoln's small size and self-sufficiency have led to the college being accused of insularity. Lincoln's food is outstanding, among the best in the university. Sporting achievement is impressive for a college of this size, in part a reflection of its good facilities, with its football team winning Cuppers – one of the oldest football cup competitions in the world.

Magdalen

Magdalen College, Oxford OX1 4AU
01865 276063 (admissions)   admissions@magd.ox.ac.uk   www.magd.ox.ac.uk
Undergraduates: 415   Postgraduates: 184

Perhaps the most beautiful college in Oxford or Cambridge, Magdalen is known around the world for its tower, its deer park and its May morning celebrations – when students threw themselves off Magdalen Bridge into the river Cherwell. This practice has now been banned after shallow water resulted in a large number of injuries. The college has shaken off its public school image to become a truly cosmopolitan place, with a large intake from overseas and an increasing proportion of state school pupils. Magdalen's record in English, history and law is second to none, while its science park at Sandford is bound to bolster its reputation in these subjects. The college is academically very strong and topped the Norrington Table in 2010 for the first time, with over half of the finalists last year achieving Firsts. Library facilities are excellent, especially in history and law. First-year students are accommodated in the Waynflete Building and are allocated rooms in subsequent years by ballot. Undergraduates can be housed in college for the full length of their course. Rents are not cheap compared to other colleges, but there is always financial help on offer. Sets in cloisters and in the palatial New Buildings are particularly sought after. Magdalen is also conveniently placed between the city centre and East Oxford, where there is a plethora of pubs and restaurants and a lively music scene. The college bar is one of the best in Oxford and the college is a pluralistic place, proud of its drama society and choir. In recent years the college has become particularly strong at rowing. Elsewhere, enthusiasm on the sports field makes up for a traditional lack of athletic prowess.

Mansfield

Mansfield College, Oxford OX1 3TF
01865 270920 (admissions)   admissions@mansfield.ox.ac.uk   www.mansfield.ox.ac.uk
Undergraduates: 210   Postgraduates: 98

Mansfield's graduation to full Oxford college status in 1995 marked the culmination of a long history of development since 1886. Its spacious, attractive site is fairly central, close to the libraries, the shops, the University Parks and the river Cherwell. With just over 200 undergraduates, the community is close-knit, although this can verge on the claustrophobic. Recent moves to increase intake numbers may change that. The less intimidating atmosphere of Mansfield is, perhaps, helped by its strong representation of state-school students; the highest ratio in the university. First and third years live in college accommodation while second-years live in private houses nearby. The library is open 24 hours and the JCR is among the largest of any college, while Mansfield students share Merton's excellent sports ground and have numerous college teams. In recent years the college has produced many student journalists and contributes many performers to theatre and music productions. The twice-termly champagne and chocolate parties held in the chapel are hugely popular and very cheap. Despite its former theological background, students are not admitted on the basis of religion and can read a wide variety of subjects. Mansfield is home to the Oxford Centre for the Environment, Ethics and Society (OCEES) and the American Studies Institute backs onto its gardens, evidence of the strong links between Mansfield and the USA, which is reflected by some 35 visiting students annually. It also spearheads the Oxford FE Initiative, which encourages applications to the university from further education colleges.

Merton

Merton College, Oxford OX1 4JD
01865 276299 (admissions)   admissions@admin.merton.ox.ac.uk   www.merton.ox.ac.uk
Undergraduates: 313   Postgraduates: 313

Founded in 1264 by Walter de Merton, Bishop of Rochester and Chancellor of England, Merton is one of Oxford's oldest colleges and one of its most prestigious. Quiet and beautiful, with the oldest quad in the university, Merton has high academic expectations of its undergraduates, consistently reflected in a position at or near the top of the Norrington Table. It is currently in third place. History, English, physics, PPE and chemistry all enjoy a formidable track record. The medieval library is the envy of many other colleges. Accommodation is some of the cheapest in the university, of a good standard and offered to students for all three years. Merton's food is well-priced and among the best in the university; formal hall is served six times a week. Kitchens are provided for second years who live in off-site accommodation while Merton's many diversions include the Merton Floats, its dramatic society, the Neave (Politics)

Society, an excellent Christmas Ball and the peculiar Time Ceremony, which celebrates the return of GMT. Sports facilities are excellent, although participation tends to be more important than the final score.

New College

New College, Oxford OX1 3BN
01865 279512 (admissions)   admissions@new.ox.ac.uk   www.new.ox.ac.uk
Undergraduates: 421   Postgraduates: 244

New College is actually rather old (founded in 1379 by William of Wykeham), large and much more relaxed than most expect when first confronting its daunting facade. It is a bustling place, as proud of its excellent music and its bar as of its strength in classics, chemistry, music and maths. The college came fifth in the Norrington Table last year. Traditionally in the bottom third of colleges for attracting state-school students, the college has been making particular efforts to increase this proportion, inviting applications from schools that have never sent candidates to Oxford. The Target Schools Scheme, designed to increase applications from state schools, is well established. All first, second and fourth-year students can live in college and almost all of the third-years who want to live in usually can. The college's library facilities are impressive, especially in law, classics and PPE. The sports ground is nearby and includes good tennis courts. Women's sport is particularly strong, especially on the river. A sports complex, named after Brian Johnston, opened in 1997, at St Cross Road. The sheer beauty of New College remains one of its principal assets and the college gardens are a memorable sight in the summer, especially the other-worldly Mound in the heart of the college. In spite of these traditional charms, the college has strong claims to be considered admirably innovative. Music is a feature of college life, and the college has some of the best practice facilities in the university. The Commemoration Ball, held every three years, is a highlight of Oxford's social calendar.

Oriel

Oriel College, Oxford OX1 4EW
01865 276522 (admissions)   admissions@oriel.ox.ac.uk   www.oriel.ox.ac.uk
Undergraduates: 305   Postgraduates: 159

In spite of its reputation as a bastion of muscular privilege, Oriel is a friendly, centrally-located college with a strong sense of identity. In recent years the college has succeeded in ridding itself of its image of being home to the archetypal "Tory boy" characters. Academic pressure is relaxed by Oxford standards and it tends to inhabit the middle reaches of the Norrington Table, though it climbed to 11th last year. The well-stocked library is open 24 hours a day. The college is traditionally described as having "a strong crew spirit" reflecting its traditions on the river, though the last few years have not been quite so glorious for the Oriel crew. Other sports are well catered for, even if their facilities are considerably farther away than the boathouse, which is only a short jog away. Accommodation is of variable quality, but Oriel can provide rooms for the duration of the course – be it three years or four – for those students who require them. Extensive accommodation is one mile away off the Cowley Road and at the Island Site on Oriel Street. Oriel also offers a lively drama society, a Shakespearian production taking place each summer in the front quad. College meals are cheap, with students charged little more than £6 for three meals a day in hall.

Pembroke

Pembroke College, Oxford OX1 1DW
01865 276412 (admissions)   admissions@pmb.ox.ac.uk   www.pmb.ox.ac.uk
Undergraduates: 359   Postgraduates: 145

Although its alumni include such extrovert characters as Dr Johnson and Michael Heseltine, Pembroke is stereotypically one of Oxford's least dynamic colleges. The college is historically poor financially, though its modern art collection draws in visitors and revenue. Mid-table in terms of exam results, the college has Fellows and lecturers in almost all the major university subjects. Pembroke will be able to accommodate all undergraduates when the new extension is opened in 2012, and the Sir Geoffrey Arthur building on the river, ten minutes' walk from the college, offers excellent facilities; in addition to 100 student rooms there is a concert room, computer room and a multigym. College food is reasonable, with formal hall three times a week. Rugby and rowing are strong, with Pembroke usually behind only Oriel and Magdalen on the river, and squash and tennis courts are available at the nearby sports ground. The college's netball, football and hockey teams all reached the finals of college cup competitions. Over the past few years Pembroke's intake has had among the lowest proportion of state-school students in the university, though is running access schemes to improve this ratio.

Queen's

Queen's College, Oxford OX1 4AW
01865 279161   admissions@queens.ox.ac.uk   www.queens.ox.ac.uk
Undergraduates: 345   Postgraduates: 134

One of the most striking sights of the High Street, Queen's has now shed its exclusive "northern" image to become one of Oxford's liveliest and most attractive colleges. The college's academic record is average, although results have improved recently and it is now placed 14th in the Norrington Table. Modern languages, chemistry and mathematics are reckoned among the strongest subjects. Queen's does not normally admit undergraduates for the single honour schools of theology (without philosophy), computer science or geography, and is seen as strong in history and politics. The library is as beautiful as it is well stocked. All students are offered accommodation, first years being housed in modernist annexes in east Oxford, and the college is in the process of converting all rooms into en-suite facilities – at the moment it is about half en suite in the main college. Queen's can be insular and is largely apolitical, but has a strong college enthusiasm for sport, particularly rugby and netball. The college's beer cellar is one of the most popular in the university and the JCR facilities are also better than average. An annual dinner commemorates a student who is said to have fended off a boar by thrusting a volume of Aristotle into its mouth. Postgraduates are accommodated in St Aldate's House, a modern building close to the centre of town.

St Anne's

St Anne's College, Oxford OX2 6HS
01865 274840 (admissions)   enquiries@st-annes.ox.ac.uk   www.st-annes.ox.ac.uk
Undergraduates: 426   Postgraduates: 252

Architecturally uninspiring (a Victorian row of houses with concrete "stack-a-studies" dropped into their back gardens), St Anne's makes up in community spirit what it lacks in awesome grandeur. One of the largest colleges, it has a relatively high proportion of state-school students. A women's college until 1979, its academic standing has fluctuated, having been in last place in the Norrington Table in the middle of the last decade, but now scoring around mid-table. PPE is particularly strong. The library, which is now open 24 hours, is very well-stocked and is rich in law, Chinese and medieval history texts. The college has a strong presence in the university journalism scene and its football teams usually do very well. Accommodation is guaranteed to all undergraduates, and the college also offers help to students wishing to live out in their second year, of whom there are usually only about ten. It is situated to the north of the city centre, although not as far out as St Hugh's. Three new accommodation blocks contain 150 student rooms, including four for disabled students, while the older rooms have been refurbished. Half of all rooms are en suite.

St Catherine's

St Catherine's College, Oxford OX1 3UJ
01865 271703 (admissions) admissions@stcatz.ox.ac.uk www.stcatz.ox.ac.uk
Undergraduates: 499 Postgraduates: 250

Arne Jacobsen's modernist design for "Catz", one of Oxford's youngest and largest undergraduate colleges, has attracted much attention as the most striking contrast in the university to the lofty spires of Magdalen and New College. Close to the Law, English and Social Science faculties, the university science area and the pleasantly rural Holywell Great Meadow, St Catherine's is nevertheless only a few minutes' walk from the city centre. Academic standards are especially high in mathematics and physics. The well-liked Wolfson library is open till midnight on most days. Rooms are small but tend to be warmer than in other, more venerable colleges, and are now available on site for first, second and third years. There is an excellent theatre, as well as an on-site punt house, gym and squash courts. The college is host to the Cameron Mackintosh Chair of Contemporary Theatre, currently held by Sir Trevor Nunn. Previous incumbents include Kevin Spacey, Arthur Miller and Sir Ian McKellen. St Catherine's has one of the best JCR facilities in Oxford.

St Edmund Hall

St Edmund Hall, Oxford OX1 4AR
01865 279011 (admissions) admissions@seh.ox.ac.uk www.seh.ox.ac.uk
Undergraduates: 411 Postgraduates: 191

St Edmund Hall – "Teddy Hall" – has one of Oxford's smallest college sites but also one of its most populous. The college offers students the chance to live in its medieval quads right in the heart of the city. With the male/female ratio nearly equal (despite there anomalously being twice as many men as women last year) the college is shedding its image as a home for "hearties", and the authorities have gone out of their way to tone down younger members' rowdier excesses. Nonetheless, the sporting culture is still vigorous and the college usually does well in rugby, football and hockey. The college is also known across the university for its "bops" – the name given to student discos. Academically, Teddy Hall tends to yo-yo between the middle and the bottom of the Norrington Table. It is currently 23rd out of 30. But the college has some impressive names among its fellowship as well as a marvellous library, originally a Norman church. It hosts three annual prizes for journalism, including a £500 award for a student from St Edmund Hall. College accommodation is reasonable and can be offered for three years, either on the main site or in North or East Oxford. The college has three annexes, one near the University Parks, and two on Iffley Road, where many of the rooms have private bathrooms. Hall food is better than average, especially after the arrival of a new chef last year.

St Hilda's

St Hilda's College, Oxford OX4 1DY
01865 286620 (admissions)   college.office@st-hildas.ox.ac.uk www.st-hildas.ox.ac.uk
Undergraduates: 402   Postgraduates: 166

October 2008 marked a milestone for St Hilda's and the university as a whole, as the college welcomed its first mixed sex intake. Although the college, founded in 1893, lasted more than 100 years as an all-female institution, the governing body voted in 2006 to admit men. Male students now make up nearly half of the first year in incoming years. The college has long languished at the bottom end of the Norrington Table, though is slowly rising towards mid-table, but is a distinctive part of the Oxford landscape and is usually well represented in university life. The 65,000-volume library is growing fast and accommodation for readers was extended in 2005. St Hilda's also boasts one of the largest ratios of state-school to independent undergraduates in Oxford. Accommodation is guaranteed to first years and finalists and there are plans to renovate and expand the bar and common room and further improve disabled access, to be finished in the summer of 2011. The JCR has its own punts, which are available free for college members and their guests. Many of the rooms offer some of the best river views in Oxford. Social facilities are limited, but this is expected to change with the influx of men, though whether there is any link between this and the introduction of new widescreens televisions is not clear. The standard of food is high and the college has recently stopped fining students for serious misbehaviour, asking them to do community service instead.

St Hugh's

St Hugh's College, Oxford OX2 6LE
01865 274910 (admissions)   admissions@st-hughs.ox.ac.uk   www.st-hughs.ox.ac.uk
Undergraduates: 419   Postgraduates: 205

One of the lesser-known colleges, St Hugh's was criticised by students in 1986 when it began admitting men. There is now an equal male/female ratio, a better balance than at most Oxford colleges. Like Lady Margaret Hall, St Hugh's picturesque setting is a bicycle ride from the city centre. It is an ideal college for those seeking a place to live and study away from the madding crowd, and is well liked for its pleasantly bohemian atmosphere and beautiful gardens. Academic pressure remains comparatively low. After a brief jump up the Norrington Table last year the college is now back in the lower regions at 19th, though music is particularly strong. St Hugh's guarantees accommodation to undergraduates for all three years, although the standard of rooms is variable. Sport, particularly football, is taken quite seriously. As the college enjoys extensive grounds compared to most colleges, there is space for a croquet lawn and tennis courts. The college will celebrate its 125th anniversary this summer. Construction of a new building for the study of China will start in 2012 after a £10-million donation from a Hong Kong businessman.

St John's

St John's College, Oxford OX1 3JP
01865 277317 (admissions)   admissions@sjc.ox.ac.uk   www.sjc.ox.ac.uk
Undergraduates: 395   Postgraduates: 217

St John's is one of Oxford's powerhouses, excelling in almost every field and boasting arguably
the most beautiful gardens in the university. Founded in 1555 by a London merchant, it is richly
endowed and makes the most of its resources to provide undergraduates with an agreeable
and challenging three years. The work ethic is very much part of the St John's ethos, and
academic standards are high, with English, chemistry and history among the traditional
strengths, though all students benefit from the impressive library. The college is usually
challenging for the top spot in the Norrington Table though fell to fourth in 2010. It also has
one of the highest proportions of state-school students in Oxford. As might be expected of a
wealthy college, the accommodation is excellent and guaranteed for three or four years,
boosted by the completion of a brand new quad with en-suite rooms and a new gym, café and
law library. The college's riches allow it to subsidise accommodation costs to a large degree, as
well as providing generous book grants and prizes. St John's has a strong sporting tradition and
offers good facilities, but the social scene is relatively limited. As befits such an all-round strong
college, entry is fiercely competitive. The college is very close to two of Oxford's landmark
pubs: the Eagle and Child and the Lamb and Flag.

St Peter's

St Peter's College, Oxford OX1 2DL
01865 278863 (admissions)   admissions@spc.ox.ac.uk   www.spc.ox.ac.uk
Undergraduates: 341   Postgraduates: 94

Opened as St Peter's Hall in 1929, St Peter's has been an Oxford college since 1961. Its
medieval, Georgian and 19th-century buildings are in the city centre and close to most of
Oxford's main facilities. Though still young, St Peter's is well represented in university life and
has pockets of academic excellence, rising to tenth in the Norrington Table in 2004, although it
has since fallen far back into the bottom half, languishing in 27th. History tutoring is
particularly good, but there are no Fellows in classics at the college. Accommodation is offered
to students in their first and third years. Although previously prohibited from cooking on the
main site, students now have a kitchenette with limited facilities. Student rooms vary from
traditional ones in college to new purpose-built rooms a few minutes' walk away. The college's
facilities are impressive, including one of the university's best JCRs. The college has a proud
sporting heritage, being particularly strong at rugby and rowing. St Peter's is known as one of
Oxford's most vibrant colleges socially. It is strong in acting and journalism, and has a recently
refurbished bar, although the college has recently suffered from a severe shortage in funding.

Somerville

Somerville College, Oxford OX2 6HD
01865 270619 (admissions)   secretariat@some.ox.ac.uk   www.some.ox.ac.uk
Undergraduates: 395   Postgraduates: 84

The announcement, early in 1992, that Somerville was to go co-educational sparked an
unusually acrimonious and persistent dispute within this most tranquil of colleges. Protests

were doomed to failure, however; the first male undergraduates arrived in 1994 and now account for half the students as peace has returned. The college's atmosphere appears to have survived the momentous change, although the culture of protest reappeared when a number of students refused to pay the Government's tuition fees in 1998. The college has relatively strong state-school representation. Accommodation, including 30 small flats for students, is of a reasonable standard, and was supplemented by a new 68-room building this year, so that all first, third and fourth-year students can live in, as well as around three-quarters of second-years. There are kitchens in all college buildings, but hall food is towards the cheaper end of the university. Sport is strong at Somerville and the women's rowing eight usually finishes near the head of the river. The college's hockey pitches and tennis courts are nearby. The 120,000-volume library is open 24 hours a day and is the second largest college library as well as one of the most beautiful in Oxford. The college also has an active music society and strong drama presence, as well as the perk of having Wi-Fi internet throughout the college.

Trinity

Trinity College, Oxford OX1 3BH
01865 279860 (admissions)   admissions@trinity.ox.ac.uk   www.trinity.ox.ac.uk
Undergraduates: 308   Postgraduates: 106

Architecturally impressive and boasting beautiful lawns (which you can actually walk on), Trinity is one of Oxford's least populous colleges, admitting some 80 undergraduates each year. It is ideally located, beside the Bodleian, Blackwell's bookshop and the White Horse pub, a short stroll from the University Parks and the town centre. Cardinal Newman, an alumnus of Trinity, is said to have regarded Trinity's motto as "Drink, drink, drink". Academic pressure varies, but the college had recently made impressive steps up the ranks of the Norrington Table of academic performance, though fell to 25th out of 30 last year, despite a fair share of Firsts, especially in arts subjects. Trinity has shaken off its reputation for apathy, and whilst members are active in all walks of university life, the college has its own debating and drama societies, as well as sharing a fierce rivalry with neighbouring Balliol. Usually, all undergraduates are given a room on the main site in their first and second years, with the majority of third and fourth years living in a purpose-built block a mile and a half north of the main site. Students rate the food highly and the atmosphere is famously close-knit at so intimate a college.

University

University College, Oxford OX1 4BH
01865 276959 (admissions)   admissions@univ.ox.ac.uk   www.univ.ox.ac.uk
Undergraduates: 362   Postgraduates: 216

University is the first Oxford college to be able to boast a former student in the Oval Office: former President Clinton was a Rhodes Scholar at University in the late 1960s. The college is probably Oxford's oldest – a claim disputed by Merton – though highly unlikely to have been founded by King Alfred, as legend claims. Academic expectations are high and the college prospers in most subjects, and it is currently sixth in the Norrington Table. Physics, PPE and maths are particularly strong. That said, University has fewer claims to be thought a powerhouse in the manner of St John's, arguably its greatest rival. Students who are accepted to read courses with a mathematical element are invited to a free week-long maths course just before the beginning of their first term, providing a head-start in their studies. Accommodation is guaranteed to undergraduates for all three years, with third years lodged in an annexe in north Oxford about a mile and a half from the college site on the High Street, although the vast majority of third years choose to live out in rented accommodation. Sport is strong and University has been well represented and successful on the rugby field in the last few years, but the college has a reputation for being quiet socially. Students from the state sector are poorly represented, despite a generous bursary scheme, though last year's intake saw a 10 per cent shift to the state sector following the college's proactive access schemes.

Wadham

Wadham College, Oxford OX1 3PN
01865 277545 (admissions)   admissions@wadh.ox.ac.uk   www.wadh.ox.ac.uk
Undergraduates: 452   Postgraduates: 149

Founded by Dorothy Wadham in 1609, Wadham is known in about equal measure for its academic track record – the college generally ranks just above mid-table – and its leftist politics. The JCR – or student union as both the JCR and MCR have rebranded themselves – is famously dynamic and politically active, although the breadth of political opinion is greater than its left-wing stereotype suggests. Wadham students are notoriously trendy, although some in the university find the atmosphere at the college slightly forced. That said, the college is very strong on admitting students from state schools. And for somewhere supposedly unconcerned with such fripperies, its gardens are surprisingly beautiful. The somewhat rough-hewn chapel is similarly memorable. The college has a good 24-hour library. Accommodation is guaranteed for at least two years and there are many large, shared rooms on offer. Journalism, music and drama play an important part. Highlights in the social calendar are Queer Festival, a riotous celebration of all things gay, and Wadstock, the college's open-air summer music festival.

Worcester

Worcester College, Oxford OX1 2HB
01865 278391 (admissions)   admissions@worc.ox.ac.uk   www.worc.ox.ac.uk
Undergraduates: 429   Postgraduates: 168

Worcester is to the west of Oxford what Magdalen is to the east: an open, rural contrast to the urban rush of the city centre. The college's rather mediocre exterior conceals a delightful environment, including some characteristically muscular Baroque Hawskmoor architecture, a garden and a lake. The college has been rising up the Norrington Table and is currently eighth this year. The 24-hour library is strongest in the arts. Accommodation, guaranteed for two years and provided for the majority of third years, varies in quality from ordinary to conference standard in the Canal Building. More en-suite accommodation, next to the new gym, is now available. Sport plays an important part in college life, as befits the only college with playing fields on site. Worcester's hockey team is not quite what it once was, but the college has had five successful rowing teams since the first term of 2010–11 and has had recent successes in football and cricket. Formal halls are available four nights a week and cost just £3. Like Magdalen and New, it is home to the Commemoration Ball once every three years, a highlight of the Oxford social calendar. Of the 2011 intake, 55 per cent will be from the state system (fairly representative for the college), and 61 per cent will be female.

Cambridge College Profiles

Christ's

Christ's College, Cambridge CB2 3BU

01223 334983 (admissions)   admissions@christs.cam.ac.uk   www.christs.cam.ac.uk

Undergraduates: 440   Postgraduates: 111

Christ's strength lies in its location, right in the middle of the city. It is one of the few colleges that is just as convenient distance-wise for the arts faculties as it is for scientists and architects (a five-minute walk). All first and third years, and most second years, live in college, which makes for an intimate and cosy atmosphere. Rooms on offer vary from the gothic splendour of some of the old buildings to the more modern New Court "Typewriter", which has been recently refurbished, offering students en-suite accommodation and private balconies. The college has a visual arts centre where the college's artist in residence works, and a newly refurbished gallery and performance space, the Yusuf Hamied Centre. Christ's Films – widely considered to be one of the best film societies in the university – and the Christ's Amateur Dramatics Society are active student groups. Sport flourishes and the football team has won Cuppers more time than any other college. The playing fields, shared with St Catharine's, are situated on Barton Road, about two miles away. Christ's prides itself on its academic strength, though has slipped down the Tompkins Table to 12 last year. Over a decade ago it was a steady first. In 2010 some 63 per cent of students accepted came from the state sector and women make up about 40 per cent of the students. Christ's is one of the last Cambridge college to give "easy offers", as low as two E grades at A-levels. The college is confident of its ability to identify potential high-flyers at interview and, in effect, prepared to circumvent A-levels as the principal criteria for entry to ease the pressure on good applicants and allow them to read around their subject. However, "easy offers" are rare and applicants need "an outstanding record of GCSE grades and strong support from your school". Christ's has a reputation for being dominated by hard-working medics, natural scientists and mathematicians, although it is also strong in history and English. Notable alumni include Charles Darwin and the poet John Milton.

Churchill

Churchill College, Cambridge CB3 0DS

01223 336202 (admissions)   admissions@chu.cam.ac.uk   www.chu.cam.ac.uk

Undergraduates: 500   Postgraduates: 255

Students at Churchill claim they are the most unpretentious of Cambridge colleges – and are proud of the fact the college allows its students to walk on the grass. This informality stems from the youth of the college, as well as its relatively high state-school intake. But lack of spires does not signal lack of success: last year the college received its best ever results and jumped to third on the Tompkins Table. Founded in 1958 to help meet "the national need for scientists and engineers and to forge links with industry", the college has a noticeably high proportion of scientists and men: only one in three students are female. Compared to the breathtaking architecture of other Cambridge colleges, Churchill's modern and functional architecture strikes many as ugly, with some students saying the "1960s brutalism is something you get used to". Another perceived flaw is its distance from the city centre – the college is a 15-minute walk from the centre of the City. Others argue that the distance offers much-needed breathing space, and rate the college's spacious and leafy grounds. One undeniable advantage is Churchill's ability to provide every undergraduate with a room in college for all three years, with a lauded feature being the heated window seats that keep Siberian winds at bay. There are extensive on-site playing fields, and the college does well in rugby, hockey and rowing. The university's only student radio is based here, and frequently wins national awards for best student radio station. The College Archive Centre houses the papers of both the college's namesake, Winston Churchill, and former prime minister Margaret Thatcher.

Clare

Clare College, Cambridge CB2 1TL
01223 333246 (admissions)   admissions@clare.cam.ac.uk   www.clare.cam.ac.uk
Undergraduates: 490   Postgraduates: 258

Though the second oldest college in Cambridge, Clare is far from austere. It occupies a quiet yet central position behind Caius, in the shadow of King's College Chapel and looking onto "the Backs". It is also one of the oldest of the colleges, founded in 1326. Despite these accomplishments, Clare is known among students as one of the friendliest and most welcoming places to study, with an active bar, frequent live music and comedy in Clare Cellars, a magnet for students all across town. Accommodation is guaranteed for all three years, either in college – where life centres around the 17th-century Old Court – or nearby hostels. The college has recently finished the Gillespie Centre, which houses undergraduates and provides conference facilities. The college has made systematic attempts to raise the proportion of state-educated students. Clare's extracurricular life is a big attraction. Music thrives, and the choir records and tours regularly. The student acting group, the Clare Actors, are well-known in college, whilst Clare Comedy provides a night of stand-up every month. One of the few complaints is that its playing fields, which are shared with Peterhouse and the graduate college, Clare Hall, are a 15-minute bicycle ride away. Clare isn't known for its sporting prowess: instead, emphasis is placed on participation and "the social elements of sport".

Corpus Christi

Corpus Christi College, Cambridge CB2 1RH
01223 338056 (admissions)   admissions@corpus.cam.ac.uk   www.corpus.cam.ac.uk
Undergraduates: 273   Postgraduates: 185

One of the oldest Cambridge colleges, Corpus Christi's small size inevitably makes it one of the more intimate colleges. Some argue that allows for a cohesive community, others feel it can become a goldfish bowl. Although small, it is traditionally broadly based academically. Mixed with the old architecture, however, is a state-of-the-art undergraduate library – which has improved study facilities in the college – and a new student centre, both of which opened recently. The college's formal halls have a good reputation and canteen food is "always edible" according to students. Students are offered a range of accommodation, from the old-fashioned to the modern: all undergraduates are allocated a room in college or neighbouring hostels for at least three years. Some students dislike the college's policy of allocating rooms partly on the basis of academic results. There is a fairly even social balance at Corpus: the latest data showed 60 per cent of undergraduates at the college came from the state sector. The sporting facilities, at Leckhampton (just over a mile away), are among the best in the university and include a popular outdoor swimming pool. The size of the college means that its sporting reputation owes more to enthusiasm than success, however. Drama is also well catered for, with The Fletcher Players performing a number of plays each term, and the college owns The Playroom, the university's best small theatre. Music is strong at Corpus — although some students complain about the practice rooms, the college has one of the best student-run choirs and a beautiful chapel in which to practice.

Downing

Downing College, Cambridge CB2 1DQ
01223 334826 (admissions)   admissions@dow.cam.ac.uk   www.dow.cam.ac.uk
Undergraduates: 445   Postgraduates: 222

Hidden away behind the bustle of Regent Street, close to the city centre yet off the tourist trail, lies Downing College. Its unusual neo-Classical quadrangle and beautiful architecture opens up magically from an unassuming front gate. Founded in 1800 for the study of law, medicine and natural sciences, these are still thought to be the college's strong subjects. Indeed Downing is often called "the law college", and also has something of a reputation for hard-playing, hard-drinking rugby players and oarsmen. The college has many successful sports teams – with its own on-site tennis, netball and squash courts, a gym and plenty of open space (The Paddock), whilst it is also one of the best on the river. First and third years generally live on site, with second years offered houses on nearby Lensfield Road. The library, opened in 1993, has won an award for its architecture. There is a good mix between students with state and independent school backgrounds among new undergraduates. The student-run bar/party room has improved college social life, and meals are of a high standard, as is formal hall, which is often held in candlelight. For those of a less sporting persuasion, meetings of the student debating society and the Blake Society, named after alumnus Quentin Blake, are important events in the student calendar. Music at the college is strong, and a new student theatre, providing a venue for drama, music and exhibitions, opened in 2010.

Emmanuel

Emmanuel College, Cambridge CB2 3AP
01223 334290 (admissions)   admissions@emma.cam.ac.uk   www.emma.cam.ac.uk
Undergraduates: 513   Postgraduates: 160

On average the most successful college academically, Emmanuel, more commonly known as "Emma", topped the Tompkins Table again last year. Despite this, it is keen to present itself as the "friendly" Cambridge college and entertainments at its (literally) ship-shaped bar are famous university-wide, as are its ducks. The college is proud of students' achievements in sport and music and has one of the most popular of the smaller May Balls. Despite its academic success, and being one of the wealthiest of the colleges, Emma has an unpretentious atmosphere: students and fellows share an open-air pool in the fellows garden, the college bar is stylish and strikingly modern. The library has seen a recent extension. For the last few years Emma has fairly consistently kept the state to independent student ratio at about 60:40, and around half of all undergraduates are women. All students are guaranteed accommodation for the duration of their course. Second years can choose to stay on site or nearby in college-owned houses. With self-catering facilities limited, most students eat in hall and the college chefs were recently voted best in the university. Although formal hall is good, most popular is the Sunday brunch: a late-morning affair with fry-ups or pastries and the Sunday papers. The college offers expedition grants to undergraduates every year, and has a large hardship fund. In the summer, the college gardens, with tennis courts and an outdoor swimming pool, offer a welcome haven from exam pressures. The sports grounds are excellent, if some distance away, and the women's rowing team have excelled in recent years.

Fitzwilliam

Fitzwilliam College, Cambridge CB3 0DG
01223 332030 (admissions)   admissions@fitz.cam.ac.uk   www.fitz.cam.ac.uk
Undergraduates: 487   Postgraduates: 229

Based in the city centre until 1963, Fitzwilliam now occupies a large, modern site on the Huntingdon Road, a ten-minute bicycle ride from the centre. Despite its lack of architectural splendour ("multi-storey car park" is a common comparison) the flower-filled quads are a well-kept secret. "Fitz" was established in 1869, with the aim of widening access to the university. They are proud of this tradition, and have consistently attracted a larger than average proportion of talented applicants from the state sector. The college is notably "unstuffy", with a good college bar, excellent ENTS events (attracting big-name acts) and a strong sporting reputation. The football and rugby teams have enjoyed great success, and there are extensive and well-kept sports facilities close by, including a gym, football, rugby, cricket, hockey and tennis grounds – as well as squash courts on site. Music also thrives at the college: Fitz is the only college in Cambridge to have access to a professional string quartet. Food lacks a certain something, but self-catering facilities include the rare use of ovens, meaning avid bakers need not miss out. The college has a 250-seater auditorium for performances, and brand new state-of-the-art library and IT centre, designed by the award-winning architect Edward Cullinan. Undergraduates are guaranteed college accommodation for three or four years, either on site or in nearby housing, and its newly built accommodation is spacious and bright.

Girton

Girton College, Cambridge CB3 0JG
01223 338972 (admissions)   admissions@girton.cam.ac.uk   www.girton.cam.ac.uk
Undergraduates: 551   Postgraduates: 168

Students at Girton readily admit: "You've probably never heard of Girton, half of Cambridge students haven't." Its anonymity is due to its distance from the city centre. Admittedly, the centre is only a 15-minute bicycle ride away, but in Cambridge terms that is as long a commute as you can get and in the (frequent) wind and rain can be an unwelcome start to the day. However, its comparative isolation inevitably encourages a strong community spirit, and students get to enjoy its beautiful grounds away from the tourists and the relative bustle of the city. Girton stands in 50 acres and all facilities, including an indoor swimming pool, gym, squash and tennis courts are on site, as well as an orchard through which to meander if academic pressure proves too much. There is no question of overcrowding: rooms are available for the entire course. The majority of second-year students live in Wolfson Court (near the University Library, closer to town). Some find that the long corridors remind them of boarding school, but accommodation at the college, which includes a number of self-contained houses on site, is noticeably cheaper than some other colleges. Since becoming coeducational in 1977, the college has maintained a balanced admissions policy. At least 60 per cent of the undergraduates admitted are from state schools, and just under half are women. Girton also has one of the highest proportion of women Fellows in any mixed college. The college is active in most sports and particularly strong in football, and many students go on to represent the University. Given its comparative isolation, many people eat and socialise in college. The food is reported to be excellent.

Gonville and Caius

Gonville and Caius College, Cambridge CB2 1TA
01223 332440 (admissions)   admissions@cai.cam.ac.uk   www.cai.cam.ac.uk
Undergraduates: 559   Postgraduates: 234

Gonville and Caius College – to confuse the outsider, the college is usually known as Caius (pronounced "keys") – is among the most beautiful of Cambridge's colleges, as well as one of the most central. It has an excellent academic reputation, especially in medicine and history, although maths and law are also highly rated. Caius also has one of the largest and most architecturally impressive student libraries in Cambridge, housed in the Cockerell Building next door to the college. Accommodation, though guaranteed for three years, varies in quality depending on how lucky you are. Most first years are housed in Harvey Court, a five-minute walk away across the river, which is currently under renovation. Many second years are flung out to houses near the train station, a 10-15 minute bicycle to main faculties. Adjacent to Harvey Court is the £13-million Stephen Hawking Building, named after the college's most famous fellow, which opened in October 2006. Providing en-suite accommodation for 75 students and eight fellows, the building boasts some of the highest-standard student accommodation in Cambridge. Third years live in the idyllic surroundings of the old courts. An ongoing gripe is that undergraduates are obliged to eat in hall most nights of the week, having to purchase 36 meal tickets a term. There is formal hall every night of the week, for which the food is no different from informal hall, but students wear gowns, and dine with fellows by candlelight. The college is working to diminish its public school reputation – more than 60 per cent of new students now come from state schools. Academically, the college has been a strong performer, but slipped out of the top third of the Tompkins Table last year. Caius has one of the best and most competitive boat clubs in the university, and has won the "bumps" numerous times over the last few years.

Homerton

Homerton College, Cambridge CB2 8PH
01223 747252 (admissions) admissions@homerton.cam.ac.uk www.homerton.cam.ac.uk
Undergraduates: 607   Postgraduates: 452 PGCE and other graduate courses

Homerton's origins were in 18th-century London, and it moved to Cambridge in 1894. Although the college has been part of the university for over 30 years, where it is known primarily as a teaching college, in 2010 it was awarded full college status. Homerton now accepts students onto a wide range of courses offered by the university, although it continues to specialise in education, including teacher training – through the BA degree and the postgraduate certificate in education (PGCE). Homerton was recently voted the "friendliest college in Cambridge", and its position, a mile from the city centre in its own large grounds, does not stop Homertonians from being among the most active in university life. That said,

there are some great facilities on site and some popular societies. The Music Society –
comprising of an orchestra, swing band, choir and even a steel-pan group – hold regular
concerts, whilst the Amateur Dramatic Society performs several times throughout the year. All
first years have rooms in college in modern accommodation blocks. In the second year,
accommodation may be in college or in private rented houses, but final-year students can live
in if they wish. Over two thirds of students come from state schools, and there is a 50:50 ratio of
women to men, rare for any other teacher training course.

Hughes Hall

Hughes Hall, Wollaston Road, Cambridge CB1 2EW
01223 334897 (admissions)   admissions@hughes.cam.ac.uk   www.hughes.cam.ac.uk
Undergraduates: 113   Postgraduates: 427

Hughes Hall admits mature undergraduates over the age of 21 and affiliated students (who
already have a good honours degree from another university). The college is the oldest
graduate college in the university, founded in 1885 for the training of graduate women
teachers. Since then it has become a lively and cosmopolitan community of 500 mature
undergraduate and graduate students studying for nearly all the degrees Cambridge offers. It
has a large international community, and supports the applications of overseas students.
Accommodation within the college is available for all single undergraduates and affiliated
students throughout their course, though family accommodation can be difficult to get hold of.
Despite its reputation as the "invisible college" (hardly anyone knows where it is), it is
centrally located and next door to the city's main gym and swimming pool. It also boasts a new
accommodation block, new library and attractive gardens. Hughes Hall forms a close-knit
community, with a well-frequented bar, and the MCR (student council) lay on free tea and
cakes twice a week.

Jesus

Jesus College, Cambridge CB5 8BL
01223 339455 (admissions)   undergraduate-admissions@jesus.cam.ac.uk
www.jesus.cam.ac.uk
Undergraduates: 515   Postgraduates: 251

For those of a sporting inclination Jesus is perhaps the ideal college. Within its spacious
grounds there are football, rugby and cricket pitches, as well as three squash courts and no less
than ten tennis courts, while the Cam, and the university boat houses, are just a few hundred
yards away. With these facilities, it is hardly surprising that sports, in particular rowing, rugby
and hockey, rate high on many students' agendas. That said, sporting prowess is far from the
whole story. The music society thrives, and has extensive practice facilities. Although Jesus
lacks a theatre of its own, the college is active in university drama and the ADC theatre is a
three-minute walk. On the academic front, the fellows-to-undergraduates ratio is generous.
There is an excellent and stylish new library which is open 24 hours. Accommodation is
another plus, and the college recently spent £10 million renovating some quarters. Rooms in
college are guaranteed for all first and half of third-year students, whilst all other students live
in college houses, just over the road, which are the envy of students from other colleges.
Regardless of where you are placed though, you are likely to have good lodgings. Approaching
60 per cent of new undergraduates are state educated and the college is keen to encourage

more applications from the state sector. The college grounds – particularly The Chimney walkway to the porter's lodge – are attractive and the college boasts some of the oldest buildings anywhere in the university, with parts dating to the 12th century. It is also ideally located for city centre shops and the delights of the King Street, famous for its plethora of pubs.

King's

King's College, Cambridge CB2 1ST
01223 331255 (admissions)   undergraduate.admissions@kings.cam.ac.uk
www.kings.cam.ac.uk
Undergraduates: 430   Postgraduates: 225

Despite being founded to absorb Eton boys into Cambridge, King's is now one of the most accessible colleges for state school pupils and ethnic minorities. It has a reputation for its radical leftist values which, though clearly still thriving, are not as typical as the stereotype might suggest. There has been fierce debate in recent years as to whether the communist flag should remain on a wall in its bar. Nonetheless, King's has done away with many Cambridge traditions. Gone are gowns, a fellows' "High Table" at dinner (though they still sit separately) and superior rooms to reward good results. Formal halls are banned, and May Balls replaced by the more casual June Events. This doesn't deter the tourists, who flock there in droves. The college was one of the first of the all-male colleges to admit women, and is actively involved in an initiative to increase the number of candidates from socially and educationally disadvantaged backgrounds. The college has a reputation for accepting a high proportion of state-school applications, usually over 70 per cent. The students' union is active politically, campaigning on issues such as top-up fees and the arms trade. The college has fewer undergraduates than the grandeur of its buildings might suggest, one result being that accommodation is guaranteed, either in college or in hostels. With the highest ratio of fellows to undergraduates in Cambridge, it is not surprising that King's has a strong academic reputation. The world-famous chapel and choir form the heart of an outstanding music scene – stroll past the 15th-century chapel some evenings to hear them practising.

Lucy Cavendish

Lucy Cavendish College, Cambridge CB3 0BU
01223 330280 (admissions)   lcc-admissions@lists.cam.ac.uk   www.lucy-cav.cam.ac.uk
Undergraduates: 142 (women only)   Postgraduates: 132

Lucy Cavendish pitches itself as the college for "smart, inspirational women" and is the only all-mature female college in the country. Since its creation in 1965, Lucy Cavendish has given hundreds of women over the age of 21 the opportunity to read for Tripos subjects. A number of its students had already started careers and/or families when they decided to enter higher education. Around 20 per cent of students are over 40 years of age, and some students are in their 60s. The college has a number of bursaries available, including some that give preference to single parents and applicants from the north-west of England. The college has particularly strong provision for the teaching of medicine and veterinary medicine and has a good reputation for social sciences and English literature. Accommodation is provided for all who request it, either in the college's three Victorian houses or in its three modern residential blocks. The college's small size enables all students to get to know one another within an intimate and informal atmosphere, although some find it a little too quiet: the college bar only really comes to life on a Thursday after formal hall. However, others appreciate a more relaxed, egalitarian atmosphere, with the lack high table in the dining hall being a prime example. The college has its own annual women's politics and literature festival, Women's Word. All the fellows are women, and there is a well-established network of university teachers for subjects not taught in college.

Magdalene

Magdalene College, Cambridge CB3 0AG
01223 332135 (admissions)   admissions@magd.cam.ac.uk   www.magd.cam.ac.uk
Undergraduates: 379   Postgraduates: 146

As the last college to admit women (1988), Magdalene used to have a lingering image as the home to hordes of public school hearties. However, times are changing: now the number of female undergraduates just exceeds the number of male undergraduates, and more than half of new undergraduates come from the state sector. With the most expensive May Ball ticket in Cambridge and a daily formal hall by candlelight, it certainly knows how to play "Brideshead". That said, the sporty emphasis, on rugby and rowing in particular, is undeniable. The nearby playing fields are shared with St John's and the college has its own Eton fives court. Magdalene's academic standing has improved of late – previously the college languished towards the bottom of the Tompkins Table, but it has steadily improved and finished fifth last year. Students are heavily involved in university-wide activities from drama to journalism, as well as sport. Accommodation is provided for all undergraduates, either in college or in one of 21 houses and hostels, all within two minutes' walk. Magdalene is proud of its river frontage, the longest in the university, which is especially memorable in the summer when students take to the "beach" to relax. Students enthuse about supportive academic staff and friendly porters, but gripe about the poor canteen food. One attractive prospect for undergraduates is that they may also be eligible for travel grants from the college, ranging from £50 to £2,000.

Murray Edwards

Murray Edwards College, New Hall, Cambridge CB3 0DF
01223 762229 (admissions)   admissions@murrayedwards.cam.ac.uk
www.murrayedwards.cam.ac.uk
Undergraduates: 373 (women only)   Postgraduates: 113

Murray Edwards College was until two years ago known as New Hall. The college was established in 1954 to allow more young women to study in Cambridge, and unsurprisingly became known as "New Hall", remaining officially unnamed for more than 50 years. In 2008 however, Ros Smith, a New Hall graduate, and her husband, Steve Edwards, gave the college a £30-million endowment, and, at last, a new name. One of three remaining all-women colleges, Murray Edwards enjoys a largely erroneous reputation for feminism and academic underachievement. The college is particularly proud of its collection of contemporary women's art, the second largest in the world, and students are politically active. Unlike many colleges, Murray Edwards has no religious leanings and thus no chapel. Although modern – the college's signature building is the "dome", the central building where students take their meals – the grounds are lovely. There are also practice rooms for musicians and an art room with dark room facilities for the artistically inclined. The college is known for its unusual split-level bar, but many students choose to socialise elsewhere. Accommodation has improved in recent years, with new rooms, many en suite, now on offer. Sport is a good mixture of high-fliers and enthusiasts, with grounds, shared with Fitzwilliam, half a mile away. It is another "hill" college, meaning a bicycle and a strong disposition is a must.

Newnham

Newnham College, Cambridge CB3 9DF

01223 335783 (admissions)   admissions@newn.cam.ac.uk   www.newn.cam.ac.uk

Undergraduates: 385 (women only)   Postgraduates: 185

Newnham has long had to battle with a blue-stocking image. Its entry in the university prospectus used to insist that it was "not a nunnery" and that the atmosphere in this all-women college was no stricter than elsewhere. It even has a "Newnham Nuns" drinking club to make the point. Newnham was founded in 1871 to help women to reach their full academic and personal potential in what was then an all-male university. The college still has all-women fellows, and Newnham is in the perfect location for humanities students, with the lecture halls and libraries of the Sidgwick Site just across the road. Sylvia Plath is perhaps the college's most famous alumna. Nearly all students live in for all three years, and room rents are the same across the board, which means students can have luxuries from a balcony to a chaise longue without worrying about the cost. Newnham students are anything but insular and are some of the most active in the social, sporting and artistic life of the university. As well as being blessed with the largest and most beautiful lawns in Cambridge (upon which students can both walk and sunbathe), Newnham has its playing fields and tennis courts on site. The boat club has been notably successful, while the college competes to a high standard in tennis, cricket and a number of minority sports.

Pembroke

Pembroke College, Cambridge CB2 1RF

01223 338154 (admissions)   adm@pem.cam.ac.uk   www.pem.cam.ac.uk

Undergraduates: 465   Postgraduates: 203

Another college with a reputation for public school dominance, Pembroke's image is changing: today, well over half of its intake come from state schools. Rowing and rugby still feature prominently, but with women undergraduates recently outnumbering men for the first time, its traditional reputation is giving way to a more relaxed atmosphere. Around two thirds of all undergraduates live in college, including all first years. The rest are housed in fairly central college hostels, though the standards of these are variable. That said, the college has recently completed a new student accommodation block that contains a gym, music rooms, and a new art room. Academically, Pembroke is towards the top of the Tompkins Table, steadily featuring in the top ten over the last decade, with traditional strengths in engineering and natural sciences. The New Cellars venue lends itself to plays, parties and gigs. The famed Pembroke Players generally stage one play a term in the Old Reader, which also doubles as the college cinema, and many Pembroke students are involved in university dramatics. The Old Library is a popular venue for classical concerts. Indeed music is a Pembroke strength. Nestled in one of the quads is the college chapel, designed by Sir Christopher Wren. In a city of memorable college gardens, Pembroke's are among the best.

Peterhouse

Peterhouse, Cambridge CB2 1RD
01223 338223 (admissions)   admissions@pet.cam.ac.uk   www.pet.cam.ac.uk
Undergraduates: 273   Postgraduates: 124

The oldest and smallest of the undergraduate colleges, Peterhouse has for many years worked hard to change its unenviable old reputation as a Conservative, male-dominated, public school college. The male–female ratio is now about 60:40, and over 55 per cent of undergraduates come from state schools. The college's diminutive size inevitably makes for an intimate atmosphere, but this does not mean that its undergraduates never venture beyond the college bar. Peterhouse is known above all as "the history college", and while history is indeed seen as a traditional strength, other societies are influential. The Peterhouse Politics Society has 900 university-wide members, while the Heywood Society (the resident dramatic society), the Perne Club (an intellectual society), the scientific Kelvin Club, and the Peterhouse Music Society are all very active. Academically, the college is generally a mid-table performer, though it reached 7th in the Tompkins Table in 2010. The 13th-century candle-lit dining hall provides what is by common consent one of the most impressive formal halls in the university. The college's rents are famously affordable – and most first years are housed in a row of houses just beside college or in the more modern William Stone Building. During the remaining years students live on site or in college hostels, most within ten minutes' walk. The sports grounds are shared with Clare and are about a mile away, although the college teams have a less than glittering reputation, not surprisingly, given its size. Too intimate for some, Petreans are fiercely loyal.

Queens'

Queens' College, Cambridge CB3 9ET
01223 335540 (admissions)   admissions@queens.cam.ac.uk   www.queens.cam.ac.uk
Undergraduates: 536   Postgraduates: 380

There is a strong case for claiming that Queens' is the most tightly knit college in the university. With all undergraduates housed in college for the full three years, a large and popular bar and outstanding facilities, including Cambridge's first college nursery, it is easy to see why. More than half of new undergraduates come from the state sector, and about 45 per cent of undergraduates are women. The architecture is probably the most eclectic in the university, from the medieval cloisters and the sundial in Old Court, to the 1970s Cripps Court. They are linked over the river Cam by the Mathematical Bridge, designed by Sir Isaac Newton, under which the college-owned punts are moored. In addition to three excellent squash courts, Lyon Court is also home to Fitzpatrick Hall, a multipurpose venue containing Cambridge's best-equipped college theatre and the hub of Queens' renowned social scene. The college generally hangs around the middle of the Tompkins Table, and is known instead for its contribution to the Footlights and university journalism. The amateur dramatics society, BATS, produces some of the best in-college theatre productions. There is a gym and a dance studio on site. The playing fields (one mile away) are shared with Robinson. Stephen Fry was a notable graduand.

Robinson

Robinson College, Cambridge CB3 9AN
01223 339143 (admissions)   apply@robinson.cam.ac.uk   www.robinson.cam.ac.uk
Undergraduates: 421   Postgraduates: 130

Robinson is one of the youngest colleges in Cambridge and admitted its first students in 1979. Its unspectacular architecture has earned it the unfortunate nickname "the car park". On the other hand, having been built with one eye on the conference trade, what Robinson lacks in grand architecture, it makes up for with excellent facilities. Rooms are more comfortable than most, and the majority have their own bathrooms and balcony. Almost all students live in college or in nearby houses, and the college is one of the few with rooms adapted for disabled students. Academically, Robinson tends to be found in the middle of the Tompkins Table. One in four fellows are women, one of the highest proportions in any mixed college. Its youth and admissions policy (the college typically accepts around 60 per cent from state schools) ensure that Robinson has one of the more unpretentious atmospheres. The auditorium is the largest of any college and is a popular venue for films, plays and concerts. The sports fields (shared with Queens') are home to excellent rugby and hockey sides, and the boat club is also successful. The atmosphere at the optional twice-weekly formal halls are described by students as "very down to earth". The college has two newly built graduate buildings providing state-of-the-art facilities as well as 48 new graduate rooms.

St Catharine's

St Catharine's College, Cambridge CB2 1RL
01223 338319 (admissions)   undergraduate.admissions@caths.cam.ac.uk
www.caths.cam.ac.uk
Undergraduates: 482   Postgraduates: 174

Known to everyone as "Catz", this medium-sized, 17th-century college stands opposite Corpus Christi on King's Parade. The principal college site, with its distinctive three-sided main court, though small, provides accommodation for all its first and third years. Rooms are small, but the cheapest in Cambridge. The majority of second years live in four- or five-room flats at St Chad's Court, a ten-minute walk away. Once not considered one of the leading colleges academically, its status is much changed. Having been top of the Tompkins Table in 2005, the college has hovered around the top ten ever since. It has a reputation as a friendly place. About half of the students are women, and the split between independent and state-school undergraduates accepted to the college is around 40:60. A new library and JCR have improved the facilities considerably, and there is a strong musical tradition. College social life centres on the large bar, which has been likened, among other things, to a ski chalet or sauna. In 2006 St Catharine's proudly announced that it was the first college to be awarded Fair Trade status. With a reputation for being sporting rather than sporty, Catz is one of the few colleges that regularly puts out three rugby XVs, last year provided two blues for the Boat Race, has a history of success at hockey and is the only Cambridge college with its own world-class Astroturf pitch. The playing fields are a ten-minute walk away.

St Edmund's College

St Edmund's College, Mount Pleasant, Cambridge CB3 0BN
01223 336086 (admissions)   admissions@st-edmunds.cam.ac.uk
www.st-edmunds.cam.ac.uk
Undergraduates: 154   Postgraduates: 269

St Edmund's is primarily a graduate college, with over half its students coming from overseas. Students say this diversity gives the college a unique atmosphere. The college is set in quiet grounds and is conveniently placed to the north-west of the city centre. The college buildings currently house more than 200 single students, and some of the accommodation has been constructed specifically for students with physical disabilities. There is brand new accommodation block for couples and in addition there are a small number of maisonettes suitable for students with children or married couples. A new building with an additional 70 student rooms opened in 2006, and the college has recently invested in a new library, teaching rooms, a gym and music practice rooms. In recent times, St Edmund's students have become regulars in the university sports team, earning an impressive number of "blues" (awarded for competing in a varsity match against Oxford), whilst a number of the college's international students also represent their own countries as well. The college bar may be sparsely populated, but it is an ideal place for mature students seeking a quiet life.

St John's

St John's College, Cambridge CB2 1TP
01223 338703 (admissions)   admissions@joh.cam.ac.uk   www.joh.cam.ac.uk
Undergraduates: 615   Postgraduates: 334

Second only to Trinity in size and wealth, St John's has an enviable reputation in most fields and is sometimes resented for it. The wealth translates into excellent accommodation in college, as well as book grants and a new 24-hour library. St John's straddles the River Cam, linked by the magnificent Bridge of Sighs and its chapel spire is the highest point until Ely Cathedral. Its riches ensure the best possible facilities, both academic and social, and access and travel grants are available to all. Its May Ball, a biennial end-of-year party, was once voted the "seventh-best party in the world". St John's has a formidable academic record, and English and natural sciences have been recent strengths. However, a reputation for heartiness persists and the female intake is below average at just below 40 per cent. St John's receives relatively few applications from state-school students, and the latest figures saw the intake of state students at around 52 per cent, among the lowest among the colleges, and some students say they find the atmosphere "posh" and the college's events "terribly formal". The boat club has a powerful reputation, but rugby, hockey and cricket are all traditionally strong. In such a large community, however, all should be able to find their own level. Extensive playing fields shared with Magdalene are a few hundred yards away, and the boathouse is extremely good. The college film society organises popular screenings in the Fisher Building, which also contains an art studio and drawing office for architecture and engineering students. Music is dominated by the world-famous choir. Excellent as the facilities are, some students find that the sheer size of St John's can be daunting, making it hard to settle into. Others argue that such a large college provides a diverse atmosphere where "everybody can find their niche".

Selwyn

Selwyn College, Cambridge CB3 9DQ
01223 335896 (admissions)   admissions@sel.cam.ac.uk   www.sel.cam.ac.uk
Undergraduates: 403   Postgraduates: 159

Selwyn is one of the less assuming colleges, but nonetheless a strong choice. It has a relatively unpressured atmosphere behind "the Backs", and near the Sidgwick site where most humanities are taught, making it an ideal position for arts and humanities students, though engineering is also a perceived strength. Its position also means it is far from town, and though many students were once forced to live away, new accommodation blocks mean everyone is housed within 400 yards of the centre quad. It also hides some of the most beautiful college gardens, which are a riot of colour in spring. In recent years it has consistently appeared in the top ten of the Tompkins Table, coming first in 2008 (and sixth last year). One of the first colleges to admit women (1976), now almost half of Selwyn's undergraduates are female. Its state–independent ratio among new undergraduates stands at around 70:30. Food has improved enormously in recent years. The college was a leader in IT provision, being one of the first to provide all college rooms with online connections, and there are two well-stocked computer rooms. As well as the usual college groups, the music society is especially well supported. Selwyn bucks the trend for a summer ball or June event, and hosts the popular Snow Ball each December. In sport, the novice boat crews have done well in recent years, as have the hockey and badminton sides, but the emphasis is as much on enjoyment as achievement. The grounds are shared with King's and are three quarters of a mile away.

Sidney Sussex

Sidney Sussex College, Cambridge CB2 3HU
01223 338872 (admissions)   admissions@sid.cam.ac.uk   www.sid.cam.ac.uk
Undergraduates: 380   Postgraduate: 170

Students at this small, central college are forever the butt of jokes about Sidney being mistaken for the branch of Sainsbury's over the road. Despite its location in the heart of the city, the college's large private gardens award the college an unexpectedly tranquil environment behind the redbrick walls. All students are housed either in college or one of 11 nearby hostels. The college's unpretentious atmosphere is cultivated by the students, half of whom are women. Despite its size, Sidney has an active social life, boasting one of the few student-run bars in the university and maintaining fortnightly "bop" dances like many of the larger colleges. The college choir has produced critically acclaimed recordings, and tours regularly in the UK and overseas. Sports are taken less seriously, with enthusiasm and enjoyment the focus of the students' sporting endeavours. Exam results at the college improved steadily for a number of years, although the last two years have seen a decline: the college fell from 9th, its best score in the Tompkins Table in 2006, to 29th in 2008, but rose to 18th in 2010. Sports grounds are shared with Christ's and are a ten-minute bicycle ride away. Sidney's size means that the college is a tight-knit community, although some students find such insularity suffocating rather than supportive.

Trinity

Trinity College, Cambridge CB2 1TQ
01223 338422 (admissions)   admissions@trin.cam.ac.uk   www.trin.cam.ac.uk
Undergraduates: 734   Postgraduates: 328

The legend that you can walk from Oxford to Cambridge without ever leaving Trinity land typifies Cambridge undergraduates' views about the college, even if it is not true. Indeed, the college is almost synonymous with size and wealth – it is the largest and wealthiest of all Cambridge colleges. Founded by Henry VIII, its endowment is almost as big as the other colleges' put together. There was a view that every Trinity student was an arrogant public schoolboy. Though less true than it was, the number of students from the state sector has been historically low – the figure has risen from 38 per cent in 2007, but only 43 per cent of acceptances in 2010 were from state schools, and only 36 per cent of undergraduates are women. Being rich, Trinity offers book grants to every student as well as generous travel grants. The rooms are amongst the cheapest at the university as they are subsidised by the college, and are also known for being spacious. The huge number of rooms at Trinity means students can stay in residence for the duration of their course. Consistently strong academically, last year the college slipped down to second position in the Tompkins Table. Trinity has a well-established reputation as a centre of excellence for sciences and maths, but is also strong in a number of arts subjects. Keen to dispel a reputation for being overly serious and academic, students have set up a new Cocktail Society. Christopher Wren designed the college's iconic library, which backs onto the river. Trinity rarely fails to do well in most sports, with cricket in the forefront. The playing fields are half a mile away.

Trinity Hall

Trinity Hall, Cambridge CB2 1TJ
01223 332535 (admissions)   admissions@trinhall.cam.ac.uk   www.trinhall.cam.ac.uk
Undergraduates: 400   Postgraduates: 240

Trinity Hall or "Tit Hall" is one of the oldest and smallest colleges in Cambridge, resulting in a remarkably close community of students. The outstanding performance of its oarsmen has ensured the prevailing view of Trinity Hall as a "boaty" college, but it is also known for its drama, music and bar. The Preston Society is one of the better college drama groups, and stages regular productions. Weekly recitals keep the music society busy. The size of the bar (tiny) is inversely proportional to the number of people who frequent it (many). Not surprisingly, many undergraduates rarely feel the need to go elsewhere for their entertainment. The college is strong academically, and at fourth in the Tompkins Table in 2010, it reversed an unusually low position in the recent past. It has equal numbers of students studying arts and sciences. Just over half of the undergraduates are women, and in recent years the college has increased the number of state-school students at the college. Over 55 per cent of new undergraduates come from the state sector. All first years and approximately half the third years live in college, which is situated on "the Backs" behind Caius. The remainder take rooms either in two large hostels close to the sports ground, or in college accommodation about five minutes' walk away. The college offers a number of travel bursaries and hardship funds for current students.

Wolfson

Wolfson College, Barton Road, Cambridge CB3 9BB
01223 335918   ugadministrator@wolfson.cam.ac.uk   www.wolfson.cam.ac.uk
Undergraduates: 124   Postgraduates: 510

Wolfson, although primarily a graduate college, has around 120 mature or affiliated undergraduates. Wolfson is one of three colleges that admit students for the graduate course in medicine. The average age is 27 and life is enriched by the high proportion (about 50 per cent) of overseas students, reflected in popular societies and events, such as the salsa night. It thus likes to call itself "the most cosmopolitan college in Cambridge". The relationship between senior and junior members is informal; common rooms, facilities and social activities are equally open to both. The college has a relaxed atmosphere. The college regularly hosts senior academic visitors, journalists and specialists, many of whom give open talks at the college. Wolfson is situated in west Cambridge, close to the University Library and the arts faculties – or as the students say, nearer to the M11 than the Cam. The location, however, means the green fields and popular pathway to nearby Grantchester are a short hop away. The main buildings of Wolfson College were built in the 1970s around attractive garden courts. The college has accommodation for most students who want to live in college. There is also some accommodation for couples.

13 University Profiles

The following profiles contain valuable information about each university. Each profile contains contact details, including the postal address, the telephone number for admission enquiries, email or web addresses for admissions and prospectus enquiries, the main university web address, the address of the students' union website and any university grouping that the institution is affiliated to (Russell Group, etc.). In addition, each profile provides:

The Times **rankings** These figures are taken from the main league table. See chapter 4, *The Top Universities*, for this table and the sources of the data. The headings follow those in the main league table.

Undergraduates The first figure is for full-time undergraduates. The second figure (in brackets) gives the number of part-time undergraduates. The figures are for 2009–10, and are the most recent provided by HESA.

Postgraduates The first figure is for full-time postgraduates. The second figure (in brackets) gives the number of part-time postgraduates. The figures are for 2009–10, and are the most recent provided by HESA.

Mature students The percentage of first degree entrants who were 21 or over at the start of their studies. The figures are from 2009–10, and are from HESA.

Overseas students The number of undergraduate overseas students (both EU and non-EU) as a percentage of full-time undergraduates. The figures relate to 2009–10, and are based on HESA data.

Applications per place The number of applicants per place for 2010 as calculated by UCAS.

From state-school sector The number of young full-time undergraduate entrants from state schools or colleges in 2009–10 as a percentage of total young entrants. The figures are published by HESA.

From working-class homes The number of young full-time undergraduate entrants in 2009–10 whose parental occupations are skilled, manual, semi-skilled or unskilled (NS-SEC classes 4–7) as a percentage of total young entrants. The figures are published by HESA.

Accommodation The information was obtained through a survey made of all university accommodation services, and their help in compiling this information is gratefully acknowledged.

Undergraduate fees and support Full details of the major changes in funding and financial support for students starting in 2012–13 were not available at the time this book went to press in spring 2011. Most (but not all) English universities had announced their proposed fees and many had outlined their proposed support packages, and we give information based on these announcements. However, all proposals were awaiting approval from the Office for Fair Access (OFFA). OFFA will confirm arrangements by 11 July 2011. **It is essential that you check university websites for full details of fees and related support packages for the latest information**. For universities in Northern Ireland and Scotland, the devolved governments had not confirmed their policies for fees in 2012–13 at the time of going to press, while in Wales, although the policy is known, only one university (Aberystwyth) has announced its fees. Again, it is essential to check university websites for details. Universities will also offer a variety of scholarships and bursaries, for example, in particular subjects or to help people from particular places. There is not space in this book to give details of such awards, and, again, you are advised to check university websites for details. For the principles behind the funding system, see chapter 7, *The Cost of Studying*.

Comments on campus facilities apply to the universities' own sites only. Newer universities, in particular, operate "franchised" courses at further education colleges, which are likely to have lower levels of provision. Prospective applicants should check out the library and social facilities before accepting a place away from the parent institution.

For the first time this year we include profiles on the two major suppliers of part-time degrees, the Open University and Birkbeck College. However, we do not give profiles to separate business and medical schools, specialist colleges or institutions that only offer postgraduate degrees, such as Cranfield University (**www.cranfield.ac.uk**) and London Business School (**www.lbs.ac.uk**). Specialist institutions such as the Royal College of Music (**www.rcm.ac.uk**) and St George's, University of London medical school (**sgul.ac.uk**) could not fairly be compared with generalist universities. Their omission is no reflection on their quality, simply a function of their particular roles. A number of colleges with degree-awarding powers also do not appear because they have yet to be granted university status. However, at the end of the book, we list higher education colleges with their addresses and websites.

The University of Wales, founded in 1893, remained a federal university until 2007. It is now the degree-awarding authority to accredited higher education institutions in Wales. In addition it plays an active role in promoting Welsh language and culture. See **www.wales.ac.uk**.

University of Aberdeen

Buoyed by record applications, Aberdeen has launched a major reform of its offer to students, covering extra-curricular activities as well as the structure of its courses. The new range of "Sixth Century Courses" includes cross-disciplinary degrees such as risk in society, sustainability and the digital society. They provide the option of "sustained study programmes" in a language, computing or a business-related subject. The aim is to give graduates broader knowledge and more intellectual flexibility.

The university marked the early years of its sixth century with the recruitment of high-quality academics and a series of big capital projects. Aided by one the most successful fundraising schemes at any UK university, Aberdeen has spent £28 million on a sports centre that opened in 2009 and £57 million on a futuristic new library that will open in 2011. Student services had already been transformed and the redeveloped Butchart Centre has given the Students' Association a new social centre on campus.

The university registered some good results in the 2008 Research Assessment Exercise, when more than half of the work submitted was judged to be "world-leading" or internationally excellent. Health services research and theology, divinity and religious studies produced the best results in the UK, while computer science and informatics, anthropology, English and history also did particularly well. Research income grew by more than a third over five years, cementing Aberdeen's ambitions to be recognised among the top 100 universities in the world.

The 32 per cent growth in applications in 2010 was among the biggest in Scotland and Aberdeen maintained the momentum in 2011, with an 8 per cent increase while the other ancient universities north of the border were in decline.

Aberdeen considers itself a "balanced" university because roughly half of its students study medicine, science or engineering, half the arts or social sciences. Even on traditional degree programmes, students can try out three or four subjects before committing themselves at the end of their first or even second year. The modular system, covering more than 650 first-degree programmes, is so flexible that the majority of students change their intended degree before graduation. The mixture propelled Aberdeen into the top 20 in the National Student Survey in 2010, with 100 per cent satisfaction in English and Iberian studies and close to that mark in anatomy, physiology and pathology.

Medicine, law and divinity head Aberdeen's traditional strengths – the university established the English-speaking world's first chair in medicine in 1497, and has produced its share of advances since. The Institute of Medical Sciences, which has

---

King's College
Aberdeen AB24 3FX

01224 272090/91 (admissions)
sras@abdn.ac.uk
www.abdn.ac.uk
www.ausa.org.uk
Affiliation: none

ABERDEEN
Edinburgh
Belfast
London
Cardiff

The Times Rankings
Overall Ranking: **42**

Student satisfaction:	=12	(81%)
Research quality:	=33	(1.9)
Entry standards:	41	(332)
Student–staff ratio:	=37	(15.8)
Services & facilities/student:	48	(£1,421)
Expected completion rate:	86	(80.6%)
Good honours:	38	(67.4%)
Graduate prospects:	=32	(69.4%)

brought together all Aberdeen's work in this area, boasts state-of-the-art laboratory facilities. Another £20 million has been invested in the Suttie Centre, which opened in 2009 as a new teaching and learning centre for medical education and clinical skills. Education is now also considered among Aberdeen's strengths, while biological sciences have developed considerably in recent years, becoming second only to the social sciences in terms of size. Biomedicine is particularly strong, and the university's links with the oil industry show in geology's high reputation.

Today's university is a fusion of two ancient institutions which came together in 1860. With King's College dating back to 1495 and Marischal College following almost a century later, Aberdeen likes to boast that for 250 years it had as many universities as the whole of England. The original King's College buildings are the focal point of an appealing campus, complete with cobbled main street and some sturdily handsome Georgian buildings, about a mile from the city centre.

Medicine is at Foresterhill, a 20-minute walk away, adjoining the Aberdeen Royal Infirmary. Buses link the two sites with the Hillhead residential complex. Almost a third of all students come from the north of Scotland, but taking one in six from outside Britain ensures a cosmopolitan atmosphere. Students from England and the 120

nationalities from further afield are generally prepared for Aberdeen's remote location and, although the winters are long, the climate is warmer than the uninitiated might expect. As the energy capital of Europe, transport links are good. Students find the city lively and welcoming but expensive: the JobLink service does provide a good selection of part-time jobs.

Student facilities are good and include the Butchart Centre and the students' centre – The Hub – which brings together dining and retail outlets with support services, and the careers service. There is also a city centre bar and first-class sports facilities, which have improved still further with the opening of the Aberdeen Sports Village, part-funded by the City Council and Sports Scotland. The university ICT network has over 1,500 computers for student use. A £20-million phased investment in accommodation added over 500 new single study en-suite bedrooms at Hillhead in 2008, and all new undergraduates are guaranteed a place.

Undergraduate Fees and Support

» Fees 2012–13:   awaiting Scottish Government policy.
» Fees for Scottish and EU students 2011–12   No fee
» Fees for Non-Scottish UK-domiciled students 2011–12   £1,820
                                                  £2,895 (medicine)
» Fees for international students 2011–12   £10,500–£13,200
                                                £24,000 (medicine)
» Scholarships based on circumstances or by competition.
» Check the university's website for the latest information.

Students

Undergraduates:	**10,295**	**(1,315)**
Postgraduates:	**2,565**	**(1,360)**
Mature students:	**17.2%**	
Overseas students:	**17.5%**	
Applications per place:	**5.8**	
From state-sector schools:	**79.5%**	
From working-class homes:	**25.6%**	

For detailed information about fees, grants and bursaries and how they work, see chapter 7.

Accommodation

Number of places and costs refer to 2010–11
University-provided places: about 2,720
Percentage catered: 14%
Catered costs: £129.56–£149.04 a week (38 weeks).
Self-catered costs: £65.00–£119.48 a week (38–50 weeks).
First-year students are guaranteed accommodation.
International students: as above.
Contact: studentaccomm@abdn.ac.uk

University of Abertay Dundee

Abertay has been reeling from the double suspension of its long-serving Principal and his deputy, who was subsequently reinstated and given the top job. But nothing has dented the university's popularity: a 24 per cent increase in applications in 2010 had been outstripped when the official deadline passed for courses beginning in 2011. Abertay doubled in size during the 1990s and has grown further since up-front tuition fees were abolished for Scottish students. There are now more than 4,700 students, mainly in Dundee, but with several hundred in locations as far afield as Malaysia, Canada and China. There have been dramatic improvements to a dropout rate at less than 8 per cent – almost half the benchmark for the university's courses and entry qualifications. Almost a quarter of the undergraduates come from socially deprived areas and practically all attended state schools. More than a third come from working-class homes.

The former Dundee Institute of Technology had already established its academic credentials when university status arrived in 1994, with teaching in economics rated more highly than in some of Scotland's elite universities. Subsequent assessments were solid, but economics, engineering and environmental sciences were given the highest possible rating in later inspections. More recently, Abertay was awarded three of only nine degree accreditations for computer games and computer arts courses awarded by Skillset, the Government-sponsored training council for the creative industries. The university has been accredited as the first Interactive Media Academy in the UK and also the first national Centre for Excellence in Computer Games Education. Staff and students in the Institute for Art, Media and Computer Games work with industrial partners from across the broadcast, inter-active and wider digital media sectors. The university even has a partnership with Peking University on computer games.

Research is not being ignored. Abertay is proud of its record in establishing a series of specialist centres, in areas as diverse as wood technology, urban water systems, bioinfor-matics, earth systems and environmental sciences. The university opened Europe's first research centre dedicated to computer games and digital entertainment, and a major environmental science centre. Earth systems and environmental sciences, and general engineering, mineral and mining engineering produced the best scores in the latest research assessments. Those for law and psychology were the best at any post-1992 university north of the border.

Abertay plays to its strengths with a limited range of courses, and is not shy about

Bell Street
Dundee DD1 1HG
01382 308080

sro@abertay.ac.uk
www.abertay.ac.uk
www.abertayunion.com
Affiliation: million+

DUNDEE
Edinburgh
Belfast
London
Cardiff

The Times Rankings
Overall Ranking: **101**

Student satisfaction:	**n/a**	
Research quality:	**=79**	(0.3)
Entry standards:	**=97**	(252)
Student–staff ratio:	**73**	(19.4)
Services & facilities/student:	**68**	(£1,268)
Expected completion rate:	**110**	(74.2%)
Good honours:	**99**	(51.0%)
Graduate prospects:	**81**	(57.7%)

its achievements. A high-tech approach permeates all four of the university's schools, while spending on libraries and computers is among the highest in Britain, providing one computer for every four students.

Based mainly in the centre of Dundee, all the university's buildings are within 15 minutes' walk of each other. The buildings are modern and functional, with new facilities being added gradually, from the £6-million student centre, which opened in 2005, to the innovative White Space facility, the university's flagship creative learning and working environment, where students study alongside industry professionals. A 500-bed student village opened at the start of the academic year in 2010 and work is nearing completion on new premises for a £5-million Business Prototyping Project to support the UK's creative industries.

Entrance requirements have been rising, although for most courses other than high-demand areas such as computer games, they are still modest. Well-qualified A-level students are eligible for direct entry into second year. Degrees are predominantly vocational, with more subjects being added every year. Forensic science, mental health nursing, visual communications and media design, computer arts, and sports coaching and development have been followed recently by the likes of creative sound production, and ethical hacking and countermeasures. All courses can be taken on a part-time basis, and the aim is for new programmes to offer students the chance to spend at least 30 per cent of their time in industry.

The university's revamped degree scheme means that undergraduates take a maximum of eight modules a year. First-year students are assessed by coursework alone in the first semester, with examinations at the end of the year. Students can complete a Certificate of Higher Education after one year, a diploma after two, an ordinary degree after three, or honours in four years. Abertay is piloting a new problem-based learning approach among first-year students focusing on real-world issues and learning by doing rather than sitting in lectures.

Dundee has a large student population and is improving as a place for young people where the cost of living is modest. More than 30 per cent of the undergraduates are over 21 on entry, many living locally. This lifts the pressure on university-owned beds sufficiently that all first years have priority for accommodation.

Undergraduate Fees and Support

» Fees 2012–13:   awaiting Scottish Government policy.
» Fees for Scottish and EU students 2011–12   No fee
» Fees for Non-Scottish UK-domiciled students 2011–12   £1,820
» Fees for international students 2011–12   £9,500
» Scholarships and bursaries based on circumstances or by competition.
» Check the university's website for the latest information.

Students

Undergraduates:	**3,385**	**(345)**
Postgraduates:	**305**	**(165)**
Mature students:	**31.4%**	
Overseas students:	**16.1%**	
Applications per place:	**2.9**	
From state-sector schools:	**97.9%**	
From working-class homes:	**36.7%**	

For detailed information about fees, grants and bursaries and how they work, see chapter 7.

Accommodation

Number of places and costs refer to 2011–12
University-provided places: 668
Percentage catered: 0%
Self-catered costs: £54.11–£104.00 a week (38, 42 or 51 weeks).
New first years are given priority provided conditions are met.
Some residential restrictions.
International students: prioritised by distance from Dundee.
Contact: accommo@abertay.ac.uk

Aberystwyth University

Aberystwyth consistently registers by far the highest student satisfaction levels of any university in Wales and was again among the top five in the UK in the 2010 National Student Survey. Accounting and sports science both registered 100 per cent satisfaction levels, with biology, physical geography and environmental science not far behind.

The oldest of the Welsh universities, Aberystwyth changed its title from the University of Wales, Aberystwyth, to emphasise its independence from the University of Wales and is now awarding its own degrees. It has long prided itself on a modern outlook: it was among the pioneers of the modular degree system and allowed students flexibility between subjects even before that. Uniquely in the UK, every student is offered the opportunity of a year's work experience in commerce, industry or the public sector, either at home or abroad. Those who have taken advantage of the scheme have achieved better than average degrees and enhanced their employment prospects.

Aber is always heavily oversubscribed even though the number of places has increased. Over a third of the UK students are from Wales. An agreement to collaborate with Bangor University in a range of subjects, from business to science, emphasises teaching in Welsh. An attractive seaside location does the university no harm when the applications season comes around. The demand for places has grown substantially in each of the last four years, with a 13 per cent increase in 2010 followed by an even larger increase in the latest round of applications.

The university has grown significantly in recent years and a £1.5-million Student Welcome Centre, opened in 2009, has brought together services such as the fees office and student support services that were previously distributed around the campus or in town. A purpose-built sports and exercise science centre has been added on the Penglais campus, which overlooks the town, and a new student health centre and crèche will open soon. A new building for the highly rated international politics department opened in 2006 and a £10-million Visualisation Centre followed in 2007, providing virtual reality facilities for academic and industrial partnerships. A new psychology department is the latest addition.

Almost 95 per cent of the undergraduates come from state schools or colleges – a far higher proportion than the mix of subjects would imply – and a third are from working-class homes. The dropout rate remained above 10 per cent in the latest survey but is still one of the lowest in Wales.

The Institute of Biological, Environmental and Rural Sciences (IBERS),

---

King Street,
Aberystwyth, Ceredigion
SY23 2AX

01970 622021 (admissions)
ug-admissions@aber.ac.uk
www.aber.ac.uk
www.aberguild.co.uk
Affiliation: University Alliance

The Times Rankings
Overall Ranking: **43**

Student satisfaction:	=4	(84%)
Research quality:	=33	(1.9)
Entry standards:	=54	(298)
Student–staff ratio:	=57	(18.1)
Services & facilities/student:	50	(£1,404)
Expected completion rate:	50	(86.3%)
Good honours:	70	(58.5%)
Graduate prospects:	=90	(55.1%)

established in 2008 following a merger with the Institute of Grassland and Environmental Research, has over 300 staff and an annual budget in excess of £25 million, making it one of the largest groups of scientists and support staff working in this field in Europe. It caters for more than 1,000 undergraduate and research students with a remit to look for creative solutions to some of the major challenges facing the world in sustainable land use, climate change, renewable energy and the security of food and water supplies. The institute, which won a Queen's Anniversary Prize for its work in 2010, gives Aber the widest range of land-related courses in the UK. Two new buildings are being built: one providing research and teaching facilities on the Penglais campus and the other a new Phenomics facility on the Gogerddan campus.

International politics produced the best results in the 2008 research assessments, with 40 per cent of work rated world-leading. Computer science, geography and earth sciences, Welsh, and theatre, film and television also did well.

Entrance scholarships and bursaries are available in a range of subjects, even though Welsh students have been spared the full impact of top-up fees. Aber boasts one of higher education's most informative websites and also publishes a 12-page guide for parents. There is 24-hour access to the computer network, and the four university libraries are complemented by the National Library of Wales.

The town of Aberystwyth is compact and travel to other parts of the UK slow, so applicants should be sure that they will be happy to spend three years or more in a tight-knit community. The students' guild is the largest entertainment venue in the region and the prize-winning arts centre has been extended at a cost of £3.5 million. The seaside town of 25,000 people was placed among the top ten university locations in the UK in one 2009 survey and in the top three by another. There is plenty of out-of-season accommodation to supplement the university's 3,700 places, all of which are now online. Sports facilities are good for the size of institution. A 400-metre running track has just been added to 50 acres of pitches, a refurbished swimming pool, a climbing wall and specialist outdoor facilities for water sports.

Undergraduate Fees and Support

» Fees 2012–13:   £9,000
  (Welsh Assembly expected to pay fees above £3,375 for Welsh students)
» Fees for international students for 2011–12   £9,500
» Scholarships and bursaries based on circumstances or by competition.
» Check the university's website for the latest information.

Students

Undergraduates:	**6,840**	**(2,190)**
Postgraduates:	**1,000**	**(775)**
Mature students:	**8.8%**	
Overseas students:	**12.7%**	
Applications per place:	**3.7**	
From state-sector schools:	**94.3%**	
From working-class homes:	**33.3%**	

For detailed information about fees, grants and bursaries and how they work, see chapter 7.

Accommodation

Number of places and costs refer to 2011–12
University-provided places: 3,631
Percentage catered: 15%
Catered costs: £94.64–£108.58 a week (31 or 37 weeks).
Self-catered costs: £78.07 – £102.23 a week (37 weeks).
First years are guaranteed accommodation if conditions are met.
International students: accommodation guaranteed for students classed as overseas for fees.
Contact: www.aber.ac.uk/residential
accommodation@aber.ac.uk

Anglia Ruskin University

Applications to Anglia Ruskin were up by more than 50 per in 2010 and there had been another substantial rise when the official deadline passed for entry in 2011. The university has invested more than £80 million in five years in the latest learning environments, particularly for health and social care. Further developments costing £124 million are planned for the next five years. Recent additions have included a new student centre on the larger of the university's two main sites, in Chelmsford, which houses support services as well as union facilities, and enhanced teaching and practice facilities for the arts, law and social sciences at the second main site in Cambridge.

The two very different locations are far enough apart to limit contact, although electronic networking and a central administration mean that key academic facilities are available throughout the university. The university has more than 22,000 full and part-time students, who are taught primarily on the two main campuses, but also through a growing network of regional and international partners. Already one of the largest universities in the east of England, Anglia Ruskin has signed up to deliver higher education courses in Peterborough, Harlow and King's Lynn in partnership with local further education

colleges. Three out of four graduates go on to work in the region.

Anglia was the last university to retain a polytechnic title, but discarded it in 2005 to avoid confusion among employers and overseas applicants. The former APU took the name of John Ruskin, who founded the Cambridge School of Art, which evolved into the university. It has since acquired the former Homerton College School of Health Studies in Cambridge, after a long period of partnership, and added a new health and social care building in Chelmsford, with bespoke counselling rooms, simulated hospital wards, operating theatres, and a complementary medicine suite. The 22-acre Rivermead campus also boasts an impressive business school and a sports hall, as well as the £15-million Marconi Building, completed in 2008, which includes a mock courtroom for law students.

At the same time, the university has made considerable strides in becoming more "green", reaching an internationally recognised standard for its environmental impact and being awarded the Carbon Trust Standard for reduced carbon emissions. Anglia Ruskin was in the top ten in the Green League 2010, compiled by People and Planet.

Nearly all the students attended state schools or colleges and almost 40 per cent are from working-class homes. The dropout rate has improved substantially in the latest survey. At below 12 per cent, the current

---

Chelmsford Campus:
Bishop Hall Lane,
Chelmsford CM1 1SQ
Cambridge Campus:
East Road,
Cambridge CB1 1PT
0845 271 3333 (enquiries)
contact via website
www.anglia.ac.uk
www.angliastudent.com
Affiliation: million+

The Times Rankings
Overall Ranking: **108**

Student satisfaction:	=106	(70%)
Research quality:	=92	(0.2)
Entry standards:	96	(254)
Student–staff ratio:	109	(22.7)
Services & facilities/student:	95	(£1,101)
Expected completion rate:	74	(82.4%)
Good honours:	79	(56.9%)
Graduate prospects:	=86	(55.5%)

projection is less than half the rate of three years ago.

There have been good reports, under the new healthcare assessments, for nursing and midwifery and allied health professions. But Anglia remained among the bottom ten universities in the National Student Survey published in 2010. Ophthalmics, history, languages and building produced the best results, but the score for cinematics and photography was unusually low.

Only 71 academics were entered for the Research Assessment Exercise in 2008, but almost a third of their work was considered world-leading or internationally excellent. All but one of the nine subject areas had some top-rated research, with history, English and psychology producing the best grades. Psychology produced the best results among the new universities.

Each undergraduate has an adviser to help compile a degree package which looks at the chosen subject from different points of view to maximise future job prospects. There is also an employer mentoring scheme for second-year undergraduates planning for the transition from study to work. Each student is carefully matched with a mentor from their chosen career field who volunteers time to provide skills-building, support and encouragement.

Employers play a part in planning courses which are integrated into a modular system which extends from degree level to professional programmes, including a modest selection of vocational two-year Foundation degrees. The Business School, for example, has developed a work-based course with Barclays Bank, where the students are sponsored and salaried for all three years of their course. The programme is now being offered to other businesses in order to aid retention and staff development.

The social scene varies between the two campuses, but the university now has two art galleries and a theatre. There is limited collaboration with Cambridge University on the Cambridge Centre for Cricketing Excellence, and a base for Anglia Ruskin's Rowing Club. Some students find Chelmsford dull, but the social scene is said to be improving. Neither base is far from London by train.

Undergraduate Fees and Support

- » Fees for UK/EU students 2012–13: £8,300
  Foundation degree £7,500
- » Fees for International students 2011–12 £9,500–£10,500
- » Anglia National Scholarship (limited number: household income below £25K)
  fee waiver of £6,800 over three years plus services including option of laptop, books, or accommodation costs help.
- » Bursary for those who do not receive Anglia National Scholarship household income less than £25K, £1,200 a year; household income £25K–£35K: £500.
  Choice between fee waiver and institutional services.
- » Check the university's website for the latest information.

Students

Undergraduates:	**11,330**	**(7,600)**
Postgraduates:	**1,490**	**(1,630)**
Mature students:	**37.9%**	
Overseas students:	**13.3%**	
Applications per place:	**4.5**	
From state-sector schools:	**97.3%**	
From working-class homes:	**39.1%**	

For detailed information about fees, grants and bursaries and how they work, see chapter 7.

Accommodation

Number of places and costs refer to 2011–12

University-provided places: Cambridge, 797 plus 291 referral rooms; Chelmsford, 511

Percentage catered: 0%

Self-catered costs: Cambridge: £73–£127 a week; Chelmsford: £90–£98 a week.

Most first years are accommodated. Distance restrictions apply. International students: conditions and deadline apply.

Contact: cambaccom@anglia.ac.uk

essexaccom@anglia.ac.uk

Aston University

Aston was the first university outside the elite Russell and 1994 groups to announce £9,000 fees for 2012. Professor Julia King, the vice-chancellor, was a member of the Browne Review, which recommended higher fees, and she said that Aston's strong record for graduate employment justified the charges. Small and lively, set in the heart of Birmingham, the university has remained resolutely specialist in science and technology, business and languages, concentrating on the sandwich degrees which have served its graduates so well in the employment market. But it is now aiming for "sustainable growth in key areas" to provide financial security and the size necessary to boost research performance and become a top-ten university.

Aston did break into the top 20 in *The Times* table, although it has slipped back recently, mainly due to less favourable staffing levels and lower spending on student facilities. Despite some modest growth, the university still has fewer than 8,000 full-time undergraduates. But, with healthy funding from industry and commerce, Aston has been investing in its future, boosting staffing in business, engineering and languages, and developing the campus with a £215 million programme of improvements. An impressive new library, with glazed façade, opened in

2010. The Woodcock Sport Centre, including a Grade II listed swimming pool, is due for completion by Summer 2011.

Applications have grown in recent years, despite consistent increases in entry grades. There was a big increase in 2010, but the start of 2011 saw a drop of more than 18 per cent. New undergraduates take 12 study skills modules before the formal start of their course, covering areas such as essay writing.

Business and management led the way in the 2008 Research Assessment Exercise, with health subjects also producing good grades from a smaller submission. The university submitted far more staff for assessment than in 2001 but, while 45 per cent of the work in the four subject areas was judged to be world-leading or internationally excellent, the results placed Aston near the bottom of the tables of pre-1992 universities.

As befits a one-time college of advanced technology, Aston is strong in the sciences, although the highly rated business school accounts for almost half of the students. A £20-million extension to the business school has seen an increase in staff from 80 to over 120.

There is a wide range of combined honours programmes for those who prefer not to specialise. More than 80 per cent of Aston graduates – far more than the national average – go straight into jobs, often returning to the scene of work placements, which have become the norm for seven out of

Aston Triangle
Birmingham B4 7ET

0121 204 4444 (course enquiries)
ugenquiries@aston.ac.uk
www.aston.ac.uk
www.astonguild.org.uk
Affiliation: none

The Times Rankings
Overall Ranking: **36**

Student satisfaction:	=48	(77%)
Research quality:	=49	(1.3)
Entry standards:	=35	(370)
Student–staff ratio:	=46	(17.1)
Services & facilities/student:	42	(£1,525)
Expected completion rate:	=25	(91.7%)
Good honours:	=43	(66%)
Graduate prospects:	16	(74.8%)

ten undergraduates. At the forefront of employer-led degrees, Aston was awarded £1.6 million to set up a Foundation Degree Centre to establish new courses and explore other ways of delivering qualifications. The Foundation degree in electrical power engineering has attracted several large companies, while others include hearing aid technology and pharmaceutical technology.

The university's dropout rate has been improving and, at a little over 7 per cent in the latest statistics, is well below the national average for Aston's subjects. Socially, the intake is diverse, with more than a third of the undergraduates coming from working-class homes. Nearly one student in five comes from Birmingham and about four in ten are from the West Midlands more broadly. More than half of the undergraduates are from ethnic minorities.

The 40-acre campus, a ten-minute walk from the centre of Birmingham, is barely recognisable from the university's early days. Recent building programmes have brought all Aston's residential and academic accommodation onto one carefully landscaped site. Almost half of the undergraduates live on campus, with places guaranteed for first years. A new phase of construction for residential accommodation began in 2008 and will have added 2,400 en-suite rooms by 2014. More than half of them became available in 2010. Recent developments in sporting facilities have included the addition of a new gymnasium, while an £8-million Academy of Life Sciences merges research with private practice in eye care and brain imaging. Another £4 million has been spent upgrading the IT and computing network.

Aston was among the pioneers of "smart cards", giving students access to university facilities and enabling them to make purchases on campus, once they have money in their accounts. There is plenty of opportunity to use them in a buzzing social scene, which most students find to their taste. The guild of students has always been very active, both socially and politically.

Undergraduate Fees and Support

- » Fees UK/EU students 2012–13   £9,000
  Fees for sandwich placement year   £1,000
- » Fees for International students 2011–12   £11,700–£14,700
- » Aston is planning a financial support package of bursaries and fee waivers. It is expected that over 45 per cent of Aston students will be entitled to some form of fee discounts.
- » Scholarships and bursaries based on circumstances or by competition are available.
- » Check the university's website for the latest information.

Students		
Undergraduates:	**7,415**	**(660)**
Postgraduates:	**1,950**	**(875)**
Mature students:	**9.9%**	
Overseas students:	**21.3%**	
Applications per place:	**7.1**	
From state-sector schools:	**91.2%**	
From working-class homes:	**37.1%**	

For detailed information about fees, grants and bursaries and how they work, see chapter 7.

Accommodation

Number of places and costs refer to 2011–12

University-provided places: 2,307

Percentage catered: 0%

Self-catered accommodation: range £72 (standard) – £125 (en-suite deluxe) a week.

First years are guaranteed accommodation if they fulfil requirements and apply by the deadline.

International fee-paying students: as above.

Contact: accom@aston.ac.uk; www.aston.ac.uk/accommodation

Bangor University

Bangor has the "fairest" workload of any UK university, according to polls of students published in 2009 and 2010, and it moved into the top 30 for overall satisfaction levels in the latest National Student Survey. Undergraduates in biology, Celtic studies, chemistry, education, history and modern languages gave particularly high marks in the 2010 survey. The "small and friendly" nature of the university and the city no doubt helped – students have given it high marks for security.

Bangor's community focus dates back to a 19th-century campaign which saw local quarrymen putting part of their weekly wages towards the establishment of a college. The School of Education and Lifelong Learning continues the tradition with courses across North Wales, but the university has also built a worldwide reputation in areas such as environmental studies and ocean sciences. Like Aberystwyth and Swansea, it is another part of the University of Wales to have asserted its independence by taking the title of Bangor University and awarding its own degrees.

The 2008 research assessments identified world-leading work in all Bangor's 19 subject areas. The university claimed the grades for accounting and finance to be the best in the UK, with electronic engineering second and both sports science and Welsh in the top ten in their respective subjects. Teaching assessments were impressive, with half of the subjects rated as excellent. There is a high proportion of small-group teaching and tutorials, as well as one of Britain's largest peer guiding schemes, which sees senior students mentoring new arrivals.

Bangor merged with a nearby teacher training college, Colleg Normal, in 1996, and that site is now part of the university. The 22 academic schools are grouped into five colleges: arts, education and humanities; business, social sciences and law; natural sciences; health and behavioural sciences; and physical and applied sciences. All schools are within walking distance of each other, apart from ocean sciences, which is two miles away in Menai Bridge.

The university estate has been redeveloped, with the addition of a £5-million environmental sciences building, while a £3.5-million Cancer Research Institute is attracting specialists of international repute. A combination of private funds and a £5-million European grant was used to establish a new Business Management Development Centre on a waterfront site. A £35-million Arts and Innovation Centre is due to open in 2013, forming a bridge between the university's upper campus and the nearby science site. Part-funded by the Welsh Assembly, it will include a new students' union and an innovation hub, as well as teaching and performance spaces that

---

Bangor
Gwynedd LL57 2DG

01248 382017 (admissions)
admissions@bangor.ac.uk
www.bangor.ac.uk
www.undeb.bangor.ac.uk
Affiliation: none

The Times Rankings

Overall Ranking: **57**

Student satisfaction:	=24	(79%)
Research quality:	=45	(1.5)
Entry standards:	65	(288)
Student–staff ratio:	=91	(20.7)
Services & facilities/student:	96	(£1,091)
Expected completion rate:	82	(81.1%)
Good honours:	77	(57.1%)
Graduate prospects:	=72	(59.7%)

will include a 500-seat theatre and an outdoor amphitheatre.

Based little more than a stone's throw from Snowdonia with its attractions for sports enthusiasts, Bangor is an expanding centre for Welsh-medium teaching. Although a majority of students come from outside Wales – there is a strong link with Ireland, for example – more than a quarter of the students speak the language and one of the halls of residence is Welsh-speaking. The university also has a flourishing international exchange programme. Finland is a favourite destination for forestry and environmental science students; biologists tend to head for the USA.

Bangor does better than most traditional universities when judged against access benchmarks. More than 95 per cent of the students come from state schools or colleges, and nearly one in three come from working-class homes. The university is spending £2.8 million a year on bursaries and scholarships. There are 40 merit scholarships of up to £3,000 for students who excel in the University's annual entrance scholarships examinations, sports scholarships worth up to £2,000 per year and £5,000 excellence scholarships in several subject areas. The university's Talent Opportunities Programme, which operates in schools across North Wales, targets potential applicants from lower socio-economic families, who have little or no history of going on to university. Applications have increased steadily in recent years. The demand for degree places was up by almost 20 per cent at the start of 2011 – comfortably the biggest increase at any university in Wales.

There is a strong focus on student support – the Peer Guide Scheme supports new students in the transition to university life, while the pioneering dyslexia unit offers individual and group support throughout students' courses. Six new halls of residence opened in 2008 and another five followed 12 months later. The work was part of a £35-million upgrade at the main university accommodation site. Bangor is also one of the most cost-effective places in which to study – one survey made it the second-cheapest university in the UK.

Undergraduate Fees and Support

» Fees 2012–13: to be announced; able to charge up to £9,000, with Welsh Assembly expected to pay fees above £3,375 for Welsh students.
» Fees for international students 2011–12   £9,600–£11,800
» Scholarships and bursaries based on circumstances or by competition.
» Check the university's website for the latest information.

Students

Undergraduates:	**7,350**	**(1,335)**
Postgraduates:	**1,690**	**(1,075)**
Mature students:	**22.0%**	
Overseas students:	**9.0%**	
Applications per place:	**4.2**	
From state-sector schools:	**95.1%**	
From working-class homes:	**33.5%**	

For detailed information about fees, grants and bursaries and how they work, see chapter 7.

Accommodation

Number of places and costs refer to 2011–12
University-provided places: approx 2,184
Percentage catered: 0%
Self-catered costs: £71–£95 (standard); £101–£112 (en-suite or larger rooms) a week (40-week contract).
All first-year students are guaranteed places.
International students: as above.
Contact: accommodation@bangor.ac.uk
www.bangor.ac.uk/accommodation/

University of Bath

Bath is nearing the end of a four-year expansion and refurbishment of its campus that has cost more than £100 million. It has added further facilities for teaching and research, as well as extra student accommodation and social space, including a new student centre which opened in October 2010. Bath is a relatively small university with just over 9,000 full-time undergraduates and nearly 5,000 postgraduates. The university enjoys both an attractive location and a high academic reputation – it has never been out of the top 20 in *The Times* League Table. However, it has not seen the sharp growth in demand for places experienced by many of its peers in recent years. Applications were flat at the start of 2011 and grew by only 2 per cent in the boom year of 2010.

Students like the community feel of campus life, and one of the lowest dropout rates in Britain suggests that they are well supported. The library is open 24 hours a day, seven days a week. Few can fail to be impressed by the magnificence of the city's architecture. The modern campus on the edge of Bath, with some undistinguished buildings dating from its origins as a technological university in the 1960s, is hardly in the same league. But the 200-acre site has pleasant grounds and is functional, with academic, recreational and residential facilities in close

proximity. More lecture theatres and computer laboratories have eased the pressure on teaching space and 468 new study bedrooms have also been added recently. A rolling programme to refurbish and update all the teaching facilities is well under way. The central Parade now features a lively and contemporary café, while a new building opened in April 2010 provides additional research and teaching space, as well as a new postgraduate centre.

Research is Bath's greatest strength: 60 per cent of the work submitted for the 2008 Research Assessment Exercise was judged to be world-leading or internationally excellent. Social work and social policy, business and management, physics, pharmacy and maths did particularly well, but there were good results in a number of areas. The university's research grants and contracts portfolio is worth around £100 million. Bath was also in the top 30 universities in the 2010 National Student Survey. Sports science produced the best results, but pharmacology, toxicology and pharmacy, Iberian studies, and civil and mechanical engineering all showed high levels of satisfaction.

Most courses have a practical element, and assessors have praised the university for the work placements it offers. The majority of students take courses with placements or a period of study abroad, which helps to produce consistently outstanding graduate employment figures. Entrepreneurship is

---

Claverton Down
Bath BA2 7AY

01225 383019 (admissions)
admissions@bath.ac.uk
www.bath.ac.uk
www.bathstudent.com
Affiliation: 1994 Group

The Times Rankings
Overall Ranking: **12**

Student satisfaction:	=20	(80%)
Research quality:	=21	(2.2)
Entry standards:	10	(459)
Student–staff ratio:	=39	(16.1)
Services & facilities/student:	28	(£1,682)
Expected completion rate:	5	(96.4%)
Good honours:	13	(76.6%)
Graduate prospects:	=9	(77.9%)

actively encouraged among the students through a number of initiatives and projects. A recent success story involved two students who set up their own frozen yogurt range, Arctic Farm, which is now on the shelves of Harrods.

The university's other great claim to fame lies in its sports facilities, which were already among the best in Britain before the addition of a £35-million training village, funded with National Lottery money. The campus acquired a 50-metre swimming pool by this route, to which it added an indoor running track, a multipurpose sports hall, eight indoor tennis courts, an indoor jumps and throws hall, air pistol and fencing sale, a judo dojo and even a simulated bobsleigh and skeleton start area, as used by Amy Williams, 2010 Olympic gold medallist for the skeleton. There is a strong tradition in competitive sports: the university pioneered sports scholarships more than 20 years ago. There are also courses to do the facilities justice, as recognised in a near-perfect score for teaching quality in sport and leisure. The university has begun to charge students for more of its facilities, but they still represent an exceptional resource. The campus will also host the British Paralympics team and the Malaysian Olympic team in the run up to London 2012.

Students – nearly a quarter of whom were educated at independent schools – may find the campus quiet at weekends and struggle

to afford some of Bath's attractions, but they value its location. When they tire of the beauty of Bath, the nightlife of Bristol is only a few minutes away by public transport. The two cities have a combined student population of more than 50,000. The award-winning students' union is very active and the university has been upgrading its student support services, for example through the introduction of a new virtual learning environment and establishment of a centrally based one-stop centre for student services. More than nine out of ten students surveyed say they would recommend the university to family and friends.

Undergraduate Fees and Support

» Fees for UK/EU students 2012–13:   £9,000
» Fees for International students 2011–12:   £11,600–£14,800
» A package of financial support and widening participation activity to be announced. .
» Scholarships and bursaries based on circumstances or by competition are available.
» Check the university's website for the latest information.

Students		
Undergraduates:	**9,310**	**(540)**
Postgraduates:	**1,680**	**(3,075)**
Mature students:	**8.3%**	
Overseas students:	**21.8%**	
Applications per place:	**6.8**	
From state-sector schools:	**75.5%**	
From working-class homes:	**19.0%**	

For detailed information about fees, grants and bursaries and how they work, see chapter 7.

Accommodation
Number of places and costs refer to 2011–12
University-provided places: 3,372
Percentage catered: 3%
Catered cost: £170–£180 a week.
Self-catered cost: £85–£140 a week.
First years guaranteed accommodation if conditions are met, and applications received by 13 July.
International students: as above. Exchange students are housed on a reciprocal basis.
Contact: www.bath.ac.uk/accommodation/enquiry/

Bath Spa University

Bath Spa is one of a number of "teaching-led" universities created since the millennium under Government reforms. But it is far from new in other respects and not without research strengths. The history of the predecessor colleges goes back 160 years, and it boasts some famous alumni, including Body Shop founder Anita Roddick and Turner Prize winner Sir Howard Hodgkin. Its Newton Park headquarters, four miles outside the World Heritage city of Bath, is in grounds landscaped by Capability Brown in the eighteenth century, with a handsome Georgian manor house owned by the Duchy of Cornwall as its centrepiece.

In recent years, the new university has undertaken its biggest-ever building programme to cater for growing student numbers. Applications grew by 17 per cent in 2010 and by almost as much in the current round. With around 8,800 students, it is still comparatively small, but the range of courses has been growing steadily. At Newton Park, the base for all students except those taking art and design subjects, the students' union has practically doubled in size, a library extension has added about 120 workstations and £4.8 million has been spent on an impressive university theatre with a 200-seat auditorium. The Creative Writing Centre is housed in the 14th-century gatehouse, part of the original St Loe's Castle and a scheduled ancient monument. Significant further development is planned at Newton Park starting in 2011, encompassing teaching, social and residential facilities that will enable another 600 students to be housed on campus. The university is in a strong financial position and is one of the few higher education institutions with no borrowing on its balance sheet.

A second campus at Sion Hill, in Bath itself, which houses the Bath School of Art and Design, has recently undergone a £6-million redevelopment and boasts facilities that are among the most modern in the country. Meanwhile, the university has established a postgraduate centre at Corsham Court, a 16th-century manor house near Chippenham that previously housed the Bath Academy of Art, and there is a teacher training centre on the site of Culverhay School, in Bath. About a third of the students are postgraduates, including a large cohort training to be teachers.

Bath Spa has been awarding its own degrees since 1992 – much longer than some of the other new arrivals on the university scene – and now also has the power to award research degrees. Results in all the National Student Surveys have been good, especially for teaching quality. Music, history, geography and business studies produced the best results in 2010. The university was designated a national centre for excellence in

---

Newton Park
Newton St Loe
Bath BA2 9BN

01225 875609 (admissions)
admissions@bathspa.ac.uk
www.bathspa.ac.uk
www.bathspasu.co.uk
Affiliation: million+

The Times Rankings
Overall Ranking: **84**

Student satisfaction:	=73	(75%)
Research quality:	=79	(0.3)
Entry standards:	60	(293)
Student–staff ratio:	98	(21.1)
Services & facilities/student:	115	(£741)
Expected completion rate:	=37	(89%)
Good honours:	31	(69.0%)
Graduate prospects:	113	(46.5%)

teaching and learning in the creative industries, bringing significant investment in facilities in the Schools of Music and Performing Arts, Humanities and Cultural Industries and Bath School of Art and Design. Half of the subjects in which the university entered the 2008 Research Assessment Exercise (art and design, communication, cultural and media studies, English, history and music) were judged to have some world-leading work.

Despite a setting that would seem to be a magnet for applicants from independent schools, 95 per cent of the home intake is state-educated and 34 per cent are from working-class homes. Two thirds of the students are female, reflecting the arts and social science bias in the curriculum, and 25 per cent are over 25. The latest projected dropout rate, at a little over 9 per cent, is significantly better than the national average for the university's courses and entry grades. There are about 500 overseas students from a variety of countries.

The university has a number of partner colleges in the region, both in the further education and private sectors, where a range of two-year Foundation degrees are delivered. The latest of these include musical theatre, professional musicianship, contemporary circus and physical performance, and further education management. Many students then progress to the university campuses to complete an honours degree. About 85 per cent of first years attending Bath Spa itself are offered hall places and more places are available off-campus through a partnership with Unite, a private company specialising in student accommodation. Students like the "small and friendly" atmosphere, which the university is anxious to retain in spite of the temptation to go for more substantial growth. Sports facilities are not extensive, but a new gym in the students' union has improved them, and a number of the university's sports teams fare well in local competitions. The countryside – on and off campus – is a major draw.

Undergraduate Fees and Support

» Fees for UK/EU students 2012–13 £9,000
  Foundation degree £6,000–£7,800
» Fees for International students 2011–12 £9,690–£10,315
» A package of financial support and widening participation activity worth more than double current spending to be announced.
» Scholarships and bursaries based on circumstances or by competition are available.
» Check the university's website for the latest information.

Students

Undergraduates:	**5,120**	**(510)**
Postgraduates:	**735**	**(2,435)**
Mature students:	**19.9%**	
Overseas students:	**3.0%**	
Applications per place:	**6.2**	
From state-sector schools:	**95.2%**	
From working-class homes:	**34.6%**	

For detailed information about fees, grants and bursaries and how they work, see chapter 7.

Accommodation

Number of places and costs refer to 2010–11
University provided places: 1,083 in halls; 123 in Accredited Independent Housing
Percentage catered: 0%
Self catered: £79–£118 a week; £135 (studio flat) for 40 or 45 weeks.
First years are housed provided requirements are met. Students with a disability or medical condition have priority.
International students: as above; Homestay option available
Contact: http://housing.bathspa.ac.uk;
accommodation@bathspa.ac.uk

University of Bedfordshire

By 2012, Bedfordshire will have ploughed £140 million into its estate since taking over De Montfort University's Bedford campus and establishing a new identity in 2006. The move made the former Luton University the main provider of higher education in a relatively prosperous county. The new university has see-sawed in *The Times* League Table, but the demand for places has increased dramatically. The 35 per cent rise in applications in 2010 was one of the largest at any university and the start of 2011 saw further growth of 15 per cent.

With five campuses to its name, the new university is expanding and developing. It has already spent £60 million on the two main campuses, adding a well-equipped media arts centre and an impressive learning resources centre in Luton. A new campus centre comprising a 280-seat auditorium and a students' union, as well as a new accommodation block completes the Bedford redevelopment.

Work is now underway on developments costing another £74 million in Luton. A new campus centre opened in 2010, with teaching and exhibition space as well as the students' union, information desks, and the careers and employment centre. New £40-million student halls are being built nearby and are on schedule to be ready for the 2011–12 intake. The accommodation will comprise 850 flats, complete with en-suite facilities, phone and high-speed internet access. The third phase of the redevelopment programme is a £15-million postgraduate and continuing professional development centre ready in 2012, and new student accommodation which should be ready a year later.

Although there are partner colleges in Bedford, Dunstable and Milton Keynes, the bulk of the students remain in Luton. The centrepiece of the campus, in the midst of the shopping area, is the striking atrium which leads into the learning resources centre.

The Bedford campus, once a teacher training college, is a 20-minute walk from the town centre in a "self-contained leafy setting". It houses the Faculty of Education, Sport and Tourism, with 3,000 students, making it the UK's largest provider of physical education teacher training, as well as a national centre for other subjects at primary and secondary level.

There is also an attractive management centre and conference venue at Putteridge Bury, a neo-Elizabethan mansion three miles outside Luton. Nursing and midwifery students in the growing Faculty of Health and Social Sciences are based at the Butterfield Park campus, near Luton, which opened in 2008, or at the even newer Oxford House development, in Aylesbury, Buckinghamshire. There are additional teaching facilities at Stoke Mandeville and Wycombe General hospitals. A postgraduate medical school is

---

Park Square
Luton
Bedfordshire LU1 3JU

0844 848 2234
enquiries via website
www.beds.ac.uk
www.ubsu.co.uk
Affiliation: million+

The Times Rankings
Overall Ranking: **106**

Student satisfaction:	=78	(74%)
Research quality:	=92	(0.2)
Entry standards:	116	(187)
Student–staff ratio:	=69	(19.1)
Services & facilities/student:	55	(£1,368)
Expected completion rate:	103	(76.2%)
Good honours:	=111	(44.4%)
Graduate prospects:	63	(61.2%)

run in partnership with Hertfordshire and Cranfield universities, as part of the Government's £1-billion investment in healthcare across Bedfordshire and Hertfordshire.

Courses in the new university are largely vocational. The portfolio of two-year Foundation degrees, for example, is among the largest in the country, stretching from animal management and graphic design to animation for industry and sustainable construction. The university pioneered electronic assessment, with more than 10,000 students in disciplines from accountancy to biology tested by computer. Bedfordshire also hosts a national centre of excellence in personal development planning and employability, which aims to link student learning with life after university.

Almost all of Bedfordshire's entrants are from state schools and nearly 47 per cent come from working-class backgrounds. Four in ten undergraduates are over 20 on entry, many taking access courses to bring them up to degree or diploma standard, and about a third take part-time courses. The numbers entering through Clearing have dropped from nearly one in three to only one in ten, but the latest projected dropout rate of nearly 20 per cent remains high, taking into account the university's courses and entry qualifications. Surprisingly high numbers – nearly a fifth – are from outside the EU, many taking postgraduate courses.

The university celebrated much-improved results in the 2008 Research Assessment Exercise, registering at least some world-leading work in earth systems and environmental science, social work, social policy and administration, sport, tourism and leisure, English language and literature, and communications, cultural and media studies. Scores in the National Student Survey slipped in 2010 after two years of improvement. The highest satisfaction levels have been in marketing, journalism and human resource management.

Neither Luton nor Bedford is particularly famous for its social scene, but both have their share of pubs, clubs and restaurants and London is only half an hour away by train. The university cannot guarantee first-year students accommodation, but helps them find alternative housing where necessary. While those in Luton are improving, the impressive sports facilities in Bedford are set to host athletes for the 2012 Olympics.

Undergraduate Fees and Support

- » Fees for UK/EU students 2012–13   to be announced
- » Fees for International students 2011–12   £9,300
- » A package of financial support and widening participation activity to be announced.
- » Scholarships and bursaries based on circumstances or by competition are available.
- » Check the university's website for the latest information.

Students

Undergraduates:	**9,545**	**(4,870)**
Postgraduates:	**3,195**	**(1,585)**
Mature students:	**41.9%**	
Overseas students:	**17.2%**	
Applications per place:	**4.5**	
From state-sector schools:	**99.0%**	
From working-class homes:	**46.7%**	

For detailed information about fees, grants and bursaries and how they work, see chapter 7.

Accommodation

Number of places and costs refer to 2011–12

University-provided places: about 2,110

Percentage catered: 0%

Self-catered costs: £97.50–£140.00 a week.

First years cannot be guaranteed a place but help is available to find alternative housing in the private sector.

International students: as above.

Contact: www.beds.ac.uk/studentlife/accommodation

studentservices.bedford@beds.ac.uk

accommodation@beds.ac.uk

Birkbeck, University of London

Birkbeck does not appear in the overall ranking of universities published in this *Guide* because, as a specialist provider of part-time higher education, it cannot be compared fairly with other institutions on some of the measures. But the college has become an increasingly popular and prestigious choice for Londoners of all ages. That trend may accelerate with the introduction of more generous support for part-time students from 2012, although Birkbeck will not be immune from charging higher fees. The college chose not to announce details of its proposals to the Office for Fair Access at the same time as most other universities, but said that fees would be pro-rata, according to the time spent on the course, with a possible maximum of £9,000 for full-timers.

Founded in 1923, Birkbeck, University of London specialises in flexible evening higher education, enabling its students to combine their studies with work, family or other commitments. There will be over 90 part-time undergraduate degree courses to choose from in 2012. The college encourages applications from people without traditional qualifications and there is a flexible policy for entry at undergraduate level. Students aged over 21 are not asked for formal qualifications, but the college makes its own assessment of skills and knowledge, on the basis of interviews and/or short tests.

The Labour Government's removal of funding for students returning to take a different qualification cost Birkbeck 40 per cent of its income and student numbers. The college reorganised into a smaller number of "super-schools", increased its recruitment activity and set about improving the student experience. The strategy appears to be succeeding and has brought the college a nomination for a leadership award. Among the innovations has been the introduction of full-time undergraduate degrees. A surprisingly wide range of subjects will be available in 2012, from criminology to the history of art, psychology and planetary science. Most are in the arts and social science, but the 15 degrees include law and environmental management. Students apply for full-time courses through UCAS, rather than direct to the college, as is the case for the part-time portfolio. Birkbeck took only 152 students onto a narrower programme of full-time courses in 2010 but, with only 450 applications, it represented a better-than-average chance of entry to a high-quality degree course.

There are now 19,000 students at the college, which is the University of London's main base for flexible, non-residential teaching. Undergraduate teaching takes

Malet Street
Bloomsbury
London WC1E 7HX

0845 601 0174 (general enquiries)
info@bbk.ac.uk
www.bbk.ac.uk
http://bbk.ukmsl.net
Affiliation: 1994 Group

Edinburgh
Belfast
Cardiff
LONDON

The Times Rankings
The available data do not match the data used to rank the other full-time universities, so Birkbeck could not be included in the League Table this year.

place mainly in the evening and students take four years to gain a degree. Birkbeck did not appear in the 2010 National Student Survey because not enough students responded, but its undergraduates have been among the most satisfied in the UK in previous years. The My Birkbeck Student Centre acts as a front door to all the college's student support services, from help in choosing courses and submitting applications to information about financial support and study skills. It is open late and at weekends, referring those who require more in-depth professional support to the appropriate service, as well as providing information via the **www.bbk.ac.uk/mybirkbeck** website.

Nine out of ten academics at the college are researchers as well as teachers. More than half of the work submitted to the 2008 Research Assessment Exercise was considered world-leading or internationally excellent. Earth Sciences, psychology, history, classics and archaeology and history of art, film and visual media were rated in the top five nationally. Its research strength has helped Birkbeck to a place among the top 200 universities in the world, according to the 2010 *Times Higher Education* world rankings.

Birkbeck is located in the heart of the University of London, in Bloomsbury, close to the university's Senate House headquarters and main facilities. Almost £20 million has been spent consolidating the college's buildings and bringing them under one roof. Teaching also takes place in Stratford, east London, where there is a unique partnership with the University of East London. A new shared £33-million university building in Stratford will welcome its first cohort of students in 2013. University Square, Stratford is the first shared project of this kind in the capital, allowing a broad mix of 3,400 adults to take a wide variety of courses throughout the day and evening.

The main campus is easily accessible by tube, mainline stations, bus and cycle routes. It is next door to the University of London Union (ULU), where facilities include the Energy Base, which offers a 60-station gymnasium with cardio theatre, a 33-metre swimming pool and two studios. Through ULU, a wide range of sports clubs is available for students. As most Birkbeck students already live and work in the capital they do not need university accommodation, but those who do can apply to the University of London Accommodation Office (ULAO).

Undergraduate Fees and Support

» Fees for UK/EU students 2012–13   £4,500–6,750
(on the basis of students studying for four years at 75% intensity, equivalent to £6,000–£9,000 full-time fees.)
» Fees for International students 2011–12   £11,334
» Birkbeck is planning a generous financial support package.
» Flexible payment options for courses and variation in study patterns to help costs.
» Check the university's website for the latest information.

Students

Undergraduates:	10	(14,230)
Postgraduates:	870	(3,565)
Mature students:	97.4%	
Overseas students:	n/a	
Applications per place:	3.0	
From state-sector schools:	n/a	
From working-class homes:	n/a	

For detailed information about fees, grants and bursaries and how they work, see chapter 7.

Accommodation

As the courses provided are part-time, the university has a limited number of places in the intercollegiate halls of residence, and these are normally reserved for full-time international students. For further accommodation information see:
www.bbk.ac.uk/mybirkbeck/services/facilities/accommodation

International students should also contact
www.bbk.ac.uk/prospective/international/accommodation

University of Birmingham

Birmingham is the original "redbrick" university and remains a source of great civic pride in the second city. To those outside the West Midlands, however, it has been a quiet achiever, lacking the glamour of some of its Russell Group counterparts. The university recruited Professor David Eastwood, chief executive of the Higher Education Funding Council for England, to maximise its undoubted potential. He has said he wants Birmingham to be "the best of the rest" after Oxbridge and the top London colleges.

There are plans for more postgraduates, greater investment in research and major changes to the university's estate. The university is the national hub for a new STEM programme, a national initiative to promote interest in science, technology, engineering and maths among young people and enhance higher level skills in the workplace. It has also become the first link in a chain of Cancer Research UK Centres, while a £60-million fundraising campaign launched in 2009 will support projects ranging from research into brain injury, ageing and clean energy to scholarships and a centre for heritage and cultural learning.

Students come to Birmingham from more than 150 countries. Entry standards are high, averaging the equivalent of more than ABB at A level. With over six applicants for each place, they are likely to remain so, but aspiring students still flock to the largest open days in Britain each June. There is also an additional open day for upper sixth-formers in September.

The university's enduring reputation is based on its research, with 16 per cent of the work submitted for the 2008 Research Assessment Exercise regarded as world-leading. Birmingham took satisfaction from the broad range of subjects in which it produced good results, with music, physics, computer science, mechanical engineering, European studies, primary care, cancer sciences, psychology and law all doing well. The university is now going to partner with Nottingham University on a range of research projects.

Birmingham finished in the top 30 in the 2010 National Student Survey, faring better than most of the big city universities. Planning produced a rare 100 per cent satisfaction score, while American studies, chemical engineering, French, geology, human geography, physics and medical subjects were the other top performers. Birmingham encourages interdisciplinary study, for example allowing undergraduates to combine technology with subjects ranging from Latin or modern Greek to the management of floods and other natural disasters.

In recent years, the university has spent £200 million on its estate, adding a student facilities building at the Medical School, a

---

Edgbaston
Birmingham B15 2TT

0121 415 8900 (admissions)
admissions@bham.ac.uk
www.bham.ac.uk
www.guildofstudents.com
Affiliation: Russell Group

Edinburgh
Belfast
BIRMINGHAM •
Cardiff
London

The Times Rankings
Overall Ranking: **26**

Student satisfaction:	=24	(79%)
Research quality:	=21	(2.2)
Entry standards:	20	(421)
Student–staff ratio:	=31	(15.4)
Services & facilities/student:	14	(£1,969)
Expected completion rate:	14	(93.9%)
Good honours:	25	(72.9%)
Graduate prospects:	=23	(71.8%)

new home for Sport and Exercise Sciences and a well-equipped learning centre, as well as upgrading student accommodation. In the latest phase, the Muirhead Tower has been extensively refurbished to house the College of Social Sciences. The Bramall concert hall and music department will open in 2012 and there are plans for further sports facilities and a new central library. The university is also investing £3.5 million on an employability initiative which will include internships and mentoring by some of the university's most successful alumni.

The 230-acre campus in leafy Edgbaston is dominated by a 300-foot clocktower, which is one of the city's best-known landmarks, and boasts its own station. Dentistry is located in the city, while part of the School of Education is in Selly Oak, a mile from the Edgbaston campus. Drama is also located there, along with the BBC Drama Village, which is part of a strategic alliance between the university and the corporation.

Most of the halls and university flats are conveniently located in an attractive parkland setting near the main campus. There are more than 4,000 university-owned beds, following a ten-year programme of expansion, and accommodation in the private sector is also plentiful.

The campus is less than three miles from the centre of Birmingham, but the area has plenty of shops, pubs and restaurants of its own. With its own nightclub among the facilities on campus, some students do not even stray that far, but the city is acquiring a growing reputation among the young, which is helping to make the university even more popular. Some 40 per cent of Birmingham graduates choose to make the city their home.

Student facilities on campus are on a par with the best in the country, and include a medical practice. An outdoor pursuits centre is by Coniston Water, in the Lake District. Birmingham has traditionally been concerned with the body as well as the mind, and the voluntary Active Lifestyles Programme attracts 4,000 students to 150 different courses. Tutors with national qualifications run classes from beginner to advanced level and National Lottery funding will extend the range of sporting choice yet further. Birmingham has ranked in the top four in British Universities and College Sports competitions for the past 15 years.

Undergraduate Fees and Support

» Fees for UK/EU students 2012–13 £9,000
» Fees for International students 2011–12 £11,340–£14,650
£26,590 (clinical)
» Students with household income below £16K, award of £4,300 or partial fee waiver. Tapered support for household income £16K–£42K.
» Scholarships and bursaries based on circumstances or by competition are available.
» Check the university's website for the latest information.

Students

Undergraduates:	**17,260**	**(1,615)**
Postgraduates:	**6,195**	**(5,055)**
Mature students:	**8.1%**	
Overseas students:	**10.1%**	
Applications per place:	**7.9**	
From state-sector schools:	**81.0%**	
From working-class homes:	**23.3%**	

For detailed information about fees, grants and bursaries and how they work, see chapter 7.

Accommodation

Number of places and costs refer to 2011–12
University-provided places: 4,267
Percentage catered: 42%
Catered costs: £109.50–£165.50 a week
Self-catered costs: £77.50–£133.50 a week
All first years are guaranteed housing (subject to conditions).
International students: as above
Contact: ugradaccomm@bham.ac.uk
www.birmingham.ac.uk/students/accommodation

Birmingham City University

Birmingham City University has never looked back since adopting its new name in 2007. Applications were up substantially for the third year in a row at the start of 2011. Improved grades have doubled the university's research income, leading to the establishment of 11 new research centres. The transformation of the university's facilities has continued, although the Government's plans for a high-speed rail terminal in Birmingham appear to have scuppered its most ambitious project by taking the intended site of a new city-centre campus.

The switch from the previous identity as UCE Birmingham (in turn originally the University of Central England) was designed to emphasise the university's location, reinforce its close links with the city and give the university a stronger identity. The Vice-Chancellor's strategy has been to build on the university's traditionally close links with business and the professions. An emphasis on employability is underlined by a £300,000 project to create "future-proof" graduates with training and education resources to help develop skills and knowledge for the workplace. High-powered visiting lecturers and an innovative iLearning strategy contribute to this agenda.

The annual satisfaction survey goes to half of the student body, and the results are taken seriously: a recent exercise led to the introduction of internet tutorials in engineering and new help with research for undergraduates in law and social science. The prize-winning Student Academic Partners scheme has spawned a formal agreement between the university and the students' union to improve the student experience.

The university has a proud record of extending access to higher education: over 44 per cent of its students come from working-class homes and 97 per cent attended state schools or colleges. The drop-out rate has improved slightly in the latest figures but, at 17.5 per cent, remains slightly worse than the national average for the university's courses and entry grades. About half of the full-time students come from the West Midlands, many from ethnic minorities. The university also has one of the largest programmes of part-time courses in Britain, making it the biggest provider of higher education in the region. Entrance is through the network of associated further education colleges, which run foundation and access programmes.

Eight campuses straggle across the city, but about half of students are concentrated on the modern City North Campus at Perry Barr. The planned city-centre campus in the Eastside district, near Millennium Point, already had planning permission and was intended to form the centrepiece of a sustained programme of capital investment.

Perry Barr
Birmingham B42 2SU

0121 331 5595 (enquiries)
choices@bcu.ac.uk
www.bcu.ac.uk
www.birminghamcitysu.com
Affiliation: million+

The Times Rankings
Overall Ranking: **87**

Student satisfaction:	=95	(73%)
Research quality:	=92	(0.2)
Entry standards:	=89	(263)
Student–staff ratio:	=94	(20.9)
Services & facilities/student:	40	(£1,554)
Expected completion rate:	=95	(78.7%)
Good honours:	91	(53.7%)
Graduate prospects:	44	(67.7%)

If the rail project goes ahead, an alternative site will be sought for the creative and performing arts, media, technology and design. The relocation of engineering and computing to Millennium Point in 2001 provided a new focus for the university. Facilities in the £114-million Lottery-funded centre are open to the public. The Birmingham School of Acting also moved into £4-million purpose-built facilities at Millennium Point in 2007.

The Edgbaston campus has been refurbished for the Faculty of Health, with a prize-winning library, IT suites, teaching facilities and recreational space. The Birmingham Institute of Art and Design spreads over four campuses from Gosta Green and the impressive listed Venetian gothic fine art campus at Margaret Street, both in the city centre, to Bourneville. This facility was refurbished at a cost of £20 million and occupies part of the Cadbury village. The largest institute of its kind outside London, it also includes the world famous and newly refurbished School of Jewellery in the city's famous Jewellery Quarter.

One of the university's best-known features is its Conservatoire, housed in part of Birmingham's smart convention centre. Courses from opera to world music have given it a reputation for innovation. Teacher education courses consistently produce among the best scores in Ofsted inspections.

The university was awarded a national centre for excellence in teaching and learning for health and social care.

The university has been increasing its portfolio of high-tech degree courses like electronic commerce, communications and network engineering, and electronic systems. The 2008 Research Assessment Exercise recorded some world-leading work in all seven areas covered by the university's submission. In art and design, 30 per cent were given the top grade, placing Birmingham City in the top ten for the subject.

University-owned accommodation is guaranteed for first years, and there is a relatively cheap and plentiful private housing sector. The Pavilion, adjacent to the City North Campus, has added £4.5 million of conference facilities and a £10-million sports village opened in 2010. The city's student scene is highly rated and has been charted in a Lonely Planet guide.

Undergraduate Fees and Support

» Fees for UK/EU students 2012–13   £7,500–£8,200
    Specialist courses (including Conservatoire)   £9,000
    Foundation degree   £6,000
    Sandwich year out   £1,500
» Fees for International students 2011–12   £9,600–£11,050
    £13,750 (Conservatoire and acting)
» A package of financial support and widening participation activity to be announced.
» Check the university's website for the latest information.

Students

Undergraduates:	**15,335**	**(5,275)**
Postgraduates:	**1,605**	**(2,620)**
Mature students:	**29.6%**	
Overseas students:	**7.4%**	
Applications per place:	**5.7**	
From state-sector schools:	**97.2%**	
From working-class homes:	**44.7%**	

For detailed information about fees, grants and bursaries and how they work, see chapter 7.

Accommodation

Number of places and costs refer to 2011–12
University-provided places: 2,485
Percentage catered: 0%
Self-catered costs: £83.00–£109.50 a week (40–43 weeks).
Accommodation guaranteed for first years if conditions are met.
International students are guaranteed accommodation.
Contact: www.bcu.ac.uk/accommodation
accommodation@uce.ac.uk

University of Bolton

Bolton has enjoyed two years of healthy growth in applications – a welcome return to the boom years that followed the granting of university status in 2005. The university now has a single campus in the centre of the town, as well as a branch campus in the United Arab Emirates that is part of a longer-term internationalisation strategy. The rationalisation of sites in Bolton has provided additional and enhanced teaching space, facilities to interact with industry and a new students' union.

The university traces its roots back as far as 1824 to one of the country's first three mechanics institutes. There are now more than 9,000 students but there are no plans for further dramatic growth. The university sees itself as a regional institution, with three quarters of the students coming from the North West, many through partner colleges. But the international dimension includes long-established links in Malaysia, China, Zambia, Malawi and Vietnam, as well as a regular contingent of overseas students from 60 different countries. The Ras as Khaimah campus opened in 2008, offering a range of undergraduate and postgraduate courses identical to those taught at Bolton. The £1-million development near Dubai has 270 students and is intended to take 700 within five years. Students at Bolton will also have the opportunity to study in the UAE for part of their degree course.

Student satisfaction scores improved a little in 2010 without matching the early days of the National Student Survey, when Bolton almost made the top ten. It has since dropped into the bottom half of the table on this measure, although there was a good score in 2009 for maths and statistics. At the other end of the scale, design students were among the least satisfied in the whole survey. The university has done better in the International Student Barometer, which tracks the views of overseas students at UK institutions.

The university is not research-driven, but engineering, architecture and the built environment, social work and social policy all contained some world-leading research in the 2008 assessments. A centre for research and innovation in materials which opened in 2003 is to be the first of a series of "knowledge exchange zones". Bolton is not one of the new breed of "teaching-only" universities; it has been accredited for research degrees for more than ten years and acquired its new status under the old rules. About 1,500 of the students are postgraduates, taking qualifications up to and including PhDs.

The £11.3-million building programme at the Deane campus has included a design studio and three floors of teaching and learning space where students work on actual

Deane Road
Bolton BL3 5AB

01204 903903 (course enquiries)
enquiries@bolton.ac.uk
www.bolton.ac.uk
www.ubsu.org.uk
Affiliation: million+

The Times Rankings
Overall Ranking: **114**

Student satisfaction:	=95	(73%)
Research quality:	=92	(0.2)
Entry standards:	109	(222)
Student–staff ratio:	85	(20.4)
Services & facilities/student:	116	(£625)
Expected completion rate:	115	(66.2%)
Good honours:	110	(45.7%)
Graduate prospects:	116	(45.4%)

briefs for companies seeking design solutions, an Innovation Factory housing, among others, special effects laboratories and a product design studio. Also included within this development is a new social learning zone which includes a students' union bar and social facilities, a computer access room and new students' union offices and advice centre. Now completed, this combined student services covers floor space equivalent to the size of a football pitch. A multifaith chaplaincy opened in 2010, with a resources area, a quiet room and a prayer room. A swimming pool and sports complex built in partnership with the local authority is due to be completed in February 2012 and will offer students access to the pool, gym, sports courts, teaching facilities and equipment, physiotherapy and rehabilitation facilities, an NHS surgery and emergency walk-in centre. The 702 reasonably priced residential places go a long way in an institution with a high proportion of home-based students. Almost half of the undergraduates are over 21 at entry.

The university exceeds all the access measures designed to widen participation in higher education: nearly all the students are state-educated, 52 per cent are from working-class homes and the proportion from areas without a tradition of higher education is almost twice the national average for Bolton's subjects and entry qualifications. The downside – and an important one – is that the dropout rate remains the highest in England. The university has an action plan to bring the rate down to the national average for its courses and qualifications by 2012 but, while the latest projection represents some improvement, still almost 28 per cent of undergraduates who entered in 2008 are projected to leave without a qualification.

Undergraduate Fees and Support

» Fees for UK/EU students 2012–13:

Classroom-based courses	£6,300
Studio-based and resource-intensive courses	£7,200
Laboratory and specialist courses using dedicated facilities	£8,400

» Fees for International students 2011–12 £8,400

» The university estimates that around 70 per cent of students will pay £7,200; many students on £8,400 courses likely to be eligible for fee waivers of up to £1,200 from the Government's Science, Technology, Engineering & Mathematics (STEM) funding.

» A range of scholarships and other support activity to be announced.

» Check the university's website for the latest information.

Students

Undergraduates:	**4,120**	**(3,610)**
Postgraduates:	**555**	**(965)**
Mature students:	**49.9%**	
Overseas students:	**7.4%**	
Applications per place:	**4.1**	
From state-sector schools:	**99.8%**	
From working-class homes:	**52.3%**	

For detailed information about fees, grants and bursaries and how they work, see chapter 7.

Accommodation

Number of places and costs refer to 2011–12

University-provided places: 702

Percentage catered: 0%

Self-catered costs: £2,840 annually (40 weeks); £71 a week. There is a £200 discount if the full rent is paid in one lump sum.

All first years are generally accommodated.

International students: accommodation is secured for these students.

Contact: accomm@bolton.ac.uk

Bournemouth University

Once a university that gloried in the absence of traditional academic disciplines, Bournemouth has been subtly changing its image. It has appointed 150 academics in three years to "facilitate the transformation of its staff profile and foster the development of an academically-led culture". Research moved up the agenda with a £1-million investment in 80 PhD studentships – only three universities showed more improvement in the last set of research assessments – and the aim is to increase undergraduates' entry qualifications. The university rose 27 places up *The Times* League Table in four years but fell back four places in the last two years.

Bournemouth's forte has always been in identifying gaps in the higher education market and then filling them with innovative programmes. Degrees in public relations, retail management, scriptwriting and tax law are among the examples. The university also boasts the National Centre of Computer Animation. The mix has been popular with students: applications increased substantially over a number of years, although they were down by more than 10 per cent at the start of 2011. Attendance at open days tripled in four years.

The university claims a number of firsts in its growing portfolio of courses, notably in tourism, conservation and media-related programmes. It was no surprise to find Bournemouth among the pioneers of two-year Foundation degrees. Now much expanded, the courses are being delivered in further education colleges from Somerset to Wiltshire, supporting the needs of business in the creative arts, media and tourism. One even serves soldiers based around the world, who are studying business and management via the internet to boost their employment prospects when they leave the military.

A majority of undergraduates take sandwich courses, and 70 per cent do work placements. The result is that nearly four out of five graduates went straight into jobs at the time of the latest survey. The retail management degree notched up eight successive years of full employment and is still running at over 90 per cent. Virtually all students take up the offer of personal development planning, both online and with trained staff, while 1,400 first years also take advantage of peer-assisted learning, receiving advice and mentoring from more experienced undergraduates.

Accounting and journalism achieved high levels of satisfaction in the National Student Survey published in 2010, but the university's overall scores slipped and it remained in the bottom half of the table overall. Media courses are a particular strength, with entry requirements well above the average for Bournemouth – itself now among the highest in the post-1992 universities. State-of-the-art

Fern Barrow
Talbot Campus
Poole
Dorset BH12 5BB

08456 501501 (enquiries)
askBUenquiries@
  bournemouth.ac.uk
www.bournemouth.ac.uk
www.subu.org.uk
Affiliation: University Alliance

The Times Rankings
Overall Ranking: **=62**

Student satisfaction:	=78	(74%)
Research quality:	=70	(0.4)
Entry standards:	=56	(297)
Student–staff ratio:	114	(23.6)
Services & facilities/student:	69	(£1,260)
Expected completion rate:	44	(87.0%)
Good honours:	=49	(63.6%)
Graduate prospects:	64	(61.1%)

equipment includes a motion capture facility for real-time animation, which is used in teaching and available for use by outside companies. The university was designated as England's only centre for excellence in media practice.

In the 2008 Research Assessment Exercise, eight of the ten subject areas contained at least some world-leading research, with art and design, and communication, cultural and media studies producing the best grades. The results have tripled Bournemouth's research grant and the university won a £6-million research grant, its largest ever, to establish an Industrial Doctorate Centre in Computer Animation with the University of Bath.

New teaching and residential accommodation has been added in recent years, with more to come. There is a wide range of accommodation, from around 2,300 places in university halls to shared houses. Students based in halls of residence in Poole enjoy a millionaire's view of Poole Harbour. Recent developments include a new Executive Business Centre, which is a focus for services to local companies and £1.5 million has been spent on improvements to information technology. There are now two campuses – the original Talbot site in Poole and a campus in Bournemouth – with partner colleges in Bridgwater, Yeovil, Bournemouth and Poole, Dorchester, Salisbury and Weymouth.

The southern seaside location and the subject mix attract more middle-class students than most new universities, although almost 95 per cent attended state schools and colleges. Students are discouraged from bringing cars, but many still do. The campuses are served by a subsidised bus service. The area has plenty to offer students during the summer season. Although it naturally becomes less lively in the winter months, Bournemouth no longer shuts up when the tourists go home. The students' union's Old Fire Station bar is the favourite among many nightlife options. Bournemouth is becoming the UK's latest surfing hotspot and other water sports are catered for in Poole Harbour. The university is also benefiting from the Lottery-funded *Free your Fitness* campaign, which gives students to opportunity to take up a new sport or return to one that they have dropped.

Undergraduate Fees and Support

» Fees for UK/EU students 2012–13 £8,200
  Flagship degrees, for example in computer animation,
  journalism, television production, tourism £9,000
  Foundation degrees £6,000
» Fees for International students 2011–12 £9,500–£11,5000
» A package of financial support and widening participation
  activity to include fee waivers, bursaries and accommodation
  bursaries and special support for those leaving care to be
  announced.
» Check the university's website for the latest information.

Students		
Undergraduates:	**12,345**	**(3,320)**
Postgraduates:	**1,465**	**(1,180)**
Mature students:	**21.6%**	
Overseas students:	**6.0%**	
Applications per place:	**6.8**	
From state-sector schools:	**94.8%**	
From working-class homes:	**31.0%**	

For detailed information about fees, grants and bursaries and how they work, see chapter 7.

Accommodation

Number of places and costs refer to 2010–11
University-provided places: about 2,910 (2,310 in halls; 600 head tenancy)
Percentage catered: 0%
Self-catered costs: £78–£95 a week.
The university expects to offer all first years a place to live.
Residential restrictions apply.
International students: guaranteed if conditions are met.
Contact: accommodation@bournemouth.ac.uk

University of Bradford

Bradford has been a leading light in the green movement in higher education, with its "ecoversity" programme addressing issues of sustainable development in all the university's practices, including the curriculum. The most visible sign will be the opening in 2011 of The Green, a sustainable student village catering mainly for first-year and international students. The development is part of a £70-million modernisation plan that includes a £7-million investment in new and upgraded teaching facilities. Another project produced the distinctive four-storey Atrium, which has brought together all student support services in a single, open-plan social space.

The university is at the heart of a new "Learning Quarter", an area of education institutions and creative and knowledge-based industries, which is levering in over £40-million worth of investment to the area. Still a relatively small university of little more than 10,000 undergraduates, Bradford has carved out a niche for itself with mature students, who now make up over a quarter of all undergraduates. They relish the vocational slant and the accent on work experience and placement courses, which regularly place Bradford towards the top of the graduate employment tables. More than half of the undergraduates are from working-class homes – by far the biggest proportion of any pre-1992 university. Demand for places has recovered after a difficult period: applications were up by 15 per cent at the start of 2011 and admission requirements have been rising.

Nearly 20 per cent of the university's students are from overseas, many of them taught in partner institutions in locations as diverse as Poland, India, Iceland and Hong Kong. Nearer home, there are alliances with a number of further education colleges to help boost participation in a region where it is well below the national average. The colleges offer Foundation degrees in areas such as public sector administration, community justice, engineering technology and enterprise in IT. Perhaps the best known is in health and social care, where the university was already expanding opportunities locally, bringing about a fourfold increase in enrolments by young women from South Asian families.

The relatively small, lively campus is close to the city centre. Health students have their own building a few minutes' walk away, while a shuttle bus service runs to the highly rated management school two miles away in a 14-acre parkland setting. The eventual aim is to develop a health and science quarter, with the School of Health Studies housed in its own building on campus. Improvements in recent years have included upgraded laboratories for chemical and forensic

Richmond Road
Bradford
West Yorkshire BD7 1DP

0800 073 1225 (freephone)
course-enquiries@bradford.ac.uk
www.bradford.ac.uk
www.ubuonline.co.uk
Affiliation: University Alliance

The Times Rankings
Overall Ranking: **=62**

Student satisfaction:	=48	(77%)
Research quality:	54	(1.0)
Entry standards:	83	(268)
Student–staff ratio:	=50	(17.5)
Services & facilities/student:	71	(£1,258)
Expected completion rate:	=97	(78.6%)
Good honours:	76	(57.5%)
Graduate prospects:	=32	(69.4%)

science, and new sports facilities including a gym and climbing wall and an improved sports hall.

The university maintained its recent improvements in the National Student Survey in 2010, remaining in the top 50 with good results in anatomy, business, geography, history, ophthalmics and nursing. Bradford is harnessing the power of technology: it operates an online social network for prospective students before they even apply to the university. A so-called "e-induction" acts as a preparation for university life, while those who do win a place are offered a "self-audit" that gauges new students' levels of confidence in different academic areas and allows them to develop an action plan with their personal tutor.

Some 80 per cent of the work submitted for the 2008 Research Assessment Exercise was placed in the top two categories, although more than a third of the academics were not entered. Social work and social policy, politics, civil engineering and pharmacy produced the best results. Politics includes the university's best-known offering of peace studies, which has acquired an international reputation, while the human studies programme, which combines psychology, literature and sociology with philosophy, is another imaginative construct.

The university has launched suites of ICT and media studies courses to add to those in e-commerce and internet computing, computer animation and special effects, interactive systems and video games design. Computer-assisted learning is increasing in many subjects, making use of unusually extensive IT provision and a new wireless network. Some courses feature online assessment and the use of laptops in lectures.

More southerners are being attracted to Bradford's status as Britain's cheapest student city. Places in halls are reasonably priced and all have internet connections. Another 1,000 places will be added when The Green opens. There is particularly good provision for disabled students, who account for 6 per cent of the university population. Bradford's senior management group includes a Director of Student Engagement to ensure that the student voice is heard in future developments.

Undergraduate Fees and Support

» Fees for UK/EU students 2012–13 £9,000
» Fees for International students 2011–12 £9,800–£12,350
» A package of scholarships, bursaries and widening participation support at a cost of £5 million to be announced.
» Scholarships based on circumstances or by competition are also available.
» Check the university's website for the latest information.

Students		
Undergraduates:	**8,505**	**(1,535)**
Postgraduates:	**1,365**	**(1,770)**
Mature students:	**29.3%**	
Overseas students:	**18.0%**	
Applications per place:	**4.2**	
From state-sector schools:	**94.3%**	
From working-class homes:	**52.4%**	

For detailed information about fees, grants and bursaries and how they work, see chapter 7.

Accommodation

Number of places and costs refer to 2011–12
University-provided places: 1,026
Percentage catered: 0%
Self-catered costs: £85.55 (town house) – £93.00 (en suite) a week (42-week contracts).
All first-year undergraduate students are guaranteed accommodation (terms and conditions apply).
Contact: halls-of-residence@bradford.ac.uk
www.brad.ac.uk/accommodation

University of Brighton

With plans to include entrepreneurship in the curriculum, Brighton is increasing its focus on the careers of its graduates. Employability skills as well as career planning and development, are already built into every course, while leadership skills, management training and enterprise are available as modules or in workshops. Courses are designed in collaboration with employers in the public and private sectors, and many include work placements or a sandwich year. Three quarters of the courses are endorsed by professional associations. The employment-focused approach is popular with applicants: numbers were up again at the start of 2011.

A series of new developments have been completed recently. Languages and literature students, as well as those in the School of Education, moved into the new Checkland Building on the Falmer campus, which now also boasts a £7.3-million sports centre. Meanwhile, at the Moulsecoomb site, the £23-million Huxley Building, with its living roof, has provided a new home for pharmacy and biosciences.

Brighton came of age as one of the first new universities to be awarded a medical school, but is equally well known for imaginative initiatives. It has set up a centre in Hastings and runs a number of schemes, both to draw people from the region into higher education and to help them with practical problems. The £28.5-million medical school, run jointly with neighbouring Sussex University, is training 128 doctors a year and has proved popular with applicants. Brighton was already heavily engaged in other health subjects, such as nursing and midwifery. The medical school's headquarters, on the Falmer campus, has also provided a new base for applied social sciences, such as criminology and applied psychology, which are among the university's most sought-after degrees.

The two universities have been collaborating since Brighton was a polytechnic. There is a joint research building for science policy and management studies, and a joint accord guarantees the offer of a place to all suitably qualified applicants from the Channel Island of Jersey. Brighton does the same for applicants from Sussex and leads a Learning Network for the county. Almost a third of undergraduates now come through these accords.

Brighton was again one of the top new universities in the 2008 Research Assessment Exercise. Art and design produced the best results, with two thirds of the work submitted considered world-leading or internationally excellent. Business management, sports studies and mechanical and aeronautical engineering also did well. Geography and environmental science, medicine and sports science achieved the best scores in the latest National Student Survey.

Mithras House
Lewes Road
Brighton BN2 4AT

01273 600900 (switchboard)
enquiries@brighton.ac.uk
www.brighton.ac.uk
www.bsms.ac.uk
www.ubsu.net
Affiliation: none

The Times Rankings
Overall Ranking: **=69**

Student satisfaction:	=63	(76%)
Research quality:	=55	(0.9)
Entry standards:	=61	(290)
Student–staff ratio:	=64	(18.8)
Services & facilities/student:	109	(£959)
Expected completion rate:	73	(82.5%)
Good honours:	=59	(61.4%)
Graduate prospects:	=86	(55.5%)

Brighton's strengths in art and design – recognised in the award of national teaching centres in design and creativity – have been at the forefront of the university's rising popularity. But the university also has a growing reputation in areas such as sport and hospitality, as well as scoring well in teacher education rankings. It was the first university to achieve an "outstanding" rating from the Office for Standards in Education for management and quality assurance across the full range of primary, secondary and post-compulsory teacher education courses.

The Design Council's national archive is lodged on campus, and the four-year fashion textiles degree offers work placements in the USA, France and Italy, as well as Britain. Teaching facilities include a flight simulator, a fully functional newsroom for the university's sports journalists, modern clinical skills laboratories for pharmacy, and a custom-designed culinary arts studio. At Eastbourne there is a new library and extensive sports and leisure facilities, including a sports centre with three gymnasia and a dance studio, a refurbished swimming pool and fitness facilities. Sport science laboratories and 354 en-suite residential places have been added, and improvements made to the learning resources centre, lecture theatres and refectory.

Four sites house the five faculties. Art and design has the prime location opposite the Royal Pavilion, with sports science, service management and the health professions at Eastbourne and the other subjects at Falmer and Moulsecoomb, the university's head-quarters. The university has a cosmopolitan air, with more overseas students, and a more middle-class UK intake than most of the former polytechnics. More than a quarter of undergraduates are over 21 on entry, often attracted by strongly vocational courses. Personal tutors advise on combinations within the modular degree scheme.

Students have taken to the "managed learning environment", an interactive service providing online access to teaching materials and other information, known as Studentcentral. Most also like Brighton, although the cost of living is high. There is a lively social scene. Eastbourne is also surprisingly popular, and both towns offer plentiful accommodation to supplement the university's stock, which is being expanded considerably.

Undergraduate Fees and Support

» Fees for UK/EU students 2012–13   £9,000
    Foundation degrees at partner colleges   £7,000–£8,300
» Fees for International students 2011–12   £9,960–£11,580
    £23,678 (medicine)
» Students in the National Scholarship Programme will receive £3,000 (year 1), £2,000 (other years); Sussex Accord Plus students eligible for £2,000 bursaries.
» Check the university's website for the latest information.

Students

Undergraduates:	**13,505**	**(3,495)**
Postgraduates:	**1,530**	**(2,475)**
Mature students:	**26.6%**	
Overseas students:	**11.3%**	
Applications per place:	**6.0**	
From state-sector schools:	**92.8%**	
From working-class homes:	**34.7%**	

For detailed information about fees, grants and bursaries and how they work, see chapter 7.

Accommodation

Number of places and costs refer to 2010–11

University-provided places: 2,000; 208 in private sector university-managed houses or flats.

Percentage catered: 43%

Catered costs: £126– £138 a week.

Self-catered costs: £80 –£127 a week.

First years have priority for housing if conditions are met.

International students: guaranteed accommodation if conditions are met.

Contact: accommodation@brighton.ac.uk

University of Bristol

Bristol is the most popular multi-faculty university in Britain, judged in terms of applications per place – just over ten hopefuls vie for every degree slot. It has long been a natural alternative to Oxbridge, favoured particularly by independent schools, whose pupils take more than a third of the places. In order to broaden the intake, departments are encouraged to make slightly lower offers to the most promising applicants from schools and colleges with poor records at A level. Applications were down in 2010, when most universities registered big increases, but had practically levelled out at the start of 2011, with competition remaining intense.

Bristol's academic credentials are not in doubt – it broke into the top 30 in the QS World University Rankings for 2009. But it has found it difficult to attract working-class teenagers, who fear that they would be out of place socially, if not academically. In 2009–10 only just over 15 per cent came from a working-class home – one of the lowest proportions outside Oxbridge. Tiny numbers are recruited from the schools in the bottom half of the A-level league tables and few come from Scotland or the north of England, but £1 million a year is being spent on efforts to recruit more widely. In a new effort to broaden the intake, every student who qualified for free school meals will be spared

the £9,000 fees that other undergraduates will pay. There will be a sliding scale of reductions for those from only slightly more affluent homes.

Overall entry standards remain among the highest at any university and there are no plans to ape the growth plans of some of its rivals, but there has been modest expansion to nearly 13,000 full-time undergraduates and the university has continued to live up to expectations in assessments of teaching and research. Almost two thirds of the work submitted for the 2008 Research Assessment Exercise was rated in the top two categories, with epidemiology and public health, health services research, chemistry, mathematics, drama, mechanical engineering and economics producing the best results. There are 33 Fellows of the Royal Society and similar numbers in other learned societies.

Bristol was given the best rating among the small group of universities seeking to demonstrate their creditworthiness to the money markets. The university celebrated its centenary in 2009 and launched a new fundraising campaign with a target of £100 million by 2014. The previous campaign helped the university to create new chairs and embark on a number of building projects, including a well-appointed centre for the highly rated chemistry department, for example, which allowed new medical science laboratories to be constructed in the department's former premises. Both

---

Senate House
Tyndall Avenue
Bristol BS8 1TH

0117 928 9000 (admissions)
ug-admissions@bristol.ac.uk
www.bristol.ac.uk
www.ubu.org.uk
Affiliation: Russell Group

The Times Rankings
Overall Ranking: **13**

Student satisfaction:	=48	(77%)
Research quality:	=7	(2.8)
Entry standards:	9	(467)
Student–staff ratio:	11	(13.5)
Services & facilities/student:	11	(£2,055)
Expected completion rate:	6	(96.0%)
Good honours:	8	(80.8%)
Graduate prospects:	11	(77.7%)

chemistry and medical sciences were chosen to house national teaching and learning centres, and the university was also awarded four centres to train doctoral scientists and engineers.

An impressive sports complex with a well-equipped gym has been developed at the heart of the university precinct, where academic developments have included the £11-million Centre for Nanoscience and Quantum Information, which opened in 2008 It contains some of the "quietest" labs in the world, with extremely low levels of vibrational and acoustic noise, and tight controls on temperature and air movement. The first stage of a programme of refurbishment for the university's library facilities was completed in 2009 and there are plans for a new boathouse and a health and fitness centre. Facilities at the underused students' union building have been improved and planning approval has been obtained for a major new centre for biological sciences as part of an ambitious, ongoing investment plan.

The city is one of the most attractive in Britain, as well as possessing a vibrant youth culture. An academic think tank named it European City of the Year in 2009. It is also relatively prosperous, offering job opportunities to students and graduates alike. The university merges into the centre, its famous gothic tower dominating the skyline from the junction of two of the main shopping streets. Despite its hills, Bristol is England's first Cycling City and was the only UK city to be shortlisted for the European Green Capital Award 2010.

The current students' union is less of a social centre than in some universities, partly because of the intense competition from nightclubs. Most students enjoy life in Bristol, although the high cost of living can be a serious drawback. The dropout rate is among the lowest in Britain. Parts of the city suffer from the same security concerns as any big conurbation, but the university won a police-approved Secured Environments award for its crime protection work.

Undergraduate Fees and Support

» Fees for UK/EU students 2012–13 £9,000
    For students with household income £15K or below £3,500
    For students with household income £20K or below £4,500
    For students with household income £25K or below £6,000
» Fees for International students 2011–12 £12,400–£15,550
    £28,700 (dentistry, medicine)
» For students in the Access to Bristol scheme with household income of £25K or below a full fee waiver and maintenance bursary of £3,750.
» Increased funding for university hardship funds.
» Scholarships and bursaries based on circumstances or by competition are available.
» Check the university's website for the latest information.

Students		
Undergraduates:	**12,590**	**(1,825)**
Postgraduates:	**4,125**	**(1,650)**
Mature students:	**5.0%**	
Overseas students:	**11.8%**	
Applications per place:	**10.2**	
From state-sector schools:	**60.0%**	
From working-class homes:	**14.2%**	

For detailed information about fees, grants and bursaries and how they work, see chapter 7.

Accommodation

Number of places and costs refer to 2010–11
University-provided places: about 3,964
Percentage catered: 46%
Catered costs: £108–£192 a week.
Self-catered costs: £61–£133 a week.
First years are guaranteed one offer of accommodation provided conditions are met.
International students: accommodation is guaranteed provided conditions are met.
Contact: www.bristol.ac.uk/accommodation/

Brunel University

Brunel has invested more than £300 million in teaching, research and sporting facilities in recent years. The building programme has included a £6.5-million outdoor sports complex and a £7-million indoor athletics and netball centre, making a fitting home for the former Borough Road College and its illustrious sporting traditions, as well as serving the modern-day university. There is also a hugely extended university library, increased residential accommodation, more catering and social amenities and enhanced teaching and research facilities. A new accommodation complex comprising 1,188 en-suite rooms, 40 specially adapted rooms for students with disabilities and 112 studio flats opened in 2008. Other developments include a new engineering and design annex and a student facilities complex, featuring an atrium entrance that opens onto a dining area, bars, the students' union and retail outlets.

For the first time since its early years, the whole university is located on the main Uxbridge campus. But there is still plenty of scope for development. Still less than 50 years old, Brunel has over 14,000 full-time students who share a spacious, but hitherto uninspiring, main campus that had an isolated feel despite affording easy access to central London.

In recent years, Brunel has introduced more variety into a portfolio of degrees that was once given over almost entirely to sandwich courses. Many undergraduates still take four-year degrees that incorporate work placements, but new developments have tended to be conventional three-year arts, humanities or sports programmes. There has also been significant growth in courses specialising in new technologies, such as multimedia design and broadcast media, as well as health and social care. Other innovations include creative writing, journalism, sonic arts, aviation engineering and pilot studies, motorsport engineering and games design.

Work placements and the inclusion in degree courses of skills modules (such as oral and written communication, business and computer literacy) in degree courses have helped maintain a consistently good record in the graduate employment market. Many courses are validated by professional institutions. A recent survey placed Brunel graduates 13th in the UK for average starting salaries. At more than £22,000, the figure was almost £3,000 above the national average.

Substantial investment in research centres and academic recruitment produced significant improvements in the latest Research Assessment Exercise, when Brunel registered one of the biggest increases in the numbers of staff entered. Almost nine out of ten academics were assessed, compared with

---

Uxbridge
Middlesex UB8 3PH

01895 265265 (admissions)
admissions@brunel.ac.uk
www.brunel.ac.uk
www.brunelstudents.com
Affiliation: none

The Times Rankings
Overall Ranking: **51**

Student satisfaction:	=95	(73%)
Research quality:	=42	(1.6)
Entry standards:	44	(325)
Student–staff ratio:	=82	(20.2)
Services & facilities/student:	39	(£1,558)
Expected completion rate:	43	(87.8%)
Good honours:	45	(65.7%)
Graduate prospects:	76	(59.3%)

barely more than six out of ten in 2001. With 43 percent of the work submitted judged to be world-leading or internationally excellent, the outcome was a 54 per cent increase in Brunel's research allocation from the Higher Education Funding Council for England. The extra money is being invested in 40 senior academic posts.

Recent reviews of NHS-funded health programmes, including physiotherapy and occupational therapy, have been satisfactory and Brunel also scored well in its last institutional audit. Sporting excellence is also being maintained, with four graduates winning Olympic medals in 2008 and several students competing in the games – notably Montell Douglas, who broke the British 100 metres record on the day before she graduated. Brunel has also been selected as a pre-training site for the 2012 Olympics and is likely to be a training base for international teams in the run-up to the London Games.

More than a third of the undergraduates are from working-class homes – significantly more than the national average for the subjects on offer – and more than half come from ethnic minorities. There is a large contingent of international students, who benefit from a £100,000 scholarship programme. The level of applications has been rising, despite increased entry scores, which now average 320 points. There was a surprise drop in 2010, when most universities were recording big increases, but at the start of 2011, applications were up by almost 9 per cent – well above the national average. The projected total of less than 10 per cent leaving without a qualification is much better than the UK average for Brunel's subjects and entry grades, and an improvement on previous years.

Student union facilities are good and students like Brunel's intimacy, although the university has not done well in National Student Surveys. It was among the bottom 20 universities in the 2010 survey, although aerospace engineering, design, history and physiotherapy students were among the most satisfied in the country. The university's residential stock has been greatly increased and all new undergraduates are now guaranteed accommodation on campus. Brunel has also won awards for its provision for disabled students and for its placement service.

Undergraduate Fees and Support

» Fees for UK/EU students 2012–13 £9,000
   Placement year £1,000
» Fees for International students 2011–12 £10,300–£12,600
» Over 300 National Scholarship awards: £2,000 fee waiver and £1,000 university service vouchers; 380 Access Scholarships for students from under-represented groups or who are mature: vouchers £1,000 (year 1), £1,500 (year 2), £2,000 (year 3).
» Scholarships and bursaries based on circumstances or by competition are available.
» Check the university's website for the latest information.

Students

Undergraduates:	**10,460**	**(625)**
Postgraduates:	**3,695**	**(1,630)**
Mature students:	**14.6%**	
Overseas students:	**12.9%**	
Applications per place:	**5.8**	
From state-sector schools:	**95.7%**	
From working-class homes:	**37.8%**	

For detailed information about fees, grants and bursaries and how they work, see chapter 7.

Accommodation

Number of places and costs refer to 2011–12
University-provided places: 4,549
Percentage catered: 0%
Self-catered costs: £90.86–£115.78 a week (36 weeks).
All new full-time first-year students are eligible for on-campus accommodation.
International students: as above.
Contact: www.brunel.ac.uk/life/accommodation
accom-uxb@brunel.ac.uk

University of Buckingham

Britain's only private university describes itself as the country's smallest and friendliest – a claim borne out by the last three National Student Surveys, in which Buckingham students emerged as the most satisfied in England. Business, economics and politics all produced unusually high levels of satisfaction in 2010, but every subject satisfied at least 90 per cent of final-year undergraduates.

Even before the latest rise in fees elsewhere, Buckingham claimed to be no more expensive than other universities because its intensive two-year degrees cut maintenance costs and accelerate entry into employment. Total fees for UK undergraduates taking the two-year degree from September 2011 are now £18,720, and there are further discounts for payment in advance. Overseas students pay £30,570 and there is a range of scholarships for both home and overseas candidates.

The university, which celebrates its 35th anniversary in 2011, has no ambitions to follow its peers into the mass higher-education market: it values the personal approach that comes with having fewer than ten students to each member of staff, when the UK average is 17. One-to-one tutorials, which have all but disappeared outside Oxbridge and are by no means universal there, are common at Buckingham. The average teaching group contains about six students. However, it is enjoying modest growth – enough to get it back into *The Times* League Table for the first time in more than a decade. Only its absence from the Research Assessment Exercise (which is open only to state-funded institutions) prevented the university from finishing even higher in the table.

A Conservative-backed experiment of the 1970s, Buckingham is now an accepted part of the university system. Although in 1992 it installed Baroness Thatcher as Chancellor, the university has no party political ties. Dr Terence Kealey, a biochemist from Cambridge University, became the latest Vice-Chancellor in April 2001, declaring an ambition for Buckingham to "one day" challenge the cream of American higher education. He has recruited a number of high-profile libertarians, including Chris Woodhead, the former Chief Inspector of Schools.

The university's degrees carry full currency in the academic world and teaching standards are high. Education courses now have accreditation from the Training and Development Agency for Schools. Student numbers have increased by 25 per cent over the past three years, and were set to rise again at the start of 2011 when Buckingham enjoyed an unprecedented 87 per cent increase in applications.

The university runs on calendar years,

Hunter Street
Buckingham MK18 1EG

01280 814080
info@buckingham.ac.uk
www.buckingham.ac.uk
www.buckingham.ac.uk/
life/social/su
Affiliation: none

The Times Rankings
Overall Ranking: **21**

Student satisfaction:	1	(88%)
Research quality:		(n/a)
Entry standards:	=74	(273)
Student–staff ratio:	1	(8.9)
Services & facilities/student:	104	(£1,041)
Expected completion rate:	=30	(90.8%)
Good honours:	113	(43.6%)
Graduate prospects:	1	(87.5%)

rather than the traditional academic variety, although some courses give the option of entering in July or September. Most degree courses run for two 40-week years, minimising disruptive career breaks for the many mature students. Over 60 per cent of the students are from overseas, but the proportion from Britain has been growing. Students have the option of a three-year degree in the humanities and other schools are now following suit.

Recent additions to the subjects on offer in Buckingham include a BSc in business enterprise and Masters programmes in international financial services, security and intelligence studies. Masters programmes in biography, military history and decorative arts are now taught in London. A new BA in art history and heritage management offers the opportunity of a term at the British Institute in Florence. The most striking development, however, has been the postgraduate medical school launched in 2008 with a two-year MD in clinical medicine. The course attracts overseas medical graduates who find it difficult to secure junior doctor posts as a result of Government restrictions.

Campus facilities have improved considerably in recent years, although they cannot compare with those available at traditional universities. Buckingham operates on two sites, within easy walking distance of each other. An academic centre containing computer suites, lecture theatres and student facilities provides a focal point that was missing previously. A new six-acre site was acquired recently to make room for future expansion.

The social scene is predictably quiet, given the size of the university and the workload, especially at weekends. There is a university cinema and the town of Buckingham is pretty, with a good selection of pubs and restaurants. Milton Keynes or Oxford are near, although Buckingham has no rail station. A good bus service operates throughout the week with extra buses at weekends.

Undergraduate Fees and Support

» Fees for UK/EU students for full degree course starting in September 2011 will be £18,720. Note that the course only lasts two years (eight terms). Also term fees from January 2013 still to be confirmed, so total cost may be higher.
» Fees for International students for full degree course starting in September 2011 will be £30,570. Note that the course only lasts two years (eight terms). Also term fees from January 2013 still to be confirmed, so total cost may be higher.
» Scholarships and bursaries based on circumstances or by competition are available.
» Check the university's website for the latest information.

Students		
Undergraduates:	**800**	**(45)**
Postgraduates:	**455**	**(35)**
Mature students:	**52.4%**	
Overseas students:	**59.8%**	
Applications per place:	**4.2**	
From state-sector schools:	**86.8%**	
From working-class homes:	**n/a**	

For detailed information about fees, grants and bursaries and how they work, see chapter 7.

Accommodation

Number of places and costs refer to 2011–12
University-provided places: 521
Percentage catered: 0%
Self-catered accommodation: £975–£1,696 a term (4 terms); £1,096 (typical standard room a term).
All new first-year students are guaranteed accommodation if they apply by the deadline.
International students: same as above.
Contact: accommodation@buckingham.ac.uk

Buckinghamshire New University

Two huge increases in applications followed the establishment of Buckinghamshire New University in 2007, but another big rise (of more than 18 per cent) at the start of 2011 suggests that its popularity is about more than mere novelty. The first phase of a £200-million campus redevelopment was completed in 2009, and students have been responding enthusiastically to a portfolio of innovative courses and an attractive package of financial support and extra-curricular benefits for students.

The redevelopment allows most students to be based at the main campus in High Wycombe – the exception being those taking nursing, who have moved into a new building in nearby Uxbridge. The prize-winning Gateway Building at High Wycombe has transformed the town-centre campus with improved teaching, social and administrative space. The complex includes a new sports hall, gym, treatment rooms and sports laboratory, which are available to the public as well as to students. At the same time, collaboration with two of the world's biggest IT companies is developing one of the most advanced student networks in UK higher education.

Sport is an important part of life at the new university, which partners the London Wasps rugby union team in a relationship which trades coaching for Bucks students for courses for Wasps players. But the university's main aim is to contribute to the social and economic life of the region, embracing workplace learning and close ties with local businesses. Employees of the bed company, Dreams, which is based in High Wycombe, take a new Foundation degree in retail management while at work, for example. A further innovation in 2010 was the establishment of the National School of Furniture with local employers and further education colleges, offering qualifications from certificate level to PhD.

Bucks has also won awards for its training of commercial pilots and its courses for music industry management. Other Foundation degrees include animation and visual effects, protective security management and sports coaching and performance, all run at partner colleges.

There are over 9,000 full and part-time students, 83 per cent of whom are taking first degrees and 45 per cent of whom are over 25. Nearly 60 per cent of the students are female. Academic departments are divided into two faculties: Design, Media and Management, and Society and Health. The extensive nursing provision has growing links with the Imperial College London Health-care Trust, including a joint appointment designed to promote innovation. The child nursing

Queen Alexandra Road
High Wycombe
Buckinghamshire
HP11 2JZ
0800 0565 660 (enquiries)
advice@bucks.ac.uk
www.bucks.ac.uk
www.bucksstudent.com
Affiliations: Guild HE, million +

The Times Rankings
Overall Ranking: **110**

Student satisfaction:	=108	(69%)
Research quality:	=105	(0.1)
Entry standards:	112	(212)
Student–staff ratio:	106	(22.3)
Services & facilities/student:	46	(£1,467)
Expected completion rate:	=79	(81.8%)
Good honours:	=106	(49.3%)
Graduate prospects:	111	(48.8%)

courses have the best rating in the London area. Only 26 staff were entered for the 2008 Research Assessment Exercise – half of them in art and design, which registered the only world-leading research. However, an institutional audit expressed "broad confidence" in academic standards.

The projected dropout rate for undergraduates entering in 2008 improved to 13 per cent, considerably lower than at most comparable institutions and 3 percentage points better than the national average for its subjects and entry qualifications. Nor was this achieved by neglecting the Government's widening participation agenda: almost all the entrants are from state schools or colleges, and nearly 40 per cent are from working-class homes. The university has a particular focus on student support, devoting more than a third of its fee income to bursaries under the previous fee regime – one of the biggest proportions in England. A new mission statement stresses the university's determination to "put students first".

However, one disappointment has been consistently low scores in the National Student Survey, which has left Bucks in the bottom ten for the last four years. The extensive building work on the main campus may have been a factor. Only law and social work satisfied more than 80 per cent of final-year undergraduates in 2010, when language students registered a particularly low score.

The university's own annual survey, carried out by independent academics, has been more complimentary. And the courses and lecturers attracted some of the most positive verdicts of any university on a national student reviews website.

Beyond the campus, High Wycombe might not be an iconic student destination, but it has the usual range of pubs and clubs for a medium-sized town and central London is only 40 minutes away by train. The university has opened an art gallery in the main shopping centre to showcase students' work, as part of its efforts to maintain a strong relationship with the town.

Undergraduate Fees and Support

» Fees for UK/EU students 2012–13

New business degree	£6,000
Majority of degrees	£7,500
Art, design and production-based courses using workshops or studios	£8,000

» Fees for International students 2011–12 £8,500–£9,300
» Students in the National Scholarship Programme will receive £6,000 over three years as vouchers redeemed against fees, accommodation or a similar institutional service, or a cash bursary of up to £1,000 a year.
» A package of widening participation activity to be announced.
» "Big Deal" package which encourages participation in a range of sporting, recreational and social activities.
» Check the university's website for the latest information.

Students

Undergraduates:	**5,020**	**(3,555)**
Postgraduates:	**270**	**(515)**
Mature students:	**35.9%**	
Overseas students:	**10.3%**	
Applications per place:	**4.6**	
From state-sector schools:	**96.9%**	
From working-class homes:	**39.7%**	

For detailed information about fees, grants and bursaries and how they work, see chapter 7.

Accommodation

Number of places and costs refer to 2010–11
University-provided places: 780
Percentage catered: 0%
Self-catered costs: £85–£108 a week (42 or 44 weeks)
First-year students cannot be guaranteed accommodation.
Residential restrictions apply.
International students: priority allocation for first years.
Contact: accom@bucks.ac.uk

University of Cambridge

Cambridge already had the highest entry standards of any UK university when it became the first to announce plans to use the new A* grade for admissions. As a result, the standard offer for entry in 2012 will be AAA* at A level. The only good news for applicants is that, for most degrees, the top grade can come in any subject. The bad news is that there will still be additional tests, such as Cambridge's own STEP papers, in a number of subjects.

Until 2001, Cambridge had also enjoyed an unbroken run at the top of *The Times* League Table, and even now it is practically inseparable from first-placed Oxford. The university produced the best results in the 2008 Research Assessment Exercise and the university still tops far more of our subject tables than any of its rivals. Nearly a third of its research was considered world-leading and over 70 per cent was rated in the top two categories. Cambridge topped the QS World University Rankings in 2010, overtaking Harvard on more research-oriented criteria than are used in *The Times* table. It scores particularly well in the sciences, but has shown growing strength in other areas.

At first, Cambridge students did not respond in sufficient numbers for the university to be included in the National Student Survey. But the 2010 results put Cambridge in the top five in the UK, with undergraduates in classics, geography, languages, philosophy, politics, psychology and sociology particularly satisfied. The tripos system was a forerunner of the currently fashionable modular degree, allowing students to change subjects (within limits) midway through their courses. Students receive a classification for each of the two parts of their degree.

More students now come from state schools than the independent sector – a trend the university is keen to continue – but the proportion of working-class undergraduates remains low, at little more than 10 per cent. Summer schools, student visits and, in some colleges, sympathetic selection procedures are helping to attract more applications from comprehensive schools and further education colleges. Although Cambridge will charge the full £9,000 undergraduate fee in 2012, there will be £6,000 fee waivers for the poorest students and additional bursaries according to parental income below a threshold of £42,600.

The application system has been simplified slightly, with candidates no longer required to complete an initial Cambridge form, as well as their UCAS form. However, they are still sent the Supplementary Application Questionnaire, after they have submitted their UCAS form, covering the applicant's academic experience in more detail.

The Old Schools
Trinity Lane
Cambridge CB2 1TN

01223 333308 (admissions)
admissions@cam.ac.uk
www.cam.ac.uk
www.cusu.cam.ac.uk
Affiliation: Russell Group

The Times Rankings
Overall Ranking: **2**

Student satisfaction:	=4	(84%)
Research quality:	1	(4.1)
Entry standards:	1	(559)
Student–staff ratio:	6	(11.7)
Services & facilities/student:	3	(£2,895)
Expected completion rate:	1	(98.7%)
Good honours:	2	(88.3%)
Graduate prospects:	3	(85.5%)

A lively alternative prospectus, available from the students' union, used to say there was no such thing as Cambridge University, just a collection of colleges. Where applications are concerned, this is still true, as it is to some extent socially. Making the right choice of college is crucial, both to maximise the chances of winning a place and to ensure an enjoyable three years if you are successful. Applicants can take pot luck with an open application if they prefer not to opt for a particular college. But, though the statistics show that this route is equally successful, only a minority takes it. Most teaching is now university-based, especially in the sciences, and a shift of emphasis towards the centre has been taking place more generally.

Cambridge boasts numerous successful partnerships with the private sector, several of which benefit undergraduates as well as researchers. The university was also chosen for a Government-sponsored partnership with the Massachusetts Institute of Technology to promote entrepreneurship and, more recently, was selected to host one of five Academic Health Science Centres to lead biomedical innovation.

A £1-billion funding appeal to mark the university's 800th anniversary, in 2009, reached its target two years early, making Cambridge the first university outside the USA to raise such a sum. The money has gone into bursaries and scholarships, professorships and teaching posts, and new buildings for research, teaching and student accommodation. The latest major donation was from David Harding, the founder of Winton Capital Management, who has pledged £20 million to the Cavendish Laboratory. Such is the scale of development that almost £500-million worth of building is either planned or under construction, with longer-term plans for expansion to the west of the city.

With around four applicants for each place – fewer still if you choose your subject carefully – the competition for places appears less intense than at the popular civic universities, but the real difference is that nine out of ten entrants have at least three A grades at A level. The pressure does not end there: the amount of high-quality work to be crammed into eight-week terms can prove a strain, although the projected dropout rate of 1.3 per cent is the lowest at any university.

Undergraduate Fees and Support

» Fees for UK/EU students 2012–13   £9,000
» Fees for International students 2011–12   £10,829–£18,000
     £26,632 (medicine) plus College fees (£4,400–£5,200)
» A bursary of £3,500 for students whose parental annual income is less than £25K, tapered down to earnings of £42.6K, payable either as a grant or fee waiver. Enhanced support will provide fee waivers of £6,000 to students with low-income backgrounds.
» Scholarships and bursaries based on circumstances or by competition are available.
» Check the university's website for the latest information.

Students

Undergraduates:	**12,080**	**(1,115)**
Postgraduates:	**5,890**	**(1,665)**
Mature students:	**4.0%**	
Overseas students:	**16.1%**	
Applications per place:	**4.8**	
From state-sector schools:	**59.3%**	
From working-class homes:	**12.6%**	

For detailed information about fees, grants and bursaries and how they work, see chapter 7.

Accommodation

See chapter 12 for information about individual colleges.

Canterbury Christ Church University

Applications to this former Church of England college have practically doubled since it became a university in 2005. It now has 18,000 students and has become the largest provider of higher education to the public services in Kent, particularly for teaching, health and social care, nursing and policing. The teacher training courses, which are among the biggest in the UK, are rated "outstanding" by Ofsted.

There is a network of campuses across Kent, the most populous county in England but, until recently, one of the most sparsely provided with higher education. The purpose-built campus at Broadstairs, for example, focuses on arts and media courses such as commercial music, digital media, photography, and child and youth studies. There is an imposing country house outside Tunbridge Wells, mainly for postgraduates, as well as a newly expanded Medway site at Chatham that is shared with Greenwich and Kent universities and offers education and health programmes at a variety of levels, from foundation degree to postgraduate. The University Centre at Folkestone, also developed in partnership with Greenwich, offers performing and visual arts.

The majority of the students, however, are at the university's Canterbury headquarters. The main campus, which dates from 1962, is a few minutes' walk from the city centre, but the university has several buildings in other parts of Canterbury. A £35-million library and student services centre, with specialist teaching and IT facilities, opened in 2009. It includes a café, two garden terraces, an atrium and multipurpose floor space for public events, conferences, exams, teaching and exhibitions. The Sidney Cooper Gallery, in the heart of the city, hosts exhibitions and workshops from visiting artists as well as work from students before the best goes on to be exhibited in London galleries.

The Church of England link was underlined with the installation of the Archbishop of Canterbury as the university's first Chancellor. A residential course for church music has recently been developed at the Canterbury campus.

Scores in the National Student Survey dropped in 2010, but still met the average for all institutions. American studies registered a rare 100 per cent satisfaction rate in 2010, when geography, history and languages also produced particularly good scores. Canterbury Christ Church was one of the new "teaching-led" universities, but was given the power to award research degrees in 2009. The university entered staff in seven areas in the 2008 Research Assessment Exercise. The best grades came in education and music, both of which had 10 per cent of

---

North Holmes Road
Canterbury CT1 1QU

01227 782900 (admissions)
admissions@canterbury.ac.uk
www.canterbury.ac.uk
www.ccsu.co.uk
Affiliation: Cathedral Group

The Times Rankings
Overall Ranking: **88**

Student satisfaction:	=78	(74%)
Research quality:	=92	(0.2)
Entry standards:	101	(247)
Student–staff ratio:	62	(18.6)
Services & facilities/student:	101	(£1,067)
Expected completion rate:	59	(84.5%)
Good honours:	88	(54.5%)
Graduate prospects:	55	(63.3%)

their work assessed as world-leading.

The subject mix, with an emphasis on health subjects and education, means that seven out of ten students are female. Nearly 97 per cent of the undergraduates are state-educated and more than a third come from working-class homes. The dropout rate improved significantly in the latest projections and, at 12 per cent, is now better than average for the university's courses and entry qualifications. Graduates' job prospects are relatively good, with three quarters going straight into employment and only 6 per cent unemployed six months after completing a degree.

All campuses are interconnected by a high-speed regional data network, providing access to online teaching and learning materials, the student web portal and email. A new student and staff support service – i-zone – was introduced in 2009, and can be accessed online or via staff at the i-zone desks. The new Drill Hall Library at Medway provides 110,000 items, 400 computers and 280 study spaces. The bookshop on the Canterbury campus has been refurbished and extended, with a new "grab and go" café opposite.

Social and sports facilities naturally vary between the campuses, although the students' union is present on all of them. A new sports centre in Canterbury includes a fitness suite and a hall big enough for eight badminton courts. There is also a tennis court and netball court on campus and the university also has facilities at Polo Farm Sports Club close to the city. There are 12 acres of playing fields about a mile from the main campus.

Accommodation is available to all first years who want it. The pressure is eased to some extent because more than 60 per cent of the students come from Kent, many of them taking part-time courses. Another 204 single, en-suite student bedrooms and ten three-bedroom family houses will be available in 2012 close to the main campus, where a student centre with a café bar, internet café and office space for the students' union will also open. The existing North Holmes campus' Student Building will be remodelled for music students' use, providing more rehearsal space.

Undergraduate Fees and Support

- » Fees for UK/EU students 2012–13   to be announced
- » Fees for International students 2011–12   £9,150–£9,405
- » A package of financial support and widening participation activity to be announced.
- » Scholarships and bursaries based on circumstances or by competition are available.
- » Check the university's website for the latest information.

Students		
Undergraduates:	**8,510**	**(5,060)**
Postgraduates:	**1,640**	**(2,770)**
Mature students:	**27.4%**	
Overseas students:	**8.0%**	
Applications per place:	**4.6**	
From state-sector schools:	**96.4%**	
From working-class homes:	**39.2%**	

For detailed information about fees, grants and bursaries and how they work, see chapter 7.

Accommodation

Number of places and costs refer to 2011–12

University-provided places: 1,570

Percentage catered: 0%

Self-catered costs: £78.50–£167.00 a week.

Accommodation guaranteed for first years if conditions are met.

International students: as above.

Contact: accommodation@canterbury.ac.uk

www.canterbury.ac.uk/support/accommodation

Cardiff University

Cardiff is long established as the front-runner in Welsh higher education and a leading player in the UK and beyond. It is a member of the Russell Group of 20 research-led universities and has two Nobel Laureates on its staff. The university now has more than 27,000 students and nearly 6,000 staff. A third of the students come from Wales, but the 3,000 from overseas testify to Cardiff's international reputation.

The 2008 Research Assessment Exercise rated almost 60 per cent of the submitted work in the top two categories, with 33 of the 34 subject areas containing some world-leading research. Journalism, media and cultural studies, English, city and regional planning, and business produced the best results.

Teaching quality is also highly rated, with courses accredited by 41 different professional bodies. An audit by the Quality Assurance Agency complimented the university on its "powerful academic vision and well-developed and effectively articulated mission to achieve excellence in teaching and research". Student support services, including counselling facilities and the help offered to dyslexics, were among the features singled out for praise.

Cardiff has been a consistent performer in the National Student Survey, finishing just outside the top 25 in 2010. It was rated best in the UK for dentistry, ophthalmics, pharmacy and biomedical science, and in 22 subjects more than 90 per cent of final-year undergraduates declared themselves satisfied. Cardiff was the first Welsh university to be awarded the Frank Buttle Trust Quality Mark which recognises support for students who were in public care.

Many full-time degrees share a common first year, and the modular system of courses makes undergraduate study flexible thereafter. Recent additions at degree level include marine geoscience, an MMath degree and a new portfolio of computing courses.

The university occupies a significant part of the civic complex around Cathays Park in the Welsh capital. The five healthcare schools at the Heath Park campus share a 53-acre site with the University Hospital of Wales. A new Medical Education Centre is due for completion in 2011 on the Heath Park campus. Named the Cochrane Building in honour of a Cardiff pioneer in medical research, it will offer a new library, clinical skills and simulation laboratories and seminar space to students. In recent years, there has been major investment in new buildings and equipment, and extensive refurbishment. Current projects include a £4-million extension for the School of Biosciences and there are plans for an entirely new campus for research.

Library services are being transformed in

Cardiff
Wales CF10 3XQ

029 2087 4455 (enquiries)
enquiry@cardiff.ac.uk
www.cardiff.ac.uk
www.cardiffstudents.com
Affiliation: Russell Group

The Times Rankings
Overall Ranking: **35**

Student satisfaction:	=37	(78%)
Research quality:	=33	(1.9)
Entry standards:	25	(406)
Student–staff ratio:	28	(15)
Services & facilities/student:	52	(£1,374)
Expected completion rate:	=19	(93.0%)
Good honours:	=34	(68.5%)
Graduate prospects:	=17	(73.6%)

order to improve access to resources, increase the range of electronic resources, extend self-service provision and improve the environment for the study of rare collections. A new IT working environment gives students online access to information about their studies and social life, from reading lists and timetables to social events and networking groups. The campus is also wireless enabled, with over 1,300 access points throughout the university.

Other recent developments include the establishment of the International Academy of Voice, providing individual training for opera stars of the future, while the School of Earth, Ocean and Planetary Sciences has invested in its own research vessel for a programme of research and teaching voyages. In 2009, Cardiff Business School launched a state-of-the-art trading room which allows students to gain the practical skills needed for life at the Stock Exchange.

Entry requirements have been rising, despite recent expansion, and the graduate employment record is good. The university has been bucking the national trend with increases in applications in science, technology, engineering and maths, but the overall demand for places was down significantly at the start of 2011. One undergraduate in seven comes from an independent school, but still more than one in five have a working-class background. The projected dropout rate is comfortably the lowest in Wales, at a little over 6 per cent.

With nearly 5,200 study bedrooms, the university can accommodate all first years. Rents are among the lowest in the UK, according to a National Union of Students survey. The city of Cardiff is popular with students. The main residential site at Talybont boasts a "sports village", and there is also a city-centre fitness suite and a sports ground available to students. The university is continuing to update its sports facilities across the three sites, one being an upgrade of the floodlit grass training pitch with a new synthetic pitch. It is to be an official training centre for Olympic football at the 2012 Games.

Undergraduate Fees and Support

» Fees 2012–13: to be announced; able to charge up to £9,000, with Welsh Assembly expected to pay fees above £3,375 for Welsh students.
» Fees for international students 2011–12   £10,700–£13,750   £24,500 (medicine, dentistry)
» Scholarships and bursaries based on circumstances or by competition are available.
» Check the university's website for the latest information.

Students

Undergraduates:	**16,835**	**(3,280)**
Postgraduates:	**4,050**	**(3,390)**
Mature students:	**12.0%**	
Overseas students:	**10.5%**	
Applications per place:	**6.8**	
From state-sector schools:	**85.2%**	
From working-class homes:	**22.9%**	

For detailed information about fees, grants and bursaries and how they work, see chapter 7.

Accommodation

Number of places and costs refer to 2010–11
University-provided places: 5,171
Percentage catered: 5.2%
Catered costs: £74–£88 a week.
Self-catered costs: £65–£91 a week.
All first years (except Clearing students) are guaranteed accommodation if conditions are met.
Policy for international students: as above
Contact: residences@cardiff.ac.uk

University of Wales Institute, Cardiff (UWIC)

The University of Wales Institute in Cardiff has an international reputation for sport, but other areas are also benefiting from a £50-million programme of improvements. The £20-million Cardiff School of Management opened on the Llandaff campus in 2010, offering improved facilities for business, hospitality and tourism. A new campus centre, with a shop and catering facilities, was also added in 2010, along with an Information Zone for student services such as accommodation. The Cyncoed campus already had a new student centre with a nightclub and all the normal catering and leisure facilities.

UWIC's scores improved in the 2010 National Student Survey and were better than average for post-1992 universities. Computer science, aural studies and initial teacher training produced the best results. International students appear particularly satisfied. Accounting, food studies and social work produced good scores, but sociology students were among the least satisfied in any subject in the UK. UWIC was the top university in the UK in seven categories, including overall satisfaction, in the 2010 International Student Barometer. There was a 12 per cent increase in applications at the start of 2011, which was well above the UK average.

Two thirds of UWIC's 13,000 students are Welsh, half of them from Cardiff or the Vale of Glamorgan. Some 95 per cent attended state schools and nearly 40 per cent come from working-class homes. The dropout rate has improved in the latest survey and is better than the average for Wales, but the latest figure of almost 15 per cent is still higher than the UK average for UWIC's subjects and entry grades.

UWIC is one of Britain's leading centres for university sport, with team performances to match some excellent facilities. In recent years, the Institute has had British university champions in gymnastics, trampolining, athletics, rugby union, rugby league, boxing, squash, archery, weightlifting and judo. More than 300 past or present students are internationals in 30 sports. Fourteen of them appeared at the New Delhi Commonwealth Games, bringing home three medals. The £7-million National Indoor Athletics Centre is UWIC's pride and joy, but other facilities are also of high quality.

Academically, the large Cardiff School of Art and Design is the star performer, with 70 per cent of the work submitted to the 2008 Research Assessment Exercise rated either world-leading or internationally excellent. Sport also registered some world-leading research and all six teacher training courses are rated as excellent by Estyn, the school inspectorate. UWIC also did well in the Higher Education Academy's satisfaction

---

Cardiff Institute
Western Avenue
Cardiff CF5 2YB

029 2041 6070 (enquiries)
uwicinfo@uwic.ac.uk
www.uwic.ac.uk
www.uwicsu.co.uk
Affiliation: University
   Alliance

Edinburgh
Belfast
London
CARDIFF

The Times Rankings
Overall Ranking: **=71**

Student satisfaction:	=63	(76%)
Research quality:	=79	(0.3)
Entry standards:	=84	(267)
Student–staff ratio:	=91	(20.7)
Services & facilities/student:	59	(£1,354)
Expected completion rate:	58	(84.7%)
Good honours:	=84	(55.3%)
Graduate prospects:	89	(55.3%)

survey of postgraduate research students.

Entrance requirements are generally modest, but the menu of largely vocational courses means that many students come with qualifications other than A levels. Just over a fifth are mature students and more than 1,000 are international students from 143 different countries. Many are among the 23 per cent of students who are postgraduates – the largest proportion in Wales. UWIC courses are also taught at partner colleges in Kuala Lumpur, Singapore and Dhaka.

The three Cardiff sites are all within three miles of the city centre. The Cyncoed campus, which houses education and sport, is the centre of activity, particularly for first-year students. As well as the new student centre, the athletics centre is there, together with a multitude of outdoor facilities and also the Welsh Sports Centre for the Disabled. Student facilities, including the Institute's largest bar, have been upgraded recently. A £2-million learning centre opened in 2005; the IT suite has 250 computers available 24 hours a day.

Howard Gardens is the home of fine art, while the Llandaff campus hosts design, engineering, food science and health courses. The student centre at Llandaff includes a dyslexia support unit among a number of advice and representation services, and a learning centre with more than 300 computers.

Students tend to like Cardiff as a city, and UWIC's enterprising union does its best to make their time there as lively as possible. It owns a nightclub and bar in the city centre to add to the campus choices. During term-time, the UWIC Rider bus service links all the campuses with other parts of Cardiff at a cost to students of £4.67 a week in 2010–11, down on the previous year. The 929 UWIC hall places, plus rooms in privately run residences, accommodate most first years, but recent expansion means that some have to rely on the private sector. UWIC is the only university to have been awarded the Government's Charter Mark four times, the judges commenting particularly on the level of satisfaction among students.

Undergraduate Fees and Support

» Fees 2012–13: to be announced; able to charge up to £9,000, with Welsh Assembly expected to pay fees above £3,375 for Welsh students.

» Fees for international students 2011–12   £8,200–£9,400
                                                    £11,400 (podiatry)

» Scholarships and bursaries based on circumstances or by competition are available.

» Check the university's website for the latest information.

Students		
Undergraduates:	**7,550**	**(775)**
Postgraduates:	**1,325**	**(3,430)**
Mature students:	**22.6%**	
Overseas students:	**11.8%**	
Applications per place:	**4.0**	
From state-sector schools:	**94.6%**	
From working-class homes:	**38.4%**	

For detailed information about fees, grants and bursaries and how they work, see chapter 7.

Accommodation
Number of places and costs refer to 2011–12
University-provided places: 929
Percentage catered: 34%
Catered cost: £115–£125 a week (£78.50–£88.50 outwith term).
Self-catered costs: £79.00–£97.50 a week.
First-year students have no guarantee, terms and conditions apply.
International students: accommodation is reserved, subject to availability and if conditions are met.
Contact: accomm@uwic.ac.uk

University of Central Lancashire (UCLan)

A big university at the heart of England's newest city of Preston, UCLan has spent £120 million on its campus as student numbers have doubled – and still the building continues. A £17-million indoor sports centre and a £12.5-million building for forensic science and chemistry were due to open in the spring of 2011. New facilities for business, computing, dentistry, health, media, nuclear science, pharmacy, psychology and sport have been opened in the last five years, in addition to the award-winning students' union building. The campus also boasts Europe's largest 3D lecture theatre and the library has been upgraded. The dental school was one of the first to open in over a century, while the architecture degree launched in 2009 was the first new such course for ten years.

Close links with a wide range of employers allow students to undertake short-term internships and longer term work placements to gain essential work experience and enhance their employability skills. The Futures Centre brings together advice on careers and work placements, employability and enterprise course electives, business start-up and self-employment services. For the last three years, the university has produced the most graduate business start-ups in the North West and is in the top five nationally.

There is also an international dimension to UCLan. Travel bursaries enable students to undertake periods of overseas work experience and they have the opportunity to study a range of world languages, including Arabic, Chinese, Japanese and Russian. The university is also actively engaged in international research collaborations and has a base in China, where a team is conducting research in nanotechnology. UCLan was the only UK university to break into the QS World University Rankings in 2010.

A former polytechnic, UCLan has a high reputation in some apparently unlikely fields. Astrophysics benefits from two observatories in Britain and a share in the Southern African Large Telescope, its academics working closely with NASA. Linguistics and journalism produced the best results in the 2008 Research Assessment Exercise, when 17 areas contained work considered world-leading or internationally excellent. The university has since invested £10 million in ten research centres in areas as diverse as philosophy and nuclear science. The Confucius Institute promotes and supports the development of Chinese language and culture throughout the North West region.

UCLan opened a £10-million campus in Burnley in 2009, in partnership with Burnley College, which offers a number of the university's degree and Foundation degree

Preston

Lancashire PR1 2HE

01772 892400 (enquiries)
cenquiries@uclan.ac.uk
www.uclan.ac.uk
www.yourunion.co.uk
Affiliation: million+

The Times Rankings

Overall Ranking: **61**

Student satisfaction:	=37	(78%)
Research quality:	=70	(0.4)
Entry standards:	=92	(260)
Student–staff ratio:	59	(18.4)
Services & facilities/student:	29	(£1,642)
Expected completion rate:	83	(80.9%)
Good honours:	94	(52.8%)
Graduate prospects:	75	(59.6%)

courses. A Centre for Outdoor Education has been developed at Llangollen, in North Wales, enabling the university to launch a degree in the subject. A West Cumbrian Campus, in Westlakes, has been redeveloped to boost nuclear skills training. Areas of research will include environmental sciences, sustainable development, epidemiology and genetics. Ranked as the fourth greenest university in the UK, UCLan has become one of only five higher education institutions to hold both ISO 14001 certification and the Carbon Trust Standard. The university runs modules in sustainability and was the first in the UK to install solar trackers.

Electives are used to broaden the curriculum, so that up to 11 per cent of students' time is spent on subjects outside their normal range. Scores in the National Student Survey have been steady, with satisfaction ratings in forensics and archaeology, journalism, physical geography and environmental science all in the top six for 2010. Cinematics and photography, design studies, fine art, psychology, sociology and tourism, transport and travel were all rated in the national top 20. The university reluctantly opted for £9,000 fees, promising a "comprehensive student package" to ensure that UCLan remains accessible to all.

Over four out of ten Central Lancashire students come from working-class homes. A high proportion are local people in their twenties or thirties, many of whom come through the well-established lifelong learning networks run in colleges throughout the North West. Almost 20 per cent of the university's students are taught in colleges but, unlike some institutions involved in "franchising", Central Lancashire has won official praise for the quality of its external programmes. Applications were up by 22 per cent in 2010 and the 6 per cent rise at the start of 2011 was well above the national average.

Preston's social scene may not compare with Manchester or Liverpool, but neither do the security risks, and the cost of living is low. The students' union boasts one of the biggest student venues in the country. Its "Feel" club nights have won national recognition. UCLan commands great loyalty among its students. Rents for the nearly 2,000 places in university accommodation are among the lowest in Britain and the 60-acre Preston Sports Arena has some of the best outdoor facilities in higher education.

Undergraduate Fees and Support

» Fees for UK/EU students 2012–13   £9,000
» Fees for International students 2011–12   £9,450–£10,450
» A package of financial support and widening participation activity to be announced.
» Scholarships and bursaries based on circumstances or by competition are available.
» Check the university's website for the latest information.

Students		
Undergraduates:	**17,700**	**(9,960)**
Postgraduates:	**1,470**	**(3,165)**
Mature students:	**29.5%**	
Overseas students:	**9.2%**	
Applications per place:	**4.3**	
From state-sector schools:	**97.7%**	
From working-class homes:	**43.7%**	

For detailed information about fees, grants and bursaries and how they work, see chapter 7.

Accommodation

Number of places and costs refer to 2011–12

University-provided places: around 2,000

Percentage catered: 0%

Self-catered costs: £83 (standard) – £95 (en suite) a week (42 weeks).

The Student Accommodation Service will assist all first years to find suitable accommodation either in university owned/leased halls of residence, private sector registered halls, or shared houses.

International students: as above.

Contact: www.uclan.ac.uk/study/accommodation/index.php

University of Chester

The picturesque Roman city of Chester is one of those places that outsiders probably always expected to have its own university. Indeed, William Gladstone was among the founders of the first Church of England teacher training college there in 1839. Although it took until 2005 for that college to achieve university status, it had been building up a solid reputation in a number of subjects beyond education. Applications were up by more than 20 per cent at the start of 2011, following a string of increases that has taken the demand for places far above that in pre-university days.

The main campus is only a short walk from the centre of Chester, a 32-acre site boasting manicured gardens and a number of new developments. A new students' union is just one of a stream of improvements, including the opening of a second campus in the city in 2007. A third base was added in 2010, following the purchase of historic County Hall in Chester, which now houses the faculties of Health and Social Care and Education and Children's Services.

The Warrington campus, which has eight halls of residence, focuses on the creative industries and public services. It has seen the addition of state-of-the-art production facilities in collaboration with Granada Television and a new bar. The university has also signed a partnership agreement with the BBC, which is intended to open up new employment opportunities in the media industry and develop new talent as a result of the transfer of parts of the corporation to Salford in 2011. The library has been extended to three times its original size and a business centre opened for students and local firms. The campus is expected to be the focus of future developments to accommodate a modest increase in student numbers.

Chester was among the top ten universities in the first National Student Survey but has since slipped into the bottom half of the table. Overall satisfaction levels dropped in the 2010 survey, but archaeology, English, Spanish, maths and theology all achieved outstanding results in the 2009 survey. Chester was the first of the universities created in 2005 to be granted the power to award research degrees. Four of the ten subject areas entered for the 2008 Research Assessment Exercise contained at least some world-leading work. History was the most successful, with nearly half of its submission placed in the top two categories.

With more than 14,500 students, including part-timers, Chester is among the biggest of the new universities established in 2005. Over a fifth of the undergraduates are over 20 on entry and two thirds are female. Nearly all are state-educated, and almost 40 per cent have working-class roots. The projected dropout rate of 15 per has improved, but is

Parkgate Road
Chester CH1 4BJ

01244 512528 (admissions)
enquiries@chester.ac.uk
www.chester.ac.uk
www.chestersu.com
Affiliation: Cathedral Group

The Times Rankings
Overall Ranking: **=71**

Student satisfaction:	**=63**	(76%)
Research quality:	**=105**	(0.1)
Entry standards:	**=74**	(273)
Student–staff ratio:	**49**	(17.2)
Services & facilities/student:	**97**	(£1,085)
Expected completion rate:	**93**	(79.2%)
Good honours:	**72**	(57.9%)
Graduate prospects:	**54**	(63.4%)

still above the national average for the university's courses and entry standards. About a third of the undergraduates take combined honours degrees and many courses of all types include a period of extended work experience. There is also a limited range of Foundation degrees, mainly in health subjects but now including courses in business or leadership and management for RAF personnel. The Foundation degree in mortuary science is the first of its kind, as is one for guide dog trainers. Even the more traditional degrees have been designed to support the practical and vocational demands of the professions. Initial teacher training courses have been rated "outstanding" by Ofsted.

A student contract of the type that is set to become universal in the higher education sector sets out clear conditions on the offer of a place, as well as detailing the university's responsibilities. Students promise to "study diligently, and to attend promptly and participate appropriately at lectures, courses, classes, seminars, tutorials, work placements and other activities which form part of the programme." The university undertakes to deliver the student's programme, but leaves itself considerable leeway beyond that.

However, Chester offers considerable support and facilities for its students. It was the first UK university to receive the maximum five-star rating from the British Quality Foundation for its student support and guidance and its careers and employability departments.

There are extensive sports facilities at Warrington and especially on the main campus at Chester, catering partly for the large physical education programme.

Most first years are offered one of the growing number of hall places, although there is not yet enough university accommodation to make this a guarantee. Student union facilities form the basis of the social scene on both campuses, but Chester has more to offer for those looking further afield.

Undergraduate Fees and Support

» Fees for UK/EU students 2012–13   £9,000
» Fees for International students 2011–12   £7,920–£9,270
» A package of financial support and widening participation to include around 200 National Student Scholarships of £3,000 a year;
  students with household income of less than £25K, £1,000 as fee waiver, cash payment or discount on university accommodation;
  students from targeted partner schools and colleges with household income less than £42K eligible for £1,000 as fee waiver, cash payment or discount on university accommodation.
» Scholarships and bursaries based on circumstances or by competition are available..
» Check the university's website for the latest information.

Students		
Undergraduates:	**7,440**	**(3,740)**
Postgraduates:	**815**	**(2,585)**
Mature students:	**21.9%**	
Overseas students:	**1.6%**	
Applications per place:	**7.2**	
From state-sector schools:	**97.5%**	
From working-class homes:	**39.2%**	

For detailed information about fees, grants and bursaries and how they work, see chapter 7.

Accommodation
Number of places and costs refer to 2010–11
University-provided places: approx 1,040
Percentage catered: 40%
Catered costs: £70.70–£139.65 a week.
Self-catered costs: £70.00–£99.75 a week.
First years cannot be guaranteed accommodation.
International students: guaranteed accommodation if they apply by the advertised date.
Contact: www.chester.ac.uk/campus-life/accommodation

University of Chichester

Chichester is the smallest of the nine universities created in 2005, but it features consistently among the leading modern universities in league tables. It headed the post-1992 foundations in the National Student Survey in successive years before slipping slightly in 2010. History, English and imaginative writing still showed very high levels of satisfaction and the university's overall scores remained above average. The university also slipped down the order in *The Times Higher Education* student experience survey, having been the top-rated modern university in 2009. Applications have also been rising, although there had been only a modest 1 per cent increase at the start of 2011.

The university traces its history back to 1839, when the college that subsequently bore his name was founded in memory of William Otter, the education-minded Bishop of Chichester. It became a teacher training college for women, who still account for two thirds of the places. Two further stages preceded university status – 20 years as the West Sussex Institute of Higher Education, following an amalgamation with the nearby Bognor Regis College of Education, and then seven as University College Chichester. The Chichester campus – now the larger of two – continues to carry the Bishop Otter name,

signifying a continuing link with the Church of England.

The two faculties operate on both sites, one covering business, arts and the humanities; the other sport, social sciences and education. The portfolio of some 300 courses ranges from adventure education to humanistic counselling, fine art and the psychology of sport and exercise. The PE teacher training course is the largest in the country – the university now trains one in five PE teachers in England – and is highly rated by Ofsted. Sport was the only area in which the university registered any world-leading work in the 2008 Research Assessment Exercise, but history and drama, dance and performing arts also produced good results.

The university is financially stable, having reported a surplus of more than £2 million last year. It holds nearly £10 million in reserves and considers itself one of the best placed institutions to deal with the challenges of the future. It has embarked on capital investment projects in Bognor Regis that will cost £13 million, the majority of which will be spent transforming the Dome into a business and research centre and creating a new learning and resource centre.

The Alexandra Theatre, in Bognor, is used as a base for the musical theatre programme and there are links, too, with the Chichester Festival Theatre. The Mathematics Centre, at Bognor, has an international reputation, working with over 30 countries as well as

---

Bishop Otter Campus
College Lane
Chichester
W. Sussex PO19 6PE

01243 816002 (admissions)
admissions@chi.ac.uk
www.chi.ac.uk
www.chisu.org
Affiliation: Cathedral
Group

The Times Rankings
Overall Ranking: **54**

Student satisfaction:	=12	(81%)
Research quality:	=92	(0.2)
Entry standards:	=61	(290)
Student–staff ratio:	44	(16.6)
Services & facilities/student:	=88	(£1,148)
Expected completion rate:	39	(88.8%)
Good honours:	90	(54.0%)
Graduate prospects:	96	(54.4%)

teaching the university's own students. It has become a focal point for curriculum development in Britain and elsewhere. Chichester runs short courses for education ministries in countries as diverse as Bhutan, Russia and the Seychelles.

Graduate employment rates have been good for a number of years. In the last survey published, only 4 per cent were thought to be jobless, but the relatively high proportion starting off in non-graduate work pushes Chichester down our table on this measure. About 18 per cent of the 5,000 students are over 20 on entry. Almost all are state educated and the proportions from working-class homes and areas of low participation in higher education are both close to the national average for the university's courses and entry grades, despite the comfortable south coast location. The projected dropout rate remained below 8 per cent in the latest survey, approaching half the benchmark figure. The university runs summer taster sessions and has a series of partnerships with schools in the Channel Islands and Sussex to encourage a broader intake. Courses are also run in collaboration with Isle of Wight College.

Both of the university's campuses are within ten minutes' walk of the sea and the 647 residential places are roughly equally divided between them. There is a university bus service linking the two and students' union bars at each. Sports facilities are good and competitive teams surprisingly successful for such a small university. The university was chosen to provide training facilities for competitors in athletics, boxing, road cycling and table tennis before the 2012 Olympic Games. The Barbados team will be taking advantage of Chichester's expertise in sports science and medicine in the run-up to the Games.

The small cathedral city of Chichester is best known as a yachting venue and, while Bognor's days as a leading holiday resort are well in the past, it is said to have the longest stretch of coastline in the south where all types of water sports are available. Both locations offer a good supply of private housing and some student-oriented bars. Much of the surrounding countryside has been designated an area of outstanding natural beauty.

Undergraduate Fees and Support

- » Fees for UK/EU students 2012–13 £8,500
- » Fees for International students 2011–12 £8,775–£9,990
- » Students with household income below £25K, £2,500 each year as bursary or fee waiver; with a household income of £25K–£42K, £1,000 each year as bursary or fee waiver.
- » Scholarships and bursaries based on circumstances or by competition are available.
- » Check the university's website for the latest information.

Students

Undergraduates:	**3,375**	**(725)**
Postgraduates:	**260**	**(870)**
Mature students:	**18.1%**	
Overseas students:	**2.4%**	
Applications per place:	**5.1**	
From state-sector schools:	**96.6%**	
From working-class homes:	**34.5%**	

For detailed information about fees, grants and bursaries and how they work, see chapter 7.

Accommodation

Number of places and costs refer to 2011–12
University-provided places: 647
Percentage catered: 66.5%
Catered costs: £116.41 (twin) – £155.05 (single, en suite) a week (37 or 40 weeks).
Self-catered costs: £91.00 (shared) – £128.10 (en suite) a week (37 or 40 weeks).
First years are accommodated on a first come, first served basis.
International students: as above.
Contact: www.chi.ac.uk/accomm/index.cfm

City University London

City expects to be "significantly more selective" in 2012, when it will charge undergraduate fees of £9,000. It has promised to invest heavily in new academic staff and student related facilities in return. City will offer over 70 National Student Scholarships each year, and invest more than £1 million a year in outreach and retention activities such as maths tutoring, master-classes, summer schools and subject-specific events.

Marketing itself as the "international university in the heart of London", City has added the name of the capital to its title to make the most of its greatest asset. Students come from more than 150 different countries to study on the borders of the financial district. Once a college of advanced technology, City now has roughly a quarter of its students taking business courses, another quarter health and community subjects and the remaining half law, computing, mathematics, engineering, journalism and the arts .

The university is focused on business and the professions, reaping the benefits with consistently good graduate employment figures. City's graduates play their part, with nearly 2,000 of them offering practical help to current students through an online careers network. Courses have a practical edge, and many of the staff hold professional, as well as academic, qualifications.

Student numbers doubled during the 1990s, partly due to the incorporation of colleges of radiography and nursing and midwifery. There are now more than 17,000 students, and because around a fifth of them are from outside the EU and around 40 per cent are postgraduates, City is one of the universities that are least dependent on Government funding. City is among the most popular universities in London, with over eight applications for each undergraduate place. There was a 7.5 per cent rise in applications at the start of 2011, the latest in a series of above-average increases.

A number of interdisciplinary centres have been launched to increase collaborative teaching and research, as well as to build stronger links between industry and academia. These include the Centre for Creativity in Professional Practice, the Centre for Information Leadership, the Centre for Performance at Work and the City Collaborative Transport Hub.

Development is continuing at the university's Islington headquarters. Some £20 million went into an impressive new building for the School of Social Sciences, the students' union has been refurbished and £12 million invested in a new School of Arts with well-equipped recording and television studios. The School of Engineering and Mathematical Sciences added four new interactive classrooms and a modern electronics laboratory in 2009, and the library

---

Northampton Square
London EC1V 0HB

020 7040 5060
contact via website
www.city.ac.uk
www.culsu.co.uk
Affiliation: none

has been renovated at a cost of £2.3 million, giving students more space, upgraded technology and better support.

The £42-million Cass Business School, which opened in 2002, is one of City's great strengths. It has 3,000 students and is ranked among the top 50 business schools in the world. Based in the heart of the financial district, it has built up an impressive cadre of visiting practitioner lecturers who find it easy and convenient to visit. City has links with 50 European universities and many more further afield, and many students spend a year of their course abroad.

The university boosted its legal provision by incorporating the Inns of Court School of Law in 2001. The City Law School, which includes the university's original department, was the first in London to offer a "one-stop shop" for legal training, from undergraduate to professional courses.

City is also working with Queen Mary, University of London, in a range of subjects, starting with medicine and other health subjects, journalism and engineering. The two universities jointly host a national centre for teaching and learning in nursing and midwifery. Journalism is highly regarded and the university has launched the UK's first graduate school of journalism in new £12-million facilities. There is a flourishing sub-degree programme for adults, which ranges from sitcom writing to e-business.

City has a particularly high reputation in music, where it is associated with the Guildhall School of Music and Drama. Together with nursing and midwifery, music achieved the university's best results in the 2008 Research Assessment Exercise. Social work and social policy also produced good results. Like other universities in London, City has struggled to make an impression in the National Student Survey, finishing low down the table in 2009. Aerospace engineering and music received high marks for teaching, while finance and mathematics produced high overall satisfaction levels.

Official performance indicators show the dropout rate falling steadily. It is now below 11 per cent and better than average for the subjects and entry qualifications. City has a better record than most of its peers for widening participation in higher education, with four out of ten undergraduates coming from working-class homes. The students' union is popular, but sports facilities are poor by current standards, although the indoor sports centre is conveniently located.

Undergraduate Fees and Support

» Fees for UK/EU students 2012–13   £9,000
» Fees for International students 2011–12   £10,000–£11,500
» Details of a package of financial support, including matched funding for 70 National Scholarships, and widening participation and retention activity to be announced.
» Scholarships and bursaries based on circumstances or by competition are available.
» Check the university's website for the latest information.

Students		
Undergraduates:	**7,955**	**(2,100)**
Postgraduates:	**4,420**	**(2,745)**
Mature students:	**22.9%**	
Overseas students:	**20.8%**	
Applications per place:	**8.7**	
From state-sector schools:	**91.9%**	
From working-class homes:	**39.6%**	

For detailed information about fees, grants and bursaries and how they work, see chapter 7.

Accommodation

Number of places and costs refer to 2011–12
University-provided places: 1,141
Percentage catered: 0%
Self-catered costs: £170–£247 a week.
Accommodation is guaranteed for first years if conditions are met.
Residential restrictions apply.
International students: preference is given to new overseas students.
Contact: accomm@city.ac.uk
www.city.ac.uk/studentcentre/housing

Coventry University

Coventry is in the throes of a £160-million investment to rejuvenate its 33-acre campus close to the city centre. Much of the ten-year programme involves student facilities such as the showpiece turreted library, which cost £20 million and is almost entirely naturally ventilated and lit. The latest development is a brand new Students' building, containing the new students' union offices, a live music venue to fit up to 800 people, three floors of informal study space, convenience stores and restaurants. Work has also started on the new home for the faculty of engineering and computing, which is due to open in September 2012.

The campus is now fully Wi-Fi enabled and there are 2,400 PCs for student use. The university has already added other facilities, including more residential accommodation, a £7-million arts centre and a sports centre, during a decade in which student numbers doubled to more than 20,000.

Coventry traces its origins back to 1843 with the foundation of the College of Design and its links with the motor industry of the Midlands were reflected in its earlier title of Lanchester Polytechnic, named after a leading engineering figure. It has adopted an innovative approach to computer-assisted learning, supported by an expanded computer network. The university was chosen to house national centres of excellence in teaching for e-learning in health and social care, as well as in maths, and transport and product design.

The university has a focus on employment, which is reflected in a predominantly vocational curriculum. The Start-Up Café encourages business networking and local employers are engaging with the programme of work-based learning. The Add+vantage scheme covers a wide range of skills and helps students gain work-related knowledge and prepare for a career.

The majority of students exercise their right to take "free-choice modules" that cover the full range of university provision, with IT skills and languages particularly popular. Coventry has been building up its portfolio of courses, introducing eye-catching degrees in subjects such as ethical hacking and network security, disaster management, forensic chemistry, criminology and boat design.

The 2010 National Student Survey showed 100 per cent satisfaction in human and social geography for the second year in a row, with good scores in medical subjects, biology and dance. The university's overall score improved but still left it in the bottom half of the table. Research grades improved in the 2008 assessment exercise, when small amounts of world-leading work were recognised in seven of the sixteen areas in which the university made submissions. Art

---

Priory Street
Coventry CV1 5FB

024 7615 2222 (admissions)
studentenquiries@coventry.ac.uk
www.coventry.ac.uk
www.cusu.org
Affiliation: million+

The Times Rankings
Overall Ranking: **76**

Student satisfaction:	=78	(74%)
Research quality:	=92	(0.2)
Entry standards:	=54	(298)
Student–staff ratio:	=35	(15.7)
Services & facilities/student:	86	(£1,158)
Expected completion rate:	=100	(77.6%)
Good honours:	=59	(61.4%)
Graduate prospects:	=70	(59.9%)

and design and electrical and electronic engineering produced the best results. Design benefits from a revolutionary £1.6-million digital modelling workshop, sponsored by the Bugatti Trust, which provides full-scale vehicle modelling facilities for students as well as researchers.

Among the initiatives to improve the student experience has been the introduction of tangible rewards for excellent teaching and further development of electronic learning. The Centre for Academic Writing offers advice on essays and theses, with group sessions and one-to-one appointments, while the Maths Support Centre includes a statistics advisory service and specialist support service for students with dyslexia.

More than most universities, Coventry is a creature of its city, and the civic-minded approach of the university has created many town–gown links. The 20-acre Coventry University Technology Park has benefitted both the university and the city. It houses the TechnoCentre and the £3-million Enterprise Centre as well as the Coventry and Warwickshire New Technology Institute. The university's main buildings open out from the ruins of the bombed cathedral, as university and public facilities mingle in the city. Student residences are in easy walking distance of the campus and city centre.

However, the university has now opened a business-oriented campus in London, which enrols its first undergraduates in 2011.

A three-year degree in global business management will include a workplace project and a period of study abroad. The campus, close to Liverpool Street station, also offers one-year top-up programmes giving international students entry into the final year of a BA degree.

Students in Coventry welcome the relatively low cost of living there. Just over 40 per cent of the undergraduates have working-class backgrounds, many from areas of low participation in higher education. Applications have been healthy and were up by slightly more than the national average at the start of 2011, following a big rise in 2010. The projected dropout rate had improved significantly in the latest survey, and, at 15 per cent, is a little better than the national average for the university's courses and entry qualifications.

Undergraduate Fees and Support

» Fees for UK/EU students 2012–13:

Foundation degrees and most part-time courses up to £4,800	
Classroom-based courses	£7,500
Studio and activity-based courses	£7,900
Laboratory-based courses	£8,300
Specialist courses	£9,000

» Fees for International students 2011–12   £9,060–£9,380
» Details of financial support and widening participation activity to be announced.
» Scholarships for students from low-income backgrounds as cash and fee waivers.
» Check the university's website for the latest information.

Students

Undergraduates:	**13,450**	**(5,575)**
Postgraduates:	**2,250**	**(2,065)**
Mature students:	**22.4%**	
Overseas students:	**14.1%**	
Applications per place:	**4.3**	
From state-sector schools:	**97.1%**	
From working-class homes:	**40.8%**	

For detailed information about fees, grants and bursaries and how they work, see chapter 7.

Accommodation

Number of places and costs refer to 2011–12
University-provided places: 2,725 (includes 540 beds on Nomination Agreements)
Percentage catered: 22%
Catered costs: £110 a week (10 meals).
Self-catered costs: £92–£140 a week.
First-year students are guaranteed housing provided conditions are met.
International students: as above.
Contact: www.coventry.ac.uk/cu/accommodation

University of Cumbria

One of the largest counties without a university of its own put that right through the amalgamation of a former teacher training college and an arts institute, with the addition of the two Cumbrian campuses of the University of Central Lancashire. The new University of Cumbria was divided between Carlisle, Penrith, Ambleside and Lancaster, as well as running a specialist teacher education centre in east London. There are partnerships with the four further education colleges in the county to provide higher education locally. The university is to open a base of its own at Furness College, in Barrow in Furness, and has already established Learning Gateway West, another teaching centre, at the Energus Building in Workington.

The new university, which has more than 12,000 students, was finally established in 2007, after a series of false starts. It is the largest provider of higher education in Cumbria by a considerable margin and growing in popularity. Applications were up by 3 per cent at the start of 2011, following much bigger increases in the two previous years. However, these successes were tempered by financial problems, which led to plans to "mothball" the Ambleside campus and cut a number of courses.

The university's headquarters is in Carlisle, but the biggest of the component parts is the former St Martin's College, which was founded in Lancaster by the Church of England in 1964 to train teachers and expanded during the 1990s with the addition of a nursing college. It forms the new university's main base, a ten-minute walk from Lancaster town centre. The Gateway, a £9.2-million development, opened in 2009 providing a range of student services and there is a modern library and excellent sports facilities, including a £2.5-million sports complex, gymnastics centre and fitness centre. The Ambleside campus, which has an outdoor studies centre and a new learning resources centre, was also part of St Martin's.

There are two main sites in Carlisle, the larger of which is in a parkland setting close to the River Eden. The second campus, closer to the city centre, boasts a new Learning Gateway, an innovative multi-media learning resource centre, and a sports centre with a four-court sports hall and well-equipped fitness room. The former Cumbria Institute of the Arts can trace its history in Carlisle back to 1822, eventually becoming the only specialist institute of the arts in North West England and one of only a small number of such institutions in the country. The creative arts are one of the main areas for development in the university's initial planning.

A lengthy review was still taking place as the *Guide* went to press into the future of the other main campus, at Newton Rigg, a mile

---

Fusehill Street
Carlisle
Cumbria CA1 2HH
01524 384360/694
contact via website
www.cumbria.ac.uk
www.thestudentsunion.
org.uk
Affiliations: Cathedral Group,
Guild HE

The Times Rankings
Overall Ranking: **=82**

Student satisfaction:	=103	(71%)
Research quality:	115	(0)
Entry standards:	=89	(263)
Student–staff ratio:	41	(16.3)
Services & facilities/student:	57	(£1,361)
Expected completion rate:	57	(84.8%)
Good honours:	=82	(55.8%)
Graduate prospects:	=47	(66.2%)

outside Penrith. Acquired from the University of Central Lancashire, it is set in landscaped gardens overlooking the fells, and caters mainly for agriculture and forestry. A former agricultural college, it has broadened into related areas such as environmental management and other subjects not directly related to land-based industries. Courses include outdoor education and leadership, sport, forensic science and conservation biology. Library and learning resource facilities have been improved and residential accommodation expanded. There are also two farms, one adjacent to the campus and a working hill farm 15 miles away within the National Park.

Plans for a £160-million development of its estate, including a new campus in Carlisle, have been shelved. But the university is anxious to maintain a "Cumbria-wide presence" and is not planning to close Newton Rigg. There are three faculties: Arts, Business and Science; Education; and Health and Wellbeing. Building on its heritage, it is one of the biggest teacher training centres in the UK.

Cumbria made its debut in the lower reaches of *The Times* League Table, but is now out of the bottom 30. However, the university was bottom of the initial rankings from the 2008 Research Assessment Exercise, recording only a small amount of world-leading research in theology, divinity and religious studies. And, after some improvement in National Student Survey, scores slumped again in 2010, plunging the university into the bottom 10. Drama, complementary therapies and nursing produced by far the most satisfied students.

The early focus of the university has been on attracting more students from a region of low participation in higher education, as well as on serving the social and economic needs of the county. Almost all the undergraduates are from state schools and colleges and more than 40 per cent are from working-class homes. The proportion from areas without a tradition of higher education is also well above the national average for the university's subjects and entry grades.

Undergraduate Fees and Support

- » Fees for UK/EU students 2012–13   £8,400
- » Fees for International students 2011–12   £8,550
- » A package of financial support and widening participation activity to be announced.
- » Bursary on partial grant: household income up to £50K: £500.
- » Scholarships and bursaries based on circumstances or by competition are available.
- » Check the university's website for the latest information.

Students		
Undergraduates:	**5,615**	**(4,080)**
Postgraduates:	**1,075**	**(1,640)**
Mature students:	**29.3%**	
Overseas students:	**1.2%**	
Applications per place:	**3.5**	
From state-sector schools:	**97.8%**	
From working-class homes:	**43.7%**	

For detailed information about fees, grants and bursaries and how they work, see chapter 7.

Accommodation

Number of places and costs refer to 2010–11

University-provided places: 821

Percentage catered: 65%

Catered costs: £90.95–£103.95.

Self-catered costs: £71–£90 a week.

First years are guaranteed halls accommodation if Cumbria is first choice.

International students: guaranteed halls accommodation if conditions are met.

Contact: www.cumbria.ac.uk/FutureStudents/Accommodation

De Montfort University

An emphasis on research paid off spectacularly for De Montfort in the 2008 Research Assessment Exercise, when the university achieved the best results of any post-1992 university. Some 43 per cent of the work submitted was rated world-leading or internationally excellent. Almost all the subject areas contained some world-leading research and in the case of English language and literature the proportion reached an outstanding 40 per cent. Communication and media studies and drama, dance and performing arts also produced excellent results. However, the university has suffered a big drop in the latest *Times* League Table with declines on several indicators, notably graduate prospects.

Accolades in the previous RAE laid the foundations, helping to bring in annual research income of about £10 million a year in external research grants and contracts. Much of the successful work took place in the Institute of Creative Technologies, which acts as a catalyst for research that defies the traditional boundaries of computer science, the digital arts and humanities, and is already exciting the interest of the business world.

Another £3.7 million was spent on creative technology studios, which feature video, audio and radio production suites, recording studios and laboratories with the latest broadcast and audio analysis technology. A Performance Arts Centre for Excellence (PACE) had already opened, allowing the university to deliver innovative teaching for students of dance, drama and music technology.

Once a network of campuses spreading far beyond Leicester, De Montfort is concentrating its efforts on its original base, investing £143 million in a more manageable estate. From September 2011, the entire institution will be on one campus for the first time since it became a university. The last piece in the jigsaw will see nursing and midwifery move into new premises for the health and life sciences. Four further education colleges across the East Midlands are associates, linked into the university's network and offering its courses.

Other campus developments include the diversion of part of the ring road to allow the university to open up the 15th-century Magazine Gateway building, which will become the focal point of a university quarter with public open spaces and new links to the city centre. A prize-winning building for business and law, which opened in 2010, is at its heart. The Hugh Aston Building, which cost £35 million and caters for around 6,000 students, includes a court room, law library, dedicated law clinic and bookshop, as well as more conventional teaching facilities. Elsewhere, the 24-hour library has been remodelled with wireless

The Gateway
Leicester LE1 9BH

08459 454647 (enquiries)
enquiry@dmu.ac.uk
www.dmu.ac.uk
www.demontfortstudents.com
Affiliation: University
Alliance

The Times Rankings
Overall Ranking: **85**

Student satisfaction:	=37	(78%)
Research quality:	=60	(0.6)
Entry standards:	=94	(259)
Student–staff ratio:	=50	(17.5)
Services & facilities/student:	99	(£1,080)
Expected completion rate:	=79	(81.8%)
Good honours:	=102	(49.8%)
Graduate prospects:	103	(52.8%)

networks and rooms equipped with audio-visual and IT facilities, and new game development studios have been installed to enable students to see their work in 3D.

The professional accounting courses achieved "premier" status in a worldwide accreditation scheme, and the university was awarded a national teaching centre for drama, dance and theatre studies. Recent results in the National Student Survey have been good, with human resource management, aural and oral science, fine art and management studies all finishing in the top three in the UK. Business studies, psychology, journalism and music technology also did well in 2010.

De Montfort enjoyed one of the biggest increases in applications of any university in 2010 – approaching 30 per cent – but the demand for places was down in 2011.

Among the recent additions to the portfolio of courses is a BSc in green energy technology and another in public and community health, tackling issues such as increases in sexually transmitted infections and obesity. Others include a new Foundation degree for community development and regeneration, and a BSc in evaluating practice for students who wish to further their study after completion of the Foundation degree in children, families and community health.

The dropout rate has improved considerably: at less than 14 per cent, it is now around the national average for the university's courses and entry grades. De Montfort has abandoned semesters and gone back to a three-term year, partly because it believed the prospect of imminent assessment encouraged some students to give up at Christmas in their first year. The university has a proud record for widening access to higher education with over 40 per cent of students coming from working-class homes. It was one of the first to set up an employment agency to help students find part-time work as well as find careers upon graduation. Strong links with local business and industry manifest themselves in courses such as the BSc in media production, run in conjunction with the BBC.

Accommodation difficulties have been addressed, with the addition of new halls within walking distance of lectures, although all first years cannot be guaranteed housing. Rents in the private sector are among the lowest in England.

Undergraduate Fees and Support

» Fees for UK/EU students 2012–13 £9,000
» Fees for International students 2011–12 £9,250
» A package of financial support and widening participation and retention activity to be announced. Expected to help 40 per cent of students with cash bursaries up to £6,000 over three years.
» Academic scholarships of £1,000 a year; bursaries of £1,000 a year for students on access courses.
» Check the university's website for the latest information.

Students		
Undergraduates:	**14,915**	**(3,470)**
Postgraduates:	**1,165**	**(2,905)**
Mature students:	**22.0%**	
Overseas students:	**5.0%**	
Applications per place:	**5.7**	
From state-sector schools:	**97.7%**	
From working-class homes:	**41.2%**	

For detailed information about fees, grants and bursaries and how they work, see chapter 7.

Accommodation

Number of places and costs refer to 2011–12
University-provided places: around 3,100
Percentage catered: 0%
Self-catered costs: £85–£159 a week.
First years cannot be guaranteed accommodation.
International students: new students are guaranteed accommodation.
Contact: housing@dmu.ac.uk

University of Derby

Derby sees itself as a prototype for the modern university, providing courses at all levels in a variety of ways. While accepting that Derby will never scale the heights in league tables such as ours, the university has set itself the target of becoming the pre-eminent university of its type by 2020. Its yardsticks are student satisfaction, employ-ability, service to business and flexibility, all delivered cost effectively. Applications were up by 22 per cent at the start of 2011 and by 38 per cent a year earlier – both among the biggest increases at any university.

The university takes pride in its record for widening access and has pitched its fees for 2012 accordingly. They will range from £6,995 for most courses to £7,995 for about one degree in five, in specialist subjects. Higher entry grades have coincided with the recruitment of more students from affluent families, but still almost four in ten under-graduates are from working-class homes and two in ten are from areas of low participation in higher education – well above the national average for the courses and entry qualifica-tions. However, the latest projected dropout rate was more than 24 per cent, also well above the benchmark figure for the university.

Campus developments are continuing: a £21-million art, design and technology building opened in 2007 and £5 million has been spent on refurbishing the nearby Britannia Mill where social science courses and some health-related courses are based. This is all part of a £75-million estates strategy that has created a university quarter for the city of Derby. The second campus in Buxton is based in what used to be the Devonshire Royal Hospital and provides an ideal centre for courses in spa, outdoor recreation and hospitality management, as well as further education programmes. The landmark building, which has a bigger dome than St Paul's Cathedral, houses a training restaurant, a beauty salon and a health spa, as well as more conventional teaching facilities. A new sports centre opened in Buxton in 2011.

There are two main sites in Derby: an extended academic campus at Kedleston Road, two miles from the city centre, and a residential campus close to the city's entertainment district. Kedleston Road caters for most of the main subjects including all business, computing, science, humanities and law courses. The Markeaton cluster hosts arts, technology and some social science and health courses. The students' union, multi-faith centre and main sports facilities are here. The £1.5-million clinical skills suite was built to NHS "Red Book" standards, featuring hospital wards, counselling rooms and diagnostic radiography facilities. The site's three tower blocks have been

---

Kedleston Road
Derby DE22 1GB

01332 590500 (admissions)
askadmissions@derby.ac.uk
www.derby.ac.uk
www.udsu.co.uk
Affiliation: million+

Edinburgh
Belfast
DERBY
London
Cardiff

The Times Rankings
Overall Ranking: **107**

Student satisfaction:	=73	(75%)
Research quality:	=105	(0.1)
Entry standards:	100	(250)
Student–staff ratio:	=86	(20.5)
Services & facilities/student:	53	(£1,373)
Expected completion rate:	111	(73.2%)
Good honours:	101	(50.1%)
Graduate prospects:	=104	(52.3%)

refurbished in a £13.5-million project, which will make them more energy efficient with the installation of photovoltaic panels and wind turbines. A new all-weather sports pitch was added in 2009. The university has acquired the 550-seat Derby Theatre to house theatre arts programmes as well as continuing as a producing theatre. Students have access to the main auditorium as well as their own 112-seat studio theatre.

The sites are within ten minutes walk of each other as well as being linked by free shuttle buses and the UniBus service, which also connects with the train station and the city centre. The university also has a centre in Chesterfield to teach nursing.

A Foundation programme allows students to begin work at a partner college before transferring to the university. Derby has also awarded more work-based qualifications than any other UK university. Business and management is by far the university's biggest academic area, but work placements are encouraged in all relevant subjects. The accent on employability continues through the "Skillbuilder" career development programme, which covers a range of transferable skills to give graduates an edge in the employment market. Derby is at the forefront of development of a Higher Education Achievement Record that students can make available electronically to prospective employers.

Derby has been quick to adopt new teaching methods, pioneering the use of interactive video for a national scheme. Distance learning is a growth area, either online or through Derby's nine regional centres. Prospective students can even sample a virtual open evening. A variety of courses, from Foundation degrees to postgraduate qualifications, are available online. The university won an award for the imaginative use of distance learning.

The university spent £30 million in five years to maintain its guarantee of accommodation for all first years and has improved student facilities. Students seem to appreciate the university's efforts because Derby comes out well in its own satisfaction surveys, although this has not been reflected in the national equivalent. Scores have improved in the National Student Survey, but the university remained in the bottom half of the table in 2010. History, teacher training, English, law, marketing, music and the performing arts recorded the best results.

Undergraduate Fees and Support

» Fees for UK/EU students 2012-13:

Classroom-based courses	£6,995
Resource -intensive courses	£7,495
Specialist "signature courses"	£7,995

No charge for course "extras".

» Fees for International students 2011-12   £9,250-£9,500
» A package of financial support and widening participation activity to be announced.
» Check the university's website for the latest information.

Students			Accommodation
Undergraduates:	**10,700**	**(3,690)**	Number of places and costs refer to 2011-12
Postgraduates:	**755**	**(2,330)**	University-provided places: 2,500
Mature students:	**34.4%**		Percentage catered: 0%
Overseas students:	**10.3%**		Self-catered costs: £73.50-£102.06.
Applications per place:	**5.5**		First-year students are guaranteed accommodation if they apply
From state-sector schools:	**96.8%**		before 31 July.
From working-class homes:	**37.9%**		Policy for international students: as above.
			Contact: www.derby.ac.uk/halls

For detailed information about fees, grants and bursaries and how they work, see chapter 7.

Student Living – tel: 01332 594111 (126 Nuns St, Derby, DE1 3LQ)

University of Dundee

Dundee has enjoyed a surge in popularity in recent years. Applications doubled in a decade and a 15 per cent increase at the start of 2011 compared favourably with the university's competitors, some of which were experiencing a drop in demand for places. Dundee describes itself as "Scotland's most enterprising university" and, while there would be other claimants to that title, it has certainly been among the liveliest in recent years. A long series of good quality ratings and the acquisition of education, nursing and art colleges, which doubled its size and greatly increased its scope, have been complemented by high-profile research successes, especially in medicine and the life sciences.

The university now has over 16,000 students, over 60 per cent of whom are undergraduates, including a healthy number from overseas. It has been looking outwards to achieve the "critical mass" which experts regard as essential to break into the higher education elite, appointing many new professors in recent years.

A £200-million campus redevelopment designed by the leading architect, Sir Terry Farrell, is now complete. Almost £40 million of this was spent on wireless-networked student residences. The IT facilities include a superfast broadband network and are among the best in the UK, allowing the latest technologies to be used to enhance teaching. Education and social work moved into a new teaching block on the main campus in 2008, and there have been extensions to the library and the sports centre. Best-known for life sciences, where research into cancer and diabetes is recognised as world-class, the university has already opened new buildings for interdisciplinary research, applied computing and clinical research.

Set in 20 acres of parkland, the medical school is the one of the few components of the university outside the compact city-centre campus – while some of the nursing and midwifery students are 35 miles away in Kirkcaldy. Biochemistry is the flagship department, housed in a complex that includes the £13-million Wellcome Trust Building and the Sir James Black Centre, which cost £21 million. Its academics were the first in Britain to be invited to take part in Japan's Human Frontier science programme and are now the most-quoted researchers in their field.

More than half the work submitted for the 2008 Research Assessment Exercise was rated world-leading or internationally excellent. Dundee recorded the best results in Scotland for art and design, civil engineering, biological and laboratory-based clinical sciences. The university has also produced consistently good scores in the National Student Survey. In 2010, there was

---

Nethergate
Dundee DD1 4HN

01382 383838 (enquiries)
contactus@dundee.ac.uk
www.dundee.ac.uk
www.dusa.co.uk
Affiliation: none

The Times Rankings
Overall Ranking: **40**

Student satisfaction:	=12	(81%)
Research quality:	=45	(1.5)
Entry standards:	39	(353)
Student–staff ratio:	17	(14.3)
Services & facilities/student:	58	(£1,355)
Expected completion rate:	78	(81.9%)
Good honours:	=34	(68.5%)
Graduate prospects:	38	(68.9%)

100 per cent satisfaction in environmental science, geography, pharmacology and town and regional planning, with high scores in accounting, anatomy and physiology, education, English, history, medicine, philosophy and life sciences.

Vocational degrees predominate, helping to produce the university's consistently good graduate employment record. The university sends more graduates into the professions than any other institution in Scotland, and only Oxbridge graduates came out ahead of Dundee's in a national survey of starting salaries. Most degrees include a career planning module and an internship option, and students are now provided with their own personal development website. Among the new courses introduced recently are dual qualifying law (Scots and English), digital interaction design and business computing. The highly rated design courses are taught at the former Duncan of Jordanstone College of Art.

There has been an emphasis on opportunities for women ever since Dundee's separation from St Andrews University in 1967, and the addition of teacher training has increased the female majority. Two thirds of Dundee's students are from Scotland and nearly one in ten from Northern Ireland. One in five come from areas with little tradition of higher education and more than a quarter are from working-class homes. They enjoy a welcoming atmosphere and a cost of living which is lower than in most university cities. Private accommodation is plentiful for those who are not housed by the university. Applicants have access to MyDundee, an online portal not only giving further information about the university during the application process and to prepare them for the academic year, but also an extensive virtual learning environment which all students can access.

The city is profiting from recent regeneration programmes and becoming more fashionable. The university has been at the heart of a successful campaign to bring an outpost of the Victoria and Albert Museum to Dundee by 2014 (its first outside London). Spectacular mountain and coastal scenery are close at hand, but social life tends to be concentrated on the students' union, which is one of the largest and most active in Scotland.

Undergraduate Fees and Support

» Fees 2012–13: awaiting Scottish Government policy.
» Fees for Scottish and EU students 2011–12 No fee
» Fees for Non-Scottish UK-domiciled students 2011–12 £1,820
  £2,895 (medicine)
» Fees for international students 2011–12 £9,200–£13,700
  £16,750–£25,500 (medicine)
» Scholarships and bursaries based on circumstances or by competition are available.
» Check the university's website for the latest information.

Students

Undergraduates:	**8,980**	**(1,750)**
Postgraduates:	**1,810**	**(3,650)**
Mature students:	**29.3%**	
Overseas students:	**9.5%**	
Applications per place:	**6.4**	
From state-sector schools:	**90.5%**	
From working-class homes:	**25.4%**	

For detailed information about fees, grants and bursaries and how they work, see chapter 7.

Accommodation

Number of places and costs refer to 2011–12
University-provided places: 1,587
Percentage catered: 0%
Self-catered costs: £101.29–£117.95 a week.
First-year students are guaranteed accommodation if conditions are met. No residential restrictions.
International students are guaranteed accommodation if conditions are met.
Contact: residences@dundee.ac.uk
www.dundee.ac.uk/studentservices/residences

Durham University

Long established as a leading alternative to Oxford and Cambridge, Durham has a collegiate structure and picturesque setting that attracts a largely middle-class student body. However, although nearly four out of ten undergraduates come from independent schools, the university has been attracting more applicants from non-traditional backgrounds. All those who receive an offer are invited to a special open day to see if Durham is the university for them. Since around 80 per cent come from outside the northeast of England, most are seeing the small cathedral city for the first time.

Undergraduates apply to one of 14 colleges, all of which have been mixed since 2004. The newest, Josephine Butler College – a self-catering college with around 400 bedrooms – accepted its first intake of students in 2006. Colleges range in size from 300 to 1,100 students and are the focal point of social life, although all teaching is done in central departments. There are significant differences in atmosphere and student profile, ranging from the historic University College, in Durham Castle, to modern buildings on the city's outskirts and on the Queen's Campus, 23 miles away at Stockton-on-Tees.

Durham has been among the top 20 universities for student satisfaction for the last four years. English recorded an overall satisfaction rate of 100 per cent in 2010, while classics and ancient history, law, physics, history and theology all scored highly. Winning a place is far from easy – entrance requirements are among the highest in Britain – but the dropout rate of less than 2 per cent is also among the lowest in any university. Durham has seldom been out of the top ten in *The Times* League Table and has been moving up the world rankings, finishing in the top 100 in both the QS and *Times Higher Education* rankings.

More than 60 per cent of the work submitted for the 2008 Research Assessment Exercise was rated world-leading or internationally excellent. Applied maths, archaeology, and theology and religion achieved among the best results in the UK. Music, English, and geography and environmental science also did well. The Calman Learning Centre, on the Science Site, incorporates lecture theatres, seminar and conference facilities and a "techno café". The site will also see the opening of a landmark "Gateway" development, containing a new law school and student services centre, in 2012.

As the third-oldest university in England, Durham is generally quite traditional. Wherever possible, teaching takes place in small groups and most assessment is by written examination. However, the establishment of the Queen's Campus in

---

University Office
Old Elvet
Durham DH1 3HP

0191 334 6128 (admissions office)
admissions@dur.ac.uk
www.dur.ac.uk
www.dsu.org.uk
Affiliation: 1994 Group

The Times Rankings
Overall Ranking: =6

Student satisfaction:	=12	(81%)
Research quality:	=7	(2.8)
Entry standards:	5	(487)
Student–staff ratio:	=29	(15.3)
Services & facilities/student:	6	(£2,231)
Expected completion rate:	3	(96.7%)
Good honours:	10	(79.4%)
Graduate prospects:	8	(80.4%)

Stockton-on-Tees broke the mould. Initially a joint venture with Teesside University, Stockton is now home to a wide range of courses including applied psychology, biomedical sciences, business and business finance, anthropology and primary education. The campus has also seen the fulfilment of Durham's long-held ambition to restore the medical education it lost when Newcastle University went its own way 45 years ago. An innovative joint project allows students to do the first two years of their training at Stockton, concentrating on community medicine, before transferring to Newcastle to complete their degree.

Significant investment has been made to improve social facilities for the 2,000 students on the Queen's Campus, and £5.5 million has been earmarked for improved sporting facilities, relocating some of the university's elite sports activities as part of a strategy to increase integration between Durham and Stockton. The university's aim is for the campus to be equal in academic status to Durham City, focusing on interdisciplinary research and covering the full range of research, taught postgraduate and undergraduate study. The strategy would see both student and staff numbers at the campus double.

The university dominates the city of Durham to an extent which sometimes causes resentment, but adds considerably to the local economy. The 2009 National Student Housing Survey rated Durham top for private sector accommodation and second for halls of residence. For those looking for nightlife, or just a change of scene, Newcastle is a short train journey away. Sports facilities are excellent, and Durham is among the premier universities in national competitions: it came sixth in national student championships in 2009–10. Among the alumni are the current and former England cricket captains, Andrew Strauss and Nasser Hussain, and rugby World Cup winner, Will Greenwood. The university hosts centres of excellence in cricket, rowing and fencing, and offers a range of sports scholarships. Nine out of ten students take part in sport on a regular basis and Durham's College Sport programme is the largest intra-mural competition in the UK. Some 380 teams compete in 15 sports every week.

Undergraduate Fees and Support

» Fees for UK/EU students 2012–13 £9,000
» Fees for International students 2011–12 £11,970–£15,300
» Details of a programme of scholarships and bursaries to be announced to ensure students recruited with the greatest merit and potential, regardless of background.
» Scholarships and bursaries based on circumstances or by competition are available.
» Check the university's website for the latest information.

Students

Undergraduates:	**11,215**	**(175)**
Postgraduates:	**3,075**	**(1,620)**
Mature students:	**5.9%**	
Overseas students:	**9.5%**	
Applications per place:	**6.8**	
From state-sector schools:	**59.2%**	
From working-class homes:	**16.8%**	

For detailed information about fees, grants and bursaries and how they work, see chapter 7.

Accommodation

Number of places and costs refer to 2011–12
University-provided places: 4,751
Percentage catered: 67%
Catered costs: £142.74 (38 weeks) – £154.00 (33 weeks).
Self-catered costs: £117.79 (38 weeks, Durham); £111.24 (38 weeks, Queen's campus).
All full-time students become members of one of the university's colleges or societies and are allocated housing if they want it. International students: first years are guaranteed housing.
Contact: admissions@dur.ac.uk

University of East Anglia

UEA has been one of the big winners in the National Student Survey, finishing in the top ten every year in published results. Nine out of ten final-year undergraduates were satisfied overall in 2010. Media studies and sociology both achieved 100 per cent satisfaction levels, while pharmacy and occupational therapy were both top in their field. Physiotherapy, speech and language therapy, drama and psychology also registered extremely high scores. Students appear to like the scale of this relatively small campus university, as well as the quality of its courses, and the news appears to be getting through to many sixth-formers: applications were up by nearly 17 per cent on the 2010 figure, which itself represented the biggest increase at any pre-1992 university.

The university has been engaged in an ambitious building and refurbishment programme on the 320-acre site on the outskirts of Norwich. It has included the provision of 700 more en-suite student bedrooms, a new health centre and the extension and refurbishment of the central library, catering facilities and students' union. The Square, the university's social centre, has been regenerated and new buildings added for the schools of Nursing and Midwifery and Medicine, as well as for an INTO English language centre for overseas students. A £3.9-million extension to the Sportspark opened recently, together with a new lecture theatre and seminar building. In keeping with the university's strong "green" credentials, a biomass generator facility has been provided that should reduce the university's carbon emissions dramatically.

Some of the broad subject combinations that the university pioneered from its origins in the 1960s – such as development studies and environmental sciences – are highly regarded in the academic world. With successive 5* ratings for research followed by a good result in the 2008 Research Assessment Exercise, environmental sciences is the flagship school. The Climatic Research Unit and the Government-funded Tyndall Centre for Climate Change Research are among the leaders in the investigation of climate change. The university was at the centre of international controversy regarding climate data manipulation, but enquiries on two continents proved the allegations to be groundless, though a lack of openness was criticised. UEA contributed more than any other university in the world to the 2007 Nobel Prize-winning Intergovernmental Panel on Climate Change.

History of art and culture and media did even better in the latest RAE, with half of their research considered world-leading. Art history has the benefit of the Sainsbury Centre for the Visual Arts, perhaps the

---

Norwich NR4 7TJ

01603 591515 (admissions office)
admissions@uea.ac.uk
www.uea.ac.uk
www.ueastudent.com
Affiliation: 1994 Group

The Times Rankings

Overall Ranking: **27**

Student satisfaction:	=7	(83%)
Research quality:	=30	(2.0)
Entry standards:	32	(386)
Student–staff ratio:	=24	(14.9)
Services & facilities/student:	27	(£1,688)
Expected completion rate:	=32	(90.2%)
Good honours:	=29	(69.6%)
Graduate prospects:	49	(66.1%)

greatest resource of its type on any British campus. The centre, which has been refurbished and extended, houses a priceless collection of modern and tribal art, in a building designed by Norman Foster. Creative writing is another star-studded area, with authors Andrew Cowan, Giles Foden and Lavinia Greenlaw taking up where Andrew Motion and the late Malcolm Bradbury left off.

Health studies have been among UEA's fastest-developing areas. The university was awarded one of the first new medical schools for 20 years, graduating its first doctors in 2007, and has since added pharmacy and speech and language therapy degree courses.

Almost nine out of ten undergraduates come from state schools or colleges, and over a quarter have a working-class background. Most have the opportunity of work experience as part of their course. An academic adviser guides all students on their options under the modular course system and monitors their progress through to graduation. The university is proposing to focus even more on employability when £9,000 fees are introduced in 2012. Almost a third of undergraduates are expected to benefit from fee waivers or bursaries of up to £3,000 and there will be scholarships of £1,500 for students who achieve three A grades at A level or the equivalent.

Dropout rates have fluctuated, but the latest projected figure of less than 9 per cent was below the national average for the university's subjects and entry standards. Most students come from outside the region, although there is an unusually large contingent of mature students for a traditional university, who tend to be more local. UEA opened University Campus Suffolk in 2007, in partnership with Essex University, with a main site in Ipswich and smaller bases in Bury St Edmunds, Great Yarmouth, Lowestoft and Otley.

The university is situated in parkland, with easy access to the medieval city of Norwich, which has been voted one of the best small cities in the world. The Sportspark boasts an Olympic-sized swimming pool, fitness and aerobics centres, athletics track, climbing wall, courts and pitches. The university was chosen as the base for the English Institute of Sport in the East.

Undergraduate Fees and Support

» Fees for UK/EU students 2012–13 £9,000
» Fees for International students 2011–12 £11,000–£13,700
£23,250 (medicine)
» Students with household income up to £30K, are eligible for fee waivers on a sliding scale.
» Entrants to Science Foundation Year programmes with household income of less than £42.6K eligible for £4,500 fee waiver.
» Excellence Scholarships worth £1,500 in the form of a fee waiver for students achieving AAA or equivalent.
» Check the university's website for the latest information.

Students		
Undergraduates:	**10,275**	**(2,735)**
Postgraduates:	**2,275**	**(1,360)**
Mature students:	**18.3%**	
Overseas students:	**12.1%**	
Applications per place:	**6.2**	
From state-sector schools:	**88.3%**	
From working-class homes:	**27.6%**	

For detailed information about fees, grants and bursaries and how they work, see chapter 7.

Accommodation

Number of places and costs refer to 2011–12
University-provided places: 3,457
Percentage catered: 0%
Self-catered costs: £2,058.84–£3,926.16 (38 weeks)
First years are guaranteed accommodation if conditions are met.
Distance restrictions.
International students (non EU) are guaranteed accommodation if conditions are met.
Contact: accom@uea.ac.uk
www.uea.ac.uk/accommodation

University of East London

East London (UEL) will charge the full £9,000 undergraduate tuition fee in every subject from 2012. The university says the fee level reflects the degree of investment required to deliver the quality of teaching and facilities that its students expect and deserve, following the reduction in government teaching grant. It is also promising a "generous package" of scholarships and bursaries to help with living costs and ensure that potential students are not deterred from accessing higher education.

The university has spent more than £190 million on its Docklands campus, and is now unrecognisable from its early days as a pioneering polytechnic. Student residences and recreational facilities sit side by side with academic buildings in a prize-winning waterside development for more than 7,000 students. The final pieces in the jigsaw were the business school and Knowledge Dock, a support centre for local companies, and a £40-million student village by the Royal Albert Dock, which added 800 more beds. The campus has helped to attract substantial growth in applications to UEL – there was a 31 per cent increase in 2010 and another 13 per cent rise at the start of 2011. Student numbers have almost doubled since 2001, with students coming from 120 countries.

The capital's first new campus for 50 years gave the university a new focal point, with its modern version of traditional university features like cloisters and squares. The United States Olympic team is to be based at UEL for the 2012 Games. The logistical and operational team will use a new £21-million sports and academic centre at the Docklands campus, called the Sports Dock, which is due to open at the end of 2011. UEL's new Vice-Chancellor, Professor Patrick McGhee, has said that that the university's Olympic and Paralympic involvement, together with its location and the diversity of its students, give it a unique role in the area's regeneration.

The university's original Stratford campus is also being redeveloped, with a new library and learning centre, student residences and facilities for part-time and evening courses. The Great Hall in University House boasts a high-tech, 230-seat fully retractable lecture theatre, while the health and bioscience laboratories have been refurbished. The new Cass School of Education has now opened and law is next on the development agenda. A unique partnership project between UEL and Birkbeck, University of London, will see a new campus open in Stratford in 2013. The Stratford Island University Centre will house a selection of departments from each university and incorporate a range of flexible teaching and administrative spaces, alongside dedicated spaces for subjects including law, performing arts, dance, music and information technology.

Stratford Campus
Water Lane
London E15 4LZ

020 8223 3333 (admissions)
study@uel.ac.uk
www.uel.ac.uk
www.uelunion.org
Affiliation: million+

The Times Rankings
Overall Ranking: **115**

Student satisfaction:	=106	(70%)
Research quality:	=70	(0.4)
Entry standards:	115	(200)
Student–staff ratio:	=111	(23.3)
Services & facilities/student:	108	(£998)
Expected completion rate:	107	(74.5%)
Good honours:	=111	(44.4%)
Graduate prospects:	112	(48.6%)

All but one of the nine subject areas in which UEL entered the 2008 Research Assessment Exercise contained at least some world-leading research. In communication, culture and media studies, the proportion was 20 per cent, with another 60 per cent of work rated internationally excellent. Art and design and sociology also produced good results. Teacher training courses have been given good marks by the Office for Standards in Education. Accounting, English studies and law achieved the best results in what was overall a poor set of scores in the 2010 National Student Survey, which left UEL towards the bottom of the satisfaction league table.

UEL's focus is more concerned with extending access to higher education than competing with the elite universities. Barely more than half of new first years arrive with A levels and a majority are over 21 on entry – many choosing to start courses in February. Many degrees are vocational and employers are closely involved in course planning. Almost 1,000 businesses, including many in the City or Canary Wharf, are involved in mentoring programmes and/or a work-based learning initiative which offers accredited placements.

Almost half of UEL's students come from working-class homes and over 98 per cent are state-school educated, many from the area's large ethnic minority populations. A successful mentoring scheme for black and Asian students has become a model for other institutions, while a guidance unit advises local people considering returning to education. UEL is also strong on provision for disabled students and houses the Rix Centre for Innovation and Learning Disability. The projected dropout rate has been improving – the latest figure of 14.5 per cent is better than the national average for UEL's courses and entry qualifications.

University-owned accommodation is not plentiful, although there are now more than 1,200 bedspaces overall and the rents are good value for London. Priority is given to disabled students and those living furthest away. The social mix means that UEL has not been the place to look for the archetypal partying student lifestyle, although the Docklands campus is beginning to change this. Sports facilities and new students' union premises have been added at both Stratford and Docklands.

Undergraduate Fees and Support

» Fees for UK/EU students 2012–13   £9,000
» Fees for International students 2011–12   £9,300–£13,200
» Details of a package of bursaries and scholarships, on top of what it currently provides, and enhanced graduate employability programmes to be announced.
» Scholarships and bursaries based on circumstances or by competition are available.
» Check the university's website for the latest information.

Students

Undergraduates:	**13,720**	**(4,975)**
Postgraduates:	**4,315**	**(3,920)**
Mature students:	**57.9%**	
Overseas students:	**12.5%**	
Applications per place:	**3.7**	
From state-sector schools:	**98.4%**	
From working-class homes:	**47.2%**	

For detailed information about fees, grants and bursaries and how they work, see chapter 7.

Accommodation

Number of places and costs refer to 2010–11
University-provided places: 1,200
Percentage catered: 0%
Self-catered costs: £101–£125 a week (39 weeks)
First years not guaranteed accommodation; priority given to disabled students and to those living furthest away.
International students: same as above.
Docklands Campus 020 8223 5093/4
dlres@uel.ac.uk

Edge Hill University

Edge Hill surprised many observers with its decision to charge £9,000 undergraduate fees in all subjects. But the university insists that, after losing 95 per cent of its teaching grant, it had no choice if it was to continue enhancing its students' learning experience. Based at Ormskirk, near Liverpool, the university has been one of the fastest growing in the UK, as well as one of the newest. It has more than doubled its complement of students since the millennium to reach 25,000, although only 8,000 of them are on full-time undergraduate courses. Applications increased three-fold in a decade, culminating in a 31 per cent rise in 2010. Rapid growth often does universities no favours in rankings, but Edge Hill moved 22 places up *The Times* League Table in the last two years and has remained in the top 80 in the new edition.

There are plans for significant expansion with the recent purchase of land adjoining the existing site, but the next generation of students will have to make do with improvements to the current campus. Some £130 million has been spent on it already and more is on the way. A £14-million home to house the Faculty of Health, the SOLSTICE e-learning centre and a 900-seat theatre were completed in 2007. A £8-million Business School opened in 2009, when additional student residences also came on stream.

Although university status arrived only in 2005, Edge Hill has been training teachers since the 19th century. Having moved to its 75-acre landscaped campus in the 1930s, it has long since expanded into other subjects, but it remains the largest provider of secondary teacher training and courses for classroom assistants. It has also won the lion's share of funding to deliver further training for qualified secondary school teachers.

A £5-million expansion of resources for the performing arts opened in 2005 and there are industry-standard facilities for animation, TV and other media areas. SOLSTICE (which stands for Supported Online Learning for Students using Technology for Information and Communication in their Education) is recognised officially as a national centre of excellence in teaching and learning. It has a particular focus on learning in the workplace, but is involved with curriculum development and delivery in all three of the university's faculties.

Other big recruiters are health, business, sport and media courses. Nursing, midwifery and other health care programmes have been commended by inspectors and the unversity's primary and secondary teacher training courses have been rated as outstanding by Ofsted. Courses are determinedly job-related – three quarters of graduates leave with professional accreditation. A recent addition is Chinese studies as a joint honours programme with English or business.

St Helens Road
Ormskirk
Lancashire L39 4QP

01695 575171
enquiries@edgehill.ac.uk
www.edgehill.ac.uk
www.edgehillsu.com
Affiliation: none

The Times Rankings

Overall Ranking: **77**

Student satisfaction:	=24	(79%)
Research quality:	=105	(0.1)
Entry standards:	=92	(260)
Student–staff ratio:	=60	(18.5)
Services & facilities/student:	94	(£1,107)
Expected completion rate:	94	(79.1%)
Good honours:	98	(51.1%)
Graduate prospects:	56	(63.2%)

All students have a personal tutor, as well as access to counsellors and financial advice. Satisfaction levels have been consistently above average in the National Student Survey, with particularly good scores for students' personal development. Physical geography and environmental science produced 100 per cent satisfaction in 2010, with geography, history, imaginative writing, nursing, creative arts and subjects allied to medicine all exceeding 90 per cent.

Beyond Ormskirk, there are seven satellite campuses in Liverpool, Manchester and other parts of the North West to facilitate local learning. The largest is based in the grounds of University Hospital Aintree, where students in the Faculty of Health can see at first-hand how a busy hospital runs. In addition, a range of further education colleges in the North West teach the university's Foundation degrees.

Edge Hill has one of the highest proportions of state-educated students in England – 99 per cent. Over four in ten undergraduates have a working-class background and almost a quarter come from areas without a tradition of higher education – far above the national average for the university's courses and entry qualifications. The projected dropout rate has increased in the latest survey, but 14.5 per cent is still below the university's benchmark.

Before the fees went up, Edge Hill won an award for a student finance support package that rewarded achievement, as well as encouraging students to complete their studies, rather than simply offering incentives for enrolling. The university is proposing to expand the Excellence Scholarship Scheme with the income from increased fees, spending at least £100,000 on awards in sport, the performing arts, volunteering and the creative arts.

The university has been rated among the cheapest in the UK for accommodation and overall cost of living. There are now over 1,000 hall spaces, although first years aren't guaranteed housing. The £3.9-million Sporting Edge complex, which was part funded by a Lottery grant, is open to staff, students and the local community. The university was chosen as a pre-Olympic training centre for athletics, road cycling and archery.

Undergraduate Fees and Support

» Fees for UK/EU students 2012–13   £9,000
» Fees for International students 2011–12   £9,900
» Details of a package of financial support, including matched funding for over 110 National Scholarships, and widening participation and retention activity to be announced.
» Excellence Scholarships on entrance, including competitive awards for "Determination, Commitment and Achievement" in sport, performing arts, creative arts, volunteering.
» Check the university's website for the latest information.

Students

Undergraduates:	**8,140**	**(6,605)**
Postgraduates:	**900**	**(9,675)**
Mature students:	**26.8%**	
Overseas students:	**2.4%**	
Applications per place:	**4.5**	
From state-sector schools:	**99.0%**	
From working-class homes:	**44.0%**	

For detailed information about fees, grants and bursaries and how they work, see chapter 7.

Accommodation

Number of places and costs refer to 2010–11
University provided places: 1,045
Percentage catered: 29%
Catered costs: £87 a week (38–40 weeks)
Self-catered costs: £54–£93 a week (40 weeks)
First years cannot be guaranteed housing. Residential restrictions apply.
Students designated overseas for fees are guaranteed accommodation if conditions are met.
Contact: www.edgehill.ac.uk/study/accommodation

University of Edinburgh

Edinburgh retains a special status in Scotland, where the university is regarded as the nearest thing to Oxbridge north of the border. Despite having to play second fiddle to St Andrews in our League Table recently, it is seldom far from the top ten in the UK and was in the top 20 universities in the world in the latest QS World University Rankings. The presence of more than 6,000 international students testifies to its worldwide reputation.

Edinburgh is the largest university in Scotland, with around 26,000 students. The university's buildings are spread around the city, but most border the historic Old Town. These include the university's main library, which has been redeveloped at a cost of £60 million. The science and engineering campus is two miles to the south.

Competition for places is greater than ever: almost 12 applications for each place in 2010. However, as in many of the leading universities, applications were down 15 per cent in 2011 after a slight decrease the previous year as well.

Like Oxbridge, Edinburgh has been trying to widen its intake. More than £32 million has been raised for 200 access bursaries of at least £1,000 a year. Other measures include an eight-week summer school for teenagers from local schools and support for students in the transition to higher education and later in their courses. The university has always attracted a high proportion of middle-class candidates – many from England – and is a favourite in independent schools, whose students take about three places in ten. Selection guidelines aim to look more broadly at candidates' potential. The university reduced its minimum entry requirements to consider a wider pool of candidates and place more weight on references and personal statements. It also gives extra credit in some oversubscribed programmes to applicants from Scotland and the north of England, from Teesside to Cumbria.

The university, which is a member of the Russell Group of 20 leading UK research universities, has stepped up its fundraising activities. They have already contributed to a new informatics building, as well as to the development of a "BioQuarter", a ground-breaking collaboration between the university and a number of public bodies that is intended to consolidate Scotland's reputation as a world leader in biomedical science. In 2010, the author J.K. Rowling gave £10 million to the university to set up a new research clinic for multiple sclerosis patients.

The Business School has relocated to the heart of the main campus and a new research centre has been established for the study of Islamic civilisation and issues relating to Islam in Britain. Elsewhere an £80-million redevelopment of the university's Easter

---

Old College
South Bridge
Edinburgh EH8 9YL

0131 651 1905 (admissions)
sra.enquiries@ed.ac.uk
www.ed.ac.uk
www.eusa.ed.ac.uk
Affiliation: Russell Group

The Times Rankings
Overall Ranking: **15**

Student satisfaction:	=63	(76%)
Research quality:	=4	(3.0)
Entry standards:	12	(442)
Student–staff ratio:	=18	(14.4)
Services & facilities/student:	12	(£2,043)
Expected completion rate:	22	(92.5%)
Good honours:	7	(81.3%)
Graduate prospects:	21	(72.4%)

Bush site is nearing completion. A vet school building, a research building for the recently incorporated Roslin Institute and a cancer centre will open in 2011. Around the same time, a new building to house the MRC Centre for Regenerative Medicine will open at Little France.

Almost two thirds of the work submitted for the 2008 Research Assessment Exercise was rated as world-leading or internationally excellent, the highest proportion in Scotland. The university's entry was among the largest in the UK and produced strong results across the board. The College of Medicine and Veterinary Medicine was the star performer, with all of the work in hospital-based clinical subjects rated at the international level and 40 per cent at the highest grade. Informatics, linguistics and English literature also produced outstanding results.

Scores in the National Student Survey improved considerably in 2010, placing Edinburgh among the top 30 universities. There was 100 per cent satisfaction in archaeology and sociology, and very high scores in theology, human and social geography, subjects allied to medicine, psychology and nursing. Departments organise visiting days in October for those thinking of applying and in the spring for those holding offers, as well as the annual open day in June. New undergraduates generally take three subjects in both their first and second years. Every student has a Director of Studies to help them narrow down the selection of a final degree and give personal advice when necessary.

A new £4.5 million extension to the University's Centre for Sport and Exercise was unveiled in 2010, adding to the already impressive sports facilities. Considerable sums have also been spent making the university more accessible to the 1,600 disabled students. All students are issued with a smart card for access to university facilities. The students' union operates on several sites.

The city is a treasure-trove of cultural and recreational opportunities. Most students thrive on Edinburgh life, even though the cost of living can make it difficult to do it justice. Some scientists complain of isolation, although there is a regular bus link with the main university area around George Square. Plentiful residential accommodation means first years are guaranteed an offer of housing.

Undergraduate Fees and Support
» Fees 2012–13: awaiting Scottish Government policy.
» Fees for Scottish and EU students 2011–12 No fee
» Fees for non-Scottish UK-domiciled students 2011–12 £1,820
  £2,895 (medicine)
» Fees for international students 2011–12 £12,050–£15,850
  £15,850–£33,200 (medicine)
» Scholarships and bursaries based on circumstances or by competition are available.
» Check the university's website for the latest information.

Students

Undergraduates:	**17,305**	**(655)**
Postgraduates:	**5,580**	**(2,155)**
Mature students:	**9.2%**	
Overseas students:	**17.6%**	
Applications per place:	**11.9**	
From state-sector schools:	**70.8%**	
From working-class homes:	**18.6%**	

For detailed information about fees, grants and bursaries and how they work, see chapter 7.

Accommodation
Number of places and costs refer to 2011–12
University-provided places: about 6,300
Percentage catered: about 30%
Catered costs: £113–£226 a week
Self-catered costs: £58–£127 a week.
First years are guaranteed an offer of accommodation providing they fulfil requirements. Residential restrictions apply.
International students: accommodation guaranteed if conditions are met.
Contact: www.accom.ed.ac.uk

Edinburgh Napier University

For two years in a row, Edinburgh Napier has enjoyed among the biggest increases in applications at any UK university. At the start of 2011, growth was more than 25 per cent, following an astonishing 45 per cent rise in the previous year. Although partly fuelled by UK-wide changes in art and design and nursing qualifications, the unprecedented demand for places is a reflection of the university's growing popularity.

With over 14,000 students from 115 different countries, Napier is now one of Scotland's biggest. The university attracts nearly 3,000 international students, who make up more than 20 per cent of the intake. Professor Dame Joan Stringer, who was the first woman to lead a university north of the border, has set Napier a target of becoming "one of the leading modern universities in the United Kingdom". A £100-million redevelopment programme is well underway to help achieve that ambition.

The latest phase has seen the reopening of the Sighthill campus with new facilities that bring the Faculty of Health, Life and Social Sciences together on a single site. Students will benefit from a learning resource centre, clinical skills laboratories, an environmental chamber and biomechanics laboratory, a crime scene scenario room, as well as integrated sports facilities. The new gym and sports centre include a large fitness suite and a sports hall that will be available to the local community as well as students and staff.

Once Scotland's first and largest polytechnic, the university is named after John Napier, the inventor of logarithms. The tower where he was born still sits among the concrete blocks of the Merchiston campus in the city's main student district. The 500-seat computing centre is open all hours, and students have access to online lecture notes and study aids via WebCT. There are fully networked libraries at each campus, and a multimedia language lab and adaptive technology centre for students with special needs.

The Craiglockhart campus houses Scotland's biggest business school and features a glass atrium housing a cyber café and two spherical lecture theatres with a total of 600 seats, as well as a new fitness suite. The Edinburgh Skillset Screen and Media Academy, run in partnership with Edinburgh College of Art, reflects the university's strong reputation in film education. The university is also planning a new 725-bed student residence in the city centre, which should be ready in Summer 2013. There are several smaller sites, mainly in the leafy south of Edinburgh, ranging from a converted church to a former school, as well as outposts in Melrose and Livingston.

An International College, launched in

Craiglockhart Campus
Edinburgh EH14 1DJ

08452 606040 (switchboard)
info@napier.ac.uk
also contact via website
www.napier.ac.uk
www.napierstudents.com
Affiliation: million+

The Times Rankings
Overall Ranking: =71

Student satisfaction:	=63	(76%)
Research quality:	=79	(0.3)
Entry standards:	58	(296)
Student–staff ratio:	=101	(21.6)
Services & facilities/student:	=91	(£1,133)
Expected completion rate:	106	(75.5%)
Good honours:	62	(61.3%)
Graduate prospects:	=35	(69.3%)

EDINBURGH
Belfast
London
Cardiff

2007, offers overseas students a dedicated service, with pastoral and recruitment activities, as well as support for Edinburgh Napier's programmes in China, Hong Kong and India. Closer to home, the university has developed significantly through partnerships with colleges. The development of approximately 2,000 college "articulation routes" has enabled students to use their college qualifications to gain direct entry into year two or three of a university degree. Widening participation is high on the university's list of priorities: more than a third of the undergraduates come from working-class homes.

Most of Edinburgh Napier's avowedly vocational courses include a work placement, and the close relationship with industry and commerce helps to produce consistently good graduate employment figures. The modular course system allows movement between courses at all levels and has allowed students the option of starting courses in February, rather than September.

Edinburgh Napier has been held up as a model to other universities trying to reduce non-completion rates. The university uses its own students to mentor newcomers, runs bridging programmes and offers pre-term introductions to staff and information on facilities, as well as running summer top-up courses in a variety of subjects. The Confident Futures programme helps students make the transition to higher education and teaches employability skills and personal development. However, the latest projected dropout rate of more than 15 per cent, is above the UK average for the subjects on offer.

Nine Institutes of Research Excellence have recently been established at Edinburgh Napier each offering expertise in different areas. Library and information management achieved by far the best results in the 2008 Research Assessment Exercise, when just over a fifth of the university's submission was considered world-leading or internationally excellent. The University's Building Performance Centre was awarded the Queen's Anniversary Prize in 2009 for "innovative housing construction for environmental benefit and quality of life".

The dispersed nature of the university does nothing for the social scene, although Edinburgh is hardly dull. Some students find life too quiet in the evenings and at weekends, although the students' association, in partnership with local clubs, organises regular party nights in the city centre.

Undergraduate Fees and Support

» Fees 2012–13:   awaiting Scottish Government policy.
» Fees for Scottish and EU students 2011–12   No fee
» Fees for non-Scottish UK-domiciled students 2011–12   £1,820
» Fees for international students 2011–12   £9,310–£10,820
» Scholarships and bursaries based on circumstances or by competition are available.
» Check the university's website for the latest information.

Students

Undergraduates:	**9,645**	**(1,960)**
Postgraduates:	**1,105**	**(1,390)**
Mature students:	**46.3%**	
Overseas students:	**21.4%**	
Applications per place:	**5.0**	
From state-sector schools:	**94.6%**	
From working-class homes:	**34.9%**	

For detailed information about fees, grants and bursaries and how they work, see chapter 7.

Accommodation

Number of places and costs refer to 2011–12
University-provided places: 956
Percentage catered: 0%
Self-catered costs: £96–£99 average cost a week.
First years and direct entrants undergraduates are guaranteed a place provided requirements are met. Residential restrictions apply.
International students: as above.
Contact: accommodation@napier.ac.uk

University of Essex

Essex will charge £9,000 fees in all subjects from 2012, but is promising to invest significantly in scholarships and bursaries to preserve the breadth of its intake. It will make the change from a position of strength: the 24 per cent increase in applications in 2010 was one of the biggest at any pre-1992 university and the start of 2011 saw another 8 per cent rise. The university has acquired a reputation for high-quality research, especially in the social sciences, which led to a strong set of results in the 2008 Research Assessment Exercise (RAE). Essex has also been doing well in the National Student Survey.

There are little more than 11,000 full-time students, about a fifth of whom are post-graduates. The student population is unusually diverse for a traditional university, with high proportions of mature and overseas students. More than a third of the undergrad-uates are from working-class homes and almost 96 per cent went to state schools or colleges – both higher figures than the subject mix would suggest.

Sociology and politics led the way in the latest RAE where almost two thirds of the work submitted by the university was found to be world-leading or internationally excellent. Both politics and sociology produced the best results in the country, while the newly formed Essex Business School ranked second in the UK for accounting and finance. Philosophy achieved a 100 per cent approval rating in the 2010 National Student Survey, while biology, economics, drama, linguistics and politics were all in the top ten in their field. An overall satisfaction rate of 88 per cent represented a big improvement on the previous year and placed Essex among the top 20 universities.

The university has been building up its science departments – the biological sciences department is now one of its largest. Computer science is also strong and a BSc in computer games and internet technology shows Essex keeping pace with changing demands in graduate employment. But improvements in the university's academic performance could not disguise the fact that the glass and concrete campus, set in 200 acres of parkland on the outskirts of Colchester, was showing distinct signs of wear and tear. The university has been carrying out major refurbishments at the same time as expanding student facilities.

The incorporation of the East 15 Acting School, in Loughton, enhanced the university's provision in theatre studies, and was the university's first venture beyond Colchester. There has been heavy investment in a third campus, in Southend, which opened in 2007, offering courses in business, health education and the arts. It also includes health

---

Wivenhoe Park
Colchester
Essex CO4 3SQ

01206 873666 (enquiries)
admit@essex.ac.uk
www.essex.ac.uk
www.essexstudent.com
Affiliation: 1994 Group

The Times Rankings
Overall Ranking: **41**

Student satisfaction:	=37	(78%)
Research quality:	=25	(2.1)
Entry standards:	50	(307)
Student–staff ratio:	34	(15.6)
Services & facilities/student:	34	(£1,594)
Expected completion rate:	47	(86.7%)
Good honours:	67	(59.3%)
Graduate prospects:	77	(58.6%)

and dental facilities, the latter staffed by senior dental students from Barts and the London School of Medicine and Dentistry. The Gateway Building has become a focal point of the town centre, while a £5-million church restoration produced rehearsal space and a theatre.

Another regional project sees Essex collaborating with the University of East Anglia on University Campus Suffolk, which offers courses in Ipswich and at smaller centres across the county. Essex degrees are also taught at Writtle College, near Chelmsford, the Colchester Institute and South East Essex College, in Southend.

Essex announced a capital development programme in excess of £200-million in the lead-up to its 50th anniversary in 2014. A new teaching centre and gym opened on its Colchester Campus last year and student accommodation was expanded at Southend. A new Student Centre and library extension at Colchester and a new library and learning centre at Southend are planned for coming years. The Colchester library has already been extended once and is open for over 84 hours a week, with the Large Reading Room open all hours, Monday to Thursday, and seven days a week in the summer term. Sustainable energy and technology are being used whenever possible, with recent projects featuring ground source heat pumps and a wind turbine. Work is set to start on the £10-million transformation of the historic Wivenhoe House into the UK's first country house hotel to be run and staffed by students, supervised by industry professionals.

Essex champions academic breadth, and students follow a common first year before specialising. They may take four or five different subjects before committing themselves to a particular degree. Social and sporting facilities are good, following a £1.4-million extension of the Sports Centre, as well as the refurbishment of the students' union bars and nightclub. Some 40 acres of land are devoted to sports facilities.

First years new to Colchester are guaranteed university accommodation, which in 2009 won the "best halls of residence" category in the National Student Housing survey. All university accommodation is now networked to the IT system and equipped with telephones giving free access to the internal phone system. Some ground-floor flats have been adapted for disabled students.

Undergraduate Fees and Support

» Fees for UK/EU students 2012–13 £9,000
» Fees for International students 2011–12 £10,750–£12,750
» Details of a package of targeted bursaries and scholarships to support the most able students, regardless of social background, and outreach activities to be announced.
» Scholarships and bursaries based on circumstances or by competition are available.
» Check the university's website for the latest information.

Students		
Undergraduates:	8,870	(2,135)
Postgraduates:	2,335	(1,140)
Mature students:	22.1%	
Overseas students:	21.1%	
Applications per place:	5.3	
From state-sector schools:	95.9%	
From working-class homes:	38.9%	

For detailed information about fees, grants and bursaries and how they work, see chapter 7.

Accommodation

Number of places and costs refer to 2011–12

University-provided places: 4,061

Percentage catered: 0%

Self-catered costs: £65.38 (South Towers) – £112.07 (South Court en suite) a week.

New first years living outside the borough of Colchester are guaranteed accommodation if conditions are met.

International students: new students are guaranteed accommodation if conditions are met.

Contact: admit@essex.ac.uk

University of Exeter

Exeter was one of the first universities to plump for the maximum undergraduate fee from 2012, having decided that £9,000 was needed to direct resources at widening participation, fair access and improving the student experience. The university remains in the top ten in *The Times* League Table, which it entered for the first time last year, despite slipping two positions. Good results in the National Student Survey and the Research Assessment Exercise (RAE) were largely responsible. There was a surprisingly large drop in applications for courses beginning in 2011, but selection remains highly competitive – especially in English literature, drama, law, history and psychology.

Exeter is one of the strongest performers in the National Student Survey, featuring in the top ten since the survey began. The university maintained this record in 2010, with an overall satisfaction rate of 88 per cent. There was a 100 per cent satisfaction among final-year classics and theology undergraduates, while accounting, drama and politics all produced extremely high scores.

The 2008 RAE saw Exeter move up the pecking order of research universities, with most of its work judged to be world-leading or internationally excellent despite a much larger submission (involving 95 per cent of academics) than most of its peers. English, classics, archaeology, and accounting and finance did particularly well. The successes produced one of the biggest increases in research funding at any English university.

Exeter boasts one of the most attractive settings of any university, and is currently investing more than £270 million on its main campus. This includes £130 million for student residences, substantial investment in the business school and new facilities for biosciences. The jewel in the crown of the new developments is the Forum, a new £48-million student services centre which will include an extended library and more learning, social and retail facilities. Most of this work will be complete by 2012.

Almost a third of the undergraduates come from independent schools – a much higher proportion than the national average for Exeter's subjects, although this figure has been dropping. Professor Steve Smith, the Vice-Chancellor, has put broadening the social mix at the top of his agenda, particularly targeting schools and colleges in the rural South West. Location is partly responsible for the relatively rarefied social mix. Lacking a large centre of population and despite sophisticated shopping and a lively entertainment scene, South West cathedral cities are not what every teenager is looking for. Nevertheless, the city has been attracting new businesses like the Met Office and benefiting from major investment such as the £235-million Princesshay shopping centre.

Northcote House
The Queen's Drive
Exeter, Devon EX4 4QJ

01392 263855 (admissions)
ug-ad@exeter.ac.uk
www.exeter.ac.uk
www.pcmd.ac.uk
www.exeterguild.org
www.fxu.org.uk
Affiliation: 1994 Group

The Times Rankings
Overall Ranking: **10**

Student satisfaction:	=7	(83%)
Research quality:	=12	(2.6)
Entry standards:	13	(439)
Student–staff ratio:	=66	(19)
Services & facilities/student:	17	(£1,948)
Expected completion rate:	4	(96.5%)
Good honours:	5	(82.8%)
Graduate prospects:	=29	(70.3%)

A £100-million campus near Falmouth, in Cornwall, has helped boost applications. Shared with University College Falmouth, the campus offers Exeter degrees in bioscience, geography, English, history and politics plus a range of degrees, such as mining engineering that are not available in Exeter. The latest development in Cornwall is a £30-million Environment and Sustainability Institute that will help put the university at the forefront of environmental and climate change research.

The other big development of recent years was the opening of Peninsula College of Medicine and Dentistry, in association with Plymouth University. Recruitment has been strong and Peninsula was the only successful bidder for a new dental school in 2006. The four-year Bachelor of Dental Surgery has an annual intake of 64 science graduates or health service professionals.

Arabic and Islamic studies have benefited from support from the Middle East. Exeter's longstanding international focus is exemplified by the growing range of four-year programmes "with international study" and by its 180 partner universities worldwide. All students are offered tuition in foreign languages and even some three-year degrees include the option of a year abroad.

Career management skills are built into degree programmes and students can gain work experience through the university's employability and business project programmes. The Employability and Graduate Development Service has been expanded to increase the work experience and placement opportunities available to students. The university's Exeter Award provides official recognition of all the extra-curricular activities that students undertake to enhance their employability. There is a particularly strong record of voluntary activities.

The main Streatham campus, close to the centre of Exeter, has a lively social scene. The highly rated departments of education and sport and health sciences are a mile away at the St Luke's campus. Some £11 million has been invested in sports facilities, which are among the best in the country. Exeter is one of only nine UK universities to have indoor tennis facilities to national competition standards and a new £2-million cricket centre opened in 2009. Exeter is one of the UK's top sporting universities and was placed tenth in the 2009–10 national rankings.

Undergraduate Fees and Support

» Fees for UK/EU students 2012–13 £9,000
» Fees for International students 2010–11 £12,200–£14,500
£13,200–£21,500 (medicine)
» A package of fee waivers, bursaries and outreach activities including National Scholarship partial fee waiver of £3,000 for students with a household income below £16K. UK Access to Exeter bursaries of £1,500 – £750 on a sliding scale for students with household income up to £35K.
» Check the university's website for the latest information.

Students

Undergraduates:	**12,335**	**(180)**
Postgraduates:	**3,840**	**(1,360)**
Mature students:	**8.4%**	
Overseas students:	**16.5%**	
Applications per place:	**7.2**	
From state-sector schools:	**70.9%**	
From working-class homes:	**20.8%**	

For detailed information about fees, grants and bursaries and how they work, see chapter 7.

Accommodation

Number of places and costs refer to 2011–12
University-provided places: 5,016
Percentage catered: 32%
Catered costs: £119.00–£196.42 a week (31 weeks)
Self-catered costs: £77.63–£129.00 a week (40, 44 or 51 weeks).
Unaccompanied first years are guaranteed accommodation provided conditions are met.
International students: as above.
Contact: accommodation@exeter.ac.uk

University of Glamorgan

Glamorgan, which has taken to adding Cardiff and Pontypridd to its title, is investing £130 million in new facilities to enhance the experience of its students. The latest developments include a £15-million expansion for health, science and sport students, new halls of residence and specialised teaching facilities. The university has already added a new students' union building on the Treforest campus, a new home for the Law School in a listed building and the £35-million ATRiuM campus in the heart of Cardiff.

The university has been growing in popularity, with the 12 per cent increase in applications just the latest in a series of rises. The opening of the ultra-modern ATRiuM building in 2007 made a crucial difference, increasing the demand for courses based in the capital by more than 60 per cent. The university's Cardiff School of Creative and Cultural Industries offers an "eclectic mix of teaching and research in the theory and practice of media, design and the arts". Students there also have access to 1,206 rooms in privately run halls of residence.

The new development followed a merger with the Royal Welsh College of Music and Drama, with its conservatoire courses. Most of Glamorgan's 21,000 students still remain on the Treforest campus, 20 minutes by train from Cardiff, overlooking the market town of Pontypridd. Others take Glamorgan courses in five overseas centres or in a growing number of further education colleges across Wales. Four have become accredited colleges, guaranteeing places on degree courses if students meet set conditions, while Merthyr Tydfil College has become the university's Faculty of Further Education.

The university produced good results in the 2008 Research Assessment Exercise, albeit from a low entry in most subjects. Almost a third of the work submitted was judged to be world-leading or internationally excellent, with English and nursing and midwifery doing especially well.

Originally based in a large country house, Glamorgan now has a large, modern campus. The Law School moved to new premises on the main campus in 2008 with upgraded facilities including a moot courtroom, while accommodation for mathematics and computing has had a £5-million refurbishment. The Faculty of Health Sport and Science are on the Glyntaff site, a short walk from the main campus. They are housed in new buildings and restored tramsheds, a reminder of the industrial past of the area. The popular Institute of Chiropractic is one of only two university-based centres for training chiropractors in the UK.

The business school is the largest in Wales, and the university was among the first providers of Foundation degrees. The range of two-year courses has since expanded

---

Pontypridd
Mid Glamorgan CF37 1DL

08456 434 030 (enquiries)
contact via website
www.glam.ac.uk
www.glamsu.com
Affiliation: University
  Alliance

The Times Rankings
Overall Ranking: **93**

Student satisfaction:	=78	(74%)
Research quality:	=70	(0.4)
Entry standards:	71	(279)
Student–staff ratio:	=82	(20.2)
Services & facilities/student:	56	(£1,362)
Expected completion rate:	108	(74.4%)
Good honours:	75	(57.6%)
Graduate prospects:	97	(54.3%)

rapidly, covering subjects as diverse as football and rugby coaching, surveying and costume construction. The vocational approach pays dividends for graduate employment, which is consistently good, although the projected dropout rate is above average for the university's courses and entry qualifications, at more than 20 per cent, despite considerable improvement in the latest figures. Glamorgan exceeds all its access benchmarks: almost 40 per cent of undergraduates come from working-class homes and 14 per cent are from areas with no tradition of higher education. Three quarters of the 17,000 campus-based students are from Wales, but a healthy 3,700 are from outside the UK.

The university did well in the early rounds of the National Student Survey, but has since slipped into the bottom half of the table. There were some good scores in 2010, however: combined studies, geography, history, philosophy, creative writing, law, maths, nursing and environmental science all recorded satisfaction levels of more than 90 per cent. The Faculty of Advanced Technology has been designated a centre of excellence for Wales, while three National Partnership awards testify to high standards in course design and delivery. Degrees in computer forensics, computer games development, lighting and design technology and aerospace courses are all designed with the involvement of employers.

Many of the 12,150 full-time undergraduates live around Pontypridd, while others choose Cardiff, which is both livelier and a better source of accommodation. However, the Pontypridd campus has been developing. There is also a modern a recreation centre as well as the new students' union.

The sports facilities were good enough for Glamorgan to have been awarded the 2001 British University Games and have continued to improve since then. The university hosts one of six centres of excellence in cricket and its playing fields have been used for training purposes by leading football and rugby teams. Glamorgan is successful in student competitions, especially in rugby, and offers a number of sports bursaries for students with international potential. There is also a wide range of health and fitness classes for those with lower aspirations.

Undergraduate Fees and Support

» Fees 2012–13: to be announced; able to charge up to £9,000, with Welsh Assembly expected to pay fees above £3,375 for Welsh students.
» Fees for international students 2011–12   £9,800
» Scholarships and bursaries based on circumstances or by competition are available.
» Check the university's website for the latest information.

Students

Undergraduates:	**12,150**	**(4,990)**
Postgraduates:	**1,980**	**(1,950)**
Mature students:	**33.8%**	
Overseas students:	**13.2%**	
Applications per place:	**3.7**	
From state-sector schools:	**98.0%**	
From working-class homes:	**39.1%**	

For detailed information about fees, grants and bursaries and how they work, see chapter 7.

Accommodation

Number of places and costs refer to 2011–12
University-provided places: 1,206
Percentage catered: 0%
Self-catered accommodation: £84 (standard) – £105 (premium) a week (39 weeks); £140 (studio flat, 42 weeks).
First-year students are offered accommodation. Local restrictions apply.
International students are guaranteed housing.
Contact: accom@glam.ac.uk

University of Glasgow

More distinctively Scottish than its rivals in Edinburgh or St Andrews, almost half of Glasgow's students come from within 30 miles of the city and two thirds are from north of the border. There was always a high proportion of home-based students, but the university also attracts students from 126 countries. They seem to enjoy the experience, for they voted Glasgow third in the UK in i–graduate's independent International Student Barometer. British students are also pretty satisfied – Glasgow was in the top ten in the National Student Survey published in 2010, with 90 per cent of all final-year undergraduates giving their seal of approval. The five 100 per cent satisfaction ratings – in electrical and electronic engineering, genetics, human and social geography, microbiology and nursing – were the most at any university. In addition, students in computing science, veterinary sciences, comparative literature and theatre, film and television were the most satisfied in the UK.

Glasgow enjoys the rare distinction of having been established by Papal Bull, and began its existence in the Chapter House of Glasgow Cathedral in 1451. Since 1871 it has been based next to Kelvingrove Park in the city's fashionable west end on the Gilmorehill campus, with its 104 listed buildings – more than any other British university. A new student centre opened in 2008, with student services and catering facilities.

Education occupies a separate campus nearby, while the Vet School and outdoor sports facilities are located at Garscube, four miles away. A £15-million small animal hospital for the Vet School opened in 2009, with state-of-the-art facilities including a radioactive iodine unit for cats, and an underwater treadmill. The centre will have 11,000 visits annually from all over the UK, and has already won two architecture awards. The environmental research building has also won awards as one of the "greenest" in Scotland.

Glasgow has adopted an increasingly outward-looking style in recent years, marked by the launch of the Commonwealth Scholarship scheme in 2008, which celebrates the city's success as host of the 2014 Commonwealth Games by offering 53 students from developing countries the chance to study at the university. The Centre for International Development, which is the first of its kind in Scotland and the largest in the UK, has helped to secure more than £20 million of research income. The university also has a campus at Dumfries, which is taking liberal arts and teacher education degrees to southwest Scotland.

Not that Glasgow is a stranger to innovation: it was the first university in Britain to have a school of engineering, for

---

University Avenue
Glasgow G12 8QQ

0141 330 6062 (enquiries)
student.recruitment@
   glasgow.ac.uk
www.gla.ac.uk
www.theguu.com
www.qmu.org.uk
Affiliation: Russell Group

The Times Rankings
Overall Ranking: **22**

Student satisfaction:	=7	(83%)
Research quality:	=18	(2.3)
Entry standards:	=22	(408)
Student–staff ratio:	=20	(14.5)
Services & facilities/student:	10	(£2,085)
Expected completion rate:	=45	(86.8%)
Good honours:	21	(73.7%)
Graduate prospects:	22	(72.1%)

example, and the first in Scotland to have a computer. It has now appointed Scotland's first Gaelic language officer and the country's first chair of Gaelic to promote both learning opportunities and cultural events. Glasgow is a member of the Russell Group of 20 leading research universities. More than half of the work submitted for the 2008 Research Assessment Exercise was considered world-leading or internationally excellent. Art history was the most highly rated in the UK and the Vet School joint top in its field, while the university finished in the top ten in 18 subject areas. The Business School has been rated among the world's top 100 business schools.

Almost half of the university's applications are for arts or sciences degrees, reflecting the popularity of a flexible system of study where students can delay choosing a subject in which to specialise until the end of their second year. Applications have been growing but, as in most of the older universities in Scotland, there was a decline at the start of 2011. The projected dropout rate had improved in the latest statistics but, at almost 13 per cent, is above the average for the subjects on offer and entry qualifications. Overseas recruitment has remained strong, as Glasgow has moved into the top 80 in the QS World University Rankings.

The Club 21 programme, which provides students with paid work experience placements, involves more than 100 employers from Santander to T-Mobile, some of whom sponsor undergraduates at £1,000 a year, as part of an arrangement to forge closer links with local business. Nearly a quarter of the students are from working-class homes. The university operates a number of access initiatives, including the Top Up programme, which has been working with schools in the West of Scotland since 1999, and the Talent Awards, 50 annual awards of £1,000 a year for academically able entrants who could face financial difficulties in taking up a place at Glasgow.

Most students like the combination of campus and city life, with the added bonus that Glasgow has been rated among the most cost-effective cities in which to study. Undergraduates have the choice of two students' unions, plus a sports union supporting 46 clubs and activities.

Undergraduate Fees and Support

- » Fees 2012–13: awaiting Scottish Government policy.
- » Fees for Scottish and EU students 2011–12 No fee
- » Fees for Non-Scottish UK-domiciled students 2011–12 £1,820
  £2,895 (medicine)
- » Fees for international students 2011–12 £11,500–£15,000
  £22,500 (veterinary medicine)
  £27,000 (medicine)
  £32,000 (dentistry)
- » Scholarships and bursaries based on circumstances or by competition are available.
- » Check the university's website for the latest information.

Students

Undergraduates:	**15,465**	**(4,535)**
Postgraduates:	**3,630**	**(1,970)**
Mature students:	**14.4%**	
Overseas students:	**8.8%**	
Applications per place:	**6.7**	
From state-sector schools:	**86.9%**	
From working-class homes:	**24.5%**	

For detailed information about fees, grants and bursaries and how they work, see chapter 7.

Accommodation

Number of places and costs refer to 2011–12

University-provided places: 3,521

Percentage catered: 6.7%

Catered costs: £132.93–£147.07 a week.

Self-catered costs: £75.11–£121.59 a week.

First years are guaranteed accommodation if conditions are met. Deadline applies.

International students: first years are guaranteed accommodation if conditions are met. 20% of returners are also housed.

Contact: accom@gla.ac.uk

Glasgow Caledonian University

Glasgow Caledonian has spent more than £70 million developing modern facilities on a single campus that does justice to a university of more than 17,000 students. But its ambitions extend well beyond Glasgow, having become the first Scottish university to open a campus in London and by operating an engineering college in Oman. Although a leader in Scotland on widening participation in higher education, Caledonian is also among the top dozen post-1992 universities in *The Times* League Table.

Over 80 per cent of the buildings on the main campus are new or have been upgraded, and improvements are still being made. The Govan Mbeki health building combines teaching and research facilities and includes a virtual hospital, where students can hone their clinical and interpersonal skills. The Saltire Centre, which has brought all library and student services together for the first time, has study spaces for 1,800 students. The compact, modern city-centre campus is a big advantage for the university. Sports and social facilities have been among the priorities in the building programme and a learning café combines enhanced-learning technology with an informal cyber-café atmosphere.

Applications have been booming. There was an increase of more than 40 per cent in 2010, buoyed by changes in the applications process for nursing, and a rise of 6.6 per cent at the start of 2011 was well above the UK average. Caledonian is among the top universities for attracting students from areas without a tradition of higher education, and more than a third of its undergraduates come from working-class homes.

The projected dropout rate has been improving. The university puts the latest rate at 16 per cent, but this is still above the UK average for Caledonian's courses and entry qualifications. Caledonian has introduced a series of measures designed to improve retention. Telltale signs are monitored, such as non-attendance at lectures, and better academic, social and financial support offered to those at risk of dropping out.

Degrees in all areas are strongly vocational, and are complemented by a wide portfolio of professional courses. A high proportion of students choose sandwich courses, which help to boost graduates' prospects in the employment market. In a move to secure the university's long term sustainability and deliver growth and innovation during a challenging time for higher education, the university has announced plans to consolidate core strengths and areas of academic excellence from its existing six schools into three larger ones – Health and Life Sciences;

Cowcaddens Road
Glasgow G4 0BA

0141 331 8681 (enquiries)
studentenquiries@gcu.ac.uk
www.gcu.ac.uk
www.caledonianstudent.com
Affiliation: University
    Alliance

GLASGOW
Edinburgh
Belfast
London
Cardiff

The Times Rankings
Overall Ranking: **75**

Student satisfaction:	=48	(77%)
Research quality:	=79	(0.3)
Entry standards:	52	(302)
Student–staff ratio:	=94	(20.9)
Services & facilities/student:	72	(£1,257)
Expected completion rate:	89	(79.7%)
Good honours:	36	(68.4%)
Graduate prospects:	82	(57.3%)

Engineering, Computing and the Environment; and Business, Law and Social Sciences.

Half of the 14 subject areas in which the university entered the 2008 Research Assessment Exercise contained at least some world-leading work, with 30 per cent of all researchers judged to have produced world-leading or internationally excellent work. Health subjects registered the best results and entered the largest numbers for assessment. The university has among the most extensive health programmes in Britain and produced particularly good results in rehabilitative health sciences, which covers long-term health conditions such as arthritis and strokes.

Business is the other big area, the Caledonian Business School boasting more undergraduates than any other institution in Scotland, with almost 1,000 in each year group. The university pioneered subjects such as entrepreneurship and risk management, and offers highly specialist degrees, such as tourism management, fashion marketing and consumer protection.

The new London campus provides a range of specialist postgraduate courses and professional development programmes in business, finance and risk, retailing and tourism from the heart of the City. There are no plans to offer undergraduate courses. Caledonian College of Engineering, in Oman, has been open for more than a decade, predating the current vogue for overseas campuses. The university also offers a physiotherapy degree in the Gulf state. Its international network includes partners in Bangladesh, China, India, Pakistan and South America. The most significant of these involves joint degrees with the University of Jinan, in China's Shandong province.

The legacy of Queen's College, which catered mainly for women, has continued with Caledonian registering one of the highest proportions of female students at any university in Britain. There are also 4,000 mature students and the largest number of part-timers in Scotland. Indoor sports facilities have improved – the Arc contains two spacious gyms, multipurpose halls, a health spa and hairdressing salon – but there is no university-owned provision for outdoor sports. The diversity of the student population has an impact on the social scene, but Glasgow is a famously lively city. The university is consistently rated top in Scotland for international student experience, according to independent education researchers, i-graduate.

Undergraduate Fees and Support

» Fees 2012–13:   awaiting Scottish Government policy
» Fees for Scottish and EU students 2011–12   No fee
» Fees for Non-Scottish UK-domiciled students 2011–12   £1,820
» Fees for international students 2011–12   £9,700–£14,500
» Scholarships and bursaries based on circumstances or by competition are available.
» Check the university's website for the latest information.

Students		
Undergraduates:	**11,275**	**(3,285)**
Postgraduates:	**1,665**	**(1,445)**
Mature students:	**35.6%**	
Overseas students:	**6.4%**	
Applications per place:	**6.5**	
From state-sector schools:	**96.9%**	
From working-class homes:	**36.8%**	

For detailed information about fees, grants and bursaries and how they work, see chapter 7.

Accommodation

Number of places and costs refer to 2010–11

University-provided places: 660

Percentage catered: 0%

Self-catered costs: £83.46–£96.21 a week.

Students under 19 living outside the Glasgow area have priority for accommodation.

International students: non-EU students given priority if conditions are met.

Contact: www.gcu.ac.uk/study/undergraduate/accommodation

University of Gloucestershire

Gloucestershire is investing £5 million in new teaching accommodation and social space after closing two campuses and dividing its courses between the university's three remaining sites. The reorganisation, in response to financial problems that saw the departure of the Vice-Chancellor, has maintained the full range of subjects and added a media hub with new studio areas for fine art, photography and specialist design. One casualty is a London campus for teacher training, which only opened in 2003. The other is the Pittville campus, in Cheltenham, whose art and design students have transferred to the nearby Francis Close Hall, which they will share with a new Institute of Education and Public Services, covering education, health and social care.

The headquarters at Park campus is the main base for the Faculty of Business, Education and Professional Studies, which includes accounting and law. Sport and exercise sciences, playwork, leisure, tourism, hospitality and event management will continue to be based at the Oxstalls campus in Gloucester, which will also house the Countryside and Community Research Institute, the largest rural research centre in the UK.

Gloucestershire has a longstanding focus on green issues, topping the Green League of Universities in 2008 for its all-round environmental performance and finishing second in 2010. There are allotments for students, diplomas in environmentalism and an International Research Institute in Sustainability that brings together researchers from around the world, undertaking work for agencies such as UNESCO. Students are discouraged from bringing cars to university and bus fares between campuses are subsidised. This approach may have been a factor behind a series of increases in applications, which have continued in subjects such as biology, TV production and marketing. However, the overall demand for places has stalled recently, with applications dropping in the boom year of 2010 and showing another fall at the start of 2011.

One of the more recent additions to the list of universities, Gloucestershire was the first for more than a century to have formal links with the Church of England. Although its religious origins have been played down in recent years and students of all faiths are welcomed, the university includes church appointees on its governing body. Lord Carey, the former Archbishop of Canterbury, was its first Chancellor. This did not prevent the university dropping theology at degree level as part of a curriculum review, although the subject is now taught by distance learning.

The Park Campus
The Park
Cheltenham GL50 2RH

0844 8011100 (prospectus)
admissions@glos.ac.uk
www.glos.ac.uk
www.yourstudentsunion
   .com
Affiliations: Cathedral
   Group, million+

The Times Rankings
Overall Ranking: **65**

Student satisfaction:	=63	(76%)
Research quality:	=92	(0.2)
Entry standards:	88	(264)
Student–staff ratio:	=88	(20.6)
Services & facilities/student:	60	(£1,320)
Expected completion rate:	63	(84.2%)
Good honours:	=51	(63.0%)
Graduate prospects:	=79	(57.8%)

Before university status in 2001, Cheltenham and Gloucester College of Higher Education had been the product of a merger between a church college and the higher education wing of a college of arts and technology. After considerable expansion during the 1990s, there are now just over 9,000 students, including 2,530 part-timers, and over 1,000 academic and support staff. The university prides itself on a good range of work placements, which include Airbus and Renault.

The main campus is on the attractive site of the former College of St Paul and St Mary, a mile outside Cheltenham. There has also been considerable development of the Gloucester campus, on the site of a former domestic science college which became part of the university in 2002. Although middle-class Cheltenham is a world away from more working-class Gloucester socially, the two centres are only seven miles apart and students are not as isolated as they are in some split-site institutions.

Gloucestershire did not quite repeat the success it enjoyed in the previous research assessments when the exercise was repeated in 2008. Some world-leading research was found in five of the 12 areas in which the university submitted work, with the small education entry producing the best results. But less than 20 per cent of all work reached the top two categories. Results in the National Student Survey improved again in 2010 and are now close to the national average. However, education and cinematics and photography were the only areas to register 90 per cent satisfaction ratings among final-year undergraduates.

The university's intake is diverse, with over 95 per cent of undergraduates from state schools and more than a third from working-class homes. The projected dropout rate has improved dramatically, with the latest projection of less than 8 per cent well below the national average for the university's subjects and entry qualifications. The well-equipped Gloucester campus, where participation in higher education has always been low, focuses particularly on access initiatives.

The sports facilities include a sports hall, gym and tennis courts. First years are given preference for the 1,350 hall places, and the university assures its students that it has access to enough private sector places to meet their needs. At both sites facilities overall are improving.

Undergraduate Fees and Support

- » Fees for UK/EU students 2012–13   £8,250
- » Fees for International students 2011–12   £8,800
- » Details of a package of financial support, including bursary of £1,000 for students from compact partner institution with household income below £25K and a contribution towards accommodation costs to students with household income below £25K, to be announced.
- » Check the university's website for the latest information.

Students		
Undergraduates:	**5,985**	**(1,080)**
Postgraduates:	**1,225**	**(1,430)**
Mature students:	**21.3%**	
Overseas students:	**5.1%**	
Applications per place:	**4.4**	
From state-sector schools:	**95.5%**	
From working-class homes:	**36.1%**	

For detailed information about fees, grants and bursaries and how they work, see chapter 7.

Accommodation
Number of places and costs refer to 2010–11
University-provided places: about 1,350
Percentage catered: 0%
Self-catered costs: £78–£106 a week.
First-year undergraduates have priority for halls.
International students: first-year undergraduates are guaranteed accommodation if conditions are met.
Contact: accommodation@glos.ac.uk

Glyndŵr University

The former North East Wales Institute of Higher Education took the name of the medieval Welsh prince Owain Glyndŵr, who championed the establishment of universities throughout Wales in the early 15th century, when it was awarded university status in 2008. The new university is based on two campuses in Wrexham and one at Northop, in Flintshire, on the site of the former Welsh College of Horticulture. The Flintshire campus is the first university presence in the county, and £1.7 million has been invested to make it a centre of excellence for land and animal-based studies.

Glyndŵr has 3,700 full-time students and another 4,300 part-timers, all of whose qualifications will continue to be awarded by the University of Wales. Nearly 60 per cent of the undergraduates are over 20 on entry and a third of all students are from overseas, many from other EU countries, India or China. As NEWI, there were only two applications per place – a lower ratio than at any UK university. But Glyndŵr enjoyed the customary boost that accompanies a change of status, and sustained it with another 13 per cent in applications at the start of 2011.

The new university has embarked on a series of academic developments, including the opening of a £2-million Centre for the Child, Family and Society, based on a Scandinavian concept to allow those working in the field of child development to hone their skills in both an academic and practical manner. The Advanced Composite Training and Development Centre, a partnership with Airbus, followed in October 2010. Research carried out at the centre will help to improve the efficiency of aircraft and will feed into the university's undergraduate engineering courses, which have been developed in association with Airbus. The Centre for the Creative Industries opened in 2011 with new TV, radio and online production studios for students from disciplines such as art and design, media and computing. It will play a key role in the university's new television degree, and is also the new home of BBC Cymru Wales in North East Wales.

Fewer than half of the undergraduates are school-leavers and nearly all of them are state-educated. Almost half are from working-class homes – easily the biggest proportion in Wales and far in excess of the UK average for the university's subjects and entry grades. Glyndŵr also has the largest proportion of disabled students in Wales and was nominated for an award for its provision for them. There is a dedicated centre for students with disabilities that assesses students' needs before they embark on a course. Sports science, education and English all produced outstanding ratings in the National Student Survey published in 2010, but they were not repeated elsewhere in the

---

Mold Road
Wrexham
N. Wales LL11 2AW

01978 293439 (student enquiries)
sid@glyndwr.ac.uk
www.glyndwr.ac.uk
www.glyndwr.ac.uk/
  en/Ourstudentsupport/
  StudentsGuild/
Affiliation: none

The Times Rankings
Overall Ranking: **=102**

Student satisfaction:	=78	(74%)
Research quality:	=105	(0.1)
Entry standards:	108	(231)
Student–staff ratio:	=107	(22.5)
Services & facilities/student:	33	(£1,598)
Expected completion rate:	=104	(76.1%)
Good honours:	105	(49.4%)
Graduate prospects:	51	(65.5%)

university. A drop in the overall score placed Glyndŵr close to the bottom ten in the table.

Among the recent additions to the portfolio of courses have been a Foundation degree in floristry and floral design, and degrees in mobile computing and therapeutic childcare. The university has even launched a degree in equestrian psychology, examining the way in which horses learn and investigating their bond with humans. Only Cardiff has a better graduate employment rate among universities in Wales.

Glyndŵr entered only 27 academics for the 2008 Research Assessment Exercise, but almost a quarter of their work was judged to be world-leading or internationally excellent. Computer science and materials both reached the top grade for a small proportion of their work, and the university's research funding more than doubled as a result.

The two campuses in Wrexham are within five minutes' walk of each other. Most courses are taught at the larger Plas Coch site, next to the Wrexham FC ground. The first phase of a new student accommodation complex, with 156 rooms, opened in September 2010 adjacent to the Plas Coch site, and is the result of a partnership with the football club. The university's art school is based at the Regent Street campus, nearer the town centre.

The modern sports centre, in Wrexham, is one of the features of the university. There are two floodlit artificial pitches with different surfaces, including an international standard hockey pitch, a human performance laboratory and indoor facilities that include a sports hall with a 1,000 square-metre sprung floor. The centre has hosted a number of big sporting events, as well as conferences.

Bursaries of up to £1,000 a year are available for all UK students, dependent on family income, and entrants to full-time courses with more than 300 UCAS points are eligible for one-off scholarships of another £1,000. Two thirds of the students are from the local area, many living at home, which inevitably affects the social scene. But Wrexham is not without nightlife, and both Manchester and Liverpool are within reach for those in search of more sophisticated shopping or clubbing.

Undergraduate Fees and Support

» Fees 2012–13: to be announced; able to charge up to £9,000, with Welsh Assembly expected to pay fees above £3,375 for Welsh students.

» Fees for international students 2011–12   £7,500

» Scholarships and bursaries based on circumstances or by competition are available.

» Check the university's website for the latest information.

Students			Accommodation
Undergraduates:	**3,060**	**(3,805)**	Number of places and costs refer to 2011–12
Postgraduates:	**640**	**(500)**	University-provided places: 615
Mature students:	**57.8%**		Percentage catered: 0%
Overseas students:	**33.5%**		Self-catered costs: £69.50 (shared) – £130.00 (superior en suite)
Applications per place:	**2.2**		a week (37 weeks).
From state-sector schools:	**99.0%**		First-year undergraduates are guaranteed accommodation.
From working-class homes:	**54.5%**		International students: guaranteed housing.
			Contact: accommodation@glyndŵr.ac.uk

For detailed information about fees, grants and bursaries and how they work, see chapter 7.

www.glyndŵr.ac.uk/en/Ourstudentsupport/Accommodation/

Goldsmiths, University of London

Dubbed the "campus of cool" in a Brand Council exercise, Goldsmiths is best known for excellence in the arts, but it stresses that it brings the same creative approach to a wider range of subjects, spanning humanities, social sciences, computing and teacher training. Alumni include Mary Quant and Damien Hirst among many other famous names, such as Antony Gormley, Julian Clary, Malcolm McLaren and Linton Kwesi Johnson. Graduates of the college have won the Turner Prize no fewer than six times.

There is another side to Goldsmiths, however, in its tradition of community-based courses, which predates membership of the University of London. Evening and other part-time classes are still as popular as conventional degree courses and many subjects can be studied from basic to postgraduate levels. A history of providing educational opportunities for women is reflected in one of the largest proportions of female students in the British university system – nearly two thirds at the last count.

Determinedly integrated into its southeast London locality, the campus has a cosmopolitan atmosphere. Around 30 per cent of new undergraduates are over 20 on entry (many of them at least 25), with a strong representation from the area's ethnic minorities, and there is a growing cohort of overseas students. The age profile helped Goldsmiths to a rise in applications of more than 11 per cent in 2010, but there had been a decline at the start of 2011.

The campus is a mixture of old and new. The latest addition, a prize-winning building for media and communications facilities and the Institute for Creative and Cultural Entrepreneurship, opened in September 2010. The Rutherford Building, containing library and IT services, also won an award from the Royal Institute of British Architects, and a Grade II listed former baths building has been converted to provide more space for research and art studios. The Ben Pimlott Building, which features a dramatic metal "scribble" by the acclaimed architect Will Alsop, contains state-of-the-art studio facilities and two multidisciplinary centres for interaction between the arts and social sciences.

Although dominated by the arts, Goldsmiths' portfolio of subjects stretches through the humanities and social sciences as far as computing and psychology. More than half of the work submitted for the 2008 Research Assessment Exercise was considered world-leading or internationally excellent. Indeed, it was among the top ten universities for the proportion of work (22 per cent) placed in the highest category. Sociology was rated joint top in the UK,

Lewisham Way
New Cross
London SE14 6NW

020 7919 7766 (admissions)
admissions@gold.ac.uk
www.gold.ac.uk
http://goldsmithsstudents.
  org
Affiliation: 1994 Group

while communication, cultural and media studies, music and art and design all did well.

There are only 6,500 full-time students and around 1,500 part-timers at Goldsmiths. Undergraduates have declared themselves generally satisfied in the National Student Survey although, in common with other London universities, really high scores have been hard to come by. Only social work satisfied 90 per cent of final-year undergraduates in 2010, although anthropology, English and modern languages came close. Employment prospects are good, especially for an institution with such a high proportion of students taking performing arts subjects, where a period of unemployment after graduation is commonplace. However, the projected dropout rate of 17 per cent is above average for the courses and entry qualifications.

Student politics has survived at Goldsmiths to an extent not seen at many universities – the union building was given the name Tiananmen – while a college in which Alex James and Graham Coxon, from Blur, are just two of a number of successful rock alumni cannot fail to have a thriving music scene. The union has a strong tradition in volunteering and an award-winning newspaper, and in recent years have been winners of several Sound Impact Awards, in recognition of work on ethical and environmental issues.

The surrounding area enjoyed a mini-boom before the recession as a prime location for loft apartments. Although sky-high prices put them way beyond the reach of the student housing market, there are plenty of more reasonably priced options in the vicinity. There are over 1,000 residential places within walking distance of the campus – not enough to guarantee accommodation for all first-years, but overseas students can be housed throughout their course. Sports enthusiasts have been less well provided for, although there is a well-equipped and affordable gym on campus. There is also a swimming pool and indoor complex in Deptford, but the main pitches are eight miles away. Goldsmiths expects to make more of a contribution to the cultural programme than the sporting one at the 2012 Olympic Games.

Undergraduate Fees and Support

» Fees for UK/EU students 2012–13   £9,000
» Fees for International students 2011–12   £10,500–£14,100
» Ten £9,000 fee waivers for best students from Lewisham; a further £3,000 as bursary or fee waiver to all students awarded National Scholarships;
    for students from local boroughs with household income below £50K, £750; from areas of low participation, £1,000 as bursary or fee waiver;
    £500 fee waiver for all English students from low-income background.
» Scholarships and bursaries based on circumstances or by competition are available.
» Check the university's website for the latest information.

Students		
Undergraduates:	**4,905**	**(605)**
Postgraduates:	**1,595**	**(865)**
Mature students:	**28.9%**	
Overseas students:	**13.4%**	
Applications per place:	**7.0**	
From state-sector schools:	**89.9%**	
From working-class homes:	**31.6%**	

For detailed information about fees, grants and bursaries and how they work, see chapter 7.

Accommodation

Number of places and costs refer to 2010–11

University-provided places: 971 (college halls); 51 studio flats through McMillan Student Village (private hall provider)

Percentage catered: 0%

Self-catered costs: £91.50–£124.00 a week (studio flats in McMillan Student Village are £161.35–£202.02 a week)

Priority is given to new full-time students; distance restrictions apply.

International students will be given priority.

Contact: www.goldsmiths.ac.uk/accommodation

University of Greenwich

Greenwich has the most satisfied students of any post-1992 university in London. After a series of improvements, the university finished in the top quarter of all universities in the 2010 National Student Survey. Maths and pharmacy both recorded 100 per cent satisfaction rates, while law and civil, chemical and other engineering courses were all in the top three in the country. The successes were reflected in sharp growth in the demand for places: applications were up by almost a third in 2010 and approaching a fifth at the start of 2011 – both among the largest increases in England.

The university claims to have "one of the grandest university settings in the world", and it is hard to argue. Its move, completed in 2002, into the former Royal Naval College buildings designed by Sir Christopher Wren provided a campus worthy of one of the most desirable titles of any university. Its name has always conjured up images of history and science in equal measure, and the main campus is now part of a World Heritage Site. Wren's baroque masterpiece is being used, with the former Dreadnought Hospital, to teach over half the university's students in humanities, business, law, maths, computing and maritime studies. Four halls provide around 2,300 residential places.

Greenwich draws primarily from southeast London and Kent. The prize-winning Medway campus, centred on the former naval base at Chatham, has been developed in partnership with Kent and Canterbury Christ Church universities. New student accommodation for an additional 140 students opened there in 2008, together with an improved café for Greenwich students in the main Pembroke building. Greenwich put £20 million into the campus, which houses one of the first new schools of pharmacy for 20 years, as well as the schools of science and engineering, the Natural Resources Institute, nursing and some business courses. A joint learning resources centre serves the Chatham Maritime campus and Kent's neighbouring premises. Another shared facility has improved teaching facilities and expanded student services, the campus having already exceeded the original target of 6,000 students. A new BSc in paramedic science combines learning in the workplace, as part of an ambulance crew, with academic study, assessments and laboratory exercises.

Other schools are situated at Avery Hill, a Victorian mansion on the outskirts of southeast London, where a £14-million sports and teaching centre opened in 2006, with a new gym and refurbished café following in 2008. As well as a sports hall and 220-seat lecture theatre, there are laboratories for health courses that replicate NHS wards. A neighbouring building is now the main base for the School of Health and Social Care. The

Old Royal Naval College
Park Row,
Greenwich
London SE10 9LS

0800 005 006 (course enquiries)
courseinfo@greenwich.ac.uk
www.gre.ac.uk
www.suug.co.uk
Affiliation: million+

The Times Rankings
Overall Ranking: **99**

Student satisfaction:	=24	(79%)
Research quality:	=79	(0.3)
Entry standards:	111	(215)
Student–staff ratio:	=111	(23.3)
Services & facilities/student:	64	(£1,290)
Expected completion rate:	88	(79.8%)
Good honours:	109	(46.7%)
Graduate prospects:	94	(54.7%)

campus also contains a student village of 1,300 rooms, as well as teaching accommodation for the social sciences, architecture, landscape and construction, and the large education faculty, which is one of the few to offer both primary and secondary teacher training courses. The Avery Hill TV studio has also been refurbished to meet current industrial standards.

The university has also bought a large site in Greenwich town centre, where it plans to invest £76 million in a new library and a new home for the School of Architecture and Construction. The development will increase student numbers in the town by about 20 per cent.

The university achieved mixed results from a large entry to the 2008 Research Assessment Exercise, which showed a quarter of the work reaching world-leading or internationally excellent levels. The small mechanical, aeronautical and manufacturing engineering group produced by far the best results, but architecture and history also did well. A fifth of the university's income is from research and consultancy – the largest proportion at any former polytechnic. Despite the recession, externally sponsored research and consultancy income has leapt by a massive 60 per cent in two years, to an annual figure of £15.3 million. Including other funding from government sources, the university's total research revenues have almost doubled since 2007–08.

Eleven associated colleges in Kent and London teach the university's courses, while strong links with institutions in Europe and further afield provide a steady flow of overseas students, as well as exchange opportunities for those at Greenwich. The university is the UK's top recruiter of students from India, and also takes large numbers from Mauritius and Nigeria among a total of 5,000 international students.

A commitment to extending access is reflected in a high proportion of mature students. Almost 98 per cent of undergraduates are state-educated, and over half come from working-class homes. Both figures are significantly higher than the national average for Greenwich's courses and entrance requirements. The downside has been the dropout rate. The latest projection of 17 per cent is marginally higher than the university's benchmark.

Undergraduate Fees and Support

» Fees for UK/EU students 2012–13   to be announced
» Fees for International students 2011–12   £9,375
» A package of financial support and widening participation activity to be announced.
» Scholarships and bursaries based on circumstances or by competition are available.
» Check the university's website for the latest information.

Students

Undergraduates:	**15,655**	**(7,005)**
Postgraduates:	**3,680**	**(2,465)**
Mature students:	**47.6%**	
Overseas students:	**12.8%**	
Applications per place:	**5.0**	
From state-sector schools:	**97.9%**	
From working-class homes:	**55.5%**	

For detailed information about fees, grants and bursaries and how they work, see chapter 7.

Accommodation

Number of places and costs refer to 2010–11
University-provided places: 2,300
Percentage catered: 0%
Self-catered costs: £90.16–£160.16 a week.
First years are guaranteed a place. Conditions apply.
International students: new students get priority.
Contact: www.gre.ac.uk/about/accommodation;
accommodation-AH@gre.ac.uk (Avery Hill)
accommodation-GM@gre.ac.uk (Greenwich)
accommodation-ME@gre.ac.uk (Medway)

Heriot-Watt University

Heriot-Watt is investing £10 million to boost its teaching and research in business and technology as part of a commitment to become a world-leading university within ten years. The university is already Scotland's most international institution, with a campus in Dubai and a total of almost 12,000 students in approved learning centres overseas or taking distance learning courses in 150 different countries. Overseas students also fill a third of the places on the university's Edinburgh campus – one of the biggest proportions in the UK.

Heriot-Watt's strengths lie in the physical sciences, mathematics, engineering and in the built environment, where it provides more graduates each year than any other Scottish university. Concentration on these areas is fitting for a university which commemorates James Watt, the pioneer of steam power, and George Heriot, financier to King James VI. The university has fostered interdisciplinary teaching and research, with a battery of employment-related degrees.

Heriot-Watt is also one of the most commercially diversified universities in Britain, with almost 70 per cent of its income from non-government funding, in particular research income generated from business and industry. The research park was the first of its kind in Europe, providing direct access to expertise for a range of companies based there. The university also has a £6.5-million project to transfer knowledge and expertise to Scottish businesses by providing a network of academic expertise, and by promoting business interaction and income generating partnerships.

More than half of the work in a larger-than-average submission for the 2008 Research Assessment Exercise was rated world-leading or internationally excellent. Mathematics produced by far the best results, but there were good grades, too, in petroleum engineering, physics, general engineering, the built environment, and art and design. The results helped propel the university seven places up *The Times* League Table last year and into the top 40, although it has slipped back a little this year.

The last institutional review of the university's quality produced the top grade of "broad confidence". Heriot-Watt has also done well in the National Student Survey, with scores rising sharply in 2010. Economics registered a 100 per cent satisfaction rating, and psychology students were the most satisfied in the UK. Civil engineering, chemistry and business studies also contributed strongly to an overall satisfaction rate of 87 per cent.

The main Edinburgh campus, in the Riccarton area of the city, close to the airport and 20 minutes drive from the city centre, still has a modern feel more than 40 years after it

---

Edinburgh Campus
Edinburgh EH14 4AS

0131 449 5111
enquiries@hw.ac.uk
www.hw.ac.uk
www.hwunion.com
Affiliation: none

EDINBURGH
Belfast
London
Cardiff

The Times Rankings
Overall Ranking: **44**

Student satisfaction:	=63	(76%)
Research quality:	41	(1.7)
Entry standards:	40	(335)
Student–staff ratio:	=69	(19.1)
Services & facilities/student:	26	(£1,732)
Expected completion rate:	53	(85.4%)
Good honours:	37	(68.0%)
Graduate prospects:	39	(68.8%)

opened. The university remains small in terms of full-time students – there are about 7,500 on the Edinburgh campus, with another 1,800 in Dubai taking business, engineering, science, technology or textiles and design courses. Numbers in the Gulf state are expected to rise to 3,000 at the end of 2011. Heriot-Watt won an award from the Scottish Council of Development and Industry, partly for its support for international students.

Science, engineering, management and languages are located on the Edinburgh campus. The Scottish Borders Campus in Galashiels, 35 miles south of the capital, specialises in textiles, fashion, textiles design and management. Heriot-Watt and Borders College have signed a partnership agreement for a long-term collaboration to deliver higher and further education in the historically under-provided region, both institutions now sharing £34 million of new campus facilities. In addition, there is a postgraduate campus at Stromness in Orkney, which is home to the International Centre for Island Technology.

The subject mix serves graduates well: Heriot-Watt is seldom far from the top of the graduate employment league tables. The latest projected dropout rate of less than 9 per cent is well below the UK average for the university's subjects and entrance qualifications. More than half of the undergraduates are from Scotland, and just under 20 per cent from other parts of Britain. Over 90 per cent of them are from state schools and colleges, but the proportion from working-class backgrounds is slightly below average for the courses and entry qualifications.

The Edinburgh campus has an attractive parkland setting, with the students' union at its heart and halls of residence conveniently placed. Students have complained that the six-mile journey to the city centre leaves them isolated, but there are frequent bus services. Sports enthusiasts are well provided for, and representative teams do well. Hearts, one of Edinburgh's two Scottish Premier League football clubs, have their sports academy on campus, which is used by students and local people as well as the young professionals. Music also thrives: there is a professional musician-in-residence and a number of music scholarships, as well as a varied programme of events.

Undergraduate Fees and Support

» Fees 2012–13:   awaiting Scottish Government policy.
» Fees for Scottish and EU students 2011–12   No fee
» Fees for Non-Scottish UK-domiciled students 2011–12   £1,820
» Fees for international students 2011–12   £10,120–£12,760
» Scholarships and bursaries based on circumstances or by competition are available.
» Check the university's website for the latest information.

Students		
Undergraduates:	**5,920**	**(360)**
Postgraduates:	**1,820**	**(3,200)**
Mature students:	**17.8%**	
Overseas students:	**24.7%**	
Applications per place:	**6.7**	
From state-sector schools:	**90.4%**	
From working-class homes:	**29.7%**	

For detailed information about fees, grants and bursaries and how they work, see chapter 7.

Accommodation
Number of places and costs refer to 2011–12
University places provided: 1,624
Percentage catered: 19%
Catered costs: £119.84–£131.87 a week.
Self-catered costs: £86.29 (standard) – £103.93 (en suite) a week.
All new first years are guaranteed accommodation provided conditions are met and applications in place by 22 August.
International students: as above.
Contact : halls@hw.ac.uk
www.hw.ac.uk/student-life/campus-life.htm

University of Hertfordshire

Hertfordshire has become a model for the "business-facing" university, serving the needs of local employers and improving the job prospects of its students in the process. The university even runs the local bus service and plays an important role in steering the local economy, helping it to *Times Higher Education* magazine's award for the Entrepreneurial University of the Year in 2010. Hertfordshire has not followed the pack on tuition fees either, charging less than £8,000 for most courses. Degrees are divided into three bands, from £7,400 to £8,500.

A purpose-built £120-million campus, close to the existing Hatfield headquarters, opened in 2003, bringing the university together for the first time and providing outstanding facilities. The de Havilland campus, named after the aircraft manufacturer which once occupied the site, houses business, education and the humanities. It has a 24-hour learning resources centre, £15-million sports complex and 1,600 networked, en-suite residential places. The two sites are linked by cycleways, footpaths and university-owned shuttle buses.

As Hatfield Polytechnic, the university's reputation was built on engineering and computer science, but health subjects now account for by far the largest share of places. An innovative degree in paramedic science was Britain's first, its students using the UK's largest medical simulation centre to train how to treat patients in emergency situations. The university is still hoping for a medical school, although its last bid was not successful. A new School of Pharmacy and a postgraduate medical school have strengthened its position. Increased research activity resulted in the establishment of the Health and Human Sciences Institute.

Art and design is also growing, particularly the multimedia courses. In 2005, the university launched a School of Film, Music and New Media and in 2007 built a £10-million media centre, with the latest technology for the teaching of music, animation, film, television and multimedia, based on the College Lane campus. This includes one of the largest art galleries in the eastern region, which mounts regular public exhibitions, while a 460-seat auditorium enhances the cultural programme. An Automotive Centre has upgraded the teaching facilities for that branch of engineering, as well as boosting interaction with industry.

The university has been trying to widen its base through collaboration with local further education colleges, where Foundation degrees will cost £5,800 in 2012. The intake is more diverse than might be expected, given the location and subject mix: 40 per cent of undergraduates come from working-class homes and almost all are state-educated. The

---

College Lane
Hatfield
Herts AL10 9AB

01707 284800 (admissions)
contact via website
www.herts.ac.uk
www.uhsu.co.uk
Affiliation: University Alliance

HATFIELD
Edinburgh
Belfast
Cardiff
London

The Times Rankings
Overall Ranking: **64**

Student satisfaction:	=63	(76%)
Research quality:	=79	(0.3)
Entry standards:	103	(244)
Student–staff ratio:	=60	(18.5)
Services & facilities/student:	30	(£1,636)
Expected completion rate:	=66	(83.9%)
Good honours:	54	(62.1%)
Graduate prospects:	=72	(59.7%)

projected dropout rate improved in the latest survey to 13.5 per cent, better than the national average for the subject mix and entry grades.

Applications rose by 36 per cent in 2010 and were up by 3 per cent – around the national average – at the start of 2011. Many Hertfordshire students include work placements in their degrees, the close links with employers sometimes bringing in valuable research and consultancy contracts, and contributing to a consistently good graduate employment record. The university runs Graduate Futures, a programme offering graduates lifelong support on employment and career development issues.

There has been steady improvement in scores in the National Student Survey. Hertfordshire was only just below the national average in 2010, with the most satisfied students in creative writing, communications, pharmacy, physiology and human resource management.

Hertfordshire produced some of the best results of any post-1992 university in the 2008 Research Assessment Exercise, when approaching half of its submission was judged to be world-leading or internationally excellent. History, nursing and midwifery, engineering and computing collected the highest grades. The results helped the university to a rise of 16 places in two years in *The Times* League Table, although it has slipped back one place this year.

The award-winning library and resource centre on the main campus offers 24-hour access to hundreds of computer work-stations. A second centre on the de Havilland campus provides another 1,100 workstations. The StudyNet information system has been a leader in its field, giving all staff and students their own storage space. Students can use it for study, revision or communication, as well as to access university information.

In September 2009, the university opened the "Forum", a new student venue on the College Lane campus. It includes an auditorium for live gigs and club nights, a nursery, a convenience store and a multi-storey car park, as well as quiet areas. A £15-million sports complex, the Hertford-shire Sports Village, boasts some of the best university-based facilities in Britain. Although principally for student use, it is also open to local residents.

Undergraduate Fees and Support

» Fees for UK/EU students 2012–13   £7,400-£8,500
   Foundation degrees at partner colleges   £5,800
» Fees for International students 2011–12   £9,000-£10,000
» A package of financial support and widening participation activity to be announced.
» Scholarships and bursaries based on circumstances or by competition.
» Check the university's website for the latest information.

Students

Undergraduates:	**17,535**	**(4,115)**
Postgraduates:	**2,925**	**(3,075)**
Mature students:	**23.9%**	
Overseas students:	**13.9%**	
Applications per place:	**· 6.3**	
From state-sector schools:	**97.6%**	
From working-class homes:	**40.4%**	

For detailed information about fees, grants and bursaries and how they work, see chapter 7.

Accommodation

Number of places and costs refer to 2010–11
University-provided places: 3,300
Percentage catered: 0%
Self-catered costs: £70–£115 a week.
First years are guaranteed accommodation if conditions are met.
International students: as above.
Contact: Accommodation@herts.ac.uk

University of the Highlands and Islands

The University of the Highlands and Islands (UHI) is the only institution to be added to the complement of UK universities this year. As a federation of 13 colleges and research institutions stretching north and west from Perthshire to the Western Isles and Shetland, it is also the most unusual. UHI has waited almost 20 years for university status – indeed, its establishment was recommended in 1990 in a report to the Highland Regional Council which envisaged that the process might take four years. The region has waited a lot longer than that for a university: the UHI website says that Perth was first identified as a suitable location for a university in 1425.

The university's development has come in stages since its establishment was formally recommended in 1992. As the UHI Millennium Institute, it became a higher education provider in 2001 and received degree-awarding powers in 2008. University status finally came in February 2011, by which time it had 8,000 students spread around its many campuses. It makes its debut in *The Times* League Table in the bottom ten, but some data – notably on staffing levels – will be refined in future years.

The 13 colleges spread from Dunoon in the south to the village of Scalloway, the ancient capital of the Shetland Islands, in the north. But that does not begin to do justice to the university's network of campuses. Argyll College, for example, has 13 sites on the mainland and on islands such as Arran, Islay and Mull. UHI provides educational opportunities at more than 50 learning centres located throughout the Highlands and Islands, Moray and Perthshire. Some colleges are relatively large and located in the urban centres of the region such as Perth, Elgin and Inverness. Others are smaller institutions, including some whose primary focus is research. The university insists, however, that all have a student-centred culture and an individual approach.

Several of the colleges are in spectacular locations. Lews Castle College, in Stornoway, in the Outer Hebrides, for example, is set in 600 acres of parkland. It claims "possibly the UK's most attractive location to study art" for its harbourside location in North Uist. Sabhal Mòr Ostaig UHI is the only Gaelic-medium college in the world, set in breathtaking scenery on the Isle of Skye. The West Highland College is in Fort William, close to Ben Nevis, and offers a course in adventure tourism management. The Scottish Association for Marine Science is located along the beautiful Argyll coastline near Oban and offers an option to spend a semester in the Arctic at Svalbard as part of a degree in marine science.

UHI's priority is to give students living in

Executive Office
Ness Walk
Inverness IV3 5QS

01463 279 000 (general enquiries)
contact via website
www.uhi.ac.uk
www.uhisa.org.uk
Affiliation: none

The Times Rankings
Overall Ranking: **111**

Student satisfaction:		n/a
Research quality:	=92	(0.2)
Entry standards:	=81	(269)
Student–staff ratio:		n/a
Services & facilities/student:	113	(£888)
Expected completion rate:	116	(57.2%)
Good honours:	=51	(63%)
Graduate prospects:	109	(49.5%)

the region local access to learning and research relevant to their needs and to those of local employers. More than 2,500 people have graduated in the last 12 months with a broad range of qualifications, from higher national certificates and diplomas and degrees to professional development awards. The university is widely acknowledged as a major asset to the regional economy, helping to create and sustain businesses, as well as championing local culture and the environment. But the university also attracts students from further afield with a wide choice of locations, extensive use of information technology, including online materials and video conferencing, and small class sizes. Many courses are also available by online distance learning

The university offers more than 100 undergraduate courses, all tailored to the needs of the region. Degree courses intended to lead to careers in renewable engineering, tourism and hospitality, health care, and children's services are among the options for 2012. A new degree in childhood practice will launch in 2011, catering for daycare managers in children's services and nurseries. Those planned for 2012 include archaeology, fine art textiles, music business, tourism and hospitality practice, environment and sustainability studies, and electrical and energy engineering. Existing courses such as audio engineering, health studies with rural health or health and welfare, and adventure

tourism management have added an honours year of study.

UHI became the first higher education institution to publish a Gaelic language plan in 2010, setting out plans to provide students with unique opportunities to learn Gaelic, improve existing skills, or study for qualifications entirely through the language. There is now a growing community of students with Gaelic skills throughout the UHI network. The university's mission statement is published in five languages, of which Gaelic is the first, and staff are offered a one-day Gaelic Awareness course.

Environmental science produced the best results and made by far the largest submission in the 2008 Research Assessment Exercise, but there was some world-leading research in Celtic studies and archaeology. There are a dozen research centres specialising in everything from agronomy to Nordic studies, diabetes and rural childhood.

Undergraduate Fees and Support

- » Fees 2012–13: awaiting Scottish Government policy.
- » Fees for Scottish and EU students 2011–12 · No fee
- » Fees for Non-Scottish UK-domiciled students 2011–12 £1,820
- » Fees for international students 2011–12 £7,200–£8,580
- » Scholarships and bursaries based on circumstances or by competition are available.
- » Check the university's website for the latest information.

Students		
Undergraduates:	**3,310**	**(3,720)**
Postgraduates:	**90**	**(385)**
Mature students:	**70.8%**	
Overseas students:	**2.6%**	
Applications per place:	**n/a**	
From state-sector schools:	**100.0%**	
From working-class homes:	**41.9%**	

For detailed information about fees, grants and bursaries and how they work, see chapter 7.

Accommodation

On-site halls of residence are available at four of the partner colleges. The other colleges provide lists of local lodgings or private rented accommodation. Some international students prefer to stay with host families.

Contact: Perth College UHI: pc.enquiries@perth.uhi.ac.uk

Sabhal Mòr Ostaig UHI: trusadh@smo.uhi.ac.uk

Lews Castle College UHI: enquiries@lews.uhi.ac.uk

NAFC Marine Centre UHI: www.nafc.ac.uk/Accommodation.aspx

University of Huddersfield

Official performance indicators for higher education have shown Huddersfield living up to its mission to help produce a more diverse student population. More than four out of ten full-time students are from working-class homes – far in excess of the national average for the university's courses and entry qualifications – and the numbers coming from areas without a tradition of higher education are among the highest in the country. The university has opened satellite centres in Barnsley and Oldham to widen participation further.

Imaginative conversions and new buildings have finally allowed the university to come together on one town-centre campus. The university capitalised on Huddersfield's industrial past to ease the strain on facilities that were struggling to cope with expansion which reached 13 per cent a year at its peak. Canalside, a refurbished mill complex, provided extra space for mathematics and computing, and education occupies another mill site – this time a £4-million re-creation of the original. The university has created "pocket parks" and a landscaped area along the reopened Narrow Canal to provide additional green space. Human and health sciences have also acquired new premises, and an additional £4 million has been spent on a new students'

union, allowing drama courses to take over the existing union complex. The new union includes alcohol-free social areas to encourage participation by those overseas students and ethnic minorities who would otherwise avoid the facilities. The latest additions include a striking creative arts building, which cost some £16 million. A similar sum was spent on a new business school, which opened in September 2010.

The 19th-century Ramsden Building – the historical heart of the university, in use for 125 years – has now been refurbished and there are high-tech facilities behind its carefully preserved exterior. Over the next 18 months the university plans to invest some £58 million in facilities including a new sport, learning and leisure complex and improvements to teaching, learning and research space.

A tradition of vocational education dates back to 1841, and the university has a long-established reputation in areas such as textile design and engineering. But there are less obvious gems such as music and social work, as well as teacher training, for which Huddersfield was awarded a national centre of excellence.

Scores in the National Student Survey improved in 2010, although the university remained in the bottom half of the table. Anatomy, physiology and pathology recorded a 100 per cent satisfaction rate, while initial teacher training, nursing and

---

Queensgate
Huddersfield
West Yorkshire HD1 3DH

0870 901 5555 (prospectus)
prospectus@hud.ac.uk
www.hud.ac.uk
www.huddersfield
   student.com
Affiliation: University
   Alliance

The Times Rankings
Overall Ranking: **59**

Student satisfaction:	=48	(77%)
Research quality:	=92	(0.2)
Entry standards:	=74	(273)
Student–staff ratio:	=52	(17.6)
Services & facilities/student:	47	(£1,439)
Expected completion rate:	=100	(77.6%)
Good honours:	=80	(56.1%)
Graduate prospects:	31	(69.5%)

history were close behind. The university's own satisfaction surveys suggest that students value the friendliness and helpfulness of staff. The dropout rate had been improving, but the latest projection of 20 per cent is higher than the national average for Huddersfield's courses and entry qualifications.

Most of the areas in which Huddersfield entered the 2008 Research Assessment Exercise contained at least some world-leading work. A third of the university's submission was placed in the top two categories, with music producing by far the best results and social work also doing well. The results brought a 45 per cent increase in research funding. A flourishing relationship with industry produces more private income than is achieved in many larger institutions, as well as influencing courses. The university has sealed partnerships recently with the National Physical Laboratory, the Food and Environment Research Agency and the Royal Armouries in developments that it expects to benefit undergraduates as well as researchers.

The most popular courses are in human and health sciences. Many arts and social science courses have a vocational slant. History, for example, includes a compulsory work placement module, while politics features a six-week placement, which often takes students to the House of Commons. The university's chancellor, the actor Sir Patrick Stewart, coaches drama students in his capacity as professor of performing arts. A third of the students in all subjects take sandwich courses, one of the highest proportions in Britain, and more than 4,000 have some element of work experience. The approach has been paying off in terms of graduate employment figures and applications, which were up by 14 per cent at the start of 2011 following a big increase in the previous year.

Most residential accommodation is now concentrated in the Storthes Hall Park student village, but additional housing is available at Ashenhurst, just over a mile from the campus. Recent developments mean that there are enough residential places to guarantee accommodation to first years, and private housing is cheap and plentiful in Huddersfield. Town–gown relations are good and most students like the town's friendly atmosphere, although they tend to base their social life on the students' union.

Undergraduate Fees and Support

» Fees for UK/EU students 2012–13   £7,950
» Fees for International students 2011–12   £10,750–£11,750
» A package of financial support and widening participation activity to be announced.
» Scholarships and bursaries based on circumstances or by competition are available.
» Check the university's website for the latest information.

Students		
Undergraduates:	**12,380**	(5,685)
Postgraduates:	**1,395**	(2,675)
Mature students:	**30.6%**	
Overseas students:	**5.1%**	
Applications per place:	**4.8**	
From state-sector schools:	**98.2%**	
From working-class homes:	**43.4%**	

For detailed information about fees, grants and bursaries and how they work, see chapter 7.

Accommodation

Number of places and costs refer to 2011–12

University-provided places: 1,711 in privately-owned halls

Percentage catered: 0%

Self-catered costs: £70–£99 a week.

First years are guaranteed accommodation provided conditions are met.

International students: as above.

Contact: www.digstudent.co.uk; www.digashenhurst.co.uk

University of Hull

Hull recorded one of the biggest ever rises in applications at a traditional university in 2009, so it did well to attract another big increase in 2010. The demand for places had flattened out at the beginning of 2011, but at a much higher level than previously. A string of excellent performances in the National Student Survey will have done the university no harm. Hull has been near the top for overall student satisfaction in every round of the survey, and made the top 20 again in 2010. American studies, history and archaeology, English and modern languages all returned extremely good scores, while French studies produced a satisfaction rating of 100 per cent.

The university and the city have always commanded loyalty among students, who appreciate the modest cost of living and ready availability of accommodation, as well as the quality of courses. Research plaudits have been more elusive, however. Hull had the lowest proportion of world-leading research among England's older universities in the 2008 exercise. Health subjects, geography and environmental science, and drama, dance and performance achieved the best grades. An Institute for Learning encourages academics to put research findings into practice, developing training courses and developing the university's interest in lifelong learning.

A longstanding focus on Europe shows in the wide range of languages available at degree level, with the purpose-built Language Institute heavily used by students of all subjects. Strength in politics is reflected in a steady flow of graduates into the House of Commons. The Westminster Hull Internship Programme (WHIP) offers a year-long placement and month-long internships for British politics and legislative studies students. A new Legal Advice Centre, staffed by law students, provides guidance and advice to the public.

After years of relative stability, Hull expanded rapidly, both on its spacious home campus and through mergers. First it added nursing to its portfolio of courses with the acquisition of the former Humberside College of Health, then it took in University College Scarborough. Finally the university bought the adjacent campus of the former Humberside (now Lincoln) University. The main academic development has been the establishment of a medical school in conjunction with York University, which takes 150 students a year and handles its own admissions. Hull's patient development, in collaboration with the local health authority, of a postgraduate medical school was rewarded with the award of a traditional school housed in a landmark building on the former Humberside (West) campus. The West campus also contains a Business Quarter, incorporating the Business School

---

Cottingham Road
Hull HU6 7RX

01482 466100 (admissions)
admissions@hull.ac.uk
www.hull.ac.uk
www.hyms.ac.uk
www.hullstudent.com
Affiliation: none

The Times Rankings
Overall Ranking: **53**

Student satisfaction:	=12	(81%)
Research quality:	=52	(1.1)
Entry standards:	=48	(309)
Student–staff ratio:	=80	(20.1)
Services & facilities/student:	73	(£1,244)
Expected completion rate:	68	(83.4%)
Good honours:	97	(52.0%)
Graduate prospects:	52	(64.6%)

and a new Enterprise Centre to support local business.

The original 94-acre main campus has also seen considerable development, with improvements to social facilities, new buildings for languages and chemistry, a Graduate Research Institute and a state-of-the-art sport, health and exercise science laboratory. The campus, with its art gallery and highly automated library, is less than three miles from the centre of Hull. In early 2010 the university opened a history centre in partnership with the city council, telling the story of the city over the centuries. It attracted 10,000 visitors in its first six weeks. The university spent more than £13 million in the summer of 2010 upgrading the teaching facilities and student accommodation, as well as bringing together student welfare and other advice services.

The Scarborough campus has also seen investment, with new laboratories for music technology and digital arts, and a renovated café bar. A new enterprise lab opened on the campus in 2010, helping new start-up firms and existing businesses to harness their innovations. Student union facilities and teaching rooms have also been refurbished. Hull has always maintained a roughly equal balance between science and technology and the arts and social sciences, but the Scarborough campus has tipped the scales towards the arts.

Nearly 95 per cent of the undergraduates are state-educated – one of the highest proportions at any pre-1992 university – while just over a third are from working-class homes. The projected dropout rate of 13 per cent is close to the benchmark for the university's courses and entry qualifications.

Student leisure facilities, which were always good but becoming crowded, have been upgraded as part of the campus building programme. The students' union, which has been rated among the best in Britain, has been refurbished and features the popular "Asylum" nightclub. New football pitches have been added recently on campus and the Sports and Fitness Centre has been attracting praise. Halls of residence in both Hull and Scarborough were refurbished in 2010.

Undergraduate Fees and Support

» Fees for UK/EU students 2012–13   £9,000
» Fees for International students 2011–12   £10,290–£12,495
     £23,268 (medicine)
» A package of financial support, including fee waivers and accommodation support, and widening participation activity to be announced.
» Scholarships and bursaries based on circumstances or by competition are available.
» Check the university's website for the latest information.

Students

Undergraduates:	**12,375**	**(7,325)**
Postgraduates:	**2,165**	**(1,210)**
Mature students:	**21.3%**	
Overseas students:	**10.4%**	
Applications per place:	**4.2**	
From state-sector schools:	**94.6%**	
From working-class homes:	**34.9%**	

For detailed information about fees, grants and bursaries and how they work, see chapter 7.

Accommodation

Number of places and costs refer to 2010–11
University-provided places: 2,601 (owned stock); 150 (leased/associated stock)
Percentage catered: 49%
Catered costs: £78.96–£126.63 (31 weeks).
Self-catered costs: £52.36–£88.83 a week (34–50 weeks).
Unaccompanied first years are guaranteed accommodation if conditions are met.
International students: as above.
Contact: www2.hull.ac.uk/student/accommodation.aspx

Imperial College of Science, Technology and Medicine

Regularly in the top four in *The Times* League Table, London's specialist university of science, engineering and medicine is also in the top ten of both the QS and *Times Higher Education* world rankings. Over 6,000 academic staff include 68 Fellows of the Royal Society, 68 Fellows of the Royal Academy of Engineering and 78 Fellows of the Academy of Medical Sciences. Imperial's submission for the 2008 Research Assessment Exercise contained a higher proportion of world-leading or internationally excellent work (73 per cent) than any other university's submission. The college achieved the best results in the UK for pure mathematics, chemical engineering, civil engineering, mechanical, aeronautical and manufacturing engineering, and history of science.

Imperial is not recommended for academic slouches, but tough entrance requirements ensure that they are a rare breed in any case. The projected dropout rate of almost 9 per cent is low, but still more than twice the national average for the courses and entry qualifications. Competition for places is high. There were nearly 15,000 applications for less than 2,500 places in 2010 and there was no fall in demand at the start of 2011. Even in subjects that struggle for candidates elsewhere, entrants

average better than two As and a B at A level. More than a third of the undergraduates are from independent schools – one of the highest proportions at any university and considerably more than the national average for Imperial's courses. Just over a third of the almost 15,000 students are from outside the EU.

Medicine has been the main area of development recently: mergers with the St Mary's, Charing Cross and Westminster, and Royal Postgraduate medical schools produced one of the biggest faculties of medicine in the UK. In 2007, Imperial formed the UK's first Academic Health Science Centre in partnership with Imperial College Healthcare NHS Trust in order to translate research advances into patient care. The partnership was named as one of the UK's five Academic Health Science Centres in 2009, denoting international excellence in biomedical research, education and patient care. The medical school has teaching bases attached to a number of hospitals in central and west London, and facilities at Hammersmith are currently being redeveloped to accommodate the AHSC. Imperial is also collaborating with Nanyang Technological University, in Singapore, to jointly deliver undergraduate medicine degree courses overseas from 2013.

Engineering degrees last four years and lead to an MEng. The college has been expanding its range of European exchanges, with a variety of prestigious technological institutions available for courses such as the

---

Exhibition Road
South Kensington
London SW7 2AZ

020 7589 5111 (switchboard)
contact via website
www.imperial.ac.uk
www.imperialcollege
  union.org
Affiliation: Russell Group

The Times Rankings
Overall Ranking: **4**

Student satisfaction:	=48	(77%)
Research quality:	=4	(3)
Entry standards:	3	(519)
Student–staff ratio:	4	(10.9)
Services & facilities/student:	1	(£3,971)
Expected completion rate:	28	(91.2%)
Good honours:	=14	(76.2%)
Graduate prospects:	2	(86.7%)

MSci in physics. The growing business school is Imperial's main concession to the academic world beyond science, technology and medicine. There is also an environmental research campus at Silwood Park, 25 miles west of London.

Scientists and engineers can develop and broaden skills by taking humanities or business modules. Many of the courses offered involve placements and students are actively encouraged to seek summer internships. The Undergraduate Research Opportunities Programme provides opportunities for "hands-on" experience of the research activities of college staff and postgraduates. It is especially popular in the summer vacation, when students can be paid bursaries and international undergraduates can participate without needing a work permit. The Careers Advisory Service's award-winning website has section dedicated to aiding international students, as well as supplementing the normal advice for home students.

Imperial celebrated its centenary in 2007 and has left the University of London to trade on its global reputation. It has been redeveloping and expanding facilities on its main campus, in the heart of South Kensington's museum district. Construction of a new sports centre, a second complex of halls of residence and refurbishments to the central library were completed in 2009 and a refurbished students' union bar and nightclub in September 2010.

Imperial's specialisms have the effect of making it one of the most male-dominated university institutions in Britain, although the number of female students doubled during the 1990s and now stands at more than a third. The social scene has improved and Imperial claims to have the largest selection of clubs and societies in the country. Outdoor sports facilities are remote, but there is a well-equipped sports centre at the South Kensington campus offering students free gym and swimming facilities.

Student satisfaction levels are well above the national average and particularly good for London, where many universities have struggled in the National Student Survey. Civil engineering, mechanical engineering, biology and medicine produced the best results in the survey published in 2010. There were high levels of satisfaction on the quality of teaching, the library and IT resources and personal development, but more concern about academics' feedback on students' work.

Undergraduate Fees and Support

» Fees for UK/EU students 2012–13   £9,000
» Fees for International students 2011–12   £22,450–£23,800
                                     £26,250–£39,150 (medicine)
» A package of financial support and widening participation activity to be announced.
» Scholarships and bursaries based on circumstances or by competition are available.
» Check the university's website for the latest information.

Students

Undergraduates:	**8,580**	**(0)**
Postgraduates:	**4,950**	**(1,335)**
Mature students:	**7.5%**	
Overseas students:	**35.3%**	
Applications per place:	**6.0**	
From state-sector schools:	**62.1%**	
From working-class homes:	**18.7%**	

For detailed information about fees, grants and bursaries and how they work, see chapter 7.

Accommodation

Number of places and costs refer to 2011–12
University-provided places: 2,497
Percentage catered: 0%
Self-catered costs: £57.48–£236.42 a week.
First-year undergraduates are guaranteed accommodation if application received by 29 July.
International students: as above.
Contact: accommodation@imperial.ac.uk

Keele University

Keele has set itself the goal of becoming the "ultimate 21st-century campus university" and is committing more than £70 million of public and private investment to provide the necessary facilities. The university has opted for £9,000 undergraduate fees in pursuit of that goal, but has promised financial support of at least £1,000 a year to the poorest third of its 2012 entrants. The guarantee would cover all students from the lowest socio-economic groups admitted in 2009, when Keele was also far more successful than other universities with similar courses and entry qualifications at recruiting from areas of low participation in higher education. The university has been trying to broaden its intake by targeting 12 and 13-year-olds with a special website, as well as running masterclasses in local schools and hosting a summer school.

The university is currently developing the Keele Distinctive Curriculum in time for 2012–13 entry, and is committed to breadth of study. The curriculum will build on the current degree structure, combining core academic activities with a purposeful range of co-curricular activities. At present, the majority of the degree programmes are dual honours degrees, with single honours in professional subjects like health and law. Popular combinations include criminology and psychology, geology and physical geography, history and politics, and biology and forensic science. More unusual pairings include geology and music, and mathematics and sociology. Students have a choice of over 500 degree combinations, most giving the opportunity of a semester abroad.

An emphasis on research since an improved set of results in the 2001 assessments brought limited success in the 2008 exercise. A total of 46 per cent of the work submitted was judged to be world-leading or internationally excellent, but Keele was still towards the bottom of the traditional universities on this measure. The most successful subjects were history and music, with some world-class work in primary care, physics, applied mathematics, business and management, law, social policy and administration, politics, Russian and English language and literature.

Green issues have been rising up the university's agenda as it achieved the Carbon Trust Standard. Within five years, the university aims to have at least halved its reliance on external energy supplies, and a number of initiatives are being developed to ensure that Keele gains international recognition for expertise in sustainability. A degree in environment and sustainability was introduced in 2009 and all undergraduates can take a module in sustainability or environmental studies.

However, health subjects have been the

Keele
Staffordshire ST5 5BG

01782 734005 (admissions)
undergraduate@keele.ac.uk
www.keele.ac.uk
www.kusu.net
Affiliation: none

The Times Rankings
Overall Ranking: **45**

Student satisfaction:	=20	(80%)
Research quality:	51	(1.2)
Entry standards:	47	(310)
Student–staff ratio:	=20	(14.5)
Services & facilities/student:	83	(£1,185)
Expected completion rate:	=32	(90.2%)
Good honours:	=57	(61.6%)
Graduate prospects:	45	(67.5%)

main focus of development in recent years. First degrees in physiotherapy and nursing and midwifery were added to the well-established postgraduate medical school. Keele also offers a five-year undergraduate medical course. Some 130 students each year are taught in new facilities on the Keele campus, at the University Hospital of North Staffordshire NHS Trust, three miles away, and at the Associate Teaching Hospital at the Shrewsbury and Telford Hospitals NHS Trust in Shropshire. Students take the new Keele undergraduate degree programme, which is in the process of validation by the GMC. New improved facilities for pharmacy and the natural sciences opened in 2010.

All Keele's courses are modular, with the academic year divided into two 15-week semesters, with breaks at Christmas and Easter. The university remains small by modern standards – under 7,000 full-time undergraduates, despite 75 per cent growth during the 1990s. The proportion of postgraduates has also been growing, with 20 per cent of students now taking higher degrees. Applications for undergraduate places were up by 27 per cent in 2010 and by more than 30 per cent at the start of 2011 – both among the biggest rises at any pre-1992 university.

Keele has an excellent record in the National Student Survey, with 89 per cent of final-year undergraduates satisfied in 2010, placing it on the verge of the top ten on this measure. The best results were in anatomy, physiotherapy, nursing, chemistry, biology, biochemistry, forensic science, geology, physical geography and environmental science. The projected dropout rate improved in the latest survey to 7 per cent – well below the national average for the university's subjects and entry qualifications.

The cost of living in the Potteries and the surrounding area is relatively low. But nearly two thirds of the undergraduates live on the attractive 617-acre campus, which inevitably dominates the social scene as well as providing part-time employment for hundreds of students. More than £2 million was spent during 2009–10 improving the halls of residence and adding to student social space. The sports facilities have benefited from a new all-weather pitch, and the leisure centre has refurbished its fitness suite.

Undergraduate Fees and Support

» Fees for UK/EU students 2012–13 £9,000
» Fees for International students 2011–12 £9,990–£11,800
£19,570–£22,900 (medicine)
» Financial support will include a £3,000 National Scholarship (fee waiver of £2,000 plus £1,000 cash bursary) for the most-disadvantaged 10 per cent of the 2012 intake; a £1,000 cash bursary for all other students with a household income below £25K.
» Scholarships and bursaries based on circumstances or by competition are available.
» Check the university's website for the latest information.

Students

Undergraduates:	**6,750**	**(1,500)**
Postgraduates:	**790**	**(1,425)**
Mature students:	**15.0%**	
Overseas students:	**7.0%**	
Applications per place:	**7.1**	
From state-sector schools:	**91.6%**	
From working-class homes:	**33.1%**	

For detailed information about fees, grants and bursaries and how they work, see chapter 7.

Accommodation

Number of places and costs refer to 2011–12
University-provided places: 3,200
Percentage catered: 0% (optional meal plan available)
Self-catered costs: £68–£115 a week.
First years are guaranteed accommodation on campus if Keele is first or firm choice university.
International students: guaranteed accommodation for the duration of their course. Deadlines apply.
Contact: accomenq@keele.ac.uk

University of Kent

Kent has capitalised sensibly on its position near the Channel ports, specialising in international programmes, as well as in the flexible degree structures that have been the hallmark of most 1960s universities. Styling itself "the UK's European university", Kent now has postgraduate sites in Brussels and Paris, as well as giving many undergraduates the option of a year abroad. Partnerships with over 100 European universities make Kent one of the UK's most enthusiastic participants in the EU's Erasmus exchange programme, providing its undergraduates with study or work opportunities in countries from Spain to the Czech Republic.

The university has been broadening its horizons at home as well, assuming a regional role. Access courses throughout the county allow students to upgrade their qualifications to university standard, but the main focus is on the Medway towns, where Kent is involved in ambitious projects with Greenwich and Canterbury Christ Church universities and Mid-Kent College. The Medway campus, based in the old Chatham naval base, has already exceeded its target of 6,000, a third of whom are Kent students. A new School of Pharmacy is the main feature of a £50-million development. It now has more than 550 undergraduates.

The original low-rise campus, set in 300 acres of parkland overlooking Canterbury, is tidy rather than architecturally distinguished. The student centre has a nightclub big enough to attract big-name bands, as well as a theatre, cinema and bars. The university has another base in Tonbridge serving part-time students, of whom there are 3,000 across Kent, mainly taught in associate colleges. Entry grades for full-time degrees have been rising in most subjects. Offers are pitched according to the UCAS points tariff, although those taking A levels are expected to pass at least three subjects (one of which may be general studies).

Applications have been increasing, partly thanks to the Medway development. The demand for places was down slightly at the start of 2011, but this followed three successive big increases. Kent is strongest in the social sciences, although biosciences, philosophy, and drama, dance and theatre studies took pride of place in the old system of teaching assessments, each registering a maximum score. The university takes teaching standards seriously, encouraging all academics to take a postgraduate certificate in higher education. Kent academics have been awarded national teaching fellowships in each of the last four years.

The university was also much more successful in the 2008 research assessments than in previous exercises, with more than half of its submission placed in the top two categories – 30 per cent of research in social

---

Canterbury
Kent CT2 7NZ

01227 827272 (admissions)
information@kent.ac.uk
www.kent.ac.uk
www.kentunion.co.uk
Affiliation: none

Edinburgh
Belfast
Cardiff London
CANTERBURY

The Times Rankings
Overall Ranking: **39**

Student satisfaction:	=24	(79%)
Research quality:	=42	(1.6)
Entry standards:	42	(329)
Student–staff ratio:	=18	(14.4)
Services & facilities/student:	62	(£1,311)
Expected completion rate:	40	(88.6%)
Good honours:	=55	(61.9%)
Graduate prospects:	=66	(60.7%)

policy was considered world-leading. Kent has since been awarded ten prestigious Erasmus Mundus joint doctoral fellowships in the humanities. The university has been building up its science departments, among which computing is particularly well regarded, but still a majority of the students take arts or social sciences. Graduates of all disciplines fare well in the employment market – the university regularly features among the top 20 for graduate starting salaries. It is also in the top 20 in the National Student Survey, with 100 per cent satisfaction in electrical and electronic engineering and molecular biology and biochemistry. There were good scores, too, in American studies, chemistry and forensic science, comparative literary studies, modern languages and psychology.

The university has a more mixed intake than many in the south of England: over nine out of ten undergraduates are from state schools and a over quarter come from working-class homes. Kent has opted for £9,000 undergraduate fees, but has promised fee waivers and bursaries to preserve access for such groups. Significant numbers of American and European students give the university a cosmopolitan feel and campus security is good, although some complain that Canterbury itself is expensive and limited socially.

Undergraduates on the main campus are attached to one of four colleges, although they do not select it themselves. The colleges act as the focus of social life, and include academic as well as residential facilities. They provide accommodation for all first years. Among £100 million of completed or planned capital developments has been an expansion of sports facilities and residential accommodation at the Parkwood student village, bringing the total number of residential places to 4,300. The most recent developments on the main campus have included a new School of Arts building, the Canterbury Innovation Centre and a new sports pavilion. Future developments on the Medway campus, which now has 600 residential places, will include an expanded presence in the dockyard part of the site to accommodate the School of Arts there.

Undergraduate Fees and Support

» Fees for UK/EU students 2012–13   £9,000
» Fees for International students 2011–12   £11,230–£13,400
» A package of financial support and widening participation activity to be announced.
» Scholarships and bursaries based on circumstances or by competition are available.
» Check the university's website for the latest information.

Students		
Undergraduates:	**12,915**	**(3,415)**
Postgraduates:	**1,655**	**(1,275)**
Mature students:	**14.3%**	
Overseas students:	**13.9%**	
Applications per place:	**5.5**	
From state-sector schools:	**93.0%**	
From working-class homes:	**28.3%**	

For detailed information about fees, grants and bursaries and how they work, see chapter 7.

Accommodation

Number of places and costs refer to 2011–12
University-provided places: 4,981
Percentage catered: 16%
Catered costs: £115–£129 a week.
Self-catered costs: £95–£138 a week.
First years are guaranteed accommodation provided applications received before 31 July.
International students: as above
Contact: hospitality-enquiry@kent.ac.uk

King's College London

One of the oldest and largest of London University's colleges, King's has been cementing its reputation among the elite of British higher education. Ranked among the top 25 universities in the world, it is Europe's largest centre for the education of doctors, dentists and other healthcare professionals and home to six Medical Research Council centres. Sixty per cent of the work submitted to the 2008 Research Assessment Exercise was judged to be world-leading or internationally excellent, with cardiovascular medicine, dentistry, nutritional sciences, philosophy, languages and the Centre for Computing in the Humanities among the leaders in their fields.

Applications were up by 3 per cent at the start of 2011, following a much bigger increase in 2010. About one student in five is from outside the European Union, many of them among the 9,500 postgraduates. King's has done well in the National Student Survey and saw a big rise in satisfaction levels in 2010, placing it in the top 30. Biology, history and archaeology, biomedical sciences, pharmacy and Iberian languages produced the best results. An institutional audit by the Quality Assurance Agency gave King's the highest mark, stressing the excellence of the student support services.

King's is now concentrated on four main campuses close to the Thames, within walking distance of each other. The original Strand site and the Waterloo campus, which includes the largest university building in London, house most of the non-medical departments. Nursing and midwifery and some biomedical subjects are also based at Waterloo, while medicine and dentistry are mainly at Guy's Hospital, near London Bridge, and in the St Thomas' Hospital campus, across the river from the Houses of Parliament. A fifth site, at Denmark Hill, in south London, houses the Institute of Psychiatry and more medicine and dentistry. Information services centres on each campus provide students with integrated library and computing facilities. There are over 1,600 PC workstations and computer rooms are open 24 hours a day, seven days a week. An extensive wireless internet also covers much of the college.

King's has recently acquired the east wing of the iconic Somerset House, and is now in the second phase of a £1-billion programme which is transforming its estate. A £40-million redevelopment of the Grade I listed King's Building provided new teaching facilities, wireless internet access, social and catering facilities. The conversion of the former Public Record Office in Chancery Lane created the largest new university library in Britain since World War II. A donation of £4 million by a graduate allowed the spectacular Maughan Library to be equipped with 1,600 networked reader places.

Strand
London WC2R 2LS

020 7836 5454 (enquiries)
thecompass@kcl.ac.uk
www.kcl.ac.uk
www.kclsu.org
Affiliation: Russell Group

The Times Rankings
Overall Ranking: **24**

Student satisfaction:	=48	(77%)
Research quality:	=21	(2.2)
Entry standards:	11	(447)
Student–staff ratio:	8	(12)
Services & facilities/student:	19	(£1,924)
Expected completion rate:	17	(93.7%)
Good honours:	=18	(75.3%)
Graduate prospects:	6	(82.6%)

Once known primarily for science, King's now excels in a wide range of subjects in nine schools of study, including such unusual features as Britain's only department devoted entirely to Portuguese – one of four language departments rated internationally outstanding in the latest research assessments. War studies is another unusual and well-regarded department.

Graduates enjoy one of the best employment rates in the UK and typically, also earn among the highest starting salaries. Although King's has slipped in this year's *Times* League Table, it is in the top five for graduate prospects. The college's central location means King's students are in an enviable position for accessing opportunities for work experience.

More than a quarter of the undergraduates come from independent schools, despite the college's efforts to widen its intake. Among the medical courses, for example, are successful programmes catering for mature students and school-leavers who have attended London comprehensives with generally poor A-level results. Much of the teaching is in small groups and every student is allocated a personal tutor.

Student facilities on the Strand and Guy's campuses have been upgraded recently and the active students' union, which runs bars, cafes and a nightclub, puts on an extensive programme of events. The college is well provided with accommodation places in a variety of residences, in busy central locations as well as quieter, residential areas. There are 2,623 places in university provided housing, 175 in Liberty Living residencies and 724 in the University of London Intercollegiate halls. Some of the outdoor sports facilities are a long way from the college, but are accessible by train. They have facilities for all the main sports, while there are also rifle ranges, two gyms and a swimming pool.

Undergraduate Fees and Support

» Fees for UK/EU students 2012–13   £9,000
» Fees for International students 2011–12   £13,250–£16,800
                                           £31,150 (medicine)
» Financial support will include 116 National Scholarships (£3,000 matched fee waiver);
King's STEM Enterprise Scholarships of £9,000 fee waiver and £1,000 cash bursary for up to 30 students with household income below £25K;
King's Living Bursaries of £1,000 for students with full maintenance grant, and £500 for partial grant;
£9,000 first year fee waiver for up to 85 students and Access to the Professions programme.
» Scholarships and bursaries based on circumstances or by competition are available.
» Check the university's website for the latest information.

Students

Undergraduates:	**12,400**	**(2,570)**
Postgraduates:	**5,580**	**(3,945)**
Mature students:	**18.1%**	
Overseas students:	**16.5%**	
Applications per place:	**9.1**	
From state-sector schools:	**71.7%**	
From working-class homes:	**24.2%**	

For detailed information about fees, grants and bursaries and how they work, see chapter 7.

Accommodation

Number of places and costs refer to 2010–11
University-provided places: 2,623; 724 intercollegiate.
Percentage catered: 17.9% King's Residences; 100% intercollegiate
Catered costs: £116.48 King's Residence; £122.50–£227.50 intercollegiate a week
Self-catered costs: £71.19–£144.41 (40 weeks); £255.00 single studio.
New full-time undergraduate students are guaranteed the offer of one year in accommodation if specific conditions are met.
International students: priority for new students.
Contact: 020 7848 2759; www.kcl.ac.uk/accomm

Kingston University

Kingston's mission is to be an inclusive university, open to all who can benefit from higher education. It has one of the most ethnically mixed student populations of any UK university and many undergraduates are the first in their family to experience higher education. Kingston has been one of the UK's fastest-growing universities over recent years. Applications had increased by twice the national average at the start of 2011, enabling the university to reduce the numbers recruited through Clearing. The university is revitalising its four campuses, opening three impressive new buildings as part of a £123-million programme which will run to 2018. The new facilities, which include multiple projection systems, video conferencing, interactive displays and built-in voting systems, have won plaudits from staff and students alike. The centrepiece is the £20-million John Galsworthy Building at the heart of the Penrhyn Road campus, which incorporates lecture theatres, flexible teaching space and information technology suites as well as a "Knowledge Centre" giving students a spacious setting, including at a laptop bar, in which to do course work.

There have been extensive upgrades of the library facilities on each campus. Learning resource centres bring together library, computing and multimedia facilities to encourage interactive and group learning. There are bookable study rooms with multimedia facilities and specially equipped spaces dedicated to meeting the needs of disabled users. The main LRCs are open 24 hours a day during term weekdays and a high-tech self issue system makes borrowing resources much quicker and easier.

The university markets itself as in "lively, leafy London", making a virtue of its suburban location southwest of central London as well as its proximity to the bright lights. Two of its four campuses are close to Kingston town centre; another, two miles away, is at Kingston Hill; the fourth is in Roehampton Vale, where a site once used as an aerospace factory now contains a new technology block. A flight simulator and the university's own Learjet as well as a Foundation degree in aeronautical engineering continue the tradition. Kingston boasts the third largest engineering faculty in London, behind Imperial College and Brunel.

Elsewhere, new buildings under way include a new home for the Business School and extensive refurbishment at the Knights Park site, home to the Faculty of Art, Design and Architecture. Other developments include a three-storey teaching extension at the Faculty of Engineering's Roehampton Vale site. The university also contributed to the £11-million cost of the Rose Theatre, where students and staff use performance and exhibition space.

River House
53–57 High Street
Kingston upon Thames
Surrey KT1 1LQ

0844 855 2177 (application enquiries)
aps@kingston.ac.uk
www.kingston.ac.uk
www.kusu.co.uk
Affiliation: million+

KINGSTON
UPON THAMES

The Times Rankings
Overall Ranking: **97**

Student satisfaction:	=78	(74%)
Research quality:	=79	(0.3)
Entry standards:	104	(243)
Student–staff ratio:	79	(19.9)
Services & facilities/student:	87	(£1,155)
Expected completion rate:	87	(80.4%)
Good honours:	=55	(61.9%)
Graduate prospects:	=104	(52.3%)

Approaching a third of the university's submission to the 2008 Research Assessment Exercise was rated world-leading or internationally excellent. The star performance was in history of art, architecture and design, where half of the submission was at least internationally excellent. In nursing, 15 per cent of the work reached the top level, and in business and management studies, the proportion was 10 per cent, making Kingston the highest-rated new university in the field.

Nursing is part of the Faculty of Health and Social Care Sciences, a collaboration with St George's Hospital Medical School, which now has more than 4,000 students and also covers midwifery, radiography, physiotherapy, social work, paramedic science and biomedical sciences. A new £420,000 purpose-built pharmacy practice laboratory opened in 2009. Radiotherapy students are among the first in the country to hone their clinical skills in a simulated cancer treatment room. The Centre for Paramedic Science serves as a hub for course delivery and a raft of revolutionary research projects positions the two institutions at the forefront of paramedic education. The Royal Marsden School of Cancer Nursing and Rehabilitation launched a new collaboration with the faculty in 2010.

Over a quarter of Kingston's places go to mature students and around 40 per cent to those from working-class families – both groups with low completion rates nationally.

Students get extra support in their first year. The latest projected dropout rate is just over 15 per cent, lower than the national average for the subjects on offer. Results in the National Student Survey are around the average for London universities. Medical technology produced a second successive 100 per cent satisfaction rating in 2010, when nursing, biology, mathematics and English all scored well.

Students like the university's location, although they complain about the high cost of living. A "one-stop shop" deals with student issues ranging from careers and accommodation to complaints and financial advice. Over £20 million has been spent on halls of residence and Kingston's sports facilities have improved. A new £2.65-million sports pavilion, designed to suit both able-bodied and disabled users, and an upgraded sports ground opened in 2010.

Undergraduate Fees and Support

» Fees for UK/EU students 2012–13 £8,500

   Foundation degree £6,000

   Pharmacy and studio-based art and design £9,000

» Fees for International students 2011–12 £9,950–£11,000

» A package of financial support and widening participation activity to be announced. It will include matching funding for more than 520 National Scholarships; Kingston scholarships for other first generation entrants with household income below £25K.

» Check the university's website for the latest information.

Students		
Undergraduates:	**18,270**	**(2,085)**
Postgraduates:	**3,405**	**(3,325)**
Mature students:	**26.7%**	
Overseas students:	**11.7%**	
Applications per place:	**5.9**	
From state-sector schools:	**96.5%**	
From working-class homes:	**40.5%**	

For detailed information about fees, grants and bursaries and how they work, see chapter 7.

Accommodation

Number of places and costs refer to 2011–12

University-provided places: 2,360; private hall: 214

Percentage catered: 0%

Self-catered costs: £96.00–£120.25 a week (university provided); £148.50–£175.00 (private hall).

Offers accommodation to many first-years who make Kingston their firm choice.

International students: offered places if conditions met, subject to availability.

Contact: www.kingston.ac.uk/accommodation/

Lancaster University

Lancaster broke into the top ten for the first time in last year's *Times* League Table and it has moved up another place in the latest edition. Students are more satisfied, entry grades have gone up and a higher proportion of undergraduates achieved top-class degrees. Having celebrated its 45th birthday and almost completed a £300-million makeover of its campus, Lancaster has been expanding its overseas activities in line with its ambition to be truly international. The campus hosts students from more than 100 countries, but there will soon be more graduating with the university's degrees in India, Malaysia and Pakistan than in Lancaster itself. The university has opened a campus near Delhi in partnership with an Indian group and in the latest development, is offering dual degrees with COMSATS Institute of Information Technology, in Pakistan.

At home, recent campus developments will increase its capacity by up to 50 per cent. A £10-million building for the Lancaster Institute for the Contemporary Arts has brought together art, music and theatre studies with the university's public art gallery, concerts and theatre. Still a relatively small institution, Lancaster has established itself in among the leading research universities, with Vice-Chancellor Professor Paul Wellings

chairing the 1994 Group. It is a member of the N8 Group of northern research universities and is amongst the highest-placed institution in the northwest in league tables.

Lancaster has done well in all six National Student Surveys. Linguistics, physics and astronomy all recorded 100 per cent satisfaction ratings in 2010, when English, history, law, sociology and human and social geography all did well. The university has also won nine National Teaching Fellowships since the scheme was launched in 2000.

Lancaster did not quite repeat the scale of success achieved in the 2001 Research Assessment Exercise in 2008, but more than 60 per cent of its work was rated as world-leading or internationally excellent. Physics was the star performer, with the best results in the country, but there were good results in health studies, computer science, art and design, management and sociology. Specialising in environmental research, Lancaster has won both a Queen's Anniversary Prize and the *Times Higher* research project of the year award for the development of water-saving techniques which help farmers in some of the world's driest regions.

A new 24-hour student learning space at the centre of the campus will provide students with flexible learning environments and social space with up-to-date technology. Infolab 21, the £15-million centre of excellence in information communication

Bailrigg
Lancaster LA1 4YW

01524 592028 (admissions)
ugadmissions@lancaster.ac.uk
www.lancaster.ac.uk
www.lusu.co.uk
Affiliation: 1994 Group

The Times Rankings
Overall Ranking: **9**

Student satisfaction:	=12	(81%)
Research quality:	=9	(2.7)
Entry standards:	24	(407)
Student–staff ratio:	14	(13.8)
Services & facilities/student:	23	(£1,825)
Expected completion rate:	=15	(93.8%)
Good honours:	22	(73.6%)
Graduate prospects:	=23	(71.8%)

technology, acts as a technology transfer and incubation facility and houses a training facility for high-tech businesses. Other recent developments include a leadership centre for the highly rated Management School.

Lancaster is another of the campus universities which has always championed a flexible degree structure. Most undergraduates can broaden their first-year studies by taking a second or third subject. The final choice of degree comes only at the end of that year. Combined degree programmes, with 200 courses to choose from, are especially popular. The degree portfolio now includes medicine, with students taking a five-year course following the Liverpool University curriculum. New developments include a research centre specialising in bipolar disorder and a new Centre for Organisational Health and Wellbeing.

The projected dropout rate of 6 per cent is lower than the average for the subjects on offer. Lancaster also exceeds expectations for the recruitment of state-school students and the proportion from working-class homes is only marginally below the benchmark for the university's courses and entry grades.

Students join one of eight residential colleges on campus, which become the centre of most students' social life. Most house between 800 and 900 students in self-catering accommodation and each has its own bar and social facilities. The pioneering 800-room

Eco Residence, which opened in 2008, has won an environmental award. As part of the developments, Cartmel and Lonsdale colleges have transferred to the New Alexandra Park area of the campus with enhanced social facilities.

The campus has been praised by students, especially for its refurbished lecture theatres and academic areas. Lancaster itself is a ten-minute bus ride away. Both the campus and city have been rated among the safest in the UK. Sports facilities are good and conveniently placed. A £20-millon sports centre will open in 2011, and feature a climbing wall built to Chancellor Sir Chris Bonington's specifications. For the outdoor life, the Lake District is within easy reach and there is a "trim trail" through the woodland surrounding the campus. Road and rail communications are good, but Lancaster is inevitably more limited than larger university centres in terms of off-campus life.

Undergraduate Fees and Support

» Fees for UK/EU students 2012–13   £9,000
» Fees for International students 2011–12   £11,425–£14,580
» A package of financial support and widening participation and retention activity to be announced.
» Scholarships and bursaries based on circumstances or by competition.
» Check the university's website for the latest information.

Students

Undergraduates:	8,180	(600)
Postgraduates:	1,940	(1,405)
Mature students:	4.8%	
Overseas students:	15.5%	
Applications per place:	4.6	
From state-sector schools:	92.1%	
From working-class homes:	25.5%	

For detailed information about fees, grants and bursaries and how they work, see chapter 7.

Accommodation

Number of places and costs refer to 2011–12
University-provided places: 6,600 (plus about 1,000 places in university-managed houses)
Percentage catered: 5%
Catered costs: £109.48 (standard) – £141.33 (en suite).
Self-catered costs: £73.85–£105.60 a week; £126 for flats or studios.
All first years are normally accommodated; no formal guarantee for Insurance, Clearing and late applicants.
International students are guaranteed accommodation.
Contact: CRO@lancaster.ac.uk

University of Leeds

The rise of Leeds as a shopping and clubbing centre has added to the attractions of a university which has long been one of the giants of the higher education system. It is the third most popular UK university in terms of applications, but even so the demand for places was flat at the start of 2011. Leeds scaled back its campus development plan and cut a number of academic posts to cope with a looming deficit, but is still spending heavily on new facilities that are designed to propel it into the top 50 universities in the world. It rose 14 places in the QS World University Rankings in 2009.

Like all its fellow members of the Russell Group of research-led universities, Leeds will charge £9,000 for undergraduate tuition in 2012. But it expects a third of UK and EU students to benefit from subsidies, which they can choose to take as fee waivers, bursaries or accommodation discounts. An unusually wide range of degrees gives applicants more than 500 undergraduate programmes to choose from, with over 2,000 academic staff teaching 33,000 students, including more than 9,000 postgraduates.

The university occupies a 98-acre site within walking distance of the city centre. The buildings are a mixture of Victorian and modern. The latest developments are The Edge – a new swimming pool and 200-station fitness centre, which is one of the largest at any UK university – a high-spec hall of residence, a childcare centre and new buildings for the schools of earth and environment and law.

Leeds is part of the Worldwide Universities Network, which brings together 16 research-led universities to collaborate on research, postgraduate degree programmes and continuing professional development. There is a thriving study abroad programme and the university has links with over 200 universities around the world. A free-standing language unit caters for casual learners as well as specialists.

Leeds operates a modular course system, enabling its students to take elective modules or combine complementary subjects. Almost a quarter now take joint honours or interdisciplinary combinations such as nanotechnology, women's studies or international studies. The university was chosen to house a national centre of excellence in interdisciplinary teaching and another in assessment and learning in medical practice settings.

The 2008 Research Assessment Exercise scores showed improvement since 2001, with over 60 per cent of the university's submission rated as world-leading or internationally excellent. Electrical and electronic engineering produced the best results in the country, with social work and social policy, English, Italian, geography and

---

Leeds
West Yorkshire LS2 9JT

0113 343 2336 (enquiries)
contact via website
www.leeds.ac.uk
www.leedsuniversityunion.
 org.uk
Affiliation: Russell Group

The Times Rankings
Overall Ranking: **30**

Student satisfaction:	=37	(78%)
Research quality:	=25	(2.1)
Entry standards:	=22	(408)
Student–staff ratio:	=24	(14.9)
Services & facilities/student:	49	(£1,416)
Expected completion rate:	24	(92.1%)
Good honours:	12	(76.7%)
Graduate prospects:	50	(65.8%)

nursing also highly rated. Income from research grants and contracts continued to grow in 2009–10, increasing by 6 per cent to £119 million. Leeds also has 17 national teaching fellows – more than any other university in England.

The Quality Assurance Agency gave Leeds the best possible verdict on its academic processes in 2008. Scores in the National Student Survey published in 2010 slipped back for the second year in a row, but are still in line with the average for all universities. Pharmacologists and aural and oral scientists were 100 per cent satisfied for the third year running, while biology, social studies and zoology produced the best of the remaining results. The verdict on learning resources was especially positive, thanks to one of the largest libraries at any UK universities and an extensive IT network.

Sports and social facilities are first rate. Leeds teams regularly excel in competition and the university hosts one of five centres of cricketing excellence. Sustainability is a key strategic aim of the university, and Leeds has won a number of environmental awards, including the 2009 Green Gown Award for continuous improvement and a place among the top 25 in the People and Planet Green League.

National statistics show just more than a quarter of the undergraduates coming from independent schools and over a fifth come from working-class homes. The projected dropout rate has improved and, at less than 8 per cent, is only slightly above the national average for the university's courses and entry grades. The already large students' union, famous for its long bar and big-name rock concerts, has been extended to cope with the latest phase in the university's expansion. It was named the NUS Students' Union of the Year 2009–10 and is the UK's only gold accredited students' union under a national evaluation scheme. In 2010–11, £1 million is being spent on the union building to provide better services and more space for students to socialise.

Town–gown relations are generally good, although residents in Headingley, the main student area for both of the city's universities, have complained about the impact on their neighbourhood. The wider local community benefits from 2,000 student volunteers.

Undergraduate Fees and Support

» Fees for UK/EU students 2012–13 £9,000
» Fees for International students 2011–12 £11,800–£15,600
 29,750 (medicine)
» Students with household income below £25K: £3,000 fee waiver, cash award or accommodation discount; with household income £25K–£42.6K: sliding scale; and with no household income: up to £6,000 in year 1, £3,000 in years 2 and 3.
» Scholarships and bursaries based on circumstances or by competition.
» Check the university's website for the latest information.

Students

Undergraduates:	**22,595**	**(1,485)**
Postgraduates:	**6,935**	**(2,565)**
Mature students:	**7.4%**	
Overseas students:	**8.0%**	
Applications per place:	**7.1**	
From state-sector schools:	**74.2%**	
From working-class homes:	**21.6%**	

For detailed information about fees, grants and bursaries and how they work, see chapter 7.

Accommodation

Number of places and costs refer to 2011–12
University-provided places: 7,900
Percentage catered: 23%
Catered costs: £102–£161 a week.
Self-catered costs: £74–£139 a week.
Single first years are guaranteed a place provided conditions are met.
International students: guaranteed to full fee-paying undergraduates if conditions are met.
Contact: www.leeds.ac.uk/accommodation

Leeds Metropolitan University

Leeds Met took the bold step of charging only two thirds of the £3,000-a-year maximum allowed when top-up fees were introduced in 2006. Having suffered the financial consequences, it will not be doing the same in 2012, although its £8,500 undergraduate fee will again be below the maximum. The university says this is the least it needs to replace lost Government funding, establish schemes to support the retention and success of students, and support a wide range of activities to improve social mobility.

Promotional ventures, such as the sponsorship of professional rugby league, and penalties for the misreporting of student numbers left the university with considerable financial problems. But the arrival of Professor Susan Price as Vice-Chancellor has injected a note of optimism. Student satisfaction scores shot up in 2010, taking the university well clear of the foot of the National Student Survey table. For the second year in a row, physiotherapists were 100 per cent satisfied with their course and there were extremely good results in aural and oral science, nursing and nutrition. Applications were up by 11 per cent at the start of 2011, following an even bigger increase in 2010.

Leeds Met has a longstanding reputation for widening participation in higher education: it is one of the largest providers of Foundation degrees and has almost 28,000 students, including part-timers. A quarter of the students come from the Yorkshire and Humberside region, and around one in five is over 20 on entry. More than 90 per cent are state-educated and almost a third come from working-class homes. A Regional University Network of 24 further education colleges, which stretches from Belfast to Stamford via Glasgow, enables students to take Leeds Met courses locally.

Some 2,500 students come from 90 countries outside the UK, including 200 from Africa. Only just over half all undergraduates are taking conventional full-time degrees, such is the popularity of sandwich and part-time courses. The projected dropout rate of 16 per cent has improved but is still above average for the university's courses and entry qualifications. As part of its efforts to widen access, Leeds Met runs a course for sixth-formers from the region, awarding UCAS points for those who complete successfully. There is also a wide range of summer schools, including one for Asian women and one for Afro-Caribbean boys.

There are two bases in Leeds: the Civic Quarter campus, close to the city centre, and the Headingley campus, three miles away in the 100 acres of park and woodland of Beckett Park. The latter boasts outstanding

Civic Quarter
Leeds
West Yorkshire LS1 3HE

0113 812 3113 (enquiries)
www.experience.leedsmet.ac.uk
www.lmu.ac.uk
www.leedsmetsu.co.uk
Affiliation: million+

The Times Rankings
Overall Ranking: **=104**

Student satisfaction:	=103	(71%)
Research quality:	=92	(0.2)
Entry standards:	=84	(267)
Student–staff ratio:	=88	(20.6)
Services & facilities/student:	111	(£941)
Expected completion rate:	72	(82.6%)
Good honours:	93	(52.9%)
Graduate prospects:	=86	(55.5%)

sports facilities, including the £2-million Carnegie Regional Tennis Centre, as well as teaching accommodation for education, informatics, law and business. Over 7,000 students take part in some form of sporting activity, and there is a range of £2,000 sports scholarships. The university has been named a UK centre for coaching excellence.

The Civic Quarter campus is the subject of a £100-million development programme. A futuristic lecture theatre complex next to Leeds Civic Hall now houses the business school. The former BBC building has reopened as Old Broadcasting House, while next door Broadcasting Place has become the new home of the Faculty of Arts and Society. In the first developments of their kind, a new stand has been built at the Headingley rugby ground, with classrooms, coaching facilities and social space for use by the university and the two professional clubs, and a new pavilion at the adjacent Test and County Cricket ground has similar multi-use facilities. It hosts students on media, events management and hospitality courses.

Relatively few academics were entered for the 2008 Research Assessment Exercise, but nearly a third of their work was judged to be world-leading or internationally excellent. Communication, cultural and media studies, sport and library and information management produced the best results. Students are included on the committees that design and manage courses.

A growing emphasis on educational technology is enhanced by a £20-million learning resources centre. More than 400 computers, audiovisual presentation studios and study areas are available all hours. Contacts with small and medium-sized businesses have been carefully fostered as part of the university's successful attempts to maintain a good record in graduate employment. Like its older neighbour, Leeds Met is benefiting from the city's growing reputation for nightlife, but it is making its own contribution with a famously lively entertainments scene. With 4,500 bed spaces, those who accept places before Clearing are guaranteed university accommodation. Carnegie Village, a self-contained residential facility on the Headingley campus, has added to the places available. The Athletic Union hosts 32 clubs and came second in the BUCS competitions in 2009–10. A season pass for both the Headingley campus and Civic Quarter facilities cost £100 in 2010–11.

Undergraduate Fees and Support

» Fees for UK/EU students 2012–13   £8,500
» Fees for International students 2011–12   £10,500–£11,500
» A package of financial support, including match funding the National Scholarship Programme, and widening participation and retention activity to be announced.
» Scholarships and bursaries based on circumstances or by competition.
» Check the university's website for the latest information.

Students		
Undergraduates:	**17,710**	**(5,710)**
Postgraduates:	**1,745**	**(2,705)**
Mature students:	**20.5%**	
Overseas students:	**4.5%**	
Applications per place:	**5.8**	
From state-sector schools:	**93.2%**	
From working-class homes:	**36.9%**	

For detailed information about fees, grants and bursaries and how they work, see chapter 7.

Accommodation

Number of places and costs refer to 2011–12

University-provided places: 4,500

Percentage catered: 0%

Self-catered costs: £82–£145 a week (41–51 weeks).

First years with Conditional Firm or Unconditional Firm offers guaranteed accommodation.

International students: guaranteed accommodation if conditions are met.

Contact: www.leedsmet.ac.uk/accommodation

University of Leicester

Leicester has been enjoying a period of unprecedented success, after many years living in the shadow of the big city universities. Consistently among the leaders in the National Student Survey, it has become a fixture in the top 20 of the *Times* League Table. The university has shown the scale of its ambitions with a £1-billion development plan. The Queen opened the university's new £32-million library in 2008 and another £16 million has been spent on a new students' union that includes the only O2 Academy at a UK university.

Applications have risen substantially over several years, although they had slipped back a little at the start of 2011. The same applied to Leicester's scores in the 2010 student survey, although the university still finished in the top ten. American studies, chemistry, geology, molecular biology, politics and physics produced the best results. The university has been trialling the use of social media to improve feedback in an attempt to increase satisfaction levels even more. A new web technologies facility opened in 2010 to keep staff up to date with the latest developments in e-learning and web technologies more generally.

Although Leicester will celebrate its 90th anniversary in 2011, it only approaches the size of other big city universities by dint of rapid growth in postgraduate and distance learning programmes. The 9,185 full-time undergraduates based on the main campus represent just over half of the student population. Professor Sir Robert Burgess, the Vice-Chancellor, has focused on strengthening research, and Leicester entered a much larger proportion of its academics than many of its peers in the 2008 Research Assessment Exercise. As a result of the large entry, less than half of the university's submission was considered world-leading or internationally excellent, but there was a big increase in research funding. The star performer was the small department of museum studies, which produced the highest proportion of world-leading research in any subject at any UK university, with almost two thirds of its work placed in that top category.

Leicester has the most socially diverse intake of any university in our top 20, partly as a result of initiatives such as a summer school for local teenagers. An £8-million scholarship programme is designed to keep it that way, offsetting the impact of £9,000 undergraduate fees. Among the elements will be £3,000 scholarships for students from disadvantaged backgrounds and £2,000 awards for those who achieve three As at A level, or the equivalent. Nearly nine out of ten undergraduates come from state schools and more than a quarter come from working-class homes. The 7 per cent projected dropout rate falls below the national average for the

---

University Road
Leicester LE1 7RH

0116 252 5281 (admissions)
admissions@le.ac.uk
www.le.ac.uk
http://leicesterunion.com
Affiliation: 1994 Group

The Times Rankings
Overall Ranking: **=17**

Student satisfaction:	=4	(84%)
Research quality:	=33	(1.9)
Entry standards:	27	(399)
Student–staff ratio:	22	(14.7)
Services & facilities/student:	21	(£1,891)
Expected completion rate:	21	(92.7%)
Good honours:	41	(66.8%)
Graduate prospects:	26	(71.5%)

university's courses and entry grades.

Leicester was awarded national centres of excellence for teaching and learning in geography, genetics and physics. The university also has a long-established reputation in space science, with Europe's largest university-based space research facility, including the £52-million National Space Centre.

The medical school, which allows graduates in the health and life sciences to qualify in four years, has among the most modern facilities in Britain. The siting of a medically based interdisciplinary research centre at the university was another indication of strength. The genetics department, where DNA genetic finger-printing was discovered, has helped make Leicester's academics among the most cited in Britain, according to the Scopus database, which monitors research.

Other than clinical medicine which is taught at the city's three hospitals, all teaching and much residential accommodation is concentrated in a leafy suburb a mile from the city centre. Its location, adjacent to one of Leicester's main parks, is popular with students. The new library has doubled the available space and brought the total number of workspaces to 1,500.

The students' union already ran one of the most popular university nightclubs. Its new building features a spectacular new atrium with communal social space for students and improved catering and retail facilities, extra space for student societies, and increased provision for welfare and support services.

Extensive residential accommodation includes a £21-million 600-bed en-suite development. First years are guaranteed a residential place and many second and third-year students also live in hall, although the majority choose to live in the reasonably priced private accommodation available nearby. The main sports facilities are conveniently located: in 2009–10, students paid £60 a year to use them.

As a city, Leicester is not one of the most fashionable student destinations, but its ethnic diversity makes for a rich cultural experience. It is big enough to provide all the normal sports and entertainment opportunities, but also offers events such as the biggest Diwali celebrations outside India.

Undergraduate Fees and Support

» Fees for UK/EU students 2012–13 £9,000
» Fees for International students 2011–12 £10,750–£13,750
£24,895 (medicine)
» Annual scholarships of £3,000 for those from disadvantaged backgrounds; of £2,000 for grades AAA or equivalent (not medicine); of £1,250 for meeting course requirements (not medicine); 150 £1,000 one year scholarships for those from local colleges.
» Check the university's website for the latest information.

Students

Undergraduates:	**9,185**	**(1,220)**
Postgraduates:	**3,325**	**(3,740)**
Mature students:	**9.8%**	
Overseas students:	**15.0%**	
Applications per place:	**7.3**	
From state-sector schools:	**89.4%**	
From working-class homes:	**26.4%**	

For detailed information about fees, grants and bursaries and how they work, see chapter 7.

Accommodation

Number of places and costs refer to 2011–12
University-provided places: 4,634
Percentage catered: 32%
Catered costs: £109.90–£168.00 a week (30 weeks).
Self-catered costs: £79.80–£161.00 (42 weeks).
First-year students are guaranteed accommodation if conditions are met.
International students: as above, with priority to those returning.
Contact: www.le.ac.uk/accommodation

University of Lincoln

Lincoln achieved the biggest rise of any university in last year's *Times* League Table and has gone up another seven places in the latest edition, on the back of higher entry standards, more satisfied students and a better completion rate. The opening of an impressive purpose-built campus alongside a marina in the centre of Lincoln in 1996 brought about the most dramatic transformation of any university in recent times. Humberside University, as it had been, even gave its new location pride of place in its title. Five years later it went a step further, selling the previous headquarters campus in Hull and becoming the University of Lincoln. While not moving out of Hull entirely, the university has concentrated its activities there on a much smaller city-centre site.

The switch has paid undoubted dividends, helping to attract high-quality academics. The number of professors grew from eight to 87 in four years. Student applications have increased for most of the last decade, despite rising admission requirements. Although the demand for places was down at the start of 2011, this followed an increase of almost 20 per cent in 2010. New science laboratories, sports facilities, an architecture school, a library in a converted warehouse and a students' union and entertainment venue in a former railway engine shed have taken the cost of the development in Lincoln to over £100 million, and another £30 million has been committed to complete the main campus. A £6-million performing arts centre contains a 450-seat theatre and three large studio spaces, while the Human Performance Centre is a regional facility for excellence in sport, coaching and exercise science. The latest developments are the new School of Engineering, the relocation of the Lincoln Business School to its own dedicated building and the opening of the Enterprise building – a one-stop-shop for students to get careers advice, enhance their CVs or find work, as well as for graduates who are supported in setting up their own businesses.

The various projects have won two regeneration awards. The campus now has slightly more than 1,000 bedspaces, while purpose-built private developments in close proximity to the university now provide well over 2,000 further residential places. Only the School of Health and Social Care remains in Hull, following the transfer of art and design degree provision in the city to Hull College.

Lincoln initially concentrated on social sciences, but the university now has a much wider range of courses. Following the acquisition of former art and design and agriculture colleges from De Montfort University in 2001, the university now has more than 8,000 students in and around Lincoln. The School of Architecture has over 400 students. Art and design is based in the

---

Brayford Pool
Lincoln LN6 7TS

01522 882000 (enquiries)
contact via website
www.lincoln.ac.uk
www.lincolnsu.com
Affiliation: University
Alliance

The Times Rankings
Overall Ranking: **55**

Student satisfaction:	=24	(79%)
Research quality:	=62	(0.5)
Entry standards:	=63	(289)
Student–staff ratio:	=75	(19.7)
Services & facilities/student:	76	(£1,202)
Expected completion rate:	51	(86.1%)
Good honours:	=73	(57.7%)
Graduate prospects:	85	(55.9%)

city centre, while animal, biological and equine studies are at Riseholme Park, a 1,000-acre site ten minutes outside Lincoln. Riseholme has been chosen as one of the training centres for equine events ahead of the 2012 Olympic Games.

The university was determined to achieve a high-profile return in the Research Assessment Exercise in 2008 to match a sharp rise in its research income over recent years. Lincoln entered more of its academics for assessment than many institutions in its peer group and improved on previous results, with 28 per cent of its submission judged to be world-leading or internationally excellent. The result was a £2-million boost in research grants. Communication, cultural and media studies and computer science and informatics produced the highest grades. The university has also had successes in applied research and knowledge transfer, notably with the National Centre for Food Manufacturing, based in Holbeach, which specialises in the production of chilled foods.

All students take the Effective Learning Programme, which uses computer packages backed up by weekly seminars to develop necessary study skills, and produce a detailed portfolio of all their work. Some degrees can be taken as work-based programmes, with credit awarded for relevant aspects of the jobs. Lincoln was the first university to win a Charter Mark for exceptional service.

Results in the National Student Survey have improved and reached the average for all universities in 2010. Accounting boasted the most satisfied students in the country, while fine art and tourism and marketing ranked second in the UK. Business studies and management, design, sociology and journalism were all in the top ten for their subject.

Almost 41 per cent of the undergraduates come from working-class homes and the improved dropout rate of 11 per cent is below the average for the subjects on offer, given the entry standards. The city is adapting to its increasing student population with new bars and clubs, although the social scene there is not the prime draw for students.

Undergraduate Fees and Support

» Fees for UK/EU students 2012–13 £9,000
» Fees for International students 2011–12 £10,395–£11,460
» A package of financial support, including scholarships and bursaries, to be announced.
» Check the university's website for the latest information.

Students

Undergraduates:	**8,415**	**(2,115)**
Postgraduates:	**540**	**(1,005)**
Mature students:	**21.5%**	
Overseas students:	**5.9%**	
Applications per place:	**4.2**	
From state-sector schools:	**97.7%**	
From working-class homes:	**40.4%**	

For detailed information about fees, grants and bursaries and how they work, see chapter 7.

Accommodation

Number of places and costs refer to 2010–11
University-provided places: Lincoln, 1,037; Riseholme Park, 180
Percentage catered: 13% (Riseholme Park only)
Catered costs: £91–£129 a week (half-board)
Self-catered costs: £90–£104 a week.
Student accommodation prioritised by distance within application date.
International students are given detailed information and assistance.
Contact: www.lincoln.ac.uk/accommodation

University of Liverpool

Liverpool is investing more than £230 million in new and upgraded teaching and research facilities over the next five years. An additional £10 million is being spent on improving the university's estate and infrastructure. The main library has already been expanded and refurbished at a cost of £17 million, a one-stop shop established for student services, and sports facilities have been renovated and extended. A £9-million refurbishment of the Guild of Students should be complete in 2012.

A £25-million project, due for completion in September 2011, will create 15 centralised teaching laboratories which will be used across a variety of science-based subjects. The laboratories, several of which will accommodate more than 200 students, will be focused on undergraduate teaching and will facilitate the introduction of innovative new teaching modules that promote interdisciplinary science. The School of Environmental Sciences has taken delivery of a custom-built coastal research vessel which is supporting both teaching and research.

More than half of the work submitted for the 2008 Research Assessment Exercise was judged to be world-leading or internationally excellent. Computer science, materials, architecture, English and history produced particularly good results. Another £70 million

is going on an interdisciplinary research facility that will accommodate 600 researchers and help to cement Liverpool's international standing in work to combat infectious diseases, cancer, and digestive diseases. A Centre for Personalised Medicines has opened in the old Liverpool Royal Infirmary, developing treatments tailored to a patient's individual genetic make-up. One of Europe's largest facilities for training dentists opened in 2007, marking the start of another big investment programme following the award of an additional 125 dental places from 2009.

There has been substantial investment in new educational technology, helping to cope with the demands of extra undergraduates. The university was awarded a national centre of excellence to develop professionalism in medical students. Full-time numbers throughout the university are almost exactly balanced between the sexes. Pharmacy and nursing produced 100 per cent satisfaction in the 2010 National Student Survey, when Liverpool registered above-average scores overall. There were also extremely good results in animal science, archaeology, biology, classics, Irish studies, and physics and astronomy. Liverpool was also the most popular Russell Group university of the 11 participating in the latest satisfaction survey for international students. Total applications were up by 12 per cent at the start of 2011.

Liverpool is developing a growing

Liverpool L69 3BX

0151 794 5927 (enquiries)
contact via website
www.liv.ac.uk
www.lgos.org.uk
Affiliation: Russell Group

The Times Rankings
Overall Ranking: **31**

Student satisfaction:	=48	(77%)
Research quality:	=33	(1.9)
Entry standards:	26	(401)
Student–staff ratio:	9	(13.2)
Services & facilities/student:	9	(£2,088)
Expected completion rate:	=30	(90.8%)
Good honours:	27	(71.5%)
Graduate prospects:	=29	(70.3%)

international presence and opened a new university in Suzhou, China, in partnership with Xi'an Jiaotong University, in 2006. Chinese students can complete the latter part of their studies in Liverpool, while Liverpool-based students are offered work experience at Suzhou Industrial Park, which is home to 53 "Fortune 500" companies. From September 2011, students in electrical engineering and electronics, computer science and maths will have the opportunity to spend a year studying in China. The university is planning further collaborations with universities in Chile, Mexico and Spain that will allow Liverpool students to complete part of their degree at one or more of these institutions via a range of options such as projects or placements. Students will have access to a full range of support services while abroad.

Liverpool was among the first traditional universities to run access courses for adults without traditional qualifications. The proportion of undergraduates from working-class homes is the highest among the civic universities. The projected dropout rate improved again in the latest survey. At less than 7 per cent, it is comfortably below the national average for the courses and entry grades. The university will commit 30 per cent of the additional income it receives from £9,000 fees to bursaries, scholarships and outreach activities. Among the existing scholarships are 30 in memory of John Lennon, mainly for Merseyside residents.

The university has one of the largest careers resources centres in the UK and runs an internship programme that gives students access to local, regional and national employers. The Careers Service was ranked first in the 2010 High Fliers survey.

Some £45 million has been invested in the new Eco Residences, which are due to open in September 2011, and the nearly 4,000 bedspaces are enough to guarantee accommodation to all first years. The suburban setting of the main halls complex means the focus of social life is on the Guild of Students, but there is no shortage of nightlife. The main Sports Centre is on campus, but the university has opened a new gym on the halls site. The Sports Centre now has a team of professional sports development officers, responsible for elite athlete support and student club development.

Undergraduate Fees and Support

» Fees for UK/EU students 2012–13   £9,000
» Fees for International students 2011–12   £10,500–£13,500
                      £20,500 (dentistry and medicine)
» Details of financial support, including bursaries and fee waivers of £2,000–£3,000 per year, and widening participation and retention activity to be announced.
» Scholarships and bursaries based on circumstances or by competition.
» Check the university's website for the latest information.

Students		
Undergraduates:	**13,950**	**(2,645)**
Postgraduates:	**2,390**	**(1,605)**
Mature students:	**14.2%**	
Overseas students:	**11.3%**	
Applications per place:	**7.2**	
From state-sector schools:	**84.7%**	
From working-class homes:	**25.2%**	

For detailed information about fees, grants and bursaries and how they work, see chapter 7.

Accommodation
Number of places and costs refer to 2011–12
University-provided places: 3,657
Percentage catered: 59%
Catered costs: £114.10–£129.15 a week.
Self-catered costs: £82.95–£93.80 a week.
First-year students are guaranteed accommodation if requirements are met.
International students: as above.
Contact: accommodation@liverpool.ac.uk
www.liv.ac.uk/accommodation

Liverpool Hope University

Liverpool Hope continues to opt out of league tables after finishing at the bottom of our table on its only appearance in *The Times Good University Guide*. It has improved some scores since then, but the university believes that the criteria used in league tables are biased in favour of wealthier institutions with a longer history. It insists that its objections "can't be summed up in one sentence". Hope even hides its application rates from public view, although it admits that they fell in 2008 and 2009.

Hope is a unique ecumenical institution formed from the merger of two Catholic and one Church of England teacher training colleges in 1980. The two churches' leading figures on Merseyside described the union as a "sign of hope", unintentionally providing the name for one of the nine new universities created in 2005. It describes itself as "teaching led, research informed and mission focused". The university is opening its own joint Church of England and Roman Catholic academy in September 2011, replacing two comprehensive schools. There are also partnerships with the Royal Liverpool Philharmonic Orchestra, Liverpool Tate and the National Museums Liverpool to develop cultural programmes and new curricular areas such as art history and curating.

Student satisfaction rates have slipped in the last two years, leaving the university in the bottom 20. There was 100 per cent satisfaction in geography and environmental science, but no other subject reached 90 per cent. Most students opt for combined subject degrees, choosing after the first year whether to give them equal weight or to go for a major/minor arrangement. The university has significantly increased its national recruitment profile, with nearly 60 per cent of students now coming from beyond Merseyside. Entry standards have increased, with the average UCAS points topping 300 in 2010.

Hope undergraduates can register for the Service and Leadership Award, which is credit-rated and runs alongside their degree work. The award recognises service work, learning and leadership development. Students can volunteer locally, within the region or internationally as part of Global Hope, the university's award winning overseas charity.

More than a quarter of the academics were entered for the 2008 Research Assessment Exercise – a higher proportion than at most comparable institutions. Theology was again the top scorer, although a small amount of world-leading work was found in applied social sciences. Overall, only 12 per cent of the university's submission reached the top two grades – placing it among the bottom five on this measure.

Hope Park
Liverpool L16 9JD

0151 291 3295 (admissions)
admission@hope.ac.uk
www.hope.ac.uk
www.hopesu.com
Affiliation: Cathedral Group

Edinburgh
Belfast
LIVERPOOL
London
Cardiff

The Times Rankings
Liverpool Hope blocked the release of data from the Higher Education Statistics Agency and so we cannot give any ranking information.

Nearly 30 per cent of the undergraduates are over 20 on entry and female students outnumber their male counterparts by more than two to one. Hope comfortably exceeds all of the official benchmarks for widening participation in higher education. Almost all the undergraduates are state educated, approaching a half are from working-class families and almost one in five is from an area with little tradition of higher education – one of the highest proportions in England. This is partly the result of the Network of Hope, which brings university courses to sixth-form colleges across the northwest of England, in areas where there is limited higher education. Single honours and Foundation degrees are taught in Bury and Blackburn. The projected dropout rate had jumped to 11 per cent in the latest survey but, having improved in recent years, remains well below the national average for the courses and entry qualifications.

The university's own premises are now concentrated on two sites in Liverpool, with a residential outdoor education centre set in 20 acres of woodland in the heart of Snowdonia, North Wales. The main campus – Hope Park – is three miles from the city centre in the suburb of Childwall, while the creative and performing arts are based at the more central Creative campus in Everton, where a new performance centre opened in 2010. It houses one of only three Steinway Schools in England, as well as practice rooms, recording spaces and a theatre. The £5-million main library, on the Hope campus, has 270,000 items and 700 study spaces, with electronic access from other sites.

Other recent campus developments have included a Centre for Education and Enterprise, which supports local business as well as hosting the Faculty of Education. More than £1 million has been spent on a new food court and a dedicated library and reading room has opened on the Creative campus. Plans for this campus were completed in 2010 with the opening of the Angel Field, a Renaissance-style garden which includes an outdoor performance area. Sports facilities have been improving and the students' union building has been upgraded. The university has a range of residential accommodation, some of it provided by a private firm, and is able to guarantee places for overseas students and first years who apply before Clearing.

Undergraduate Fees and Support

- » Fees for UK/EU students 2012–13   less than £9,000
- » Fees for International students 2011–12   £7,120–£8,400
- » A package of financial support and widening participation and retention activity to be announced.
- » Scholarships and bursaries based on circumstances or by competition.
- » Check the university's website for the latest information.

Students

From state-sector schools:	**98.3%**
From working-class homes:	**45.8%**

Accommodation

Number of places and costs refer to 2011–12
University-provided places: 1,098
Percentage catered: 0%
Self-catered costs: £78 (shared); £98–£104 (en suite) a week.
First years are guaranteed accommodation if Liverpool Hope is their first choice and they apply before Clearing.
International students: housing is subject to availability, but demand is usually met.
Contact: accommodation@hope.ac.uk

Liverpool John Moores University (LJMU)

Liverpool John Moores (LJMU) was the first post-1992 university to announce that it would charge undergraduate fees of £9,000 in 2012. It said the maximum fee was necessary to maintain a high quality experience for its students and promised them a "distinctive, life changing experience worth the financial commitment". The university will use some of the fee income to improve student facilities and enhance its prize-winning WoW (world of work) initiative, which embeds employment skills in the curriculum, offering internships, work placements, extra staff support and personal learning tools. Work-related learning is included in every degree and undergraduates are encouraged to master eight transferable skills, applicable to a wide range of professions and careers.

The programme has been shaped and steered by leading companies and business organisations. More than 100 local employers have trained as WoW skills verifiers, working with LJMU to give students invaluable "real-world" interview experience in the sector they want to work in after they graduate. All students will have their skills verified through an employer-validated statement in future.

Naming itself after a football pools millionaire set a pattern of innovation for LJMU. Early examples included Britain's first student charter, which became a template for others. The university also launched the first degrees in sports science and criminal justice, and the first distance learning degree in astronomy. It has been investing £180 million to transform its three campuses by 2013. An Art and Design Academy opened in 2009 and a £25-million life sciences building opened in 2010. A new home for the Liverpool Screen School, the Faculty of Business and Law, and a new Professional Centre, costing £37 million, is on schedule to open in spring 2012.

There is a learning resource centre in each of the three campuses and a state-of-the-art media centre that is open all hours. The university's Virtual Learning Environment enables students to access most teaching materials and a range of other support features online. Student numbers have increased substantially in recent years, although applications were down a little at the start of 2011. Scores in the National Student Survey have been below average and declined in 2010.

Mainly concentrated in an area between Liverpool's two cathedrals, the university is now one of Britain's biggest with almost 26,000 students in the city and another 4,500 taking LJMU courses overseas. Arts and science courses occupy separate sites within easy reach of the city centre, with the IM Marsh campus three miles away for

---

Roscoe Court
4 Rodney Street
Liverpool L1 2TZ

0151 231 5090 (course enquiries)
courses@livjm.ac.uk (enquiries)
www.livjm.ac.uk
www.l-s-u.com
Affiliation: University
  Alliance

The Times Rankings

Overall Ranking: **100**

Student satisfaction:	=78	(74%)
Research quality:	=70	(0.4)
Entry standards:	=89	(263)
Student–staff ratio:	=94	(20.9)
Services & facilities/student:	77	(£1,200)
Expected completion rate:	84	(80.8%)
Good honours:	68	(59.2%)
Graduate prospects:	108	(50.5%)

education and community studies. It was announced in 2011 that this campus would close, with courses moved to the main campus. Nearly half of the students are drawn from the Merseyside area. A "learning federation" embracing four further education colleges in St Helens, Southport and Liverpool itself adds to the regional flavour.

A growing research reputation is a source of particular pride: LJMU was one of only two new universities to have a subject – sports science – rated internationally outstanding in the 2001 Research Assessment Exercise. There is now a national centre of excellence in teaching and learning in PE, dance, sport and exercise sciences. The new life sciences building houses the School of Sports and Exercise Sciences and the School of Natural Sciences and Psychology. Facilities include appetite laboratories, psychology testing labs, neuroscience labs, an indoor 70-metre running track, physiology suites and a chronobiology lab.

A third of the research assessed in 2008 was rated as world-leading or internationally excellent, with 12 of the 17 subject areas having some work in the top category. The built environment, electrical and electronic engineering, general engineering and sport-related studies produced the best results. The university did well in areas such as astrophysics and biological anthropology, traditionally older university territory. A

£1.6-million maritime centre features the UK's most advanced 360-degree ship-handling simulator.

The university's efforts to extend access to higher education are successful: there are significantly more state-educated undergraduates than average for the subjects offered and over four in ten are from working-class homes. A new range of scholarships and bursaries will accompany the new fees in 2012. Among them will be the John Lennon Imagine Awards, match-funded through a gift of £260,000 from Yoko Ono, which help students who have either been in local authority care or who are estranged from their parents. LJMU also has a wide range of disability support services and has been addressing concerns about its dropout rate, which is now close to the official benchmark for the university.

Student facilities have been improving. The university has partnerships with private accommodation providers, so that all new students are guaranteed accommodation, even if they enter through Clearing.

Undergraduate Fees and Support

» Fees for UK/EU students 2012–13   £9,000
» Fees for International students 2011–12   £10,050–£10,750
» Details of financial support and widening participation and retention activity to be announced.
» Scholarships and bursaries based on circumstances or by competition.
» Check the university's website for the latest information.

Students

Undergraduates:	**16,615**	**(4,385)**
Postgraduates:	**2,035**	**(2,820)**
Mature students:	**18.6%**	
Overseas students:	**9.4%**	
Applications per place:	**5.7**	
From state-sector schools:	**95.2%**	
From working-class homes:	**41.0%**	

For detailed information about fees, grants and bursaries and how they work, see chapter 7.

Accommodation

Number of places and costs refer to 2011–12
University-provided places: 3,300 plus 15,000 through Liverpool Student Homes.
Percentage catered: 0%
Self-catered costs: £69–£114 a week.
All new students are guaranteed a place in university accommodation, even if applying through Clearing.
International students: as above
Contact: accommodation@ljmu.ac.uk
www.ljmu.ac.uk/accommodation

University of London

The federal university is Britain's biggest by far, with more than 120,000 students, despite the loss of Imperial College in 2007. The majority study at colleges in the capital but such is the global prestige of the university's degrees that over 50,000 students in 180 different countries take University of London International Programmes.

The university, which celebrates its 175th anniversary in 2011, consists of 19 self-governing colleges and ten smaller specialist research institutes. Its students have access to some joint residential accommodation, sporting facilities and the University of London Union. But most identify with their college.

Other prestigious colleges have considered following Imperial in going their own way and applied for their own degree-awarding powers to hold in reserve, but they remain bound together by the London degree. Reforms to the university's governance have given the colleges more autonomy and look to have staved off further departures for now.

The following colleges – some of which have dropped the word "college" from their title to underline their university status – have separate entries in this chapter. Each also appears in the main university league table, with the exception of Birkbeck, whose overwhelmingly part-time provision does not lend itself to a full comparison on the measures used in our *Guide*.

Birkbeck College
Goldsmiths, University of London
King's College London
London School of Economics and Political Science
Queen Mary
Royal Holloway
School of Oriental and African Studies
University College London

Many of London's teaching hospitals have now merged with colleges of the university:
» King's College now incorporates Guy's and St Thomas' (the United Medical and Dental Schools of Guy's and St Thomas').
» Queen Mary now incorporates St Bartholomew's and the Royal London School of Medicine and Dentistry.
» University College now incorporates the Royal Free Hospital Medical School and the Eastman Dental Hospital.

In addition, the School of Slavonic and Eastern European Studies is now part of University College.

Senate House
Malet Street
London WC1E 7HU

020 7862 8000
enquiries@london.ac.uk
www.london.ac.uk
www.ulu.co.uk

Edinburgh
Belfast
Cardiff
LONDON

Enquiries: to individual colleges, institutes or schools.

Ten colleges do not have separate entries in the *Guide*. These are listed below, with postal, telephone and electronic contacts.

Central School of Speech and Drama

Eton Avenue
London NW3 3HY
020 7559 3912 (admissions)
admissions@cssd.ac.uk
www.cssd.ac.uk
555 undergraduates. Acting and theatre practice.

Courtauld Institute of Art

Somerset House, Strand
London WC2R 0RN
020 7848 2645 (degree programmes)
ugadmissions@courtauld.ac.uk
www.courtauld.ac.uk
150 undergraduates. History of art degree.

Heythrop College

Kensington Square
London W8 5HN
020 7795 4202 (admissions enquiries)
enquiries@heythrop.ac.uk
www.heythrop.ac.uk
515 undergraduates. Degrees in theology and philosophy.

Institute of Education

20 Bedford Way
London WC1H 0AL
020 7612 6000 (switchboard)
info@ioe.ac.uk
www.ioe.ac.uk
540 undergraduates; mainly postgraduate education courses.

London Business School

Regent's Park
London NW1 4SA
020 7000 7000 (switchboard)
webenquiries@london.edu
www.london.edu
Postgraduate MBA and other courses.

London School of Hygiene and Tropical Medicine

Keppel Street
London WC1E 7HT
020 7299 4646 (admission enquiries)
registry@lshtm.ac.uk
www.lshtm.ac.uk
Postgraduate medical courses.

Royal Academy of Music

Marylebone Road
London NW1 5HT
020 7873 7393 (registry)
registry@ram.ac.uk
www.ram.ac.uk
330 undergraduates. Degrees in music.

Royal Veterinary College

Royal College Street
London NW1 0TU
0020 7468 5147 (undergraduate admissions)
enquiries@rvc.ac.uk
www.rvc.ac.uk
1,535 undergraduates. Degrees in veterinary medicine.

St George's, University of London

Cranmer Terrace
London SW17 0RE
020 8725 2333 (admissions enquiries)
enquiries@sgul.ac.uk
www.sgul.ac.uk
4,590 undergraduates. Degrees in medicine.

School of Pharmacy

29–39 Brunswick Square
London WC1N 1AX
020 7753 5831 (enquiries)
registry@pharmacy.ac.uk
www.pharmacy.ac.uk
735 undergraduates. Degrees in pharmacy. From 2012 the School of Pharmacy is to merge with University College London.

London Metropolitan University

London Met is back in the *Times* League Table for the first time in six years. Although it reappears at the bottom of the ranking, the university that students will join in 2012 will be very different to the one that these figures portray. The new Vice-Chancellor, Professor Malcolm Gillies, and a new board of governors are taking drastic action to tackle well-publicised financial difficulties and prepare for the new fees regime. The university found that 80 per cent of its 28,000 students were on just 80 of the 557 courses and many of the rest had intakes of less than ten. As a result, there are proposals to cut university's portfolio to about 160 courses, with consequent reductions in the numbers of staff and students.

Under the proposals, undergraduates entering in 2012 will pay fees ranging from £4,500 to £9,000, according to the course. An average less than £7,000 would make London Met the cheapest place in the country to take many degrees. The aim is to make the university financially sustainable while maintaining diversity of its intake. London Met specialises in extending higher education boundaries to bring in groups who are under-represented at traditional universities. More than a third of the students are Afro-Caribbean and the proportion of mature students is among the highest in England. Almost 58 per cent come from working-class homes, far above the average for the courses and entry qualifications.

The proposed changes are part of a "radical overhaul of undergraduate education" planned for 2012. It includes a move to year-long modules consisting of 30 weeks of timetabled teaching. Over a year, students will typically study four modules worth 30 credits each and receive a minimum of 60 teaching hours per module. The university expects first-year students to have 12 hours of teaching a week, giving more opportunity for development and guidance. Student support services, from admission to careers advice, were remodelled and there is a particular emphasis on academic and pastoral counselling on entry and at other key points of courses. But the projected dropout rate had risen to more than 26 per cent at the time of the latest survey – the second-highest rate in England.

London Met has also been in the bottom four for student satisfaction for the last two years. Maths and statistics produced by far the best results, but no other subjects satisfied 90 per cent of final-year undergraduates. The new administration has promised a "renewed focus on student satisfaction and the quality of student learning". There has been increased investment in the campus, with more study zones, and a £13.5-million

---

166–220 Holloway Road
London N7 8DB

020 7133 4200 (enquiries)
admissions@londonmet.ac.uk
www.londonmet.ac.uk
www.londonmetsu.org.uk
Affiliation: million+

The Times Rankings
Overall Ranking: **116**

Student satisfaction:	111	(65%)
Research quality:	=79	(0.3)
Entry standards:	110	(221)
Student–staff ratio:	=75	(19.7)
Services & facilities/student:	114	(£885)
Expected completion rate:	113	(68.3%)
Good honours:	=102	(49.8%)
Graduate prospects:	115	(45.5%)

refurbishment programme. A newly refurbished library on the Holloway Road site has more computers, informal learning spaces, technobooths and teaching rooms, as well as a café. There is also a new head-quarters for the students' union on the site. At the same time, the university has been working hard to reduce its carbon footprint. A 12 per cent reduction led to the award of the Carbon Trust Standard in 2011.

Earlier developments saw four "business-related" departments join together to form the London Metropolitan Business School which, with 10,000 students, is one of Europe's largest. An "international medical degree" was launched in September 2008, through the University of Health Studies, in Antigua. The course, lasting five years, will be based in London and graduates will complete the United States Medical Licensing Examination, enabling them to practise in America.

Since its establishment from the merger of London Guildhall and North London universities, the level of UK applications to London Met has been uneven, although overseas recruitment has remained healthy. There had been a slight decline in the demand for places at the start of 2011, but this followed a 6 per cent increase in 2010. The university's sites are centred on the City of London and north London's Holloway Road. A graduate school, designed by Daniel Libeskind, opened soon after the merger, and an impressive £30-million science centre followed in 2006. This features a "superlab" of 280 workstations that is Europe's largest, as well as a multipurpose gym and sports therapy facilities.

London Met entered more academics than most former polytechnics in the 2008 Research Assessment Exercise, when almost a quarter of the work submitted was placed in the top two categories. About half of the 21 subject areas contained some world-leading research, with architecture, media studies, education and social studies producing the best results. Education, maths and statistics and sociology had the most satisfied undergraduates.

Residential accommodation is limited, but many of London Met's students live at home. Sports facilities are still not extensive, although competitive teams are successful. However, the social scene is lively, particularly in north London.

Undergraduate Fees and Support

» Fees for UK/EU students 2012–13   £4,500–£9,000
    Average fee expected to be £6,643.
» Fees for International students 2011–12   £10,080
» Details of financial support and widening participation and retention activity to be announced.
» Scholarships and bursaries based on circumstances or by competition.
» Check the university's website for the latest information.

Students

Undergraduates:	**12,685**	**(4,775)**
Postgraduates:	**3,295**	**(3,580)**
Mature students:	**54.9%**	
Overseas students:	**18.9%**	
Applications per place:	**6.1**	
From state-sector schools:	**96.6%**	
From working-class homes:	**57.2%**	

For detailed information about fees, grants and bursaries and how they work, see chapter 7.

Accommodation

Number of places and costs refer to 2010–11

University-provided places: Students have access to accommodation in a wide range of halls of residences provided by specialist student accommodation providers.

Percentage catered: 0%

Self-catered costs: approximately £107–£270 a week.

The university cannot guarantee a place in halls. All students have access to halls spaces.

International students: first years given priority.

Contact: accommodation@londonmet.ac.uk

London School of Economics and Political Science (LSE)

Always one of the big names of British higher education, the LSE is in the top five social science institutions in the world, according to the QS World University Rankings. Like most of the universities at the top of the league tables, LSE did not share in the 2010 applications boom and the demand for places had dropped by almost 9 per cent at the start of 2011. But with around 14 applications for every place, competition for admission remains tougher than at any UK university. Only Oxford, Cambridge and Imperial College London have higher average entry grades. The school has added 1,000 places in recent years, having seized the chance to tackle a longstanding shortage of teaching space by acquiring former Government buildings near the school's Aldwych headquarters. However, most of the extra capacity has gone on postgraduate courses.

The school endured a difficult start to 2011, when Sir Howard Davies, the Director, resigned over the LSE's links to the Gadaffi regime in Libya. Many other universities had also been active in Libya, but Sir Howard felt that the LSE's reputation was suffering.

The school has a long history of political involvement, from its foundation by Beatrice and Sidney Webb, pioneers of the Fabian movement. Sir Howard's predecessor, Professor Anthony Giddens, was the academic face of Tony Blair's Third Way and before the 2010 General Election, 31 MPs and 42 members of the House of Lords were alumni. The tradition lives on, not only among the academics, but in a students' union which claims to be the only one in Britain to hold weekly general meetings at which every student may attend and vote.

The LSE has a cosmopolitan feel that derives from the highest proportion of overseas students at any publicly funded university. Due to national funding restrictions, only a relatively small proportion of the extra places have been for UK undergraduates. More than 30 past or present heads of state have either studied or taught at the university, as have 16 Nobel prizewinners in economics, literature and peace – including George Bernard Shaw, Bertrand Russell, Friedrich von Hayek and Amartya Sen. The latest of them is Professor Christopher Pissarides, who shared the prize for economics in 2010.

The nationals of more than 140 countries take up half of the 9,000 places. At the undergraduate level, only the much larger Manchester University has more applications from overseas. Its international character not only gives the LSE global prestige but also an unusual degree of financial independence. Less than a fifth of its income is from the Higher Education Funding Council for

---

Houghton Street
London WC2A 2AE

020 7955 7125 9 (admissions)
ug.admissions@lse.ac.uk
  (admissions)
www.lse.ac.uk
www.lsesu.com
Affiliation: Russell Group

Edinburgh
Belfast
Cardiff
LONDON

The Times Rankings
Overall Ranking: **3**

Student satisfaction:	=78	(74%)
Research quality:	3	(3.6)
Entry standards:	4	(513)
Student–staff ratio:	7	(11.8)
Services & facilities/student:	4	(£2,583)
Expected completion rate:	7	(95.7%)
Good honours:	11	(79%)
Graduate prospects:	5	(84.1%)

England, although the LSE will still be affected by cuts in Government funding.

Just under a third of British students are from independent schools – one of the highest ratios in the country and higher than the funding council's benchmark figure. Efforts are being made to attract a broader intake with Saturday classes and summer schools. The projected dropout rate of less than 5 per cent is among the lowest at any university. Scores in the 2010 National Student Survey improved from a low base, but there was still no subject in which more than 85 per cent of students were satisfied with their course. However, the percentage of leavers securing graduate-level employment is impressive.

Areas of study range more broadly than the name suggests: law, management and history are all on the curriculum and there is even a small contingent of scientists. Only Cambridge recorded higher average scores than the LSE in the 2008 assessment exercise, which saw almost 70 per cent of the work submitted rated world-leading or internationally excellent. Ninety-five per cent of the economics submission, 80 per cent in social policy and 75 per cent in law reached the top two categories.

Improvements have been made to the campus over a number of years. A £30-million Norman Foster-designed redevelopment of the Lionel Robbins Building houses a much-improved library.

The move was a welcome one since the number of books borrowed by LSE students is more than four times the national average, according to one survey. Routes between most of the buildings have been pedestrianised and a new student services centre has opened. In 2008 the Queen opened LSE's £71-million eco-friendly academic building, which helped the LSE to second place in the "Green League" of universities in 2009. It is now being refurbished and work has begun on a new student centre which is due to open in 2013.

Partying is not the prime attraction of the LSE for most applicants, who tend to be serious about their subject, but London's top nightspots are on the doorstep for those who can afford them. The 3,650 residential places offer a good chance of avoiding central London's notoriously high private sector rents.

Undergraduate Fees and Support

» Fees for UK/EU students 2012–13   to be announced
» Fees for International students 2011–12   £14,592
» A package of financial support and widening participation activity to be announced.
» Scholarships and bursaries based on circumstances or by competition.
» Check the university's website for the latest information.

Students		
Undergraduates:	**3,905**	**(95)**
Postgraduates:	**5,030**	**(535)**
Mature students:	**1.8%**	
Overseas students:	**44.9%**	
Applications per place:	**14.5**	
From state-sector schools:	**70.7%**	
From working-class homes:	**18.7%**	

For detailed information about fees, grants and bursaries and how they work, see chapter 7.

Accommodation

Number of places and costs refer to 2010–11
University-provided places: 3,650
Percentage catered: about 38%
Catered costs: from £70–£151 a week.
Self-catered costs: £77–£251 a week.
First years are guaranteed an offer of accommodation.
Policy for international students: same as above.
Contact: accommodation@lse.ac.uk
to apply online: www.lse.ac.uk/accommodation

London South Bank University (LSBU)

LSBU has invested over £50 million in the recent past in modern teaching facilities and this investment programme is continuing with a further £38 million to include a new student centre scheduled for completion in late 2012, and an Enterprise Centre to showcase the achievements of students and staff in 2013. The university was in the top ten in the last survey of graduate starting salaries. A PricewaterhouseCoopers study in 2007 found that a LSBU degree increased lifetime earnings by more than £185,000, which was nearly £26,000 more than the national average. LBSU is one of the top universities in the UK for "knowledge transfer partnerships" with firms and other outside organisations, its projects spanning construction, manufacturing, energy and environment, food, information technology, health and the creative industries.

The university will be charging £8,450 for degrees taught on campus, although Foundation courses taught in partner colleges will cost £5,950.

Over 70 per cent of students are from the capital, most of them from south London and especially from the area's wide range of ethnic minorities. Of nearly 19,000 undergraduates, over a 40 per cent are part-time and half are on sandwich courses. Fewer than half enter with traditional academic qualifications. Applications were buoyant throughout the period following the introduction of top-up fees and the start of 2010 saw another big increase, of 38 per cent.

The proportion of mature entrants is among the highest in the UK, encouraged by initiatives such as the summer school for local people to upgrade their qualifications. Six out of ten students are over 25. The Fast Track to Higher Education programme has been expanded to include English, IT and science, as well as the original mathematics. The courses, some of which are tailored to the needs of mature students and some for younger students, start at the end of June and are limited to 15 hours a week so as not to affect students' benefit entitlement.

LBSU gives a high priority to widening participation in higher education, something for which it won a London education award for its work with non-traditional learners who have no family history or aspirations to apply to university. Diploma and degree courses run in parallel so that students can move up or down if they are better suited to another level of study. The university offers a wide range of Foundation and pre-degree courses in business and accounting, law, tourism and hospitality, design and engineering, and science and technology for international students

Specialist facilities, such as the Centre for

103 Borough Road
London SE1 0AA

020 7815 6100 (course enquiries)
course.enquiry@lsbu.ac.uk
www.lsbu.ac.uk
www.lsbsu.org
Affiliation: million+

Explosion and Fire Research, show that the vocational theme carries through into research. Although the university entered only 87 academics for the 2008 Research Assessment Exercise, their average grades were among the best of the new universities. More than 40 per cent of the submission was rated as world-leading or internationally excellent, with social policy, engineering and communication, culture and media studies leading the way.

LSBU is in the midst of a 15-year programme to develop its campus in Southwark, near the Elephant and Castle, and not far from the South Bank arts complex. The nine-storey Keyworth Centre, completed in 2002, provides upgraded teaching accommodation and a focal point for the university. The flagship building "K2", opened in 2009, houses the Faculty of Health and Social Care and the Department of Education. By summer 2010, K2 will also accommodate the Centre for Efficient and Renewable Energy in Buildings, a teaching, research and demonstration resource for the built environment.

Some health students are based on the other side of London, in hospitals in Romford and Leytonstone, where there are smaller satellite campuses to supplement those in Southwark. The university now trains 40 per cent of London's nurses. It topped the list of London universities for midwifery and was rated third for nursing in

NHS London's new Higher Education Quality Assurance assessment.

The capital's attractions are on the doorstep of the main campus but, with nearly half of the students coming from working-class homes, many cannot afford them. The official projected dropout rate is nearly 30 per cent, a proportion exceeded by only one university in England. But LSBU insists that the true rate is less than half that figure because most students do complete their courses eventually; they just take longer than the standard course length.

A new hall of residence means that the university now has residential places within ten minutes' walk of the main campus, but the first years cannot yet be guaranteed housing. Sports facilities improved considerably with the launch of the Academy of Sport. Representative teams have been quite successful in recent years and sports bursaries of £3,000 are available for elite performers.

Undergraduate Fees and Support

- » Fees for UK/EU students 2012–13 £8,450
  Foundation degree £5,950
- » Fees for International students 2010–11 £9,000–£9,240
- » A package of financial support, and widening participation and retention activity to be announced.
- » Scholarships and bursaries based on circumstances or by competition.
- » Check the university's website for the latest information.

Students

Undergraduates:	**10,555**	**(8,320)**
Postgraduates:	**2,010**	**(4,060)**
Mature students:	**60.4%**	
Overseas students:	**8.2%**	
Applications per place:	**5.1**	
From state-sector schools:	**98.7%**	
From working-class homes:	**49.1%**	

For detailed information about fees, grants and bursaries and how they work, see chapter 7.

Accommodation

Number of places and costs refer to 2011–12
University-provided places: 1,400
Percentage catered: 0%
Self-catered costs: £99–£102 (standard) – £122 (en suite) a week.
First-year UK students are not guaranteed accommodation, but high priority is given to those who live outside the Greater London area.
International students: first years are guaranteed accommodation if conditions are met.
Contact: accommodation@lsbu.ac.uk

Loughborough University

Loughborough has maintained its place in the top 20 in the *Times* League Table, despite slipping four places this year. It has been one of the universities with the most satisfied students every year since the National Student Survey was launched. There was near total satisfaction in chemistry in 2010 and very high scores in anatomy, physiology and pathology, drama, geography and physics. Loughborough has also won four successive *Times Higher Education* awards for best student experience, after separate national polls of undergraduates.

The university remains best known for its successes on the sports field: as well as capturing a 30th consecutive British Universities and Colleges Championship in 2010, Loughborough was chosen as the Official Preparation Camp Headquarters for Team GB prior to the London 2012 Olympics. Past and present students and Loughborough-based athletes won a total of 44 medals at the 2010 Commonwealth Games in Delhi. If the university had been a country, it would have finished eighth in the medal table.

But the university has also enhanced its academic reputation recently, consistently finishing well up *The Times* rankings and improving its performance in the 2008 Research Assessment Exercise. Although the results were patchy, more than half of the research in art and design was considered world-leading, and there were particularly good results in architecture and sport. The Office for Standards in Education also rates Loughborough in its top category for teacher training in PE, design and science.

The university remains a major centre of engineering with more than 2,800 students in a £20-million integrated engineering complex. Loughborough provides the headquarters for the £1-billion national Energy Technologies Institute, which concentrates on low-carbon energy, as part of a consortium with Birmingham and Nottingham universities. Civil, aeronautical and automotive engineering are particularly strong, although art and design, business and sports science now all have more students than any single branch of the discipline. However, its successes have not translated into extra applications: the demand for places was flat in 2010 and had dropped by 9 per cent at the start of 2011.

The original 216-acre campus has benefited from a sustained construction programme which included a large students' union extension and a new business school, as well as the gradual refurbishment of residential accommodation. The first phase of a £68-million on-campus accommodation development opened in 2008 and further building will eventually provide another 1,300 bedspaces in four new halls.

Ashby Road
Loughborough
Leicestershire LE11 3TU

01509 263171 (switchboard)
access via website
www.lboro.ac.uk
www.lufbra.net
Affiliation: 1994 Group

The Times Rankings
Overall Ranking: **20**

Student satisfaction:	**3**	(85%)
Research quality:	**=18**	(2.3)
Entry standards:	**29**	(390)
Student–staff ratio:	**=46**	(17.1)
Services & facilities/student:	**45**	(£1,486)
Expected completion rate:	**36**	(89.2%)
Good honours:	**=29**	(69.6%)
Graduate prospects:	**37**	(69.2%)

The purchase of the adjacent Holywell Park site increased the size of the campus by 75 per cent. This will become the focus for research and collaboration with industry, including a £59-million BAE-sponsored Systems Engineering Innovation Centre. The university prides itself on a close relationship with industry, which accounts for its record haul of six Queen's Anniversary Prizes. Arts facilities are improving with the upgrading of the Cope Auditorium to serve the campus and local community. An £8-million building for Health, Exercise and Biosciences opened in 2010 and a new Design Centre, the first project in a wider master plan for the East Park area of the campus, is expected to open at the start of the 2011–12 academic year.

Most subjects are available either as three-year full-time or four-to-five-year sandwich courses, which include a year in industry. This has helped to give graduates an outstanding employment record, as well a dropout rate of only 6 per cent, which is particularly low for the subjects on offer. The university is a leader in the use of computer-assisted assessment, offering students the chance to gauge their own progress online.

However, Loughborough misses all its access benchmarks: less than a quarter of the undergraduates are from working-class homes and little more than 5 per cent are from areas of low participation in higher education. The university has promised up to £7 million in bursaries and scholarships to compensate for £9,000 undergraduate tuition fees from 2012. It expects to offer £3,000 a year in accommodation discounts and other support to students from disadvantaged backgrounds.

The programme of sports scholarships is the largest in the university system. The campus boasts a 50-metre swimming pool, national academies for cricket and tennis, a gymnastics centre and a high-performance training centre for athletics. The university also boasts the UK's only centre for disability sport and has spent £15 million on its Sports Technology Institute. SportPark, a bespoke central hub for some of the UK's leading sports bodies, allows a variety of organisations to share best practice.

Social activity is concentrated on the students' union. Loughborough is never going to be a clubber's paradise, but both Leicester and Nottingham are within easy reach.

Undergraduate Fees and Support

- » Fees for UK/EU students 2012–13   £9,000
- » Fees for International students 2010–11   £10,990–£14,400
- » Details of financial support and widening participation activity to be announced. For students from less well-off backgrounds, £3,000 including accommodation discount of £1,000.
- » Scholarships and bursaries based on circumstances or by competition.
- » Check the university's website for the latest information.

Students		
Undergraduates:	**11,280**	**(495)**
Postgraduates:	**2,475**	**(2,020)**
Mature students:	**4.0%**	
Overseas students:	**10.3%**	
Applications per place:	**6.7**	
From state-sector schools:	**82.8%**	
From working-class homes:	**22.7%**	

For detailed information about fees, grants and bursaries and how they work, see chapter 7.

Accommodation

Number of places and costs refer to 2011–12
University-provided places: 5,600
Percentage catered: 42.5%
Catered costs: £4,395.60 – £5,752.30
Self-catered costs: £2,733.90 – £5,539.80
Undergraduate first-year first-choice students are guaranteed accommodation.
International students: guaranteed housing in same residence for two years.
Contact: http://accommodation.lboro.ac.uk

University of Manchester

Always among the giants of British higher education, Manchester added to its 23 Nobel laureates in 2010, when Professor Andre Geim and Professor Konstantin Novoselov took the physics prize. With the economist Joseph Stiglitz and the scientist Sir John Sulston already on the staff, their success brought the current complement of Nobel prize-winners to four, the most at any UK university. Manchester has also appointed its first female vice-chancellor, in Dame Nancy Rothwell, a distinguished scientist who had been deputy vice-chancellor since the merger of the old Victoria University with the neighbouring University of Manchester Institute of Science and Technology in 2004.

Some departments were already administered jointly with UMIST and the two institutions only separated fully in 1993, so the new institution has been able to avoid some of the problems associated with other university mergers. A £400-million building and refurbishment programme, the largest ever in UK higher education has been completed and another £250 million of investment is planned by 2015. Work has begun on the development of the university's £30-million "Learning Commons" building, which is due to open its doors in summer 2012. It will provide more than 1,000 flexible learning spaces in Phase One, high quality IT facilities and a campus hub for student-centred activities, as well as a variety of learning support services.

Having appointed a raft of new professors, the university's aim is not only to break into higher education's "golden triangle" of Oxford, Cambridge and London, but to make Manchester one of the top 25 universities in the world by 2015. It reached the top 30 in 2010. Manchester was among the top ten universities in the 2008 Research Assessment Exercise, with almost two thirds of its submission considered world-leading or internationally excellent. There were particularly strong performances in cancer studies, nursing, biology, dentistry, engineering, sociology, development studies, Spanish, and music and drama. Google is helping to fund new research that could help blind people to find their way around the worldwide web.

Manchester reclaimed its place as the university with the largest number of applicants after the merger, although there had been no significant increase at the start of 2011. Scores in the National Student Survey improved in 2010, but were still below the national average. There was 100 per cent satisfaction in Italian and very high levels in electrical and electronic engineering, geology, zoology and physics and astronomy.

One of the priorities in the new institution's founding strategy is to broaden the undergraduate intake, with a particular

---

Oxford Road
Manchester M13 9PL

0161 275 2077 (admissions)
ug-admissions@manchester.ac.uk
www.manchester.ac.uk
www.umsu.manchester.ac.uk
Affiliation: Russell Group

The Times Rankings
Overall Ranking: **32**

Student satisfaction:	=95	(73%)
Research quality:	=12	(2.6)
Entry standards:	19	(422)
Student–staff ratio:	=31	(15.4)
Services & facilities/student:	24	(£1,802)
Expected completion rate:	18	(93.6%)
Good honours:	28	(70.6%)
Graduate prospects:	28	(70.4%)

focus on increasing recruitment from the city and its surrounding area. But it is yet to reach the national average for its courses and entry qualifications for the recruitment of state-educated students or those from working-class homes. The board of governors agreed only "very reluctantly" to charge £9,000 fees from 2012 and proposes to spend about 30 per cent of the additional income on bursaries and fee waivers of up to £3,000 a year for undergraduates from the least wealthy homes.

UMIST's legacy was a strong reputation among academics and employers alike in its specialist areas of engineering, science and management. Surveys of employers frequently placed UMIST among their favourite recruiting grounds, helping to produce an unrivalled network of industrial sponsorship. Employers have rated Manchester's careers service the best at any university. The merger also produced the largest engineering school in the UK, with a £20-million budget and 1,200 students.

A £14-million extension to the School of Chemistry, the second-largest in Britain, opened in 2007. A new £39-million research centre dedicated to Biomedical Science was opened in May 2009, making it one of the largest complexes of its kind in Europe. The business school, which provides many undergraduate courses, is among the strengths of the merged institution, as is the medical school. Its new teaching block helps to cater for 2,000 undergraduates following a problem-based curriculum.

The city's famed youth culture and the university's position at the heart of a huge student precinct already help to ensure keen competition for places – and hence high entry standards in most subjects. Sports facilities, which were already first rate, have improved still further since the city hosted the Commonwealth Games. Students get discount rates at the aquatics centre opened for the games on campus, for example. The university sports teams are also high achievers, ranking ninth overall in the BUCS league. The city's reputation for violent crime has subsided, but the students' union (which has the largest premises in the country) runs late-night minibuses, self-defence classes, and regular safety campaigns. Students tend to be fiercely loyal both to the university and their adopted city.

Undergraduate Fees and Support

» Fees for UK/EU students 2012–13 £9,000
» Fees for International students 2011–12 £11,700–£14,700
£26,800 (medicine)
» Financial support to include up to £3,000 in fee waivers and bursaries for less well-off students; enhanced outreach programme; 50% more students entering through Manchester Access Programme.
» Scholarships and bursaries based on circumstances or by competition.
» Check the university's website for the latest information.

Students

Undergraduates:	**27,105**	**(1,585)**
Postgraduates:	**7,950**	**(3,755)**
Mature students:	**9.6%**	
Overseas students:	**17.5%**	
Applications per place:	**6.5**	
From state-sector schools:	**78.6%**	
From working-class homes:	**24.4%**	

For detailed information about fees, grants and bursaries and how they work, see chapter 7.

Accommodation

Number of places and costs refer to 2011–12
University-owned/managed places: 9,200
Percentage catered: (approx) 30%
Catered costs: £4787–£6,217 (40 weeks).
Self-catered costs: £3,286–£4,760 (40 weeks).
All first years are guaranteed accommodation provided conditions are met.
International students paying overseas fees are guaranteed accommodation if conditions met.
Contact: www.manchester.ac.uk/accommodation

Manchester Metropolitan University

Manchester Metropolitan (MMU) was the second most popular university in the UK among aspiring undergraduates at the start of 2011 just behind its Manchester neighbour. A rise of more than 8 per cent in the number of applications followed the previous year's growth of 15 per cent. MMU will hope to maintain that progress, having pitched its undergraduate fees for 2012 below the level of many of its rivals. A majority of its degrees will cost £8,000 a year, with a few at £8,500. The most expensive, at £9,000 will be specialist scientific, healthcare, and art and design subjects that require intensive use of facilities, teaching and learning resources. There will be a £10-million student support scheme.

Longstanding commitments to extending access are being continued: even among the full-time undergraduates, a fifth are over 25 and almost 40 per cent come from working-class homes. With over 35,000 students, including more than 8,000 part-timers, MMU is one of the largest universities in Britain. But the giant institution boasts quality as well as quantity: more than a third of the work entered for the 2008 Research Assessment Exercise was rated as world-leading or internationally excellent. Education, English, and art and design produced the best results.

Almost 1,000 courses cover more than 70 subjects, with the menu of programmes including a growing range of two-year Foundation degrees. The university takes teaching seriously: small groups are used whenever possible and staff are encouraged to take a three-year MA in teaching. Many courses also involve work placements. MMU has more professionally accredited courses than any other university. Yet scores in the 2010 National Student Survey declined, leaving the university just outside the bottom ten. Only philosophy and human and social geography satisfied more than 90 per cent of full-time undergraduates. The projected dropout rate was close to 20 per cent in the latest survey, significantly worse than average for the subjects and entry qualifications.

Education courses have fared well in the Teacher Training Agency's performance indicators, however, especially for primary training. The university trains more teachers than any other and has launched a Centre for Urban Education to develop its expertise further. Some 800 trainees and other students taking contemporary arts and sports science are at the former Crewe and Alsager College campuses, 40 miles south of Manchester and now rebranded as MMU Cheshire. The remaining education students are based at Didsbury, five miles out of the centre of Manchester, with those taking community studies. A single Institute of Education

---

All Saints Building
All Saints
Manchester M15 6BH

0161 247 2000 (general enquiries)
enquiries@mmu.ac.uk
www.mmu.ac.uk
www.mmunion.co.uk
Affiliation: University Alliance

The Times Rankings
Overall Ranking: **98**

Student satisfaction:	**102**	(72%)
Research quality:	**=70**	(0.4)
Entry standards:	**=78**	(271)
Student–staff ratio:	**=88**	(20.6)
Services & facilities/student:	**=91**	(£1,133)
Expected completion rate:	**=95**	(78.7%)
Good honours:	**78**	(57.0%)
Graduate prospects:	**83**	(57.1%)

covers both centres.

The two Cheshire campuses are being merged into one at Crewe in the area of the town now known as the University Quadrant. A £30-million student village has already opened and arts facilities have switched to Crewe with the opening of a £6-million drama, music and dance centre. A £10-million Sport Science Centre opened in November 2010 and the Business School will open in early 2012. Exercise and sport science students will be the final group to make the six-mile move and will be based at Crewe before autumn 2011, after which only sports fields will remain at Alsager.

The five sites in Manchester will eventually be reduced to two linked campuses. The university will move from leafy Didsbury in the southern suburbs and create a £120-million "campus for the professions" in the city centre that will be one of the most environmentally sustainable in the UK, uniting provision for teachers, nurses, health and youth workers. The new site is close to the existing All Saints campus, on the university's border with Hulme and Moss Side.

New science and engineering buildings at All Saints cost £42 million – part of a £300-million building programme for the university as a whole. The large business school will benefit from a new £65-million building next to the Mancunian Way. Overseas links have expanded rapidly in recent years, with MMU offering exchange opportunities in Europe and further afield, as well as establishing teaching bases abroad. However, more than half of the students come from the Manchester area, easing the pressure on accommodation in a city of nearly 70,000 students. The university plays an important role in the region's economy, not least because 70 per cent of graduates stay and work in the North West. Its financial impact on the region has been put at £690 million a year and rising.

All first years who request accommodation can be housed, with priority for university-owned halls going to the disabled and those who live furthest from Manchester. The city's attractions do no harm to recruitment levels, but much depends on where the course is based; students at Crewe can feel isolated. Some potential applicants are daunted by the sheer size of the university, but individual courses and sites usually provide a social circle.

Undergraduate Fees and Support

» Fees for UK/EU students 2012–13   £8,000–£8,500
  Specialist science, healthcare and art & design   £9,000
» Fees for International students 2011–12   £9,030–£14,700
» Details of financial support and widening participation activity to be announced. Likely to include bursaries of up to £1,650 for students with household income below £25K.
» Scholarships and bursaries based on circumstances or by competition.
» Check the university's website for the latest information.

Students		
Undergraduates:	**23,975**	**(3,720)**
Postgraduates:	**3,210**	**(4,615)**
Mature students:	**20.8%**	
Overseas students:	**7.3%**	
Applications per place:	**5.5**	
From state-sector schools:	**96.2%**	
From working-class homes:	**38.7%**	

For detailed information about fees, grants and bursaries and how they work, see chapter 7.

Accommodation
Number of places and costs refer to 2011–12
University provided places: 3,530
Percentage catered: 3.9%
Catered costs: Manchester £98.32 a week
Self-catered costs: Manchester £79.11–£103.13 a week; Cheshire £79.11– £89.55 a week
All new full-time students will be housed if requirements are met. Local restrictions apply.
International students: as above.
Contact: www.mmu.ac.uk/accommodation/

Middlesex University

Middlesex had one of the biggest increases in applications at any university in 2010 – more than 30 per cent – but the demand for places had still grown by another 11 per cent at the start of 2011. Although helped by changes in nursing and art and design, the rises mark the culmination of a programme of reorganisation that has seen a new pattern of courses and more international recruitment. The university has rationalised its schools to focus on its strengths in business, computing and the arts. Now 23,000 strong, including part-timers, it would like to carry on growing, partly through partner colleges at home and abroad that participate in exchanges or offer Middlesex qualifications.

Overseas recruitment was Middlesex's salvation when it found UK students more difficult to attract: foreign undergraduates make up 16 per cent of its intake. A long-standing commitment to Europe sees more than 1,000 students arriving from the Continent, and even more come from further afield. There is a network of 11 regional offices, producing a student population drawn from 130 countries, which won the university a Queen's Award for Enterprise. Middlesex has its own campus in Dubai and has now become the first UK university to open a campus in Mauritius. The university's next overseas venture will be at Noida, east of the Indian capital of Delhi, where a new campus will open in October 2011. Current Indian legislation requires students at international universities to complete their course at that university's home campus, but Indian students will be able to choose between London, Dubai or Mauritius.

The highly flexible course system allows students to start some courses in January if they prefer not to wait until autumn, and offers the option of an extra five-week session in the summer to try out new subjects or add to their credits. The introduction of year-long modules have the benefit of instilling a deeper level of learning, allowing students to get to grips with a subject before assessment.

Nine out of ten students take vocational courses, including at postgraduate or sub-degree level. Media students, for example, benefit from a Skillset Academy. The business school is the biggest subject area, but almost half of the undergraduates are on multidisciplinary programmes. About 40 per cent are over 20 on entry and half of the full-timers come from London. Almost all of the British students are from state schools, 48 per cent of them from working-class homes. The projected dropout rate remained around 21 per cent in the latest survey, above the national average for the university's subjects and entry qualifications.

For some time, the university has been reducing the number of campuses dotted

---

North London Business Park
The Burroughs
London NW4 4BT

020 8411 5555 (enquiries)
contact via website
www.mdx.ac.uk
www.musu.mdx.ac.uk
Affiliation: million+

The Times Rankings
Overall Ranking: **=94**

Student satisfaction:	=103	(71%)
Research quality:	=62	(0.5)
Entry standards:	113	(207)
Student–staff ratio:	97	(21)
Services & facilities/student:	5	(£2,305)
Expected completion rate:	112	(72.4%)
Good honours:	=82	(55.8%)
Graduate prospects:	=79	(57.8%)

around London's North Circular Road. A building programme that has already cost £100 million will eventually concentrate the university on three sites in north London. A new art, design and media building, described by the Greater London Authority as "world class design" is under construction on the Hendon campus and due to be completed in time for beginning of the academic year in 2011. Some 1,600 students will move to the new building, mainly from the Cat Hill campus, which will close. More than £50 million has already been invested at Hendon on a library, learning resources centre and roofing in the main quadrangle to provide social space. New student facilities, including an entertainment venue, expanded nursery and refectory have been added to meet the demand from the extra students and staff. The campus, which boasts one of the country's few Real Tennis courts, already housed the business school, also has a new teaching and learning centre that includes biomedical, computing science, psychology and sports laboratories.

The other locations include a picturesque country estate at Trent Park, which includes a gym and multipurpose sports hall, outdoor swimming pool, outdoor fitness trail and access to the on-site training ground of Southgate hockey club. Nurses and other health students are based in four London teaching hospitals and on a campus at Archway which is shared with the University College and Royal Free Hospital medical schools. There is also a joint degree in veterinary nursing run with the Royal Veterinary College.

Results from National Student Surveys have been disappointing. Despite dramatic improvement in 2010, Middlesex remained in the bottom 20. Accounting and initial teacher training were the only areas to satisfy more than 90 per cent of final-year undergraduates. The number of residential places is planned to double in the next few years from the current 1,156 bedspaces. Priority is given to first years who live outside London and to international students. Sports facilities have been improving and now includes a "fitness pod" at Hendon with a gym and multi-purpose outdoor courts.

Undergraduate Fees and Support

» Fees for UK/EU students 2012-13   £9,000
» Fees for International students 2011-12   £10,400
» A package of financial support and widening participation activity to be announced.
» Scholarships and bursaries based on circumstances or by competition.
» Check the university's website for the latest information.

Students		
Undergraduates:	**13,460**	**(3,675)**
Postgraduates:	**2,760**	**(3,280)**
Mature students:	**38.4%**	
Overseas students:	**16.1%**	
Applications per place:	**5.9**	
From state-sector schools:	**98.8%**	
From working-class homes:	**48.4%**	

For detailed information about fees, grants and bursaries and how they work, see chapter 7.

Accommodation
Number of places and costs refer to 2011-12
University-provided places: 1,156
Percentage catered: 0%
Self-catered costs: £94-£120 a week.
Full-year students have priority; residential restrictions apply.
International students are guaranteed a room provided they apply by the deadline.
Contact: accomm@mdx.ac.uk; www.mdx.ac.uk/accommodation

Newcastle University

For the last three years, Newcastle has been named as the best university city in the UK and there have been other accolades for its nightlife and sustainability. The message appears to be getting through to sixth-formers, who applied in greater numbers than at most other Russell Group universities both in 2010 and at the start of 2011. The university will be charging undergraduate fees of £9,000 in 2012, but is proposing to spend £29 million on fee waivers and bursaries over the next five years.

Newcastle has almost completed the first phase of a £200-million programme of investment in its campus and facilities. The latest developments include an £8-million refurbishment of the students' union that is due for completion in September 2011, extra investment in library facilities, and a teaching and accommodation complex for international students taking pre-entry courses in English and academic skills. In addition, a £30-million research centre and Institute of Health and Society has brought together the world's largest group of scientists working on fundamental problems in bacteria.

The glass-fronted King's Gate building had already created a new "front door" to the university, as well as housing all the main student services and a visitor centre. New buildings have opened for music and medical sciences, and nearly 100 study bedrooms have been added on campus. Science and engineering laboratories have been upgraded, disabled access improved and thousands of students provided with internet connections in university-owned flats and halls of residence. The university's museum has been redeveloped into the £26-million Great North Museum: Hancock, taking in collections from two other university museums and its gallery.

The university has also been active overseas. A branch campus in Singapore offers degrees in naval architecture. A second campus in Johor, Malaysia, opened in 2011 and will add biomedical science to the existing medical degree in 2012. For those who prefer to come to the UK, the university does well in i-graduate's International Student Barometer for careers advice and the overall student experience.

Newcastle has also performed consistently in the National Student Survey, finishing on the verge of the top 20 in 2010, when 87 per cent of final-year undergraduates were satisfied overall. Media achieved the best results in the UK, medicine was joint first, while law, music, speech science and archaeology were all placed second. Newcastle is popular with independent schools, whose applicants take three in ten places, but the university has stepped up its already considerable efforts to broaden its

---

Kensington Terrace
Newcastle upon Tyne
NE1 7RU

0191 208 3333 (enquiries)
www.ncl.ac.uk/enquiries
www.ncl.ac.uk
www.unionsociety.co.uk
Affiliation: Russell Group

The Times Rankings
Overall Ranking: **25**

Student satisfaction:	=20	(80%)
Research quality:	=30	(2.0)
Entry standards:	21	(410)
Student–staff ratio:	=29	(15.3)
Services & facilities/student:	25	(£1,742)
Expected completion rate:	12	(94.2%)
Good honours:	17	(75.5%)
Graduate prospects:	15	(75.4%)

intake. The dropout rate, at only 5 per cent, is one of the lowest in the country.

Originally a school of medicine and surgery established in 1834, Newcastle became Durham University's medical school until going its own way in 1937. Its excellence in that area was confirmed by its selection as a national centre to disseminate best teaching practice in medicine. The school has gone back into partnership with Durham, with about a third of trainees spending their first two years at Durham's Stockton campus. Cancer research was the star performer in the 2008 Research Assessment Exercise, with 90 per cent of work considered world-leading or internationally excellent. Newcastle entered fewer academics than most members of Russell Group universities, but almost 60 per cent of its work reached the top two categories, with art and design, music, English, town planning and civil engineering all producing excellent results.

Recent additions to the portfolio of courses have included degrees in drug development and biopharmaceutical technology. Newcastle already had a number of unusual features for a traditional university, such as a fine art degree which attracts up to 15 applicants for each place. It also has a longstanding reputation for agriculture, which benefits from two farms in Northumberland. The award-winning ncl+ initiative encourages all students to develop employability skills through activities such as working as a student ambassador or writing for the university newspaper. On most courses, a career development module gives credit for work experience, volunteering or part-time employment.

The campus occupies 50 acres close to the main shopping area, civic centre and New-castle United's ground. The university also boasts an expanded and refurbished independent theatre. Tyneside has plenty more culture to offer in the riverside Sage Gateshead music centre and the BALTIC Centre for Contemporary Art.

The cost of living is reasonable and town–gown relations better than in many cities. Sport is a particular strength: a new £5.5-million sports centre supplements two older venues, which have been extensively refurbished. The main outdoor pitches are two miles away. Over £30,000 is awarded annually in sports bursaries for elite athletes.

Undergraduate Fees and Support

- » Fees for UK/EU students 2012–13 £9,000
- » Fees for International students 2011–12 £10,840–£13,905 £25,735 (medicine)
- » Up to a third of students will benefit from £2,000 a year as fee waivers and bursaries.
- » Scholarships and bursaries based on circumstances or by competition.
- » Check the university's website for the latest information.

Students		
Undergraduates:	**14,515**	**(75)**
Postgraduates:	**3,985**	**(1,675)**
Mature students:	**8.3%**	
Overseas students:	**14.4%**	
Applications per place:	**6.1**	
From state-sector schools:	**69.2%**	
From working-class homes:	**21.9%**	

For detailed information about fees, grants and bursaries and how they work, see chapter 7.

Accommodation

Number of places and costs refer to 2011–12
University-provided places: 4,609
Percentage catered: 24%
Catered costs: £102.34–£120.05 a week.
Self-catered costs: £71.89–£125.75 a week.
All single undergraduates are guaranteed a room in university-managed accommodation provided requirements are met. Local restrictions apply.
International students: as above.
Contact: web enquiry form at www.ncl.ac.uk/enquiries

University of Wales, Newport

A futuristic £35-million riverside campus that will be a focal point for the city of Newport, as well as its university, opened in 2011. The City campus will house the Business School and part of the School of Art, Media and Design. Newport is one of the largest degree providers in Wales for creative arts and education. The city council has contributed £10 million towards the development, which will be at the heart of a new Cultural Quarter designed to attract inward investment and strengthen the local economy.

Newport had already embarked on an ambitious expansion strategy before attaining full membership of the University of Wales. Full-time student numbers rose by more than 50 per cent in five years, but the demand for places really took off after the change of status from college to university. Applications were up by 12 per cent at the start of 2011, following a string of increases. Students have been attracted by a range of new courses in areas such as photography for fashion and advertising, creative therapies in education, and applied drama.

The university is pursuing closer links with the University of Wales Institute Cardiff (UWIC) and Glamorgan University, which it already partners in a number of subjects. A joint submission with UWIC in art and design was particularly successful in the 2008 Research Assessment Exercise. Newport entered only 28 staff for the RAE, but their work was highly rated compared with most of their peers in similar institutions. More than half of it was considered world-leading or internationally excellent, with mechanical engineering and social work doing especially well.

Newport also did well in the first National Student Survey, finishing in the top ten, but it has slipped down the table subsequently and was in the bottom ten in 2010. Only English reached 90 per cent satisfaction, although initial teacher training, sports science and business subjects came close. A poll of local employers was particularly positive about the university, however, and Estyn, the Welsh schools inspectorate, gave the best grades in Wales to the teacher-training courses. Newport achieved the highest possible rating in its last audit of academic processes by the Quality Assurance Agency.

The university, which was previously Gwent College of Higher Education, now has over 9,000 students, including 500 from outside the EU. Virtually all the full-time undergraduates come from state schools and four in ten come from working-class homes. The projected dropout rate of 17 per cent is much improved, but still higher than the benchmark set according to the subject mix and entry qualifications. Newport operates a

Caerleon Campus
Lodge Road
Newport
South Wales NP18 3QT

01633 432030 (admissions)
admissions@newport.ac.uk
www.newport.ac.uk
www.newportunion.com
Affiliation: University
   Alliance

The Times Rankings

Overall Ranking: **=104**

Student satisfaction:	=78	(74%)
Research quality:	=79	(0.3)
Entry standards:	=97	(252)
Student–staff ratio:	=107	(22.5)
Services & facilities/student:	102	(£1,061)
Expected completion rate:	=90	(79.5%)
Good honours:	=106	(49.3%)
Graduate prospects:	95	(54.5%)

number of access schemes, and is a partner in the University of the Heads of the Valleys Institute, a community education initiative that was launched in 2010. It is expected to provide the equivalent of 4,000 places on courses up to Foundation degrees by 2015.

Newport describes itself as a "community university" and is actively involved with a range of local businesses. It was rated the number one university in Wales for enterprise education by the Knowledge Exploitation Fund for three years in a row, helping more than 70 new start-up businesses. Among its innovations were the Corus to Campus project for redundant steelworkers previously employed by the company. Newport is also well-known for photography and film, hosting the International Film School Wales, whose graduates include double-BAFTA winner Asif Kapadia, and Justin Kerrigan, director of the cult movie, *Human Traffic*.

There will be two campuses in 2012. The smaller, Allt-Yr-Yn, campus will close during 2011, following the move of its business, art, media and design students to the new City campus. The larger Caerleon campus is further out, with impressive views, and now caters for humanities, education, health and social sciences, photography and fine art. This is also where the student village of 661 self-catered study bedrooms is located and where the Wales International Study Centre opened in 2008. Accommodation is guaranteed for students who commit to Newport by the end of August. Free buses link the campuses, which are officially among the safest in Britain: Newport was the first educational establishment to pass an industry-standard security inspection.

A well-equipped sports centre at Caerleon has transformed facilities that previously compared unfavourably with those of other universities. The city of Newport is undergoing a £2-billion regeneration programme, and has also established something of a reputation for producing successful rock bands. There are plenty of clubs and entertainment venues, but students in search of serious cultural or clubbing activity gravitate to nearby Cardiff.

Undergraduate Fees and Support

» Fees 2012–13: to be announced; able to charge up to £9,000, with Welsh Assembly expected to pay fees above £3,375 for Welsh students.
» Fees for international students 2011–12   £8,250–£9,250
» Scholarships and bursaries based on circumstances or by competition.
» Check the university's website for the latest information.

Students

Undergraduates:	**3,510**	**(3,940)**
Postgraduates:	**670**	**(1,170)**
Mature students:	**35.9%**	
Overseas students:	**2.8%**	
Applications per place:	**3.6**	
From state-sector schools:	**99.4%**	
From working-class homes:	**43.4%**	

Accommodation

Number of places and costs refer to 2011–12
University-provided places: 661
Percentage catered: 0%
Self-catered costs: £77–£89 a week.
First years are guaranteed accommodation if requirements met.
International students: same as above.
Contact: accommodation@newport.ac.uk

For detailed information about fees, grants and bursaries and how they work, see chapter 7.

University of Northampton

Northampton has been enjoying record demand for its degree places: a jump of almost 18 per cent in applications at the beginning of 2011 was one of the largest rises at any university, building on a 14 per cent increase in 2010. Consistently good results in the National Student Survey may have helped. The university matched the UK average in 2010, when history, finance, accounting and management produced the best results.

A raft of new courses, many provided by partner institutions in the UK and overseas, is helping to attract more students. In the last 12 months, a series of degrees have been approved in leather technology, midwifery, nursing and health and social care. Specialisms such as leather technology, fashion and wastes management have helped build overseas recruitment to more than 1,000 students from over 100 countries, while overall student numbers have risen to almost 14,000.

Although one of the newest universities, formed in 2005, Northampton can trace its history back to the thirteenth century. Henry III dissolved the original version, allegedly because his bishops thought it posed a threat to Oxford. The modern university originated in an amalgamation of the town's colleges of education, technology and art, and aims to "create a campus for creative technologies bringing together synergies between the arts and sciences". It has a particular focus on training for public services in the region, with students combining their studies with work placements in the community. The police and criminal justice studies Foundation degree, delivered for Northamptonshire Police Authority, for example, has been designed to prepare students for a career in policing or the criminal justice system.

The university is taking part in a national pilot to develop fast-track degrees and extended work-based equivalents. The two-year route is available in law, management, marketing and sport development; the four-year option in a range of business, finance and marketing courses. Business is the university's most popular area, but teacher training and health subjects are not far behind – the university is the region's largest provider of teachers and healthcare professionals. The School of Education was awarded the Training and Development Agency's highest grade for quality and was named an Outstanding Ofsted provider 2009–10.

Northampton was close to the bottom of the ranking for the 2008 Research Assessment Exercise, although there was some world-leading research in four of the ten subject areas, with history producing by far the best results. There are now 11 research centres, focusing on everything from

Park Campus
Boughton Green Road
Northampton NN2 7AL

0800 358 2232 (courses freephone)
study@northampton.ac.uk
www.northampton.ac.uk
www.northampton
union.com
Affiliation: million+

The Times Rankings
Overall Ranking: **92**

Student satisfaction:	=48	(77%)
Research quality:	=92	(0.2)
Entry standards:	107	(238)
Student–staff ratio:	110	(22.9)
Services & facilities/student:	=79	(£1,198)
Expected completion rate:	70	(83.1%)
Good honours:	63	(60.9%)
Graduate prospects:	102	(52.9%)

contemporary fiction to anomalous psychological processes and transitional economics in China.

The university has two sites: Park campus on the edge of Northampton and the smaller but more central Avenue campus. They are linked by a regular and free weekday bus service. Park campus is set in 80 acres of open green parkland, with accommodation, a sports hall, students' union centre and nightclub. A major expansion of the Sulgrave Building to provide new learning spaces for trainee teachers is due for completion at the end of 2011, part of a £73-million programme of improvements. The Business School is also on the Park campus.

Avenue campus, the centre for art, design, science and technology and the performing arts, hosts frequent theatre performances and exhibitions, and has its own art gallery. A recent £11-million investment saw the conversion of an adjacent Grade II-listed former school into a technology and research centre with NVision and a 3D immersive technology and visualisation facility. Another university-backed development is the iCon building in Daventry, set to open at the end of 2011. The facility will offer a base for a diverse range of innovative, green businesses.

Northampton takes its mission to widen participation in higher education seriously: almost all the undergraduates attended state schools or colleges, while just over 40 per cent come from working-class homes.

The projected dropout rate improved considerably in the latest survey and, at 14 per cent, is better than the national average for the university's courses and entry qualifications. Since many of the students are from the region, the 1,620 residential places are enough to guarantee accommodation for all first years who make Northampton their first choice.

Sports enthusiasts have a Premier League rugby club on their doorstep, as well as a more modest football club, first-class cricket and the Silverstone motor circuit. The university has added a £100,000 gym to its sports facilities, which include a sports hall and outdoor pitches. The town has a number of student-oriented bars, but the two campuses' union bars remain the hub of the social scene. Students receive a free discount card to use in Northampton's high-street and independent shops, entertainment and health venues.

Undergraduate Fees and Support

» Fees for UK/EU students 2012–13   to be announced
» Fees for International students 2011–12   £9,100
» A package of financial support and widening participation activity to be announced.
» Scholarships and bursaries based on circumstances or by competition.
» Check the university's website for the latest information.

Students

Undergraduates:	**8,170**	**(3,245)**
Postgraduates:	**925**	**(1,585)**
Mature students:	**37.8%**	
Overseas students:	**6.3%**	
Applications per place:	**5.1**	
From state-sector schools:	**97.8%**	
From working-class homes:	**41.7%**	

For detailed information about fees, grants and bursaries and how they work, see chapter 7.

Accommodation

Number of places and costs refer to 2010–11
University-provided places: 1,620
Percentage catered: 0%
Self-catered costs: £43.00 (small twin) – £97.70 (en-suite single) a week (42-week contract)
First years have priority, provided requirements are met.
International students: guaranteed housing.
Contact: www.northampton.ac.uk/study/accommodation/

Northumbria University

Northumbria consistently ranks among the leading post-1992 universities and a £136-million investment in its city centre campus has produced facilities to match. The first phase was completed in 2007, when design, law and business students moved into the new City Campus East development, which is linked to the existing main campus by an iconic new footbridge spanning the city's central motorway. Extensive developments on the west side of the campus are now complete and include a £6-million refurbishment of the library, which is open 24 hours a day, renovation of the students' union building and a £30-million sports centre. An environmental chamber allows researchers to experience conditions equivalent to anywhere in the world, and there is a 3,000-seater indoor arena.

The university has announced plans for £8,500 tuition fees in 2012, with £14.5 million a year set aside for a package of financial support that would benefit up to 40 per cent of undergraduates. Fee waivers and bursaries would save students from the poorest homes £4,000 a year and there would be £1,000 scholarships for the brightest students. The university is also promising to improve staffing levels, building on an £18-million programme to recruit more academics. Seven of the current staff have won National Teaching Fellowships.

Northumbria has attracted more than 31,000 students, one in ten of whom are from overseas. Three quarters of students are from the North East of England but numbers drawn from across the UK have been rising year on year, as have entry standards. A further 4,000 are studying Northumbria degrees in other countries. Applications were up by 13 per cent in 2010 and by another 9 per cent when the official deadline passed for courses beginning in 2011.

Entry grades for those with A levels are among the highest in the new universities, but half of the mature students enter through the Higher Education Foundation Certificate, an access course system with modules in more than 30 subjects. Free one-day taster courses run throughout the year to give local people an idea of what studying at Northumbria would be like. Over a third of the students come from working-class homes, many from areas with little tradition of higher education. The projected dropout rate has fluctuated recently. It was back above 15 per cent in the latest survey, higher than the benchmark for the university's courses and entry grades. Scores improved in the 2010 National Student Survey, when the university matched the UK average for satisfaction rates. European languages,

---

Ellison Terrace
Newcastle upon Tyne
NE1 8ST

0191 243 7420 (admissions)
er.admissions@northumbria..ac.uk
www.northumbria.ac.uk
http://mynsu.northumbria.
ac.uk
Affiliation: University
Alliance

The Times Rankings
Overall Ranking: **60**

Student satisfaction:	=48	(77%)
Research quality:	=79	(0.3)
Entry standards:	53	(300)
Student–staff ratio:	=75	(19.7)
Services & facilities/student:	84	(£1,183)
Expected completion rate:	=79	(81.8%)
Good honours:	69	(58.6%)
Graduate prospects:	43	(68.0%)

education, law, initial teacher training, maths, sociology, nursing and social policy and anthropology all registered at least 90 per cent satisfaction, while architecture students were the most satisfied in the country.

Northumbria is one of only eight institutions to hold maximum Ofsted grades for its primary training provision and one of only five to reach the highest standard for secondary provision. Its PGCE training was second only to Cambridge's in a 2010 ranking. Many degrees are available as sandwich courses, with placements of up to a year in business or industry.

The majority of subjects are based in the city centre, with health, education and community studies on the Coach Lane campus on the outskirts of the city, where £18 million has been spent upgrading facilities. Coach Lane now incorporates a learning resources centre with a fully integrated library, a clinical skills centre, where students can learn in simulated hospital environments, and new sports facilities, as well as teaching and seminar rooms.

Northumbria's best-known feature is its School of Design, which has launched a new base in London. Its students followed up recent successes with a string of awards in 2010, while the academics produced some of the university's best results in the 2008 assessment exercise. The university entered a comparatively low proportion of its academics, but more than a third of its submission was considered world-leading or internationally excellent. Architecture and the built environment, general engineering and nursing and midwifery were other high scorers. Northumbria intends to double its capacity in research and enterprise over the next five years.

Sport plays a growing role: Northumbria is consistently among the top 20 in the British Universities and Colleges Sport rankings. The sports scholarship programme has supported over 250 athletes from over 40 sports in the past ten years, some going on to success at the highest level.

Most first years are offered places in university accommodation. Two large residential developments will open in September 2011, bringing the total stock to over 4,200 places, and there is a plentiful supply of privately rented flats and houses.

Undergraduate Fees and Support

» Fees for UK/EU students 2012–13   £8,500
» Fees for International students 2011–12   £9,450–£10,150
                                                    £11,350 (physiotherapy)
» For students with household income below £16K, £4,000 in fee waivers and bursaries; for household income £16K–£25K, £3,000 in fee waivers and bursaries; academic scholarships of £1,000 a year.
» Scholarships and bursaries based on circumstances or by competition.
» Check the university's website for the latest information.

Students		
Undergraduates:	**17,570**	**(7,100)**
Postgraduates:	**3,125**	**(3,630)**
Mature students:	**19.2%**	
Overseas students:	**10.1%**	
Applications per place:	**4.6**	
From state-sector schools:	**92.2%**	
From working-class homes:	**34.0%**	

For detailed information about fees, grants and bursaries and how they work, see chapter 7.

Accommodation

Number of places and costs refer to 2011–12

University-provided places: 4,200

Percentage catered: 6%

Catered costs: £118 a week.

Self-catered costs: £70–£119 a week.

First years who need accommodation can be offered rooms. Local restrictions apply.

International students: first years are guaranteed accommodation if requirements met.

Contact: rc.accommodation@northumbria.ac.uk

University of Nottingham

Nottingham is the nearest Britain has to a truly global university, with campuses in China and Malaysia modelled on a head-quarters that is among the most attractive in Britain. The university has now been invited to establish a second Chinese campus in Shanghai. For many years Nottingham has been among the institutions with the stiffest competition for each place, and a striking new campus and extra courses has made the university even more fashionable in recent years. Growth in applications of more than 9 per cent in 2010 was higher than at most comparable universities and there had been a similar rise at the start of 2011.

The university enjoyed a spectacular rise up the pecking order of higher education. In less than 20 years, it went from being a solid civic university to a prime alternative to Oxbridge. It now has 34,000 students and is in the top 75 in the QS World University Rankings. Nottingham describes itself as "research-led", with work carried out at the university winning two Nobel prizes in 2003. Professor Sir Peter Mansfield, who won the medicine prize for research leading to the development of the MRI scanner, has spent almost all his academic career there.

About £70 million was spent on recruiting academics in advance of the 2008 Research Assessment Exercise, including 20 new research chairs. The investment paid off handsomely with sharply improved results in the RAE, which will bring long-term increases in funding. Almost 60 per cent of a large submission was judged to be world-leading or internationally excellent, with pharmacy and Spanish, Portuguese and Latin American studies producing the best results in the UK and chemistry and physics the second-best.

Physical expansion has allowed the university to take almost 1,000 more students, but new undergraduates' average A-level grades have not dropped. Once in, they tend to stay the course – the dropout rate of 4 per cent is consistently among the best in the country. The university has succeeded in broadening its intake, but still has significantly more independent school students and fewer from working-class homes than the national average for the subjects offered. There is a well-established programme of summer schools, masterclasses and support for post-16 students from backgrounds without a history of progressing to selective universities.

Consistently good results in the National Student Survey continued in 2010, when 87 per cent of final-year undergraduates were satisfied. Agriculture, law, nutrition, pharmacy, physics and theology produced the best scores after particular improvement in the grades for staff feedback – the most common cause for complaint nationally. The

---

University Park
Nottingham NG7 2RD

0115 951 5559 (enquiries)
undergraduate-enquiries@
 nottingham.ac.uk
www.nottingham.ac.uk
www.su.nottingham.ac.uk
Affiliation: Russell Group

The Times Rankings
Overall Ranking: **16**

Student satisfaction:	=24	(79%)
Research quality:	=21	(2.2)
Entry standards:	15	(428)
Student–staff ratio:	16	(14.2)
Services & facilities/student:	32	(£1,604)
Expected completion rate:	11	(94.5%)
Good honours:	24	(73.0%)
Graduate prospects:	=9	(77.9%)

university has also stepped up its efforts to give students the best possible chance in the jobs market. The Nottingham Advantage Award offers a range of extra-curricular modules, as well as providing scores of internships for graduates, who enjoy lifetime access to the Centre for Career Development.

The original University Park campus has won eight consecutive Green Flag awards for excellent parkland, the only university to do so. A mile away is the 30-acre Jubilee campus, the second phase of which opened in 2009 and features the tallest free-standing sculpture in the UK. Futuristic buildings cluster around an artificial lake and house the schools of management and finance, computer science and education, as well as 750 residential places. Further construction costing £38 million is under way to provide new buildings for mathematics, bioenergy, engineering and science, humanities and energy technologies.

The Queen's Medical School is also close to University Park, although its recently established graduate-entry outpost is in Derby. The biosciences and the new veterinary school are at Sutton Bonington, 12 miles south of the city in a rural setting. A third student services centre has opened there, so that there is now a centre on all three campuses.

Nottingham has long-standing links with the Far East, which provides the majority of its overseas students in the UK, and has a Chinese physicist, Professor Fujia Yang, as its Chancellor. The two branch campuses outside Kuala Lumpur, in Malaysia, and at Ningbo, in China, now host another 8,000 students. The purpose-built campuses have echoes of Nottingham's distinctive clock tower. Students have the opportunity to move between the three countries.

The two main campuses are within three miles of the centre of Nottingham, with a good selection of student friendly clubs. However, halls of residence and the students' union tend to be the centre of student social life. New bars, café facilities and a nightclub were included in a recent £1-million makeover. Sports facilities are excellent and expanding: a £1.6-million sports pavilion opened in 2010 at the university's playing fields adjoining the main campus.

Undergraduate Fees and Support

- » Fees for UK/EU students 2012–13   £9,000
- » Fees for International students 2011–12   £11,420–£14,970 £14,970–£20,420 (veterinary medicine), £15,780–£27,430 (medicine)
- » Details of financial support and widening participation activity to be announced. It will include bursaries, fee waivers, support for local students, disabled students, carers and students formerly in care.
- » Scholarships and bursaries based on circumstances or by competition.
- » Check the university's website for the latest information.

Students

Undergraduates:	**22,340**	**(2,325)**
Postgraduates:	**6,880**	**(2,575)**
Mature students:	**7.5%**	
Overseas students:	**15.7%**	
Applications per place:	**7.1**	
From state-sector schools:	**69.6%**	
From working-class homes:	**19.1%**	

For detailed information about fees, grants and bursaries and how they work, see chapter 7.

Accommodation

Number of places and costs refer to 2011–12
University-provided places: 7,500
Percentage catered: 50%
Catered costs: £112.97–£183.00 a week (31 weeks).
Self-catered costs: £85.50–£153.83 a week (43–44 weeks).
First years are guaranteed accommodation if conditions are met.
International undergraduates: as above
Contact: www.nottingham.ac.uk/accommodation

Nottingham Trent University

Nottingham Trent (NTU) has been consistently among the leading post-1992 universities in *The Times* League Table, as well as one of the biggest, but it has dropped 11 places this year after a larger decline than elsewhere in graduate employment prospects. Nevertheless, the university has demonstrated high quality in an unusually wide range of disciplines. Best known for fashion and other creative arts, which have the largest number of students, it also boasts one of the UK's biggest law schools, offering legal practice courses for both solicitors and barristers as well as degrees. A four-year "exempting law degree", launched in 2009, combines both phases with an extended work placement, enabling students to qualify as solicitors without paying postgraduate fees.

NTU has over 26,000 students, 5,000 of whom are postgraduates and 5,000 part-time. International students make up almost 6 per cent of the student body in Nottingham, while another 7,000 are studying overseas. Over a third of the undergraduates come from working-class homes and nine out of ten attended state schools or colleges, while the projected dropout rate of 13 per cent is close to the national average for the university's courses and entry grades.

An extensive research programme attracted a £7.65 million donation – thought to be the largest to a post-1992 university – to advance the university's work in cancer diagnosis and therapy. A new conference centre, opened in 2010, will also help to boost income and investment. The university held its own in the 2008 Research Assessment Exercise, although it entered fewer academics than some of the other leading new universities. More than a third of its submission was rated world-leading or internationally excellent, with communication, culture and media studies, social policy, engineering and biomedical sciences producing the best results.

Scores declined in the 2010 National Student Survey, leaving Nottingham Trent in the bottom half of the table. Biology, fine art, forensic science, maths and statistics, physics, sports science and creative art and design produced the best results. The university has seen a series of big rises in applications; there was a 20 per cent increase in 2010 and another 10 per cent at the start of 2011.

The extensive main city site contains a mixture of Victorian and modern buildings. An ambitious estates strategy led to a nomination for a *Times Higher Education* award in 2010. Over the past five years, the university has undertaken a £90-million regeneration of two city centre buildings. As well as substantial refurbishment, the project has added a central court building to link the two. Redevelopment work has taken place on all three of the university's campuses, ranging

---

Burton Street
Nottingham NG1 4BU

0115 848 4200 (admissions)
contact via website (prospectus)
www.ntu.ac.uk
www.trentstudents.org
Affiliation: University
   Alliance

The Times Rankings
Overall Ranking: **66**

Student satisfaction:	=78	(74%)
Research quality:	=70	(0.4)
Entry standards:	66	(287)
Student–staff ratio:	=71	(19.3)
Services & facilities/student:	51	(£1,402)
Expected completion rate:	64	(84.1%)
Good honours:	86	(54.8%)
Graduate prospects:	68	(60.6%)

from the renovation of existing facilities to the building of new lecture theatres, restaurants, reception areas, student services areas and laboratories. Art and design facilities on the City site have been upgraded, as has the Boots Library, as part of a £130-million building programme.

The schools of science and technology, education, and arts and humanities are five miles away on the Clifton campus, where computing and informatics have a new building. The university has runs a bus service linking Clifton and the city. The Brackenhurst campus, devoted to animal, rural and environmental studies, is 14 miles out of Nottingham and includes an equestrian centre with a purpose-built indoor riding area, a well-equipped veterinary nursing building and an animal unit. A new £1.5-million unit houses state-of-the-art equipment and facilities and will be used to provide veterinary nursing courses.

NTU was responsible for the largest programme of Foundation degrees when the two-year qualification was launched. Subjects ranging from food science to horticulture, screenwriting and wildlife conservation saw another big increase in applications early in 2011, bringing the numbers to almost 1,000.

The university has a strong sporting reputation and always fares well in the BUCS leagues, ranking 27th in 2009–10. The new Lee Westwood Sports Centre on the Clifton campus boasts an array of top facilities, including sports halls, studios, fitness suites and a nutrition training centre. NTU alumni include England Rugby player Nick Easter and Great Britain Hockey players Crista Cullen, Adam Dixon and Alistair Wilson.

The student body is diverse, with large numbers of mature and overseas students. With private providers adding to the university's residential stock of 4,200 beds, all first years and overseas students can be housed. Social life varies between campuses, but all have access to the city's lively cultural and clubbing scene. A late-night bus service links the main campuses and the city's new tram system serves the university.

Undergraduate Fees and Support

» Fees for UK/EU students 2012–13   to be announced
» Fees for International students 2011–12   £9,950–£10,950
» A package of financial support and widening participation activity to be announced.
» Scholarships and bursaries based on circumstances or by competition.
» Check the university's website for the latest information.

Students

Undergraduates:	**19,275**	**(2,085)**
Postgraduates:	**2,135**	**(2,960)**
Mature students:	**12.0%**	
Overseas students:	**5.9%**	
Applications per place:	**5.9**	
From state-sector schools:	**93.0%**	
From working-class homes:	**35.5%**	

For detailed information about fees, grants and bursaries and how they work, see chapter 7.

Accommodation

Number of places and costs refer to 2011–12
University-provided places: 4,200
Percentage catered: 0%
Self-catered costs: £75–£137 (44–51 weeks).
First years and new students are guaranteed accommodation if conditions are met.
International students: guaranteed accommodation if conditions are met.
Contact: www.ntu.ac.uk/accommodation
accommodation@ntu.ac.uk

The Open University (OU)

The Open University (OU) is one of the great success stories of UK higher education and a model for distance learning institutions around the world. It does not appear in *The Times* League Table because the absence of full-time undergraduates makes the OU unsuitable for comparison with other universities on some of the measures used. There are now more than 250,000 students, making it one of the largest in the world, and more undergraduates alone than there are students at any of the UK's conventional universities. The average age of new undergraduates is 32, but the demand from school leavers has grown to the point where a quarter are less than 25 years old. More than 60 per cent are female and most live in the UK, but there are now 20,000 students outside the country.

The OU was established in 1969 and the first students enrolled two years later. The university is based at Milton Keynes, in Buckinghamshire, but has regional centres in each of its 13 regions around the UK, as well as offices and exam centres in other countries. The open access principle that was a cornerstone of its foundation remains in place, most undergraduates entering without traditional qualifications. Seven out of ten students were in full-time or part-time employment in 2009–10, often working towards a qualification to progress or change their career. Over 50,000 students are sponsored by their employer, but the OU also provides financial support for those from poor backgrounds: about 47,500 received some assistance in 2009–10.

More than 7,000 tutors guide students through degrees that generally take six years to complete. The "Open Learning" system allows students to work where they choose – at home, in the workplace or at a library or study centre. They have contact with fellow students at tutorials, day schools or through online conferencing, social networks and informal study groups. Learning materials are written specifically for each module and delivered in book form, often supplemented by web-based resources, CDs and DVDs. The traditional week-long residential school that was once a feature of OU courses is now a thing of the past in most subjects, although it remains compulsory on most science and language degrees.

Also gone are the late-night television programmes that were the mainstay of teaching until 2006. The OU now produces mainstream television and radio programming aimed at bringing learning to a wider audience. In the 2009–10 academic year, more than 2,000 people bought course materials but did not enrol on a course. The 1,200 full-time academic staff have a proud research record: more than half of the work submitted for the 2008 Research Assessment

Walton Hall
Milton Keynes MK7 6AA

085 300 6090 (enquiries)
contact via website (prospectus)
www.open.ac.uk
www.open.ac.uk/ousa
Affiliation: University
    Alliance

Edinburgh
Belfast
MILTON KEYNES
Cardiff
London

The Times Rankings
The available data do not match the data used to rank the other full-time universities, so the Open University could not be included in the League Table this year.

Exercise was regarded as world-leading or internationally excellent. Art and design, computer science, geography and sociology produced the best results. The OU employs more than 500 people engaged in research and there are over 1,200 research students. It spends approximately £20 million each year on research. However, the majority of academics are part-time associate lecturers with teaching duties.

The university is divided into seven faculties and a business school, which produces more MBAs than the rest of the UK's business schools put together, as well as offering Honours and Foundation degrees. As well as degrees in a named subject, the OU also awards "Open" Bachelor degrees where the syllabus is designed by the students by combining any number of modules. Several faculties have introduced short modules worth ten credits, which are taught entirely online and start at regular intervals throughout the year. Most provide an introduction to a broader subject over a period of ten weeks. Longer modules, worth 30 or 60 credits, typically run either from October to June, or from February to October. Assessment is by both continual assessment and examination or, for some modules, a major assignment. Except in fast moving areas such as computing, there is no limit on the time taken to complete a degree.

The OU has also pioneered the use of virtual worlds in teaching and learning, with two main islands in Second Life: Open University island and OUtopia village. They are separated by a third region OU Ocean. The university also leads the universities placing material on the iTunesU site, with more than 20 million downloads by the end of 2010. The OU was one of the first universities worldwide to make eBooks available on iTunes U, adding 300 free, interactive titles by the end of 2010. The content comes from the OU's OpenLearn website which contains over 6,600 hours of free, current course materials and has had more than 14 million visits to date (**http://openlearn.open.ac.uk/**).

Undergraduate Fees and Support

» Fees vary depending upon the course, on where you live and the choices you make.
» The costs of all courses are given in the OU prospectus: www3.open.ac.uk/study/undergraduate/index.htm
» Various forms of financial help are available. Details are given at: **www3.open.ac.uk/study/explained/financial-support.shtml**

Students		
Undergraduates:	**15**	**(195,285)**
Postgraduates:	**325**	**(14,080)**

Accommodation

As the courses provided are part time, the university does not provide accommodation

Contact: www3.open.ac.uk/contact/faq.aspx?t=S&cat=1-1SOVWF

University of Oxford

Oxford continues to top *The Times* League Table, as it has since 2002, when it wrested first place from Cambridge. The oldest and probably the most famous university in the English-speaking world, Oxford remains almost inseparable from Cambridge in terms of overall quality. Both are head and shoulders above the other non-specialist universities in *The Times* table and in the view of most experts. Oxford is also among the top six universities in the world, according to the QS and *Times Higher Education* world rankings. More satisfied students and higher spending on student facilities helped keep the university ahead of its ancient rival this year, when Oxford was one of the few universities to improve its graduate employment rate.

Applications were up a little at the beginning of 2011, when the demand for places at Cambridge fell. There were still fewer than six applicants to the place – a much more favourable ratio than at some of the top universities – but nearly all are predicted at least three As at A level, or their equivalent. Gradually, there may be more postgraduates and marginally fewer UK undergraduates, making the competition for places still more intense.

The university is still struggling to broaden its intake and shake off allegations of social elitism. There was another spat with Government in 2011, when David Cameron accused Oxford of admitting only one black undergraduate. In fact, the statistic applied only to UK students declaring themselves to be black Caribbeans. The long-term growth in demand for places is due, at least partly, to more systematic attempts to get the message through to teenagers that Oxford is open to all who can meet the exacting entrance requirements. Student visits to comprehensive schools have been supplemented by summer schools, recruitment fairs and colleges' own initiatives, as well as tireless public statements of intent by the university.

For all the university's efforts to shed its *Brideshead Revisited* stereotype, however, official figures still show 45 per cent of Oxford's students coming from independent schools – the largest proportion at any university. Just one student in nine comes from a working-class home, despite the introduction of generous bursaries that will be extended when £9,000 fees are introduced in 2012. The university is planning to spend 70 per cent of the extra income on fee waivers and bursaries that will leave students from the poorest homes with only £3,500 to repay. A projected dropout rate of 2 per cent is bettered only by Cambridge.

Applications must be made by mid-October – a month earlier if you wish to be interviewed overseas. There are written tests for some subjects and you may be asked to

---

University Offices
Wellington Square
Oxford OX1 2JD

01865 288000 (admissions)
undergraduate.admissions
@admin.ox.ac.uk
www.ox.ac.uk
www.ousu.org
Affiliation: Russell Group

The Times Rankings
Overall Ranking: **1**

Student satisfaction:	2	(86%)
Research quality:	2	(4.0)
Entry standards:	2	(536)
Student–staff ratio:	3	(10.8)
Services & facilities/student:	2	(£3,249)
Expected completion rate:	2	(97.9%)
Good honours:	1	(91.2%)
Graduate prospects:	4	(85.0%)

submit samples of work. Selection is in the hands of the 30 undergraduate colleges, which vary considerably in their approach to this issue and others. Sound advice on academic strengths and social factors is essential for applicants to give themselves the best chance of winning a place and finding a setting in which they can thrive. A minority of candidates opt to go straight into the admissions pool without expressing a preference for a particular college. The choice is particularly important for arts and social science students, whose world-famous individual or small group tuition is based in college. Science and technology are taught mainly in central facilities. All subjects operate on eight-week terms and assess students entirely on final examinations – a system some find too pressurised. Overall, however, Oxford is in the top two universities for student satisfaction.

The development of a new campus on the site of the Radcliffe Infirmary will be the first fruit of a £1.25-billion fundraising campaign. Oxford's biggest capital development for more than a century will provide more student accommodation for neighbouring Somerville College, a new Mathematical Institute building and a new building for the humanities. There should be many more developments as a result of a commitment by Dr James Martin, the technology entrepreneur who was already the university's largest benefactor, to donate £50 million if others would match it. Within a year, at the height of the recession, the university had raised the matching funds, and thus gained the full £100 million.

There was never much doubt about the strength of Oxford's research, but the 2008 Research Assessment Exercise found more than 70 per cent of it to be world-leading or internationally excellent. Oxford entered more academics for assessment than any other university – twice as many as some research-based universities of similar size. There were good results in all areas, but the university was pre-eminent in several medical specialisms, as well as statistics, development studies, education and French. Oxford also attracts the largest amount of research income.

Undergraduate Fees and Support

» Fees for UK/EU students 2012–13 £9,000
» Fees for International students 2011–12 £12,700–£14,550 £26,500 (medicine) plus College fees £5,920
» First-year students with household income below £16K, £5,500 fee waiver, other years, fee waiver £3,000: household income £16K–£25K, fee waiver £3,000–£1,000.
» First-year students from the lowest income households, a bursary of £4,300, other years, £3,300; household income below £42K, bursary on sliding scale.
» College scholarships and bursaries available.
» Check the university's website for the latest information.

Students

Undergraduates:	**11,455**	**(4,625)**
Postgraduates:	**7,080**	**(1,310)**
Mature students:	**5.2%**	
Overseas students:	**10.1%**	
Applications per place:	**5.6**	
From state-sector schools:	**54.7%**	
From working-class homes:	**11.5%**	

For detailed information about fees, grants and bursaries and how they work, see chapter 7.

Accommodation

See chapter 12 for information about individual colleges.

Oxford Brookes University

Oxford Brookes is proposing to cut its entry by up to 15 per cent when it begins charging higher fees in 2012 to increase the contact time with lecturers and improve the student experience generally. The fees for honours degrees will be £9,000, but charging £6,000 for Foundation degrees at further education colleges will bring the average for all the university's courses down to £8,000. The extra income will also speed up planned improvements to the campuses and fund bursaries and fee waivers of up to £4,500 for the poorest students.

Firmly established as England's leading post-1992 university in *The Times* League Table, Oxford Brookes receives almost six applications to the place – a level of competition not unlike that at some Russell Group universities. The demand for places was up by almost 18 per cent at the start of 2011, one of the biggest increases at any university, following a substantial increase in 2010.

Brookes is particularly popular with independent schools, which provide more than a quarter of the undergraduates – by far the highest proportion among the new universities and twice the national average for the university's subjects and entry grades. However, the proportion from working-class homes, at 44 per cent, is also considerably ahead of the official benchmark. The

university has been trying to attract more students from state schools and has targeted areas in Oxfordshire and the wider region

The university's location has always been an advantage in student recruitment, but the quality of provision is the real draw. Its departments feature near the top of *The Times* rankings for several subjects. Ofsted rated primary teacher training outstanding and the university was in the top 40 in the 2010 National Student Survey. Molecular biology achieved 100 per cent satisfaction among final-year undergraduates, while publishing, philosophy, media studies, economics and health subjects all reached at least 95 per cent.

The university was awarded national centres for hospitality, leisure and tourism, and the teaching of business and undergraduate research, as well as one for teacher training in partnership with Westminster University. The *Architect's Journal* rated the department of architecture the best outside London. Oxford Brookes, was also chosen to partner Warwick University in the Labour Government's academy for gifted and talented schoolchildren.

Grades in the 2008 Research Assessment Exercise showed improvement, with more than a third of the work judged to be world-leading or internationally excellent. History, which made headlines in 2001 with a higher grade than its world-renowned neighbour, again produced the best results, but there

---

Headington Campus
Gypsy Lane
Oxford OX3 0BP

01865 484848 (enquiries)
query@brookes.ac.uk
www.brookes.ac.uk
www.thesu.com
Affiliation: University Alliance

The Times Rankings
Overall Ranking: **48**

Student satisfaction:	=24	(79%)
Research quality:	=60	(0.6)
Entry standards:	=45	(314)
Student–staff ratio:	=57	(18.1)
Services & facilities/student:	65	(£1,287)
Expected completion rate:	41	(88.5%)
Good honours:	40	(67.1%)
Graduate prospects:	58	(62.0%)

were good performances, too, in history of art and computer science.

As a polytechnic, Oxford pioneered the modular degree system that has swept British higher education. The scheme has now trimmed the 2,000 modules it once offered, but undergraduates can pair subjects as diverse as history and biology, or catering management and environmental management. Each subject has compulsory modules in the first year and a list of others that are acceptable later in the course. Students are encouraged to take advantage of a range of placement and exchange opportunities as well as subjects outside their main area of study, such as additional language modules.

There are four main sites, two of which are only a mile from the city centre and linked to each other by a footbridge. Some £150 million has been earmarked for improvements to the Headington, Wheatley and Harcourt Hill campuses over the next few years. A £132-million library and teaching building is also under construction at Gipsy Lane, the original site. This will provide social learning space that allows students to work together and engage with careers guidance, volunteering opportunities and student support services.

Maths and engineering have now joined computing and business five miles away at Wheatley. The new engineering building supports the university's status as a Government-designated regional centre for motorsport and high performance engineering. The Harcourt Hill campus at Botley, focuses on teacher education, human development and learning. Oxford Brookes finished seventh in the People and Planet Green League and has been in the top category in all four years of the environmental assessments. It was the first university to be awarded Fairtrade status.

A 25-metre swimming pool and 9-hole golf course have been added to the already impressive sports facilities which include a recently refurbished gym and climbing centre. Representative teams have a good record, with the rowers particularly successful, winning medals at three consecutive Olympic games, and the cricketers now combining with Oxford University to take on county teams. The students' union runs one of the biggest entertainment venues in Oxford. The university has 3,600 residential places – enough for all first-year undergraduates.

Undergraduate Fees and Support

- » Fees for UK/EU students 2012–13   £9,000
  Foundation degrees at partner colleges   £6,000
- » Fees for International students 2011–12   £10,600–£11,300
      £12,150 (physiotherapy)
- » Financial support and widening participation activity to include bursaries and fee waivers up to £4,500 for students from low income groups.
- » Check the university's website for the latest information.

Students		
Undergraduates:	**11,410**	**(2,845)**
Postgraduates:	**1,675**	**(2,405)**
Mature students:	**22.8%**	
Overseas students:	**15.0%**	
Applications per place:	**5.5**	
From state-sector schools:	**71.6%**	
From working-class homes:	**44.0%**	

For detailed information about fees, grants and bursaries and how they work, see chapter 7.

Accommodation

Number of places and costs refer to 2011–12
University-provided places: 3,600
Percentage catered: 15%
Catered cost: £4,846–£5,300
Self-catered cost: £3,561–£5,200 (38-week contract)
All accommodation is allocated to first year who select Oxford Brookes as Firm choice through UCAS and meet all deadlines for application.
International students: as above.
Contact: accomm@brookes.ac.uk

University of Plymouth

Now one of the UK's largest universities with over 32,000 students, Plymouth has climbed three places in the latest *Times* League Table and is firmly among the top ten post-1992 universities. It has restructured its activities to concentrate on its home city and the Vice-Chancellor, Professor Wendy Purcell, a graduate of the university in the 1980s, has declared a new mission to make Plymouth the top "enterprise university". It was named as the most enterprising organisation in the southwest in 2008 and 2009, and was short-listed for the award of Entrepreneurial University of the Year in 2010. The university's commitment to sustainability was also recognised when it was placed top of the People and Planet Green League.

Following the closure of campuses in Exmouth, Exeter and near Newton Abbot, about £120 million has been spent on the main North Hill campus in Plymouth. The library was extended and upgraded and the students' union refurbished. A £35-million arts complex opened in 2007, housing the Faculty of Arts and the Plymouth Arts Centre. Teaching facilities and residential accommodation for the education courses transferred from Exmouth, while a new building for the Faculty of Health and Social Work includes sports facilities as well as teaching space.

Plymouth opened a £1-million Immersive Vision Theatre, thought to be the first of its kind at a UK university, in 2008. Projection onto the dome gives students in a variety of subjects the feeling of being "in", rather than just observing, different types of images. The latest development saw the opening of the new School of Marine Science and Engineering, building on Plymouth's worldwide reputation in this field. With 1,400 students and 80 staff, the school is the largest of its kind in Europe. It is also the base for the new Peninsula Research Institute for Marine Renewable Energy, a joint venture with the University of Exeter. An £18-million facility which will house some of the country's most advanced wave-testing facilities is scheduled to open in 2012.

Plymouth and Exeter were already partners in the Peninsula College of Medicine and Dentistry, which has its headquarters and a second teaching building in the city. One of the new wave of medical schools, established in 2002, the Peninsula was the only successful bidder for a new dental school in the last national competition. The school, which will train 64 dentists a year, opened in 2007. With campuses in Plymouth, Exeter and Truro, along with teaching facilities in Bristol, the university's Faculty of Health and Social Work is the largest provider of nursing, midwifery and health professional education and training in the southwest.

Drake Circus
Plymouth
Devon PL4 8AA

01752 600600 (enquiries)
contact via website
www.plymouth.ac.uk
www.pcmd.ac.uk
www.upsu.com
Affiliation: University
Alliance

The Times Rankings
Overall Ranking: **58**

Student satisfaction:	=73	(75%)
Research quality:	59	(0.7)
Entry standards:	=56	(297)
Student–staff ratio:	42	(16.4)
Services & facilities/student:	63	(£1,306)
Expected completion rate:	56	(84.9%)
Good honours:	=59	(61.4%)
Graduate prospects:	53	(64.3%)

The university is also a partner in the Combined Universities in Cornwall, which is boosting further and higher education in one of the few counties without its own university. Plymouth has established a unique relationship with its 18 partner colleges, which have become a faculty of the university, sharing £3.5 million in capital investment. They spread from Cornwall to Somerset, taking in Jersey, and have 10,000 students taking university courses.

The intake reflects Plymouth's position as the working-class hub of the southwest, with almost 95 per cent of students state-educated and more than a third from the poorest social classes. The projected dropout rate of less than 12 per cent is below average for the courses and entry grades. Some 12,000 students undertake work-based learning or placements, while the new Plymouth Award recognises extra-curricular achievements through a separate item on graduates' Higher Education Achievement Report.

Plymouth was chosen to house no fewer than four national teaching centres – in health and social care placements, experiential learning in environmental and natural sciences, institutional partnerships, and education for sustainable development – all of which have now been brought into the university's core activities. There is also a national subject centre for geography, earth and environmental sciences and the Royal Statistical Society Centre for Statistical Education. No university has exceeded the 14 National Teaching Fellowships won by its academics.

Plymouth entered by far the largest number of academics of any post-1992 university in the latest research assessments – twice the proportion entered by some of its peer group. More than a third of the submission was rated world-leading or internationally excellent. Computer science produced by far the best results, but civil engineering, geography and environmental science, and art and design also did well.

A 1,300-bed student village costing £15 million, has greatly improved the university's residential stock. There is a lively social scene as well as a thriving nightlife. With excellent and recently upgraded facilities for water sports as well as an £850,000 fitness centre, the sports facilities have improved, while a range of sports scholarships and bursaries will help support high-fliers.

Undergraduate Fees and Support

>> Fees for UK/EU students 2012–13   £9,000
>> Fees for International students 2010–11   £9,104
                                    £14,000–£21,500 (medicine)
>> Financial support, including the National Scholarship scheme, scholarships and grants, and widening participation activity to be announced.
>> Check the university's website for the latest information.

Students

Undergraduates:	**19,900**	**(7,960)**
Postgraduates:	**1,340**	**(2,995)**
Mature students:	**27.7%**	
Overseas students:	**5.9%**	
Applications per place:	**3.0**	
From state-sector schools:	**94.7%**	
From working-class homes:	**33.8%**	

For detailed information about fees, grants and bursaries and how they work, see chapter 7.

Accommodation

Number of places and costs refer to 2011–12
University-provided places: 2,500
Percentage catered: 0%
Self-catered costs: £86–£135 a week.
First years are not guaranteed university provided accommodation.
International students: overseas students have priority for allocation.
Contact: accommodation@plymouth.ac.uk
www.plymouth.ac.uk/pages/view.asp?page=30

University of Portsmouth

After two boom years for applications, the demand for places at Portsmouth settled down at the start of 2011 with a small increase. Nevertheless, the university is now attracting double the numbers received a decade ago. It has always been among the leaders of its generation of universities, but a wider portfolio of courses, a modernised campus and new facilities in the city are proving a powerful draw. The university will be charging £8,500 fees in 2012 and has drawn up a range of bursaries and discounts designed to preserve access for students of all backgrounds.

The university has jumped six places in this year's *Times* League Table and is one of the few to record an improved graduate employment score. Portsmouth also has the best record of any post-1992 university in the National Student Survey. None of its peer group produced better results in 2010, when there were satisfaction levels of at least 95 per cent in biology, accounting, geology, finance, history, European languages and sports science. Forty per cent of the work submitted for the 2008 Research Assessment Exercise was considered world-leading or internationally excellent. Applied mathematics and European studies achieved particularly good results, while biomedical and biomolecular sciences also did well.

Languages are Portsmouth's traditional strength – one student in five takes a language course at some level – and the facilities rival those of many traditional universities. About 1,000 Portsmouth students go abroad for part of their course, and at least as many come from the Continent. However, it is in health subjects that the university's reputation has been growing most obviously. The new £9-million Dental Academy trains student dentists in their final year at King's College London in a team-based primary care setting, working alongside other health professionals. There is also a centre for molecular design and the UK's first dedicated brain tumour research centre. A new £1-million model pharmacy to help train pharmacists opened in 2009. Over 600 radiographers, paramedics, medical technologists, pharmacists, clinicians and social workers graduate from the university each year.

The main city-centre Guildhall campus has undergone extensive redevelopment. The £11-million library complex, integrated into its 1970s predecessor, has won a string of awards. Building work has started on a new wing to include an exhibition space, artists' studios and a 250-seat professional theatre and film screening facility open to the community. Plans are also underway for a new building in the city centre with 598 student bedrooms and additional teaching space.

University House
Winston Churchill Avenue
Portsmouth
Hampshire PO1 2UP

023 9284 8484
info.centre@port.ac.uk
www.port.ac.uk
www.upsu.net
Affiliation: University
 Alliance

The Times Rankings
Overall Ranking: **=67**

Student satisfaction:	**=24**	(79%)
Research quality:	**=62**	(0.5)
Entry standards:	**67**	(283)
Student–staff ratio:	**=86**	(20.5)
Services & facilities/student:	**81**	(£1,188)
Expected completion rate:	**=60**	(84.4%)
Good honours:	**100**	(50.9%)
Graduate prospects:	**84**	(56.7%)

Earlier developments included the aluminium-clad St Michael's Building and the eco-friendly Portland Building, with its solar panels. The Business School is housed in a £12-million building on the main campus. Other recent additions include a sports science building with laboratories, a swimming flume and two British Olympic Medical Centre accredited climatic chambers. A new £9-million building for the internationally recognised Institute of Cosmology and Gravitation opened in 2009. And following the launch of the new School of Law, a £1-million mock courtroom has been provided for law, forensics, criminology and related courses.

Teaching in all subjects is concentrated on the Guildhall campus, while much of the residential stock is a couple of miles away at Langstone. A £6.5-million student centre caters for the multicultural population of the university with alcohol-free areas and an international students' bar. There is also a new social learning space, with café, wireless internet and learning spaces for individuals and groups. Modernised sport, exercise and fitness facilities include gyms, dance studios and a sports hall.

Portsmouth has a larger working-class population and more deprivation than some applicants may realise. Three in ten undergraduates come from working-class homes, although this is still below the national average for the subjects and entry qualifications. Efforts are being made to broaden the intake further through an award-winning membership club that introduces teenagers to higher education through workshops, holiday courses and access to university facilities. The projected dropout rate has improved considerably over the last decade and, at 13 per cent is now lower than the university's benchmark.

Many students live in Southsea, which has a vibrant social scene and quirky shops. In recent years the city has seen considerable regeneration, including the retail and entertainment complex at Gunwharf dominated by the 170-metre landmark Spinnaker Tower. The cost of living is not as high as at many southern universities, and the sea is close at hand. Hall places are offered to 90 per cent of first years and they have access to a combined broadband, phone and TV service. The university runs "secure a home" days at the beginning of September to help the remaining new arrivals with house-hunting.

Undergraduate Fees and Support

» Fees for UK/EU students 2012–13 £8,500
» Fees for International students 2011–12 £9,600–£11,000
» Students with household income below £25K, a bursary of £1,000 each year and a fee waiver of £2,000 in year 1 only; bursaries also for students with household income up to £42.6K.
» Check the university's website for the latest information.

Students		
Undergraduates:	**15,705**	**(2,200)**
Postgraduates:	**1,875**	**(2,410)**
Mature students:	**17.6%**	
Overseas students:	**10.6%**	
Applications per place:	**5.4**	
From state-sector schools:	**95.2%**	
From working-class homes:	**32.4%**	

For detailed information about fees, grants and bursaries and how they work, see chapter 7.

Accommodation

Number of places and costs refer to 2011–12
University-provided places: 3,000
Percentage catered: 25%
Catered costs: £91–£117 a week (37 weeks).
Self-catered costs:£75–£119 a week (37 weeks).
Majority of first years offered university accommodation.
International, Channel Island and Isle of Man students guaranteed university accommodation subject to terms and conditions.
Contact: Student.housing@port.ac.uk
www.port.ac.uk/studentlife/accommodation/

Queen Margaret University

Scotland's first new university of the 21st century got a campus to match, when Queen Margaret University (QMU) moved into gleaming new premises in Musselburgh, to the southeast of Edinburgh, in September 2007. The "campus in the park", as it has been dubbed, was designed in consultation with students, and is one of the most environmentally sustainable in the UK, exceeding current environmental standards. The university has made sustainability a top priority, in the curriculum as well as in the way it operates. The campus has won a string of awards and QMU is particularly proud of Re:Use Project which has diverted more than 18 tonnes of serviceable household waste from landfill.

Named after Saint Margaret, the 11th-century Queen of Scotland, the institution dates back to 1875 and was originally a school of cookery for women. The college had been awarding its own degrees since 1992, but was too small to qualify for university status until 2007. Having achieved that ambition, the university made an auspicious debut in *The Times* League Table and has been outscoring many of the former polytechnics.

Queen Margaret is the smallest university in Scotland and likely to remain so. Its strategic plan promises that the university will be "smart, innovative and very clearly focused and above all relevant" to compensate for the limitations of size. There are almost 6,000 students, three quarters of whom are female. There are three faculties: Health Sciences, Business, Enterprise and Management, and Arts and Social Sciences. Restructuring of the performing arts courses has consolidated four drama degrees into one interdisciplinary programme, under the title of drama and performance. The university no longer offers conservatoire training, but the new degree draws together the university's recognised strengths in acting, screen work, community theatre, contemporary performance and playwriting to reflect the current needs of a changing profession.

Health is an area of particular strength: Queen Margaret offers courses in an unusually broad range of subjects, from dietetics, podiatry and audiology to art therapy, music therapy and health psychology. There are also courses in the field of international health which attract students from all over the world as well as a specialism in international healthcare, with students in Angola, Guatemala, Uganda, Ethiopia, Gambia, India and Cuba. Other international programmes run in Egypt, Saudi Arabia, Greece and Switzerland, and in 2008, the university opened the first UK university campus in Singapore. It is a joint venture with the East Asia Institute of Management, which had taught Queen Margaret degrees for several years.

Queen Margaret University
 Drive
Musselburgh EH21 6UU

0131 474 0000
admissions@qmu.ac.uk
www.qmu.ac.uk
www.qmusu.org.uk
Affiliation: none

EDINBURGH
Belfast
London
Cardiff

The Times Rankings
Overall Ranking: **78**

Student satisfaction:		n/a
Research quality:	=79	(0.3)
Entry standards:	=48	(309)
Student–staff ratio:	=103	(21.7)
Services & facilities/student:	98	(£1,082)
Expected completion rate:	85	(80.7%)
Good honours:	33	(68.7%)
Graduate prospects:	=60	(61.8%)

Yet all has not been plain sailing. Queen Margaret has struggled with debts and only one university had a lower average score in the 2008 Research Assessment Exercise. The demand for places has remained healthy, however. There was a 6 per cent increase at the start of 2011 to follow a 15 per cent rise in 2010. Although it has improved for the last two years, the projected dropout rate of 15 per cent is still higher than average for the university's courses and entry qualifications. Almost four undergraduates in ten come from working-class homes and just more than a third are over the age of 21 on entry.

An impressive learning resource centre, parts of which are open 24 hours a day, offers a variety of study spaces. Specialist laboratories and clinics are well equipped. The nursing simulation lab, for example, is set out exactly like a hospital ward, helping to instil students with the confidence to move on easily to a work placement or career in the NHS or private practice. There are also specially equipped rooms for podiatry, radiography, occupational therapy, physiotherapy and art therapy.

The campus is located next to Musselburgh train station, from where Edinburgh city centre is only a six-minute journey. There is also a frequent bus service from the campus to the city centre. There are 800 residential places on the campus, 474 of them standard rooms and 326 premier, or double. Other features include a students'

union building, indoor and outdoor sports facilities, a variety of catering outlets and landscaped gardens with a range of environmental features.

Undergraduate Fees and Support

» Fees 2012–13: awaiting Scottish Government policy.
» Fees for Scottish and EU students 2011–12 No fee
» Fees for Non-Scottish UK-domiciled students 2011–12 £1,820
» Fees for international students 2011–12 £10,170–£11,230
» Scholarships and bursaries based on circumstances or by competition.
» Check the university's website for the latest information.

Students

Undergraduates:	**2,915**	**(1,020)**
Postgraduates:	**400**	**(1,065)**
Mature students:	**33.6%**	
Overseas students:	**13.0%**	
Applications per place:	**7.3**	
From state-sector schools:	**94.9%**	
From working-class homes:	**37.4%**	

For detailed information about fees, grants and bursaries and how they work, see chapter 7.

Accommodation

Number of places and costs refer to 2011–12
University-provided places: 800
Percentage catered: 0%
Self-catered costs: £102.75–£108.56 a week (either 40 or 50 week contract).
First years are guaranteed accommodation. Residential and age restrictions apply.
International students: guaranteed housing.
Contact: accommodation@qmu.ac.uk
www.qmu.ac.uk/services/halls_residence.htm

Queen Mary, University of London

Queen Mary (QMUL) is aiming to be a top-ten university by 2015, and in the QS and *Times Higher Education* world rankings, which are more concerned with research, it is now in the top 150. Research is given added weight in *The Times* League Table, where QMUL is 37th this year, but it also performs well in our other categories. The university has opted for £9,000 fees from 2012 in order to meet the cost of delivering "research-informed" undergraduate degrees, as well as continuing to enhance the quality of its buildings and equipment. However, it estimates that about half of its students will benefit from bursaries and fee waivers, which will be especially generous to first years.

More than £150 million has been spent developing London University's East End base into a broadly based institution of 15,000 students and strengthening the academic staff. Some of the investment paid off in spectacularly improved grades in the 2008 Research Assessment Exercise, when almost two thirds of the work submitted was rated world-leading or internationally excellent. Linguistics, geography and drama produced the best results in their fields, with dentistry, English and several medical specialisms in the top five, propelling Queen Mary into the top 25 UK universities for research in our table.

Queen Mary has the capital's most extensive self-contained campus. It includes a state-of-the-art learning resource centre with 24-hour access and an award-winning student village with 2,000 en-suite rooms. An arts quarter, containing research facilities, a conference centre, drama studio and teaching space, was completed in 2006. A £15-million humanities building is due to open in Autumn 2011 and a BioEnterprise Innovation Centre for science companies has opened, next door to the £44-million Blizard Building – the striking home of Barts and the London School of Medicine and Dentistry, in Whitechapel. The Centre of the Cell is also located on the Whitechapel campus, the first such facility to be based within a working medical school research laboratory to give young people a glimpse of how scientists operate.

The modern setting is a far cry from the People's Palace, which first used the site to bring education to the Victorian masses, but there is still a community programme as well as conventional teaching and research. The arts-based Westfield College and scientific Queen Mary came together in 1989, but it took time to mould the new institution and overcome financial difficulties. The sale of Westfield's Hampstead base released the necessary capital to begin to modernise the Mile End Road campus. Now the historic

---

Mile End Road
London E1 4NS

020 7882 5511 (admissions)
admissions@qmul.ac.uk
www.qmul.ac.uk
www.qmsu.org
Affiliation: 1994 Group

The Times Rankings
Overall Ranking: **37**

Student satisfaction:	**=37**	(78%)
Research quality:	**=25**	(2.1)
Entry standards:	**31**	(387)
Student–staff ratio:	**=12**	(13.6)
Services & facilities/student:	**36**	(£1,582)
Expected completion rate:	**=34**	(89.4%)
Good honours:	**48**	(64.4%)
Graduate prospects:	**25**	(71.7%)

People's Palace building, which is still the college's most recognizable feature, is to be restored to host cultural events for the institution and the local community.

Queen Mary is best known for its strength in arts subjects, which boast a clutch of high-profile academics. But the medical school was rated in the top 30 in the world in 2011 and the college is also leading a national initiative to boost the number of maths graduates. Applications have risen at the rate of 7 per cent a year for most of the last decade, although they had dipped slightly at the beginning of 2011. There has been particular success in attracting overseas students, who make full use of a unit specialising in English as a foreign language and now fill about one place in six. Results have been consistently good in the National Student Survey and improved again in 2010, when 86 per cent of final-year undergraduates were satisfied. Languages, media studies, human and social geography, English and history produced the best scores.

The majority of undergraduates take at least one course in departments other than their own, under the modular course system. Most degrees are organised in units to allow maximum flexibility. Interdisciplinary study has always been encouraged: for example, medics can choose selected modules in English and drama. There is a flourishing exchange programme, which includes universities in the USA and Japan, as well as Europe. Each student has an adviser to guide them through the possibilities. Language students can use the University of London Institute in Paris, while students at Beijing's University of Posts and Telecommunications can take double degrees (awarded by their own institution and Queen Mary) without leaving China.

Queen Mary attracts students from across the UK and over 120 countries around the world and has a socially diverse intake: nearly 37 per cent come from the two lowest socio-economic classes, many of them from London's minority ethnic groups. Social life centres on the campus, which features a refurbished students' union with a subsidised health and fitness centre and a new bar, and the West End is easily accessible by tube. Students welcome the relatively low prices (for the capital) in east London, which has more to offer than many expect when they apply.

Undergraduate Fees and Support

» Fees for UK/EU students 2012–13 £9,000
» Fees for International students 2011–12 £11,300–£13,250
£16,442–£26,224 (medicine)
» QMUL bursaries of £1,500 for students with household income below £25K; of £1,200 for household income £25K–£42.6K. Over 250 National Scholarships of £1,500 fee waiver and £1,500 bursary in year 1; QMUL bursary in other years.
» Scholarships and bursaries based on circumstances or by competition.
» Check the university's website for the latest information.

Students

Undergraduates:	**11,045**	**(40)**
Postgraduates:	**2,535**	**(1,110)**
Mature students:	**15.2%**	
Overseas students:	**17.7%**	
Applications per place:	**7.7**	
From state-sector schools:	**85.7%**	
From working-class homes:	**36.6%**	

For detailed information about fees, grants and bursaries and how they work, see chapter 7.

Accommodation

Number of places and costs refer to 2010–11
University-provided places: 2,418
Percentage catered: 6%
Catered costs: £145 upwards a week.
Self-catered costs: £92–£124 a week.
First years giving Queen Mary as first choice get priority, if terms and conditions are met. Residential restrictions apply. International students given priority if conditions are met.
Contact: residences@qmul.ac.uk

Queen's University, Belfast

Northern Ireland's premier university, Queen's became a member of the Russell Group of leading UK research institutions in 2006. The university is in the midst of a major recruitment campaign to attract high-calibre academics from around the world and is investing heavily in new and updated facilities to improve the student experience and enhance its research performance. Now in the top 200 in the QS World University Rankings, the aim is to break into the top 100 in the world within four years. The 2008 Research Assessment Exercise showed some progress, with more than half of the university's submission rated as world-leading or internationally excellent, and Queen's ranked in the UK's top ten in eleven subject areas. Music, English and anthropology produced the highest grades and all branches of engineering were placed in the top ten in their respective disciplines.

In recent years the Queen's campus has been transformed. The centrepiece is the £50-million McClay Library, said to be one of the most ambitious building projects in Northern Ireland, which opened in 2009. More teaching accommodation has been added, with better access for the disabled. The university's vision for the future also includes improvements in student facilities: a student village, costing £45 million, has replaced the previous tower block residences with three-storey self-catering "villas" and a new centre for international students and postgraduates opened in 2010. A new student guidance centre has brought services together at the heart of the campus and the students' union has had a £9-million refurbishment. It now includes Enterprise SU, an area for students to improve their enterprise and employability skills. Queen's has also introduced Degree Plus – a new award providing official recognition of extra-curricular activities and achievements and to help graduates in the job market.

Scores improved in the 2010 National Student Survey, taking Queen's back into the top 40 universities. Chemistry and chemical engineering both recorded 100 per cent satisfaction rates, while physics, pharmacy, geography and environmental science, maths, management, dentistry and economics were all over 90 per cent. In its latest institutional audit by the Quality Assurance Agency, carried out in 2009, teaching at Queen's received the highest possible grade. Strictly non-denominational teaching is enshrined in a charter which has guaranteed student representation and equal rights for women since 1908. Even the teaching of theology is done through four associated colleges.

Queen's was one of four university colleges for the whole of Ireland in the nineteenth century, and still draws students from all over the island. Applications were

---

University Road
Belfast BT7 1NN

028 9097 2727 (admissions)
admissions@qub.ac.uk
www.qub.ac.uk
www.qubsu.org
Affiliation: Russell Group

The Times Rankings
Overall Ranking: **38**

Student satisfaction:	=48	(77%)
Research quality:	40	(1.8)
Entry standards:	37	(362)
Student–staff ratio:	23	(14.8)
Services & facilities/student:	20	(£1,911)
Expected completion rate:	55	(85.1%)
Good honours:	26	(71.8%)
Graduate prospects:	=32	(69.4%)

down at the start of 2011, but this followed a series of increases. The university has begun to attract more students from Great Britain, as well as boosting the numbers of overseas students. A variety of international agreements have been forged in the USA, India, Malaysia and China. However, the majority of students still come from Northern Ireland. Queen's suffers in the comparison of entry grades in *The Times* League Table because most schools in the Province limit sixth-formers to three A levels.

Students are encouraged to take language programmes from a unique "virtual" language laboratory, which provides online tuition from any computer in the university. IT facilities are good: Queen's was the first institution to meet the national target of providing at least one computer workstation for every five undergraduate students. An unusually large proportion of graduates go on to further study, which does Queen's no harm in the employment stakes. The university's reputation for research has been enhanced recently with a national award for innovation. The £30-million Centre for Secure Information Technologies leads the UK in cybersecurity research.

The city centre is not short of nightlife, but the social scene is still concentrated on the students' union and the surrounding area. Sports facilities, which include a university cottage in the Mourne mountains, are of a high standard. A £7-million

extension to the university's physical education centre helped in Queen's selection as an official training camp for the 2012 Olympics, and a £12-million enhancement of the university's outdoor sports facilities is under way. The university runs academies for football, rugby, rowing and Gaelic sports, which have strong external links. Numerous Queen's players are selected at club, provincial and national levels.

The university district is amongst the most attractive in Belfast, and is one of the city's main cultural and recreational areas. Queen's highly successful international arts festival runs each autumn, as well as an art gallery, the Brian Friel theatre and the only full-time university cinema in the UK. First years are guaranteed accommodation and there is plenty of reasonably priced private housing.

Undergraduate Fees and Support

» Fees 2012–13:   awaiting Northern Ireland Executive policy.
» Fees for UK/EU students 2011–12   £3,375
» Fees for international students 2011–12   £10,730–£13,145
                                                £14,534–£26,534 (medicine)
» Scholarships and bursaries based on circumstances or by competition.
» Check the university's website for the latest information.

Students		
Undergraduates:	**13,355**	**(3,855)**
Postgraduates:	**3,415**	**(2,080)**
Mature students:	**14.8%**	
Overseas students:	**3.7%**	
Applications per place:	**5.7**	
From state-sector schools:	**98.9%**	
From working-class homes:	**32.9%**	

For detailed information about fees, grants and bursaries and how they work, see chapter 7.

Accommodation
Number of places and costs refer to 2011–12
University-provided places: around 2,000
Percentage catered: 0%
Self-catered costs: £67.77–£96.61 a week.
First-year students are guaranteed accommodation if conditions are met.
International students: as above.
Contact: accommodation@qub.ac.uk
www.stayatqueens.com

University of Reading

Reading is another of the medium-sized campus universities that have demonstrated their appeal through the National Student Survey. Consistently in the top 20, it again satisfied almost 90 per cent of its final-year undergraduates in the results published in 2010. Agriculture, chemistry, classics, food science, history, Italian, law, maths and zoology produced the highest satisfaction rates. The university has said that to sustain the level of support and investment needed to produce such scores, it will need to charge the full £9,000 for all subjects in 2012. It claims that a package of financial support will ensure that ability and potential are the only criteria for entry.

The university is ranked among the top 200 in the world and did well in the latest Research Assessment Exercise, despite entering a much higher proportion of its academics than many of its peers. More than half of their work was considered world-leading or internationally excellent, with archaeology and art and design doing particularly well. Archaeology was the source of the last of three Queen's Anniversary Prizes, being rewarded for a unique combination of research, teaching and enterprise. There are international centres of research excellence in areas such as agriculture, biological and physical sciences, meteorology, European histories and cultures.

There are three main sites within Reading, including the original 320-acre parkland site, and the university also owns 2,000 acres of farmland at nearby Sonning and Shinfield, where the renowned Centre for Dairy Research (CEDAR) is located. To these has been added the former Henley Management College, which became the university's Business School in 2008. The Greenlands site, on the banks of the river at Henley-on-Thames, houses postgraduate and executive programmes, while undergraduates are taught in the new £35-million Business School on the main Whiteknights campus. An £11-million home for film, theatre and TV opened on the campus opened in the spring of 2011, while an Enterprise campus is scheduled to open in Shinfield in the summer, bringing together academic expertise with local and international technology-based businesses.

Reading was the only university established between the two world wars, having been Oxford's extension college for the first part of the last century, but the attractive main campus now has a modern feel. A multimillion pound student services building provides a one-stop shop for student support and welfare, and sports facilities have been extended. Watersports are a strong focus, with off-campus boathouses on the Thames and a sailing and canoeing club

---

Whiteknights
PO Box 217
Reading RG6 6AH

0118 378 8618/9
student.recruitment@
reading.ac.uk
www.reading.ac.uk
www.rusu.co.uk
Affiliation: 1994 Group

The Times Rankings
Overall Ranking: **33**

Student satisfaction:	=24	(79%)
Research quality:	=25	(2.1)
Entry standards:	=35	(370)
Student–staff ratio:	33	(15.5)
Services & facilities/student:	74	(£1,243)
Expected completion rate:	29	(91.0%)
Good honours:	39	(67.3%)
Graduate prospects:	46	(66.3%)

nearby. Representative teams have a good record in inter-university competitions and the campus was chosen as a pre-Olympics training camp for basketball and fencing.

The university's location, a bus ride away from Heathrow Airport, and an international reputation in key areas for developing countries have always ensured a healthy flow of overseas students. Overall applications were up by 4 per cent at the start of 2011, the latest in a long series of increases. About one undergraduate in six is from an independent school and more than a quarter come from working-class homes, both somewhat below average for the university's subjects and entry qualifications. The retention rate is slightly better than the university's benchmark, with 8 per cent of undergraduates expected to leave without a qualification.

Reading has been involved with a number of centres of excellence in teaching and learning, including one focusing on career management skills. All undergraduates take career management skills modules that contribute five credits towards their degree classification. The online system, which has 200 web pages of advice, exercises and information, has been bought by 30 other universities and colleges. Sessions are delivered jointly by academics and careers advisors, with input from alumni and leading employers.

The town – only a short walk from the campus – may not be the most fashionable, but it has plenty of nightlife and an award-winning shopping centre. It also offers temporary and part-time employment opportunities for students. London is easily accessible by train, but the cost of living is on a par with the capital. Two new halls of residence opened recently and there are plans for a private company specialising in student accommodation to redevelop some of the older stock. Students praise the social scene, although the high proportion of students from the southeast of England means that many go home at the weekends. The large students' union had a £500,000 refit in 2007, improving and extending its popular main venue. The union has been voted among the best in Britain, and has won numerous awards including Best Bar None status for encouraging safe drinking. It has also been known to attract some big-name bands. Students who live in town can make use of the free night bus service to take them back into Reading.

Undergraduate Fees and Support

» Fees for UK/EU students 2012–13   £9,000
» Fees for International students 2011–12   £10,896–£12,996
» A package of financial support and widening participation activity to be announced.
» Scholarships and bursaries based on circumstances or by competition.
» Check the university's website for the latest information.

Students		
Undergraduates:	**8,850**	**(485)**
Postgraduates:	**2,560**	**(2,585)**
Mature students:	**13.0%**	
Overseas students:	**13.4%**	
Applications per place:	**6.6**	
From state-sector schools:	**81.9%**	
From working-class homes:	**26.4%**	

For detailed information about fees, grants and bursaries and how they work, see chapter 7.

Accommodation

Number of places and costs refer to 2010–11
University-provided places: about 4,300
Percentage catered: 20%
Catered costs: £127–£170 (31 weeks).
Self-catered costs: £72–£132 (39 weeks).
First-year undergraduate students are guaranteed a place if conditions are met.
International students: given priority if conditions are met.
Contact: www.reading.ac.uk/life/life-accommodation.aspx

Robert Gordon University

Robert Gordon is the top post-1992 university in Scotland and second in the UK, despite slipping six places in this year's *Times* League Table. It also features in the top half of the latest National Student Survey, with 100 per cent satisfaction among social work students and extremely good rates in accounting, mechanical engineering, social studies, sociology, pharmacy and other medical subjects. The university saw a big improvement in its score for research quality, one of its weaker areas in previous years, after a much better performance in the 2008 Research Assessment Exercise. Almost a third of its submission was considered world-leading or internationally excellent, with library and information management the star performer. The University has since launched three research institutes to focus on its key strengths in business and information; innovation, design and sustainability; and health and welfare.

So close are links with the North Sea oil and gas industries that Robert Gordon used to dub itself the Energy University. But with nursing and the health sciences now equally important, it has gone for the broader soubriquet of the Professional University. The creative industries are a growth area and there is a full portfolio of courses in business, design and engineering. Flexible programmes, with credit accumulation and transfer, make for easy movement in and out of the university for an often mobile local workforce. Work placements, lasting up to a year, are the norm, helping an employment record that has been Scotland's best for several years and consistently one of the UK's leaders.

Like most new universities, especially in Scotland, RGU recruits most of its students locally, 60 per cent of them female. However, overseas student numbers have been growing sharply and the overall demand for places has been stronger than at most universities north of the border. The 27 per cent increase in applications at the beginning of 2011 was among the largest in the UK. Efforts to extend access beyond the normal higher education catchment have produced a diverse student population, with just over a third of the undergraduates coming from working-class homes and almost all attending state schools or colleges. The dropout rate has improved considerably over recent years and, at 11 per cent, matches the UK average for RGU's subjects and entry qualifications.

Robert Gordon has a pedigree in education that goes back 250 years. The School of Pharmacy is the oldest in the UK, Gray's School of Art is over 120 years old and the Scott Sutherland School of Architecture and the Built Environment has just celebrated its 50th anniversary. The university now offers about 150 degrees.

Schoolhill
Aberdeen AB10 1FR

01224 262728 (enquiries)
admissions@rgu.ac.uk
www.rgu.ac.uk
www.rgunion.co.uk
Affiliation: none

ABERDEEN
Edinburgh
Belfast
London
Cardiff

The Times Rankings
Overall Ranking: **52**

Student satisfaction:	=37	(78%)
Research quality:	=62	(0.5)
Entry standards:	59	(295)
Student–staff ratio:	=66	(19)
Services & facilities/student:	66	(£1,286)
Expected completion rate:	75	(82.2%)
Good honours:	66	(60.2%)
Graduate prospects:	12	(76.7%)

Students from the city's two universities mix easily, and there is healthy academic rivalry in some areas, despite the obvious differences. There is also a partnership with Aberdeen College, which has become an associate college of the university to encourage progression from school to higher education.

Named after an eighteenth-century philanthropist, Robert Gordon has two sites around the city. The historic Schoolhill site adjoins Aberdeen Art Gallery in the city centre, while Garthdee, where 70 per cent of undergraduates are taught, is a mile away overlooking the River Dee. The university has spent £100 million on its buildings and facilities, with Norman Foster designing the business school, while other recent develop-ments made room for art, architecture and the faculty of health and social care, which has recently launched the Centre of Obesity Research and Epidemiology. Another £170 million of improvements is planned for Garthdee over the next few years, with the aim of giving the university some of the best teaching and research facilities by 2015.

The university is pinning many of its hopes on new technology. An award-winning virtual campus was launched with an online course in e-business for postgraduates. It also enables management undergraduates to receive course materials via an intranet, and other degree and short courses are available. The new Moodle system is used across Robert Gordon's courses for both on-campus and distance learning students.

Aberdeen is a long way to go for English students, but train and air links are excellent, and the city regularly features in the top ten for quality of life. A £12-million sports and leisure centre opened in 2005, provides a centre of excellence for the region in hockey, as well as a 25-metre swimming pool, three gyms, a climbing wall and bouldering room, a café bar, three exercise studios and a large sports hall. Sport scholarships are available to budding athletes, with European and Commonwealth gold medallist swimmer Hannah Miley, amongst the university's current students. Although accommodation can be expensive in the private sector, low prices in the students' union partially compensate, and there are enough residential places to guarantee housing to first years from outside the local area.

Undergraduate Fees and Support

- » Fees 2012–13: awaiting Scottish Government policy.
- » Fees for Scottish and EU students 2011–12 No fee
- » Fees for Non-Scottish UK-domiciled students 2011–12 £1,820
- » Fees for international students 2011–12 £9,550–£11,500
- » Scholarships and bursaries based on circumstances or by competition.
- » Check the university's website for the latest information.

Students

Undergraduates:	**6,980**	**(2,515)**
Postgraduates:	**1,895**	**(2,325)**
Mature students:	**25.0%**	
Overseas students:	**12.1%**	
Applications per place:	**4.4**	
From state-sector schools:	**93.4%**	
From working-class homes:	**34.9%**	

For detailed information about fees, grants and bursaries and how they work, see chapter 7.

Accommodation

Number of places and costs refer to 2011–12
University-provided places: 1,431
Percentage catered: 0%
Self-catered costs: £60–£170 a week.
All first-year students are eligible to apply for student accommo-dation. Residential restrictions apply.
International students: given priority for accommodation.
Contact: accommodation@rgu.ac.uk
www.rgu.ac.uk/living/accommodation

Roehampton University

Fully independent since 2004, Roehampton is now making its mark as a university in its own right, after four years in a federation with Surrey University. There have been record intakes, with applications growing consistently despite rising entry requirements, and this year the university has jumped six places in *The Times* League Table. Another rise in the number of applications of almost 9 per cent at the start of 2010 was one of the biggest in London.

Roehampton has chosen not to cash in on its popularity in setting fees for 2012, however. Subject to the agreement of the Office for Fair Access, most honours degrees will cost less than £8,000 a year, while more expensive specialist programmes will carry fees of £8,250. Fees for Foundation degrees will be £7,500. The university's admirably clear statement explained that it was losing 95 per cent of its teaching grant and almost all of its capital funding so, even after making savings of 15 per cent in its own costs, it could not go lower. There were no bursaries or fee waivers in its proposals to the Office for Fair Access because these had been shown to be ineffective, but 98 per cent of a student's fee would be spent on his or her education.

Successes in the latest Research Assessment Exercise, when Roehampton entered a much higher proportion of its academics than most of its peer group, added to the university's reputation. A third of the submission was judged to be world-leading or internationally excellent, with the university producing the best results in the country for dance and doing well in anthropology and drama, theatre and performance studies.

Roehampton is a collegiate university with four distinctive colleges, which still maintain some of the traditional ethos of their religious foundations: the Anglican Whitelands, the Roman Catholic Digby Stuart, the Methodist Southlands, and the Froebel, which follows the humanist teachings of Frederick Froebel. Students need not follow any of these denominations to enrol in the colleges. The university also has a Jewish resource centre and Muslim prayer rooms.

All four colleges are based in a 64-acre campus, with stunning parkland and lakes, on or adjacent to Roehampton Lane. Whitelands is based in the eighteenth-century mansion, Parkstead House, overlooking Richmond Park, which also houses the School of Human and Life Sciences. The buildings have been refurbished with IT facilities, student accommodation, laboratories and teaching space. The colleges all have their own bars and other leisure facilities, although they are open to all members of the university.

A £6-million building, mainly for dance and PE, opened on the main campus in 2005.

Erasmus House
Roehampton Lane
London SW15 5PU

020 8392 3232 (enquiries)
enquiries@roehampton.ac.uk
www.roehampton.ac.uk
www.roehampton
  student.com
Affiliations: Cathedral
  Group; million+

The Times Rankings

Overall Ranking: **79**

Student satisfaction:	=95	(73%)
Research quality:	58	(0.8)
Entry standards:	=94	(259)
Student–staff ratio:	=64	(18.8)
Services & facilities/student:	54	(£1,369)
Expected completion rate:	77	(82.0%)
Good honours:	87	(54.7%)
Graduate prospects:	=70	(59.9%)

More recent projects include a £4-million facility for the School of Arts and a new national centre of excellence for teaching on citizenship education, human rights and social justice. Over the summer of 2009 a fully functioning newsroom was opened for journalism and media students. A 15-year programme will bring further improvements, designed to enhance the student experience and provide an environment that can be enjoyed by the local community. The plans include a new library, halls of residence, a university congregation hall, more sports facilities, a new students' union hub, cloisters, piazzas and a performing arts centre.

True to the university's origins, education remains the largest subject area, accounting for more than a quarter of the students. The Quality Assurance Agency complimented Roehampton on the accessibility of academic staff to students and the positive ways in which they responded to student needs. One example has been the provision of enhanced sports facilities on campus, with a new gym, two football pitches, running track and a multi-use games area. The sport performance and rehabilitation centre offers students, staff and local people physio-therapy, podiatry and sports massage, as well as access to physiological assessment, bio-mechanical analysis, sport psychology support and sports nutrition. The university is a high performance centre for British fencing.

Like other London universities, however, Roehampton has struggled to reach national averages for student satisfaction. Only philosophy and business studies satisfied more than 90 per cent of final-year undergraduates in the 2010 National Student Survey. More than 97 per cent of undergraduates were educated in state schools and 41 per cent come from working-class homes. The dropout rate has been coming down and the latest projection of 15 per cent is close to average for the university's courses and entry grades.

About 80 per cent of first years who want a hall place are offered one, with priority going to those who make Roehampton their first preference. Rents are not cheap for those who miss out on a place or prefer the private sector, but students like the proximity of central London and the lively and attractive suburbs around Roehampton.

Undergraduate Fees and Support

» Fees for UK/EU students 2012–13

Foundation degrees	£7,500
Most courses	£7,900
Specialist or higher-cost courses	£8,250

» Fees for International students 2011–12 £9,900

» The university is not proposing to offer fee waivers or bursaries.

» Scholarships and bursaries based on circumstances or by competition.

» Check the university's website for the latest information.

Students

Undergraduates:	5,580	(705)
Postgraduates:	935	(1,600)
Mature students:	26.2%	
Overseas students:	5.3%	
Applications per place:	3.6	
From state-sector schools:	97.4%	
From working-class homes:	41.6%	

For detailed information about fees, grants and bursaries and how they work, see chapter 7.

Accommodation

Number of places and costs refer to 2010–11
University-provided places: 1,500
Percentage catered: 0%
Self-catered costs: £93.10 (standard) – £119.70 (en suite) a week.
First years are given priority if conditions met. Local restrictions apply.
International students: guaranteed for first year
Contact: accommodation@roehampton.ac.uk

Royal Holloway, University of London

Royal Holloway has moved up three places in this year's *Times* League Table and into the top 30, with higher entry standards, more satisfied students and better graduate prospects at a time when most universities saw a decline in employment rates. It will charge £9,000 fees in 2012, but has proposed a range of student support that, unusually, includes £1 million for postgraduates so that graduates with large debts are not deterred from continuing their studies.

As the University of London's "campus in the country", Royal Holloway occupies 135 acres of woodland between Windsor Castle and Heathrow. The 600-bed Founder's Building, modelled on a French chateau and opened by Queen Victoria, is one of Britain's most remarkable university buildings. More than £100 million has been spent on the campus in the last five years, resulting in an impressive range of new and refurbished academic and social facilities. Recent projects have included a major auditorium, extensions to the School of Management and other academic buildings, an extension to the main library and new student residences, which have been praised for their comfort and eco-friendly features.

Other developments have included expansion of academic staff numbers, better student services and a portfolio of scholarships and bursaries that predated top-up fees. One offers free places or reduced fees to those who stay on for a postgraduate degree. The conversion of the huge Victorian boilerhouse into a performance space for drama and the establishment of formal links with institutions such as New York, Sydney and Yale universities, demonstrate that progress has not just been a matter of bricks and mortar. Closer to home, another link allows music students to take lessons at the Royal College of Music.

Both Bedford College and Royal Holloway, which amalgamated to form the existing college 26 years ago, were founded for women only, their legacy commemorated in the Bedford Centre for the History of Women. However, the gender balance in the student population is now roughly equal and, although still best known for the arts, Royal Holloway has a broad portfolio of subjects, including a science foundation year for those wishing to change academic direction.

Of the work entered for the Research Assessment Exercise, 60 per cent was rated world-leading or internationally excellent, cementing Royal Holloway's place among the top 25 research universities. Music was ranked top in the UK, with 90 per cent of its research in the top two categories, while biology, drama, earth sciences, economics, geography, German, media arts and

---

University of London
Egham
Surrey TW20 0EX

01784 434455 (switchboard)
admissions@rhul.ac.uk
www.rhul.ac.uk
www.surhul.co.uk
Affiliation: 1994 Group

The Times Rankings
Overall Ranking: **28**

Student satisfaction:	=48	(77%)
Research quality:	=12	(2.6)
Entry standards:	33	381
Student–staff ratio:	=35	(15.7)
Services & facilities/student:	44	(£1,505)
Expected completion rate:	23	(92.3%)
Good honours:	32	(68.8%)
Graduate prospects:	57	(63.1%)

psychology were all in the top ten in their fields.

The college has also had consistently good results in the National Student Survey, with another improvement in 2010 taking the proportion of satisfied students to 86 per cent. European languages produced a 100 per cent satisfaction rate, while history and philosophy, geology, geography, maths, molecular biology and psychology all exceeded 90 per cent. All 18 departments encourage interdisciplinary work, which is facilitated by a modular course structure with examinations at the end of every year. An Advanced Skills Programme, covering information technology, communication skills and foreign languages, further encourages breadth of study.

Royal Holloway offers a number of e-degrees and promotes numerous opportunities to study abroad, building on the international flavour of the campus and its links with many universities overseas. It is spearheading the development of the University of London Institute in Paris, allowing students to spend part of their course in France.

Applications had dipped slightly at the start of 2011, but this followed a healthy increase in the previous year that was the highest in the University of London and among the best at any pre-1992 university. The college draws over a fifth of its undergraduates from independent schools,

although the proportion coming from working-class homes has been rising. The ethnic mix is above average and the projected dropout rate of 7.5 per cent is below the official benchmark.

Nearly 3,000 students are in halls of residence, many of them in the Founder's Building itself. The college's green belt location at Egham, Surrey, 35 minutes from the centre of London by rail, ensures that social life is concentrated on an extended students' union. Sports facilities are good and have been upgraded recently – there has had considerable success with its "student talented athlete award scheme" (STARS).

Students enjoy an active cultural scene, and a thriving Community Action programme involves over 1,000 student volunteers working with local organisations and charities. A high proportion of students come from London and the Home Counties, so many go home at the weekend, but the students' union is reliably lively.

Undergraduate Fees and Support

- » Fees for UK/EU students 2012–13   £9,000
- » Fees for International students 2011–12   £11,855–£13,780
- » A package of financial support will include up to £3,000 for students from lowest income groups; year-round free accommodation for care leavers; doubling of the student hardship fund; and bursaries for mature students.
- » Scholarships and bursaries based on circumstances or by competition.
- » Check the university's website for the latest information.

Students		
Undergraduates:	**6,745**	**(550)**
Postgraduates:	**1,800**	**(440)**
Mature students:	**9.3%**	
Overseas students:	**25.1%**	
Applications per place:	**5.9**	
From state-sector schools:	**78.3%**	
From working-class homes:	**25.4%**	

For detailed information about fees, grants and bursaries and how they work, see chapter 7.

Accommodation
Number of places and costs refer to 2011–12
University-provided places: 2,922
Percentage catered: 37%
Catered costs:£80.69–£134.59 a week (30–38 weeks).
Self-catered costs: £77.97–£137.10 a week (38–50 weeks).
First years are have priority for accommodation provided conditions are met.
International students: non-EU students guaranteed accommodation.
Contact: studenthousing@rhul.ac.uk

University of St Andrews

St Andrews has been the leading Scottish university in *The Times* League Table for the last five years, reaping the benefits of outstanding scores in the National Student Survey (NSS). The university already had the highest entry standards, the best staffing levels and the lowest dropout rate north of the border. Although it has slipped two places this year, it still only just outside the top five in the UK, with some of the most satisfied students, higher entry standards and improved graduate employment prospects.

Scotland's oldest university and the third oldest in the English-speaking world, St Andrews has long been both well known and fashionable among a mainly middle-class clientele. As in most of the old universities in Scotland, there was a decline in applications at the start of 2011, but even a 10 per cent drop left more than eight applicants chasing each place.

With nearly 30 per cent of the students coming from south of the border, St Andrews has earned the nickname of Scotland's English university. But another 26 per cent come from over 100 countries farther afield, giving the university a cosmopolitan feel. Fee concessions and exchange schemes have boosted applications, particularly from the USA, which provides nearly a fifth of first-year students on its own.

Peer assessments have shown that there is top quality behind the prestige. Nearly 60 per cent of the work submitted for the 2008 Research Assessment Exercise was rated as world-leading or internationally excellent. St Andrews was joint top in the UK for philosophy and top in Scotland for physics and astronomy, German, film studies, applied maths, French and psychology.

Just under 40 per cent of undergraduates come from independent schools, when the UK average for the university's courses and entry scores is little more than 25 per cent. A dedicated schools liaison service has been trying to broaden the intake, and there is a bank of £3,000-a-year scholarships for students in need. Only three UK universities have a lower proportion of students from working-class backgrounds. Those who do come could hardly be more satisfied: the 2008 NSS showed 100 per cent satisfaction among theology and religious studies students, whilst 18 of the 28 subjects with published ratings had satisfaction levels of at least 90 per cent.

The town of St Andrews is steeped in history, as well as being the centre of the golfing world. The university at its heart accounts for nearly half of the 18,000 inhabitants. There are close cultural and social relations between town and gown. New students ("bejants" and "bejantines") acquire third and fourth-year "parents" to ease them into university life, and on Raisin Monday give their academic guardians a

---

College Gate
St Andrews
Fife KY16 9AJ

01334 462150 (admissions)
student.recruitment@st-andrews.
  ac.uk (pre-recruitment)
www.st-andrews.ac.uk
www.yourunion.net
Affiliation: 1994 Group

The Times Rankings
Overall Ranking: **=6**

Student satisfaction:	=7	(83%)
Research quality:	=12	(2.6)
Entry standards:	6	(485)
Student–staff ratio:	10	(13.3)
Services & facilities/student:	8	(£2,108)
Expected completion rate:	=15	(93.8%)
Good honours:	3	(86.7%)
Graduate prospects:	14	(76.3%)

bottle of wine in return for a receipt in Latin, which can be written on anything. Another unusual feature is that all humanities students are awarded an MA rather than a BA.

Many of the main buildings date from the fifteenth and sixteenth centuries, but sciences are taught at the modern North Haugh site a few streets away. Everything is within walking distance, but bicycles are common. Although small, St Andrews offers a wide range of courses. The university's reputation has always rested on the humanities, which have a £1.3-million research centre. An £8-million headquarters for the School of International Relations opened in 2006, with Europe's first Centre for Syrian Studies, an Institute of Iranian Studies and a Centre for Peace and Conflict Studies. St Andrews has the largest mediaeval history department in Britain and has now added film studies and sustainable development. A full range of physical sciences is also on offer, with sophisticated lasers and the largest optical telescope in Britain.

A £45-million Medical and Biological Sciences Building opened in 2010, one of the first UK medical schools whose research facilities are fully integrated with other key disciplines, including physics, biology, chemistry and psychology. A £5-million Bio-medical Sciences Research complex will follow in 2011, leading the fight against superbugs and serious viral, bacterial and parasitic diseases. Support for scholarships and medical research are among the first targets of a £100-million fundraising campaign launched prior to their marriage by Prince William and Catherine Middleton, both St Andrews graduates, to mark the university's 600th anniversary.

Students do not come to St Andrews for the nightclubs, but there is no shortage of parties in a tight-knit community. The sports facilities are excellent and more than half of all students live in halls. Self-catering accommodation for 920 students during term and three-star accommodation for golfers and other tourists in vacations was opened by Gordon Brown in 2007. Features such as the grass roof made it the first university residence to be awarded the Green Tourism Business Scheme's Gold Award. A further 250 residential places opened in 2010.

Undergraduate Fees and Support

» Fees 2012–13:   awaiting Scottish Government policy.
» Fees for Scottish and EU students 2011–12   No fee
» Fees for Non-Scottish UK-domiciled students 2011–12   £1,820
» Fees for international students 2011–12   £13,500
                                £20,500 (medical science)
» Scholarships and bursaries based on circumstances or by competition.
» Check the university's website for the latest information.

Students

Undergraduates:	**6,115**	**(1,040)**
Postgraduates:	**1,645**	**(335)**
Mature students:	**3.9%**	
Overseas students:	**33.8%**	
Applications per place:	**8.1**	
From state-sector schools:	**60.7%**	
From working-class homes:	**13.6%**	

For detailed information about fees, grants and bursaries and how they work, see chapter 7.

Accommodation

Number of places and costs refer to 2011–12
University-provided places: 4,065
Percentage catered: 47%
Catered costs: £115.92–£183.92 a week (36 weeks).
Self-catered costs: £63.64–£175.00 a week (36 weeks).
Single first-year undergraduates are guaranteed accommodation if conditions are met.
Policy for international students: as above.
Contact: accommodation@st-andrews.ac.uk
www.st-andrews.ac.uk/admissions/Accommodation

University of Salford

In the last five years, Salford has slipped below some of the new universities in *The Times* League Table, but consistently good graduate employment rates, carefully targeted courses and an emphasis on the university's location close to the centre of Manchester appeal to students. Applications have been buoyant for several years and an increase of 9 per cent at the start of 2011 disguised an even bigger rise (of 24 per cent) in applications for degree courses. The university has set fees averaging £8,400 for 2012, but is promising "one of the most generous packages of student support in the sector". Up to 30 per cent of students would qualify for scholarships and bursaries worth between £2,000 and £5,000 a year.

The university has embarked on an investment programme of £500 million that will take 15 years to complete. It will include a £47-million Arts and Media Centre on campus and a centre at the MediaCityUK development in Salford Quays – home to five BBC departments from 2011. Over 1,500 students on 39 courses will enjoy exceptional opportunities to work with professionals using the latest equipment, studios and laboratories. Salford Law School opened in 2007 in a £10-million building, and £22 million was spent on a new home for the Faculty of Health and Social Care. New acoustic laboratories opened in 2008, with a reverberation room capable of transforming the quality of sound and an anechoic chamber, which is said to be the quietest place in the world. The world's first Energy House opened in 2011 – a full-size traditional terraced house built in a laboratory for students, researchers and industry to study domestic energy consumption.

Salford stresses its business links and modern portfolio of courses, including two-year Foundation degrees. The university does well on the Government's access measures: just over four in ten undergraduates come from working-class homes and there is a high proportion from areas sending few students to higher education. The projected dropout rate has fluctuated but a dramatic improvement in the latest figures saw it almost halve to 12 per cent, well below the national average for the subjects and students' qualifications. The Student Life Directorate has been charged with improving every aspect of the student experience, even planning events for students staying at Salford over the Christmas holiday closure.

The university's growing involvement in health has seen the establishment of a national centre for prosthetics and orthotics, and Salford has a high reputation for the treatment of sports injuries. The School of Nursing and Midwifery, which received outstanding ratings from its regulatory body following a recent inspection, runs Europe's

---

Salford
Greater Manchester
M54WT

0161 295 4545
course-enquiries@salford.ac.uk
www.salford.ac.uk
www.salfordstudents.com
Affiliation: University Alliance

Edinburgh
Belfast
SALFORD
London
Cardiff

The Times Rankings
Overall Ranking: **91**

Student satisfaction:	=78	(74%)
Research quality:	=55	(0.9)
Entry standards:	=69	(280)
Student–staff ratio:	115	(23.8)
Services & facilities/student:	107	(£1,013)
Expected completion rate:	49	(86.4%)
Good honours:	=84	(55.3%)
Graduate prospects:	=90	(55.1%)

first nursing course for deaf students. There is also a BA in journalism and war studies – the only undergraduate degree in the UK to combine the two disciplines.

Engineering is the university's traditional strength, attracting many of the 3,000 overseas students. Two thirds of courses offer work placements, half of them abroad and almost all counting towards degree classifications. The tradition of sandwich courses always serves Salford well in terms of graduate employment. The Enterprise Academy scheme was commended by the EU after it helped 32 student businesses become established. Students are offered training in entrepreneurship and business skills, as well as a business mentor and an innovative scheme gives unemployed and under-employed graduates the professional training and work experience they need to join the workforce.

Online degrees have been introduced and the university has also made headlines with more unusual innovations, such as the appointment of Britain's first Professor of Pop Music. The university launched Salford Business School in 2006, formed from the merger of four existing schools, and a new Centre for Applied Archaeology has been established. Salford led the way in formally recognising interaction with business and industry as of equal importance to teaching and research. The university entered a relatively low proportion of its academics for the 2008 Research Assessment Exercise, but still had among the lowest grades of the pre-1992 universities. Architecture and business produced the best results. The university has since established nine interdisciplinary research centres and a graduate school.

There has been some improvement in scores in the National Student Survey, although satisfaction levels are still below the national average. Accounting and zoology both achieved 100 per cent satisfaction ratings, but only six other areas topped 90 per cent. The modern landscaped campus, a haven of lawns and shrubberies along the River Irwell, is less than two miles from Manchester city centre and has a mainline railway station. University House, where students go for advice and support, has recently seen a £3-million upgrade. Salford also has its own TV and radio studios. Most of the residential places are either on campus or in a student village 15 minutes' walk away.

Undergraduate Fees and Support

» Fees for UK/EU students 2012–13   £8,000–£9,000
» Fees for International students 2011–12   £9,410–£11,700
» A package of financial support will include fee waivers, bursaries and scholarships offering between £2,000 and £5,000.
» Additional scholarships and bursaries based on circumstances or by competition.
» Check the university's website for the latest information.

Students

Undergraduates:	**14,405**	**(3,050)**
Postgraduates:	**2,025**	**(2,350)**
Mature students:	**34.2%**	
Overseas students:	**10.9%**	
Applications per place:	**5.0**	
From state-sector schools:	**98.2%**	
From working-class homes:	**43.1%**	

For detailed information about fees, grants and bursaries and how they work, see chapter 7.

Accommodation

Number of places and costs refer to 2011–12

University-provided places: 1,309 plus 1,930 managed by specialist providers

Percentage catered: 0%

Self-catered costs: £63–£98 (standard); £87–£98 (en suite)

First years are guaranteed accommodation (terms and conditions apply).

International students: as above.

Contact: www.accommodation.salford.ac.uk/

School of Oriental and African Studies, London

As the major national centre for the study of Africa, Asia and the Middle East, SOAS has a global reputation in subjects relating to two thirds of the world's population. Originally only a specialist Oriental college, the school now covers a broad range of subjects. The library, which holds 1.2 million volumes, periodicals and audiovisual materials in 400 languages, attracts scholars from around the world. The £12-million Library Transformation Project has added language laboratories, music studios, discussion and research rooms, gallery space and other facilities. SOAS is in the top 50 in the QS World Rankings for the arts and humanities, and has been strengthening its academic staff in a variety of disciplines as it approaches its centenary in 2016.

The 5,400 students on campus, plus over 3,000 studying distance learning programmes, come from over 130 countries. However, two thirds are from Britain and the rest of the EU – and the proportion is higher still among the undergraduates. The school does well in the National Student Survey, remaining well above the national average in 2010. Anthropology produced by far the best results, but law and social studies also did well.

SOAS has a much wider portfolio of courses than its name would suggest, with more than 350 degree combinations on offer and 100 postgraduate programmes. Degrees are available in familiar subjects such as law, music, history and the social sciences, but with a different emphasis. There is also a more limited portfolio of Foundation programmes and language courses. Over 45 per cent of undergraduates take a language as part of their degree. The school was chosen to house a national teaching centre for languages and won a Queen's Anniversary Prize for the excellence, breadth and depth of its language teaching in 2010.

Student recruitment remains healthy, especially among independent school candidates, who account for almost a quarter of the British entrants to undergraduate courses. There were small increases in undergraduate applications in both 2010 and 2011, following strong growth over the previous decade. The main growth area is in postgraduate courses, which have helped to tackle a financial deficit.

In addition, the numbers taking distance learning courses, mainly outside the UK, have grown considerably. The transfer of the University of London postgraduate programmes previously taught by Imperial College have made SOAS one of the world's largest providers of distance learning at this level. Postgraduates are attracted by a research record which saw more than half of

---

Thornhaugh Street
Russell Square
London WC1H 0XG

020 7898 4034 (student recruitment)
study@soas.ac.uk
www.soas.ac.uk
www.soasunion.org
Affiliation: 1994 Group

The Times Rankings
Overall Ranking: **23**

Student satisfaction:	=78	(74%)
Research quality:	=30	(2.0)
Entry standards:	18	(423)
Student–staff ratio:	5	(11.1)
Services & facilities/student:	16	(£1,961)
Expected completion rate:	=45	(86.8%)
Good honours:	20	(75.0%)
Graduate prospects:	40	(68.7%)

the work submitted for the 2008 Research Assessment Exercise rated world-leading or internationally excellent. SOAS was ranked top in the UK for Asian studies and did well in anthropology, politics, history and music.

There is an option of spending one, two or three terms of a degree course in one of the school's many partner universities in Africa or Asia. More than a fifth of the British undergraduates come from working-class homes. The dropout rate has fluctuated over recent years. At 13 per cent in the latest statistics, it was significantly above the UK average for the subjects and entry qualifications at SOAS. The school will charge undergraduate fees of £9,000 from 2012, but will almost double its investment in bursaries, fee waivers and scholarships. There will also be a broader range of outreach activities, including summer schools, masterclasses and academic buddying.

SOAS is located in Bloomsbury, but in 2001 a second campus opened at Vernon Square, Islington. Less than a mile from the main Russell Square site and adjacent to two of the three student residences, it provides student-orientated facilities such as a Learning Resource Centre and an internet café. The centrepiece of the main campus is an airy, modern building with gallery space as well as teaching accommodation, a gift from the Sultan of Brunei. There is no separate students' union building, although the students do have their own recently refurbished bar, social space and catering facilities. The well-equipped and under-used University of London Union is close at hand, with swimming pool, gym and bars. The West End is also on the doorstep.

Nearly 1,000 residential places accommodate both undergraduates and postgraduates, and are within 15 minutes' walk of the school. Another 101 places are available in flats in Vernon Square. However, the school has few of its own sports facilities and the outdoor pitches are remote, with no time set aside from lectures. The ethnic and national mix has led to occasional tensions in the past, but SOAS is small enough for most students to know each other, at least by sight, and the atmosphere is normally friendly. Students tend to be highly committed – not surprising since many will return to positions of influence in developing countries – and the variety of cultures makes for lively debate.

Undergraduate Fees and Support

» Fees for UK/EU students 2012–13   £9,000
» Fees for International students 2011–12   £13,230
» Financial support and widening access package to include a 50% reduction in fees for all students from low participation neighbourhoods and support package for low income students.
» Scholarships and bursaries based on circumstances or by competition.
» Check the university's website for the latest information.

Students

Undergraduates:	**2,865**	**(100)**
Postgraduates:	**1,715**	**(540)**
Mature students:	**20.7%**	
Overseas students:	**34.3%**	
Applications per place:	**5.3**	
From state-sector schools:	**76.2%**	
From working-class homes:	**28.5%**	

For detailed information about fees, grants and bursaries and how they work, see chapter 7.

Accommodation

Number of places and costs refer to 2011–12
University-provided places: 770 (Sanctuary Management Services); 186 (intercollegiate)
Percentage catered: 20%
Catered costs: £129.50–£276.50 a week
Self-catered costs: £130.83–£228.76 a week
Priority given to first years on first come basis. Residential restrictions apply.
International students: as above, although they are a high priority.
Contact: student@sanctuary-housing.co.uk

University of Sheffield

Sheffield has cemented its position in the top 20 of *The Times* League Table and recorded high finishes in a number of subjects, following good results in the 2008 Research Assessment Exercise (RAE) and consistently high levels of satisfaction among the students. The intake is the most diverse at any of our top 20 universities: 87 per cent of undergraduates come from state schools or colleges and just more than one undergraduate in five comes from a working-class home. Although it is to charge £9,000 fees from 2012, the amount spent on student support and outreach activities will almost double to £12 million by the time the new arrangements are fully operational. The university expects more than a third of the undergraduates to benefit.

Sheffield is in the top 70 universities in the world, according to the QS World University Rankings, and attracts more than 4,600 overseas students from 124 countries. Total student numbers have reached nearly 26,000 following 14 per cent growth in three years. Applications were down by an unexpectedly large margin – nearly 16 per cent – at the start of 2011, but this followed an increase in 2010 that was the highest of any member of the Russell Group universities. A new student village and a high-tech library have added to the feeling of a university on the move. The

£23-million Information Commons, opened in 2007, operates 24 hours a day, providing 1,300 study spaces and 500 computers linked to the campus network, as well as 110,000 books and periodicals.

More than 60 per cent of the work submitted for the RAE was judged to be world-leading or internationally excellent. Politics and information studies achieved the best results in the country, while town planning, philosophy, Russian, architecture, and mechanical and aeronautical engineering were near the top for their fields.

Sheffield was on the fringe of the top ten in the National Student Survey in 2010, producing some of the best results among the big city universities. There was 100 per cent satisfaction in chemistry, computer science, theology, genetics, physical science, molecular biology, biophysics and biochemistry with several other subjects, such as dentistry, not far behind. The university was awarded national teaching centres for the arts and social sciences and for enterprise learning.

There has been sustained investment in facilities in recent years: £100 million for biological and physical sciences, medicine, engineering and social sciences, and £15 million on an advanced manufacturing research centre in which Boeing is the senior partner, and which forms the hub of a technology park. The university is the lead institution for systems engineering, smart materials and stem-cell technology in a

---

Western Bank
Sheffield S10 2TN

0114 222 8030 (admissions)
http://ask.sheffield.ac.uk/
www.shef.ac.uk
www.shef.ac.uk/union
Affiliation: Russell Group

The Times Rankings
Overall Ranking: **=17**

Student satisfaction:	=12	(81%)
Research quality:	16	(2.5)
Entry standards:	17	(426)
Student–staff ratio:	=24	(14.9)
Services & facilities/student:	41	(£1,534)
Expected completion rate:	13	(94.0%)
Good honours:	23	(73.1%)
Graduate prospects:	=17	(73.6%)

research network of European, American and Chinese universities.

The conversion of the former Jessop hospital at the heart of the campus provides a new centre for the arts and humanities, which includes a visitor information centre and café. The new Soundhouse, clad in black rubber, provides ultra-modern music practice studios, rehearsal rooms and recording facilities. Another new site adjacent to the engineering departments will house high-tech multidisciplinary facilities.

Academic buildings are concentrated in an area about a mile from the city centre on the affluent west side of Sheffield, with most university flats and halls of residence a little further into the suburbs. The main university precinct now stretches into an almost unbroken mile-long "campus".

A famously lively social scene is based on the students' union's extended facilities – voted the best in Britain for the third time in 2011 – but also takes full advantage of the city's burgeoning club life. In addition to its own popular facilities, the union owns a pub in the western suburb where most students live and the students' union is renowned for attracting some big-name bands. Town–gown relations are much better and the crime rate lower than in most big cities.

Residential accommodation is plentiful, with most of the 5,550 university-owned places within walking distance of lectures, and private housing reasonably priced as well as being available very close to lectures. First years from outside Sheffield are guaranteed accommodation. The new Endcliffe Village caters for about 3,500 students in a mix of refurbished Victorian houses and new flats. A second development will add another 1,000 places and take spending on accommodation to £200 million.

The university's excellent sports facilities have been the subject of a £6-million makeover, which includes a 170-station fitness centre and three Astroturf pitches, one of which is specifically designed for soccer. A five-year student sports strategy was launched in 2007, aiming to boost participation at various levels of the sport and recreation. Intramural football has benefited the most from this scheme with large 5-a-side, 6-a-side and 11-a-side leagues spanning all three terms, as well as regular weekend tournaments.

Undergraduate Fees and Support

» Fees for UK/EU students 2012–13 — £9,000
» Fees for International students 2011–12 — £11,490–£15,100 / £27,290 (medicine)
» Up to 200 fee waivers of £9,000 for year 1 students from low-income households who live in economically deprived areas. Bursaries or accommodation discount on sliding scale of £1,400–£500 for students with household income up to £42K.
» Scholarships and bursaries based on circumstances or by competition.
» Check the university's website for the latest information.

Students

Undergraduates:	**16,325**	**(1,760)**
Postgraduates:	**6,010**	**(1,875)**
Mature students:	**7.4%**	
Overseas students:	**12.1%**	
Applications per place:	**7.9**	
From state-sector schools:	**87.1%**	
From working-class homes:	**22.6%**	

For detailed information about fees, grants and bursaries and how they work, see chapter 7.

Accommodation

Number of places and costs refer to 2011–12
University-provided places: 5,550
Percentage catered: 10%
Catered costs: £4,674.60 – £5,765.34 (42 weeks; 31 weeks of catering).
Self-catered costs: £3,272.22 – £4,577.58 (42 weeks).
First years are guaranteed accommodation if conditions are met. International students: as above.
Contact: accommodationoffice@sheffield.ac.uk
www.shef.ac.uk/accommodation

Sheffield Hallam University

Sheffield Hallam is planning to invest £20 million over three years to enhance the experience of its students, having settled on undergraduate fees of £8,500 for 2012. Some of the money will be spent on new facilities, but most will go on new academic appointments, personal support for students and a customised employability package. Hallam proposes to spend £9 million a year by 2015 on bursaries and fee waivers and is establishing a joint outreach programme with the University of Sheffield that will focus on raising aspirations among those who might miss out on the benefits of higher education. The scheme submitted to the Office for Fair Access included waiving fees for the many Hallam students on work placements and not charging for compulsory field trips.

The university currently exceeds most of its access benchmarks, although the 35 per cent share of undergraduate places going to working-class entrants is marginally below average for the courses and entry qualifications. Over 96 per cent of the intake is from state schools, while 18 per cent come from areas that send few students to higher education. The projected dropout rate of less than 12 per cent beats the benchmark set for the university.

Hallam has two campuses, one in the heart of the city centre, near the railway station, and the other not far away in a leafy inner suburb. Developments have been continuing apace, with almost £100 million already spent on teaching and learning facilities and half as much again earmarked for the next five years. Innovative library developments take pride of place on both campuses. Business and management courses, which account for easily the biggest share of places, have their own city-centre headquarters, as does the students' union, which took over the spectacular but ill-fated National Centre for Popular Music.

While most of the development has been on the main campus, the latest stage has seen the opening of a new social centre on the Collegiate Crescent site, which houses education, health and community studies. A £14-million development that opened in 2005 has allowed the faculty of health and wellbeing to almost double in size, as extra provision is made for nursing, radiotherapy, physiotherapy and social work. The Centre for Sport and Exercise Science, with its £6-million research facility is one of the largest of its kind in Europe. The faculty is the biggest provider of health and social care training in the UK and offers the widest range of sports courses.

Another new development, combined with the refurbishment of existing city-centre buildings brought all the departments in the Faculty of Arts, Computing, Engineering and Sciences together on the main campus for the

---

City Campus
Howard Street
Sheffield S1 1WB

0114 225 5555 (enquiries)
enquiries@shu.ac.uk
www.shu.ac.uk
www.hallamunion.org
Affiliation: University Alliance

The Times Rankings
Overall Ranking: =71

Student satisfaction:	=78	(74%)
Research quality:	=70	(0.4)
Entry standards:	=63	(289)
Student–staff ratio:	78	(19.8)
Services & facilities/student:	103	(£1,056)
Expected completion rate:	65	(84.0%)
Good honours:	=57	(61.6%)
Graduate prospects:	=60	(61.8%)

first time, placing them in the heart of Sheffield's thriving cultural industries quarter. The university also launched the Sheffield Business School in 2009, bringing together academic and professional groups in business, finance, management and languages, with the university's specialisms of facilities management, food and nutrition, tourism, hospitality and events management.

Scores improved in the 2010 National Student Survey, although the university remained in the bottom half of the table. Maths and statistics achieved 100 per cent satisfaction ratings but, while nutrition and human and social geography came close to emulating this feat, physiology, European languages and technology subjects were the only others to exceed 90 per cent. Almost a third of the work submitted for the 2008 Research Assessment Exercise was rated as world-leading or internationally excellent, with planning and art and design achieving the highest grades.

Hallam traces its origins in art and design back to the 1840s and celebrated the centenary of education and teacher training in 2005. It is now one of the largest of the new universities, with more than 34,000 students, including high proportions of part-time and mature students, and more than 1,000 taught on franchised courses in further education colleges. Business and industry are closely involved in the development hundreds of courses, with almost half of the students taking sandwich course placements with employers. More than 200 "specialist flexible courses" mix part-time study, distance learning and work-based learning. The university also has a growing international dimension: it celebrated its 5,000th Malaysian graduate in 2010 and has an office in India.

A "virtual campus" offers students email accounts and cheap equipment to access the growing volume of online courses, assignments and discussion groups provided by the university, even when they are at home or on work placements. Hallam can offer all first years either university-owned, managed, or private accommodation, although the large local intake means that many live at home. Transport in the city is excellent, with both a well-run bus and tram service. Sports facilities are supplemented by those provided by the city for the World Student Games. The impressive swimming complex, for example, is on the university's doorstep.

Undergraduate Fees and Support

» Fees for UK/EU students 2012–13 £8,500
  Fee waiver for placement year on sandwich courses
» Fees for International students 2011–12 £10,080–£11,520
» Bursary on full grant: household income up to £25K: £700
» A package of financial support and widening participation activity to be announced.
» Scholarships and bursaries based on circumstances or by competition.
» Check the university's website for the latest information.

Students		
Undergraduates:	**20,820**	**(6,560)**
Postgraduates:	**3,170**	**(4,865)**
Mature students:	**18.4%**	
Overseas students:	**6.9%**	
Applications per place:	**5.7**	
From state-sector schools:	**96.7%**	
From working-class homes:	**35.0%**	

For detailed information about fees, grants and bursaries and how they work, see chapter 7.

Accommodation

Number of places and costs refer to 2010–11
University-provided places: 4,205
Percentage catered: 8%
Catered costs: £91.43 (39 weeks).
Self-catered costs: £82.74 (standard single) – £190.00 (double self-contained flat) for 42–44 weeks.
All first years offered university owned, managed, partnership or private housing.
International students: as above, providing conditions are met.
Contact: www.shu.ac.uk/accommodation

Southampton University

Southampton is promising "ground-breaking" reforms to its teaching and student support programmes in exchange for £9,000 fees from 2012. Among the proposals put to the Office for Fair Access was the introduction of personalised learning through an academic advisor for every student to guide their independent learning and progress, and a more flexible curriculum that encourages undergraduates to study a second language or explore a global challenge in another discipline. In addition, one student in five would qualify for a £3,000 fee waiver, while one in three would receive a reduction of some sort. Every undergraduate would receive the Southampton Entitlement of £300 a year to spend on services such as sports membership, access to campus arts venues and local public transport.

The university has seen the demand for places grow steadily for the last few years, following substantial investment in campus facilities and good results in the National Student Survey (NSS). But applications were down at the start of 2011, as they were at most of the leading universities. The university is now in the final phase of a £250-million programme to upgrade its six sites in Southampton and Winchester.

More than 60 per cent of Southampton's submission to the 2008 Research Assessment Exercise was considered world-leading or internationally excellent, leaving the university firmly entrenched among the research elite. The best grades came in music, sociology and social policy, computer science and nursing. Southampton is in the top 100 universities in the world, according to both the QS and *Times Higher Education* rankings and the proportion of income derived from research is among the highest in Britain.

Although the percentages of students from working-class homes and areas with little tradition of university education are lower than the national average for the subjects offered, the statistics agency considers this largely a matter of location. The university does exceed the benchmark set for the number of state school pupils, as it does for the proportion of students who have a disability. Students act as ambassadors, associates and mentors in local schools and colleges, as part of the university's existing efforts to broaden its intake.

The university again finished in the top quarter in the 2010 NSS. Biology and French recorded 100 per cent satisfaction ratings, while chemistry, geology, maths, mechanical engineering and electronic and electrical engineering were all among the leaders in their fields. Research in chemistry is among the best in Europe, according to a specialist European ranking.

The main Highfield campus is in an attractive green location two miles from the

University Road
Southampton SO17 1BJ

023 8059 4732 (admissions)
admissns@soton.ac.uk
www.soton.ac.uk
www.susu.org
Affiliation: Russell Group

The Times Rankings
Overall Ranking: **19**

Student satisfaction:	=24	(79%)
Research quality:	=25	(2.1)
Entry standards:	16	(427)
Student–staff ratio:	=12	(13.6)
Services & facilities/student:	15	(£1,966)
Expected completion rate:	=19	(93.0%)
Good honours:	=18	(75.3%)
Graduate prospects:	41	(68.3%)

city centre, adjoining Southampton Common, and has been the focus of recent development. The library has been greatly extended and a purpose-built student services centre provides learning support and other advisory facilities, most of which are backed up online for students in other areas of the university. A new social learning space, designed by students for students, opened in 2010 as part of the innovative "Create your Campus" competition, which gives students the opportunity to influence the development of their learning environment. The striking £55-million Mountbatten Building for electronics and computer science and the Optoelectronics Research Centre and the £50-million Life Sciences Building are recent additions. The uni-link transport interchange, which opened on the campus in 2010 is a major transport hub for the city, as well as for students.

The university has four sites in Southampton. The National Oceanography Centre Southampton is based in the city's revitalised dock area. A £50-million joint project with the Natural Environment Research Council, it is considered Europe's finest. The Avenue campus, near the main site, is home to most of the arts departments. Clinical medicine is based at Southampton General Hospital, where a new research centre opened in 2007.

Winchester School of Art, which has been part of the university since 1996, has also enjoyed significant recent investment in new facilities. The arts are well represented in Southampton, too, with three nationally renowned arts centres: the Turner Sims concert hall, the Nuffield Theatre and the John Hansard Gallery all based at Highfield. The university has also been expanding its international activities, for example through the Centre for Contemporary China, which originated in law, the arts and social sciences, but which now links Southampton with a number of leading Chinese universities.

Social facilities for students have been expanded and refurbished. Sports facilities are first class, with an indoor sports complex and a 25-metre swimming pool next to the students' union. The outdoor sports complex, just three miles from Highfield campus, has grass and synthetic pitches. Student housing is plentiful and first years are guaranteed an offer of accommodation..

Undergraduate Fees and Support

» Fees for UK/EU students 2012–13   £9,000
» Fees for International students 2011–12   £10,820–£13,840
      £25,500 (medicine)
» A tapered fee waiver scheme: from £3,000 for household income below £25K to £200 at £42.6K. The Access to Southampton bursary will support local students and the Southampton Entitlement is a £300 annual credit for student services and transport.
» Scholarships based on circumstances or by competition.
» Check the university's website for the latest information.

Students		
Undergraduates:	**15,165**	**(1,835)**
Postgraduates:	**4,940**	**(1,790)**
Mature students:	**10.4%**	
Overseas students:	**13.1%**	
Applications per place:	**7.1**	
From state-sector schools:	**84.5%**	
From working-class homes:	**22.1%**	

For detailed information about fees, grants and bursaries and how they work, see chapter 7.

Accommodation

Number of places and costs refer to 2010–11
University-provided places: more than 5,000
Percentage catered: 10%
Catered costs: £105.00–£154.49 a week.
Self-catered costs: £71.40–£154.49 a week (self-contained flat)
All first years are guaranteed an offer of accommodation. Conditions apply.
International students: All non-EU students are guaranteed accommodation. Conditions apply.
Contact: www.southampton.ac.uk/accommodation

Southampton Solent University

Southampton Solent will offer some of the lowest fees in England in 2012, having settled on £7,800 for all courses. The university said it was striking a fair balance between its commitment to social justice and the need to invest in improving the student experience. Vice-Chancellor Professor Van Gore said, "We do not want talented people to be put off going to university and we are determined to offer them an excellent and distinctive learning experience."

The largest of the nine universities created in 2005, Southampton Solent also has the broadest range of programmes, stretching from Foundation courses to doctorates. Over 12,000 students embrace civil and mechanical engineering, as well as media, arts and business, with a separate maritime centre capitalising on the coastal location. The subject mix explains why the former Southampton Institute is now one of the few universities with a majority of male students.

The rebranded Solent Curriculum plays to the university's strengths in vocational courses, with an eye to maintaining a good graduate employment record. There is a strong representation of "non-traditional" disciplines, such as yacht and powercraft design, computer and video games, and comedy writing and performance. A Graduate Enterprise Centre provides advice and rent-free offices for those hoping to start their own businesses, while the Warsash Maritime Centre is an internationally renowned training and research facility for the shipping and offshore oil industries.

Solent entered fewer academics for the 2008 Research Assessment Exercise than any university in England – fewer than one in ten of those eligible. But two of the three areas in which it made a submission contained some world-leading research, with art and design achieving much the best results. It was also just outside the bottom ten universities for student satisfaction in 2010, despite a second successive improvement in the National Student Survey. Accounting, publicity studies, teacher training and sociology were the only subjects with satisfaction ratings above 90 per cent.

Nevertheless, applications have been healthy and had risen by 3.6 per cent at the start of 2011, following big rises in the two previous years. Demand for places remains especially strong in marine-based courses. The university is higher education's premier yachting institution, with a world champion student team that has won the national championships four times in six years. Three new boats support courses at the new, purpose-built Watersports Centre, where some of the activities are targeted towards disadvantaged young people. The centre now

---

East Park Terrace
Southampton SO14 0YN

023 8031 9000 (main switchboard)
ask@solent.ac.uk
www.solent.ac.uk
www.solentsu.co.uk
Affiliation: million+

The Times Rankings
Overall Ranking: **109**

Student satisfaction:	=95	(73%)
Research quality:	=105	(0.1)
Entry standards:	=86	(266)
Student–staff ratio:	100	(21.5)
Services & facilities/student:	100	(£1,079)
Expected completion rate:	109	(74.3%)
Good honours:	115	(42.7%)
Graduate prospects:	114	(46.2%)

boasts seven powerboats, nine dinghies and three keelboats.

Almost a third of the students come from Hampshire and there has been a substantial increase in the proportion with working-class roots, almost reaching the national average for the university's subjects and entry qualifications. Solent's projected dropout rate improved in the last two surveys and, at just below 16 per cent, is now better than the university's benchmark. There is a special link with Guernsey, which has no higher education of its own. Colleges on the island bring students for taster courses and provide evidence of academic potential that can lead to entry on criteria other than A level.

The main campus has few architectural pretensions, but is conveniently based in the city centre within walking distance of the station. Recent investment has included a new Centre for Professional Development in Broadcasting and Multimedia Production, which includes an online editing suite, digital television studio and gallery, for use by undergraduates as well as community groups and professionals. Media, arts and society courses now attract almost as many students as the consistently popular business school.

Other recent additions include the Centre for Health, Exercise and Sports Science, which enables students to conduct the latest types of fitness testing, including ergonomic and biomechanical movement analysis. A new Centre for Football Research has opened in a development that the university said would cement its position as a leading provider for football-related academic study. New music studios feature an industry-standard recording complex, while a performance space and dance studio includes a dance floor, tiered seating and a technical viewing gallery.

Students like the location, close to the city's growing complement of bars and nightclubs, as well as to the main shopping area. There are more than 2,300 hall places, most of which are allocated to first years and almost half of which are en suite. A landlord accreditation scheme helps to guarantee standards of accommodation for those who rely on the private sector. There is the usual range of sports facilities, with a sports hall and fitness suite on campus and outdoor pitches, tennis and netball courts four miles away. Students living in hall and members of university sports clubs get free fitness classes and gym use.

Undergraduate Fees and Support

» Fees for UK/EU students 2012–13 £7,800
» Fees for International students 2011–12 £9,100
» A package of financial support and widening participation activity to be announced, plus an enhanced "employability" programme.
» Scholarships and bursaries based on circumstances or by competition.
» Check the university's website for the latest information.

Students

Undergraduates:	**10,200**	**(1,525)**
Postgraduates:	**420**	**(390)**
Mature students:	**22.2%**	
Overseas students:	**14.6%**	
Applications per place:	**4.6**	
From state-sector schools:	**96.2%**	
From working-class homes:	**38.5%**	

For detailed information about fees, grants and bursaries and how they work, see chapter 7.

Accommodation

Number of places and costs refer to 2011–12
University-provided places: 2,340 (majority are offered to first years).
Percentage catered: 0%
Self-catered costs: £86.80–£110.95 a week (41 weeks).
First years are guaranteed accommodation if conditions are met.
International students: some accommodation is set aside.
Contact: Accommodation@solent.ac.uk
www.solent.ac.uk/accommodation/accommodation_home.aspx

Staffordshire University

Staffordshire used to describe itself as a "university in the community" but it is increasingly reliant on overseas students, both at home and abroad. There are more than 5,000 students taking Staffordshire courses outside Britain, almost half of them located around the Pacific Rim, as well as a growing cohort of foreign students in the university's domestic campuses. There are dedicated admissions offices in Oman, Sri Lanka, Singapore and Macedonia, and enrolment began in Slovenia and Kosovo in 2009.

There are more than 12,000 UK students, however, and the demand for places has grown substantially over the last three years, after a period of decline. The university has dropped 12 places in the latest *Times* table after a decline in graduate prospects, a worsening of staffing levels and lower spending on facilities, but growth in applications of 25 per cent at the start of 2011 represented one of the biggest increases in the UK.

The university is based on two main sites: in Stoke-on-Trent and 16 miles away in Stafford. Both have modern halls of residence, sports centres and lively students' union venues. There has been significant investment at the Stafford campus, which features the Octagon Centre, in which lecture theatres, offices and walkways surround one of the largest university computing facilities in Europe. The New Technologies Centre boasts excellent film production facilities and there is a working broadcast newsroom. Engineering and technology are based at Stafford, where facilities, including a fully equipped television studio. The Faculty of Health is also based there and has branches in Telford and Shrewsbury.

The large Business School is based at Stoke, which also hosts the Law School, the Faculty of Arts, Media and Design and courses in sport and exercise. Developments are dominated by a £287-million plan to produce an attractive and thriving University Quarter – one of the largest collaborative projects of its kind in the UK. New science facilities are due for completion in 2011, focusing on the university's strengths in forensics, biology and psychology. There is even a 25-acre nature reserve – part of the university's sustained green commitment.

A third campus in Lichfield houses an integrated further and higher education centre, developed in partnership with Tamworth and Lichfield College, as well as 26 business start-up units. The Staffordshire University Regional Federation also involves partner colleges in delivering a range of higher education awards to around 3,000 students. A bespoke £520,000 higher education centre will open on the new Newcastle College campus in 2010.

The university is a pioneer of two-year

College Road
Stoke-on-Trent ST4 2DE

01782 292753 (admissions)
admissions@staffs.ac.uk
www.staffs.ac.uk
www.staffsunion.com
Affiliation: million+

The Times Rankings
Overall Ranking: **89**

Student satisfaction:	=48	(77%)
Research quality:	=105	(0.1)
Entry standards:	=105	(241)
Student–staff ratio:	=103	(21.7)
Services & facilities/student:	90	(£1,143)
Expected completion rate:	92	(79.4%)
Good honours:	96	(52.4%)
Graduate prospects:	=66	(60.7%)

fast-track degrees, which are now offered in accounting and finance, computing science, business, English, law and geography. Staffordshire academics will also be evaluating the national programme of accelerated degrees. There already was an extensive portfolio of two-year Foundation degrees. Many programmes are available with a January start, a popular arrangement with overseas students who often take English language courses before beginning a degree.

Staffordshire is among the leading universities for secondary teacher training courses. Results have improved in the National Student Survey, leaving Staffordshire close to the national average in 2010. Nursing and other subjects allied to medicine produced 100 per cent satisfaction rates and there were high scores in physical geography and environmental science, forensic and archaeological science, biology and geographical sciences. The university entered only a small proportion of its academics for the 2008 assessment exercise. Three of the ten subject areas had some world-leading research, with general engineering and education producing the best results. Applied research has led to the development of new products in markets as diverse as medical technology and recycling.

With 98 per cent of its undergraduates state-educated and more than four in ten coming from working-class homes, Staffordshire exceeds all the benchmarks set by the funding council for widening access to higher education. There is good provision for the 700 students with disabilities. The projected dropout rate has been improving but, at nearly 20 per cent, was back above the national average for the university's courses and entry qualifications in the latest survey.

Stoke is not the liveliest city of its size, but the University Quarter project should attract more social facilities. The campus, which is close to the railway station, is within easy reach of the city centre and has a buzzing students' union. Stafford is much the more attractive setting and offers the best chance of a residential place, but the town is quiet and the campus is a mile and a half outside it. Sports facilities are good, especially in Stafford, where there is a new £1.4-million sports centre and all-weather pitches., as well as good coaching, which has helped attract some outstanding athletes.

Undergraduate Fees and Support

» Fees for UK/EU students 2012–13   to be announced
» Fees for International students 2011–12   £9,385
» A package of financial support and widening participation activity to be announced.
» Scholarships and bursaries based on circumstances or by competition.
» Check the university's website for the latest information.

Students

Undergraduates:	**10,360**	**(7,030)**
Postgraduates:	**1,570**	**(2,265)**
Mature students:	**31.3%**	
Overseas students:	**6.6%**	
Applications per place:	**4.5**	
From state-sector schools:	**98.0%**	
From working-class homes:	**41.5%**	

For detailed information about fees, grants and bursaries and how they work, see chapter 7.

Accommodation

Number of places and costs refer to 2011–12
University-provided places: 1,036 (Stoke); 786 (Stafford)
Percentage catered: 0%
Self-catered accommodation: £74–£100 a week (36 weeks).
First years have priority, if conditions are met.
International students: have priority, if conditions are met.
Contact: Accommodation_stoke@staffs.ac.uk
Accommodation_stafford@staffs.ac.uk
www.staffs.ac.uk/courses_and_study/student_services/accommodation/

University of Stirling

Stirling has one of the most beautiful campuses in Britain and has twice recently been voted the UK's top destination for international students. It has a loch-side setting beneath the Ochil Hills and is particularly well provided for sports facilities, having been designated Scotland's University for Sporting Excellence in 2008. Stirling is home to national swimming and tennis centres, as well as a golf course and a football academy.

The university remains relatively small, with only 11,500 students, and has a strong community feel. There are no faculties, but five "core areas" have been identified: health and well-being, culture and society, environment, enterprise and economy, and sport. Philosophy produced the best results in the 2008 Research Assessment Exercise, but nursing, film, media and journalism, economics, education and history all did well.

Stirling has been one of the top performers in the National Student Survey, improving its scores in 2010, when it was on the fringe of the top ten universities with 89 per cent of final-year undergraduates satisfied overall. There was 100 per cent satisfaction in philosophy and maths and statistics, while psychology, religious studies, marketing, law, history, computer science, finance and accounting all reached at least 95 per cent. Investment is taking place in a number of academic areas, including teacher education, where there have been six new appointments to enhance a research-led approach to the subject. There are also two new chairs in sport, and a new chair in creative writing.

Stirling was the British pioneer of the semester system, which has now become so popular throughout higher education. The academic year is divided into two 15-week terms, with short mid-semester breaks. Students have the option of starting courses in February, rather than September. Successful completion of six semesters will bring a General degree; eight semesters, Honours.

The emphasis on breadth is such that there are no barriers to movement between departments. Undergraduates can switch the whole direction of their studies, in consultation with their academic adviser, as their interests develop. The modular scheme allows students to speed up their progress on a Summer Academic Programme, which squeezes a full semester's teaching into July and August. Full-time students are not allowed to use the programme to reduce the length of their course, but part-timers can use it to make rapid progress.

Applications rose by a remarkable 37 per cent in 2010 – more than twice the UK average – and there had been another big increase, of 17 per cent at the start of 2011.

Stirling Campus
Stirling FK9 4LA

01786 467044 (admissions)
admissions@stir.ac.uk
www.stir.ac.uk
www.stirlingstudentsunion.com
Affiliation: none

STIRLING
Edinburgh
Belfast
London
Cardiff

The Times Rankings
Overall Ranking: **46**

Student satisfaction:	=24	(79%)
Research quality:	=49	(1.3)
Entry standards:	51	(305)
Student–staff ratio:	=71	(19.3)
Services & facilities/student:	=79	(£1,198)
Expected completion rate:	48	(86.6%)
Good honours:	=49	(63.6%)
Graduate prospects:	=47	(66.2%)

The intake is surprisingly diverse, with just over one in ten undergraduates state-educated and nearly a third coming from working-class homes. Two thirds are from Scotland. International exchanges are common, with many students going to American, Asian and European universities each year.

The most recent campus development has been an £11-million refurbishment of the 1960s library, which has been completely reconfigured and redesigned, prompting an 80 per cent increase in usage. The School of Biological and Environmental Sciences has also been refurbished, as have the computer laboratories. The university has more than 700 computers for student use, many of them available 24 hours a day, and all rooms in halls are wired for internet use. Journalism students have the use of a high-tech newsroom. In 2009, the university launched the UK's first degree in financial journalism.

The sports facilities, which include a 50-metre pool and a golf centre with indoor facilities and a synthetic putting green, are used for teaching and research, as well as for training by elite athletes and recreation for the university community. Sports Studies are particularly popular, with 100 students in 2010 benefiting from a sports scholarships programme that is open to overseas, as well as UK students. It covers golf, swimming, disability swimming, tennis, triathlon and football.

Students appreciate the individual attention that a small campus university can offer, although some find the atmosphere claustrophobic. Stirling is not the top choice of nightclubbers, but the students' union won "Best Bar None" status for three years in a row and there is a lively social scene. The MacRobert Arts Centre offers a full programme of cultural activities, while the surrounding countryside offers its own attractions for walkers and climbers. The campus has been described by police as one of the safest in Britain, but a community policeman is based there and available to students for extra advice.

Nurses and midwives can opt to study at the Highland campus, which is based in the modern Centre for Health Science, in Inverness. There is also a Western Isles campus, located in Stornoway, where the teaching accommodation is an integral part of the Western Isles Hospital.

Undergraduate Fees and Support

» Fees 2012–13: awaiting Scottish Government policy.
» Fees for Scottish and EU students 2011–12 No fee
» Fees for Non-Scottish UK-domiciled students 2011–12 £1,820
» Fees for international students 2011–12 £10,200–£12,250
» Scholarships and bursaries based on circumstances or by competition.
» Check the university's website for the latest information.

Students		
Undergraduates:	**6,995**	**(1,115)**
Postgraduates:	**1,650**	**(1,105)**
Mature students:	**19.4%**	
Overseas students:	**8.9%**	
Applications per place:	**6.3**	
From state-sector schools:	**92.3%**	
From working-class homes:	**30.5%**	

For detailed information about fees, grants and bursaries and how they work, see chapter 7.

Accommodation

Number of places and costs refer to 2011–12
University-provided places: 2,294
Percentage catered: 0%
Self-catered costs: £67.37–£105.97 a week.
All first years are guaranteed suitable housing arranged by the university.
International students: as above.
Contact: Accommodation@stir.ac.uk

University of Strathclyde

Strathclyde has set itself the target of becoming one of the world's leading technological universities. Vice-Chancellor Professor Jim McDonald has called for improvements in research to achieve this goal, but has promised not to neglect the student experience. Even as Anderson's Institution in the 18th century, Strathclyde concentrated on "useful learning". The university promises courses that are both innovative and relevant to 21st-century needs – hence product design and innovation, energy systems or international business with modern languages.

Business and law were the main successes in the 2008 Research Assessment Exercise (RAE), when almost 60 per cent of the university's submission was rated as world-leading or internationally excellent. Pharmacy and some branches of engineering also achieved good results. The Business School, rated among the top 20 in Europe by The *Financial Times* and the only one in Scotland to be accredited by the European Quality Improvement System, is normally considered Strathclyde's main strength. The School recently announced plans to open a branch campus in Greater Noida, near Delhi. Business studies students follow a management development programme, which is designed to place them in a realistic

business environment from day one and involves work with major companies.

The engineering faculty is also the largest in Scotland. The university is heavily involved in Scotland's "pooling" arrangement for research in potentially vulnerable science subjects. There were a number of joint submissions with neighbouring Glasgow University in the RAE. However, Strathclyde is not all about business and engineering. The faculties of Education, Law, Arts and Social Sciences were brought together in 2010 in order to maximise the potential for research collaboration and be more responsive to student needs.

European focus is evident throughout the university. Many students combine business or engineering with European studies or languages to give themselves an edge in the job market. Mature students account for nearly almost 15 per cent of the places and have a special organisation to look after their interests. With nearly 22,000 students, including part-timers, Strathclyde is the third-largest university in Scotland. But when short courses and distance learning programmes are included, its numbers swell to more than 60,000.

Strathclyde actively promotes wider access, comfortably exceeding UK averages for state-educated students and the share of places going to applicants from working-class homes. The projected dropout rate had dropped below 12 per cent in the latest

---

16 Richmond Street
Glasgow G1 1XQ

0141 552 4400 (main switchboard)
access via website
www.strath.ac.uk
www.strathstudents.com
Affiliation: none

GLASGOW
Edinburgh
Belfast
London
Cardiff

The Times Rankings
Overall Ranking: **34**

Student satisfaction:	=37	(78%)
Research quality:	=42	(1.6)
Entry standards:	28	(394)
Student–staff ratio:	56	(18)
Services & facilities/student:	31	(£1,608)
Expected completion rate:	69	(83.3%)
Good honours:	=14	(76.2%)
Graduate prospects:	19	(73.0%)

survey, but is still higher than average for the university's subjects and entry qualifications.

The main John Anderson campus is in the centre of Glasgow, behind George Square and near Queen Street station. Apart from the Edwardian headquarters, the buildings are mostly modern. A former maternity hospital in the centre of the campus will eventually provide extra teaching accommodation, but a £73-million refurbishment programme is taking priority. In addition, construction of the Advanced Forming Research Centre – a world class research partnership between the University and international engineering firms – was completed in 2010 and opened near Glasgow Airport.

The university has unveiled ambitious plans to invest £350 million over the next ten years to transform the city centre campus. A range of new facilities will be added, including a Centre for Sport and Health. The Strathclyde Institute of Pharmacy and Biomedical Sciences – a centre for excellence in drug discovery and development research – already has a new headquarters. The £89-million Technology and Innovation Centre opened in 2011, enabling companies to work side-by-side with university researchers.

Strathclyde's Jordanhill campus on the west side of the city was acquired from a merger with Jordanhill College of Education in 1993. The 67-acre parkland site houses the Faculty of Education, which is breaking new ground with Scotland's first part-time teacher training degree and also offers courses in speech and language pathology, community arts, social work, sport and outdoor education. The Jordanhill site is scheduled to close, its education students moving to the main campus, creating a unified, city-centre campus by 2012.

The student village on the main campus has 1,400 bedspaces, all with network access. Another 500 residential places are nearby in the trendy Merchant City. The ten-floor union building attracts students from all over Glasgow. There are over 40 sporting clubs and teams and another 40 social, cultural and political clubs and societies, plus a student newspaper and radio station. Proximity to Glasgow's vibrant and celebrated music scene is a plus, and for those with more sophisticated tastes, there are numerous theatres and arts organisations, as well as standout museums such as the Kelvingrove, one of Scotland's top attractions.

Undergraduate Fees and Support

» Fees 2012–13:   awaiting Scottish Government policy.
» Fees for Scottish and EU students 2011–12   No fee
» Fees for Non-Scottish UK-domiciled students 2011–12   £1,820
» Fees for international students 2011–12   £11,330–£15,400
» Scholarships and bursaries based on circumstances or by competition.
» Check the university's website for the latest information.

Students		
Undergraduates:	**12,260**	**(2,500)**
Postgraduates:	**3,410**	**(3,140)**
Mature students:	**14.9%**	
Overseas students:	**7.5%**	
Applications per place:	**6.8**	
From state-sector schools:	**92.9%**	
From working-class homes:	**27.7%**	

For detailed information about fees, grants and bursaries and how they work, see chapter 7.

Accommodation

Number of places and costs refer to 2011–12
University-provided places: 1,838
Percentage catered: 0%
Self-catered costs: £76–£107 a week.
First years are offered accommodation if they live further than 25 miles from the university.
International students: as above.
Contact: student.accommodation@strath.ac.uk
www.strath.ac.uk/accommodation/

University of Sunderland

The majority of degrees at Sunderland will be available for fees of less than £8,000 in 2012, but laboratory-based science courses will cost £8,500. The university, with its strong focus on widening participation in higher education, will offer Foundation degrees at £7,000 and feels it has found a "fair and attractive" overall fees structure. It will be spending £10 million a year on student support to maintain access to its courses regardless of background.

The university has a determinedly local focus, aiming to double the number of students coming from an area which has little tradition of sending students to higher education. Only one UK university recruits a higher proportion from "low participation neighbourhoods" – at 26 per cent, well above the national average for the subjects on offer. A pioneering access scheme offers places to mature students without A levels, as long as they reach the required levels of literacy, numeracy and other basic skills. The Learning North East initiative, based on Sunderland's successful pilot for the University for Industry, even offers free taster courses to take at home.

More than four undergraduates in ten have a working-class background, and the projected dropout rate has decreased to below 15 per cent in recent years, practically matching the national average for the subjects and entry qualifications. Provision for disabled students is excellent, with award-winning information produced for those with disabilities, trained support staff in every academic school as well as in the libraries and special modules to help dyslexics. The campus also houses the North East Regional Access Centre, which assesses the learning support requirements of students with disabilities and specific learning difficulties. There is special provision among the 2,200 residential places.

Sunderland already had one of the UK's newest campuses, having taken advantage of urban regeneration programmes to transform its facilities. Now the £75-million redevelopment of the original City campus is well underway, after the opening of the £12-million CitySpace sports and social space and the new Sciences Complex and Quad. The first phase of the £12-million student village has been completed, with phase two opening in September 2011. The campus now boasts an outdoor performance area, a design centre, and the Gateway, a one-stop shop for student services.

The university's other campus at St Peter's, an award-winning 24-acre site by the banks of the Wear, houses the Business School and the faculties of Applied Sciences, Law and Arts, Design and Media. The Sir Tom Cowie campus is built around a 7th-century abbey described as one of Britain's

---

City Campus
Chester Road
Sunderland SR1 3SD

0191 515 3000 (course helpline)
student.helpline@
    sunderland.ac.uk
www.sunderland.ac.uk
www.sunderlandsu.co.uk
Affiliation: million+

The Times Rankings
Overall Ranking: **=80**

Student satisfaction:	**=37**	(78%)
Research quality:	**=62**	(0.5)
Entry standards:	**102**	(246)
Student–staff ratio:	**=37**	(15.8)
Services & facilities/student:	**93**	(£1,113)
Expected completion rate:	**=97**	(78.6%)
Good honours:	**=102**	(49.8%)
Graduate prospects:	**93**	(54.8%)

Edinburgh
Belfast
SUNDERLAND
London
Cardiff

first universities and incorporates a working heritage centre for the glass industry. A glass and ceramics design degree maintains a Sunderland tradition, while teaching and research in automotive design and manufacture serve the region's modern industrial base. The large pharmacy department is another strength and the well-equipped Faculty of Applied Sciences is one of the largest in the UK, with over 3,000 students. Sunderland now has more than 18,000 students in total, including 1,000 from outside the European Union. There are large numbers on teacher training courses and both media and sports science have been growing in popularity. Magazine, fashion and sports journalism were added in 2010.

Sunderland is making the most of the opportunity to link up with the multinational companies that have arrived on its doorstep. The Institute for Automotive and Manufacturing Advanced Practice has a team of 40 researchers and consultants working with local businesses, while nearby Nissan played an important role in designing a course in automotive product development. The media centre provides students with excellent television and video production facilities and is home to the student-run community radio station, 107 Spark FM.

The university is in the top half of the table for student satisfaction. English, modern languages and pharmacy all produced satisfaction levels of 90 per cent or more in the 2010 National Student Survey. Sunderland was less successful in the latest 2008 Research Assessment Exercise, although more than half of the 16 subject areas contained at least some world-leading work. Communication, cultural and media studies produced by the far best grades, but history and English also did well. The law department has now incorporated space law into their degree, the first module of its kind in the UK.

Sunderland itself is fiercely proud of its identity and has the advantage of a coastal location. The leisure facilities are better than one might imagine: the city has the North East's only Olympic-sized swimming pool and only dry ski slope, as well as Europe's biggest climbing wall and a theatre showing West End productions. Those in search of more cultural events or serious nightlife head for Newcastle, which is less than half an hour away by Metro.

Undergraduate Fees and Support

» Fees for UK/EU students 2012–13:

Foundation degree	£7,000
Standard courses	£7,800
Lab-based courses	£8,500

» Fees for International students 2011–12   £8,800

» A package of financial support and widening participation activity to be announced.

» Check the university's website for the latest information.

Students

Undergraduates:	**8,695**	**(7,385)**
Postgraduates:	**2,035**	**(810)**
Mature students:	**32.2%**	
Overseas students:	**18.0%**	
Applications per place:	**5.2**	
From state-sector schools:	**98.1%**	
From working-class homes:	**45.0%**	

For detailed information about fees, grants and bursaries and how they work, see chapter 7.

Accommodation

Number of places and costs refer to 2011–12

University provided places: 1,501 beds in Halls, 548 (The Forge).

Percentage catered: 26%

Catered costs: £3,280 (standard) – £5,080 (1-bed flat) plus option to purchase meal vouchers.

Self-catered costs: £1,920 (shared room) – £4,499 (en suite).

New first years are guaranteed accommodation in accordance with the university's allocation policy.

International students: as above

Contact: www.sunderland.ac.uk/residentialservices

University of Surrey

Surrey has been one of the recent success stories of the university world, rising three places in *The Times* League Table, mainly thanks to higher spending on facilities and an improved completion rate. The university has remained true to its technological history while building a strong research base and a high degree of financial independence. Recent expansion in healthcare, human sciences and performing arts has added to the traditional strengths in science and engineering. Undergraduates in most subjects undertake work placements of one (or two half) years, often abroad. As a result, most degrees last four years. The format and the subject balance combine to keep Surrey near the top of the graduate employment league. It has taken to describing itself as the "University for Jobs" to ram the point home.

The mix has been proving popular: applications grew by more than half between 2006 and 2008, despite increasing entry standards, and significant rises have continued this year and last. The university is planning to boost its numbers further through overseas ventures. An international institute in the Chinese city of Dalian, in partnership with Dongbei University, is the first of these. Nearer home, Surrey has taken in the Guildford School of Acting, with its 16 studios for dance and theatre studies, and

has launched its first degree in English literature.

All students are encouraged to enrol for a course at the European language centre, and a growing number of degrees, including a new range in engineering, have a language component. The cosmopolitan feel is enhanced by one of the largest proportions of overseas students at any university – a feat which won Surrey a Queen's Award for Export Achievement. Nearly a third of the students are from outside the UK.

More than half of the work submitted for the 2008 Research Assessment Exercise was considered world-leading or internationally excellent. Electrical and electronic engineering was ranked second in the country, while health and medical sciences, sociology and general engineering were in the top ten in their fields. Another indication of the university's research strength lies in the growing proportion of income derived from sources other than Government grants: up from 10 per cent to about 70 per cent in little over a decade. The Surrey Research Park is one of only three science parks still owned, funded and managed by the university that opened it, helping Surrey to amass one of the highest proportions of private funding at any British university.

Scores dipped in the 2010 National Student Survey, but still matched the UK average. For the second year in a row, chemical, process and energy engineering

---

Guildford
Surrey GU2 7XH

0800 980 3200 (enquiries)
ug-enquiries@surrey.ac.uk
www.surrey.ac.uk
www.ussu.co.uk
Affiliation: 1994 Group

The Times Rankings
Overall Ranking: **29**

Student satisfaction:	=48	(77%)
Research quality:	=33	(1.9)
Entry standards:	30	(388)
Student–staff ratio:	=66	(19)
Services & facilities/student:	22	(£1,870)
Expected completion rate:	27	(91.6%)
Good honours:	=43	(66.0%)
Graduate prospects:	13	(76.4%)

received a 100 per cent rating, while mechanical engineering, sociology and sound recording and audio engineering were all in the top five in their field.

Both the proportions of undergraduates from working-class homes and from areas without a tradition of higher education are lower than average for the university's subjects and entry standards, but the statistics agency has acknowledged that the explanation lies largely in the university's location. There was a big improvement in the latest projected dropout rate. At less than 7 per cent, it was significantly better than the university's benchmark.

Surrey has announced £9,000 fees from 2012, but is promising a package of financial support measures will ensure that talent and potential are the only factors that dictate attendance at the university. A university statement said maximum fees were needed to accommodate a cut of over 60 per cent in its teaching grant and a 70 per cent cut in capital funding, whilst supporting students from low-income families.

The compact campus is a ten-minute walk from the centre of Guildford. Many of the buildings date from the late 1960s, but the new business school, the newly refurbished and extended library and learning centre, and the gleaming European Institute of Health and Medical Sciences offer a striking contrast. The campus includes two lakes, playing fields and enough residential accommodation to enable all first years to live in.

A second campus, under development adjacent to the Stag Hill headquarters, houses the new postgraduate medical school and over 1,500 new residential places for students and staff. Work has begun on a new reception building with café, bar and lounge areas. The impressive Surrey Sports Park opened in 2010, with three multipurpose sports halls, tennis and squash courts, a 50-metre swimming pool, indoor climbing centre, extensive fitness suite and outdoor facilities.

The main campus is the centre of social life, and has seen recent improvements to leisure facilities including new dining and social areas. Guildford has plenty of retail, cultural and recreational facilities and the proximity of London (35 minutes by train) is an attraction to many students, although it also helps account for the high cost of living.

Undergraduate Fees and Support
» Fees for UK/EU students 2012–13 £9,000
» Fees for International students 2011–12 £11,000–£13,750
» A package of financial support, including bursaries and fee waivers, and widening participation activity to be announced.
» Scholarships and bursaries based on circumstances or by competition.
» Check the university's website for the latest information.

Students			Accommodation
Undergraduates:	**8,865**	**(1,330)**	Number of places and costs refer to 2010–11
Postgraduates:	**3,525**	**(1,700)**	University-provided places: 4,851
Mature students:	**18.5%**		Percentage catered: 0%
Overseas students:	**18.0%**		Self-catered costs: £61–£131 a week.
Applications per place:	**5.6**		All first years are guaranteed a place.
From state-sector schools:	**92.9%**		International non-EU students are guaranteed accommodation
From working-class homes:	**28.0%**		for the whole of their course. Remaining places are allocated to
			final year students.

For detailed information about fees, grants and bursaries and how they work, see chapter 7.

Contact: www.surrey.ac.uk/Accommodation

University of Sussex

Sussex has celebrated its 50th anniversary by surging into the top 20 in *The Times* League Table, after moving up 21 places in two years. The latest rise of seven places was again the biggest by any university in the top half of the ranking. The university's reputation was enhanced by good results in the 2008 Research Assessment Exercise, when almost 60 per cent of an unusually large submission was rated as world-leading or internationally excellent. But it has benefited this year from improved satisfaction levels, a better completion rate and higher spending on facilities. The university, which is also rated in the top 100 in the world by *Times Higher Education*, now generates more than a third of its income from private sources, largely in research contracts.

There has been dramatic improvement in Sussex's performance in the National Student Survey over the past four years, propelling the university into the top 15 for satisfaction levels. The results in 2010 showed at least 95 per cent satisfaction in anatomy and physiology, psychology, physics, philosophy, English, biology and human and social geography. Applications increased by 29 per cent in 2010 and at the start of 2011 by another 19 per cent, both well above the national average.

Sussex will charge fees of £9,000 in 2012, but is promising an unusually wide-ranging package of student support that includes a work-study programme to help students earn money, funded work placements and three years' aftercare for graduates to help them into a career. Proposals submitted to the Office for Fair Access also include means-tested support of at least £1,000 a year, plus a £2,000 fee waiver for first years or the equivalent in rent reduction to help them live on campus.

The university was already aiming to improve the student experience with the Sussex Plus initiative, which provides recognition for students' voluntary work and other extracurricular activities. Other career-focused initiatives include an internship placement scheme and a leadership training programme. As part of a focus on flexible learning, the library, which has undergone a £6-million redevelopment, has introduced 24-hour opening during term.

The interdisciplinary approach that has always been Sussex's trademark has been re-examined to adapt this 1960s concept for the 21st century. Arts and social science students take the biggest share of places, but the life sciences are not far behind. The School of Business, Management and Economics, which opened in 2009, offers a portfolio of undergraduate and postgraduate business and management programmes.

Sussex is committed to taking candidates with no family tradition of higher education

---

Sussex House
Brighton BN1 9RH

01273 876787 (enquiries)
ug.enquiries@sussex.ac.uk
www.sussex.ac.uk
www.bsms.ac.uk
www.ussu.info
Affiliation: 1994 Group

The Times Rankings
Overall Ranking: **14**

Student satisfaction:	=12	(81%)
Research quality:	17	(2.4)
Entry standards:	34	(380)
Student–staff ratio:	=39	(16.1)
Services & facilities/student:	38	(£1,569)
Expected completion rate:	=25	(91.7%)
Good honours:	6	(82.7%)
Graduate prospects:	=35	(69.3%)

and has much larger numbers of mature students than most of its peer group of institutions. The proportion of working-class students is significantly lower than the national average for the university's subjects and entry grades, but this is attributed to the university's south coast location. The projected dropout rate has been improving and, at 8 per cent, remains below the university's benchmark.

The campus is located within the newly created South Downs National Park, four miles from the centre of Brighton, with excellent transport links into town. The university is currently completing a £100-million campus development plan, which will refurbish Sir Basil Spence's original buildings and add new ones. A striking new teaching building has opened and work is under way on a £29-million academic building which will provide a mix of lecture theatres, study and teaching space, and a social centre. The Gardner Centre is being brought back to life as the Attenborough Centre for the Creative Arts, an interdisciplinary arts hub for the university and the wider community that will open in 2012.

Student accommodation has also been upgraded and a new residential complex at the north end of campus will open in July 2011. This provides more than 4,000 bedspaces, including many en suite. All first-year students are guaranteed a place in university-managed accommodation if they meet the deadline for applications. Sussex has always attracted overseas students in large numbers and has seen big increases recently. Three times in recent years it has been voted the best university experience in England in the International Student Barometer.

Relations with neighbouring Brighton University are good. The two institutions succeeded in a joint bid for a medical school, which opened in 2003 and has since recorded big increases in applications. The Brighton and Sussex Medical School is split between the Royal Sussex County Hospital and the two universities' Falmer campuses.

There is no shortage of social events on campus and Brighton has plenty to offer. Sports facilities are good enough to house pre-Olympic training. Sports scholarships are available to outstanding athletes, including four reserved for basketball and hockey players.

Undergraduate Fees and Support

» Fees for UK/EU students 2012–13 £9,000
» Fees for International students 2010–11 £10,900–£14,640
  £23,678 (medicine)
» First Generation Scholars scheme for students whose parents did not go to university, or from low-income families, to give at least £1,000 a year plus £2,000 first-year fee waiver or the equivalent in rent reduction, and academic and employability support.
» Check the university's website for the latest information.

Students		
Undergraduates:	**8,310**	**(1,325)**
Postgraduates:	**2,000**	**(940)**
Mature students:	**18.2%**	
Overseas students:	**11.7%**	
Applications per place:	**5.6**	
From state-sector schools:	**88.1%**	
From working-class homes:	**23.8%**	

For detailed information about fees, grants and bursaries and how they work, see chapter 7.

Accommodation

Number of places and costs refer to 2011–12
University-provided places: 4,217
Percentage catered: 0%
Self-catered costs: £67–£125 a week.
First-year students are guaranteed accommodation if conditions are met.
International students: given priority providing conditions are met.
Contact: housing@sussex.ac.uk
www.sussex.ac.uk/study/ug/location/accommodation

Swansea University

Swansea's attractive coastal location and easy access from outside Wales have helped to make it a popular choice for students. Applications rose by nearly 20 per cent in 2010, when those from overseas were up by nearly half, although there was a big reversal in 2011. Most of those who take up places seem to enjoy their time there: Swansea has won awards for the best student experience in the UK and has become established among the best performers in the National Student Survey. Scores dipped in 2010, but until then the university had been in and around the top 25 in every year of the survey. It remained well in the top half of the table, with biology, civil end chemical engineering, classics, economics, German and Scandinavian studies, mechanical engineering, biophysics and sports science all registering satisfaction levels of more than 90 per cent.

Swansea became independent of the University of Wales in 2007 and students now receive a Swansea degree. Independence is intended to reflect confidence in the future, as well as helping with international recruitment and research partnerships. There are now about 500 degree courses in the modular scheme, and undergraduates are encouraged to stray outside their specialist area in their first year.

The university has links to more than 100 partner institutions worldwide and offers many degrees that include opportunities to study abroad. Popular study-abroad summer programmes allow students to experience living and studying in India, China, and the USA. The university has won more than £100 million in European funding for some of its projects, including Graduate Opportunities Wales, which steers students towards small firms through industrial placements and vacation jobs.

The most important academic development, however, came with the opening of the School of Medicine and the subsequent development of a full four-year graduate entry medical degree, launched in 2009. Previous entrants spent half of their course in Cardiff, but the new degree is linked to a new NHS University Health Board and the £50-million Institute of Life Science. The institute is home to Blue C, one of the few supercomputers in the world dedicated to life science research. The Physics Department is involved with CERN's Large Hadron Collider experiment, and was part of the first team to trap antimatter in the form of antihydrogen.

Recent developments include the announcement of a £21.6-million Centre for NanoHealth to be located on the Singleton campus and the opening of a £1.2-million facility in the university library for the Richard Burton Archives. Other additions to the campus include the £4.3-million Digital

---

Singleton Park
Swansea SA2 8PP

01792 295111 (admissions)
admissions@swansea.ac.uk
www.swansea.ac.uk
www.swansea-union.co.uk
Affiliation: none

The Times Rankings
Overall Ranking: **49**

Student satisfaction:	**=48**	(77%)
Research quality:	**=45**	(1.5)
Entry standards:	**=45**	(314)
Student–staff ratio:	**43**	(16.5)
Services & facilities/student:	**70**	(£1,259)
Expected completion rate:	**=34**	(89.4%)
Good honours:	**=73**	(57.7%)
Graduate prospects:	**69**	(60.3%)

Technium Building, for media and communication studies. The School of Engineering houses a £250,000 flight simulator. The university plans to develop a science and innovation campus within Swansea Bay and the Western Valleys region.

Despite its international links, Swansea has not forgotten its local responsibilities. The Department of Adult and Community Education teaches mature students in locations throughout the Valleys and elsewhere in South Wales. Compacts with the region's schools encourage students in areas of economic disadvantage to aspire to higher education.

Swansea makes a particular effort to cater for disabled students, which are coordinated through a £250,000 assessment and training centre. Other access measures have been only partially successful: fewer than 8 per cent of the students come from areas of low participation in higher education, although the 95 per cent share of places going to applicants from state schools and colleges is higher than the UK average for the university's courses and entry grades. The projected dropout rate is below the benchmark set for the university, at less than 10 per cent.

The attractive parkland campus two miles from the centre of Swansea overlooks the sea and offers ready access to the Gower Peninsula, the UK's first Area of Outstanding Natural Beauty. Apart from Singleton Abbey, the neo-Gothic mansion which is the administrative hub, most of the buildings are modern. The 1,800 computers available for student use represent one of the best ratios at any university. The university has recently opened two new halls of residence, providing a further 350 study bedrooms that takes the total to over 3,300.

The university's £20-million Sports Village includes a 50-metre pool, a warm-up pool, athletics track, all-weather pitches, indoor athletics training centre and gym, which attract top performers. The swimming pool is the Wales National Pool, one of only five facilities in the UK to be awarded Intensive Training Centre status. Student activities are mainly focused on campus, but the city has a good range of leisure facilities, including the new LC2 Leisure Centre, which includes Wales' largest indoor water-park and the world's first deep water standing wave machine – the Boardrider.

Undergraduate Fees and Support

» Fees 2012–13: to be announced; able to charge up to £9,000, with Welsh Assembly expected to pay fees above £3,375 for Welsh students.
» Fees for international students 2011–12   £9,800–£12,600
» Scholarships and bursaries based on circumstances or by competition.
» Check the university's website for the latest information.

Students

Undergraduates:	**10,245**	**(2,035)**
Postgraduates:	**1,500**	**(560)**
Mature students:	**17.9%**	
Overseas students:	**8.1%**	
Applications per place:	**4.3**	
From state-sector schools:	**95.1%**	
From working-class homes:	**31.9%**	

For detailed information about fees, grants and bursaries and how they work, see chapter 7.

Accommodation

Number of places and costs refer to 2011–12
University-provided places: about 3,300
Percentage catered: 6%
Catered costs: £103 – £108 a week.
Self-catered costs: £73 (standard) – £108 (en suite) a week.
First-year students holding a firm offer are guaranteed accommodation if conditions are met.
International students: offered up to 3 years.
Contact: www.swansea.ac.uk/accommodation/
accommodation@swansea.ac.uk

Swansea Metropolitan University

Although university status arrived only in 2008, Swansea Met can trace its history back more than 150 years. However, it does not appear in the main league table or in any of the subject tables because the new university has again instructed the Higher Education Statistics Agency not to release data on its performance. Those figures that are available suggest that it would have appeared in the lower reaches of the table, but not right at the bottom.

The 25 academics entered for the 2008 Research Assessment Exercise represented the smallest submission at any UK university but there was some world-leading research in three of the four subject areas in which the university was assessed. Engineering produced the best results. Every faculty has a research director, and a series of research centres is planned.

Similarly, results in the National Student Surveys have been disappointing. Although scores improved slightly in 2010, Swansea Met still ranked around the bottom 20 universities. Only initial teacher training satisfied 90 per cent of the final-year undergraduates.

Swansea Met is divided into four faculties: Applied Design and Engineering, Art and Design, Humanities, and Business and Management. Of more than 6,500 students, just over half are full-time undergraduates, almost half of whom are studying education or the humanities, and a third of whom are over 21 on entry. Surprisingly, given the mix of subjects, more of them are male than female. Two thirds of the undergraduates come from within 45 miles of Swansea, but there is also a long-established tradition of overseas recruitment, which accounts for almost 7 per cent of the places.

Based around the centre of Swansea, the new university is gradually developing an urban campus. There are four sites close to the city centre and another high above the city, overlooking Swansea Bay, for education and the humanities. The main Mount Pleasant campus is the largest in terms of student numbers, hosting design and engineering, business and leisure courses. Its automotive engineering degrees – especially those focused on motorsport – are probably now the best-known feature of the university.

The nearby Dynevor site has seen the most recent development, with £12.5 million spent on such ventures as an impressive new building for the Faculty of Art and Design, which was rated excellent in the (now dated) teaching quality assessments. All the faculty's students undertake an "external project" with a company or outside organisation, which has improved employment prospects in a notoriously difficult group of subjects.

**Mount Pleasant
Swansea SA1 6ED**

01792 481010 (admissions)
enquiry@smu.ac.uk
www.smu.ac.uk
www.metsu.org
Affiliation: none

The Times Rankings

Swansea Metropolitan blocked the release of data from the Higher Education Statistics Agency and so we cannot give any ranking information.

The two smaller sites are the former college of art, which focuses on the university's internationally rated work on architectural stained glass, and the former BBC building, where the music technology degree is located.

The university has recently completed the full acquisition of the Alexandra Road building in Swansea city centre. The building, opened in 1887, was previously home to the city's Central Library but will now be redeveloped into an Institute for Sustainable Design, housing the University School's of Industrial Design and Architectural Glass.

University status arrived at an opportune moment for, while other universities in Wales were experiencing a serious downturn in applications in 2008, its decline was the smallest in the Principality. Swansea Met shared in the applications boom of 2010, with an 18 per cent increase, and the 3 per cent decline at the start of 2011 was smaller than elsewhere in Wales.

Efforts to widen participation in higher education are high on the new university's agenda. About four undergraduates in ten have a working-class background and a high proportion come from areas with little tradition of higher education. Almost all the students are state educated. However, the projected dropout rate is well above average for the university's courses and entry grades, with 23 per cent not expected to complete their course in the expected time.

The university's finances are graded at the highest level by the Welsh funding council and are in the top five in the UK. It is also in the top category of the People and Planet Green League for environmental sustainability. Employability and entrepreneurial skills are embedded into every programme and Swansea Met ranks as the best in Wales for producing successful graduate start-up businesses.

There are over 300 residential places – not enough for all first years – but private housing is plentiful and reasonably priced. The city has seen considerable development recently and has a good range of pubs and clubs. The university's sports facilities are not extensive, but the nearby Gower Peninsula, officially an Area of Outstanding Natural Beauty, is a prime location for surfers and walkers.

Undergraduate Fees and Support

» Fees 2012–13: to be announced; able to charge up to £9,000, with Welsh Assembly expected to pay fees above £3,375 for Welsh students.
» Fees for international students 2011–12 £8,000
» Scholarships and bursaries based on circumstances or by competition.
» Check the university's website for the latest information.

Students

From state-sector schools:	**98.6%**
From working-class homes:	**40.6%**

For detailed information about fees, grants and bursaries and how they work, see chapter 7.

Accommodation

Number of places and costs refer to 2010–11
University-provided places: over 300
Percentage catered: 0%
Self-catered costs: £52.50 (twin) – £70.50 (en suite) a week (40 weeks).
First years cannot be guaranteed accommodation. Residential restrictions apply.
International students: guaranteed accommodation if conditions are met and application received by 31 August.
Contact: accommodation@smu.ac.uk; 01792 482082

Teesside University

Teesside will charge fees of £8,500 a year for all its degrees from 2012, but any qualifications below that level, including Foundation degrees, will cost £6,000. The university said these sums were necessary not only to cover its costs after serious spending cuts, but also to enhance the quality of students' learning experience and allow for further investment in the campus. Teesside has always had a diverse intake and Vice-Chancellor Professor Graham Henderson said that for many students, the associated package of grants, scholarships, loans and other support measures would make higher education much more accessible and affordable.

Teesside was *Times Higher Education*'s University of the Year for 2009, the first post-1992 institution to win the award, for its "outstanding regional economic strategy and strong financial performance." But if that sounds less than wholeheartedly student-focused, above-average results for a post-1992 university in the National Student Survey (NSS) suggest otherwise. The university's mission statement promises a "vibrant and effective learning community" with high academic standards that is committed to social inclusion, as well as benefiting the local economy.

The 2010 NSS showed 100 per cent satisfaction in physiotherapy, but history was the only other subject over 90 per cent. Teesside has also done well in the International Student Barometer. Middlesbrough has never been considered the most fashionable student destination, but the number of international students has soared and total applications were up by more than a quarter in 2010. There had been another 16 per cent increase at the start of 2011.

Teesside has long been among the leading new universities for the proportion of leavers going into graduate-level jobs or further training. The university also improved its grades in the 2008 Research Assessment Exercise, albeit with only a small proportion of its academics submitting work. Computer science and history achieved the best results, while overall 30 per cent of the research was considered world-leading or internationally excellent. Five research-led institutes will focus on digital innovation, health, culture, social science and technology.

Official performance indicators also show the university well ahead of the access benchmarks calculated by the Higher Education Statistics Agency. It takes more undergraduates than any other UK university (around three in ten) from areas of low participation in higher education, while almost half come from working-class homes. The projected dropout rate has improved enormously and, at 11 per cent, is now well below the national average for the courses and entry qualifications.

---

7 Borough Road
Middlesbrough TS1 3BA

01642 218121 (switchboard)
enquiries@tees.ac.uk
www.tees.ac.uk
www.utsu.org.uk
Affiliation: University
Alliance

The Times Rankings
Overall Ranking: **=80**

Student satisfaction:	**=24**	(79%)
Research quality:	**=92**	(0.2)
Entry standards:	**=78**	(271)
Student–staff ratio:	**74**	(19.5)
Services & facilities/student:	**82**	(£1,186)
Expected completion rate:	**99**	(78.0%)
Good honours:	**95**	(52.6%)
Graduate prospects:	**59**	(61.9%)

Over 3,000 students are taking Teesside courses at local further education colleges, which are also involved in the growing range of full-time and part-time two-year Foundation degrees. The university has higher education centres attached to five partner colleges in the Tees Valley and a new £13-million campus will open in Darlington in September 2011. The Passport scheme offers help and guidance to students considering going to university while the prize-winning Meteor scheme gives primary school children a taste of higher education.

There are almost 25,000 undergraduates, two thirds of them taking part-time courses, and more than a third of undergraduates are over 20 on entry. The 9,000 health students are by far the largest group in the university, but Teesside is also strong in niche subjects such as computer games design and animation, sport and exercise, forensic science and health-related courses. A new four-year MEng in civil engineering is to be launched in September 2011, while the new BSc in environmental health has a particular focus on food safety.

More than £130 million has been spent in recent years on the town-centre campus. A £17-million sport and health sciences building, with dentistry training and a hydrotherapy pool, opened in 2010. Recent developments include a centre for creative technologies, for computing, media and design students, and an Institute of Digital Innovation, which supports Middlesbrough's bid to become a Digital City. Over 70 new companies were created with university support in 2009-10, many incubated on campus as graduate business start-ups. Computer provision is generous, with 2,700 work-stations available for student use. Specialist facilities for those studying computer games design, animation and digital media include a new digital sound and TV studio which can create special effects.

Middlesbrough has more nightlife than sceptics might imagine, and the booming student population has attracted new pubs, cafés and student-orientated shops. The cost of living is another attraction: university rents are reasonable and the lively students' union has twice won the title of Students' Union of the Year. Outdoor sports facilities include a watersports centre on the River Tees and Elite Athlete bursaries are available. Mima, the Middlesbrough Institute of Modern Art, is putting the town on the cultural map, and there is a full programme of Culture on Campus events.

Undergraduate Fees and Support

» Fees for UK/EU students 2012–13 £8,500
   Foundation degree £6,000
» Fees for International students 2011–12 £9,750
» A package of grants, scholarships, loans and other support measures to be announced.
» Check the university's website for the latest information.

Students

Undergraduates:	**8,915**	**(15,550)**
Postgraduates:	**1,715**	**(2,455)**
Mature students:	**33.5%**	
Overseas students:	**5.2%**	
Applications per place:	**3.6**	
From state-sector schools:	**99.1%**	
From working-class homes:	**49.6%**	

For detailed information about fees, grants and bursaries and how they work, see chapter 7.

Accommodation

Number of places and costs refer to 2011–12
University-provided places: 1,149
Percentage catered: 0%
Self-catered costs: £52.50–£90.00 a week (residences, 37 weeks); £60–£65 a week (managed housing, 38 weeks)
University managed residences are reserved exclusively for first years.
International students: as above.
Contact: 01642 342255; accommodation@tees.ac.uk; www.tees.ac.uk/accommodation

Trinity St David, University of Wales

No sooner had the new University of Wales Trinity Saint David welcomed its first students than further, more subtle, changes were taking place. A new "strategic alliance" for post-16 education has been formed with Swansea Metropolitan University and three further education colleges in the area. The new arrangements will not compromise the independence of the university, which will be admitting students under its new name for the first time in 2012.

In the whole of England and Wales, only Oxford and Cambridge were awarding degrees before Lampeter, which claimed to be the smallest publicly funded university in Europe before the merger. The former University of Wales, Lampeter is continuing to make a virtue of its size in the new collegiate set-up by stressing its friendly atmosphere and intimate teaching style. With the former Trinity University College 23 miles away in Carmarthen, Lampeter will remain a quiet, rural outpost.

The new institution constitutes a more substantial academic unit, with greater financial security, to serve West Wales. The Welsh Assembly Government and the Higher Education Funding Council for Wales have invested £18 million in the merger to produce a "distinctive and unique curriculum with a strong emphasis on Welsh cultural heritage and bilingualism". The aim is to serve the region, but also to attract students from all around the world through the Confucius Centre, the Islamic Studies Centre and the Welsh American Academy.

The new title echoes Lampeter's original name of St David's College. As the University of Wales, Lampeter, applications had been dropping, but that trend was reversed with a 30 per cent increase in 2010. The number of entrants had already doubled in 2009, as more candidates accepted their offers. Those who go are enthusiastic about Lampeter: as an independent institution, it recorded high levels of satisfaction in every year of the National Student Survey, finishing in the top 20 in 2009.

Based on an ancient castle and modelled on an Oxbridge college, St David's College was established to train young men for the Anglican ministry. The original quadrangle remains and the chapel is in daily use. There have been significant changes in recent few years – notably a big expansion in distance learning and the introduction of such subjects as Chinese studies, anthropology, IT, management, and film and media studies.

Arts-dominated Lampeter is best known for theology, but archaeology produced the best results by far in the 2008 Research Assessment Exercise. The small campus includes a mosque for the growing number of

---

Lampeter Campus
Lampeter
Ceredigion SA48 7ED

01570 422351 (switchboard)
contact via website
www.trinitysaintdavid.ac.uk
www.tsdsu.co.uk
Affiliation: Cathedral Group

The Times Rankings
Overall Ranking: **90**

Student satisfaction:	=73	(75%)
Research quality:	=55	(0.9)
Entry standards:	99	(251)
Student–staff ratio:	63	(18.7)
Services & facilities/student:	85	(£1,170)
Expected completion rate:	102	(76.6%)
Good honours:	108	(48.8%)
Graduate prospects:	=72	(59.7%)

Muslim students attracted by the well-endowed programme of Islamic studies. Media studies, which benefits from a well-equipped media centre for film and television students, is also growing in popularity. A new research centre opened in 2008, housing the Founders' Library collections and the historical archives.

As a university college, Trinity did not qualify for inclusion in this *Guide*, although it was part of the University of Wales. With 2,200 students, including part-timer, it was hardly large, but still twice the size of Lampeter. Established in 1848, it is affiliated to the Church in Wales, but recruits students of all faiths and none. Trinity has a long history of teacher training, with arts and social studies the only other faculty. Results in the National Student Survey were not as good as Lampeter's, but reached the average for Wales. The same cannot be said of the 2010 scores, which placed both halves of the new university well in the bottom half of the UK table under their old identities. Only theology satisfied more than 90 per cent of final-year undergraduates, although history and philosophy came close.

A new suite of art and design courses is being offered in association with Coleg Sir Gar, one of the partners in the new alliance. The subjects include digital illustration, ceramics and jewellery, graphic communication, photography and textiles.

Lampeter is deep in Welsh-speaking rural West Wales, like its new partner, the university has strong bilingual policies. The university also takes Welsh to a wider audience, with the only university course teaching the language over the internet. Although only four hours from London and two from Cardiff, Lampeter's geographical position could be a problem for the unprepared. The town has just 4,000 inhabitants, with among the lowest crime rates in Britain, and the nearest station is more than 20 miles away.

Carmarthen is a county town of 18,000 people with reasonably priced accommodation for the few first-year students who fail to secure a place in one of the three halls of residence. Less remote as well as larger than Lampeter, it has a railway station and is not far from the end of the M4 for car drivers. Both locations are within reach of the sea and stunning countryside.

Undergraduate Fees and Support

» Fees 2012–13: to be announced; able to charge up to £9,000, with Welsh Assembly paying fees above £3,375 for Welsh students.
» Fees for international students 2011–12   £9,348
» Scholarships and bursaries based on circumstances or by competition.
» Check the university's website for the latest information.

Students

Undergraduates:	**2,645**	**(2,120)**
Postgraduates:	**725**	**(610)**
Mature students:	**42.5% (25.6%)***	
Overseas students:	**16.1%**	
Applications per place:	**2.4 (2.8)***	
From state-sector schools:	**93.9% (98.3%)***	
From working-class homes:	**32.5% (43.4%)***	

*First figure for Lampeter, second figure for Trinity College.

For detailed information about fees, grants and bursaries and how they work, see chapter 7.

Accommodation

Number of places and costs refer to 2010-11
L refers to Lampeter, CM to Carmarthen
University-provided places: 500 (L), 512 (CM)
Percentage catered: 0% (L), 44% (CM)
Catered costs: £98 a week; meals for 5 days (CM).
Self-catered costs: £64.60–£82.50 a week (L); £78 a week (CM).
First years can normally be placed in university accommodation.
International students: guaranteed housing for first year.
Contact: www.trinitysaintdavid.ac.uk/en/studentlife/accommodation/

University of Ulster

Ulster is in the top 20 universities in terms of applications and registered another 3 per cent increase in 2011, after a healthy rise the previous year. The university's reputation was further enhanced by its strong performance in the 2008 Research Assessment Exercise. Nearly half of its submission was rated as world-leading or internationally excellent, with the university ranked in the top three for biomedical sciences, Celtic studies, and nursing and midwifery. Research at Ulster generates over £30 million for the Northern Ireland economy.

Plans to transfer activity from the Jordanstown to Belfast campus and expand student numbers on the Magee campus are at an advanced stage. With more Irish students now choosing to stay in the Province to study, there is scope for expansion in Magee, despite the fact that Ulster already has over 25,000 students, including almost 9,000 part-timers.

There are four campuses – at Coleraine, Jordanstown (seven miles outside Belfast), Magee in Londonderry, and in Belfast city centre. Each campus has a distinct character and while some courses are offered at more than one campus, there is a degree of specialisation across the campuses. Belfast concentrates on art and design, architecture and hospitality and tourism management. Jordanstown concentrates on business and management, the built environment, computing and engineering, health and sports sciences and social sciences. At Coleraine there is a focus on the environmental and life sciences, humanities and services management, whist at Magee there is a concentration on the creative and performing arts, nursing and social work, computing and engineering, business and management and social sciences. The Magee campus will be intimately involved in Londonderry's activities as the UK City of Culture in 2013. Magee is a major component in the cultural life of the city, being home to teaching, performance and research of international excellence in the creative arts, including music, dance and drama.

All undergraduates complete their studies on a single campus which each have well-equipped learning resource centres. Accommodation is guaranteed for first-year students at all four campuses. The university matched the UK average for satisfaction levels in the 2010 National Student Survey, with sociology scoring 100 per cent and tourism, transport and travel, accounting, finance and law also achieving good scores.

In 2009, the university announced ambitious £250-million capital development plans which will see most of the activity currently based at Jordanstown transferred to the university's Belfast campus, where it

---

Cromore Road
Coleraine
Co. Londonderry
BT52 1SA

028 701 23456
(switchboard)
enquiry via website
www.ulster.ac.uk
www.uusu.org
Affiliation: none

COLERAINE
Edinburgh
Belfast
London
Cardiff

The Times Rankings
Overall Ranking: **56**

Student satisfaction:	=37	(78%)
Research quality:	=52	(1.1)
Entry standards:	=86	(266)
Student–staff ratio:	45	(17)
Services & facilities/student:	43	(£1,515)
Expected completion rate:	=60	(84.4%)
Good honours:	65	(60.4%)
Graduate prospects:	99	(53.9%)

has acquired a substantial additional site in the city's Cathedral Quarter. Jordanstown will be retained and developed further as Ireland's only dedicated sports campus. The university is already well positioned in this regard having won 33 sporting titles across the island of Ireland in 2009–10. Over £20 million has already been invested here in a new high performance sports centre. Facilities include an indoor sports hall, outdoor and indoor sprint tracks, a strength and conditioning suite, water recovery area and sports science and sports medicine facilities.

A further expansion in student numbers is planned and will be concentrated at Magee where the university has recently signed an option agreement which will see Ulster almost double its footprint in the city. Plans for expansion at Magee include an Institute of Health and Wellbeing and an Institute of Sustainable Technologies. Magee also houses a Centre of Intelligent Systems and the historic Foyle Arts Centre. Further expansion is also planned in the schools of creative arts, computing and electronics as well as nursing.

Coleraine is home to the £11-million Centre for Molecular Biosciences. Building on its expertise, the university also introduced a new programme in pharmacy. Ulster has a strong commitment to widening access and is consistently among the top ten universities in terms of admitting students from the less advantaged socio-economic groups. The projected dropout rate had improved in the latest survey but, at nearly 16 per cent, was still higher than the benchmark calculated according to the university's subjects and entry grades. A range of scholarships is available including sports scholarships and others for high achievers in economically relevant subjects such as engineering, computing, science and economics.

The university's contingent of inter-national students includes many from the Republic of Ireland as well as further afield. The eLearning at Ulster programme provides an alternative mode of study, offering courses online to students all over the world. With more than half of Ulster's students home based, the university is not always the focus of social life. The exception is the Coleraine campus, although many gravitate towards the nearby seaside towns of Portrush and Portstewart.

Undergraduate Fees and Support

» Fees 2012–13: awaiting Northern Ireland Executive policy.
» Fees for UK/EU students 2011–12 £3,375
» Fees for international students 2011–12 £9,225
» Scholarships and bursaries based on circumstances or by competition.
» Check the university's website for the latest information.

Students

Undergraduates:	**15,410**	**(5,205)**
Postgraduates:	**1,540**	**(3,880)**
Mature students:	**21.0%**	
Overseas students:	**9.5%**	
Applications per place:	**5.9**	
From state-sector schools:	**99.9%**	
From working-class homes:	**49.4%**	

For detailed information about fees, grants and bursaries and how they work, see chapter 7.

Accommodation

Number of places and costs refer to 2010–11
University-provided places: 2,308
Percentage catered: 0%
Self-catered costs: average £76.64 a week (37 weeks).
First-year students are guaranteed accommodation if conditions are met.
International students: same as above.
Contact: accommodation@ulster.ac.uk
www.accommodation.ulster.ac.uk/

University of the Arts London

Expensive courses, a central London location and the loss of virtually all its Government teaching grant made £9,000 fees inevitable at the University of the Arts London from 2012. The university said that even after two years of efficiencies, it needed £8,600 fees just to stand still. The remainder would help it increase access initiatives and improve the student experience. The collection of world-famous art, design, fashion and media colleges that constituted the London Institute became a university in 2005. With over 20,000 further and higher education students spread through 17 sites around central London, it is Europe's largest arts university. Unlike the other new foundations of that year, it has a research remit and is already becoming a powerful "brand".

The five component colleges became six when Wimbledon College of Art joined in 2006, bringing an international reputation in theatre design and the UK's largest school of theatre. The founding members, which continue to use their own names and enjoy considerable autonomy, were Camberwell College of Arts, Central Saint Martins College of Art and Design, Chelsea College of Art and Design, London College of Fashion and London College of Communication (formerly the London College of Printing). From September 2011, the University is offering one Foundation course across Camberwell, Chelsea and Wimbledon.

Big changes were already under way before the change of title was agreed: a £70-million development programme has produced prestigious new premises for Chelsea College next door to the Tate Gallery, on Millbank, with extensive workshop facilities, studios and an impressive new library. Another £32 million was spent on new headquarters for the College of Communication at the Elephant and Castle, south of the Thames, where a newly built Special Archives and Collections Centre includes the archives of the filmmaker Stanley Kubrick. The college now has Film Academy status.

London's largest open air art gallery was launched in 2008 on the Parade Ground at the heart of the Chelsea College of Art and Design, and final-year students' work is also showcased online at a virtual degree show. The next major project will bring Central Saint Martins together on one site for the first time, when it moves to the new King's Cross development. Published assessments have barely done justice to the eminence of the colleges, although the 2008 Research Assessment Exercise saw half of the university's submission rated as world-leading or internationally excellent.

---

272 High Holborn
London WC1V 7EY

0207 514 6197 (enquiries)
admissions@arts.ac.uk
www.arts.ac.uk
www.suarts.org
Affiliation: none

Edinburgh
Belfast
Cardiff
LONDON

The Times Rankings
Overall Ranking: **=82**

Student satisfaction:	112	(64%)
Research quality:	=33	(1.9)
Entry standards:	73	(276)
Student–staff ratio:	=82	(20.2)
Services & facilities/student:	=88	(£1,148)
Expected completion rate:	=37	(89.0%)
Good honours:	46	(64.8%)
Graduate prospects:	101	(53.1%)

Chelsea and London College of Fashion were jointly awarded a national teaching centre for the arts, focusing on practice-based teaching and learning. All the colleges make good use of visiting lecturers, who keep students abreast of current developments in their field. Two university staff were awarded National Teaching Fellowships in 2010. Yet Arts London had the lowest score in the UK in the 2010 National Student Survey, the third time in four years that it had been in this position. Cosmetic science, media studies and the performing arts were the only subjects to score more than 70 per cent satisfaction, while the 21 per cent satisfaction rate in marketing may have been the lowest score in the entire survey.

The figures have not affected applications, which have risen every year since the university was established: there was a massive 43 per cent increase in 2010 and another 15 per cent rise at the start of 2011. The university has been running weekend classes and summer schools in an attempt to broaden the intake, as well as organising a national event to help students with their portfolios, and the proportion of undergraduates from working-class homes is now over a quarter. The projected dropout rate has been improving and, at 10 per cent, is now better than average for the subjects on offer.

Students have access to the largest art and design specialist careers information centre in the country, while the pioneering Emerging Artists Programme continues to support graduates in the early years of their careers. The university held the first ever recruitment festival tailored to the needs of creative graduates in 2010, providing access to hundreds of industry professionals for networking opportunities and advice.

The colleges vary considerably in character and facilities, although a single students' union serves them all. The university's student hub, which provides a central place for students to work, socialise and share ideas, as well as housing student services such as housing and careers, moved to a new, centrally located building in 2010. The university is not overprovided with residential accommodation, although there are 13 residences spread around the colleges, providing more than 2,400 beds. House-hunting workshops help those who have to rely on an expensive private housing market. The university owns no sports facilities, although it has arranged student discounts with a number of providers.

Undergraduate Fees and Support

» Fees for UK/EU students 2012–13 — £9,000
» Fees for International students 2011–12 — £12,700
» Under the National Scholarship Programme (NSP) around 300 awards of £3,000 for year 1 and £1,000 for other years; £1,000 for students from low-income groups who do not qualify for the NSP. Details to be confirmed.
» Check the university's website for the latest information.

Students

Undergraduates:	**12,760**	**(450)**
Postgraduates:	**2,360**	**(855)**
Mature students:	**21.8%**	
Overseas students:	**35.1%**	
Applications per place:	**7.6**	
From state-sector schools:	**90.0%**	
From working-class homes:	**29.4%**	

For detailed information about fees, grants and bursaries and how they work, see chapter 7.

Accommodation

Number of places and costs refer to 2011–12
University-provided places: 2,438
Percentage catered: 0%
Self-catered costs: £119–£190 a week.
First-year students are offered accommodation if conditions are met. Priority for disabled students and those from outside London.
International students: guaranteed if conditions met.
Contact: www.arts.ac.uk/housing/
accommodation@arts.ac.uk

University College London

Such is the breadth and quality of provision at University College London (UCL) that, although part of the University of London, it can fairly describe itself as one of the top multi-faculty institutions in Europe. It ranks in the top five both in *The Times* League Table and in the QS World University Rankings. UCL's excellence is built on a history of pioneering subjects that have become commonplace in higher education: modern languages, geography and fine arts among them. It will charge £9,000 undergraduate fees in 2012, but is promising an "ambitious and innovative" programme of student support and outreach initiatives to maintain access to UCL for students from poor backgrounds. Another important change in 2012 will be a new requirement for a foreign language GCSE at grade C or above, although students will be allowed to reach this standard at UCL if they have not taken a language at school.

The 2008 Research Assessment Exercise provided further confirmation of UCL's academic power, with two thirds of its submission judged to be world-leading or internationally excellent. The top scorers were economics, which saw 95 per cent of its work rated in the top two categories, and computer science and informatics, immunology and infection, environmental sciences and history of art, all of which had at least 80 per cent at this level. Architecture, chemical engineering, cancer studies, law, philosophy and psychology also produced outstanding results.

Comfortably the largest of London University's colleges, UCL has grown rapidly in the past two decades and can now award its own degrees. It took in a number of specialist schools and institutes at the end of the 1990s. UCL's medical school, with 11 associated teaching hospitals, is now a large and formidable unit. Its credentials were strengthened still further with the announcement that UCL will be a founding partner in the new UK Centre for Medical Research and Innovation to be constructed adjacent to St Pancras Station. The centre will undertake cutting-edge research to advance understanding of health and disease. In 2012 London University's School of Pharmacy, located close by, will become part of UCL.

The various acquisitions mean that there are now outposts in several parts of central and north London, as well as plans for an archaeology and conservation campus in Qatar, but the main activity remains centred on the original impressive Bloomsbury site. UCL is pioneering the idea of education for global citizenship, ensuring students are given the opportunity and encouragement to explore academic ideas from different cultural perspectives and to work on problems of international importance, as

Gower Street
London WC1E 6BT

020 7679 2000 (main switchboard)
contact via website
www.ucl.ac.uk
www.uclu.org
Affiliation: Russell Group

The Times Rankings
Overall Ranking: **5**

Student satisfaction:	=37	(78%)
Research quality:	=4	(3.0)
Entry standards:	8	(477)
Student–staff ratio:	2	(9.7)
Services & facilities/student:	7	(£2,207)
Expected completion rate:	10	(94.9%)
Good honours:	4	(83.2%)
Graduate prospects:	7	(81.1%)

well as contributing to their local community and the university's social and cultural life.

UCL has done better than most London universities in the National Student Survey, with 87 per cent of final-year undergraduates expressing satisfaction in the results published in 2010. There was 100 per cent satisfaction in archaeological science, while classics, modern languages and pharmacy all produced high scores. A growing number of degrees take four years, and most are organised on a modular basis.

About 9,000 of UCL's students – almost a third – are from overseas, nearly half of them postgraduates. The proportion is likely to rise further in the coming years. All first-year students are helped to make the academic and social adjustment to university life through UCL's Transition Programme, which includes a variety of activities such as peer mentoring and workshops. UCL stresses its commitment to teaching in small groups, especially in the second and subsequent years of degree courses. The projected dropout rate of 5 per cent is better than the national average for UCL's courses and entry grades. Applications were down slightly at the start of 2011 but, with nearly nine applicants chasing each place, entry will remain highly competitive.

UCL is conscious of its traditions as a college founded to expand access to higher education, but the 35 per cent share of places going to independent school students is one of the highest in Britain. Around one undergraduate in five has a working-class background. Concerted attempts are being made to broaden the intake with summer schools for state-school students, outreach activities and campus-based programmes. UCL is sponsoring a new academy, which it sees as part of its contribution to the local community.

The academic pace can be frantic but, close to the West End and with its own theatre and recreational facilities, there is no shortage of leisure options. Students also have immediate access to London University's under-used central students' union facilities. Residential accommodation is plentiful and of a good standard. Indoor sports and fitness facilities are close at hand, but the main outdoor pitches, though good enough to attract professional football clubs, are a (free) coach ride away in Hertfordshire. Hockey players have access to Astroturf pitches at the Old Cranleighans ground, in Thames Ditton.

Undergraduate Fees and Support

» Fees for UK/EU students 2012–13 £9,000
» Fees for International students 2010–11 £13,410–£7,560
£26,190 (medicine)
» A package of financial support and widening participation activity to be announced.
» Scholarships and bursaries based on circumstances or by competition.
» Check the university's website for the latest information.

Students		
Undergraduates:	**12,060**	**(700)**
Postgraduates:	**7,500**	**(2,960)**
Mature students:	**12.1%**	
Overseas students:	**31.6%**	
Applications per place:	**8.6**	
From state-sector schools:	**64.1%**	
From working-class homes:	**21.1%**	

For detailed information about fees, grants and bursaries and how they work, see chapter 7.

Accommodation

Number of places and costs refer to 2011–12
University-provided places: 4,545 (including 819 intercollegiate places)
Percentage catered: 30%
Catered costs: £151.76–£170.38 a week (39 weeks).
Self-catered costs: £90.86–£189.00 a week (39 weeks).
First years are guaranteed accommodation if conditions are met.
International students: as above.
Contact: Residences@ucl.ac.uk
www.ucl.ac.uk/admissions/accommodation

University for the Creative Arts (UCA)

England's newest university is the product of a merger between two well-established arts institutes straddling Kent and Surrey. Indeed, the first version of its title was the unwieldy University for the Creative Arts at Canterbury, Epsom, Farnham, Maidstone and Rochester, although the multiple locations have since been dropped. The constituent colleges all date back to Victorian times, but university status arrived only in 2008. The site of each college is on the map below: Canterbury (1), Epsom (2), Farnham (3), Maidstone (4) and Rochester (5).

With about 6,000 students, UCA is already sizeable by the standards of specialist institutions. Applications for 2010 were up by more than 30 per cent and there has been another small rise at the start of 2011. With these figures, the university's original plan to grow to 9,000 students by 2017 would not seem unrealistic if Government policy allowed. A new campus in Kent is expected by 2017, complementing the university's ambitious expansion aims.

By far the largest enrolment is at Farnham, in Surrey, where more than 2,000 students take courses in art, design, cinematics and communications. There is a purpose-built student village with 350 rooms in the centre of town and two galleries, as well as teaching space and a library and learning centre. The campus boasts Oscar and BAFTA winners in animation in its pre-university days. It is now home to research centres in animation, crafts and sustainable design. Courses range from pre-degree Foundation courses in art and design to degrees in film production, motoring journalism and three-dimensional design.

The other four sites are of similar size in terms of student numbers. The second base in Surrey, at Epsom, specialises in fashion, graphics and new media, although it offers general art and design courses at further education level. Degrees include music journalism and fashion promotion and imaging. There is a modern library and learning resource centre for more than 1,200 students, a bar and café on campus and three halls of residence, the latest of which opened in 2010. A new £5.9-million teaching block, which will be ready for the start of the 2011 academic year, will include learning and resource facilities, a 200-seat auditorium and a digital media centre. Photovoltaic cells on the roof and solar water heating will ensure that at least 20 per cent of the energy it uses is generated on site.

The largest of the three Kent campuses is at Rochester, which offers a full range of art and design, including fashion, photography and specialist design courses. The purpose-built campus is set on a hillside overlooking

---

UCA Canterbury
New Dover Road
Canterbury
Kent CT1 3AN

01252 892883 (enquiries)
admissions@ucreative.ac.uk
www.ucreative.ac.uk
www.uccasu.com
Affiliation: Guild HE

The Times Rankings
Overall Ranking: **=102**

Student satisfaction:	**110**	(66%)
Research quality:	**=62**	(0.5)
Entry standards:	**=81**	(269)
Student–staff ratio:	**=101**	(21.6)
Services & facilities/student:	**35**	(£1,583)
Expected completion rate:	**54**	(85.2%)
Good honours:	**92**	(53.3%)
Graduate prospects:	**107**	(50.8%)

the city centre and River Medway. Halls of residence with 214 places are close to the campus, which has studio space, library and learning resource centre and a gallery.

The Maidstone campus is in parkland, ten minutes from the centre of town, with another gallery and extensive library. The integrated teaching and research facilities include a multi-user video editing facility and video studio, printmaking area, animation resources and a specialist photography resource. Courses for more than 900 students encourage interdisciplinary study. So many aspiring students had to be rejected in 2010 that a new broadcast media degree was launched in January 2011 to accommodate some of the disappointed applicants.

At Canterbury, the accent is on architecture, but there are also degrees in fine art, interior design and more general art and design. The modern site is close to the city centre and contains purpose-built studios, workshops and lecture theatres. The Canterbury School of Architecture is the only such school to remain within a specialist art and design institution, encouraging collaboration between student architects, designers and fine artists.

The university offers four-year degrees, incorporating a Foundation year, as well as the three-year format and two-year Foundation degrees, which can be topped up to produce Honours. However, results in the National Student Survey have been poor in all five years of polling, as they have been for art and design generally. The 2010 scores left the university marooned in the bottom three. Only architecture satisfied more than 80 per cent of final-year undergraduates and no other course reached even 70 per cent.

Many staff are practitioners as well as academics and the colleges have produced a string of famous graduates, such as Tracy Emin, Karen Millen and Zandra Rhodes, who has now become the university's Chancellor. There is also a strong research culture, although UCA had only limited success in the 2008 Research Assessment Exercise. Thirty per cent of the university's submission was considered world-leading or internationally excellent, but this left it well down the ranking for art and design.

Undergraduate Fees and Support

- » Fees for UK/EU students 2012–13   to be announced
- » Fees for International students 2011–12   £10,660
- » A package of financial support and widening participation activity to be announced.
- » Scholarships and bursaries based on circumstances or by competition.
- » Check the university's website for the latest information.

Students

Undergraduates:	**5,195**	**(240)**
Postgraduates:	**270**	**(105)**
Mature students:	**17.8%**	
Overseas students:	**10.2%**	
Applications per place:	**5.2**	
From state-sector schools:	**97.2%**	
From working-class homes:	**38.4%**	

For detailed information about fees, grants and bursaries and how they work, see chapter 7.

Accommodation

Places and costs refer to 2010–11
University-provided places: 1,127
Percentage catered: 0%
Self catered costs: £51.90 (shared) – £114 (en suite) a week.
Priority is given to disabled students (new and returning) and new full-time students by distance.
International students: guaranteed housing if application received by mid June
Contact: accommodation@ucreative.ac.uk; www.ucreative.ac.uk

University of Warwick

The most successful of the first wave of 1960s new universities, Warwick was derided by many in its early years for its close links with business and industry. Few are critical today. Gordon Brown described it as "one of the great universities, absolutely central to the industrial, scientific and technological future of our country". Research was very highly rated in the 2008 assessments, but the university's mission statement still stresses the extension of access to higher and continuing education and community links. The university will charge £9,000 undergraduate fees from 2012, but students from the poorest backgrounds would receive up to half of that amount in fee waivers and bursaries.

There is a smaller proportion of independent school students than at most of the leading universities – around a quarter – although this does not translate into large numbers of working-class undergraduates. The share of places going to students from the lowest social classes and the representation from areas sending few young people to higher education are both a little below the national average for Warwick's subjects and entry qualifications. But the mix helps to produce one of the lowest dropout rates in Britain at less than 5 per cent. Warwick puts almost a third of its income from top-up fees into bursaries and financial support – one of the highest proportions among the old universities.

Almost two thirds of the work submitted for the 2008 Research Assessment Exercise was considered world-leading or internationally excellent, placing Warwick among the top ten universities. Film and television studies, and horticultural research achieved two of the top scores for any subject at any university, while pure maths, French and Italian were in the top three. There were particularly high grades, too, for economics, applied maths, and theatre, performance and cultural studies.

The university was a late starter in the National Student Survey, due to opposition from the students' union, but is now in the top 20. English studies, German, accounting, finance, mechanical, production and manufacturing engineering, media studies, operational research, physics and astronomy, classics, European languages, history, French studies, history and archaeology, and psychology all produced good scores. Warwick was awarded a national teaching centre in theatrical performance, in partnership with the Royal Shakespeare Company, and is collaborating with Oxford Brookes University on another centre to "reinvent" undergraduate research. It has also been funded to help devise a blueprint for improving the undergraduate curriculum in research-led universities. The science park is among the most successful in the UK.

Coventry CV4 7AL

024 7652 3723 (admissions)
ugadmissions@warwick.ac.uk
www.warwick.ac.uk
www.warwicksu.com
Affiliation: Russell Group

Edinburgh
Belfast
COVENTRY
Cardiff
London

The Times Rankings
Overall Ranking: **8**

Student satisfaction:	=20	(80%)
Research quality:	=9	(2.7)
Entry standards:	7	(480)
Student–staff ratio:	15	(14.1)
Services & facilities/student:	13	(£1,998)
Expected completion rate:	8	(95.5%)
Good honours:	9	(80.7%)
Graduate prospects:	20	(72.5%)

The university invested shrewdly in business, science and engineering and there is now a thriving graduate entry medical school, with more than 2,000 students and new professional courses in implant dentistry. Warwick is also one of the few leading universities to embrace two-year Foundation degrees, running courses in education and community enterprise, the latter taught by a local further education college.

With over eight applicants for every place on conventional degree courses, many departments stick rigidly to offers averaging more than an A and two Bs at A level. Applications have been buoyant but, like most of the universities at the top of *The Times* League Table, Warwick did not see a big increase at the start of 2010, when the rise was only 0.5 per cent and initial data on 2011 applications show a 9 per cent fall in applications. Warwick has built up its numbers in science and engineering, however, as other universities have struggled to fill their places. The business school has grown rapidly, with a new £15-million extension, while chemistry and physics have acquired new facilities.

The recent impressive financial investment is set to continue to 2015 with another £150 million being spent on campus infrastructure. A second significant extension to students' union facilities opened in 2010 and an £8-million extension to the Warwick Arts Centre, which attracts over 250,000 visitors a year, has just been completed. A new Centre for Mechanochemical Cell Biology, an analytical science research facility for the physics and chemistry departments, and a £2.5-million refurbishment programme in engineering are currently underway.

There is also a £12.5-million building that houses a digital laboratory for manufacturing and engineering research, and a clinical trials unit. The university will also benefit from one of the largest donations ever from a member of staff, after Professor Lord Bhattacharyya made a £1-million commitment and has asked that it be put towards research.

The 750-acre campus is three miles south of Coventry, where many students choose to live, and three times as far from Warwick. University accommodation is plentiful, and more is in the pipeline, designed with environmental friendliness in mind. The sports facilities are both extensive and conveniently placed on campus.

Undergraduate Fees and Support

» Fees for UK/EU students 2012–13 £9,000
  Degrees to widen access , e.g. Warwick 2+2 degrees £6,000
» Fees for International students 2011–12 £12,325–£16,000
» Students with household income below £25K, fee waivers and bursaries up to £4,500; details to be confirmed.
» Scholarships and bursaries based on circumstances or by competition.
» Check the university's website for the latest information.

Students

Undergraduates:	**11,900**	**(7,220)**
Postgraduates:	**4,700**	**(5,045)**
Mature students:	**9.1%**	
Overseas students:	**20.2%**	
Applications per place:	**8.3**	
From state-sector schools:	**76.6%**	
From working-class homes:	**19.0%**	

For detailed information about fees, grants and bursaries and how they work, see chapter 7.

Accommodation

Number of places and costs refer to 2011–12
University-provided places: 6,282 (on campus); 1,750 (head leasing)
Percentage catered: 0%
Self-catered costs: £76–£145 a week (30, 37, 39 and 50 week contracts).
First-year undergraduates are prioritised for campus accommodation (terms and conditions apply).
International students as above
Contact: www.warwick.ac.uk/accommodation

University of West London

The former Thames Valley University has changed its name to reflect its new, narrower geographical focus. Having tried the expansion route, the university has decided to concentrate most of its activities on its original home in Ealing, where the main building has been refurbished. The university has said that, because of these changes, it is refusing to release data on its performance and so does not appear in the main league table or in any subject tables. It may hope that a change of identity has the same positive impact as Luton's switch to the University of Bedfordshire had for that institution. Although applications have been more than healthy in the past two years, Thames Valley was still associated in the public mind with past shortcomings.

The Slough campus, where the university built an award-winning learning resources centre designed by Richard Rogers, closed in the summer of 2010. Its 1,000 full-time students, two thirds of whom are on pre-registration nursing courses, have moved to the Reading campus, leaving just part-time business courses and some post-registration nursing in Slough, at a different site. The restructuring will not alter the aim to become the country's leading university for employer engagement, with an accent on the creative industries and entrepreneurship.

The Reading campus, a former college site that is still being redeveloped, has been mainly concerned with further education with some locally focused higher education. Now, however, it may host social work degrees transferred from Reading University, as well as the new nursing portfolio. The Ealing campus has a more traditional university feel and has been refurbished and upgraded at a cost of almost £10 million. The landmark Paragon Building in Brentford, not far from the Ealing campus, will remain the headquarters of one of the largest healthcare faculties in Britain. It contains 850 residential places, as well as teaching facilities.

The university has recovered from a traumatic period at the end of the 1990s, following official criticism of academic standards and a collapse in student demand. The university is virtually unrecognisable from those dark days, having seen an extra-ordinary 56 per cent increase in applications in 2010 – the most at any university in England and one of the biggest rises ever. This was followed by another increase of more than a third at the start of 2011.

Courses are now concentrated in three faculties – Arts, Professional Studies, and Health and Human Sciences. Many further education programmes are being extended into degrees or professional qualifications. Amid the reconstruction, new honours degrees have been launched in areas such as video production, 3D design, computing and

St Mary's Road
Ealing
London W5 5RF

0800 036 8888 (admissions)
learning.advice@uwl.ac.uk
www.uwl.ac.uk
www.westlondonsu.com
Affiliation: million+

Edinburgh
Belfast
Cardiff
LONDON

The Times Rankings
West London blocked the release of data from the Higher Education Statistics Agency and so we cannot give any ranking information.

information systems. The portfolio of two-year Foundation degrees is growing, with employers such as Compaq, Ealing Studios and the Savoy Hotel Group helping to provide courses. Some are run in conjunction with Stratford-upon-Avon College – one of a number of partner institutions.

Nursing courses are popular and well regarded, while the School of Hospitality and Tourism is recognised by the Académie Culinaire de France for its culinary arts programmes. The London College of Music, which is part of West London, has some of the longest-established music technology courses in the country. The university had been improving its scores in the National Student Survey, but slumped by five percentage points in 2010, when most universities enjoyed increases, finishing in the bottom five. Only psychology achieved a satisfaction rate of more than 90 per cent, with biology coming closest to that mark. Cinematics and photography, communications and information studies and creative arts were all below 40 per cent.

A policy of open access puts the university at a disadvantage on other measures in our ranking. The projected dropout rate had also been improving, but was back up to 26 per cent in the latest survey, well above the norm for universities with similar entry requirements and curriculum. Three quarters of the students are over 24, and about 60 per cent are female. Almost half of the undergraduates come from working-class homes. The university is also very ethnically diverse with only one third of undergraduates of white, European origin.

West London improved its ratings considerably in the 2008 Research Assessment Exercise, but entered only a small proportion of its academics. Only nursing and midwifery was judged to have world-leading research.

The town-centre sites in Brentford and Ealing are linked by a free bus service, and Ealing is within easy reach of central London. Almost half of the students are from the capital or Berkshire, and there is an unexpectedly large contingent of international students.

Residential accommodation is growing and the Paragon building won *Building* magazine's Major Housing Project of the Year award. However, students relying on private housing find the cost of living high. Sports facilities are limited, but there is a football ground and cricket pitch close to the Ealing campus.

Undergraduate Fees and Support

» Fees for UK/EU students 2012–13   to be announced
» Fees for International students 2011–12   £8,150–£9,540
» A package of financial support and widening participation activity to be announced.
» Scholarships and bursaries based on circumstances or by competition.
» Check the university's website for the latest information.

Students

From state-sector schools:	**98.7%**
From working-class homes:	**49.6%**

For detailed information about fees, grants and bursaries and how they work, see chapter 7.

Accommodation

Number of places and costs refer to 2011–12
University-provided places: 839
Percentage catered: 0%
Self-catered costs: from £127 a week (incl. utilities and internet).
First years are allocated housing on a first come, first served basis.
International students: same as above.
Contact: uas@uwl.ac.uk
www.uwl.ac.uk/students/student_life/Accommodation.jsp

University of the West of England, Bristol (UWE)

The University of the West of England (UWE) is the largest provider of higher education in the southwest of England and one of the most popular post-1992 universities, both in terms of total applications and the proportion who subsequently choose to study there – one in four. Applications were up by 15 per cent in 2010, although there was only a small rise at the start of 2011. The university enjoyed a series of increases over the past decade. UWE is planning a £150-million extension and development of its main campus, eventually closing some outlying sites, but few of the changes will affect those admitted in 2012.

UWE has sometimes found itself in trouble for missing its benchmarks for widening access to higher education, but it has broadened its intake considerably in recent years. The proportion of independent school entrants has dropped to just 11 per cent – still a figure exceeded by only one new university – while the share of places going to students from working-class homes is around a third. UWE has one of England's largest bursary schemes, with annual awards of £1,000 going to about a third of its students. At 17 per cent, the projected dropout rate had been coming down, but is still well above the national average for the university's subjects and entry qualifications.

The university's scores slipped in the 2010 National Student Survey, but were still close to the national average. There were particularly high levels of satisfaction in history, drama, architecture, human and social geography and mathematical sciences. Unusually, the university trains and pays its 900 student representatives – the biggest such network in the country – while a development programme helps new students settle in and supports them throughout their studies. More than half of the students come from the West Country and there are close links with business and industry. These provide guest lecturers, professors involved in practice, and thousands of part-time jobs and work placements for students, as well as helping to ensure that the curriculum is up-to-date and relevant. Most recent strong links include CERN in Geneva, Hewlett Packard and the BBC.

A tradition of vocational education regularly helps the university to a healthy graduate employment record. The entrance system credits vocational qualifications and practical experience equally with traditional academic results. Law received a commendation from the Legal Practice Board and the degree in architecture and planning won a similar accolade from the Royal Town Planning Institute for bringing together the two disciplines in one joint-honours course

---

Frenchay Campus
Coldharbour Lane
Bristol BS16 1QY

0117 965 6261 (switchboard)
contact via website
www.uwe.ac.uk
www.uwesu.org
Affiliation: University Alliance

The Times Rankings
Overall Ranking: **=67**

Student satisfaction:	=63	(76%)
Research quality:	=62	(0.5)
Entry standards:	72	(278)
Student–staff ratio:	=91	(20.7)
Services & facilities/student:	61	(£1,317)
Expected completion rate:	76	(82.1%)
Good honours:	53	(62.2%)
Graduate prospects:	62	(61.4%)

giving dual professional qualifications. UWE is one of just four universities recognised by the Forensic Science Society for the quality of courses in the subject. It has some 85 undergraduate and postgraduate courses with professional accreditation.

Only two new universities entered more academics than UWE in the 2008 Research Assessment Exercise. More than a third of the work was judged to be world-leading or internationally excellent. Physiotherapy and other health subjects, media studies and general engineering produced the best results.

For the moment, there are four sites in Bristol itself, mainly around the north of the city. Only Bower Ashton, which has new studio space and media suites for its art, media and design students, is in the south. The main campus at Frenchay, four miles out of the city centre, has already doubled in size and is to expand again after the purchase of adjoining land. It includes the largest exhibition and conference centre in the southwest, allowing it to stage major careers fairs for its students and enhance links with employers. The St Matthias campus is to close and its social sciences and humanities courses transferred to Frenchay over the next two years. Glenside campus is home to midwifery, nursing, occupational therapy, physiotherapy and radiography.

A network of 15 colleges stretches into Somerset and Wiltshire, offering UWE programmes. Hartpury College, near Gloucester, has become an associate faculty of the university, specialising in agriculture, equine studies and other land-based courses, and there are university centres in hospitals in Bath and Swindon that concentrate nursing and allied health professions.

Bristol is a hugely popular student centre: an attractive and lively city, but not cheap. University accommodation has become more plentiful in recent years, with over 4,000 places available, including nearly 2,000 in a new £80-million student village on the Frenchay campus. Sports facilities were a bone of contention for students, but a new sports complex opened in 2006 as part of a £300-million investment programme, which is one of the largest in UK higher education. It has been chosen as a pre-Olympics training site for badminton, fencing, table tennis, indoor volleyball and wrestling.

Undergraduate Fees and Support

» Fees for UK/EU students 2012–13   to be announced
» Fees for International students 2011–12   £10,500
» A package of financial support and widening participation activity to be announced.
» Scholarships and bursaries based on circumstances or by competition.
» Check the university's website for the latest information.

Students		
Undergraduates:	**20,135**	**(6,110)**
Postgraduates:	**1,710**	**(4,885)**
Mature students:	**20.2%**	
Overseas students:	**8.2%**	
Applications per place:	**4.8**	
From state-sector schools:	**88.5%**	
From working-class homes:	**33.9%**	

For detailed information about fees, grants and bursaries and how they work, see chapter 7.

Accommodation

Number of places and costs refer to 2010–11
University-provided places: about 4,000
Percentage catered: 0%
Self-catered costs: £91.00–£132.59 a week (41 or 42 weeks).
First-year students are guaranteed housing in university-approved accommodation provided requirements are met. International students are offered accommodation where possible.
Contact: accommodation@uwe.ac.uk

University of the West of Scotland (UWS)

West of Scotland appears in *The Times* League Table this year for the first time since shortly after the university was formed in 2007. The university blocked the release of data while some of the statistics related to Paisley University and Bell College, in Hamilton, the merger partners. Its position in the bottom five is considerably lower than that occupied by Paisley alone on its last appearance. But Scotland's largest new university has been enjoying massive growth in demand for places. Increases in applications of 57 per cent in 2010 and 32 per cent at the start of 2011 were both the biggest in the UK.

The exceptional figures were fuelled mainly by the move to an all-graduate nursing profession – the School of Health, Nursing and Midwifery is the largest north of the border – degrees in subjects such as computer animation, commercial music, computer games technology, sports studies and music technology have all been popular. The university is planning improvements of £250 million to its four campuses, with local provision within reach of nearly 40 per cent of Scots. An £80-million redevelopment of the Ayr campus will be complete by September 2011, when a highly energy-efficient new teaching building will open, while a

new student residences complex in Paisley should be ready by September 2012.

Research grades improved in the 2008 assessments, although UWS made only a small submission. A quarter of the work was rated as world-leading or internationally excellent, with biomedical sciences and social policy and social work producing the best results. As a Scottish institution, the university is not required to participate in the National Student Survey and is one of three not to do so.

UWS continues its parent institutions' proud records in attracting under-represented groups onto courses. Almost all the students are state educated and approaching 40 per cent are from working-class homes. Unfortunately, however, dropout rates have been high – and the latest projection of 27 per cent is more than twice the benchmark set according to the subject mix and entry qualifications. Paisley introduced measures to address the problem, including a personal tutor system, strengthened counselling support and attendance monitoring. Access measures are continuing, with hundreds of youngsters aged 14 and 15 attending the "University Experience" to sample a week of student life.

UWS's four bases are in Ayr, Dumfries, Hamilton and Paisley. Among the first developments were the £5.5-million library and student support services in Dumfries, a £2-million engineering centre at Hamilton

Paisley Campus
Paisley
Renfrewshire PA1 2BE

0141 848 3000 (switchboard)
info@uws.ac.uk
contact via website
www.uws.ac.uk
www.sauws.org.uk
Affiliation: million+

The Times Rankings
Overall Ranking: **112**

Student satisfaction:		n/a
Research quality:	=105	(0.1)
Entry standards:	=105	(241)
Student–staff ratio:	=80	(20.1)
Services & facilities/student:	75	(£1,232)
Expected completion rate:	114	(67.9%)
Good honours:	114	(43.1%)
Graduate prospects:	78	(58.3%)

and a £1-million employment centre for students across all campuses, which has its hub at the Paisley campus. The new Ayr campus, which is being developed in partnership with the Scottish Agricultural College (SAC), will create an innovative learning environment, one of the most environmentally sustainable in the UK, for over 4,000 students. The new campus is adjacent to an 18th-century mansion that houses the West of Scotland Management Centre.

Paisley is Scotland's largest town, while Hamilton ranks fifth. Both draw a high proportion of the students from the local area, many on part-time courses. Paisley numbers have grown rapidly in recent years, but staffing levels compare favourably with most new universities. There are around 1,100 international students, thanks to a growing number of Chinese and Indian nationals and long-established links with over 50 EU institutions.

Courses are strongly vocational, with business, multimedia and health subjects by far the most popular choices. There are close links with business and industry and all students are offered hands-on computer training. Paisley was the first UK university approved by Microsoft, Macromedia and Cisco, and has the status of Microsoft Academic Professional Development Centre. A games development laboratory, supported by Sony, is part of a £300,000 package of investment in multimedia and games facilities.

Paisley pioneered credit transfer in Scotland, including credit for non-academic achievement, and the modular course system covers day, evening and weekend classes. Most students either take sandwich degrees or have work placements built into their courses, earning an average of £10,000 in the process, but the impact on graduate employment has been less than elsewhere.

Over £9 million was invested in Paisley's facilities in UWS's early years. The 20-acre town centre campus now hosts a new library and learning resource centre, a £5-million students' union building, and recently up-graded indoor and outdoor sports facilities. More housing is scheduled for completion in 2012. The Dumfries campus, operated in partnership with Glasgow University, has over 400 students. The Hamilton campus contains teaching facilities, a students' union, an upgraded leisure centre and some accommodation. The Centre for Engineering Excellence is the newest addition.

Undergraduate Fees and Support

» Fees 2012–13:   awaiting Scottish Government policy.
» Fees for Scottish and EU students 2011–12   No fee
» Fees for Non-Scottish UK-domiciled students 2011–12   £1,820
» Fees for international students 2011–12   £10,000–£10,500
» Scholarships and bursaries based on circumstances or by competition.
» Check the university's website for the latest information.

Students

Undergraduates:	**8,885**	**(6,800)**
Postgraduates:	**795**	**(945)**
Mature students:	**42.4%**	
Overseas students:	**5.6%**	
Applications per place:	**2.3**	
From state-sector schools:	**98.7%**	
From working-class homes:	**38.8%**	

For detailed information about fees, grants and bursaries and how they work, see chapter 7.

Accommodation

Number of places and costs refer to 2011–12
University-provided places: 1,088 (732 at Paisley; 200 at Ayr; 156 at Hamilton)
Percentage catered: 0%
Self-catered costs: £65–£105 a week (depending on location).
First-year students have priority (conditions apply).
International students: single students guaranteed housing if conditions are met and applications received by 27 July.
Contact: www.uws.ac.uk/accommodation

University of Westminster

Westminster hit the headlines in the 2008 Research Assessment Exercise, when it was rated top in the UK for media studies with one of the highest proportions of world-leading research (60 per cent) in any subject. More than a third of all the work submitted by the university was rated in the top two categories, resulting a doubling of Westminster's research grants. Art and design, architecture and biomedical sciences all achieved good grades. The successes helped the university to a 14 per cent rise in applications at the start of 2011, well above the national average at that time, building on a 13 per cent rise in 2010. Westminster has also gone up four places in the latest *Times* League Table, with higher spending on student facilities and more students achieving firsts and upper-second class degrees.

The university is about to embark on an extensive redevelopment programme of its Harrow campus, costing £38 million. This will include a new student centre with catering facilities and a student learning and social space. The internationally recognised School of Media, Arts and Design will remain at Harrow. The School of Electronics and Computer Science has been consolidated onto a single site in the West End, and this has been followed by a merging of the Harrow Business School with the Westminster Business School – also onto a single site in the West End. The School of Life Sciences, based at the New Cavendish Street site near the BT Tower, has recently invested £2 million in modernising its laboratories .

The greenfield Harrow campus, designed for 7,500 students, boasts a high-tech information resources centre with good facilities for the highly rated media studies courses. The West End sites provide the perfect catchment area for part-time undergraduates, who account for about a quarter of the 17,000 under-graduate places. However, not all of Westminster's students are Londoners. Over 5,000 come from overseas – among the highest proportions among the post-1992 universities – and Westminster has the largest number of ethnic minority students in Britain. Westminster courses are also taught in nine overseas countries, from Sri Lanka to Uzbekistan, a characteristic which won the university a Queen's Award for Enterprise.

The university has launched a £5-million appeal to restore its main Regent Street building, which it claims as the birthplace of British cinema. It opened The Gallery, a new art and exhibition space, in the building in 2010. The historic headquarters building, near the BBC's Broadcasting House, houses social sciences, humanities and languages. Westminster claims to offer one of the widest ranges of language teaching of any British university.

---

309 Regent Street
London W1B 2UW

020 7915 5511 (enquiries)
course-enquiries@
    westminster.ac.uk
www.westminster.ac.uk
www.uwsu.com
Affiliation: none

The Times Rankings
Overall Ranking: **96**

Student satisfaction:	=108	(69%)
Research quality:	=62	(0.5)
Entry standards:	=74	(273)
Student–staff ratio:	=46	(17.1)
Services & facilities/student:	67	(£1,273)
Expected completion rate:	=90	(79.5%)
Good honours:	=80	(56.1%)
Graduate prospects:	=90	(55.1%)

The university is heading a €1-million European research project to explore the relationship between scarcity and creativity in the built environment. The university's growing interest in health subjects includes a range of courses in complementary medicine, including a BSc in acupuncture.

Westminster weaves work-related skills into its degree programmes and the dropout rate is now below 17 per cent – and better than average for the university's subjects and entry standards. But scores in the 2010 National Student Survey were among the lowest in the country for the fourth successive year, featuring in the bottom 15 universities. Only history and tourism, transport and travel had satisfaction rates of more than 85 per cent among final-year undergraduates.

More than four out of ten undergraduates are from working-class homes – a much higher proportion than the national average for the subjects offered. The university also exceeds its benchmark for the admission of students from state schools and colleges. However, those from lower participation neighbourhoods are under-represented. Westminster had the largest scholarship programme of its kind before the latest rise in fees, offering up to £4,000 a year to the brightest entrants, as well as bursaries for all those receiving a maintenance grant. The university was among the last to disclose its fees for 2012, but it was expected to increase its scholarship and bursary programme as part of its submission to the Office for Fair Access.

Westminster's students, like those at all the London universities, complain of the high cost of living, particularly for accommodation. The university has added considerably to its residential stock in recent years, with the opening of a £6-million block of halls in Harrow and the refurbishment of its Marylebone halls, but there is no way round the capital's inflated housing market at some stage. The Harrow campus is lively socially, but those based on the other campuses tend to be spread around the capital. Sports facilities are also dispersed, with playing fields and a boathouse in Chiswick, west London. Smoke Radio, Westminster's student radio station, won two awards in 2010.

Undergraduate Fees and Support

» Fees for UK/EU students 2012–13   £9,000
» Fees for International students 2011–12   £10,500
» A package of financial support and widening participation activity to be announced.
» Scholarships and bursaries based on circumstances or by competition.
» Check the university's website for the latest information.

Students

Undergraduates:	**12,290**	**(4,885)**
Postgraduates:	**3,160**	**(3,625)**
Mature students:	**30.2%**	
Overseas students:	**17.4%**	
Applications per place:	**4.6**	
From state-sector schools:	**95.4%**	
From working-class homes:	**43.9%**	

For detailed information about fees, grants and bursaries and how they work, see chapter 7.

Accommodation

Number of places and costs refer to 2011–12
University-provided places: 1,279
Percentage catered: 0%
Self-catered costs: £86.10 – £181.30 a week.
First-year students have priority. Residential restrictions apply.
International students: as above.
Contact: studentaccommodation@westminster.ac.uk
www.westminster.ac.uk/study/student-accommodation

University of Winchester

Winchester stresses its "human scale", with just more than 6,000 students and an emphasis on providing a supportive community for students to unlock their potential. The approach appears to have struck a chord: applications were up by 14 per cent at the start of 2011, well above the national average increase for the second year in a row. After successive finishes around the top 30 in the National Student Survey, however, in the last two years the university has dropped to a mid-table position. Dance, academic studies in education, history and social work all achieved a satisfaction rating of over 95 per cent in 2010, while American and Australasian studies, English studies and sports science also did well.

The university, which will charge fees of £8,500 for all degree courses from 2012, traces its history as an Anglican foundation back to 1840 and has occupied its King Alfred campus since 1862. The compact site is on a wooded hillside overlooking the cathedral city, a ten-minute walk away, with views of the surrounding countryside. A second centre occupies a large 18th-century rectory in nearby Basingstoke and concentrates on lifelong learning. It offers Foundation and Honours degrees in management.

Known as King Alfred's College until 2004, the university is still best-known for teacher training, which accounts for about a third of the places. Ofsted rates the teacher training courses as outstanding. It is one of the largest providers of primary school training in England, but courses on the main campus also span business, arts, humanities, health and social care, and social sciences. Degrees range from choreography and dance, through social work, business, accounting, law, media and teacher training to ethics and spirituality. Ancient, classical and medieval studies, modern liberal arts, sociology and vocal and choral studies were added in 2010. Global history and politics, criminology, and a range of new psychology programmes were among the innovations for 2011. Archaeology and theatre development are new degrees planned for 2012 entry.

Winchester improved on already respectable grades in the 2008 Research Assessment Exercise, when it was ranked second among the new universities in history, with over half of its submission considered world-leading or internationally excellent. Overall, more than a third of the university's work reached the top two categories and there was some world-leading research in four of the six subject areas.

The university is particularly proud of its low dropout rate, although the latest official projection of 13.5 per cent was marginally higher than the national average for Winchester's courses and entry qualifications. Over 95 per cent of the British students are

Winchester

Hampshire SO22 4NR

01962 827234
course.enquiries@winchester.ac.uk
www.winchester.ac.uk
www.winchester
  students.co.uk
Affiliations: Cathedral Group,
  Guild HE

The Times Rankings

Overall Ranking: **=69**

Student satisfaction:	=73	(75%)
Research quality:	=70	(0.4)
Entry standards:	=69	(280)
Student–staff ratio:	55	(17.7)
Services & facilities/student:	106	(£1,017)
Expected completion rate:	=66	(83.9%)
Good honours:	64	(60.5%)
Graduate prospects:	98	(54.0%)

state-educated and over a third are from working-class homes. The fee package for 2012, put to the Office for Fair Access, included fee waivers of £2,000 a year for students from under-represented social groups who "can demonstrate academic achievement". Male undergraduates are heavily outnumbered and there are about 150 overseas students from a range of countries. Winchester students can take advantage of exchange schemes with American universities in Maine, Oregon and Wisconsin, as well as with Beppu University in Japan.

The main campus is well equipped, with its theatrical performance spaces, sports hall and fitness suite now supplemented by the £3.5-million Winchester Sports Stadium, which opened in 2008. Open to local people as well as students, the stadium has an Olympic standard 400-metre eight-lane athletics track with supporting facilities for field events and also a floodlit all-weather pitch. There are six performing arts studios in a new building that opened in the spring of 2010 on the King Alfred campus. The two-storey building offers the latest technology for student productions.

An award-winning University Centre opened in September 2007, transforming the students' union, adding a nightclub, cinema, catering facilities, a bookshop and a super-market at a cost of £9 million. A "learning café" creates an informal working space with networked PCs and wireless internet access. An award-winning extension to the library made room for 200,000 books, 450 study spaces and 150 computers.

A £12-million student village, a short walk from the main campus, provides more than 700 residential places. The business school is also located on the West Downs campus. A second village, with en-suite rooms arranged in cluster flats with shared kitchen facilities, opened in September 2010. Winchester guarantees campus accommodation to first year full-time undergraduates, overseas students and students with medical needs as long they apply by the deadline. Students value the close-knit atmosphere and find the city is livelier than its staid image might suggest, with a number of bars catering to their tastes. Southampton is not far for those who hanker after the attractions of a bigger city, and London is only an hour away by train.

Undergraduate Fees and Support

» Fees for UK/EU students 2012–13   £8,500
» Fees for International students 2011–12   £9,200
» Support to include fee waivers of up to £2,000 for students from under-represented groups who can demonstrate significant academic achievement; increased outreach; developing employability skills.
» Scholarships and bursaries based on circumstances or by competition.
» Check the university's website for the latest information.

Students

Undergraduates:	**4,150**	**(890)**
Postgraduates:	**195**	**(1,195)**
Mature students:	**17.3%**	
Overseas students:	**5.8%**	
Applications per place:	**5.3**	
From state-sector schools:	**95.3%**	
From working-class homes:	**34.5%**	

For detailed information about fees, grants and bursaries and how they work, see chapter 7.

Accommodation

Number of places and costs refer to 2010–11
University-provided places: 1,274 on campus; 212 off campus
Percentage catered: 14.5%
Catered costs: £3,770.90 (term-time only).
Self-catered costs: £3,556.00 – £5,042.10 (40 weeks).
First years are guaranteed accommodation if conditions are met.
International students: non EU, as above.
Contact: housing@winchester.ac.uk

University of Wolverhampton

Wolverhampton is one of a small group of universities that have refused to release information on their performance after finishing towards the bottom of league tables. Just outside the top 100 on its last appearance in *The Times* League Table, its student satisfaction and dropout rates have improved and it might have finished higher this time. A statement on the university's website says that tables such as ours disadvantage universities like Wolverhampton and do not represent a fair picture of their strengths. As a result, it is missing from both the main ranking and all the subject tables.

Wolverhampton's success in widening participation in higher education is such that it is one of only four British universities with just over 50 per cent of students coming from working-class homes. Almost all the students are from state schools and almost one in five comes from an area of low participation in higher education. The university draws two thirds of its 23,000 students from the West Midlands, although it has a growing contingent from overseas. A third of the places are filled by mature students and its four campuses have a cosmopolitan feel, with about the same proportion coming from the region's ethnic minorities.

The university pioneered the high street "higher education shop" and more recently, a dedicated Student Finance Support Unit and Student Gateway Service, bringing all student support together in one convenient location. Big outreach programmes take courses into the workplace. The four campuses each have their own learning centres and are linked by a free bus service. Two are in the city, while sport and performance, education and part of the School of Health and Wellbeing are based in Walsall. The original site is in the heart of the city centre. A purpose-built campus at Telford in Shropshire focuses on business and engineering in a county with no higher education institution of its own.

Wolverhampton has been investing millions of pounds in an infrastructure programme known as "New Horizons". The project has seen £26 million spent on the City campus, notably on the flagship Millennium City Building, and a teaching and administration building. A 350-bed student village has opened on the Walsall campus, together with a Lottery-supported sports hall offering elite training facilities for judo and a Sports Science and Medicine Centre which are being used to train Olympic contenders. A £12-million building for the School of Education and the Institute for Learning Enhancement opened in 2008. At Telford the £7-million e-Innovation Centre has already won awards for the support it offers to

Wulfruna Street
Wolverhampton WV1 1LY

01902 321000 (enquiries)
enquiries@wlv.ac.uk
www.wlv.ac.uk
www.wolvesunion.org.uk
Affiliation: million+

The Times Rankings
Wolverhampton blocked the release of data from the Higher Education Statistics Agency and so we cannot give any ranking information.

e-businesses. Work is under way on the new Performance Hub at the Walsall campus, which is due to be completed in July 2011.

The projected dropout rate is now just below the benchmark for a university with Wolverhampton's entry grades and subjects, at 16 per cent. The university runs a national teaching centre focusing on retention, progression and achievement. Teacher-training courses are rated in the top four in the country by Ofsted, and Wolverhampton academics have been awarded six National Teaching Fellowships by the Higher Education Academy. The university was ranked in the bottom 40 in the 2010 National Student Survey having maintained its overall score from the previous year. Music, dance, pharmacology, toxicology and pharmacy and fine art were the only subjects that satisfied 90 per cent or more of the students.

The university claims a number of firsts for its academic programmes, pioneering interactive multimedia communication degrees, as well as offering one of the first degrees in British sign language and one of the first in virtual reality design and manufacturing. It was the first university to be registered under the British Standards for the quality of its all-round provision. The university stresses innovation and enterprise in its work with students and businesses, encouraging student start-up companies and leading a project to develop student placements in these companies for those who wish to become entrepreneurs. The Flying Start Programme for Sports Business is the first of its kind in the UK, providing a series of specialist workshops.

Research is mainly applied, serving the needs of business and industry, as well as underpinning teaching at all levels. The main strengths are in applications of computing and biomedical science, including ground-breaking work on brain tumours. The university was ranked fourth in the UK for statistical cybermetrics and sixth for computational linguistics in the 2008 Research Assessment Exercise. A relatively low proportion of the academics were entered for assessment, but 30 per cent of their research was considered world-leading or internationally excellent.

Social facilities vary between sites. Wolverhampton has a growing nightlife and the university has been voted the friendliest in the West Midlands. The cost of living is reasonable and Birmingham is now only a metro tramride away.

Undergraduate Fees and Support

» Fees for UK/EU students 2012–13	£8,500
» Fees for International students 2011–12	£9,450
» A package of financial support, including around 400 National Scholarships, and widening participation activity to be announced.	
» Scholarships and bursaries based on circumstances or by competition.	
» Check the university's website for the latest information.	

Students

From state-sector schools:	**99.5%**
From working-class homes:	**53.1%**

For detailed information about fees, grants and bursaries and how they work, see chapter 7.

Accommodation

Number of places and costs refer to 2011–12
University-provided places: 2,048
Percentage catered: 0%
Self-catered costs: £2,468–£3,615 (37 weeks).
First-year students are offered accommodation provided requirements are met. Residential restrictions apply.
International students: same as above.
Contact: accommodationservices@wlv.ac.uk

University of Worcester

Worcester has the most ambitious development plans of all the new universities created in 2005. A second campus in the heart of the city opened in September 2010 and a unique library and history centre – the first joint public and university library in Britain – will open in early 2012. On top of this the university is investing in a state-of-the-art sporting arena for the city, designed with disability sport in mind, to open in 2012 in time for the Olympics.

At the start of 2011, applications were up by 9 per cent, following healthy increases in the previous nine years, making the university one of the fastest growing in Britain. Business courses have been particularly popular and there have been big increases, too, in physical education, sports studies, forensic science, marketing, pre-hospital and emergency care, journalism, social work and advertising.

First as a post-war emergency teacher training college and later as a university college, the institution has always been the only provider of higher education in Herefordshire and Worcestershire. The university remains strong in education and also in nursing and midwifery – a mix that explains an overwhelmingly female student population. Former Home Secretary, Jacqui Smith, trained as a teacher there. But the six academic departments also cover applied sciences, geography and archaeology, a business school and arts, humanities and social sciences. Degrees range from animal biology to sports coaching and computing.

The 23 academics entered for the 2008 Research Assessment Exercise represented the smallest contingent from any university in England. Only English had any world-leading research, although there are pockets of excellence such as the National Pollen and Aerobiology Research Unit, which produces all of Britain's pollen forecasts. Results in the first four National Student Surveys were more positive, placing Worcester in the top 40, but results in 2009 and 2010 declined, leaving the university just outside the bottom 40. In 2010 the most satisfied students were in nursing, which scored 96 per cent. No other subjects recorded scores over 90 per cent.

Nearly one in four undergraduates come from working-class homes. The projected dropout rate has declined to around 15 per cent, but is still slightly above average for the university's subjects and entry qualifications. As well as the normal range of bursaries, the university offers £1,000 scholarships for academic achievement in the first year of a course and for extra-curricular activities such as voluntary work.

The St John's campus occupies a parkland site a 15-minutes walk from the city centre. The university has undertaken to continue improving the campus including a

---

Henwick Grove
Worcester WR2 6AJ

01905 855111 (admissions)
admissions@worc.ac.uk
www.worc.ac.uk
www.worcsu.com
Affiliation: Guild HE

The Times Rankings
Overall Ranking: **=94**

Student satisfaction:	**=78**	(74%)
Research quality:	**=105**	(0.1)
Entry standards:	**=78**	(271)
Student–staff ratio:	**105**	(21.9)
Services & facilities/student:	**110**	(£956)
Expected completion rate:	**=60**	(84.4%)
Good honours:	**89**	(54.4%)
Graduate prospects:	**65**	(60.8%)

£7-million science facility which houses state-of-the-art teaching laboratories and the National Pollen and Aerobiology Research Unit, a £1-million digital arts centre and drama studio, and a third-generation Astroturf pitch. Sport plays an important part in university life: a well-appointed sports centre also provides employment opportunities for students, while competitive teams are successful and the facilities for casual participants extensive. A mobile 3D motion analysis laboratory has been used by the England and Wales Cricket Board. Modest sports scholarships are offered in partnership with Worcestershire County Cricket Club, Worcester Wolves Basketball Club and Worcester Hockey Club. The basketball team have been national champions for three years in succession.

The new City campus occupies the site of the old Worcester Royal Infirmary. It includes teaching, residential and conference facilities and is home to the Worcester Business School. The new library and history centre is next to the campus and will be open to all students and members of the public. There are buses that run between the two campuses, as well as a cycle route. Halfway between the two sites are further new facilities, including specialist art rooms, dance studios, teaching spaces and the planned Worcester Arena. The university also has a number of partner colleges around the region offering Worcester courses.

Social life revolves around the students' union, which also has a "job pod" to help members find work experience and part-time jobs. The cathedral city is not large, but is safer than many university locations, and has its share of pubs and clubs that cater for a growing student clientele.

Undergraduate Fees and Support

- » Fees for UK/EU students 2012–13 — £8,100
  Foundation degrees at partner colleges — £6,000
- » Fees for International students 2011–12 — £9,000
- » A package of financial support and widening participation activity to be announced.
- » Scholarships and bursaries based on circumstances or by competition.
- » Check the university's website for the latest information.

Students

Undergraduates:	**5,720**	**(1,975)**
Postgraduates:	**520**	**(1,330)**
Mature students:	**28.4%**	
Overseas students:	**5.8%**	
Applications per place:	**4.5**	
From state-sector schools:	**97.3%**	
From working-class homes:	**39.6%**	

For detailed information about fees, grants and bursaries and how they work, see chapter 7.

Accommodation

Number of places and costs refer to 2011–12
University-provided places: 970 university-owned; 200–230 university-managed
Percentage catered: 0%
Self-catered costs: £75–£127 a week.
First-year students are guaranteed accommodation, on a first come, first served basis, if conditions are met.
International students are accommodated if conditions are met.
Contact: accommodation@worc.ac.uk

University of York

York has slipped out of the top ten in *The Times* League Table this year by a mere three points, but is in the top 100 in both the main world rankings. The university has decided that, with just over 15,000 students, it is too small to maintain that standing, play a leading role in the economy of the region and satisfy the growing demand for its places. In an audacious move for a highly selective university, York is expanding campus to accommodate up to 50 per cent more students and strengthen its research capability. This initiative, along with its academic excellence, social inclusion and research record, helped make York the *Times Higher Education* University of the Year for 2010.

The first building on the campus extension – a new residential college for 600 new students – opened in 2009. New buildings for computer science, law, management and theatre, film and television welcomed their first students in 2010. The campus expansion will take 10 to 15 years to complete and eventually contain housing for an additional 3,300 students, as well as more academic buildings, sports facilities and a performing arts and community complex. A £21-million "hub" for Heslington East opened in 2010 and a second residential college for 650 students will follow in 2012.

Expansion into new subjects has already started. The first intake of undergraduates in law and in writing, directing and performance in theatre, film and television will graduate in 2011. The university believes that, with six applicants for every place, other departments can grow at the same time as retaining or achieving a place in the top ten for their subject. The new subjects helped York achieve 14 per cent growth in applications in 2010, a feat not matched at the start of 2011, however, when applications declined.

Medicine was introduced in 2003 in partnership with Hull University. York also runs its own nursing and midwifery programmes. The university has done well in the National Student Survey, both in its own right and at the medical school, which is assessed separately. York has finished in the top 30 universities in all six years of polling. Archaeology, biology, chemistry, molecular biology, biophysics and biochemistry, and physical geography and environmental science all produced particularly high levels of satisfaction in the 2010 results. Around 11 per cent of the current student population are international, and around 29 per cent are postgraduates.

Entrance requirements are high and the dropout rate of only 4 per cent is among the lowest in the country. Eight out of ten undergraduates are state educated and over 21 per cent come from working-class homes, just less than the national average for York's

---

Heslington
York YO10 5DD

01904 323533 (admissions)
ug-admissions@york.ac.uk
www.york.ac.uk
www.hyms.ac.uk
www.yusu.org
Affiliation: 1994 Group

The Times Rankings
Overall Ranking: **11**

Student satisfaction:	**11**	(82%)
Research quality:	**=9**	(2.7)
Entry standards:	**14**	(437)
Student–staff ratio:	**=24**	(14.9)
Services & facilities/student:	**18**	(£1,946)
Expected completion rate:	**9**	(95.4%)
Good honours:	**16**	(75.6%)
Graduate prospects:	**42**	(68.2%)

subjects and entry qualifications. Every student has a supervisor responsible for their academic and personal welfare. Extra-curricular courses include language and computer literacy training, as well as courses on personal effectiveness, financial management, active citizenship and an introduction to accounting. The business community is involved at every level. Undergraduates can also take the "York Award", comprising a range of courses, work placements and voluntary activities which aim to prepare students for the world of work. Over 600 students work as volunteer teaching assistants in local schools through the award-winning York Students in Schools programme.

York was among the top ten institutions in the 2008 Research Assessment Exercise, when more than 60 per cent of the work submitted was judged to be world-leading or internationally excellent. The university was ranked top in the UK for English and health services research, joint top for sociology, and among the leaders for linguistics, and nursing and midwifery.

The current campus occupies 200 acres of landscaped parkland, a mile outside the historic, picturesque city centre. Students join one of eight colleges, which mix academic and social roles. Most departments have their headquarters in one of the colleges, but the student community is a deliberate mixture of disciplines, years and sexes. Nursing apart, only archaeology and medieval studies are located off campus, sharing a medieval building in the centre of the city.

Social life on campus is lively. There are television and radio stations, as well as several newspapers and magazines, to keep students abreast of campus issues. Sports facilities are good, and include a 50-station fitness suite, four sports halls, and dance studio. Plans are in hand as part of the campus expansion to establish the York Sports Village, which will feature a 25-metre pool, learner pool, 100-station gym, full-size 3G Astroturf pitch and three further five-a-side pitches. The existing campus also contains extensive playing fields and the River Ouse fosters a strong rowing tradition. Cultural events abound in the city, which is also famous for a high concentration of pubs. The club scene has improved, but students still head for Leeds for the top names.

Undergraduate Fees and Support

» Fees for UK/EU students 2012–13   to be announced
» Fees for International students 2011–12   £12,000–£15,600
   £23,268 (medicine)
» A package of financial support and widening participation activity to be announced.
» Scholarships and bursaries based on circumstances or by competition.
» Check the university's website for the latest information.

Students		
Undergraduates:	**9,670**	**(1,160)**
Postgraduates:	**3,510**	**(930)**
Mature students:	**8.0%**	
Overseas students:	**10.9%**	
Applications per place:	**6.3**	
From state-sector schools:	**79.4%**	
From working-class homes:	**21.6%**	

For detailed information about fees, grants and bursaries and how they work, see chapter 7.

Accommodation

Number of places and costs refer to 2011–12
University-provided places: 4,540
Percentage catered: 16%
Catered costs: £109.90 a week
Self-catered costs: £85.82–£118.02 a week.
First-year single undergraduates are provided with accommodation if terms and conditions are met.
International students: as above.
Contact: accommodation@york.ac.uk
www.york.ac.uk/accommodation

York St John University

York St John was one of a handful of universities to charge less than the £3,000 maximum when top-up fees were introduced in 2006. It has avoided the maximum again for 2012, although undergraduates will still pay £8,500 for all full-time degrees, and a package of fee waivers, bursaries and scholarships has been submitted to the Office for Fair Access. The university has slipped five places in this year's *Times* League Table, but it has seen applications increase by almost 40 per cent in two years, so it is confident of maintaining enrolments under the new fee regime.

One of the four universities designated in 2006, York St John is a Church of England foundation that dates back almost 170 years. The eight-acre site faces York Minster across the city walls and is a five-minute walk from the city centre. Now serving over 6,000 students, the campus has seen £75 million of development in recent years and more is planned. The Fountains Learning Centre, which has 500 computer workstations, an internet café and lecture theatre, provides a striking entrance to the university. Another new teaching development, mainly for health and life sciences, opened at the end of 2008 and is intended to be a signature building linking the university quarter with the city centre. De Grey Court, which cost £15.5 million, won a prize at the Royal Institute of British Architects Awards in 2009.

York Diocesan Training School opened in 1841 with one pupil on the register, in whose honour the current students' union is named. Divided between York and Ripon for most of its existence, the institution diversified beyond teacher training in the 1980s and decided at the start of this decade to concentrate all its teaching on York. The university's mission statement says its provision is "shaped" by the York St John's church foundation, although it welcomes students of all beliefs.

Education and theology remains the biggest faculty, with 1,700 students taking programmes in teacher education, education studies, theology and religious studies. Health and life sciences are not far behind in terms of size, with 1,600 full-time students and 200 part-timers studying health courses such as physiotherapy and occupational therapy, as well as psychology and sport. The York St John Business School, launched in May 2008, engages with a range of local and regional small to medium-sized enterprises, as well as offering the normal range of undergraduate and postgraduate courses.

The Faculty of Arts, which was formed in 2001, has been one of the main points of expansion, especially in degree programmes such as film and television, media and American studies. The university was

---

New Mayor's Walk
York YO31 7EX

01904 876598 (information hotline)
admissions@yorksj.ac.uk
www.yorksj.ac.uk
www.ysjsu.com
Affiliations: Cathedral Group,
Guild HE

The Times Rankings
Overall Ranking: **86**

Student satisfaction:	=63	(76%)
Research quality:	=105	(0.1)
Entry standards:	68	(282)
Student–staff ratio:	99	(21.2)
Services & facilities/student:	78	(£1,199)
Expected completion rate:	52	(85.6%)
Good honours:	71	(58.3%)
Graduate prospects:	106	(51.8%)

awarded a national centre for excellence in creativity, based on its work in English and theatre studies, although funding for such programmes has now ceased. It provided an enriched curriculum in the creative arts. Another music technology suite has been added and performance spaces include two dedicated TV studios, digital non-linear edit suites, digital imaging equipment and equipment for sound manipulation. Yorkshire Television and Tyne Tees Television have established a joint newsroom on campus. There are also facilities available for set design and construction and prop and costume making.

Satisfaction levels varied widely in the National Student Survey published in 2010. More than 90 per cent of final-year undergraduates in theology and religious studies and anatomy, physiology and pathology were satisfied with their courses. However, the proportion was just 52 per cent for media studies, and only 55 per cent in design studies. Drama, dance and performing arts was the most successful field in the 2008 Research Assessment Exercise and the only one to contain world-leading research.

Seven out of ten students are female – one of the highest proportions in the university system. More than 94 per cent of them attended state schools or colleges, while almost a third are from working-class homes. The projected dropout rate could not be compiled in the latest official survey, but the previous year's figure of 9 per cent represented considerable improvement and was well below the national average for the university's courses and entry qualifications.

Relatively high numbers of locally based mature students ease the pressure on residential accommodation. As a result, first years who want to live in university-owned accommodation are usually able to do so. More self-catering accommodation for 500 students, costing £10 million, opened in September 2009. Sports facilities are not extensive, but York is popular as a student city with a growing range of clubs as well as, supposedly, a pub for every day of the year.

Undergraduate Fees and Support

» Fees for UK/EU students 2012–13   £8,500
» Fees for International students 2011–12   £8,500–£11,600
» A package of bursaries and scholarships to be announced. Fee waivers based on household income: below £10K, £2,000 a year; £10K–£20K, £1,250 a year; £20K–£30K, £750 a year.
» Scholarships and bursaries based on circumstances or by competition.
» Check the university's website for the latest information.

Students

Undergraduates:	**3,885**	**(1,095)**
Postgraduates:	**285**	**(610)**
Mature students:	**16.8%**	
Overseas students:	**2.9%**	
Applications per place:	**5.6**	
From state-sector schools:	**94.3%**	
From working-class homes:	**32.0%**	

For detailed information about fees, grants and bursaries and how they work, see chapter 7.

Accommodation

Number of places and costs refer to 2011–12
University-provided places: 1,334
Percentage catered: 11%
Catered costs: £124 (semi-catered package) a week (33 weeks).
Self-catered costs: £76–£132 a week (44–48 weeks).
First years choosing university as first choice are guaranteed accommodation. Residential and age restrictions apply. International students: guaranteed housing.
Contact: accommodation@yorksj.ac.uk

Colleges of Higher Education

This listing gives contact details for higher education institutions not mentioned elsewhere within the book. All the institutions listed below offer degree courses, some providing a wide range of courses while others are specialist colleges with a limited range of courses and a small intake. Those marked * are members of GuildHE (**www.guildhe.ac.uk**). Fees are given only for English institutions that announced 2012–13 fees (subject to OFFA approval) before mid-May 2011.

Arts University College, Bournemouth*

Wallisdown, Poole, Dorset BH12 5HH
01202 533011
www.aucb.ac.uk
Fees 2012–13: £8,600

Bishop Grosseteste University College*

Lincoln LN1 3DY
01522 527347
www.bishopg.ac.uk
Fees 2012–13: £7,500

BPP University College of Professional Studies

Aldine House, Aldine Place,
122-4 Uxbridge Road, London W12 8AW
0845 0775566
www.bppuc.com

Conservatoire for Dance and Drama

Tavistock House, Tavistock Square
London WC1H 9JJ
020 7387 5101
www.cdd.ac.uk
Consists of eight Schools, six in London, including RADA

Glasgow School of Art

167 Renfrew Street, Glasgow G3 6RQ
0141 353 4500
www.gsa.ac.uk

Harper Adams University College*

Newport, Shropshire TF10 8NB
01952 820280
www.harper-adams.ac.uk
Fees 2012–13: £9,000

Leeds Trinity University College*

Brownberrie Lane
Leeds LS18 5HD
0113 283 7100
www.leedstrinity.ac.uk
Fees 2012–13: £8,000; Foundation £4,250

Liverpool Institute for Performing Arts*

Mount Street, Liverpool L1 9HF
0151 330 3000
www.lipa.ac.uk

Newman University College*

Genners Lane, Bartley Green,
Birmingham B32 3NT
0121 476 1181
www.newman.ac.uk

Norwich University College of the Arts*

Francis House, 3–7 Redwell Street
Norwich, Norfolk NR2 4SN
01603 610561
www.nuca.ac.uk
Fees 2012–13: £8,500

Ravensbourne*

6 Penrose Way, London SE10 0EW
020 3040 3500
www.rave.ac.uk

Rose Bruford College of Theatre and Performance *

Burnt Oak Lane, Sidcup, Kent DA15 9DF
020 8308 2600
www.bruford.ac.uk

Royal Agricultural College*

Cirencester, Gloucestershire GL7 6JS
01285 652531
www.rac.ac.uk
Fees 2012–13: £9,000

Royal College of Art
Kensington Gore, London SW7 2EU
020 7590 4444
www.rca.ac.uk

Royal College of Music
Prince Consort Road, London SW7 2BS
020 7589 3643
www.rcm.ac.uk
Fees 2012–13: £9,000

Royal Northern College of Music
124 Oxford Road, Manchester M13 9RD
0161 907 5200
www.rncm.ac.uk

Royal Scottish Academy of Music and Drama
100 Renfrew Street, Glasgow G2 3DB
0141 332 4101
www.rsamd.ac.uk

Royal Welsh College of Music and Drama
Castle Grounds, Cathays Park
Cardiff CF10 3ER
029 2034 2854
www.rwcmd.ac.uk

St Mary's University College*
Waldegrave Road, Strawberry Hill
Twickenham TW1 4SX
020 8240 4000
www.smuc.ac.uk
Fees 2012–13: £8,000

St Mary's University College*
191 Falls Road, Belfast BT12 6FE
028 9032 7678
www.stmarys-belfast.ac.uk

Stranmillis University College
Stranmillis Road, Belfast BT9 5DY
028 9038 1271
www.stran.ac.uk

Trinity Laban Conservatoire of Music and Dance
Music:
King Charles Court
Old Royal Naval College,
Greenwich, London SE10 9JF
020 8305 4300
Dance:
Creekside, London SE8 3DZ
020 8691 8600
www.trinitylaban.ac.uk

University Campus Suffolk
Waterfront Building, Neptune Quay
Ipswich IP4 1QJ
01473 338000
www.ucs.ac.uk
Fees 2012–13: £8,000; Foundation: £7,500

University College Birmingham*
Summer Row, Birmingham B3 1JB
0121 604 1000
www.ucb.ac.uk
Fees 2012–13: £7,800

University College Falmouth*
incorporating **Dartington College of Arts**
Woodlane, Falmouth, Cornwall TR11 4RH
01326 211077
www.falmouth.ac.uk
Fees 2012–13: £9,000

University College Plymouth St Mark and St John* (Marjon)
Derriford Road, Plymouth, Devon PL6 8BH
01752 636700
www.marjon.ac.uk
Fees 2012–13: £7,800

Writtle College*
Chelmsford, Essex CM1 3RR
01245 424200
www.writtle.ac.uk
Fees 2012–13: £8,000

Index